Sherwood Anderson's Memoirs
A Critical Edition

ANDERSON, Sherwood. Sherwood Anderson's Memoirs; a Critical Edition, newly ed. from the original manuscripts by Ray Lewis White. North Carolina, 1969. 579p il bibl 73-80019. 15.00

CHOICE   JUNE '70
Language & Literature
English & American

With the *Memoirs* White has now completed his editing of Anderson's autobiographical trilogy. Like its companions, *A Story Teller's Story* (CHOICE, Feb. 1969) and *Tar: A Midwest Childhood* (CHOICE, Mar. 1970) in the current Case Western Reserve series of Anderson reprintings, this is a critical edition newly edited from original manuscripts. Unfinished at Anderson's death in 1941, the 1942 *Memoirs* were hastily put together by Anderson's friend, the music and literary critic, Paul Rosenfeld, from 3,000 pages of largely unorganized and unedited manuscript. Though Anderson's final intentions must remain conjectural, White is surely correct in removing essays written and published in the 1920's which Rosenfeld included to achieve continuity, in replacing the many passages he rewrote with Anderson's original prose, and in reducing the repetitiousness of the original edition. With considerably more thoroughness, accuracy, and humility, White has produced not a "corrected" version of the 1942 edition, but a new transcription of this central source of study of Anderson's life and the literary movements in which he participated.

PS
3500
A549
A51
1969

Ray Lewis White, assistant professor of English at Illinois State University, has also edited *The Achievement of Sherwood Anderson: Essays in Criticism, Return to Winesburg: Selections from Four Years of Writing for a Country Newspaper,* and *A Story Teller's Story: A Critical Text.* Mr. White is the author of *Gore Vidal.*

SHERWOOD ANDERSON'S MEMOIRS

A Critical Edition

Newly Edited
from the Original Manuscripts
by

RAY LEWIS WHITE

THE UNIVERSITY OF NORTH CAROLINA PRESS
CHAPEL HILL

For Eleanor, as Sherwood wished

ACKNOWLEDGMENTS

I wish to thank the following individuals for contributing through scholarship and friendship to the making of this book: Henry Adams, Illinois State University; Karl Anderson, Chicago; Mary Anderson, Marion, Virginia; Carlos Baker, Princeton University; James Ray Blackwelder, Western Illinois University; Richard Bond, Illinois State University; Charles Chappell, Virginia Polytechnic Institute; Malcolm Cowley, Sherman, Connecticut; Bernard Duffey, Duke University; Herbert Eldredge, University of Colorado; Maxwell Geismar, Harrison, New York; Clarence Gohdes, Duke University; Robert H. Goldsmith, Emory and Henry College; Judith I. Hall, Rochester, New York; C. Hugh Holman, The University of North Carolina at Chapel Hill; Howard Mumford Jones, Harvard University; David Kesterson, North Texas State University; A. Sidney Knowles, North Carolina State University; William V. Miller, Ball State University; Amy Nyholm, The Newberry Library; William L. Phillips, University of Washington; Patricia Powell, Harold Ober Associates; Charles Pridgeon, Marietta College; Walter B. Rideout, University of Wisconsin; H. Blair Rouse, University of Arkansas; Stanley Shuman, Illinois State University; Lawrence W. Towner, The Newberry Library; Gore Vidal, New York and Rome; Ivan von Auw, Jr., Harold Ober Associates; Howard Webber, Press of Case Western Reserve University; James M. Wells, The Newberry Library; and Maude N. White, Abingdon, Virginia.

I am especially grateful for the work of the late Paul Rosenfeld, who was completely devoted to Sherwood Anderson; for the invaluable research of William Alfred Sutton of Ball State University; and for the continuing friendship, biographical knowledge, and direct help of Mrs. Sherwood Anderson.

CONTENTS

ILLUSTRATIONS

❦❦❦

INTRODUCTION

If the flow of any dynamic life is reducible to simple pattern, then the pattern of Sherwood Anderson's life is a recurrence of enthusiastic acceptance and quickly following rejection, beginning with his dramatic abandonment of a career in manufacturing. Coming in 1912, when he was thirty-six, this sudden walking away from his Ohio business and family responsibilities—however he might later interpret or motivate it—marked clearly the rejection of convention and the acceptance of flamboyant artistic life. The Chicago Renaissance group into which Anderson was welcomed in mid-life gave him a deep knowledge of life among the artists and stimulated the creation of his masterpiece, the classic *Winesburg, Ohio* (1919).

When the Chicago Renaissance died of dispersion of talent, the great satisfaction from creating *Winesburg* made Sherwood Anderson anxious to accept the new literary renaissance of New York which in the early 1920's promised great achievement. That promise unfulfilled, Anderson had in 1923 to reject New York in order to rid himself of another responsibility, a second marriage. The forced escape to Reno for over a year let Anderson reject his present troubles in order to embrace an investigation into his origins, a project that became *A Story Teller's Story* (1924), Anderson's first autobiography.

In *A Story Teller's Story,* Sherwood Anderson created the "legends" that became forever entangled with the facts of his life. The childhood poverty, the colorful father and the suffering mother, the growing artistic sense, the glorious escape from business—all became background to carry Anderson into assumed closeness to the New York literati. The sophistication of *A Story Teller's Story* contrasts sharply with a second memoir, *Tar: A Midwest Childhood* (1926), a tender autobiographical novel written in 1925–26, when Sherwood Anderson had accepted a third marriage, acquired financial success from the novel *Dark Laughter* (1925), and had rejected the literary life of New Orleans for the quiet, almost backwardly simple existence among the mountain people of southwest Virginia.

In almost a "return to Winesburg," Anderson accepted his peaceful life as a country newspaper editor in the Virginia highlands until 1930, when the effects of the Depression and the movement for labor organization called him back into the American mainstream. When a third divorce, in 1932, and a fourth marriage, in 1933, gave Anderson once again a rejection-acceptance experience, the results were more fortunate than in his past: marriage to Eleanor Copenhaver of Marion, Virginia, proved satisfying and lasting, and a new memoirs project promised Sherwood Anderson more complete artistic fulfillment than he had enjoyed since the writing of *Winesburg, Ohio*. From 1933 to his death in 1941, Sherwood Anderson wrote fully, honestly, and beautifully of his own life.

I

Eleanor Copenhaver Anderson deserves credit for encouraging her husband to write his memoirs. As national secretary of the Young Women's Christian Association, Eleanor Anderson, in her deep concern for the labor movement, drew her husband out of his period of unhappy self-absorption in 1932 and convinced him that his writing—especially of his own history —could be socially as well as artistically important. For Sherwood Anderson believed that his own life was exemplary of a common American experience—the rejection of "success" in order to search for great meaning, to be found with enormous effort, if found at all.

Sherwood Anderson and Eleanor Copenhaver were married July 6, 1933; and, later in July, Anderson began the first writing that eventually became his memoirs. Convinced that his rejection of business in 1912 was the turning point of his life and, by its nature, an object lesson for an economically distressed nation, Anderson started a long study of his first great escape. Entitled "Trumpeter," the result, a corrected typescript of seventy-nine pages, tells of Anderson's growing vague disenchantment with his Ohio products-distribution company, his slow knowledge that beauty instead of false "service" was the ideal of the good life, his almost deranged groping for a sense of meaning, and his determination to escape. "Trumpeter" is historically invaluable even though, as a fragment, its story ends just before Anderson's 1912 escape.

Having abandoned "Trumpeter," Anderson, in August, 1933, began a more comprehensive autobiography. The stimulus may have been a suggestion by Roger Sergel that Anderson write of his country house; a request by Maxwell Perkins, of Charles Scribner's Sons, that Scribner's become Anderson's publisher and that he write either a novel or a continuous narrative; or the serialization of Gertrude Stein's *The Autobiography of Alice B. Toklas* in *The Atlantic Monthly* from May through August, 1933. Sherwood Anderson's plan was to make "a story of my own experience in the American literary world, people met, what has hurt and what has helped me in my own particular effort to produce beautiful literature here." The work, to be called "I Build My House," would be "a sort of carrying on of *A Story Teller's Story* into a later-day experience, people met, etc."

The house was "Ripshin," built by Anderson in rural Grayson County, Virginia, in 1926–27. "The book," he further explained, "must however be more than the physical house. There is this stone one here might be a symbol—American earth, American men and women met and loved, the house that is a man's self built."

The manuscript of "I Build My House," apparently not all extant, at one time consisted of almost twenty thousand words and indicates Anderson's plan to discuss his friends in New York and New Orleans; the industrialization of his boyhood home town, Clyde, Ohio; his labor in factories; and the building of "Ripshin." There are two valuable sections of the work incorporated in the present book—"I Build My House" and "Meeting Horace Liveright." The project given up, Anderson for two years wrote the social criticism of *Puzzled America* (1935) and a final novel, *Kit Brandon* (1936).

In 1936, Sherwood Anderson again decided to write autobiographically; and again, as with *Tar*, the work was to be third-person narration. On May 26, 1936, Anderson wrote in his diary that he had conceived the idea for a book on "The Good Life," a work, he described the next day, "something like Stein's book but more honest." On June 18, he named the book to Maxwell Perkins as "Rudolph's Book of Days" and explained that it would contain much about the famous people whom he had known:

I would want to write the book without absolute time sequence, partly as history, but most of all as one man's impression of a world of publishers, artists, actors, painters, musicians, sculptors, etc. I think, Perkins, that my life, so looked at, has been a peculiarly rich one in those impressions and contacts. My persistent wandering has taken me all over America. I believe I can make the book big and rich.

For there is also a connection with the radicals, impressions of figures in that world got from contacts too. I would ask you, there at Scribner's, not to reveal that it is so frankly autobiographical. Let them say so if they wish when the book is a fact. It is very rich material, and I am loaded with it.

In preparation for the discussion of celebrities, Anderson made, apparently for this work, a casual list of famous friends. Taking twenty-four sheets, Anderson listed in alphabetical order and by place met the following friends—an astonishing range of acquaintance:

Catalog

A

Anderson, Earl	
Anderson, Irwin	
Anderson John	
Anderson, Karl	
Anderson, Margaret	Chicago
Anderson, Marion	
Antony, Mark	New Orleans

B

Basso, Hamilton	New York
Bazalgette, Leon	Paris
Bentley, Alys	New York
Barry, Griffin	New York
Blair, Mary	New York
Blum, Jerome	Chicago, New York
Bourne, Randolph	New York
Boyd, Ernest	New York
Bromfield, Louis	Paris
Broun, Heywood	New York
[Browne,] Ellen Von Volkenburg	
Browne, Maurice	Chicago, Little Theatre, Fine Arts
Bryant, Louise	New York breakfast

C

Caldwell, Erskine	
Cary, Lucian	Chicago
Church, Ralph	California
Clafflin, Majol	Chicago
Clark, Barrett H.	New York
Commins, Saxe	New York
Cook, George Cram	
With Cook in empty room	
Copenhaver, Laura	
Crowninshield, Frank	New York
Cummings, E. E.	New York

D

Daugherty, George	Chicago
Dean, Harriet	Chicago
Deeter, Jasper	Hedgerow [Theatre]
Dell, Floyd	Chicago

Dos Passos, John	New York
Dreiser, Theodore	St. Luke's Place, New York

E

Eastman, Max	New York
Emerson, John	
Emmett, Burton	
Emmett, Mary Pratt	New York
Esherick, Wharton	Mobile
Ethridge, Mark	

F

Faulkner, Bill	New Orleans
Faÿ, Bernard	Paris
Feibleman, James	New Orleans
Finley, Marietta	Indianapolis
Ficke, Arthur	Chicago
Frank, Jerome	Chicago, Washington
Frank, Waldo	New York
Waldo Frank's house. Walk downtown.	
Freud—Krafft-Ebing	Chicago
Friend, Julius	New Orleans
Fuller, Henry	Chicago

G

Gay, Marguerite	Paris
Galantière, Lewis	Chicago
Gallimarde	New York
Geddes, Norman Bel	New York
Glaspel, Susan	New York
Gold, Michael	New York, San Francisco, New Orleans

H

Hackett, Francis	Chicago
Hansen, Harry	Chicago
Hartley, Marsden	Chicago
Head, Cloyd	Chicago
Heap, Jane	New York
Hecht, Ben	Chicago
Hemingway, Ernest	Chicago
Howard, Sidney	New York
Huebsch, Ben	New York
Huffaker, Lucy	New York

J

Jones, Jeff	New York
Jones, Llewellyn (Susan)	Chicago
Jones, Margaret	Chicago
Jones, Robert Edmund	New York

K

Kahn, Otto H.	New York
Kemp, Harry	New York
Kenton, Edna	Chicago
Komroff, Manuel	New York
Koskull, Baroness Marie Louise	Europe
Kreymborg, Alfred	New York

L

Langner, Lawrence	
Lawson, John Howard	Paris
Lewis, Lloyd	Chicago
Lewisohn, Ludwig	New York, Paris
Light, James	New York. Directed "Triumph."
Liveright, Horace	
Liveright, Otto	
Long, Maurice	Washington
Loos, Anita	New York, New Orleans
Loving, Pierre	New York, New Orleans

M

McBride, Henry	New York
McCall, Jake	Chicago
Macgowan, Kenneth	New York
Mackaye, Percy	Marion
Marin, John	New York
Markham, Kirah	Chicago
Masters, Edgar Lee	Chicago
Millay, Edna St. Vincent	Paris
Millay, Norma	New York
Moore, Cyril	Preston, England
Morris, Mary	New York
Morrow, Marco	Chicago
Mumford, Lewis	New York

N

Nathan, George Jean	New York
Norgeldt, Brör and Margaret	Chicago

O

O'Brien, Edward	New York, Oxford
O'Brien, Frederick	New York, San Francisco
O'Donnall, Pat	New Orleans
O'Neil, Raymond	Paris, Chicago
O'Neill, Eugene	House of, day at house, Sea Island Beach

P

Perkins, Max	New York
Peters, Rollo	New York
Phillips, Miriam	Hedgerow
Pinckney, Josephine	Charleston
Provincetown beginning 1916	

R

Reed, John	New York
Robeson, Paul	New York
Robinson, Boardman	New York
Romili, Rita	New York
Rosenfeld, Paul	New York
Russell, Bertrand	New York

S

Sandburg, Carl	Chicago
Sayler, Oliver M.	New York
Schevill, Ferdinand	Chicago
Scott, Evelyn	New York
Seldes, Gilbert	New York
Sergel, Roger	Pittsburgh, Chicago
Shipman, Evan	New York
Sinclair, Upton	Los Angeles
Smith, Justin	Chicago
Smith, Pop	Chicago
Smith, T. R.	New York
Steele, Wilbur Daniel	Oxford
Stein, Gertrude	Paris
Stettheimer, Ettie	New York
Stewart, Bill	*Today*
Stevens, Covey	Chicago
Stieglitz, Alfred	New York

T

Taggard, Genevieve	New York
Thayer, [Scofield]	Of *Dial*

But the proposed new book—sometimes called "Cousin Rudolph"—begun in great enthusiasm and amazement at the wealth of material, was abandoned in the fall of 1936 when Anderson had written perhaps thirty thousand words. The reason? "I have decided," Anderson sadly recorded, "that I cannot write any more about myself and must devote myself to objective writing." But, fortunately, the writing of autobiography did continue, for, also in 1936, Anderson wrote the short essay "Pastoral" and a new piece on the building of "Ripshin."

Again, in late February, 1937, Sherwood Anderson made a false start on his memoirs. While ill at Corpus Christi, Texas, he began dictating to Eleanor an introductory essay for *Plays, Winesburg and Others* (1937). But instead of adhering to his set task, Anderson began dictating his life story. The resulting fragmentary manuscript of 119 pages, known as "Autobiographical," discusses the writing of *Winesburg, Ohio,* Earl Anderson, business slickness, Stella Anderson, advertising days, and robbery in Chicago.

A genuine start on the memoirs came in May and June, 1937, when

Sherwood Anderson wrote that he had dictated to a secretary a great deal of material. He was enthusiastic about the project, saying, "I have been working on the story of my own adventure in life. . . . I have already done about two hundred typewritten pages and have just begun. I suspect it is a job that is going to take a terrific lot of editing and cutting when I get through dictating, but I am going to plunge ahead with it now and think about that afterward."

One very special result of this effort was "We Little Children of the Arts," written August 29; and the complete writing seems to be what is known as the "Black Notebook," from which the following pieces were made into memoirs: "Rich Living," "Brother Earl," "Woman at Night," "White Spot," "Waldo Frank," and "An Explanation." This time Anderson outlined his project by subject instead of name:

To be Remembered

Ellen in the apple tree, the man stabbed at the dance.
Walks with Earl, his fate, the inability to complete.
Stella and the imagined husbands.
The woman whose man had run away in 39th Street.
The evening by the window. The talks, the bed.
Floyd Dell as talker.
Dreiser at St. Luke's Place.
The rich man who wanted his wife to be operated [on].
The painter's wife, of the flowers, the dirt and the apples.
The divorced woman and the soap ball. The fisherman.
The house at Palos. Mary and the Hearst papers. The artist.
The dirty woman.
The prostitute and the drunken advertising man.
Mama Geigans.
Jasper Deeter's axioms. "If they do evil it is because of softness, weakness. It takes strength to rise to decency in relations."
The woman in the house who continually quarreled with the maid.
The man at the ball game who suggested the story.
The woman who hid in the woods.
The woman with decorated privy.
The two men and a woman (actors) behind the thin wall.
The day with the bee hunter.
The first car, the learning to drive. The filling station man.
Sister Stella.
The man cured of a paralysis.
The woman who read on the closet seat.
Many ways of love making.

How to tell all of life by high spots.
Critic who told a story.
Woman who slept while R[udolph?] made love to her.

In October, 1937, Anderson wrote on Maurice Long; and by November he was revising a long essay on his Spanish-American War experiences, "Pick the Right War," which exists as eighty-five pages of typed, corrected material.

Anderson began in 1938 with the writing of many pieces for his memoirs. Until May, he worked on essays that remain together as an unnamed secondary group of manuscripts. Originally numbering over ninety typed and corrected pages, several parts of the group were rewritten later by Anderson; but some of the episodes are unique and are herein incorporated: "The Sandburg," "Random Notes," *"Perhaps Women,"* "A Mexican Village at Night," "Weeks," "Faulkner and Hemingway," and "Man with a Book."

On April 15, 1938, Anderson wrote of his memoirs to Maxwell Perkins: ". . . just when I will be done with it I don't know. It seems to be such a rich field that although I have written many thousands of words I seem just at the beginning." Unfortunately, Sherwood Anderson then temporarily went back to non-memoirs writing.

The year 1939 was not an active year for memoirs composition although, in April, Anderson reworked "Pastoral" and, in July, finished "Unforgotten," about his father. On November 12, he wrote an essay on meeting Tom Mooney.

Finally, in December, 1939, Sherwood Anderson rededicated himself to the memoirs by declaring: "The idea is really . . . to do an autobiography in a new way, not in the life of the teller but in lives that touch his life . . . much as I used the figure of George Willard in *Winesburg* but carrying the idea into more mature years." Now—with inspiration combined with classic form—Anderson would work steadily on the memoirs. His first effort was, apparently at this time, composing an extensive list of subjects, or "suggestions," which he marked through (items with asterisks) as he wrote of them or found them already composed:

Suggestions

*Slickness.
*Woman with Perry Williams—Grace.
*How George Daugherty lied to his wife.
*Red head in the office.

*Meeting Horace Liveright.
*Ben Hecht and the box factory man.
*John Chamberlain and Boone.
*Mama Geigans.
*Meeting a president . . . the Associated Press.
*American Spectator.
 Conversations with head of ad agency about stealing accounts.
 Party—Ben Hecht and Burton Rascoe.
 Ray Moley.
 Mrs. Walker—the robbery.
*Rich girl. Watch that struck the hour. Street car conductor.
 Jay Fenn. The talent for getting rich.
 Water and women (escape from a women's card party—soliloquy).
 Influence of writers on writers.
 Small business and professional men with tools—trying to be workmen.
 Marriage—only one.
 Taking Eleanor to the room where I wrote *Winesburg, Ohio*.
*How I got to be an advertising man.
 Pick your war.
 Mary Emmett.
 Mrs. Folger.
 Trilena White (death).
 Ferd and Lovett.
 Sandburg. Caldwell and Sandburg. His name. He's got a guitar.
 Alys Bentley.
 Maurice Long.
 The threshing crew.
 Lucile Godchaux and the poet.
 Tom Wolfe and Stark Young.
 Floyd Dell.
 What do I see with my eyes?
*The critic telling the Boone story.
 Waldo Frank.
 Boyhood illness.
 The South.
 Paul Rosenfeld.
 Stieglitz.
 Alfred Maurer.
 The old New Orleans painter. Why.
 Charles Bockler.
 Sandburg's name.
 Jacques Copeau (the robbery).
 Y. K.'s story.
 Building my house.
 I could make movies. (Trip with Mother [Copenhaver] up Scratch Gravel.

Factory closing. Boys and girls by old Ford, woman on porch, old man and woman).
I do not kiss them on the lips.
Lankes.
About letter writing (man who said, "She hasn't got a single letter of mine.").
New Orleans. *The Double Dealer.*
Fairhope. Wharton. Ann Mitchell. Florence King. Carl Zigrosser.
Gertrude Stein.
Roger Sergel.
Lewis Galantière.
Frank Lloyd Wright.
*Why we dislike the English.
Witter Bynner.
Eugene O'Neill.
American Spectator.
Joyce. Ezra Pound.
Working in the livery barn. Men. The drunk.
Ben Huebsch.
Hemingway.
Lewis Institute.
Man cured of paralysis.
In Reno—tarts in the Bull Pen.
Debauch in Paris—after World War I.
Paris with Paul.
I'll bet you a cow.
We were all poor before you came.
Floyd Dell's rehearsal.
Mike Carr and group at 57th Street, Chicago.
About feeders.
Automobile workers (how to make friends and influence people).
Going to the peace conference.
Ginn (the whipping and then the library).
Painter at Stark Young's breakfast.
Jerry Blum.
Good living (pie and cottage cheese; ham, cabbage in wine, etc., eggs).
*The delegation.
Woods and Henry Wallace.

Sherwood Anderson worked hard on his memoirs in 1940, although he did interrupt the work to write a paean to the passing American small town, *Home Town* (1940), and a soon-abandoned novel, "A Mountain Boyhood." Thus, Anderson began January by writing "Italian Poet in America" and pieces unnamed in his diary and letters. From February through May, Anderson wrote non-memoirs material; and then, on June 7, he noted, "In writing you often start one thing and it turns into another. It is happening to me in the present story." In other words, the reminiscent fiction of "A Mountain Boyhood" was inevitably turning into more autobiographical writing.

Thus, on July 1 Anderson wrote "Second Woman," followed by an unnamed piece. He was still on childhood scenes by August 1 when he talked with Stanley Young, of Harcourt, Brace and Company, who had become interested in the memoirs as news of Anderson's project spread. Harcourt, Brace did issue a contract for the book on August 22, and Anderson kept working steadily. For example, "I See Grace Again" came on August 24.

As the author had not immediately signed the issued contract, he was pleased to find that other publishers, including Scribner's, were interested in publishing his book. The encouragement resulted in rapid composition of "Old Mary, the Dogs and Theda Bara" and *"The American Spectator"* in September; "Truly's Little House" and "More about Publishers" in October; and "The Walks in New York" on November 28. Of course, Anderson was frequently completing items that cannot now be named by date. On November 28, 1940, Anderson signed the contract with Harcourt, Brace, having agreed with them that he could sell occasional items to periodicals for interim support. Thus, December was occupied with dictation of memoirs chapters.

Although early 1941 was taken up with Anderson's plans with Eleanor to visit South America as good-will representatives of the United States government, he wrote daily on the autobiography. Finally, when the Andersons sailed on February 28 aboard the *Santa Lucia,* they took the mass of collected memoirs manuscripts, dating back to 1933, with hope of finishing revision and additional writing in about nine months. On the ship Sherwood Anderson made a final outline of his book:

Final Outline

CHILDHOOD . . . Clyde. The family. Childhood sickness. The coming of the Italian workmen. Their customs. Employment. Newsboy. Water boy. Race track. First sex adventure. Being a hobo. The factories coming.

CHICAGO. City fear. Loneliness. Sickness. John Emerson. Wanderings at night. The milliner. The warehouse.

THE WAR.

COLLEGE.

BACK TO CHICAGO. The struggle to take advertising seriously. Taking the job in Cleveland. The prostitute and the money.

ELYRIA. Being a manufacturer. The resort with Perry. The woman met there. The escape.

AGAIN CHICAGO. 57th Street. Adventures in the South. Stealing the accounts. Cass Street. *Winesburg.* Its Reception. Ben Huebsch. *The Little Review. Dial* Prize. Waldo Frank's review. *Seven Arts. Old Masses.*

NEW ORLEANS. *Double Dealer.* Horace Liveright.

BUILDING MY HOUSE.

NEWSPAPER DAYS.

WAR AGAIN.

The outline complete, but the book unfinished, Sherwood Anderson died in the Panama Canal Zone, March 8, 1941.

II

Left with a literary estate to manage and over three thousand pages of confused, often variant memoirs manuscripts—some corrected, some dictated and unread, many uncopied—Eleanor Anderson chose two friends of her late husband, both very close and sympathetic to him for years, to help her edit the autobiography. Roger Sergel, of The Dramatic Publishing Company, read many of the manuscript essays and voted for or against their inclusion in a published volume; but the great part of the editorial work went to Paul Rosenfeld, the music and literary critic, who had known Sherwood Anderson for twenty-five years.

Because there was, in 1941, no really useful biographical or bibliographical study of Sherwood Anderson, Paul Rosenfeld and Eleanor Anderson faced a monumental task in choosing and editing what should be included in this last book written by him. Their aim was to present the memoirs in as complete a version as possible and as soon as possible under the contract to Harcourt, Brace and Company. Thus, Rosenfeld's editorial procedure was to take what he considered outstanding parts of the apparently finished manuscripts and typescripts and to combine these pieces with short published essays, needed for continuity, from as far back as July, 1927 ("New York," *Vanity Fair*) and May, 1930 ("A Man's Mind," *New Republic*).

But Sherwood Anderson was not writing memoirs from 1926 to 1933. Anderson's style in the late 1920's was usually impressionistic, and the later memoirs material is distinguished by Anderson's return to a more conventional narrative line and the *Winesburg* form.

Additionally, Rosenfeld, in *Sherwood Anderson's Memoirs,* published by Harcourt, Brace and Company in April, 1942, felt obliged to reorganize and rewrite Sherwood Anderson's essays. Published material, of course, could not easily be so treated; but most of the memoirs had not appeared as articles. Rosenfeld wished to make of Anderson's flowing, casual sentences and his deliberately nonchronological narration a conventional autobiography. This desire required that Rosenfeld take individual sentences and paragraphs from any location in the perhaps three thousand relevant manuscript pages and combine them in any manner he thought desirable. Moreover, Rosenfeld frequently rewrote *within* Anderson's sentences. For evidence of such rewriting, compare the following passages from Anderson's manuscripts with Paul Rosenfeld's published versions of them. (Note the wording; punctuation is "accidental.")

MANUSCRIPT	ROSENFELD VERSION
The tiny brick house, now gone, was the first of the many houses in which we Andersons had lived that stays clearly in my mind. Father and mother must have lived in several others before we came to Clyde. "Looks as though they had moved whenever the rent came due," my brother Irve once said. I have no notion of where they had married. It may have been in the village of Morning Sun, Ohio. Karl and perhaps my sister Stella were born there.	The first of the many houses in which we Andersons lived that has stayed clearly in my mind was the little brick house, now gone. It was the first in which we lived in Clyde, but father and mother must have lived in several others before we came to the town. "It looks as though they had moved whenever the rent came due," my brother Irwin once said. I have no notion of where my mother and father married. It may have been in the village at Morning Sun, in Ohio, where my older brother Karl was born. Karl and my sister Stella both beat me in the race into the world. When father married my mother he might have been a quite prosperous young man. Mother had been a bound girl, the daughter of a strange old peasant woman who had been married four times, had children by each husband—children that when she got a new man she got bound out by a custom of her time to live as a kind of semi-servant until they grew to manhood and womanhood. Our mother had been bound out to some farming family in the southern part of the state of Ohio, and our father, then
Father might have been a quite prosperous young man there. Mother had been a bound girl and must have been quite lovely. Her picture, as a young and beautiful woman, is before me on my desk as I write.	
And what a life she was to have after the picture was taken, after she stood up before some preacher to make her vows to be a faithful wife to father.	
She was all of that. She was game. Surely she must have known of some of his later surreptitious adventures in the field of love but if she ever complained I at least never heard her complaints so I must leave that phase of her character to the still night hours,	

husband and wife lying together. Married men should know what I mean.

no doubt something of a young dandy, had found her there. She must have been quite lovely. A picture of her, taken at that time, stands on my desk before me as I write.

And what a life she was to lead after the picture was taken, after she had stood up before some preacher to make her vows to be a faithful wife to my father.

She was all of that. She was game. Surely later she must have known of some of my father's surreptitious adventures in the field of love but if she ever complained, I at least never heard her and so I must leave that phase of her character to the still night hours, husband and wife lying together in their bed. Married men should know what I mean.

MANUSCRIPT

The child's life goes on for what seems to him long years in a single street of his town or in his city block. There was the house of the saloon keeper across the street from our house. The saloon keeper, a quiet tall German man, had a young wife. He left his house at daylight and returned late at night. He went silently, with bent head, along the street. There was a picket fence around his house and his wife and their one child were seldom seen. What an isolated life they seemed to lead. The wife of the saloon keeper did not go in and out of the other houses along the street and his one child, a boy of about my own age, seldom came out from behind the picket fence.

Could it have been that the saloon keeper, his wife and child were socially ostracized because of the business in which he engaged? Ours was a northern Ohio town on the edge of the West-

ROSENFELD VERSION

For what seems to him long years, a child's life goes on in a single street of his town or a block of his city. How vividly the streets along which a boy runs or walks are remembered, the houses that border them, the vacant lots between houses, the fields at the edge of town, some small stream that flows past, the streets at night in summer or on a winter night when smoke curls up out of the chimneys of small houses! In our street, it was the house of the saloon keeper that I remember first. The saloon keeper, a quiet tall German man, had a young wife. He left his house at daybreak and returned late at night. He went silently, with bent head, along the street. There was a picket fence at the front of his house and his wife and their one child were seldom seen. What an isolated life they seemed to lead. The wife of the saloon keeper did not go in and out of the

ern Reserve. There was a New England tone to the life of the town.

It was an age of temperance societies and there were two churches on our street. To sell liquor, to run a saloon was to be, I am sure, the devil's servant. Once, filled with curiosity regarding the saloon keeper's son, I ventured across the street to the picket fence before the saloon keeper's house and there was that boy. (He was always very well dressed. He did not go bare-footed. His hair was neatly combed, his face always seemed newly washed and once I heard one of the Moffitt boys, a stone hurler and my brother Karl's friend, call him a "sissy." "He is a sissy, a mother's darling," the Moffitt boy said.) The boy was sitting on the grass in the saloon keeper's yard. He had some colored marbles and was playing with them. I pressed my face into an opening between two of the pickets. "Hello," I called.

other houses in the street, and his one child, a boy of about my own age, seldom came out from behind the picket fence.

Could it have been that the saloon keeper, his wife and child, were socially ostracized because of the business in which he was engaged? It was an age of temperance societies and there were two churches on our street. To sell liquor, to own a saloon, was to be, I am sure, a devil's servant. Once, filled with curiosity, I ventured across the street to the picket fence before the saloon keeper's house and there was his boy child. He was always very well dressed. He did not go bare-footed even in the summer. His hair was neatly combed, his face seemed always newly washed and once I heard one of the Moffatt boys, a stone hurler and my brother Karl's friend, call the saloon keeper's boy a sissy.

"He is a sissy, a mother's darling," the Moffatt boy said.

The boy was sitting on the grass in the saloon keeper's front yard. He had some colored marbles and was playing with them. I pressed my face into an opening between two of the pickets.

"Hello," I said.

MANUSCRIPT

The corn field began just back of the big old frame house. It seemed big to us. They said it was a haunted house, that a certain Mamma Culver rode through the house at night on a ghostly white horse. They spoke of the clanking of chains, of groans and sighs.

We did not hear them, Mamma Culver, astride the white horse, did not come but I have no doubt that, because of her reputed inclinations to take her night rides through the walls

ROSENFELD VERSION

The corn fields began just back of the big old frame house. The house seemed big to us. The neighbors said it was haunted, that a Mamma Culver was occasionally in the habit of riding through it at midnight on a ghostly white horse. She was said to ride right through the door and walls. They spoke of the clanking of chains, of the heavy feet of the white horse on the floors, of groans and sighs. We heard none of this while we lived there. Mamma Cul-

of the house, we got it at a low price.

You went down through the corn field to the town reservoir and to Coon Creek that fed the reservoir. You went through corn fields to the Mamma Culver swimming hole and what things I learned there. It was there I learned to really swear. I found out many things (most of them I'm sure not true) about the town girls.

Young men and boys came. I learned to dive, to swim.

ver astride her white horse did not bother the house but I have no doubt that it was because of her reputed inclination to take these nightly rides through the walls of the house that we Andersons had gotten it at a low price.

You went down through corn fields to the town reservoir and Racoon Creek that fed the town reservoir. You went through corn fields to the Mamma Culver swimming hole . . . and what things I learned there! I learned to really swear. There I found out many things (most of them I am sure not true) about the town girls. Young men and boys came. I learned to swim, to dive.

MANUSCRIPT

I was living, at that time, in an apartment on the ground floor of a North Side building. It was a small apartment with but one bedroom. While I lived there in that place there was a race riot in Chicago. Gangs of young roughs rode through the streets in cars, shooting at negroes. They did not come into my neighborhood but there were several negro men, working about [a] nearby building, I knew.

I gave them the key to my apartment and they slept in there and I remember a night when there were six or eight of them lying on the floor in my little living room. I had come in late. I unlocked the door and went in. There was a small hallway and a negro man stood in the darkness with a club in his hand.

I had a distinguished visitor. The French theatre man, Mr. Jacques Copeau, had brought his company of players to New York. He had, I understood, been sent by Clemenceau. It was for the purpose of French propaganda. The World War was on but we had

ROSENFELD VERSION

Jacques Copeau, then in America with his players of the Vieux Colombier Theatre of Paris, had come to me in Chicago. He wanted to dramatize *Winesburg* and did me the honor to say that the stories were the first full rich expression of something he, a Frenchman, after living among us, had come to feel about American life.

The dramatization didn't come off. There was a little tragedy at my house, or rather at my apartment in Chicago. The apartment was a small one and was on the ground floor of a three story brick building on Division Street on the North Side in Chicago, and Copeau, while he stayed with me, slept in a small bedroom at the back. Like the office of Dr. Reefy in the play, the bedroom looked out on an alleyway and, like the alleyway in my mythical *Winesburg,* the Chicago alleyway was filled with stray cats.

Really to make the situation between myself and my guest in Chicago more clear I should go into a few details. Clemenceau was Copeau's friend and

not yet gone in. The French and the English were hard at it, trying to get us in.

Copeau had come with his company of players. He was a tall distinguished looking man and I thought a good actor and trainer of actors. He was also a maker of plays.

He had been selected to bring the company of French players for a season in New York. The venture was being backed by Mr. Otto Kahn and, during the first season, Copeau had what he and I, later when he spoke of it to me, thought a magnificent salary.

He with his company had the season in New York. I dare say Mr. Kahn got his red ribbon. At any rate, after the first season, the support of Mr. Kahn was withdrawn and Copeau, with the money got from the first season's work, carried the venture on for another year. I was at the theatre once. I saw Molière's *Doctor in Spite of Himself.* I thought it beautiful.

Clemenceau knew also our Mr. Otto Kahn.

He had got our Otto to finance the bringing of Copeau's company to New York. Otto put up the cash. I dare say the idea was to draw Americans closer to the French, to help bring us, as in the end we were brought, into the war. The company was I think to have a year in New York.

The company did play its year in New York and then, as I understood it, Mr. Kahn's financial assistance was withdrawn. Perhaps he had already got his red ribbon. I do not know but I do know that Copeau kept the company going another year. I saw his performance of Molière's *Doctor in Spite of Himself* and thought it beautiful. (What gorgeous players he had with him. I remember a certain portly Russian actress with whom I once dined. What life, what vitality . . . But never mind.)

III

But getting at the book really intended by Sherwood Anderson is now a difficult matter. The goal must be approached carefully, with explanation of each procedure undertaken by the present editor.

Transcription. The Sherwood Anderson Papers, housed at The Newberry Library in Chicago, form a well-catalogued body of many thousands of pages. The memoirs manuscripts and typescripts comprise two huge boxes of material that must be supplemented with items scattered throughout the manuscripts of several hundred individual literary works. The boxed pieces, found unorganized, had to be laid out in roughly chronological and subject-matter order. A survey of the primary pieces revealed that there were roughly three groups of manuscripts: (1) those completed and revised by Sherwood Anderson, (2) notebook pieces, some unrevised at Anderson's death, and (3) a vaguely grouped batch of memoirs and non-memoirs material.

Preliminary surveying showed that Anderson composed his memoirs rapidly, by hand or typewriter, and then rather carefully made copious additions, changes, and deletions. Thus, there are often two versions of an item: (1) holographs and (2) typed drafts with holograph corrections. Occasionally, Anderson completely rewrote items. The goal of transcribing each essay has been always to determine Anderson's latest-written or latest-corrected version.

(It must be emphasized that a "correcting" of the 1942 book was never considered, for a new transcription was necessary at all points.)

A great difficulty in correctly transcribing the memoirs was deciphering Sherwood Anderson's handwriting, but careful practice in mastering this script over several years proved helpful, as did the gracious assistance by Amy Nyholm, devoted curator of The Sherwood Anderson Papers.

A greater problem was choosing between a manuscript or typescript version of an item and the published version, Harcourt, Brace and Company having allowed Anderson to sell occasional essays to various periodicals while finishing his book. But the resolution here was simple: comparing the published with the manuscript versions revealed invariably that Anderson's work was misedited by the magazine personnel involved. Therefore, every word of the present book is taken from manuscripts and typescripts, never from published material.

Identifying for copying the pieces fugitive from the boxed items was aided by a familiarity with the body of The Sherwood Anderson Papers. As the memoirs material was not kept completely unified in 1941–42 and afterward, such important items as "Trumpeter," "Pick the Right War," "Autobiographical," and "We Little Children of the Arts" had to be copied and added to the copied boxed material.

Of course, not all of the boxed pieces could be considered memoirs material, for Anderson was in 1939–40 working on a literary textbook essay for creative writing, "The Writer's Book," and a fourth volume of collected short stories, neither of which he completed. Both of these works tended to be autobiographical, making exclusion from the memoirs a difficult choice. Some of the late autobiographical short stories, which Rosenfeld excluded from the 1942 memoirs, later appeared in *The Sherwood Anderson Reader,* edited (and often rewritten) by Rosenfeld in 1947. "White Spot" is such a piece. But fact and fancy in Sherwood Anderson are inseparable, and any apparent short story that fits into Anderson's memoirs scheme or into the known facts of his life has been incorporated into the present book. However, such an included work as

"Letters, Autographs and First Editions" may very well have been originally intended for "The Writer's Book." Only Sherwood Anderson could know that; so the present editor, in doubt, has included the item, as it was assuredly written in the last years of Sherwood Anderson's life.

The sudden ending of that life prevented Anderson from writing on every topic in his various outlines. For example, many of the people in the "Catalogue" do not appear in the finished essays. One can especially regret that Anderson did not write fully of his first childhood sexual experience; his fascinating friendship with Gertrude Stein; his third wife, Elizabeth Prall, who is never mentioned; or the details of his three trips to Europe. However, the complaint is minor when weighed against the realization that Anderson did write of every major phase of his life and of most of his own books.

When transcription was completed, the perhaps 3,000 pages of material examined yielded approximately 900 transcribed pages of potentially usable text, reduced in further editing to about 750 close-typed pages.

Organization. The preliminary organization of Anderson's manuscript and typescript essays did not obviate a more analytical laying out of the transcribed pieces. The aim here, unlike Paul Rosenfeld's, was not to make a selection of scattered sentences and paragraphs into a conventional, "unified" story but, instead, to present the essays in a form as complete as possible and as Sherwood Anderson wrote them. The organization had to be chronological and close to Anderson's final outline, but the writer's distinctive emphasis on the meaning rather than the facts of his life required that strict chronological order be discounted in favor of Anderson's intended loose structure, which considered each essay complete and separate from contiguous material. Thus, in "Stella," one of Anderson's very last works, his mother's death is established; in "New World," pre-death episodes occur; and in "My Sister Stella," the mother's death is more fully described. Such an approach is not at all foreign to Anderson's usual method of exposition; and it is doubtful that the author himself, had he lived, would have done significant "correcting" of his chronological order.

On more specific points, it must be said that the material available made use of Anderson's final outline for book headings impossible. The present headings, therefore, are the editor's. Furthermore, under the present plan, some of the chapters for the 1920's and 1930's are ambiguous as to correct location. Anderson's discussions of the South and the Negro could come any time after 1920, and the essays on Carl Sandburg and Paul Green could have been placed in the 1930's book. But here the matter of editorial judgment for tone and mood indicated for the pieces a 1920's location. The most difficult decisions of placement involved Anderson's essays on his years in advertising. Because there were three periods (1900–6, 1913–19, 1920–22), order has been established by tone whenever subject matter is unhelpful for determination.

Finally, the present prefatory material is composed of pieces written by Anderson at different times and in different moods. Arrangement of these brief essays, therefore, has been according to progression of thought and mood, revealing the various explanations and tones that Sherwood Anderson assumed for his great final work. Thus, Anderson's short summary of his biography is an invitation to join him in hearing a series of stories, sketches, and thoughts—these, for Sherwood Anderson, being the essence of a full life fully remembered.

Editing. The grand assumption—a false one—among all previous editors of Sherwood Anderson's manuscripts has been that the author knew nothing about the mechanical preparation of his writing for publication. The fact is that Anderson was by no means ignorant of paragraphing, punctuation, and grammar. True, Anderson's spelling was erratic; and the colon, semi-colon, and exclamation point are almost foreign to his script. But Sherwood Anderson knew how to write as he wanted his material read —slowly, carefully, each sentence building itself by progressive relative clauses and separate phrases into a full, often complicated structure and thought. For Anderson, then, the basic form is the comma, used to demarcate his repeating, expanding interruptions of essentially simple sentences. Only occasionally does Anderson become entangled and risk losing the reader among clauses and phrases. When that might happen, the present editor has resorted to parentheses and ellipses as the guides least likely to offend Anderson's fine simplicity of sentence movement.

Because Anderson did compose rapidly and because he never saw several of the memoirs essays in typed form, it has been necessary to add forgotten commas, to insert the most obvious occasionally omitted word, to correct infrequent verb-subject agreement, and to clarify, by punctuation if possible, a very few ambiguous sentences. Anderson's peculiar spelling is herein standardized, except for a few of his "pet" forms—*grey, Mable, practise, south, negro,* etc. Naturally, the paragraphing is Anderson's own.

Such minor problems aside, one faced the difficulty of what to do with the instances of directly repetitious matter. On the larger scale of paragraphs and brief sections, whenever repeated discussion is so exactly redundant as to offend the reader, the least explicit, usually second (and sometimes third) occurrence has been excised. For example, excluding the summary preface, Anderson told twice—in exactly similar terms—of his father's career in "graining" wood. The second episode has been cut. On the other hand, all of Anderson's comments, however variant, on such great matters as the composition of *Winesburg, Ohio* have been included.

On smaller instances of repetition, such as sentences or clauses re-explaining the nickname "Jobby," perhaps eight brief passages are omitted. The original editorial goal remains in effect: to tamper with Sherwood Anderson's words as little as possible.

However, what was to be done about whole episodes or chapters that repeat material? From "Trumpeter" in 1933 to the final essays in 1941, Anderson inevitably repeated material. The solution has been to include always Anderson's latest, most complete versions of his history. However, when two complete essays seem to fit together integrally, without any change, they are combined. Here are the instances of this process: (1) how Anderson came to socialism fits onto the end of "Trumpeter" as the discussion of Earl Anderson from "Autobiographical" fits after the false beginning on Prudence; (2) the rapist soldiers' story fits into "Pick the Right War"; and (3) two pieces each on Theodore Dreiser and Maurice Long combine into single essays on each man.

Finally, only one episode remains herein fragmentary: the manuscript of "New Word" lacks a final page. And only one chapter begins as a fragment: someone (possibly Anderson) has lost or destroyed the opening of "Faulkner and Hemingway" so that the first four words of that essay are editorial emendations.

Annotations. One great fault of the 1942 memoirs is the lack of editorial explanation of references by Sherwood Anderson. That book, of course, was never intended for annotation; but Paul Rosenfeld, having known Anderson personally for a quarter century, could surely have enlightened many still obscure points about the author's life. Perhaps, however, it is good that annotation has awaited both a correct text and the development of a body of biographical and bibliographical knowledge about Sherwood Anderson. The correct text is here provided, and the background documentation is given, *when known,* in order to provide certain categories of information: (1) basic biographical dates and names,

(2) parallel accounts in *A Story Teller's Story, Tar,* and scattered essays, (3) writings on Anderson by literary people whom he names, and (4) guides to biographical, bibliographical, and critical studies of subjects that Anderson discusses.

Space for annotation has been conserved by indicating parallel accounts or illuminating episodes in Anderson's other works by use of a simple *see.* . . . Discussions in the various full-length studies of Anderson (listed in the Bibliography), which are indexed and readily available, are seldom separately listed in notes. However, the invaluable studies of Anderson's youth by William Alfred Sutton are always listed, as are examinations of such subjects as Anderson's ideas on technology, small-town life, creative theory, Walt Whitman, and communism.

Because many aspects of Sherwood Anderson's life, especially his relationships with other writers such as Ernest Hemingway and William Faulkner, are frequently discussed in books and journals, notes attempting to list pertinent discussions have had to be selective. Also, the presentation of copious bibliographical and, sometimes, biographical information has required special grouping and convenient placing of data. The most convenient space for lengthy notes is not always near places of first mention, but requisite data soon appears. The detailed index quickly locates such major discussions and annotations.

Scholarship on Sherwood Anderson's life and works is so extensive that even a scholar completely devoted to the subject cannot "know all there is to know." The present editor can merely annotate information that he has found useful in several years of work. Needless to say, much study remains to be done. For instance, the newspaper literary supplements of the Chicago Renaissance period deserve intensive study and analysis; the continuing lack of a comprehensive biography of Sherwood Anderson is a major handicap to students of American letters; and no one has adequately studied Anderson's contributions (major) to the short story form. Perhaps the present volume will stimulate—as it surely must inform—further original study of these and other critical subjects.

IV

These memoirs, surely not here presented as Sherwood Anderson would have edited them himself but yet most sympathetically edited, deserve final comment.

First, Sherwood Anderson's repeated telling from 1924 to 1941 of certain aspects of his childhood—his rejection of business, his joyous completion of the *Winesburg* stories and his hurt at their original reception, and his absolute delight at finding in the most common lives beautiful stories to tell—should not indicate that the author had only used or limited material available for his final memoirs. Instead, one who compares these memoirs with *A Story Teller's Story* and *Tar* will discover how much more candidly and tenderly Anderson told his life as it neared his death. Surely, there can be few more wonderful tales in literature than Anderson's stories of his doomed sister Stella; the miserable poet Carnevali; the lonely old actress Mary and the dogs in the forest; and his own extended, almost mythic search—in middle life—for meaning in human existence.

Second, as these final memoirs show, Sherwood Anderson found for himself what the wise characters of *Winesburg, Ohio* learned about living. Not the outward form of "greatness" or "success," not display of fame or wealth, makes life "fortunate" at the time of death. Instead, the embracing of smallness, of suffering, of the beauty of the grotesque, of the perennial unhappiness of the creative person—this acceptance makes a good life in the modern world possible, even if that life must forever be lonely and the life's work incomplete at death.

Finally, when the definitive studies of Sherwood Anderson are completed, and when the national literature is judged honestly and well, American letters will find for Sherwood Anderson a place of enduring major importance. Anderson will then be loved and understood; others may learn from him how to write and how to live; but nowhere will Sherwood Anderson stand revealed so monumentally as in these, his memoirs.

Sherwood Anderson's Memoirs:

A Critical Edition

Preface

☙ *If there is any value in the telling,* in this fragmentary way, of my own adventures of living, the thing to be striven for is frankness. I have not begun with babyhood, moved on into childhood, young manhood, etc., not so much wanting to make the picture of the life of a man as of a certain period in American life.

My own interest is people. I have been, during most of my life, a great wanderer, the coming of the automobile being a great help in this, have lived in several states and cities, east and west, north and south, but, in so drifting, I have not sought new scenes. My joy has been in the constant little contacts with people, conversations between others overheard, sometimes sitting for hours in some little saloon in some town, visiting courts, strolling in streets, going, whenever possible, now into the home of some rich man, now to sit in the kitchen with some worker. However I cannot avoid myself. You will find here, in my book, many notes of my own reactions, to men, to women, and when these are told, I shall be trying to tell them also with all the frankness possible to me. I shall try to put down my own hatreds, moments of bitterness, moments of tenderness too. A man should occasionally, it seems to me, arise from among us, strip himself, stand naked before his fellows.

It is a temptation. It is something that, I am sure, must be in the minds of many men. There is this thing called "life." We live it, not as we intend or wish, but as we are driven on by forces outside and inside ourselves. There is something in us, sometimes gay, often malicious, brutal, selfish, at rare moments even tender, really considerate of others.

How wide my acquaintance has been but I have met few enough really tender men, men not seeking to justify their own existences. I think of men like Theodore Dreiser and Eugene O'Neill.[1] They, it seems to me, have succeeded in being, in becoming the thing I mean. I have known others, how many others, having much of it at times, and like all men who go about looking at life have found it most in unknown, unheralded men. I mean that tenderness for others that can come only from freedom from that self-consciousness that plays such havoc with most of us.

1. Whenever Anderson discusses subjects at greater length in the body of this book than in his preface, documentation is provided with the longer discussions.

[3]

To myself, and wanting a better, I use often the word "sweet" in describing these men. There is a kind of warmth, a going out to others in them. I think of the critic Mr. Burton Rascoe, that perfect gentleman and only real sophisticate I have known, Lewis Galantière, of a certain Irish owner of a huge laundry in the city of Washington, a flame of a man, Maurice Long, of Lewis Gannett, George Daugherty and Marco Morrow, of Tommy Smith and Heywood Broun.[2]

But it is foolish to go on with names. There are too many. My own life has been too rich with men admired to be calling them off here as a top sergeant would call the roll of soldiers.

It seems to me that I have been one who has dared to love men and this, for a long time, has kept me from something I have wanted to do—to speak of others, not this time fictitious characters, invented in my own imagination, but of men living in my time, of my own reactions to them (I speak here of men but I mean also women), of what I think they have done to me and of what, perhaps, I have sometimes done to them, to do this as boldly as I can.

For a long time I sought a way to do this and at last an idea came. We writers who, in America, achieve some fame find always that it is very very transitory. It is but natural that the critics, these poor devils who must consume book after book, day after day, year after year, should soon weary of those of us who persist in going on with the production of books. They grow hungry for new names and often (it is certainly understandable), having found the new man, they use him, with a kind of eager abandon, to kill off the old.

Why what funeral orations have for example been preached over me. It has happened to all of us who have persisted in going on. It is the thing that has given me the idea for my book.

"I shall write as one dead," I have told myself. "Perhaps," I have thought, "I shall go on writing on my book until I do die. I will put everyone in it."

And I have had a deliciously malicious thought about this too. My

2. Lewis Stiles Gannett (1891–   ), columnist and literary critic for the *New York Herald Tribune* (1931–56), for which Gannett reviewed Anderson's *Hello Towns!*, May 5, 1929, p. 3; and *Puzzled America,* March 30, 1935, p. 9. In the *Boston Transcript,* Gannett reviewed *Home Town,* October 23, 1940, p. 11.

Heywood Campbell Broun (1888–1939), New York newspaperman. In the *New York Tribune,* Broun reviewed *Poor White,* December 13, 1920, p. 8. In the *New York World,* he wrote of *The Triumph of the Egg,* December 6, 1921, p. 11; *Many Marriages,* February 25, 1923, p. E6; and *Dark Laughter,* September 20, 1925.

thought has been that I would spread the word about. "This is what I am doing. Look out for me."

"Is it possible," I have asked myself, "that, the word getting about, there will be a kind of fear awakened?

"Aha! I shall be treated with a new respect. Men will begin inviting me to dine about. They may even give me gifts."

The above for the more malicious side of my nature. We are all bearers of poison. You cannot come into the room where I sit without bringing me something. Sometimes you will bring me health, sometimes poison. I am like you in that respect.

I feel that I am writing out of a full life. I am a rich man, rich in men known, in adventures had. I am rich with living. I remember that Mr. Mark Twain, when he arrived at the age of seventy, made an announcement. He declared himself free of all obligations. "I have done what I could do. Now I will sit in a chair in the sun." It was something of that sort he said and I am also saying it. I shall, in my book, be malicious when I am in that mood. I shall try not to be kind, strive only to be frank.

For myself I would say this, that it seems to me that I have, all my life, been seeking. I am still seeking and what I seek is men. I was recently with a woman who asked me a question. We were with a party of other men and women and she took me aside. She was one who thought I had accomplished. It may be she was pulling my leg. She said that, in spite of the fame I had got, that, being with the others of that place (They were men and women. They ate, slept, made love, lied, cheated, were sometimes honest as I was.)—that I had not seemed to feel superior to them.

Was it true that I did not feel so? she asked.

"No," I replied. I would, of course, have said the same had I been the most egotistical man in the world.

I wanted to explain something to the woman but I couldn't. It would have taken too long. It may be that it can't be explained.

It is not a question of feeling either superior or inferior.

I was in Mexico and there I saw a dance, performed by the Indians, a religious dance. I had read D. H. Lawrence, his book *The Plumed Serpent*.[3] In it there was much said of a kind of pressing and pressing, through the feet of the dancers, down, down, down into earth. In the mind of Lawrence it seemed that the Indians, in so dancing, sought again, through

3. London: Secker, 1926; New York: Knopf, 1926.

the dance, to return, to press themselves down, into earth, into the dark mother, into a blood unity with earth.

I saw the dancers and I thought that what they wanted I did not want. I was a modern. I did not seek a return but I thought that I also, in dance or words, through a long and sometimes patient inner struggle, by also pressing and pressing, to press also myself down, not into earth but into body and spirit of men, my fellows. I have sought the artist's ruthlessness, not to hurt, to torture, but to find, to discover. I have been that, an explorer.

The blood of the pioneers has been in me but I have sought not land, not new possessions, but new roads, into men, into women.

It has been my purpose. It is for this my pen, my pencil, the keys of my typewriter have danced. If I can find them, the men and women of my land, of my time, I shall not too much mind if, occasionally, as I write, as the words dance in me, I find that, in finding, I am destroying myself.

A Dedication
and an Explanation

I am reluctant to discuss my marriages. I have had four of them. When my present wife proposed marrying me a friend asked, "Well, how do you think you will like being the seventh wife of our Henry the Eighth?"

I do not believe I can write of my own marriages, being fair to both myself and the women involved. Once I was talking of this matter to Frank Crowninshield.[4] I was in a bitter mood.

"What is the matter with me, Frank?"

"Men of your sort cannot be held down," he said. He put an arm about my shoulders.

"Such fellows as you are often wrong headed. The demands you make of life are, you know, rather terrific.

"Most men finally accept the harness life puts on them. You fellows cannot. You would die if you did.

"I'll say this for you," he added. "You do take life seriously. You believe in it. Many men come to the place where they take women merely as physical facts. Intimate contact with them is a physical necessity but it is that and nothing more.

"Fellows like yourself demand more. You keep demanding this strange thing we call 'love.' When it dies out you go. You spend your life searching for it."

My first three marriages each lasted exactly five years.[5] I have always been pretty sure that none of the women were to blame when our marriage failed. Such a man as myself, any practitioner of the arts, is a beast to live with.

We are never the same. We go away, often, for months at a time.

Well, we are there physically. We are in a house, or in a street, but we are at the same time far away.

One of us is, for example, writing a novel. For months he will be off

4. Francis Welch Crowninshield (1872–1947), editor of *Vanity Fair* (1914–35) and other Condé Nast periodicals.

5. Anderson's marriages were to Cornelia Lane (1904–16), Tennessee Mitchell (1916–24), Elizabeth Prall (1924–32) and Eleanor Copenhaver (1933–   ). This dedication is to Eleanor Copenhaver Anderson.

away from the place immediately about. Inside himself he is living another life, often having nothing to do with the people with whom he is living his own physical life. Speak to him and he will answer you but he does not really hear. You make an engagement with him. You are to meet him on a certain day, at a certain hour, in a restaurant or at a theatre. Do you think he will be there? Very likely he will not. When you made the engagement with him your words did not register on his mind. He heard but did not hear.

It was because he was not there. When you spoke to him he seemed to be sitting at his desk in a room in the house where you lived with him but in reality he was in the captain's cabin of a ship far out in the Pacific.

There was something tense going on in the cabin of the boat. There were two men and a woman in the little room. There had been a storm and the ship, a small one, had been disabled. It was drifting.

The captain of the ship, an old man, had a young wife and the mate wanted her and she had fallen in love with the mate.

The two men and the woman are having it out, there in the cabin. You see, the ship is leaking and will soon go down. It is a question of taking to boats, the boats perhaps drifting far apart.

Is the woman to go in the boat commanded by the captain or in that commanded by the mate, the man she loves?

The whole matter is to be settled now in a few minutes. It may well be that before they leave the cabin where they now sit facing each other one of the two men will be killed.

See how the woman standing there by the door, trembling, how white she is.

So . . . as the writer is watching all this, a fourth, unseen figure in the little ship's cabin, his wife comes to him. She wants to make an engagement. There is something she wants him to do for her.

"Sure. All right. Certainly I will."

Why, he did not hear her at all. Her words were blown away by a wind. They did not register on his mind.

"Why, who was this who came into the room? My wife? What is a wife? Did I marry someone? Where? When?"

It is dreadful to live with such a man. It is only possible . . . only a saint could do it.

Why, there are months and months when you are merely dust under his feet. For him you have no existence. As well, during such times, be married to one of the dummies in a store window.

Almost all of my own friends, men of the theatre, painters, musicians, have, in this matter of marriage, had the same experience I have had. They have tried and failed, tried and failed. Some of them, upon the break up of a marriage, have grown bitter. They write novels, making the woman the central character. They grow bitter and ugly about it all.

How absurd. When one of us makes a failure of marriage it is, almost inevitably, his own fault. He is what he is. He should not blame the woman.

The modern woman will not be kicked aside so. She wants children. She wants a certain security, for herself and for her children, but we fellows do not understand the impulse toward security. When we are secure we are dead. There is nothing secure in our world, out there, and as for the matter of children we are always having children of our own.

For example, someone is always asking me which one of my own stories I like best, which of all the characters I have put into books and stories I like best, and I have a pat answer for them.

"Go ask some mother who has had several children which one of them she likes best," I answer.

It is a changing shifting world, this world of the imagination in which we who work in any of the arts must live so much of our lives. We have it and then we have it not. Oh, the blank days, the black despair that sometimes descends upon us.

We grow irritable. Speak to one of us at such a time and you will probably get a sharp answer. Trust us and we may betray your trust.

No. Do not ask me to write of the women with whom I have lived in marriage. I respect them too much to do it. That I have found a woman, who, after ten years with me, can still laugh at me, who understands my wrinkles, who is there beside me, smilingly willing to forgive my idiosyncrasies, who after seeing through the years we have lived together my worst and my best, is my good fortune.

Wasn't it Napoleon who said that he would prefer to have, as one of his generals, a lucky rather than an able man?

Well I am one of the lucky ones. Good luck has always been with me. I dedicate this book to my wife.

Foreword

When I read stories of the lives of genuine great men, how they have struggled and suffered, from Abelard to Thomas Mann, Keats and Anton Chekhov in their loving and fight against disease, de Maupassant and van Gogh struggling against insanity, Herbert Spencer against poverty, Charles Darwin on his trip to the tropics in the ship *Beagle* to his long months of horrible illness, his determination and perseverance, John Brown in the insane stroke for justice to American negroes, at Harpers Ferry, Abraham Lincoln in the White House during the four terrible years of our Civil War, Dostoevski in the hour when he stood facing a firing squad and during his years in a Siberian prison camp—these men and many others in the long story of man, of his seemingly insane devotion to some art, science or idea of justice—and then look back on my own small efforts as an American story teller I have to sum up the story of my own life as a most fortunate one.

Not that I put myself among these heroic ones. I certainly do not. There will be little enough of the heroic in my story. I have enough sense too in spite of my egotism to know that I am but a minor figure among the world's artists, but when a man comes to the point of rather summing up as I am doing here and as almost all writing men eventually do, looking not forward but backward on events and people that have closely touched my own life, I am compelled to exclaim, "Oh thou fortunate one."

Fortunate to have been born an American in what may well turn out to be America's happiest period, to have been born poor and in a small town, when community life was intimate and close, to have had to work as a laborer both in factories and on farms, to have known thus from whence comes the food that has nourished my body and with what toil it is produced, to have had the mother and the always picturesque father I had, fortunate in my brothers, on the whole in my loves with women, in having been born with a talent, in friends I have made, even in my enemies.

But wait. Where are my enemies? Have I any? If I am anywhere hated perhaps I am too great an egotist to know it.

Once, when we were both young men in Chicago, Ben Hecht [6] and I were speaking of this matter.

6. Ben Hecht (1894–1964), journalist for the *Chicago News* (1911–23), who wrote of Anderson in the *Chicago Evening Post,* September 8, 1916, p. 11; "Go

"Yes, you are fortunate. You will always be a lucky man," he said. He suggested that, if I were to fall into a river, I wouldn't get wet.

"It is because of your profound egotism. It is colossal. When you are snubbed you do not know it. When someone condemns your work you simply put him down as a fool. Some of us go through terrible times of doubt that we have talent but you never do. You are one who will sail blithely through life, often doing terrible things to others without at all knowing what you are doing. Friends will stand by you. When you are pressed someone will always come to your rescue. You will always be loved more than you deserve, befriended more than you deserve. It is all because of your egotism. Why man, your egotism is so colossal that you will always be going about wearing an air of modesty and even of humility. You will even believe you are humble. Lord God, man, but you are a lucky one."

I am no doubt not quoting Ben exactly. He was always a flowery talker. I am however putting down the substance of what he said to me one night as we sat over glasses of beer in a Chicago restaurant and I have often wondered since if what Ben said was true.

I do not know. I have actually had my dark times; if I am such an egotist as Ben suggested and I must be, or why else sit down to write my memoirs, I pray God that I am in no sense also a snob.

But what is snobbishness but uncertainty? Surely the snob is but one who is afraid he is not as worthy as people think him.

And what is this egotism? If a man did not place great value upon his own life how could he be trusted in the lives of others? Isn't it just by placing great value on your own life that all life becomes important to you?

I have always, from the beginning, been a rather foxy man, with a foxiness at times approaching slickness. If you ever by chance get into a horse trade with me be a little careful. Once I had a secretary who worked with me for several years. She was about to get married. She came to say good-bye. There was a little smile playing about the corner of her mouth. She was at the door of the room in which we had long worked together.

Scholar-Gypsy!" *Story,* XIX (September–October, 1941), 92–93; *A Child of the Century* (New York: Simon and Schuster, 1954), pp. 225–32; and *Letters from Bohemia* (Garden City: Doubleday and Company, 1964), pp. 85–103. For Anderson's comments on Hecht, see *A Story Teller's Story: A Critical Text,* edited by Ray Lewis White (Cleveland: Press of Case Western Reserve University, 1968), pp. 187–88, 252; all references will be to this 1968 edition.

She stood hesitating at the door. This was when I was still half a man of business. I had been writing stories for several years, had already won some literary fame, but what fame I had was purely literary. It had brought me in, as yet, little or no money.

I was at that time very strong, could devote a certain number of hours daily to the business of advertising writing and the rest of the day and often most of the night to my literary efforts. Often, for several days at a stretch, when the writing mood had gripped me, I did not bother to sleep but I was not tired. This sort of fundamental good health that has stayed by me in spite of a good deal of abuse of my body, occasional periods of dissipation, excessive smoking always since boyhood, is but another sign that I was born under a lucky star. I had rented an office in an old building on a side street in the business district of Chicago and went there every afternoon and often at night to write. I have never developed any skill on a typewriter and, besides, when I become absorbed in writing there is always a queer internal excitement that leads me to press the keys of a typewriter too vigorously. God knows what I would do to a machine if I were ever to write a mystery or a murder story. As it is I wreck every machine I get.

And besides I like the smell of ink. I like the physical feeling of the words flowing out of a pen on the paper.

So I had engaged this woman. As no one can read my scrawl I dictated my letters and my correspondence to her from the written sheets. I dictated my stories and also my correspondence with clients of the advertising place and with publishers.

The woman was leaving me to become a wife. She stood at the door smiling. There was a wicked twinkle in her very nice eyes. She spoke with a certain hesitance.

"Mr. Anderson."

"Yes?"

"I have been working for you for nearly three years."

"Yes. It has been very nice."

"There is something I would like to say."

"Well, what the devil? What is coming?" I had begun to ask myself.

"There is something I have been wanting to say but I hardly know how to say it."

"Why go ahead, go ahead. Don't be afraid, my child."

Why look. The glance of her eyes has become very wicked.

"You will remember, Mr. Anderson, that you employed me out of a business office. You call me a child but I am past thirty. Formerly we were both employed in the same advertising office. I happen to know what you did to them."

Well, what in the devil is she driving at now?

"You got the leisure you now enjoy for your writing by stealing certain accounts from the agency. You worked your way into the confidence of these clients. You got them to sign an agreement to do their business only through you. Then you went to the president of the company. You put a gun to his head.

" 'You will do business with these clients in my way or not at all.' "

"Well!"

"I just wanted to say . . . I do not in the least blame you for what you did. There is an old saying that business is business. It is quite true. It is a sharks' game."

"Well, yes, and . . . ?"

"You see, since I have been with you . . . you know how many letters I have taken for you . . . to your clients, to your friends. I wanted to say, before I left you. . . . You see, you have continually been saying to these men with whom you do business . . . you say, 'I am no business man.' You are always playing the innocent. You put on an act of innocence. You make yourself appear naïve.

"Good God, man, don't keep it up until you believe it yourself."

She opened the door. She left me. She entered into the sacred bonds of matrimony. I thought she would probably do all right as a wife.

Slickness. It is the curse of the world, this slickness. It is in too many of our diplomats, our statesmen, governors, politicians, business is lousy with it. It invades the world of art, is in families, in groups of so-called "friends," it is everywhere.

"How can I use this man or woman? What can I make this one do for me?"

We do it under the cloak of friendship. You do it and I do it. It is a disease. When I was a small boy I heard it on all sides.

"Go it, boy. Be on the alert. Watch your chance, then push forward."

"On, onward and upward, over the shoulders of others, trample them down."

It has grown stronger, the cry, since the First World War. How could it be different? How can any man value life, after being in a modern war? Why lives are thrown away like worn out shoes. Killing becomes something glorified. Is it any wonder that so much of present day writing, of story telling, is concerned with death? Death in the morning, death at night, death to animals, death to men, death in poetry, death in prose.

But here is life, these streets, these lives that touch our lives, lives everywhere, new life always pushing up out of the wombs of women. Is it death we want?

No.

The hunger for life, the hunger for the affection that gives life, is the oldest and strongest hunger in the world.

"Life is a game. Be slick. Be foxy. Out with the other fellow. Be on the alert. Be quick on the uptake. When you see your chance, pounce."

You see, all of this is very close to me. I was an American small town boy, in a financially ruined family. I was strong, had a strong young body, was full of energy. Oh how I wanted the admiration and affection of people. I hungered and thirsted for admiration and affection. I was a boy and young man in a critical time in American life. Almost I can say that our modern industrial age, this so-called "machine age," has flowered and come into full fruit in my time.

Do you like the fruit? How does it taste to your mouth?

I had an alert, alive young mind, an alert and alive young body.

They said it to me. Everyone said it to me.

"Go it, boy! Wait your chance. Pounce."

I listened to them. I left the little town in which I had spent my boyhood and went away to the city, to Chicago.

At first things did not go well with me there. I was a common laborer, handling goods in a huge warehouse. I was lost in the mass of men, of common laboring men in the city. The work in the warehouse was too heavy for my young body. The men with whom I worked swore at me. They were all heavy, hard muscled, mature men. When I grew so weary that I fell under the heavy packages we handled they laughed at me.

"Ha! He bushed out. The kid's bushed out."

Among the intellectuals, with whom I was later to associate and most of whom had never lived the life of a common laborer, there was always a good deal of nonsense being talked. The laborer is also human, he can be decent and friendly and he can also be needlessly mean and cruel. Being poor and unsuccessful does not necessarily imply nobility.

I was so weary at night that I could not keep my grip on the rail of a street car filled with workmen going to their homes after the day's work. It was an icy cold night and my hands were nearly frozen. I was pushed off the car into the street. I hurt my hip and had to stay in bed for a month. At that time my sister and two younger brothers lived with me. The wages stopped.

There was a boy from my own Ohio town who had come to the city. It was John Emerson,[7] who years later became a well known figure in the American theatre and the first president of the actors' equity society. He was a clerk there in a Chicago warehouse and, during my illness, he came every week end and divided his weekly wages with me. I have always found such friends. Life has been a glorious adventure for me.

Do not be too cocksure that this one is hard as steel or mean or cruel. Why are you given a brain? Believe in some of the others and you will be surprised at how many will begin to believe in you. Is it preaching? All right. It is something learned the hard way.

"Education is the thing," I began to tell myself. I decided to go to night school, went night after night to a place called Lewis Institute in Chicago's West Side. I went into the warm room. The book was before me but I fell forward on my desk and slept. I was so weary I couldn't keep my eyes open.

The Spanish War came and I hurried home to enlist. Why look at this, I was proclaimed in my town a young hero. I had given up a job in the city to hurry to my country's defense.

I knew it was nonsense but what did I do? I was making life more difficult for my brothers and sisters by going away to war (there were ten times more young men ready to go than could be taken), but they wanted to glorify me and I let them. It was, for me, a chance to, at least for a time, escape from the trap in which I was caught and I looked about.

"When you see your chance, pounce. Never mind your brothers and sisters. Now and then a fellow has to look out for himself."

"Life is a game." It was becoming my watchword. The going into the war would give me a breathing spell, a chance to look about. Something might turn up.

Can a man love an abstract thing called "his country"? Lately I have begun to wonder about that. It seems to me that everything in life has to

7. John Emerson was born "Clifton Paden" at Sandusky, Ohio, May 29, 1874. He left Clyde, Ohio, in 1893 and became a motion picture producer (1914–22) for D. W. Griffith, Douglas Fairbanks, Mary Pickford, Constance Talmadge, and Paramount. Emerson died in 1956. See *A Story Teller's Story,* ed. White, pp. 22, 266; and *Letters of Sherwood Anderson,* edited by Howard Mumford Jones and Walter B. Rideout (Boston: Little, Brown and Company, 1953), Items 43, 110, 301, and 340.

begin small, that the disease of modern life is in big loose thinking. I should begin in this house in which I live, in this street in which the house stands. If I can begin a little to understand the life in others in this house, a little the lives of others in other houses in this street, the rest after that, if it is possible. . . . Let's not spread things too far, too thin.

Why I dare say our youngsters did, in a way, believe in the war cause of that Spanish War—*"Cuba Libre."*

Indeed?

How were we to know of all the slick things probably going on up there, at the top, our country taking the road to imperialism, world power, all that?

"A nice little war."

"Walk softly and carry a big stick," cried our Teddy.[8]

We see Mr. Hitler doing it now, as I sit writing these notes.

But let's pass all of that big thinking, eh? As for the war and my own part of it I hope to tell some stories of that in my book. I came home from it, safe and sound of limb and, as Walter Winchell[9] would say, "Flash" —I was in business.

I had become an advertising man and, boy, you have something there. Someone had discovered in me a certain faculty for words, at stringing words together, sometimes making them dance, march, shout, even scream in print.

"Now, be foxy, boy. Be slick. You are here among a lot of smooth ones. Here's your chance to get up a little in the world."

To be sure it wasn't all true, not by half, not by a quarter. They were just men, for the most part as puzzled and lost as I was. They were in the grip of something, the tone, the temper of an age perhaps. I was there among them for a long time.

I had got finally into business for myself, was earning a fortune. I became a promoter, organized companies, sold stock in my companies. I even established and ran for a time a little magazine of my own, writing it all. It was devoted to the pushing of my schemes.

And for a time I prospered. There I was, a bright young American business man on the make. I was growing slicker and slicker.

"It is by slickness you get there. Look at the big boys, what slick tricks they have pulled."

8. Theodore Roosevelt (1858–1919), soldier and president (1901–9). "Speak softly and carry a big stick" was Roosevelt's slogan for foreign relations.
9. Walter Winchell (1897–   ), theatrical and social gossip columnist.

It was a time in America of the glorification of the business adventurer. Our magazines were filled with articles about these men, for the most part glorifying them.

"If a man steals ten dollars put the piker in jail. If he steals a million or ten million call him 'captain.' "

That was pretty much the tone.

I had begun to get along. For a time things seemed to be opening up for me.

"Sure, I am but a little piker but I am growing."

I could go into banks, talk bankers into loaning me money. I had begun to see how money could be put to work to earn more money.

Then a curious sickness came. I had always been a passionate reader. It may be that I began to get, through my reading of the words of great men, a new conception of what a man's life might be.

I became unhappy and disturbed. There came a time of dissipation. I left the town where my factory was located and went off to some distant city. I drank. I got in with women who drank with me. I went with them to dance halls, got drunk with them. Sometimes such periods of dissipation lasted for a week end.

I remember a night in Cleveland when I wandered into a bar, connected with a small cheap hotel. We all drank together and afterward they took me to the theatre to sit in the wings, so that we could drink together later, but I wandered out upon the stage during the performance and was thrown out into an alleyway and wandered off, my clothes covered with mud.

I came back again to my business and plunged into work, was again the bright young business man. The effort to get something out of life through dissipation had proven a failure.

"Well, what is the matter with me? Am I not in the pattern of the ideal American man?"

I speak of all this to explain a little how I happened to become a writer.

There was this slickness, continual lying. Now I belonged to the local country club, played golf. There was a local literary club and I joined. We went there, sat about. Someone read a paper on some great literary figure.

Then long walks alone at night and presently in the daytime. I was at my office less and less. I had begun to neglect my business.

"What's the matter with you, man? Why this continual feeling of dirt?"

I have often wondered since how many of our successful Americans go through such periods, questioning, questioning, questioning.

How do they quiet these voices? That's what muzzles are.

All of this but to lead up to something that happened. I made a discovery.

I had a friend in the town who ran the local newspaper and one day I was in his shop talking to a workman.

"How do you like your job? Does it satisfy you?"

I had begun asking that question of every man I met.

"How do you like your job? Does it satisfy you?"

"Yes. It does."

"But why?"

The workman, an old man, looked at me and smiled. He was chewing tobacco and ran to spit in a sawdust filled box that stood over his printer's make up stone.

"It's there," he said, pointing. "When you make up a printed page there it is.

"If you live to cheat, if you make mistakes, if you do a slipshod job there it is, on the printed page, staring at you."

Why there was something I understood. It set me thinking. I had been trying to quiet my own thoughts by reading books. I kept buying books. Often when my thoughts would not let me sleep I read all night. There was a little room, in the loft of the house in which I lived, and I had made it my own private room.

I had filled it with books. I locked the door and kept the key in my pocket. I did not let my wife in there. The children did not come into the room.

I went into the room and locked the door. I walked up and down, up and down. I kept thinking of what the old printer had said.

And then one night I began to write. I wrote a little tale of something seen, or felt, something remembered out of my own experience of people.

The writing did something to me. Well, no doubt the tale I wrote that night was badly told. I can't remember.

What I do remember was a new feeling that came. In the act of writing the little tale about some other being I had for the time escaped from myself, had found something that gave me a new sense of reality, something I could not get from drinking, from going about with loose women.

I became an enthusiast. Now when I walked about in the streets of my town alone all night I kept stopping before houses.

"What is going on in that house?"

I had a passion to tear away the walls of houses. I wanted suddenly to overhear private conversations between people in their houses and there was one night when I crept through bushes to the open window of a private house.

There were a man and woman talking as they lay in bed. I crept close to the window.

I crouched there but I could not hear clearly.

I began to crawl away and then I stumbled and fell. It was very ludicrous. I fell through a bush and made a loud noise and the man in the house sprang out of his bed.

Of course I ran. I ran crashing through bushes. I jumped over a fence. Ye gods, there I was, at least in the minds of the people of the town a responsible citizen, a manufacturer, member of the country club and the local Elks Club, a supposedly well-to-do, fairly respectable man, become a Jack-the-Ripper.

They didn't catch me, didn't recognize me but I had to give that up. "You will have to be more subtle. Look and listen," I told myself. Now I had got a new passion. I wanted constantly to see more, hear more, smell, taste, feel more.

I kept writing little tales of people. I put them through experiences I had myself been through and suddenly there came a new revelation.

It was this—that it is only by thinking hard of others that you can find out anything at all of self.

Man cannot think clearly of self, cannot see himself, except through others. The self you seek, the true self you want at last to face, is hidden away.

It is in the man you just met in the street. It is in the eyes of a child. It is in a tired old woman, in a thief, it is everywhere in others.

What a discovery. Hurrah. Now I became a passionate writer. As for the business in which I was engaged I have told in another place, in *A Story Teller's Story*,[10] how one day I walked away from there, letting the others think I had become temporarily insane.

But that was only my old slickness, putting that over on them.

For to them, to those close to me at that time, it might all have seemed insane.

For what was this writing, writing, writing, thousands of pages thrown off, discarded, myself locked in the little room of my house, after writing all night, my business now quite neglected? I was not the sort of man who became a writer. I was, in every accepted sense, uneducated. I spelled badly, could not punctuate a sentence.

10. New York: B. W. Huebsch, 1924. See pp. 96–99, 215–36, in 1968 edition, ed. White.

"It is insanity. He has become insane."

"Well heavens. At last something in which I can live, still can be free, see a way of life.

"A challenge, an eternal challenge," the words of the old printer ringing in my ears.

"You put the words down and there they are.

"You print the tale you tell and there it is.

"To do perfectly the job you have now tackled would take many lifetimes but what does that matter?

"There are these shades of things to be caught, a little the stories of lives to be put down, the eternal challenge, something by which you can live."

My luck had held. I had found work at which I could keep busy all my days. Whether I ever succeeded in curing myself of the slickness I so hated in myself at last I had found a way in which it could be cured.

II

It is very difficult for me to write down facts concerning my own life. It is because I am by nature a story teller. No one ever taught me. Like such men as Erskine Caldwell, Ring Lardner [11] and other men I've known I'm a natural.

Facts elude me. I cannot remember dates. When I try to deal in facts at once I begin to lie.

I can't help it.

Once, many years ago, I sat down to write the story of my own boyhood in a middle western town.[12] I couldn't do it.

When, for example, I wrote of my own father and mother I depicted people my brothers and my sister could not recognize.

"Anyway," I said to myself, "I have made a picture of my father and mother." They were my father and mother as I felt them.

To me there is a certain music to all good prose writing. There is tone and color in words as in notes of music. When writing of another person I have always found it best to do it in my own way.

---

11. Erskine Preston Caldwell (1903–   ), sensationalist novelist of the South, famous for *Tobacco Road* (1932) and *God's Little Acre* (1933). Ringgold Wilmer Lardner (1885–1933), humorist and short story writer, discussed by Anderson in "Four American Impressions," *New Republic*, XXXII (October 11, 1922), 171–73; and "Meeting Ring Lardner," *New Yorker*, IX (November 25, 1933), 36, 38.

12. *Tar: A Midwest Childhood* (New York: Boni and Liveright, 1926). See David D. Anderson, "Emerging Awareness in Sherwood Anderson's 'Tar,'" *Ohioana*, IV (Summer, 1961), 40–42, 51.

The person also has a certain tone, a certain color. What care I for the person's age, the color of their hair, the length of their legs?

I tried to write of my own boyhood but couldn't do it so I invented a figure I called George Willard and about his figure I built a series of stories and sketches called *Winesburg, Ohio*.[13]

Later I found that there was an actual Winesburg, Ohio, but, when I gave the title to the book, I didn't know that.

I looked in a book that gave a list of Ohio towns but found no Winesburg. Perhaps the book only gave the names of towns on railroads. I am told no railroad goes to the real Winesburg.

The point is that I firmly believe that anyone reading that book is bound to have a rather sharp impression of my own youth, of what I saw and felt in the people about me.

That particular book did not sell. It was widely condemned, called "nasty" and "dirty" by most of the critics. The book was more than two years selling the first five thousand.

How strange to think that when published it was called nasty and dirty. I had felt so clean while writing it. The condemnation of the book as nasty and dirty made me ill. For a long time I went about with my head hanging.

So many people were calling me a man with a nasty mind that they almost convinced me. Pick up the book now and you will wonder what the critics were talking about.

The book has become a kind of American classic. It is used as a textbook for story tellers in many schools and colleges. Really the stories might almost be published now in the *Ladies' Home Journal*.

Many other writers are responsible for the change. We have all got a new freedom, a new license to look more directly at life.

I think the new freedom, here in America, has added immeasurably to our American health.

Many curious things happened to me in connection with that book. I had already, when I wrote it, published two novels and a book of verse.

I was in Chicago, working out there in an advertising agency, when I wrote the stories in the book. I took the stories to Mr. Floyd Dell.[14]

---

13. New York: B. W. Huebsch, 1919; all references will be to the corrected edition by Malcolm Cowley (New York: Viking Press, 1960).

14. Floyd Dell (1887–   ), novelist and journalist, left Chicago for New York in 1913. See his "Sherwood Anderson: His First Novel," *Looking at Life* (New York: Knopf, 1924), pp. 79–84; *Homecoming* (New York: Farrar and Rinehart, 1933), pp. 236–37; his review of the Anderson *Memoirs, New York Herald Tribune Books*, April 12, 1942, pp. 1–2; and "On Being Sherwood Anderson's Literary Father," *Newberry*

Floyd had been, up to that time, more or less my literary father. He had been very kind. He had taken my first novel to a publisher. He had written about my work in the *Chicago Evening Post*.

The *Post* was, at that time, the leading literary mouthpiece of the middle west. Every Friday they got out a special literary supplement. Francis Hackett had been his editor but when he went to the newly established *New Republic* Floyd got his job.[15]

He wrote praising me as a writer. He went to no end of trouble to get my novels published. I think it must have been Floyd who got Theodore Dreiser interested and Dreiser said the word that began to get my scribbling into print.

And then Floyd saw my *Winesburg* stories and condemned them.

"They are not stories," he said. "They are no good."

I am afraid I was rude to Floyd. A man gets arrogant at times. He boasts.

"Listen, man," I said. "If a passenger train comes in at a railroad station, stops for passengers, and then, after a time, goes on its way and you are not there to get aboard the train do not blame the engineer."

It was very rude of me. It was a necessary statement on my part. I felt I had to make it.

Mr. Henry Mencken, then, with George Nathan, an editor of the old *Smart Set*,[16] saw some of the stories and his reactions at that time were much the same as Dell's.

Library Bulletin, V (December, 1961), 315–21. For Anderson's comments, see *A Story Teller's Story*, ed. White, pp. 265–66, 297. On the Dell-Anderson relationship, see G. Thomas Tanselle, "Realist or Dreamer: Letters of Sherwood Anderson and Floyd Dell," *Modern Language Review*, LVIII (October, 1963), 532–37. Dell reviewed *Windy McPherson's Son* in *Masses*, IX (November, 1916), 17; and *Winesburg, Ohio* in *Liberator*, XX (September, 1919), 46–47.

15. Francis Hackett (1883–1962), literary editor of the *Chicago Evening Post* (1906–11) and associate editor of *The New Republic* (1914–22), collected his essays on Anderson in *Horizons* (New York: B. W. Huebsch, 1918), pp. 50–61. Hackett's review of *Marching Men* in *New Republic*, XII (September 29, 1917), 249–50, is reprinted in *The Achievement of Sherwood Anderson: Essays in Criticism*, edited by Ray Lewis White (Chapel Hill: The University of North Carolina Press, 1966), pp. 26–29. See also his review of *Poor White* in *New Republic*, XXIV (November 24, 1920), 330. Anderson wrote of Hackett in *Letters*, ed. Jones and Rideout, Items 34, 43, 59, and 90.

16. Henry Louis Mencken (1880–1956) was literary editor of *The Smart Set* from 1906 to 1923. In 1924, Mencken and George Jean Nathan (1882–1958) founded *The American Mercury*. For Mencken's comments on Anderson, see "America's Most Distinctive Novelist," *Vanity Fair*, XXVII (December, 1926), 88; and *Letters of H. L. Mencken*, edited by Guy J. Forgue (New York: Knopf, 1961). For Anderson's comments, see *A Story Teller's Story*, ed. White, p. 305; and *Letters*, ed. Jones and Rideout, Item 360, *passim*.

The stories wouldn't go. They were not stories, etc., etc.

And then perhaps fifteen years later I saw an article by Henry telling of how he had at once recognized the merits of the story and of how he had given me words of encouragement.

Well, it was all right with me. He thought, after the fifteen years, that he had. Our minds work like that. We can't help it.

I was at a little town in Indiana, had been sent there to write advertisements for some manufacturer.

Let us say it was a manufacturer who made medicine for gapes in chickens.

Or for blackleg or abortion in cows.

Anyway I was at a railroad station and bought a magazine and there was Mr. Waldo Frank writing in the magazine of my *Winesburg* stories.[17]

He did not say they were not stories. He praised them. He said they were clever stories, a new and healthy note in American writing.

I was at that railroad station waiting to take a train when I began reading Waldo's article. I did not take the train. Evening was coming on and I went to walk in the streets of the town and out along a country road.

It had seemed to me, for a long time, that everyone who had bought my little book had immediately written me a letter telling me how vile I was. In one New England town there had been a public burning of some three or four copies of the book purchased in an ill moment by the town librarian. Only a few days before I had got a letter from a certain woman, the wife of a friend.

I had been at her house to dine. She had written saying that since I had sat beside her at table she felt she could never again see herself as clean.

So there was Waldo Frank, saying publicly, in the pages of a magazine, that I was not dirty or filthy minded.

17. Waldo David Frank (1889–1967) apparently did not review *Winesburg, Ohio.* Anderson might have been confused by Frank's review of *Windy McPherson's Son,* "Emerging Greatness," *Seven Arts,* I (November, 1916), 73–78, reprinted in *The Achievement of Sherwood Anderson,* ed. White, pp. 20–24. See also Frank, *Our America* (New York: Boni and Liveright, 1920), pp. 136–44; *In the American Jungle* (1925–1936) (New York: Farrar and Rinehart, 1937), pp. 93–96; and "*Winesburg, Ohio* after Twenty Years," *Story,* XIX (September–October, 1941), 29–33, reprinted in *The Achievement of Sherwood Anderson,* ed. White, pp. 116–21. Frank wrote of *Dark Laughter* in *Dial,* LXXIX (December, 1925), 510–14; and Anderson wrote of Frank in *A Story Teller's Story,* ed. White, pp. 251, 272–73, 305–6, 383–85. For the correspondence, see *Letters,* ed. Jones and Rideout, Items 1–7, 9–10, 12–19, 21–27, 31, 33, 40, 43, 47, 50, *passim.*

It had grown dark when I got out of the Indiana town in which I had bought the magazine. I sat on a grassy bank beside a country road. It was one of the happiest evenings of my life. At last someone was speaking of my book I had felt so happy and clean while writing with respect.

As to what I am here trying to do it comes to the same thing. I want to write now of my own experiences in living in America. I want to speak of many people I have known.

I remember once, a good many years ago, going on a fishing trip with several men friends. Marco Morrow, later Senator Arthur Capper's right hand man out in Topeka, Kansas, publisher of Arthur's *Topeka Capitol* and a lot of farm papers, was of the party and Frank Dunn, then publisher of the *Chicago Post,* was along.

There were a half dozen of us, all except myself newspaper men, and we were staying at a fishing lodge somewhere far up in Minnesota.

The point is that the proprietor of the lodge was a man who took my fancy. He was one of the sort of men I am always making up stories about. Such stories became very real to me.

All sorts of odd absurd things happened at table up there in the fishing lodge.

Well, our host had a certain quality. Everything he said had to me a certain delightful naïveté. I began to invent speeches for him. They were all anyway things he should have said.

And then later one night, in Chicago, at a dinner table I began to report some of the man's absurd and amusing remarks. I was going good. I had the whole table laughing at some of the remarks made by that man of the Minnesota lakes and woods when a man at the end of the table caught my eye.

It was Marco and there was a look of astonishment in his eyes.

I was just about to launch forth on a new anecdote when he spoke.

"Ladies and gentlemen," he said, "we have here with us this evening the champion liar of the world. He has been telling you stories of happenings in a fishing lodge up in Minnesota. He has been using me as a stooge for some of his stories. He forgot that I was here, listening. You see, I was also one of this party of which he has been speaking. Not a one of all these happenings with which he has been amusing you really happened."

Marco arose in his place at the end of the table and bowed to me.

"Go ahead, you liar," he said. "Don't let me stop you. Don't let the truth get in your way."

Just the same and although Marco did rather take the wind out of my sails that evening (I had forgotten that he was one of the party and I had convinced myself that all the stories I was telling were true)—just the same, I swear that, although I may have been inventing some, I had really got the quality of our host at the fishing camp. If he had not said some of the things I made him say he should have said them.

III

It is difficult, impossible to write of any life without lies. Men do not live in facts. They live in dreams. And if it is difficult to write of the lives of others how much more difficult to write of your own.

But what is your own life? Is there such a thing? It seems to me that all lives merge. I am one thing as you see me and others as I seem to Jane Grey or Tom Smith or John Emerson. When one writes of self one inevitably makes self the hero.

Now it happens that I have lived in an interesting, an absorbing period. My life began at just the right time and I hope it may end at the right time, not carry on too far. It does not matter so much about physical life, ability to win foot races, hit a baseball, ride a horse over jumps, but I would like to quit living just before that terrible time when the brain, the imagination, is no longer active. My life has been so rich, so crowded, that I want to tell something about it before that time closes.

But do I want to write about my own life? No. I want to use my own life only as a kind of springboard. What difference when I was born, what women I made love to, what friends I betrayed? What is interesting is the woman loved, the friend betrayed, the friend to whom I was loyal.

The life (call it my own if you will) began I think with an ambition to be one of America's successful men. I wanted passionately to rise in the world, to make money. Rising in the world meant that to me. I have always been filled with energy, a rather vital man, restless and strong. Nowdays, if you happen to see me, to be with me, talk with me, you will find me talking with a drawl. I am inclined to drag my words, loiter through life, but do not be deceived. When I seem most at ease I am often most restless inside.

As a lad and in the small Ohio town where I spent most of my boyhood I was known by the nickname of "Jobby" and later my friend John Emerson gave me another nickname. He called me "Swatty." A swatty is an old soldier. He sits in an easy chair, in the sun, before the door of an old soldiers' home. I think the two names describe very well two sides of my nature. I want to sit and dream. I want to move restlessly about, see everything, hear everything, feel everything.

The name of "Jobby" came to me from my fellow citizens of my Ohio boyhood town because of my insatiable hunger for jobs. That was because I was so hungry for money. Very early in life I became an entrepreneur. From the man spoken of above, my life long friend Mr. John Emerson, I inherited my first job. I became, as he had been, the newsman of our town. I had a monopoly and for a time sold all newspapers that came there. I employed other boys, made a little money out of their work. There were lawns to be mown. I did not wait for spring and the coming of the new grass but, even during winter months, engaged jobs ahead for the next year. I engaged more jobs than I could do. There were no sewers in our town and back of almost all houses was a pig pen and a cow barn. Cows had to be driven to pastures and driven home at evening. I engaged to drive many cows. During my boyhood the first pavement was laid in our main street and a sewer was put down. There was a man known as "street commissioner." Someone whispered to me in the street and I went to his house, this at night. He was not at home. I sat on his front step.

He did not return to his house until after midnight but I was waiting. I got a job as water boy for the foreign workmen the pavement and sewer job brought in. Jobs that could not be handled could be sublet or even sold. Grown men of the town patted my back. "Go it, kid. You're the stuff."

"I tell you, that kid will get on."

I loved money, loved the feel of it, was hungry for it. It seemed to in some way warm me, comfort me. Money would buy warm clothes, food, safety. I wanted all of these things. I understand rich men, the hunger in them, fear in them, that makes them rich, that sharpens the accumulative faculty. The whole thing, while it lasted in me, may have been due to early poverty. I can't be sure.

There is this fact, interesting, at least to me, that I live now, for most of the year, in the country, in a very beautiful hill country and, in my country, the wooded hills, in the fall, are very beautiful but sometimes, in the early fall and when the leaves begin to turn, I do not see the beauty.

There is a dread, a fear that settles down upon me. I go blindly along, often filled with a nameless misery.

Is it because of the physical poverty of early youth? In my boyhood and in our house the fall was a time of fear. There would be no butter to spread on bread. Father, when he worked, was a house painter. There were no houses to paint. Sometimes there was lack, not only of butter, but of the bread itself. There was no money to buy wood or coal and we children went out along the Wheeling and Lake Erie Railroad tracks to pick up stray pieces of coal dropped from coal trains.

But all of this a part of many lives. Often, when the fall fear comes, I tell myself that it is because I am thinking of my mother, of how she suffered. She took in the family washing of other and more prosperous families and the winter must have been bitterly hard for her. I remember her blue cold hands, her skirts, sometimes frozen stiff so that she could take them off and stand them like skirts of wood beside the kitchen stove.

"It is thinking of the sufferings of others brings this fear," I tell myself but I lie. It is true that my own shoes were thin and broken. The wet snow crept in through holes as I ran delivering my papers but it wasn't the cold that hurt me most. I wanted really to be not only warmly but gaudily dressed. I wanted better and more richly woven clothes than other boys. My pride was hurt that I was not the best dressed boy in town.

Ambition burning in me. "I'll get rich. You'll see." It didn't come off.

So there is the outline of my story, a factual outline. Is it worth a book? I have no desire to put down, in chronological order, the incidental facts of that life but there is a loose structure, a rambling sort of house, of many rooms, occupied by many people, of which I would like to tell. My ambition to become rich, to be a big man as we, in our town, thought of big men when I was a boy, that is to say a money maker, did pass. I became interested in people and I want to make my book, my rambling house of a book, a book of people.

But here also there is something a little puzzling. It happens that I have met, in the course of the life, briefly outlined here, a good many so-called "notable" men and women, famous writers, painters, singers, actors, publishers. Whom have I not met? I have remained a restless man, always moving about. It happens that, as writer, I came into writing at a fortunate time. New paths were being made. Often nowadays my name is coupled with that of Theodore Dreiser, Sinclair Lewis, Masters, Sandburg, Eugene O'Neill and others, as, shall I say, a "pioneer." Naturally I am interested in these men met, women met, so-called "notable" men and women with many of whom I have formed friendships, but (and this fact may disappoint you who have happened to pick up this book) these notable ones are not and have not been my central interest. Some of them may or may not appear in the pages of my book and if they do appear will appear but incidentally for, in my writing, I have always written of, shall I say, "obscure" people and it is these who have given me life.

And there is also another desire. I would like to write a book of the mind and of the imagination. It happens that I have a talent, was born with it. I am an imaginative man. I believe in the imaginative life, its importance and would like to write of that. My readers therefore, those who go along with me, will have to be patient. I am going to chuck what is called "time sense." I will not, cannot, to achieve what I want, tell things in chronological order.

Rather I shall tell the tale as though you, the reader, were a personal friend. We are walking together, let's say, on a country road. The road follows a stream and the day is pleasant. We are unhurried. We stop at times to sit on a rock beside the stream. We arise and walk again and I talk.

I keep talking, love to talk. I am telling you that this thing happened to me, that that thing happened.

Do you wish I would stop talking, let you talk? Why then, dear reader, go write your own book.

I ⚘

Childhood and Young Manhood

Childhood Impressions

The tiny brick house, now gone, was the first of the many houses in which we Andersons had lived that stays clearly in my mind. Father and mother must have lived in several others before we came to Clyde. "Looks as though they had moved whenever the rent came due," my brother Irve once said. I have no notion of where they had married. It may have been in the village of Morning Sun, Ohio. Karl and perhaps my sister Stella were born there.[1]

Father might have been a quite prosperous young man there. Mother had been a bound girl and must have been quite lovely. Her picture, as a young and beautiful woman, is before me on my desk as I write.[2]

And what a life she was to have after the picture was taken, after she stood up before some preacher to make her vows to be a faithful wife to father.

She was all of that. She was game. Surely she must have known of some of his later surreptitious adventures in the field of love but if she ever complained I at least never heard her complaints so I must leave that phase of her character to the still night hours, husband and wife lying together. Married men should know what I mean.

After Morning Sun and the coming of Karl and Stella, Camden, Ohio, where my turn came, then another village, Caledonia, Ohio.[3] There are in me but faint memories of that place. I had begun to walk, even a little to go adventuring. There was that time when, offended no doubt by something Karl and Stella may have done (they may have grown weary of me tagging at their heels and have spoken sharply to me, "Oh go on home, cry baby," something of that sort) I ran away from home.

1. Irwin McLain Anderson married Emma Smith in Morning Sun, Ohio, March 11, 1873. Their first child, Karl, was born January 13, 1874. The Andersons moved to Camden, Ohio, in the summer of 1874; and their second child, Stella, was born April 13, 1875.

2. Emma Smith Anderson apparently was never a "bound girl." Born October 1, 1852, near Oxford, Ohio, she may have had little family life as a child, for her father, William H. Smith, annulled his marriage to Emma's mother on December 4, 1857. See *A Story Teller's Story: A Critical Text,* edited by Ray Lewis White (Cleveland: Press of Case Western Reserve University, 1968), p. 33; and *Tar: A Midwest Childhood* (New York: Boni and Liveright, 1926), p. 39.

3. Records show "Lawrence Anderson" was born in Camden, Ohio, September 13, 1876. The unexplained error is clearly for Sherwood Berton Anderson. Anderson describes his birth in *A Story Teller's Story,* ed. White, pp. 5, 78–81, and 87; and he remembers Camden imaginatively in *Tar* (1926), pp. 4–11. In 1877, the Andersons moved to Mansfield, Ohio; and from 1880 to 1884, they lived in Caledonia, Ohio.

I could not have run far, perhaps into a neighboring field. The town was very small. It was one of the sort of towns once described by George Ade [4] as "a town dividing two farms."

I had however decided to leave home forever, the wanderlust that was to be in me always already asserting itself.

But I have written of that in a story of childhood I called *Tar*. I told there of how I grew hungry and, no doubt having seen sheep, cows and horses grazing in fields, decided to eat grass and of how, as I went on all fours nibbling at grass and clover tops, a bee, disturbed on its clover top, stung me on the lips so that I went howling home. [5]

There is also some memory of a flood, in a creek or river that must have passed close to our house, the yellow flood water spreading all over nearby fields, of a trip holding to mother's hand to our father's harness shop, the sharp pungent smell of leather in the little shop, of a small pot bellied stove, red hot, the door open and a great piece of iron, yellow and red hot, lying on the coals. It had something to do with heating the water in a tub in which leather was put to be softened and I remember my father's grasping the hot iron in tongs and throwing it into the tub, a great cloud of steam flying up. The iron was of a sort used at that time for coupling freight cars and how father got it is still a mystery. [6]

It was a mystery that stayed in my mind and later (it might have been several years later) I questioned mother.

I was remembering how the glowing iron hissed and seemed to scream when thrown into the tub of water. I must, by the time I questioned mother, have become aware of the way in which freight cars were coupled together.

"Was he ever a railroad man, was he an engineer?"

"No child. No."

Mother was never one for explanations. She was always too busy. There were too many children to ask questions.

"But if he did not work on the railroad what right had he to it?"

There may have been a picture in my mind of father snitching it from a freight car in some railroad siding. I may have already begun to snatch

4. George Ade (1866–1944), vernacular Indiana novelist and humorist, known for his *Fables in Slang* (1899).

5. See *Tar* (1926), pp. 63–69.

6. On the father's harness shop, see *A Story Teller's Story*, ed. White, p. 79; and *Tar* (1926), pp. 11–12, 87–91.

fruit from neighboring orchards. I may have wanted to find out if father was also a snitcher.

Why what have we here, a little moralist?

There is something wrong here.

However I do remember continually questioning mother. I may have burned my hand on our kitchen stove. For some reason the heated iron thrown into the tub of water made a great impression on my child's mind. I wondered if putting the iron into the stove to be heated hurt it as touching the hot stove had hurt me.

It had seemed hurt. It had seemed to scream with pain.

"But, if he was never a railroad man what right had he to it?"

"I don't know, child. Now run and play."

That memory of little Ohio towns, before we came to Clyde, up north. The town was some twenty miles south of Sandusky Bay, that was Put-In Bay from which our Admiral Perry had once sent the stirring message "I came. I saw. I conquered." [7]

Other vague memories of the other little towns crowding in. There was a fire, half the town of Caledonia burning, people running in the streets of the town at night, fire apparatus from the larger neighboring town of Marion coming to our little town in flat cars, screaming as it neared our town. Warren Harding, who was to become president, may have come with the Marion fire fighters to help rescue us. There is a tradition that he and my father once played together in the same band. He would have been a joiner as father was. What a shame that father did not live to demand and get a government job.

As the fire raged I must have been abroad in the night streets, no doubt with my brother Karl and my sister Stella, for I remember sharply the blazing buildings and the sparks floating far up into the still night sky. The people running from houses into roadways with household goods, the great piles of such goods on the streets, chains of people passing pails of water from hand to hand, others wetting blankets from their beds and spreading them on the roofs of houses so that the flying sparks would not set fire to the houses.

Our own house, in that place, no doubt out of the path of the fire, but

7. Anderson confuses Julius Caesar and Oliver Hazard Perry, who defeated the British ships on Lake Erie in 1813 and whose real statement was: "We have met the enemy and they are ours."

the memory of this exciting evening fixing the night scenes sharply in a child's mind.

Another adventure. I was with my sister Stella and we must have wandered away from the yard of our house along a road. We had come to a rail fence by a field and there in the field before us was something going on that was strange and even terrifying to us.

There was a mother pig lying in the field near the fence and tiny pigs were coming from her. It was something my sister and I could not understand. We were at the same time curious and frightened.

"Why, look. There is another. They are alive. They are little pigs."

But how could that be, life coming thus from life? The mother pig kept groaning as though in pain.

I do not know how long my sister and I stayed there by the fence, no doubt but a few minutes as we were both frightened by what we had seen, but I do remember my sister's taking my hand and running along a road toward our house and that afterwards, when we had got safely home, that she made me promise that I would not tell mother of what we had seen and of my questioning her.

But why mightn't I tell?

"I don't know but you mustn't. You mustn't."

It was as though we also had eaten of the fruit of the tree of the knowledge of good and evil and I do not believe it could have been my promise to Stella that kept me from questioning mother. There was something else. There was this newly discovered strangeness in regard to the life in animals. It got into my dreams. Horses were coming from horses, pigs from pigs, and cows from cows. There was this amazing multiplying of life that went on. It is impossible for the man, writing of all this, to be quite sure of what could have been in the child's mind.

I do know that he wanted very much to ask his mother about it all but for some unexplainable reason he did not dare.[8]

There was (it must have been soon after the incident of the birth of the litter of pigs) the march northward to the town of Clyde.[9] Father had

8. In *Tar* (1926), pp. 110–15, Anderson describes a similar scene with his younger brother Irwin, born June 18, 1878.

9. The Andersons moved to Clyde, Ohio, in March, 1884. See William Alfred Sutton, "Sherwood Anderson: The Clyde Years: 1884–1896," *Northwest Ohio Quarterly*, XIX (July, 1947), 99–114; based on the standard biography of Anderson's early life, Sutton's "Sherwood Anderson's Formative years: 1876–1913" (Ph.D. Thesis, Ohio State University, 1943).

gone broke and his harness shop was gone, and knowing my father as I came to know him later, I am sure it must have been a bitter dose for him to take and later I was to have many explanations of his failure.

So we had gone northward to the town of Clyde, father not now a maker of harnesses for farm horses but a mere workman in another man's shop, and I do not remember the railroad journey or our arrival in the new place. I do however know that in the old place, at Caledonia, and in the town of Camden, where I was from, he was a man who would be long remembered.

They would have remembered him as a great teller of tales. While he was in Caledonia, a man of some substance there, he had joined the town band, in the neighboring larger town of Marion. He had played with Warren Harding, in that band, would have gone by train for practise in Marion, and when there was a parade to be held would have closed his shop and gone off for the day.[10]

And there would have been amateur theatricals put on, in Rising Sun, in Camden and Caledonia, as later in Clyde, and he would have been deep in all such ventures, being now a comic Irishman, now a German, now the farmer of such plays of the times, the coarse figure of the amateur play, whiskers on his chin and straw in his mouth.[11] He would never have missed anything of this sort nor would he have missed the gatherings of men at the back of the town saloons, political parades, speech makings.

As for the business of running a harness shop, the spring plowing season being on, farmers clamoring for harnesses ordered for farm horses —is a man to be a slave? Is he never to have his times of relaxation, of joy?

Of what is a man made?

The little house in Clyde was very small. How we all managed to live in it is, as I remember the house, still a mystery to me for other children would have been continually coming. More children coming and father without work. He had been brought to Clyde to work in a harness shop there but had lost his job.

It may have been due to one of the periods of depression, the two men who owned the shop, the brothers Irvin, compelled to retrench, no work

10. Irwin Anderson's band-playing is fictionalized in *Windy McPherson's Son* (New York: John Lane Company, 1916), pp. 27–33. See *A Story Teller's Story*, ed. White, p. 27.

11. See *A Story Teller's Story*, ed. White, pp. 23–26, 56–58.

coming into the shop, no harness being sold, or it may have been father's fault, his work neglected, he perhaps running off to some meeting of Civil War veterans or perhaps even a period of drinking when he could not work, but at any rate there is a winter of hardship fixed in my mind, mother struggling to in some way take father's place as the family bread-winner.

I remember that she had father paint a sign on cardboard that was hung on the front door of our house. The sign said that mother would take in family sewing but I do not remember that any sewing ever came to her.

And I remember also something else. It may have been that mother was again big with child and could not work. She would already, during that for us terrible winter, have begun taking in family washes but another child being on the way would have had to give it up and we had become objects of charity, neighbors bringing food to our door, we children half unaware of the terror of actual hunger and yet, as children are, vaguely aware of our mother's fight and sadness, tears coming suddenly to her eyes, so that we all began to cry loudly in sympathy with her, the strange long periods of silence in the house, myself, with the two older children, Karl and Stella, going along the railroad tracks that ran along the rear of our house, picking up pieces of coal dropped from trains to keep our stove in our house going, we all in the winter evenings huddled about our one stove in the little kitchen, no lamp lighted because there would have been no oil for the lamp, the crawling into bed in the darkness, all of us children in the one bed huddled close to keep warm.

Father would have been much from home during that winter. It was our hardest one. He had painted the sign announcing mother's willingness to become a sewing woman and that may have set off the artist in him. It may have been at that time that he threw up the trade of harness making to become a sign writer and he had gone off somewhere seeking signs to paint.[12]

But I have written much of my father in another book, *A Story Teller's Story,* of his vagaries and I trust a little of his charm, and must not too much repeat although, perhaps because so many of my father's characteristics are also my own, he will always be a tempting subject to me.

I have spoken of our mother's being with child and, as I write, I am wondering if it could have been during that, our hardest winter to get

12. The father as sign-painter is described in *A Story Teller's Story,* ed. White, pp. 5–7, 72–75, 94–95; and *Tar* (1926), pp. 130–31.

through, that mother was carrying my brother Earl.[13] For I am quite sure there was in me already resentment of the fact of her pregnancy, a resentment that must have been also in my brother Karl and my sister Stella, and I am also wondering, as I write, if the same resentment is not in all children born into large families among the poor.

At any rate it was a resentment that my brother Earl, the last but one of the seven children mother was to help into the world, must have felt all his life.

But I will not attempt to tell here of my brother Earl's strange fate. Here I only want to suggest that at the end of my brother Earl's life, when I went to him as he lay paralyzed and after the long years when he kept himself hidden away from the rest of us in that workmen's rooming house in the city of Brooklyn, the room that Karl when he went to him after the stroke that laid him low found filled with paintings, paintings under his bed, packed away in a closet, paintings everywhere, no one of which had ever been sold or even shown to others, when I sat beside him as he lay dying and unable to speak he took a pencil into his hand and wrote the words. "I was unwanted. You others did not want me to be born and mother did not want me," he wrote.

But I am to write of Earl's strange life in another and later part of this book. I am thinking only of the dim awareness of small children in a destitute family of a mother's pregnancy. I am quite sure that, at the time, we others (if I am correct in my timing there would have been already five of us, my brother Ray a babe in arms) would hardly have known by what mysterious process mothers become pregnant.

Perhaps however a dim feeling of the father having something to do with it. My sister and I had seen the little pigs, born of the mother pig in the field. I am however quite sure that, after the event, it was never spoken of between us. It is also possible that my brother Karl and perhaps Stella, they already going to school, would have seen the obscene drawings I later saw on the school yard fence, then may have been laughed at for the notion of children dropped into houses from the sky by large birds, knowledge I could not as yet have had.

Still the resentment in me too.

Is the feeling that comes thus to a small child, seeing the sudden new shapelessness of a mother, sensing without quite knowing of the causing

13. Ray Anderson was born May 21, 1883; and Earl Anderson was born June 18, 1885.

event, is it jealous of a mother's love to be again more widely distributed? I only know that I remember as a part of the experience that particular winter, along with resentment, that other children of the neighborhood could be more warmly clad, that they could have new shoes when the soles of mine had become loose and that my toes stuck out at holes in the toes, that they lived in warmer houses, that their fathers seemed to have a kind of substantial dignity my own father could not achieve, that along with these resentments was this other and sharper one so that when the child was born I hated it also and that, after I had been called into a room to see it, lying so small and red in the bed beside mother, I crept away into a little shed at the back of the house and had a good long lonely cry.

A Street

The child's life goes on for what seems to him long years in a single street of his town or in his city block. There was the house of the saloon keeper across the street from our house. The saloon keeper, a quiet tall German man, had a young wife. He left his house at daylight and returned late at night. He went silently, with bent head, along the street. There was a picket fence around his house and his wife and their one child were seldom seen. What an isolated life they seemed to lead. The wife of the saloon keeper did not go in and out of the other houses along the street and his one child, a boy of about my own age, seldom came out from behind the picket fence.

Could it have been that the saloon keeper, his wife and child were socially ostracized because of the business in which he engaged? Ours was a northern Ohio town on the edge of the Western Reserve. There was a New England tone to the life of the town.

It was an age of temperance societies and there were two churches on our street. To sell liquor, to run a saloon was to be, I am sure, the devil's servant. Once, filled with curiosity regarding the saloon keeper's son, I ventured across the street to the picket fence before the saloon keeper's house and there was that boy. (He was always very well dressed. He did not go barefooted. His hair was neatly combed, his face always newly washed and once I heard one of the Moffitt boys, a stone hurler and my brother Karl's friend, call him a sissy. "He is a sissy, a mother's darling," the Moffitt boy said.) The boy was sitting on the grass in the saloon keeper's yard. He had some colored marbles and was playing with them. I pressed my face into an opening between two of the pickets. "Hello," I called.

How strange. The boy quickly arose. He gathered up his marbles and ran. He ran toward the kitchen door of the saloon keeper's house.

"Mama, mama," he cried. He was indeed a sissy. Think of calling your mother "mama." No one not a sissy would do that.

My brother Irve, named for our father, was a very pugnacious lad and, even when little more than a babe, was always getting into fights. He was a climber of trees, a climber onto the roof of our house. He was a thrower of stones at windows of houses. He had thrown at a little girl passing in the street and mother had caught him in the act. She cut a switch from a bush and holding him by the collar of his shirt switched his behind.

He cried lustily.

"Ouch. Ouch," he cried, but the moment mother had released him his cries died in his throat and he ran.

He ran through our back yard. He climbed a fence. He had something in his mind. There was a boy of his own age who lived several houses away down along our street and Irve had gone to seek him. He had already been in several fights with that boy, whose name was Crawley, and he had gone to seek another. Whenever mother switched him (She did not strike hard. Her whippings did not hurt much.) he sought out the Crawley boy and pummelled him. It was a way to re-establish his self-respect. He had been held helpless in the hands of mother, had shed tears in the presence of his brothers and sisters, had been humiliated before us. The pummelling of the Crawley boy until he also shed tears and ran howling to his mother gave him back something he had lost.[14]

The stone throwers along our street were older than my brother Irve and myself. The two younger boys, Earl and Ray, were still babies. Now our hardest winter had been got through and spring had come. There was a great maple tree with a huge trunk that stood just at the sidewalk's edge and on spring days my sister Stella would be sitting at the sidewalk's edge, minding the two babies as they crawled about the yard at her feet.

The stone throwers assembled at night. They were all larger boys than Irve and myself but, sometimes, when the early spring darkness began to

14. Irwin Anderson behaves similarly in *A Story Teller's Story,* ed. White, pp. 12–21.

descend on our street or during the long twilight of summer evenings, Karl went forth to join our street's army and Irve and I tagged along.

We were told to go on home. We were pushed and, I dare say, occasionally stopped. We were reminded that the stone throwing, a contest carried on with boys from some neighboring street, was not an affair for babies but, when driven off, compelled by Karl's superior strength to return to our own yard, we did not stay. We crept back to the scene of the contest.

There was a running back and forth through back yards. There was a hiding behind fences. Stones were hurled. The forces from our street were led by the older of the two Moffitt boys. There were cries and shouts. It was all very exciting but, unlike my younger brother Irve, I was afraid. I wanted to return to the safety of our own yard but Irve would not. Already, although he was as yet in skirts, had not attained to the glory of pants, he grieved to be one of the embattled stone throwers and in his little fist was clutched a stone. Once, on a summer evening, when we were lurking thus at the edge of the battle, in the half darkness, in some neighbor's back yard and when one of the stones hurled by the real warriors had crashed through a window of some house so that both armies were fleeing from the field, Irve did throw a stone at a figure dashing past us in the half darkness as we stood behind a bush. He had hit the running boy in the face and he stopped running and came to us.

What a moment and how magnificent my brother. The boy (He might have been twelve at this time. He seemed a giant to me.) had grasped my brother by the collar of his shirt just as mother did when she switched him but now he did not cry although I was near to crying. He held my brother and shook him. Evidently he was not one of our street's forces but an enemy. He was holding my brother firmly. He shook him. He laughed.

"Why you little bastard," he said, and "Oh you go to hell," my brother gasped.

It was I thought magnificent. Such bravery! Such defiance in the very hands of the enemy. I did not know the meaning of the word "bastard" but knew it was a swear word, one of the words for saying which we occasionally had our mouths washed with soap, and my brother had sworn right back at him.

And he had won a victory. The bigger boy let go his hold on Irve's collar and laughed again. In the distance we could hear the voice of a woman, no doubt of the woman the window of whose house had been broken by the flying stone. She was scolding away in a hard voice and the enemy boy still laughing continued his flight into the darkness while Irve and I went on home, my own breast filled with pride of my brother's bravery.

The street grew longer. On Sundays horses hitched to buggies, phaetons and even to farm wagons stood tied in sheds back of the two churches and in the street. Neither father or mother went to church and I do not remember any of us children going to Sunday school while we lived in that street.

We were perhaps too poor and had no fit clothes. Mother's pride would have kept us away.

But we had begun to prosper a little. Now father had become a house painter and had an occasional house or barn to paint. He had begun speaking a new language. Now there was much talk of the fine art of mixing house paint, of how the brush should be held in the hand. There was a great passion at that time for what was called "graining." The trick was to make pine look like oak, oak like cherry, cherry like walnut. Father had got an outfit of graining tools. He practised on the doors and walls of our house. He spread a dirty brown color over a door and got out his tools. He advanced upon the door, made certain flourishes with his hand. The point was to imitate the grain of some particular wood.

"You see it is pine. It will become oak. See how perfectly the grain of oak is imitated. There is not another man in Ohio could do so perfect or beautiful a job of graining."

Now father was always coming home covered with paint. He was as I was also when, later, he sometimes took me with him to help in painting some farmer's barn. There was paint in his hair, in his eyebrows and mustache. It was on his hands, on his face. His clothes were now yellow, now brown-yellow or green.

It must have been at about this time that our mother began her career as a wash woman for I remember sharply a kind of shame that began to grow in the breasts of us children when we were sent to bring home baskets of dirty clothes or to return those washed or ironed.

We did not go, on these trips, through the street but kept, as far as possible, to alleyways, and it may well have been that the feeling of shame in us that our mother should be brought down to so low a position in the town's life was due to remarks made by other children of the street. The shame may have come at first into the minds of the two older children,

Karl and Stella, and may have been transmitted to us younger ones through them but, at any rate, it was there and I am sure that even then we had begun asking ourselves the unanswerable question.

"Why is it that this one is born into life in a big house, with a carriage at the door, with no thought of where food comes from, with warm clothes to wear, all of life to be lived in what seems to us others, outside in the cold, often in ragged clothes like little animals compelled to hunt our food from day to day . . . ? Why is it? Why is it?

"Why does our mother have to wash the dirty clothes soiled by other people?" [15]

It was not, I am sure, hatred of the others that was growing in us. It was not envy. It was a kind of shame and I am quite sure that, at a very early age, it took the form (at least it did in me) of despising my father.

It was a feeling that was to stay in me, as the hardship of our mother's life continued down to the very day of her death, and to grow into a kind of hatred. Our mother, I felt, was not made for the life she was compelled to live. She was a woman delicately built and whom I thought beautiful and I am quite sure that, even as a child, I began to want for her the things she was never to have.

Am I running ahead now? I do not know. I do know that it was only after I had become a mature man, long after our mother's death, that I began to a little appreciate our father and to understand a little his eternal boyishness, his lack of feeling of responsibility to others, his passion for always playing with life, qualities that I have no doubt our mother saw in him and that enabled her in spite of the long hardship of her life with him to remain always a faithful and, for anything I ever heard her say, a devoted wife.

She had been a bound girl, the daughter of that strange old peasant woman, our grandmother, who was married four times, having children by each of her four husbands, children that, when she got a new man she, by a custom of her time, could bind out to live, as a kind of semi-servant, until they had grown into manhood and womanhood. [16]

Our mother had been so bound out, to some farming family somewhere

15. *A Story Teller's Story* and *Tar* do not emphasize the mother's having to wash or sew to support her children.

16. Emma Smith Anderson's mother, Margaret Austry, was born September 10, 1830, in Germany and immigrated to the United States as a child. On December 22, 1851, she married William H. Smith in Butler County, Ohio. The marriage was annulled; her second marriage was to Lewis Maer, March 29, 1858. There were apparently only two marriages and no Italian ancestors for this staid Presbyterian woman. See *A Story Teller's Story,* ed. White, pp. 8–10, 78, and 187.

in the southern part of the state of Ohio, and my father, no doubt then a young dandy, had found her there and had married her. She must have worked, all of her life, even from childhood, for others, a childhood and young girlhood of washing dishes, of swilling cows, of waiting at table, a kind of half servant in a house of strangers to her own blood, only after marriage and the coming of her children to become a wash woman and if in my own life, after many attempts at living as laborer, soldier, follower of race horses, factory hand and business man, I became at last a writer I was always a writer whose sympathies went out most to the people in the little frame houses on often mean enough streets in American towns, defeated people, often with thwarted lives, it is, I am sure, all due to the feeling toward our mother that had begun to grow in me, even as a small child.

It must have been in the others of us for there is my older brother Karl.

For I am back now in the little street, the first of the American small town streets that were to stay always so sharply in my mind, up and down which my own imagination was always to play, forever digging and digging, searching for the key to the secret of lives, and there was my older brother who while we lived in that street must have been grown to be a boy of twelve or thirteen.

He who was later to become an outstanding American painter, member of the National Academy, a man of note in the world of American painters, would have been feeling something of what I have spoken of above in respect to our mother.

He would have been out searching for work to a little help to lift the load from mother and he had got a job.

And what a job.

There was on our street, in a frame house near the head of the street, where it debouched into the town's main street, a certain creature.

It was half man. It had the body of a baby and the head of a man. Its arms and legs were helpless rubbery things. It went about, was wheeled about the town and to neighboring towns in a baby carriage, a boy wheeling the carriage. It was the job my brother got and for which he was paid twenty-five cents a day.

The thing in the baby carriage was frightening to children. It sat propped in the baby carriage. It talked. It used profane words. It wheedled, it begged. It sold pencils and packages of pins and needles.

It abused those who would not give. It swore at them, called them vile words. It was petulant. It was greedy.

I remember when I first saw the thing in the carriage. I ran. There was a strange new fear in me. I ran away and as I ran I cried.

The thing in the baby carriage lived in a house. There was, I believe, an old woman and another woman, perhaps an aunt. It had to be fed with a spoon. At night it was carried into the house and put into bed. The women washed it. They fed it.

No doubt it swore at them. It abused them.

People sympathized with it. Even the poor gave it nickels, gave it dimes. The people bought from it lead pencils and needles they did not want.

It rode free on trains. It was lifted, in its baby carriage, into the luggage cars of trains. It went to other towns, my brother wheeling it about the streets of towns.

It was curiously greedy about money, was always afraid it would be robbed. It imagined itself being robbed and having no power to resist the robbers. When my brother was wheeling it through streets it suddenly began to swear violently. It went into paroxysms of weeping.

My brother took it to our county seat town and there was a certain house there it wanted to visit.

It wanted to see the women of that house, wanted to be fondled by them. The women gave it money. They took it into their arms. They let it handle their necks and their breasts.

They did it because they were sorry for it. They perhaps felt it a pitiful outcast as they were outcasts. If it was vile they felt themselves vile.

They held it. They fondled it. They gave it money.

My brother wheeled it about. He went with it to towns. He was a sensitive and a delicate boy but he went.

He went for money. He went to take some of the load for our mother. He must have often been sickened by it. He did it because he felt he must.

Piety Hill

The corn field began just back of the big old frame house. It seemed big to us. They said it was a haunted house, that a certain Mama Culver rode through the house at night on a ghostly white horse. They spoke of the clanking of chains, of groans and sighs.

We did not hear them. Mama Culver, astride the white horse, did not come but I have no doubt that, because of her reputed inclination to take her night rides through the walls of the house, we got it at a low price.

You went down through the corn field to the town reservoir and to Coon Creek that fed the reservoir. You went through corn fields to the Mama Culver swimming hole and what things I learned there. It was there I learned to really swear. I found out many things (most of them I'm sure not true) about the town girls.

Young men and boys came. I learned to dive, to swim.

There was a young man subject to fits. He was in the pool formed by damming the creek, he was near me, when one of the fits came upon him, but I was not brave. I was horribly frightened and swam and scampered rapidly away.

They dragged him out to the grassy bank of the pool. His legs and arms jerked. He made strange noises. A white froth came to his lips.

I had run naked to hide in bushes. The fit went on for a long time and my own body began to tremble. The young man who had fits got suddenly to his feet and dressing in silence walked silently away.

I was in the bushes, hiding in the bushes. I put my hands over my eyes so that I could not see but the sight of the man having the fit aroused my curiosity. I kept taking my hands away. When the young man had left, going along a path up a small hill beside a wheat field, I stayed hidden in the bushes and the other boys dipped my shirt and pants into the pool. They tied them into hard wet knots and I had to use my teeth and hands in the effort to loosen them.

There were several boys in the pool, some of my own age, the others much younger, and coming out of the pool they gathered about me. They had soft mud in their hands and with it spattered my body.

They began to dance and sang.

"Chaw beef,

"Chaw beef," they sang. There were other lines to the song. There were some words I had never heard before. Some of the boys kept running to the creek's edge to get more handfuls of the mud. There were stones mixed with the mud and the stones hurt me. The song suggested other humiliating things that might be done to me and presently I became so angry that I began to cry.

I struck out at one of the boys but he dodged away and laughed at me. I was angry at myself for crying. They kept pelting me with the mud and gravel and singing the song as they danced about me.

"Chaw beef,

"Chaw beef."

I rushed at them. I struck out. I was sobbing. There was one boy, a quite innocent one, who stood aside from the others at the creek's edge. He had taken no part in my own trouble, was fully dressed, was a small and rather sickly looking boy but as I rushed away from the others, clutching my wet clothes, I gave him a shove sending him backward into the mud.

The boy could not swim. He was a sickly little fellow and the others were pursuing me, still slinging the mud in which were mixed the small stinging stones and, as I later learned, it was only by chance that one of the older boys saw the pale sickly one about to drown in the pool and pulled him out.

So there it was, the innocent one made to suffer and come near losing his life because of the boyish cruelty of the others, myself thus tortured striking not one of my persecutors but an innocent bystander. I ran away into the bushes. I was compelled to dress in the wet clothes with the mud still on my body but presently I would grow older and bigger and would join the others in pelting some other new boy.

The corn fields were everywhere. Piety Hill, where we had now come to live, was then a little separated from the town by a creek and by low swampy land. You got to it by a kind of viaduct, a sidewalk on stilts. It was at the edge of the farm lands and the people of the hill were far from pious.

Across the street from us, when we moved to the hill, lived the McNutt boys.

They were tough. They swore and fought with one another and with the other boys along the street. Their father, who was rarely at home, traveled with a circus. He was a trapeze performer. The McNutt boys caught us. They made us play circus with them. They played clowns and had long flat paddles with which they continually beat us. When the beating hurt and we cried they also had a song they sang.

"Cry baby.

"Cry baby.

"Cry baby.

"Go home and get weaned.

"Go home and get weaned," they sang.[17]

I saw the corn fields plowed in the spring. I saw how the land rolled up under the plows. I saw the muscles working across the breasts of the horses

17. Similar incidents are described in *Tar* (1926), pp. 223–26.

as they pulled at the plows and long afterward, in a little book of verses I called *Mid-American Chants,* I tried to sing of the corn fields.

> All about me the corn—in the night the fields mysterious and vast—voices of Indians—names remembered—murmurings of winds—the secret mutterings of my own young boyhood and manhood.
>
> I sang there—I dreamed there—I was suckled face downward in the black earth of the western cornland.
>
> I remember as though it were yesterday how I first began to stand up. I sang.[18]

The ugliness of life, the strange beauty of life pressing in on a boy.

I saw the new corn push up out of the rich brown earth back of our house. I saw the crows come to pull up the young sprouts and get at the softened kernels of corn down under the earth. I saw men and boys come with shot guns. They put up scarecrows.

The black crows seemed to laugh at them. There was a sentinel crow sat on one of the arms of a scarecrow and when the men and boys came with guns he gave a warning cry. The flock of crows flew into trees at the field's edge. They sat on the limbs of the trees and laughed at the men and boys with their guns.

It seemed a kind of game and how shrewd and aware the crows seemed.

I saw the young corn push up higher and higher. Men and boys drove teams of horses up and down the rows plowing the young corn. The horses were muzzled. They could not tear the broad leaves of the corn.

And now the corn has grown higher than a boy's head. It is a forest. It is a place to hide. The boy goes along the long corn rows. There is a soft light down there under the tall corn. What sights, what warm delicious smells, smell of the corn, of the earth, of the growing pumpkins, planted in the corn. It is a place to adventure. Rabbits scurry away along the rows. The boy lies on the warm earth under the corn. He sees the little life of insects down there under the corn, hears the soft sound of broad green leaves rubbing against each other as the summer winds blow over the fields. It is a place for the boy of lovely thoughts, of escape from the rough usage of the McNutt boys. Something in him begins to sing now. He even fancies that the rustling leaves of the corn are whispering to him.

18. "Mid-American Prayer," *Mid-American Chants* (New York: John Lane Company, 1918), p. 69. Anderson here reverses the stanza order. See Walter B. Rideout, "Sherwood Anderson's 'Mid-American Chants,' " *Aspects of American Poetry: Essays Presented to Howard Mumford Jones,* edited by Richard M. Ludwig (Columbus: Ohio State University Press, 1962), pp. 149–70.

What a field for the poets of America, the corn fields. It was not until long years afterward that he was to know and become the friend of Henry Walker,[19] a true American poet of the corn fields.

And now it is time for the cutting of the corn. The tall corn stalks are set up in shocks. They are not fighting armies. They stand in rows ready to feed the nation of men.

The men come to husk out the corn. You see the piles of yellow gold on the brown earth. Here is something to make the heart glad. The corn fields, the corn fields.

There was a boy named Jimmy Moore, later in life to become a forester in the forests of the American far west. He lived alone with his mother in a house at the end of a street on Piety Hill. It was the last house along the street before the farms began. He became my first boyhood friend.

We went together into the corn fields. We went through the corn field to Coon Creek. We followed the winding of Coon Creek. We were in a little valley between low wooded hills. Pawpaws grew there. We undressed and played in the creek. We ran naked among the trees. We wanted to be monkeys and tried to swing from low hanging branch to branch. We fell and tried again.

We went to lie on the grass beside the creek. In the distance we could see a man in a corn field cutting the young corn. There were big white clouds moving slowly across a summer sky. We saw a coon come down to the creek. We were very quiet as we watched him. There were berry bushes growing near the creek and the coon reached up with his little fingered paws and picked the berries.

In the quiet of that place something began. There was Jim Moore, lying beside me on the grass at the creek's edge. He was another boy. He saw what I saw. He was not my brother, had been born of another mother and another father. He did not live in my body but in his own body. While I was having thoughts, dreaming dreams, lying there beside him, he was also having thoughts, dreaming dreams. Sometimes they were my thoughts and my dreams and sometimes he went off on his own. Such days, such a moment long remembered, the beginning of wonder about another. Questions beginning in the mind.

"What is this other like? What is he thinking now?" A curiosity about others, outside self, that was to become a growing passion, beginning on a summer afternoon, lying naked beside the boy Jim Moore, beside a creek

19. Henry Walker, unidentified.

and watching in silence a little animal picking and eating berries. The little animal was very clean. He washed the berries in the creek before eating.[20]

My father had a new occupation. He was going about selling books. He sold Grant's *Memoirs* and a book about a soldier boy named Si Klegg and I read the books.[21]

It was an occupation my father would like. It would take him into many houses. He could sit and talk to people for hours. He would tell them of his own experiences, would be invited to stay and dine. He could go into the country and stay at farmers' houses. Women would sit listening to his talk.[22]

There was a passage in Grant's *Memoirs* that would also be long remembered. He has been a failure in life but the war has come and he is in command of a regiment of soldiers. It is the first time he has had such a command.

With his regiment he is sent to a certain valley where there is an encampment of the enemy. He is marching at the head of his regiment up the hill along the road that will lead into the valley beyond.

He is suddenly afraid. He trembles with fear. Will he be able to do the right thing when it comes to the moment of battle?

Now he is doubting himself, is full of new fears. He rides at the head of his regiment over the brow of the hill and behold the enemy has fled.

The experience taught General Grant something that he says in his book he always afterwards remembered, that when he was afraid of another man it was likely the other man was also afraid of him.

The thought made a deep impression on my mind. I had begun going to school.[23] The presence of the others, boys and girls in the school room, had frightened me. Sometimes when a strange boy spoke to me I was shy and

20. Jim Moore appears in *Tar* (1926), pp. 158, 167, 225–27; and Anderson praises corn fields in *Tar* (1926), pp. 167–68.

21. Ulysses S. Grant, needing money for his retirement, published his *Personal Memoirs* in two volumes (1885–86). The story of Si Klegg must have been one of the immensely popular "dime novels" of the post-Civil War era.

22. For other of the father's tales of the Civil War, see *A Story Teller's Story*, ed. White, pp. 6–7, 28–37, 45–56; and *Tar* (1926), pp. 27–30.

23. Anderson enrolled in "C Primary" (second grade) on October 1, 1884; was not in the next grade in 1885–86; was in "D Grammar" in 1886–87 (repeated for absences, perhaps from illness); and in high school attended only September–March, 1891–92, and January–February, 1893. See *A Story Teller's Story*, ed. White, p. 115; and *Tar* (1926), pp. 127–56.

afraid. I hurried away from him without answering his greeting. The thought that others might also be shy in my presence was in some odd way a great comfort to me. What General Grant had said seemed to push open a door for me. All my life the simple thought, so simple and directly put down, was to be a help to me.

I had discovered in myself a new passion. From our house, on Piety Hill, you could go through the corn field to the town race way. You walked across the dam there, went past the engine house and up a little hill and beside another corn field there you were at the fair grounds.

It was a time when the trotting and pacing horses were in their glory and in our town as in all American towns of that time there were men who devoted their lives to the development of such horses.

At the race tracks on spring and early summer mornings there would be the one legged George Crosby, Frank Harvy, a tall silent man, there with his bay stallion, and there was Tom Whitehead who had a whole stable of horses and even went to race on the Grand Circuit.

There was the little bay gelding Doctor Fritz, the great black stallion Solarian (a dangerous one that), Doctor Robinson's gelding was there (They declared that that one was crazy. If you did not blindfold him he might suddenly go through fences. He was mad with speed. He never let up. Turned at the race track home stretch he would put the last ounce of his great strength and courage into every stride, would keep going on, if not stopped, until he dropped dead.), and there was the hotel man, Frank Welker. He did not drive but had another drive for him. His little black mare was very tiny. When she was going at speed she drew her lips back from her teeth. She seemed always to be laughing.

And there was I, a boy, hanging over the low fence in the infield by the judges' stand. How my heart beat. There was something in the sustained rhythmic swing of the legs and bodies of the horses, going at speed, that touched some secret hunger in myself, and, morning after morning, I cut away from our house alone and raced through the corn field, past the waterworks engine house to the fair grounds to catch what I could of the glorious sight before I was compelled to go off to school. I stood by the low fence trembling. I leaned far over the fence. Tears came into my eyes and a lump into my throat. It was my first love. Oh the beautiful, the courageous and aristocratic creatures. I grew sick with envy of the drivers in their high wheeled carts wheeling about the half mile track, their hands on the reins. Oh, to be such another, to hold the reins over some such beautiful beast, and what heavy sadness in my heart when the first bell rang and I had to go with dragging reluctant feet away from the race track toward the distant school.[24]

Big Fish

It must be that all children are actors. There was a boy up our street who had inflammatory rheumatism. That is what they called it. He didn't have to go to school.

Still he could walk about. He could go fishing in the creek or in waterworks pond. There was a place up at the pond where in the spring the water came tumbling over the dam and formed a deep pool. It was a good place. Sometimes you could get some good ones there.

I went down that way, on a spring morning, on my way to school. It was out of my way but I wanted to see if Walter was there.

He was, inflammatory rheumatism and all. There he was, sitting with a fish pole in his hand. He had been able to walk down there all right.

It was right then my own legs began to hurt. It was in my back too. I went on to school but, at the recess time, I began to cry. I didn't ache. The teacher, Sarah Suggett, had come into the school house yard.

She came right up to me.

"What's the matter, Sherwood?" she asked.

"I ache all over," I said. I did too.

I kept on crying and it worked all right.

"You'd better go on home," she said.

So I went. I limped painfully away. I kept on limping until I got out of the school house street.

Then I felt better. I still had inflammatory rheumatism pretty bad but I could get along better.

I got home and I told mother. I must have done some thinking on the way home.

"I'd better not say I have inflammatory rheumatism. Maybe, if you've

24. Anderson wrote of horses in *A Story Teller's Story,* ed. White, pp. 101–2, 118–25, 178–81, 195, 313–14; *Tar* (1926), pp. 175–84; "Here They Come," *Esquire,* XIII (March, 1940), 80–81. Besides the tales in *Horses and Men* (New York: B. W. Huebsch, 1923), consult Linda Carol Traynham, "The Horse as Symbol in Sherwood Anderson's Fiction" (M.A. Thesis, University of South Carolina, 1966).

got that, you swell up. I'd never noticed that Walter was swelled up," I thought.

I thought I'd better go around to where Walter was and ask him about that so I did go that way but he wasn't there.

"They must not be biting today," I thought.

I had a feeling that, if I said I had inflammatory rheumatism, mother or my brothers and my sister Stella might laugh. They did laugh at me pretty often and I didn't like it at all.

"Just the same," I said to myself, "I have got it." I began to hurt and ache again.

I went home and sat on the front steps of our house. I sat there a long time. There wasn't anyone at home but mother and the two little ones. Ray would have been four or five then and Earl might have been three.

It was Earl saw me there. I had got tired sitting and was lying on the porch. Earl was a quiet solemn little one.

He must have said something to mother for presently she came out.

"What's the matter with you? Why aren't you in school?" she asked. I came pretty near telling her right out that I had inflammatory rheumatism but I thought I'd better not. Mother and father had been speaking of Walter's case at the table just the day before.

"It affects the heart," father had said.

That frightened me when I thought of it.

"I might die," I thought. When mother asked me why I wasn't in school right away my inflammatory rheumatism got worse.

I might just suddenly die right here, my heart might stop beating. On the day before I had been running a race with my brother Irve.

We were up at the fair grounds after school and there was a half mile track up there.

"I'll bet you can't run a half mile. I bet you I could beat you running clear around the tracks," he said.

And so we did it and I beat him but afterwards my heart did seem to beat pretty hard.

I remembered that, lying there on the porch.

"It's a wonder, with my inflammatory rheumatism and all, I didn't just drop down dead," I thought.

The thought frightened me a lot. I ached worse than ever.

"I ache, ma. I don't know. I just ache," I said.

She made me go in the house and upstairs and get into bed.

It wasn't so good. It was a spring day. I was up there for perhaps an hour, maybe two, and then I felt better.

I got up and went downstairs. "I feel better, ma," I said.

Mother said she was glad. She was pretty busy that day and hadn't paid much attention to me. She had made me get into bed upstairs and then hadn't even come up to see how I was.

I didn't think much of that when I was up there but when I got downstairs and when, after I had said I felt better and she only said she was glad and nothing else and when she went right on with her work, I began to ache again.

I thought, "I'll bet I die of it. I bet I do."

I went out on the front porch and sat down. I was pretty sore at mother.

"If she really knew the truth, that I have the inflammatory rheumatism, that affects the heart so that I may just drop down dead any time, I'll bet she wouldn't care about that either," I thought.

I was getting more and more angry the more thinking I did.

"I know what I'm going to do," I thought. "I'm going to go fishing."

I thought that, feeling the way I did and if I went fishing, I might be sitting on the high bank, just above the deep pool where the water went over the dam, and suddenly my heart would stop beating.

And then of course I'd pitch forward over the bank into the pool and that if I weren't dead when I hit the water I'd drown sure.

They'd all come home to supper and they'd miss me.

"But where's Sherwood?"

Then mother'd remember that I'd come home from school feeling bad.

She'd go upstairs and I wouldn't be there. One day, during the year before, there was a child got drowned in a spring. It was one of the Wyatt children.

Right down at the end of the street there was a spring under a birch tree and there had been a barrel sunk in the ground.

Everyone had always been saying the spring ought to be kept covered but it wasn't.

So the Wyatt child went down there, playing around alone, and fell in and got drowned.

Mother was the one who had found the drowned child. She had gone to get a pail of water and there this child was, drowned and dead.

This had been on the evening when we were all at home and mother had come running up the street with the dead dripping child in her arms.

[55]

She was making for the Wyatt house as hard as she could run and she was pale.

She had a terrible look on her face. I remembered then.

"So," I thought, "they'll miss me and there'll be a search made. Very likely there'll be someone driving along the road past the waterworks pond who has seen me sitting by the pond and fishing and he'll tell how he saw me there.

"There'll be a big alarm and all the town will turn out and they'll drag the pond."

Once there was a boy swimming in waterworks pond and he got drowned and they had to drag the pond for him. I hadn't seen it but I had heard about it.

I was having a grand time, having died. Maybe, after they found me and had got me out of the deep pool, mother would grab me up in her arms and run home with me as she had run with the Wyatt child.

I got up from the porch and went around the bushes. I got my fishing pole and lit out for the pool below the dam. Mother was busy. She always was. She didn't see me go. When I got there I thought I'd better not sit too near the edge of the high bank.

By this time I didn't ache hardly at all but I thought, "With inflammatory rheumatism you can't tell," I thought.

"It probably comes and goes," I thought.

"Walter has it and he goes fishing," I thought.

I had got my line into the pool and suddenly I got a bite. It was a regular whopper. I knew that I'd never had a bite like that.

I knew what it was. It was one of Mr. Fenn's big carp.

Mr. Fenn was a man who had a big pond of his own. He sold ice in the summer and the pond was to make the ice. He had bought some big carp and put them in his pond and then, earlier that spring, when there was a big spring freshet, his dam had gone out.

So the big carp had got into our creek and one or two big ones had been caught but none of them by a boy like me.

The carp was pulling and I was pulling and I was afraid he'd break my line so I just tumbled down the high bank, holding on to the line, and got right into the pool.

We had it out there in the pool, the fish and me. We struggled. We wrestled but I got a hand under his gills and got him out. He was a big one all right. He was nearly half as big as I was myself. I had him on the bank and I kept one hand under his gills and I ran.

I never ran so hard in my life. He was slippery and now and then he wriggled out of my arms and once I stumbled and fell on him but I got him home.

So there it was. I was a big hero that day. Mother had got a wash tub and had filled it with water. She put the fish in it and all the neighbors came to look.

I had got into dry clothes and we were all at supper. I made a break. It was then I spoiled my day. I think maybe my brothers and my sister were laying for me.

They wanted to take me down, that was it. I was too chesty, they thought.

There we were, all of us, at table and suddenly father asked what had been the matter with me at school.

He had met the teacher, Sarah Suggett, on the street and she had told him how at recess time I had become ill.

"What was the matter with you?" father asked and before I thought what I was saying I let it out.

"I had the inflammatory rheumatism," I said and a shout went up. It made me sick again to hear them the way they all laughed.

It brought back all the aching again and, like a fool, I began to cry.

"Well I have got it, I have, I have," I cried and I got up from the table and ran upstairs.

I stayed up there until mother came in. I knew it would be a long time before I heard the last of the inflammatory rheumatism. I was sick all right but the aching I now had wasn't any longer in my back.[25]

A Landed Proprietor

When I was a very young boy, one of several sons in a very poor family in an American middle western town, I was, for a time, the town newsboy and among my customers in the town, to whom I delivered daily the newspaper from our nearest big city, was a certain little old woman.

She, as I was later to find out, was also very poor. She must however have had a small income from some source unknown to us but her life in her house was a very lonely one. It was a narrow penny counting life. She

25. Published (revised) as "Stolen Day," *This Week,* April 27, 1941, pp. 6, 23.

was there, living alone in a little frame house, on a street of small houses, and beside her house was a vacant lot in which grew several gnarled old apple trees. Her own house was always very clean, very neatly kept but, during the winter months, she sat all day in her kitchen. She did it to save fuel. She heated only the one room in her house.

Such old women are often very wonderful. They grow old patiently, with quiet serenity, often a strange beauty in their wrinkled old faces. They attain a beauty that seldom comes to old men. Such an old woman may carry about a worn out body, may walk with difficulty, her body may be wracked with pain but a beautiful aliveness still shines out of her old eyes and it may be because women are less defeated by modern life. I have often thought that. They have been creators. Children have been born out of their bodies. There may be in them a feeling of accomplishment we men seldom get.

"See, I have done it. Now I am old and tired but there are these others, men and women, the seeds of whom I have carried in my body. They have gone away from me now but they are alive, somewhere in the world. Here I am. I have not just lived, I have given out life."

The particular old woman of whom I speak used to call me often into her house. On cold or rainy days she stood at her kitchen door waiting for my coming. She took an evening paper and at night, sometimes, the train from the city was late. She put a lamp in her kitchen window. She called to me.

"Come in, boy. Dry yourself a little. Warm yourself by my fire." She had baked a pie or had made cookies and she gave me some. She was quite small and, as I stood by her kitchen stove, she came and put a thin old arm about my shoulders. "It is good to be young, to have your life before you," she said. She smiled at me and lights danced in her old eyes. "I am sure you will be a fine man. I feel it. I am sure of it," she added and I drank in her words. When I left her house on winter nights I found myself running joyously along through the dark night streets of our little town and when I put my hand into my coat pocket I found that, while her arm was about my shoulder, she had slipped several more cookies into my pocket.

She died and she had put my name into her will. How proud I was. She had left her house and its furnishings to a son, a mechanic living in some distant city, but the vacant lot, beside her house, in which grew the gnarled old apple trees, she had left to me.

It was a gesture. It was because my daily visits to her house had broken her loneliness. It was because, after she was gone, she wanted me to remember and think of her. It was, to me, a matter of magnificent importance. There was this will, to be probated in our court. I had got the word "probated" from a lawyer of the town to whom I also delivered a daily newspaper. My name would be read out. I would be called upon to sign a paper. I walked about the streets with my chest thrown out.

And there was something else. I had become a land owner, a landed proprietor. I took some of my boy friends to see my lot. There was a particular boy, the son of a grocer. "You see, Herman, your father may own a store but what do you own?" It was fall and there were a few small gnarled apples on the old apple trees and scattered about among tall weeds. I grew generous. "Help yourself, Herman. Put some in your pocket. It's all right with me." I filled my own pockets and took my apples home, demanding that mother make me a pie, and, when it was made, I stood over it, handing out small wedges to my brothers and sisters. This was not a family affair. It was my pie, made from the apples of my own trees that grew on my own land. How gloriously generous I had become. To be thus generous with my own property was a new and sweet feeling to me.

I took my brothers with me to see my lot but they were scornful. "Ah, it is nothing," one of them said. "Such old, no-good trees.

"And look, at the back there, where it goes down to the creek. It is all wet back there. It is a swamp."

It was something I could not stand. One of my brothers and I fought. We stood under one of my apple trees and I pummelled him while a still younger brother, little more than a babe, stood on the sidewalk before my lot and cried.

It was better with my sister who was two years older than myself and, I thought, a very sensible person. She had understanding. She praised my lot. "What fine trees," she said. "Look, the ground must be very rich. How tall the weeds have grown."

In our family we had always been moving. We went from one small frame house in the town to another. There were six of us and no two of us had been born in the same house. Perhaps we moved whenever the rent became too much overdue. I can't be sure of that.

But now I had got this piece of land and, presently, I would build a house on it, such a magnificent house. What a joy it would be to our mother. My sister and I spent hours, walking up and down through tall weeds, making our plans. "You just wait, sister. You'll see. I shall grow rich." In a town some fifty miles away oil had recently been struck. "Who knows? There may be oil down here, under this very spot on which I stand."

In a stationery store of the town I had bought a magazine devoted to house plans and I took it home. To avoid my brothers, who continued scornful ("It is just pure jealousy," I told my sister), my sister and I went upstairs into a bedroom of our house. We sat on the edge of the bed.

What plans we made. Our house continued to grow and grow. Every day we added more rooms. My sister, from time to time, began to feel, I thought, too much a co-owner and I had to rebuke her a little. It was all right for her to make suggestions but all decisions were to be left to me. I made that quite clear to her.

And then it happened. The dream faded. It blew up.

It was the same small town lawyer who had given me the word "probate" who blew it up.

"You look here, kid," he one day said to me, "about that lot that old woman left you.

"I've been looking it up," he said. He explained to me that the unpaid taxes on my lot amounted to about four times what it was worth.

"I guess you don't want to prove up on it," he said but I could not answer him. I ran away. He had his office upstairs over a shoe store in our town and I ran quickly down the stairs and through an alleyway back of stores and along residence streets until I got out into the country.

It was in the spring, on a morning in the spring, when the lawyer gave me the dreadful news and I had my morning papers to distribute but, on that morning, I did not finish delivering the papers. At the edge of town I threw them angrily into a creek. I ran into a wood.

But who can understand the sadness of a boy? I was there in that wood, not far from our town. For a time I cried and then I grew angry. So there was a thing called "taxes." You had a vacant lot given you, a fine lot, I thought, with grand trees growing on it. You had it and then you had it not. Some mysterious force you didn't understand reached down and took it away from you. You had to pay these taxes. But where would you get the money for that?

I began to blame the town in which I lived. I would leave it, I decided. If I went home there would be my brothers and when they found out that the lot that had been mine wasn't really mine they would laugh at me.

I stayed in the wood all that day, did not go to school. I made plans. When night came I would go into town and get on a train. There was a local freight that passed through town in the early evening and I would crawl into a box car and, after a time, when the town realized that I was gone for good it would be sorry. I think that, at the time all this happened to me, I must have been reading *Huckleberry Finn.*[26] For some obscure reason I decided I would go to Cairo, Illinois. I would be a bootblack on the streets there. Then I would become a steamboat captain, grow rich, return to my Ohio town a rich man, pay up the taxes on my lot, build on it a magnificent house.

I was very resolute, very determined but, in the late afternoon, it began to rain and I decided that, after all, I would put off fleeing from the town for a day or two. There were things I had to attend to. I had bought a bicycle and was paying for it on the installment plan and it was almost paid for. I would have to sell that, make myself a bootblacking outfit.

When night came I crept into town. I had begun a little to get my courage back. I went to the railroad station and there were my evening papers, in their bundle, lying against the closed door of the express office.

I had to think up an explanation of why some of my customers had not got their morning paper. That occupied my mind and also I had to think up things to say to my brothers. I ran along in the rain, distributing my papers, and when I had got into a dark residence street began talking aloud. I was making up speeches for my brothers.

"Ah, go on. Shut up. Anyway no one ever put your name in a will," I would say.

When I had got my papers delivered I could not resist going for a visit to my lot. I went and the street in which my lot stood was dark. The little frame house in which my old woman had lived was dark. Her son, the mechanic, had taken the furniture away. I stood for a time in the tall weeds, wet now by the rain, and was inclined to cry again and then, although I was frightened by the thought of the empty house, I went to the rear, to the kitchen door where, when she was alive, there had always been, on such rainy nights, a light in the window for me.

I did not stay there long. I ran away. For a time as I ran in a small town residence street in the rain I cried again and then I stopped crying. I remembered what I had planned to say to my brothers. It may be that just having said the words aloud had brought a dim realization of something that, as I grew older, would become more and more important to me.

26. For the influence of Twain on Anderson, see Seymour L. Gross, "Sherwood Anderson's Debt to *Huckleberry Finn*," *Mark Twain Journal*, XI (Summer, 1960), 3–5, 24. A valuable study of the formation of Anderson's style is Richard Bridgman, *The Colloquial Style in America* (New York: Oxford University Press, 1966), pp. 152–64, *passim*.

There was, after all, the fact that I had been mentioned in my old woman's will. Even after she had gone she had made the gesture of love and friendship to me.[27]

Upward and Onward

I had become suddenly sharp and alive. I had got a new name. Now I was no longer "Sherwood" except at home. On the streets of the town, in the stores, at the railroad station, I had become "Jobby."

I was the boy eternally seeking jobs. Oh what energy, what fire, what determination. Men stopped me on the street.

"Go it boy," they said.

Now I had become determined that someday I would be a rich man. There was our mother, still washing other people's dirty clothes. Occasionally, in the evening (we always waited until darkness came), my sister and I were compelled to again do the humiliating job of either going to get some very well-to-do family's soiled clothes or to return them washed and ironed.

I hated it. My brothers and sisters I am sure also hated it. We did not speak of it to each other but I am sure that the others had come to the same determination that I had.

There were families in the town who lived in larger and more comfortable houses. I do not believe that, at the time, there were any families in Clyde that had risen to the glory of indoor toilets or bath tubs but there was in such families no fear of hunger. The children of such families wore warm comfortable clothes. In the winter they had overcoats to wear. Boys of my own age even rose to the glory of boots with red leather tops. Such boys owned skates. They had gayly colored sleds on which to slide downhill when the snow came in the winter. Back of such a house there would at that time, inevitably, be a barn and in many a back yard there was a pig pen with its fat pig, to be killed in the fall.

Sausages to be made, hams and bacon to be cured. In the cellar of such houses there would be bins of apples, of potatoes, turnips, cabbages. There were shelves heavily burdened with often hundreds of cans of fruit, put down in the fall by the woman of the house assisted by her hired girl.

27. Published (revised) in *Rotarian,* LVIII (March, 1941), 8–10.

The rooms in such a house were all warm in the winter. There was a great base burner in what was called the "front" room. In the parlor there was an enlarged crayon portrait of the head of the house, a merchant, a lawyer, a doctor or a retired farmer. There were stoves in other rooms in such houses, even sometimes in bedrooms, while, in our house on cold days, we all clustered about the kitchen stove, the one fire in the house.

There was this to me seeming luxury in these other houses. In the barn back of the house there was a cow, driven during the summer to some pasture near the town's edge, and there were horses, to be hitched to family carriages on Sundays and on summer evenings and to gay looking sleighs in winter.

I had begun going to such houses. There was my closest friend, named Herman, the son of a grocer, a bearded kindly man with a sharp tongued wife, a leader in the local women's temperance movement. There were several sisters, warm friendly healthy girls, some older, some younger than my friend Herman.

And what a table set at that house. When I was not busy at one of my jobs running about distributing newspapers, mowing people's lawns, driving the cows belonging to some well-to-do families off to some pasture on the town's edge in the early morning and back to the barns back of the houses in the early evenings. . . .

I got twenty-five cents per week per cow and oh what a creature the cow. She is so mild. She has such large soft eyes. For months she goes along, patient, being driven off in the morning to some distant pasture and back at night. She will stand patiently while she is milked. She becomes a mother and in a few weeks her son or daughter is taken from her. When this happens she will, for a day or two, be somewhat restless, will thrust her head up and bawl loudly but in a few days she forgets. She becomes again man's most valued and patient servant, a mere machine to turn out milk.

And then, suddenly, you are driving her off to Ard's field when something strange and startling happens to her.

She falls suddenly into the mood of love. It seizes upon her. Her huge bulk is shaken with it. Now suddenly she will bolt. She throws her tail into the air and bawls loudly. Let us say you are leading her with a rope and look out. She will charge through fences. Her hind legs fly high into the air. If you are leading her along a road that follows the crest of a hill she will drag you up- and down-hill. There is the huge bulk of cow weighing perhaps eight or nine hundred pounds rampaging across country. It is late fall and it rains and darkness is coming and she has dragged up up and down down hills and through several fences and then, having torn herself free from the retaining rope, has disappeared into the darkness.

And you must get her home. You must find her. She is one of God's creatures who knows what she wants when she wants it. Let her have it and she becomes again man's most valued and patient servant.

The table at the Hurd house was piled high with food.

"Oh come on. Stay to supper," said Herman.[28]

"No. I can't."

"Sure you can."

My protests become feebler.

"No I can't."

"Yes, you can now. Now you come on. Ma has made some pie."

Herman has been in the kitchen of the Hurd house. "Ma's made corn bread. Gee, there's some swell pies. There's chicken with dumplings. Pa's brought home a big watermellon from the store."

I let myself be persuaded and how I feast. I have been told by mother that, when I am invited out to dine, I must not be a pig.

"You mustn't take the last helping in the dish.

"If there is pie do not try to get the biggest piece as you are always doing here at home. Whatever you do you must not give people the impression you are starved."

And now, at the Hurd table, Herman's father, that man of the greying beard, with the small shrewd grey eyes, in which there is at the moment shy laughter, is urging me.

"Pass your plate, boy."

"No thank you, Mr. Hurd. I have had enough."

I am trying hard to act, as mother is always saying, to act as an Anderson boy should.

"No thank you, Mr. Hurd."

But how glorious he is. He pays no attention to my protests but keeps piling high my plate.

He is a man known in the town as an agnostic, one who has his own notions of God, and occasionally, on the long summer afternoons, when I

28. Herman Hurd is interviewed by Harold Detlefsen, "Herman Hurd of Clyde, Sherwood Anderson's Boyhood Chum," *RFD News* (Bellevue, Ohio), October 8, 1962, pp. 1–2. See *A Story Teller's Story,* ed. White, p. 97; and *Tar* (1926), pp. 288–96.

am not busy at one of my jobs and when there is no school, he asks me to go with him to his farm, some miles out of our town, and I go eagerly.

We go in a wagon drawn by an old black mule named Topsy and as we go slowly along past fields of tall corn and other fields in which the wheat has already been cut and shocked he sometimes speaks of God.

"There is a God, boy. Don't doubt it," he says, "but he is not the god of the churches. He is in the field here, in that wheat stacked in that field there. He is in every growing stalk of corn. He is in the grass, in those weeds growing here beside the road. He is not, I am afraid, much in the churches. He is in you, in me, in the trees."

The kindly grey bearded grocer becomes silent and as we jog along the country road to reach his farm, little puffs of dust rising from under the hoofs of his old black mare, I am also silent, a kind of new wonder growing in me as I look at the fields and at the clump of woodland seen in the distance beyond some field. A kind of awe before the fact of life, in meadows, in corn and wheat fields, in men and women and even in the flies being whisked away from her sides by the tail of the grocer's old black mare, began growing in me.

Significant Days

It had begun. The new thing that was to change all life so significantly and even terribly, not only in our own country but in all the world, began to make itself felt even in our little Ohio town. It was to spread out over the world. What a strange hopeful creature is man. Who can doubt, for example, that when printing was first invented, men really believed that with the coming of the new art men everywhere would rush to begin reading only the finest and most uplifting of man's word put into print. Men would spend their lives reading like say such men as Shakespeare, Goethe, Dante, Milton. Such books as *Paradise Lost, Hamlet, The Divine Comedy* would begin to stand up on shelves in even the most humble dwellings. How could men know what is so obvious now, that it is much easier to spread vulgarity than true culture?

It had been on its way for a long time, the machine, that strange impersonal thing that was suddenly to make a new and even terrible world. It was perhaps implied when the first man picked up the first club to knock over some beast to feed upon.

But let me not begin here to become too highbrow, too pretentiously profound. It is not the part I have been cast to play. Away with this attempt at deep thinking. Let me get back to my real job as story teller. In a book I was to write long after the period in my own life about which I am now thinking, a book called *Poor White*,[29] I tried to tell something of what happened to one American town with the coming of modern industry. It is a book in which I tried to make a town, rather than any one individual, my central character, trying in it to tell something of the dreams of sudden wealth and power that came to men so suddenly in such a town and of how instead lives were wrecked.

In the town of my own boyhood. . . . It is by the way one American town that has remained, to this day, much as it was when I was a boy there. Boys I knew there when I was myself a boy still walk its streets. Some have risen a little in the world while others have come down. Boyhood friends are bankers there, they run little clothes pressing establishments or grocery stores or they are clerks or day laborers. It is one town into which modern industry has not much come. To be sure automobiles, rather than horses and farmers' wagons, are now parked before the main street stores. . . .[30]

Factories moving into the middle west, blatant, a rather quiet and certainly a charming city to become a mighty industrial center, a place of long miles of dreary enough streets, like that terrible Chicago West Side I was myself to know so well later, miles and miles of factories, huge fortunes piling up, C. & O. and company guards beating up labor organizers, oil and gas spurting up out of the ground in Pennsylvania and Ohio, John D. Rockefeller, the bicycle and then the automobile, presently, down at Dayton, Ohio, the Wright brothers with their queer crates, watching the flight of birds to learn how to become birdmen, new terrors in the sky in a time of new wars, what a life to be lived by an Ohio small town boy, what a time in which to live that life. If Mark Twain could speak of the sixteenth century as the most glorious of all the centuries surely he could

29. New York: B. W. Huebsch, 1920.

30. For descriptions of Clyde, Ohio, see "Winesburg, Ohio: A *Life* Artist Visits Sherwood Anderson's Town," *Life*, XX (June 10, 1946), 74–79; John H. Sullivan, "Winesburg Revisited," *Antioch Review*, XX (Summer, 1960), 213–21. For Anderson's later view of his native state, see "Ohio: I'll Say We've Done Well," *These United States: A Symposium*, edited by Ernest Gruening (New York: Boni and Liveright, 1923), pp. 109–17. *Letters of Sherwood Anderson*, edited by Howard Mumford Jones and Walter B. Rideout (Boston: Little, Brown and Company, 1953), Item 395, describes one of Anderson's last visits to Clyde.

come in his maturity to think of his own as the most terrifying of the centuries.

But he is back there now, in the Twain country, a boy there. He is driving cows to and from pastures, distributing Toledo and Cleveland daily newspapers, mowing people's lawns, filled with determination to get on. He and his brothers will lift the family up out of poverty to affluence. He is determined on that. It became the central dream of his young life.

In the meantime things are happening in my town. There was a man who came from the neighboring town of Elmore to establish a bicycle factory, later to become an automobile factory making a car called the Elmore. Later when General Motors was organized our man was bought out and went off, no doubt a rich man, to live in New York and the factory was closed. There were to be no more Elmore cars.

I was to see them running through our streets, after stopping dead, a mechanic from the factory compelled to come to get the car started again, but although the Elmore car was constantly breaking down it sold and until taken over by General Motors it sold because of the eagerness for progress of the American people, cheerfully thus financing through the experimental stage each new instrument of speed.

Now factory talk about the town stores at night, the beginning of labor unrest, myself going among the men, in and out of stores and even in and out of the town saloons to sell newspapers to the men standing by the bar.

Father often seen in one of the bars. He would become self-conscious when I came in.

"I only came in here to see a man. It is about painting his barn."

The smell of whiskey on his breath. Was I becoming a moralist so young? There was the fact of mother still at the wash tub washing people's dirty clothes. Resentment surging up in me.

"He is in here spending what money he does earn."

But money, money. I must have money. It is with money I can help to pull mother from the wash tub. She is a tall thin woman and, day by day, seems to grow thinner. Although we children do not know it, have not yet become alarmed, tuberculosis, brought on no doubt by standing over her wash tub day after day, northern Ohio winters and constantly (her clothes wet and often freezing to her body) running in and out of the steaming kitchen where she works. A rather silent woman, tall now and gaunt, who

I at least never heard complain at her lot and who in some way constantly conveyed to her sons a feeling that they were something a little special in the world.

"You will know how to make your way. Don't fear. There is something special in your very blood. You will be men of talent, someday the world will look up to you."

In some way, without the words being actually said, some such impression of her belief in us coming to us, filling our hearts with a love for her that was to last all of our lives.

But money, money, more and more money. How am I to get it?

"Money makes the mare go."

"Take care of the pennies and the dollars will take care of themselves."

There was that tailor in the town who once a month got drunk. He worked hard and steadily all through the week and then, an old hunger coming suddenly and strongly upon him, down he jumped from sitting with crossed legs on his tailor's table and seizing his hat rushed forth into the street.

The little tailor ran from bar to bar up and down the street. He began by drinking alone but, after three or four drinks, commanded others to drink with him. All through the month he had been a quiet, hard working man, not given to talk, but now he burst forth into speech. He had a wife and several children at home. He had been a soldier under General Sherman during the Civil War. His monthly sprees began always with an outbreak of love for his wife and children and ended always in the same way. At last, just able to walk, he staggered home. Earlier he had proclaimed to all his affection for his family, had rushed into one of the town grocery stores and had begun ordering groceries sent to his wife.

"I love my family. Send them a barrel of flour, a barrel of sugar, a barrel of potatoes. Send plenty. Here's the money. Here's the money. Look at it. I have plenty of money. Look, here's a ten dollar bill. Send ten dollars' worth of canned goods. Send fruit, send vegetables, send everything."

In the end a black mood came upon the little tailor. He grew angry. He was in his own house now and had begun to resent his wife and children. Once he threw a young boy of the family down a flight of stairs, injuring him for life, an act that forever afterward preyed on the poor man's mind.

He had also a daughter but I will speak of her later. She was to be a part of an adventure of my own of which I will tell.

When the little tailor had gone off on one of his sprees he began at once to call for me. General Sherman was his god and he was under the illusion that my name was "Sherman" and that I had been named for that general, an illusion that I was very careful not to dispel.

"Where is that boy? Where is that boy named Sherman? Send for him. He bears the most illustrious name in America." He was calling for me up and down the main street and in and out of the stores and saloons and presently I appeared. He thrust a dollar, two dollars, into my hand.

"Take it, boy. It is for the grand name you bear. It is a tribute to a man I love and admire. Boy, do nothing to disgrace that name. There is a great responsibility upon your shoulder, my boy. Try to bear it manfully through life."

Oh the character of our town. I could sit here at my desk writing of this for days and months. There was that boy named McClary and called Toughy—a kind of Huckleberry Finn of the town. He seemed to have no parents, lived about, sometimes sleeping in a horse stall, up at the town fair grounds, sometimes in the house of some friendly family that had for a time taken him in.

He did not have to go to school. He went hunting and fishing at all hours. Oh what a free and happy life he seemed to live.

It was with this same boy that I got into two early commercial adventures.

But dare I speak of these as purely commercial? At least one of them was the beginning in me of the practise of an art.

It was the art of the theatre, which I never followed. I had thought of a drama, to be played out on a little strip of lawn down by our railroad station.

The station was really a junction for the crossing of two railroads, a southern swinging branch of the great New York Central system, then called the Lake Shore and Michigan Central, the branch running south of the main line between Cleveland and Toledo and passing through our town and crossing there another railroad called the IB&W, now a part of the Big Four system.

There was this meeting place of trains going east and west with trains that went south and often a passenger train stood waiting some ten or fifteen minutes to pick up passengers from the other train and on pleasant days there would be passengers getting off the train to walk up and down the station platform before the little strip of lawn that had as a backdrop a flour mill.

Why I once met John L. Sullivan [31] there.

"This is the hand that shook the hand of John L. Sullivan." Alas that didn't happen to me but I did stand wide eyed while the great man with a tiny dog in his arms and a huge cigar between his lips strutted up and down before us admiring villagers.

But as to the play.

"The play's the thing."

I had thought it up, as a way to drag in sheckles, and had let Toughy in on it. No doubt I had been reading dime novels. [32] Toughy and I had fashioned two knives of wood, in our conception of the far west, sworn to kill each other at sight, and we met by chance on the little strip of lawn before the railroad platform just as the waiting passengers were strolling up and down.

We advanced toward each other.

"Ah, you are the one.

"Death to you," we both cried.

There was for a few minutes a desperate struggle, each ran with knife in hand and then, with a quick and very skillful movement, I unknifed the cur.

I had him then. My skillful move had hurled his knife aside upon the lawn and I had pounced upon it. He was there before me, unarmed, at my mercy.

However he did not run away. Although a cur at heart he was no coward. Folding his arms across his breast he stood before me.

"Go on. Kill me then. Attack, if you will, an unarmed man."

Ah what scorn in his words.

"Coward, it would be like you to do it. Go ahead."

You may be sure we had the attention of our audience by this time.

And now I, having been the author of the play, had my chance to show my real nobility. With the two knives held in my open hand I stepped toward him.

"Take your choice of the weapons," I said. "I would scorn to kill an unarmed man, even a cur like you."

And then quietly the dénouement. He pounces. Quickly he seizes not one but both of the knives. He springs upon me, knives me to the heart

31. John Lawrence Sullivan (1858–1918), boxing champion who lost his title in 1892 and who, giving up heavy drinking, became a temperance lecturer.
32. *The Last of the Mohicans* (1826) is "dramatized" as a boyhood game in *A Story Teller's Story,* ed. White, pp. 12–21.

and I fall dead, the victim of too much nobility, upon the grass while Toughy, cap in hand, runs among the applauding audience.

He collects many a nickel and dime which we divide but alas, my mother, hearing of our performance, makes me stop it. She declares it is too much like begging and I have to quit.

Oh, will women ever really understand the arts?

There was another enterprise into which I went at this time and which, in the end, when she found out about it, was squelched by mother and in this enterprise Toughy was also my partner.

Toughy had suddenly and in some mysterious way acquired a shot gun and, the summer days having come, was spending these wandering in the nearby woods and fields. He became an expert shot and began to bring in bags of rabbits and squirrels which he sold to the housewives of our town.

Toughy one day told me how he had acquired the gun and an idea for money making at once popped into my head and I proposed the partnership.

There was, at the edge of our town and facing the Maumee Pike, an early road along which pioneers had made their way from Cleveland, through Toledo and into southern Michigan, a graveyard, given special distinction because in it was buried one of the heroes of the Civil War, General McPherson.

The general, one of Ulysses Grant's most capable lieutenants, was killed before Atlanta during General Sherman's march, southward from Nashville to Atlanta and then eastward through the heart of the south, to the sea. The general's body had been brought home to our town and had been buried in our graveyard and a statue had been erected to him. The statue, of bronze and with the general's figure some eighteen or twenty feet tall, stood on a little hill facing Maumee Pike and the town and the general stood upon a pedestal. He had an arm raised and his finger was pointing, I always presumed, toward some weak spot in the enemy's front into which he was commanding his soldiers to charge.

So there the general stood and still stands but at the time of which I am now writing the McPherson farmstead also stood, also facing the Maumee Pike and close beside the graveyard. The general had left one son, known about town as Jim McPherson, a silent somewhat lonely seeming man, as I remember him, seen often going silently through the town streets, and there was also the general's widow whom I do not remember ever to have seen.

The McPherson farm extended back from the road along the side of the graveyard. It was, I believe, a rather large farm and was little worked. Perhaps the general's widow had been granted a generous pension by the government upon which she and her son could live in comfort.

At any rate there the farm was, now overgrown with weeds, and standing back from the house and half hidden by trees was a large and now unused barn.

It was into this barn that Toughy, who had become my friend, had one day wandered and he had made a discovery for there were piled upon the floor of the barn some long boxes, looking a good deal like coffins, and, filled with curiosity, Toughy had pried open the lid of one of the boxes and had found it filled with guns.

The guns were there in their boxes and having been packed in heavy grease were in good condition. They were Civil War guns and had been sent to our town by the government. There had been a plan to build a picket fence about the statue of the general, using the guns as pickets, but it had never been built.

And what a treasure. Toughy came wide eyed to tell me all about it. He took me to see the guns. We passed around the end of the graveyard, late on a spring evening, and crept through tall weeds to the barn. It was Toughy's idea that the guns could be sawed off to shot gun length. The rifling could be bored out. There was a man named Curtis in the town who had a little shop in which he could do the job.

There were the guns, with their ramrods that could also be sawed short. Toughy, it developed, had already consulted Curtis who had agreed to make the army guns into shot guns at a cost of twenty-five cents.

It was Toughy's idea that the guns had been sent to our town by the government. They had not been used. He had heard the men of the town talk of a thing called "taxes." When we had examined the guns we returned, in the half darkness of an early spring evening, to nearby bushes to have a conference. It was Toughy's notion that it would be all right for each of us to hike one of the guns and have it made into a shot gun to hunt rabbits.

"People pay taxes, don't they?" he asked. His point was that the guns were public property and he had been the one to discover them. If I would pay the fifty cents to have the guns made over, so that they would not be so cumbersome, he could see no reason why we should not both, at once, equip ourselves as hunters.

"You see, it wouldn't be stealing," he said and I agreed with him.

And then the great idea came to me.

"But why just two guns?"

Such guns, made into shot guns, could, I was sure, readily be sold to other boys of the town at fifty cents each. Toughy would get the guns, bringing them out, one or two at a time, I would find the money to pay the man named Curtis and we would both be salesmen and divide the swag.

To be sure, as we both knew, it was an enterprise that would need to be handled with caution. The source of supplies would have to be kept secret so that other boys of the town could not get at it.

And there was something else. It was a matter that did not affect Toughy, he being a free and unhampered soul, but that did profoundly affect me and the boys of the town who were to become customers.

It was again a matter of mothers, mothers in general being opposed to guns. The boys who were to be our customers would have to be sworn to keep the fact of their ownership of a shot gun a secret. When not in use such guns would have to be hidden away in barns.

And there was something else. I was quite sure that, although Toughy and I had quite convinced ourselves of our own right to the guns, they being unused government property, this government being made up of the citizenry, we ourselves being at least on the way to becoming citizens at our great discovery (we had both already heard political speeches) . . . in spite of all this there was the danger that my own mother and other mothers of the town might, in the foolish way mothers sometimes have of looking at things, call our getting of the guns stealing.

And so in the end it turned out, although for a time Toughy and I did succeed in doing quite a thriving little business in guns, it all presently leaked out and the story in some way came to mother's ears and there was, for me, an uncomfortable half hour that ended in a promise that I would give up this the fruit of my venture into the world of business.

Our Morning Roll Call

People. They parade before you at night. There was Sneaky Pete. He was a solidly built man, unmarried, who lived with his old mother. He had been a soldier of sorts but could not get into the G.A.R. Father and various veterans said he had been a bounty jumper.

He was a gay defiant man, always ready for a fight. In the spring he worked in his mother's garden but he did no other work for the rest of the year. Perhaps his mother had a small income.

He filled a basket with spring vegetables and came along the railroad track to our main street. He was intent upon trading the vegetables to some saloon keeper for a morning drink. He shouted. He laughed loudly. He sang.

"What's the use being poor when you can own the whole world for ten cents?" he shouted. Ten cents was the prevailing price of a drink of bar whisky.

It was Sneaky Pete who started our morning roll call. He became a caricature of the morals of the town. He spread terror through the town.

His mother's house was on a street out near the edge of town and in the early morning, intent on his morning drink, he went along the street to the railroad and along the tracks toward main street. It was the quiet hour, a spring summer or fall morning. Sneaky Pete swaggered along. There was a gleam in his eyes. He had a short black General Grant beard and smoked a short stemmed clay pipe. The smoke lay like a cloud in mountain forests in his beard.

It was a day of meat and potato breakfasts. The wives of the town were old fashioned fryers. There were none of the modern orange juice, toast and coffee addicts among the breakfasters of that day.

The women of the town bought cheap cuts of round steak at the local meat market. Somewhere near the outer edge of every middle western town there was a slaughter house filled with rats and flies and surrounded by a field piled high with bones of old cows. The women took the cheap steaks home and laid them on a board. They beat the steaks with a hammer. They pounded away. There was a drumming sound as of a hundred woodpeckers at work.

Sneaky Pete was far down the railroad track swaggering along. Some citizen of the town had been betrayed. It might be a man who worked in the bank, or a wash-out. It might even be a man who taught a class in the Sunday school of one of our churches.

There were in our town, as in all towns, certain women and girls. They were known as "pushovers." They were "putting out." Men met them in the evening on a side street of the town. The automobile had not come yet but almost every man in town owned a horse and buggy.[33]

33. See *Tar* (1926), pp. 227–31.

The pushover was gathered in. Alas often she was gathered in by some respectable married man of the town. The pushover was driven off into some quiet country lane. What ho.

But again, alas, someone had slipped the word to Sneaky Pete. The clerks in the stores along main street, having swept all the stores, were now sweeping the sidewalks before the stores. One of them raised his voice. The name of the man who had, he hoped, secretly met Sally Graves in the dark street down by the Seventh Day Adventist church on the night before, who had got Sally into his buggy and had driven off with her into the darkness, was now shouted over the roofs of the town.

"John Huntington."

Alas poor John. So you thought no one saw you pick up Sally, eh?

There was some clerk with a malicious streak in his make up.

"John Huntington."

The name so bawled forth floated through the quiet morning streets of the town and housewives who had been busily beating breakfast steaks quit beating. They ran quickly to kitchen doors. They were waiting for Sneaky Pete's answering voice from far down the railroad tracks.

It came.

"Sa-a-aly Graves."

There was an outburst of laughter from the clerks.

"P. T. Smith." An answering cry.

"Mary Thompson." Poor Mary had a bad leg. She went hopping about. She hopped into dark carriages with men and boys at night.

"P. T. Smith."

"Mary Thompson."

It was all very cruel. It got Sneaky Pete into endless fights but he did not mind. Well the G.A.R. wouldn't take him in. There was something wrong with his war record. He was having a good time. He was getting even. Some man of the town always slipping him the dirt of the town.

At the county seat there was a certain house run by one Moll Hunter.

So, some respectable man's foot had slipped. He had, on a certain night, gone secretly to that place. He hoped his going would remain a secret.

He was at home now, in his own house, waiting for his breakfast, but at the sound of Sneaky Pete's voice, a far carrying one, floating thus through the quiet morning streets, he trembled.

Had someone seen him slipping into that house in the darkness?

The names of respectable men were being called off. There were twenty or thirty clerks standing now before the main street stores with brooms in their hands. If his name was bawled out thus by one of the clerks it would be difficult if not impossible to name the culprit.

"A. G. Bottomly." Bottomly had told his wife that he had to go to the county seat on business.

And now, ye gods, there it was.

"A. G. Bottomly." And then the answering cry from Sneaky Pete.

"Moll Hunter."

It was something to drive a man mad. Later that day there would be a fight on main street but what did it matter to Sneaky Pete? He enjoyed fighting. He was almost always victorious in fights.

Sneaky Pete advanced along the railroad track and past the railroad station calling off names, connecting thus the names of often respectable citizens with females of ill repute. If it was spring he carried the little basket of vegetables on his arm. He was pleased with himself and with life. He was creating trouble. He was stirring up fights. He was getting even with life. He advanced to the middle of main street and turned to face the clerks standing along the street before the stores. He put a hand up to his mouth, made a trumpet of his hand. His voice rolled up the street and was followed by a loud outburst of laughter. All the men of the town whose names had not been called off in Sneaky Pete's morning roll call laughed. Women whose men were not involved giggled as they went back to their steak pounding. The old impulse in man to enjoy heartily the discomfiture of others shook the town with laughter.

Sneaky Pete was standing erect like a soldier at the foot of our main street. He had made a trumpet of his hand.

"Go-o-od Damn." His voice called up the street and as it died away was followed by the outburst of laughter. The morning roll call was at an end and three or four more citizens had been thus jerked up to start trembling under the judgment of the town.[34]

Unforgotten

One of the strangest relationships in the world is that between father and son. I know it now from having sons of my own. I am hoping they do not turn out to be writers.

34. Published (revised) in *The Sherwood Anderson Reader,* edited by Paul Rosenfeld (Boston: Houghton Mifflin Company, 1947), pp. 376–79.

It is something dreadful to have a writer for a son. How unscrupulous we writers are. I am thinking, as I write these words, of my own father, surely, as I think of him, now that he is dead, now that I am myself a father of sons, an unforgettable man.

I am thinking of the dangers of having a writer as son. We writers use everyone. We are after stories. We jerk people out of the lives in which they live, or think they live, and put them into a world we invent. We use our own lives so. Once I did an unfair mean thing to a certain man in Ohio. He was my friend and I rather sold him out. He was angry. My name began to get a little up in the world and he threatened me. He said he was going to write telling just what kind of man I was.

"Please do," I said. "Rough it up. Send the whole story to me. I've half forgotten." I pointed out that I could do the job better than he could. I meant it, too. I was a story teller and I knew I could beat him telling the story.

There are certain men who are what I call "feeders." The story teller loves such men. They go about telling little things that have happened to them. They cannot write the stories but they can tell them. Put pens into their hands and away fly the stories.

There was an Irishman I knew in Chicago who was like that. I fed on him for years and in the end I ruined him. I had got so many good stories from him, had written and sold them, that I grew ashamed. I spoke to him. "Why don't you write the stories yourself?" I said. He began trying, has been at it ever since. He can't do it. He might well have been a success in life if I hadn't got into his head the notion that he could be a writer.[35]

A man who worked for me on my farm was such a story teller. What tales he told! There is a certain naïveté in such men. They are really innocent. They look out upon life with clear innocent eyes. They tell you the most wonderful tales of things they feel, things they have done, things that have been done to them. They tell everything very clearly, with amazing innocence. The man worked for me one summer and I cleaned up on him. I got several beautiful stories, heard them from his lips, while we worked together, rushed at once into the house, put down the stories just as he had told them. Then I was a fool. At the end of the summer I told him what I had been doing and he grew afraid of me.

Or he thought I was getting too much for nothing. I should have kept

35. This "feeder" is George Daugherty, whom Anderson met in Springfield, Ohio, in 1899–1900. See Daugherty, "Anderson, Advertising Man," *Newberry Library Bulletin,* Series II, No. 2 (December, 1948), 30–43.

my mouth shut. I lost a good feeder. Now the wonderful stories he might tell to many people through me are lost.

A boy wants something very special from his father. You are always hearing it said that fathers want their sons to be what they feel they cannot themselves be but I tell you it also works the other way. I know that, as a small boy, I wanted my father to be a certain thing he was not, could not be. I wanted him to be a proud silent dignified one. When I was with other small boys and he passed along the street, I wanted to feel in my breast the glow of pride.

"There he is. That is my father."

But he wasn't such a one. He couldn't be. It seemed to me then that he was always showing off. Let's say someone in our town had got up a show. They were always doing it. At that time it would have been the G.A.R., the Grand Army of the Republic. They did it to raise some money to help pay the rent of their hall.

So they had a show, the druggist in it, the fellow who clerked in the shoe store. A certain horse doctor was always in such shows in our town and, to be sure, a lot of women and girls. They got as many in it as they could so that all of the relatives of the actors would come. It was to be, of course, a comedy.

And there was my father. He had managed to get the chief comedy part. It was, let's say, a Civil War play and he was a comic Irish soldier. He had to do the most absurd things. They thought he was funny, but I didn't think so.

I thought he was terrible. I didn't see how mother could stand it. She even laughed with the others. It may be that I also would have laughed if it hadn't been my father.

Or there was a parade, say on the Fourth of July or on Decoration Day. He'd be in that too. He'd be right at the front of it. He had got himself appointed Grand Marshall or some such office, had got, to ride in the parade, a white horse hired from a livery stable.

He couldn't ride for shucks. He fell off the horse and everyone hooted with laughter but he did not care.[36] He even seemed to like it. I remember one such occasion when he had done something ridiculous, and right out on the main street too, when I couldn't stand it. I was with some other boys and they were laughing and shouting at him and he was shouting

---

36. Such ludicrous incidents, surely spurious, form the hatred of Sam McPherson for his father in *Windy McPherson's Son* (1916), a partially autobiographical work.

back to them and having as good a time as they were. I ran away. There was an alleyway back of the stores on main street and I ran down that. There were some sheds, back of the Presbyterian church, where country people stabled horses during church on Sundays and I went in there. I had a good long cry.

Or I was in bed at night and father had come home a little lit up and had brought some men with him. He was a man who was never alone. There were always men hanging around him. Before he went broke, running a harness shop, when he had the shop, there were always a lot of men loafing in there. He went broke of course because he gave too much credit. He couldn't refuse it and I thought he hadn't any sense. I thought he was a fool. I had got to hating him. I'd be upstairs in bed in the front room of the little house we lived in and he'd bring his crowd of men friends and sit with them on the front porch of our house.

There'd be men I didn't think would want to be fooling around with him but they did. There might even be the superintendent of our schools and a quiet man who ran a hardware store in our town. Once I remember there was a white haired man who was cashier of the bank. It was a wonder to me they'd want to be seen with such a wind bag. That's what I thought he was. I know now what it was that attracted them but I didn't know then. Now I think it was because life in our town, as in all small towns, was at times pretty dull and he livened it up. He made them laugh. He could tell stories. He'd even get them to singing. If they didn't come to our house he'd get such a crowd and they'd go off, say at night, to where there was a grassy place by a creek. They'd cook food there and they'd drink beer. They'd sit about listening to him while he told his stories. I knew that most of the stories he told were lies.

He was always telling stories about himself. He'd say this or that wonderful thing had happened to him. It might be something that made him look like a fool. He didn't care. If it was a story, he'd tell it.

He was like this, let's say an Irishman came to our house. Right away father would say he was Irish. He'd tell what county in Ireland he was born in. He'd tell things that happened to him in Ireland when he was a boy. He'd make it seem so real, telling little details of his life as a boy in Ireland, that, if I hadn't known where he was born, in a county down in southern Ohio, I'd have believed him myself.

If it was a Scotchman the same thing happened. He became a Scotchman. He'd get a burr into his speech. Or he was a German or a Swede. He'd be anything the other man was.

I think now they all knew he was lying but they seemed to like him just the same. As a boy that was what I couldn't understand.

And there was mother. How could she stand it? I wanted to ask but never did. I was afraid. She was the kind you didn't ask such questions.

I'd be upstairs in my bed, in my room above the porch, and father would be telling some of his tales. There were a lot of stories about the Civil War. To hear him tell it he'd been in about every battle of the war.[37] He'd known Grant, Sherman, McPherson, Sheridan and I don't know how many others. He'd been particularly intimate with General Grant so that when Grant went east, to take charge of all the armies, he took father along.

"I was an orderly, up at headquarters, and Sam Grant said to me, 'Irve,' he said, 'I'm going to take you along with me.'"

It seems he and Grant used to slip off together sometimes and have a quiet little drink together. That's what my father said. He'd tell about the day Lee surrendered and how, when the great moment came, they couldn't find Grant.

"You know," my father said, "about General Grant's book, his *Memoirs*. You've read it, eh? You've read of how he said he had a headache and how, when he got word that Lee was ready to call it quits, he was suddenly and miraculously cured?

"Huh," said father.

"He was in the woods with me," my father declared.

"I was in there, in the woods with my back against a tree. I was pretty well corned. I had got hold of a bottle of pretty good stuff. I found it in a house.

"So I was in the woods and they were looking for Grant. He was riding along a road and had got off his horse and had come into the woods. He found me in there. He had come . . . well, nature you know. He was covered with mud.

"I had the bottle in my hand. I was sitting there with my back to a tree. What'd I care? The war was over. I knew we had them licked."

My father said that he was the one who told Grant that Lee was ready to surrender. He said he was walking along a road with the bottle hidden under a coat and that an orderly riding along the road had told him. He said the orderly knew how thick he was with Sam Grant.

37. Irwin Anderson served in the Ohio infantry from August 25, 1864, to July 1, 1865, and saw service in Tennessee, Alabama, and Georgia. See *A Story Teller's Story*, ed. White, pp. 6–7, 28–37, 45–56; and *Tar* (1926), pp. 27–30.

And then, there in the woods, he told Grant and Grant was embarrassed.

"But, Irve, look at me. I'm all covered with mud," he said to father.

And then, my father said, he and Grant decided to have a drink together. He said they took a couple of shots and then, because he didn't want Grant to show up potted before the immaculate Lee, he got to his feet and smashed the bottle against the tree.

"Sam Grant's dead now and I wouldn't want it to get out on him," my father said.[38]

That's just one of the kind of things he'd tell and of course the men, sitting and listening, knew he was lying but they seemed to like it just the same. They laughed at him but he didn't seem to care. Once some of them counted up on him. He'd been sitting with them in the evening in front of the stores or on the porch of our house, telling how many years he'd been here, how many there. To hear him tell it there wasn't a state, not a city in the whole country he hadn't been in. "I was working three years there," he'd say. He was five years in another place, ten in another. They counted up on him. Everyone called him "Major" although he wasn't a major at all.

"Major," they said, "we been figuring you up. We make it out you're a hundred and eighty years old." Do you think he cared? Not he. He laughed the same as everyone else.

We had gone broke, down and out, and do you think he ever brought anything home? Not he. If there wasn't anything to eat in the house, off visiting he'd go. He'd go visiting around at farm houses near our town. They all wanted him. Sometimes he'd stay away for weeks, mother working to keep us fed, and then home he'd come bringing, let's say, a ham. He'd got it from some farmer friend. He'd slap it on the table in the kitchen. "You bet I'm going to see that my kids have something to eat," he'd say and mother would just stand there looking at him and smiling at him. She'd never say a word about all the weeks and months he'd been away, not leaving us a cent for food. Once I heard her speaking to a woman in our street. It may be that woman had dared to sympathize with her. "Oh," she said, "it's all right. Don't you worry. He isn't ever dull like most of the men in this street. Life is never dull when my man is about."

38. See also "Tim and General Grant," *The Sherwood Anderson Reader,* ed. Rosenfeld, pp. 846–50.

I'd be up in my room and father'd be down on the porch with some of his crowd. This would be on a summer night. He'd be spinning some of his tales. Then I didn't understand but now I know he never told any lies that hurt anyone. I know now that he just wanted to give people a show, make them laugh. He knew how bitter tasting life gets to almost everyone that lives. He had I think some notion of putting a kind of color on life, touching it here and there with a bit of color. I think he wanted to wash it over with color and I think mother knew.

I was up there in my room and I was awake. I was filled often with bitterness, hearing my father go on and on with his tales, and often I wished he wasn't my father. I'd even invent another man as my father.

To be sure I wanted to protect my mother. I'd make up stories of a secret marriage, that for some strange reason never got known, as though some man, say the president of a railroad company or maybe a congressman, had got married to my mother, thinking his wife was dead and that then it turned out she wasn't.

So they had to hush it up but I got born just the same. I wasn't really the son of my father. There was a mysterious man somewhere in the world, a very dignified quite wonderful man who was really my father. You get the point. I even made myself half believe some of these fancies.[39]

And then there came a certain night. Mother was away from home when father came in and he was alone. He'd been off somewhere for two or three weeks. He found me alone in the house.

He came silently into the house and it was raining outside. It may be there was church that night and that mother had gone. I was alone and was sitting in the kitchen. I had a book before me and was sitting and reading by the kitchen table.

So in came my father. He had been walking in the rain and was very wet. He sat and looked at me and I was startled for, on that night, there was on his face the saddest look I had ever seen on a human face. For a long time he sat looking at me, not saying a word.

And then something happened to me.

There are times when a boy is so sad, he doesn't quite know why, that he thinks he can hardly bear to go on living. He thinks he'd rather die. The sadness comes mostly when it has been raining or it comes in the fall when the leaves fall off the trees. It isn't anything special. It is just sadness.

So there was father on the rainy summer night. He was sad and looking

39. Anderson's fancies about his birth are tied with his emerging imagination, as in *A Story Teller's Story,* ed. White, pp. 71–78, 81–90, and 92–96.

at him made me sad. He sat for a time, saying nothing, his clothes dripping. He must have been walking a long time in the rain. He got up out of his chair.

"You come on, you come with me," he said.

I got up and went with him out of the house. I was filled with wonder but, although he had suddenly become like a stranger to me, I wasn't afraid. We went along a street. At that time we lived in a little yellow frame house, quite far out at the edge of our town. It was a house we hadn't lived in very long. We had moved a lot. Once I heard my mother say to my father, "Well, I guess we'll have to be moving," she said. She said we were back three months on our rent and that there wasn't any money to pay it with. She didn't scold. She even laughed. She just took it as a fact that when the rent got far behind we had to move.

I was walking with my father and we went out of the town. We were on a dirt road. It was a road that led up a little hill, past fields and strips of woodland, and went on over the hill and down into a little valley, about a mile out of town, to where there was a pond. We walked in silence. The man who was always talking had stopped talking.

I didn't know what was up and had the queer feeling that I was with a stranger. I don't know now whether or not my father intended it so. I don't think he did.

The pond at the edge of the town was quite large. It was a place where a creek had been dammed and was owned by a man who sold ice in our town. We were there at the edge of the pond. We had come in silence. It was still raining hard and there were flashes of lightning followed by thunder. We were on a grassy bank at the pond's edge, when my father spoke, and in the darkness and rain his voice sounded strange. It was the only time during the evening that he did speak to me.

"Take off your clothes," he said and, still filled with wonder, I began to undress. There was a flash of lightning and I saw that he was already naked.

And so naked we went into the pond. He did not speak or explain. Taking my hand he led me down to the pond's edge and pulled me in. It may be that I was too frightened, too full of a feeling of strangeness to speak. Before that night my father had never seemed to pay any attention to me.

"And what is he up to now?" I kept asking myself that question. It was as though the man, my father I had not wanted as father, had got suddenly some kind of power over me.

I was afraid and then, right away, I wasn't afraid. We were in the pond in darkness. It was a large pond and I did not swim very well but he had put my hand on his shoulder. Still he did not speak but struck out at once into the darkness.

He was a man with very big shoulders and was a powerful swimmer. In the darkness I could feel the movement of his muscles. The rain poured down on us and the wind blew and there were the flashes of lightning followed by the peals of thunder.

And so we swam, I will never know for how long. It seemed hours to me. We swam thus in the darkness to the far edge of the pond and then back to where we had left our clothes. There was the rain on our faces. Sometimes my father turned and swam on his back and when he did he took my hand in his large powerful one and moved it over so that it rested always on his shoulder and sometimes as we swam thus I could look into his face. There would be a flash of lightning and I could see his face clearly.

It was as it was when he had come earlier into the kitchen where I sat reading the book. It was a face filled with sadness. There would be the momentary glimpse of his face and then again the darkness, the wind and the rain. In me there was a feeling I had never known before that night.

It was a feeling of closeness. It was something strange. It was as though there were only we two in the world. It was as though I had been jerked suddenly out of myself, out of a world of the school boy, out of a world in which I was ashamed of my father, out of a place where I had been judging my father.

He had become blood of my blood. I think I felt it. He the stronger swimmer and I the boy clinging to him in the darkness. We swam in silence and in silence we dressed, in our wet clothes, and went back along the road to the town and our house.

It had become a strange house to me. There was the little porch at the front where on so many nights my father had sat with the men. There was the tree by the spring and the shed at the back. There was a lamp lighted in the kitchen and when we came in, the water dripping from us, there was my mother. She was as she had always been. She smiled at us. I remember that she called us "boys." "What have you boys been up to?" she asked, but my father did not answer. As he had begun the evening's experience with me in silence so he ended it. He turned and looked at me and then he went, I thought with a new and strange dignity, out of the room.

He went to his room to get out of his wet clothes and I climbed the stairs to my own room. I undressed in darkness and got into bed. I was still in the grip of the feeling of strangeness that had taken possession of me in the darkness in the pond. I couldn't sleep and did not want to sleep. For the first time I had come to know that I was the son of my father. He was a story teller as I was to be. It may be that on the night of my childhood I even laughed a little softly there in the darkness in my bed in the room. If I did, I laughed knowing that, no matter how much as a story teller I might be using him, I would never again be wanting another father.[40]

Second Woman

There were two young girls used to parade up and down the streets of our town. They were small. They kept inviting the men and boys. One of the girls was the daughter of a man who went about exhibiting a stuffed whale.

He had the whale on a flat car. It was hitched to a freight train and hauled from town to town. How the whale was preserved I do not know. Perhaps it was but a papier-mâché whale.

He had a fence built around it and the people paid ten cents to climb up and look. He was always gone from home exhibiting the whale.

The other girl was the daughter of a drunken tailor.

The two girls, the daughter of the tailor and of the man of the stuffed whale, were always together. Every evening they were on the main street of our little town, going up and down, up and down.

They were with men. They were with young boys. They were going up and down.

There was a dark graveyard in the town where a Union general was buried. They went there with boys. There were green lanes and pastures at the edge of town. They went there.

They were walking up and down, up and down, past lighted stores, past

40. Published (revised) as "Discovery of a Father," *Reader's Digest,* XXXV (November, 1939), 21–25. On Anderson's assessing his father's character, see also *A Story Teller's Story,* ed. White, pp. 14–15, 43–44; and *Tar* (1926), pp. 11–31, 72–76, 94–107, 272–74.

the town post office, past the railroad station. Our main street sloped gently down to where the railroad crossed it and beyond the railroad the section of main street was called "Canada."

The two girls went into Canada. They were looking, expecting. The men and boys of the town did not fail them.

It was in Canada it happened. It was Sunday night and the main street was dark. Many of the people of the town were in the churches but the two girls did not go to church. They walked up and down the dark main street where men and boys were gathered in groups.

The men and boys laughed.

"There they go, the Shetland Ponies. Who will have them tonight?"

We crept along an alleyway back of the stores. I was with a bold boy, the son of a butcher. He had come to me.

"I have got it fixed," he said. "Will you come?"

I was terribly afraid. I was ashamed. I wanted to go and did not want to go. I was ashamed of my shame. I was ashamed that I was afraid.

I kept thinking of the bold boy who had invited me to go. I wanted to be as he was. He had gone right up to them, on main street, had asked them.

He had asked them what boy they wanted to come with him and the daughter of the man of the stuffed whale had spoken my name.

So he had come to me.

"She wants you to come. Will you?"

I had said I would.

But why did my heart beat so heavily? It would be for me really the first time and, although I was but a young boy, how often I had dreamed of it.

The incident of the little girl under the porch did not count.[41] Now it was to be real.

Did I dare? I walked along, through the alleyway, with the butcher's son, so bold I thought, so free from shame, and how I envied him.

We had got to the lower end of town and had crossed the railroad into Canada. Down there, all was silent, the stores dark, no men and boys standing about. We stood before one of the stores. It was an undertaking establishment, where coffins were sold.

41. An incident Anderson did not more fully narrate. On the child's sex interest, see *Tar* (1926), pp. 227–33, 239–43, 254–68.

Life and death, eh?

Would we take them to the cemetery? Well, now I was in for it. I would let the butcher's son manage.

They came, the two little things, and we walked along a dark street. I had not spoken to her, could not speak. There was a trembling sensation all over my body. My cheeks were hot. My mouth felt dry.

There seemed to be a strange silence over the town. I thought of my mother. Perhaps she had gone to church. She did occasionally. She would be sitting there, with the people, in her dress, the proud silent mother I knew.

"But she could not know. How could she know?"

I do not think I had much sense of sin, of doing a wrong.

"Would I be effective? Would I prove a good lover to the little girl who walked with me?"

This thought no doubt most in my mind. We went in silence and there was the butcher's son, with the daughter of the tailor, walking before us.

They were not silent. They kept laughing and pushing each other about.

And then, suddenly, the little girl walking with me took my hand. She put her little hand in mine. She had asked the butcher's son to ask me. She wanted me. The thought gave me a little confidence.

We went along so until we came to where another railroad crossed the street of silent dark houses in which we had been walking. We turned down along the railroad, went along the tracks, stepping on the railroad ties. We went past a dark railroad station and came to where some empty freight cars stood on a railroad siding.

It was proposed that we crawl into one of the cars. The butcher's son proposed it but the girls were afraid. They said an engine might come and take us away. They said they were afraid they would get their dresses dirty. They stood together, whispering and giggling.

So again we walked along the tracks. Again the daughter of the whale walked with me. It had become somewhat lighter. The moon was coming up.

We had got to the edge of the town and turned into a lane. It was a lane along which cows were driven from a farm back of a brick house at the edge of town to distant fields.

There was a field where I with other boys had played baseball. The cows were driven still along the narrow lane.

There was a worm fence. There were little grass covered recesses where the rails of the fence formed a v. The butcher's son with the daughter of the tailor went into one of the recesses and the daughter of the whale led me into another.

It was the great moment.

I stood in silence. She was wearing the sort of little white undergarments called "panties" and she took them off. She hung them on the fence.

She was lying on the grass.

"Come on," she whispered.

And then it happened. I had let down my own short pants. I stood there. I was terribly frightened. As I stood there, my small buttocks exposed to the moonlight, there was a sudden swishing noise and a handful of gravel, gathered from the railroad tracks and thrown with violence, struck my buttocks and I ran.

We had been followed. A young man, living in a little house beside the railroad tracks along which we had come, had seen us and, recognizing the Shetland Ponies, had crept after us.

He had crept along the narrow lane at our heels. He had dodged from one v to another along the worm fence. He had seen my little buttocks shining in the moonlight. As he had come along the railroad tracks he had gathered a handful of fine stones. He was a tall young man of twenty, the son of the section boss for the railroad.

So there I was under fire. I was wounded. A great wild cry came from my lips and clutching my pants to hold them up I ran.

I ran and I kept running but as I ran I did think of the daughter of the whale and of her white panties on the fence. Perhaps I did not want her to lose them. There is this sense of property we all have. It is bred into us early in life.

And so, as I ran along the lane, I kept crying to her.

"Get your pants," I cried. Her name was Lula.

"Get your pants, Lula. Get your pants, Lula."

It was on my lips. I could not stop it. It was a hysteria. Even when I had left her and the others far behind and was in the big field where with others I had played baseball and later when I had got into a wood and was running under trees in the moonlight I kept crying the words.

"Get your pants, Lula. Get your pants, Lula."

It was the cry that was my undoing. It was taken up by men and boys of the town. It was a desperate time for me. Men and boys cried the words at me in the streets. When there were women or girls about, clerks in the stores to which I had been sent on errands by my mother whispered it at me across the counters.

"Get your pants, Lula. Get your pants, Lula," they whispered.

It was a time of dreadful fear, of shame. Did my father, my mother, my sister, my brothers know? "I will run away," I told myself.

However I did not go and gradually the cry "Get your pants, get your pants" died away.

As for Lula and how she felt about it all I did not know. Perhaps she did not care. Perhaps she and the daughter of the tailor were like the son of the butcher who was only amused by my fright and my flight. At any rate I do not remember that I ever again spoke to the daughter of the whale. With the tailor's daughter she continued on summer evenings to walk on main street.

They walked up and down, up and down, but when I saw them on the street I dodged into a store. I hurried through the store and into the alley-way at the back. I got off the street for the night.

Third Woman

After the adventure just told I was terribly afraid of women and girls. Why, I dare say, like most school boys I now and then became enamoured of one of our town girls and I remember, faintly, several such flare-ups.

There is a picture in my mind of, say, creeping into the yard before a certain brick house at night. I hide behind bushes. There is a young school girl sitting at a piano. She is dressed in white. There is to be some sort of children's show, in the school house, or perhaps in one of the churches, and she is practising a piece she is to play on the piano.

Does she know that I admire her? It may be that even school girls, who are, as yet, little more than children, always know.

She may have noted the hungry look in my eye but I have never dared speak to her and now I do not even remember her name.

But I have this picture of myself, crouched behind a flowering bush near a window and gazing long and hungrily at her.

Things kept happening. Are all boys, at a certain age, as I was then? There was this eager lust in me, ready at any moment to flare up.

It was a winter night and I was running along alleyways, across fields at the edge of town. I was delivering evening newspapers that had come on a late train.

There was snow on the gravel and an icy crust over the snow.

I had dodged between two houses and there I was before another window. I had become a Tom-the-Peeper.

There was the living room of a small frame house and in the center of the room one of the kind of stoves known as base burners. I could see the red coals through the isinglass windows of the stove. On a table near the stove there was an oil lamp, turned low.

A young girl, quite nude, stood before the stove. She slept no doubt in some cold upper room of the little two storied house and had run down to the stove to undress. I could see clothes scattered about on chairs. She kept turning slowly, warming the back of her slender girl's body, warming the front of her body.

I stood trembling in the cold, staring, filled with inner excitement and later on other nights I again went to stand as I had stood that night—hoping.[42]

It may be that we are all like that, when we are young boys.

There were then such adventures, some of which I have used in stories of small town life.

There was a boyhood friend who had been on a visit to a town in Indiana. He kept exciting me. There had been, in the house, in the Indiana town, a cousin, some three or four years older than my boy friend, who had let him play with her body.

He kept telling of it.

"I put my hands on her breasts. She wanted me to. It would be all right. We were both sleeping upstairs in the house and her father and mother, my uncle and aunt, slept downstairs.

"I went into the room where she was lying in bed. She told me to.

"No, we didn't go all the way. She wouldn't let me. She was afraid but when I had put my hands on her she held me for a long time, tight in her arms."

The boy who had been on the visit to the Indiana town kept talking of his adventures and how wonderful it seemed to us. He told the tale over and over. It excited us, got into our dreams at night.

And then came my own adventure. I was in the main street, a slender

42. See a parallel episode in "Girl by the Stove," *Decision*, I (January, 1941), 19–22; reprinted in *The Sherwood Anderson Reader,* ed. Rosenfeld, pp. 704–7. There is a comparable scene in *Tar* (1926), pp. 231–33.

boy, of perhaps fourteen, was standing with a certain man of the town. He was a man of perhaps twenty-five, a railroad brakeman, at home for the day. He was one who liked to talk and brag of his adventures on the railroad and had found in me a good listener.

There were tales of storms at night, nights of sleet and snow when a brakeman must go out and run over the tops of moving freight cars, of the constant facing of death, of wrecks, of fights with bums and car thieves.

The man was leaning against a store front, spreading it on, and I stood, all attention, excited by his tales, when a young girl, strange in the town, passed along the street. There was a certain look in her eyes. There was a little smile on her lips. As she went past us the brakeman stopped telling his tales and punched me with his forefinger.

"Did you see that?" he asked. He declared that the strange girl had made eyes at me.

"Kid, you could get her if you dared, if you had the nerve."

He took a paper dollar from his pocket.

"I'll bet you this that you do not dare."

"Dare what?" I asked.

"Dare to go after her now, here in the street. Go up to her, walk with her, make a date with her."

The strange girl was plump and pretty. She would be of about my own age. She walked with a certain light grace. She had dark brown eyes, dark brown hair. When she had passed us she began to walk more slowly. She turned to look back.

There was a woman who had been my school teacher walking along. There was a druggist standing in the door of his drug store.

"See, she is looking back.

"I'll bet you do not dare.

"See, here is this dollar. I'll tell you what I will do. You go after her, get her, walk away with her and the dollar is yours."

The railroad brakeman was laughing at me, he was goading me because of my cowardice. I grew angry. I half ran along the street.

I was with the strange girl. I was beside her. I spoke rapidly, in a frightened voice. I thought, "If she does not consent to let me walk with her the brakeman will laugh at me, the druggist will laugh."

There were others in the streets, clerks, housewives going to stores. Two school boys I knew walked along on the opposite side of main street.

"If she turns me down they will laugh at me. Again, as in the affair in the lane with the daughter of the whale, I will be made ridiculous."

I was with the girl, walking with her. She went along without speaking.

She was smiling. There was something bold in the tilt of her little head, in her eyes, in the curl of her lips as she smiled.

"Sure you may go with me," she said at last.

"Did you not see me making eyes at you?

"I think you are a handsome boy. Come on, walk with me."

And now I was walking with her, filled with excitement. What did it matter who saw me, who laughed at me?

It became for me a time of new adventure. The new one I had got was not at all like the little daughter of the man of the stuffed whale. After all that one was so obviously just a little village pushover, a lyer on her back under hedges and in fields, the common property of small town men and boys.

Night came and I went to my new one. She was from a little village some twenty miles to the north. She told me that she lived with her grandfather and her grandmother. Her father had run away from her mother and then her mother had died.

She told me all of this in a rush of words. There was another old man, her grandfather's brother, who lived in this town and she had come to him on a visit.

It was an old man I knew. He was a teamster. He was a burner and hauler of lime. He hauled lumber and brick for building houses. He was a rather silent, stoop shouldered man, the owner of a team of well groomed, huge draft horses, who lived in a brick house on a street at the town's edge and I had often seen him driving his team through the streets. He was the owner also of a bus for hauling passengers and once he had been hired to take the baseball team, of which I was a member, to a neighboring town.

He had been dressed in his Sunday clothes on that occasion but, as on other days, when he was hauling brick or lime and was covered with white dust, he was silent.

How strange it seemed to go into that house. The teamster, it developed, lived with his old wife on the second floor, the first floor having been let out. When I had, in the afternoon, escorted the strange girl to the house she had told me that the first floor was occupied by the teamster's daughter.

She was, in fact, standing at the front door of the house that afternoon when I, with my new conquest, came along the street. She was a tall woman of perhaps forty. She stood at the front door of the house and when the girl and I came along the street and stopped at the gate to a picket fence leading into the yard of the house, she began to laugh.

"So you have got you one? You have got what you wanted?" she said, looking at the girl and laughing.

She had said that and, still laughing, with a curious high shrill laughter, had gone into the house and the girl had tried to explain.

"This is my cousin," she said. "She is a great joker."

The cousin it seemed was married to a railroad brakeman. He was one who worked with the railroad brakeman who had goaded me with pursuit of the girl.

The girl looked at me and also laughed. Already she had invited me to come to her that evening.

"I think . . . I am not sure but just the same I am pretty sure that, when her man is away, she does as she pleases with other men," she whispered.

How bold she looked at me as she said it.

"And so, you and I . . . we can do as we please. If she knew she wouldn't dare tell.

"And anyway she wouldn't care."

The new girl had said that to me. She had said it boldly, leaning toward me. She had laughed. When she had whispered the words to me, in the open street, at the gate before the house, in the afternoon, in the full light of day, other houses nearby on the street, for all the few neighbors in that part of town to which I came every day to deliver my newspapers, when she had said it, she had leaned forward, her round sun burned face near my face, so close I had thought she was about to kiss me and had drawn a little away.

And that had made her laugh again. She had boldly spoken of that too.

"Ha. You thought I was going to kiss you, here in the street, and you were afraid.

"Well you come tonight, at night. I will be upstairs. My grandfather and my grandmother there go to bed at seven."

She had pointed to a wooden stairway, the lower steps of which could just be seen at the back of the house.

"You come up the stairs. I will be waiting for you."

It had been, for me, a terrific adventure. I was a good deal frightened. I thought that the hours until eight o'clock would come would never pass.

There were my evening papers to be delivered. The train bringing them arrived at five but what if it should be late? I ran about with my papers debating with myself. At one moment I determined I would not go to her. She was too bold. In her laughter there was something too strange, too reckless.

"I will be getting myself into trouble," I thought. Although I was but fourteen I had heard many stories of boys and young men caught by girls and women.

Suddenly there was a child expected. That was it. It all began out of a kind of blind eagerness you could not control. You were with a girl and it happened.

And then, before you realized what you were in for, you were caught, forced into a marriage. On a certain street of the town, near the street in which I lived with my father, mother, brothers and sisters, there was a family of girls. There were six girls in that family and three of them had got men in that way.

It was a risk. It was something terrible. The girl was too bold. I had no doubt at all of what was about to happen.

Something in the eyes of the girl had told me.

It was in her eyes, in the way she walked, in the way she laughed.

But how lovely she was. I thought her beautiful.

What a slender strong young body. She was the sort of young girl you sometimes see who develop young.

What a lovely soft, sun burned skin she had. She had golden brown hair and little strands of it had been blown about her face as I had walked with her. She had kept putting up her plump little hand to brush it into place.

She had indicated to me, so boldly, that she liked me.

"When I saw you on the street, talking to that man, I knew at once that I wanted you to come with me."

She had said things like that, boldly laughing as she said them.

There was in me a kind of new terror, a heavy beating of the heart. How strange it seemed, being at home, at table that evening, my father and mother, my brothers and sisters, them not knowing what had happened to me, what was about to happen. I could not eat. They were all, even my mother, suddenly as strangers to me.

They were like people far off, seen through the wrong end of a telescope. They were speaking of ordinary things, about getting wild strawberries, the price of food, what someone met in the street, in some strange world of ordinary affairs, had said to one of them and what had been said in reply.

"He said and I said."

"I did not sleep last night."

"I had a headache or a toothache."

My father, who had formerly been a harness maker, with a shop of his own, but who had lost it through bad management, had now become a house painter. He smelled of paint. He was painting Mrs. Edward Smith's house. He had a mustache that drooped down over his mouth and there were spots of white paint on it. As he took bites of food he kept brushing the mustache aside with his hand. Crumbs of food clung to his mustache. He wiped it with his hand and then wiped his hand on his pants leg.

My mother was always reproving him for that.

"Don't do that, Irwin." She was the only one who called him Irwin. Others in the town called him "Teddy" and sometimes "Major." He had been in the Civil War and was forever speaking of it. Later I could not remember what the other children of the family and I called our father when we addressed him.

"We probably just called him Pa," I thought.

He paid no attention to his wife's reproof. She said he was teaching the children bad manners but he did not answer her. He was absorbed in some tale of a conversation he had with Mrs. Edward Smith in which he had got all the best of it. There were more "he said's" and "she said's." It was absurd for a woman like that to be telling a house painter his business.

What a strange world, far off, unreal.

Or was it unreal that at last I was up there in a room, on the second floor of the brick house in which lived the teamster and burner of lime, with the new and beautiful girl?

It all seemed unreal to me.

"Why should such good fortune come to me?"

It was so obvious something was about to. . . . I had been there, in that room with her, for perhaps a half hour.

It was a stuffy little room with a woven rag carpet on the floor, two rocking chairs by a small table on which was a coal oil lamp, turned low, and a couch against the wall and there were two doors besides the one leading to a back porch and the wooden stairway by which I had come up. The two doors led into two bedrooms, one occupied by the old teamster and his wife and one by the granddaughter.

The old teamster and his old wife were both in bed and asleep. They both snored. I thought they must both be having troubled dreams. Little broken sighs and muttered words came from the room. I had been met at the door by the new girl. The door to the porch was standing open when I climbed up and she stood in the doorway waiting.

She put a finger to her lips.

"Sh . . . They are asleep. Don't talk loud. They might wake up."

She had led me into the room and had seated me on the couch and immediately put her arms about my neck and kissed me.

"Do you like me?"

"Oh, I like you."

She had jumped up and gone into her own room, whispering to me that she had something to show me. She had been dressed in a tight fitting little flowered cotton dress but when she came back into the room she was dressed as I had never seen a woman dressed.

She had put on some sort of loose gown cut very low at the neck so that her hard little round breasts could be plainly seen. It was such a dress as I was to see later on women of fashion and, on the few occasions when I was to enter such places, on the women in certain houses where women were for hire.

The little plump thing came immediately to me. Was it possible that she was about to give herself without my having to ask? The thought thrilled me. There was the great difficulty—you had to ask. You had to say certain words, make the proposal. Here was something new in all my experience with girls. Well, I had been with other boys to boy and girl parties. They had played kissing games. There was one game you played in which you were called into a darkened room. The game was called "post office."

There was a girl hidden in the room and your name was announced. There was a "letter" for you in the "post office." You went in and there the girl was. She giggled and you pursued her about the room and at last caught her. You gave her a little pecking kiss.

She was a nice girl, that was it. You didn't attempt to go too far with her. Nice girls didn't go too far.

To be sure there were always stories being told by braggart boys. Oh how much of the talk among the boys I knew was concerned with girls. There was one boy, a dark skinned lad with stiff black hair, who was ambitious.

"You'll see what I am going to do when I get to be a man."

He was going to travel all over the world, go to China, Japan, India. He was going to visit every nation in the world.

"I am going to have me a woman of every nation in the world."

"And a negro woman, too?"

"Yes sir. You bet. I am going to have one of every kind there is."

It was a gigantic ambition. It was something wonderful to think about.

There were also boys who told stories about some of the nice girls.

"I was with such and such a one.

"She let me put my hand. . . ."

The suggestion was that he had gone "all the way." He didn't.

"I wouldn't do that to a nice girl."

Very likely the fellow was only bragging.

I thought I had got into something like a new strange world. It was paradise. I had become a man. I was one who had been singled out by a strange new kind of girl. She wasn't at all like that other one, the daughter of the whale man. Surely this one had not been as that one was.

That one had been free to all. She was a little rather tired silent one. She just laid herself down.

This one was firm of flesh. There was a certain freshness. She was strong. She did not just submit. She came to you.

She had taken my hand in one of her hands and had put it on one of her breasts.

"Don't you like to feel there? I like you to." She smiled boldly at me.

"Shall we do it here or shall we go somewhere else?"

Her words were like bells ringing. Was I in a dream?

Here were doors being thrown open to me. Life was suddenly becoming wonderful, glorious.

She thought perhaps we had better go out and walk.

"We will find some nice place."

The grandmother or the grandfather might awaken. There was that aunt who lived downstairs. It would be just like her to poke her nose in.

We went together out of the house, walked along a street, crossed a bridge over a creek, climbed over a fence and went across a field. It was a moonlit night. It was a night I would remember all of my life.

There was this new strange aliveness. Something in me had swept away my timidity. It seemed to me that night that every leaf on every tree in a strip of woods into which we went stood out separate and apart from every other leaf, that every blade of grass, in the meadow we crossed, separate and apart from every other blade.

We were there, in the little strip of woods, for what seemed to me a long time. We were lying quietly there.

We were walking again. We went into a graveyard. She said she wanted to lie with me on a grave.

The idea did not shock me. There was something about her that was all youth and life, defying old age and death.

She plucked a flower off the grave on which we had been lying and put it in the lapel of my coat.

We went back to the house of the teamster. We sat on the wooden stairs. There was a little garden back of the house with a grassy path. We went to lie there.

There was dew on the grass but she did not mind.

We were exhausted. We talked softly. The little back yard, back of the brick house, with its vegetable garden and the grassy path that led to an out house at the end of the garden, was, no doubt, in the daytime or when seen under ordinary circumstances, commonplace enough but on that night it was to me utterly lovely.

I wanted to sleep, to lie with her arms about me and sleep. I spoke of it to her.

"It would be nice if we could do that, if we could lie here together like this, forever."

Was it love? I was with her on the next night, and the next and the next. There was a night when it rained.

It did not matter. We were on the couch in the room upstairs. We were on the floor. I could hear the snoring of her grandfather and her grandmother. I could hear the aunt, that tall strong looking woman, moving about downstairs in the house. She went away, to that other town where she lived with another old grandfather and grandmother, and I worked and saved money to hire a horse and buggy and go there too.

When I was with her I was happy, in a kind of paradise, but when I had left her, in the daytime, when I was going about with other boys and girls, when I was with my brothers and my sister I said nothing of my adventure.

I became afraid.

"She will be having a child and I will have to marry her."

There were times when I was with her when I thought I wanted that. There was a night when we were sitting together and there was a little rumbling sound in her body.

She took my hand in one of hers. She put my hand on her little belly.

"Did you hear him?" she asked, laughing.

"It is your son, down in there, trying to call to you. He wants to call you 'daddy.' "

The words had sent a little thrill of fear through me. I had made such great plans for my life.

I was going to be a business man and grow rich. I lived with my father and mother, my brothers and my sisters in a little yellow house on one of the poorest streets of the town.

I wanted to build a great house for my mother. She was not strong and worked too hard. I wanted to buy her beautiful clothes. There was in the town a certain woman whose husband had invested money in the enterprises of a man named Rockefeller and who, every year, while doing nothing, grew richer and richer. She had got two beautiful horses and in the afternoon rode about in her carriage.

I wanted such a team and such a carriage for my mother.

I wanted to become a driver of race horses. Sometimes I thought, "I will become a business man and get rich," and again I thought, "No, I will become a famous race horse driver."

There was a man in town who owned a stable of race horses and who, at certain times of the year, went away to the races and I went often to his stables. There was a fair ground at the edge of town with a race track where the horses were trained and I went there.

The horses were going at speed and oh how beautiful they were. How I longed to be sitting in the little cart back of the horse, holding the reins, guiding, directing all of the beautiful creatures.

I was in the town. I was on the streets, was with boy friends, I was at a party at the house of some nice girl.

She who had been so free with me would be free with others.

There was that aunt and it was said that, when her husband was away from town, at his job on the railroad. . . .

But she had been so generous to me, so wonderful.

And yet. . . .

I grew more and more afraid.

"No, I must not go to her. I must not. I must not."

One day I was walking in the street and there was her aunt. She stopped me on the street.

"Have you been to see her again?

"When are you going again?

"You had better look out," she said and laughed.

She went away laughing along the street and I grew white with fright.

"I must not. I mustn't any more."

If it happened my mother would have to know, my sister, my brothers. I came at last to the taking of a resolution.

"I'll cut it out. Now I am going to cut it out."

I waited, in fear. She was in my dreams. She had become a terror to me but nothing happened and when a month, two months, three months had passed and there was no word from her I began to be proud.

I became the conquering one. I walked proudly. The other boys of the town might talk but who among them had known, had been privileged to know such an adventure as that of my own?

Stella

It must have happened in many such families, families with several boys and one girl. Our family life had been disorganized by our mother's death and there was Stella, our one sister, compelled suddenly to become a mother.

For us boys there was the life of the streets. We three older boys, Karl, Irwin and myself, were running about. We were getting jobs. It seems to me now as I look back upon that time that the men and women of the town were infinitely kind to us.

Men were speaking words of encouragement, no doubt many of them, often, the same men who sat with our father at night in some saloon. They would be buying drinks for him. They would be listening to his stories of adventure. Most of the stories would be inventions but they would be always interesting. These same men, knowing also of our father's total lack of any feeling of responsibility for his children, liking and even loving him for his gift as a talker, a little understanding him, as we could not until long years later, would at the same time have had an almost fatherly feeling toward his sons.

It was in the Irvin brothers, the brothers who had discharged father because of his drinking and his irresponsibility and into whose shop Karl was taken to learn the harness making trade, it was in the fat doctor for whom Karl, Irwin and myself all at different times worked, it was in the hardware man, the grocer, the superintendent of the town school, a large bearded man named Ginn, whose son, a boyhood friend of Karl's, became later a famous and rich corporation lawyer for the Van Schwinn Brothers and other rich corporations and individuals in Cleveland, himself a millionaire and a patron of my brother Karl's art, it was even in the saloon keepers.

"But my boy, do not be too hard on your father."

It would have been one of the saloon keepers, speaking to me as I came, engaged upon my paper selling, into his place. I had come, on the day before, into the same place and there was father, sitting with others at a little table at the back. He would have been drinking with them and telling one of his stories and I, suddenly overcome with shame for him, that he was what he was and not one of the more steady dignified men of the town, youth always passionately wanting that from the father, had hurried out, perhaps even with tears of shame in my eyes.

The saloon keeper having seen that, we would have been alone together in the bar on the next day.

"Do not think too badly of your father. He is what he is. He cannot be different. He is a good fellow. He's all right. Someday you will understand him better than you do now."

The man unable to say what he felt, feeling, no doubt, the confusion and perplexity of his own life, in relation to his own children, a little, perhaps, envying father's ability to throw all off and give himself to the moment, living so much in a world of his own invention, the man himself, being a saloon keeper and bearing the odium connected with that trade, wondering if his own sons also felt shame of their father.

"Someday you'll understand him better than you do now." Prophetic words.

"Go it kid. Money makes the mare go. You kids are going to come out all right. You'll see."

I am tempted to write on and on about this feeling, toward one family of boys, thrown suddenly out upon life by the death of a mother [43] and the irresponsibility of a father, on the part of the people of an American small town of some forty or fifty years ago, myself having been, for so large a

43. Emma Smith Anderson died May 10, 1895, after which Irwin Anderson went to Indiana, married Minnie Stevens in 1901, and apparently ignored his children until he died in a soldiers' home at Dayton, Ohio, May 23, 1919. On the mother's death, see *A Story Teller's Story,* ed. White, pp. 21, 62–63; and *Tar* (1926), pp. 162–63, 326–41.

part of my own life, a small town man, feeling as I do the great change that has come over the life of the towns with the coming of the modern hard surfaced roads, the automobile, the radio, the movies, the airplanes, the old feeling of the town as rather walled in, isolated, the one big family feeling that did prevail, wanting rather passionately to emphasize the kindness shown me and my brothers.[44]

The school teacher, a tired faced woman of forty-five, calling to me late one evening as I ran past her house.

I had been up to some deviltry in school and had been sent to the superintendent to be punished.

The school teacher was sitting on the front porch of the little frame house where she lived with her mother.

"Come here, boy."

I would have gone to her a little shame faced.

"She is going to give me hell now."

Nothing of the sort happening. Like the saloon keeper she has some difficulty in saying what is in her mind to say, in trying to say it.

"I know, boy, that you are unusually quick at your lessons. You have all this energy. You get your lessons quickly and then you get into mischief.

"All I want to say is that school, what you can get from books, can be of some importance to you later. You probably won't get to go to college. You must read a lot. Try as hard as you can to get all you can out of school while you have the chance."

The school teacher wanting to say something, not quite said, perhaps only wanting me to know that, in sending me to be punished by the superintendent, she was in no way surrendering a kind of motherly affection she had for me.

Myself vaguely feeling that, touched by it, so that to this day I remember the light in her rather tired eyes, the something infinitely tender in the timbre of her voice.

Or again the superintendent who, after school was dismissed for the day, took me across his knee and beat my behind with a strap. It was rather like the strap barbers use for strapping razors. It did not hurt too much.

And then he, that same often violently angry, big shouldered bearded

44. *Home Town* (New York: Alliance Book Corporation, 1940) is Anderson's best and final statement on his feeling for the American small town. See the complete (but revised) text in *The Sherwood Anderson Reader,* ed. Rosenfeld, pp. 740–810; and see Evelyn Kintner, "Sherwood Anderson: Small Town Man, A Story of the Growth, Revolt, and Reconciliation of a Small Town Man" (M.A. Thesis, Bowling Green State University, 1942).

man (We boys called him Faker Ginn. It was rumored that he went about peeping through keyholes to catch boys throwing spit balls when their teacher's back was turned—an unfair accusation I am sure.), he after strapping me inviting me home with him to his house. There were rows of books on shelves in his study. There was a side door.

"You see, boy, this door is always unlocked. Come here, at any time. Walk right in. Take any book you want. Take it home with you.

"Here is Dickens and Thackeray. Here is Victor Hugo, the Frenchman. Already I am told you have been to Lawyer Hurt, asking to borrow books. There are not too many libraries in this town. Come here. Get books whenever you please."

The same man going about, boasting of me.

"He has read more good books than any grown man of this town. He is educating himself thus. He is getting a better education than we could possibly give him in school."

But I must return to my sister and her peculiar plight. She had been very ambitious. She had graduated from the town high school at a very early age. She had been, always, at the top of her class.

She was beautiful. She had shining black hair, shining black eyes. Like my older brother Karl, and unlike the rest of us, she had a clear beautiful skin.

She had dreamed of going away somewhere to college, of working her way through college. In secret she wrote verses. Perhaps she might be able to win a scholarship in some college.

But now, with our mother's death, all had to be given up. Now she must stay at home, all day and every day, in our little house, while we older boys roamed the streets.

We were getting along. We were working. A little money was coming in. We could buy new suits of clothes, usually on the installment plan, five or ten dollars down, a dollar a week. We could go to parties, walk about through the streets at night with gangs of boy friends, stopping to sing before the house in which some girl lived. It was a custom among us in our town in that time.

We could go in the winter to sleigh ride parties, to spellings down in some school house. Some of the more prosperous parents of one of the boys of the several gangs to which Karl, Irve and myself belonged would own horses and surreys. We could go with one such on moonlight summer nights for drives into the country with girls.

Life having for each of us young males a certain gayety, youth—what did having to work matter? What did a little hardship matter?

Stella always at home, being mother now to the two small boys left on her hands by mother's death. They would have been as yet very small children.

Long days of it, nights of it, she confined so. It must have seemed to her that all life, all opportunity in life, was slipping away.

We, her brothers, unconscious of all this, the casual hardness of boys in us.

For her no going about on spring, fall and summer evenings with crowds of young girls of her own age, these being courted by town boys, parties organized, young girls of her own age being escorted home from church on summer evenings.

I had a passion for dancing and there was a certain Irish girl, a servant in the house of one of the more prosperous citizens of the town, who was a wonderful dancer.

There were in our town, as in all towns, what were called the "nice girls" and there were others not presumed to be nice.

They were perhaps the daughters of poor men. They did what was called "making out." They were hired girls, servants. If you wanted to go about with the nice girls you were to stay away from them, or, if you did go about with one such you did it in secret.

There was this Irish girl named Mag and I had got in with her. She was some eight or ten years older than myself. She was quick of tongue and witty. She constantly said amusing and risqué things. As in all small towns she had been checked off by the young sports of the town.

"Well that Mag. Boy she can dance. She will say anything. You can have fun with her but she is not putting out. She cannot be had."

I would be sitting with Mag on the back porch of the house where she was employed as cook. It cost two dollars to hire a horse and buggy for the evening from one of the town's two livery stables and on two or three occasions Mag and I had gone in together, putting in a dollar each. We had hired thus a horse and buggy and had driven away in the darkness, some several miles, to a place on Sandusky Bay called The Dewdrop.

It was said to be a tough place. It was a place I was to use, a long time later, as a setting for several short stories. You could dance all night in a big dance pavilion, a one eyed Civil War veteran, named Rat Gould, calling off the figures for the square dances.

"Alamen left."

"Grand right and left."

"Swing your lady high and wide.

"Marry her and you'll be tied."

Occasional fights breaking out, a drunken farm hand reeling across the dance floor to challenge some other farm hand, too attentive to his lady, Mag and I whirling about the floor. You did not have to be careful about Mag. Say whatever you wanted to say to her. On the way down to The Dewdrop she would have been telling you so-called "off color" stories.

"There was this fellow. He was a hired man on that farm. So there was the farmer's daughter and she was entertaining her best beau in the parlor. They had put out the light.

"So there was this farm hand who slept in the upstairs room in the house. He had to get up suddenly and go out, you see.

"So he was going through the room where the couple were sitting spooning in the dark. He had nothing on but his shirt. Why, the poor man was caught short. They are going to have it in court. The farmer fired him and he is suing for his wages. Lawyer Hurt has the case. He is going to make the farmer's daughter get up in court and tell all about it. He will have grand fun with her. You'll see."

There were these privileges enjoyed by the young male, to hurry out of the house, after the evening meal, to get set with Mag, hear from her lips some of the scandals of the town, go, with a crowd of other young males, on courting expeditions among the so-called "nice" girls, some of the nice girls a little angry and jealous (they couldn't go sit in the darkness on back porches of houses with young male toughs), to jump on a freight train and go to a neighboring town, eight miles away, play pool in a pool room there, flirt with girls of that town.

Your sister compelled to stay at home, evening after evening, wash the evening dishes, put the smaller children to bed.

Perhaps no young male courting her. What was the use? She was attractive, even beautiful, but there were, always, the children about, to be taken care of, watched over.

It was early on a Sunday evening, still light outside, the church bells ringing, and I was upstairs in our house. I had been off with several other boys for a Sunday afternoon tramp in the woods but now I had other plans. I had put on my new suit, combed my hair, had shined my shoes.

There was always the Sunday night hunt. Well, you did not go to church. You roamed about with other boys until time for people to emerge from church and then you went there. You stood, with other boys, at the edge of a sidewalk, under the maple trees, until the girls appeared and then, when she appeared, you stepped forth.

"May I see you home, Miss Grey?"

It was a critical moment. If she refused to let you walk with her, "turned you down," a hurt, a cry from the other young males.

"Yah! Yah! You got turned down."

There was a new young girl in town, one with blue eyes and soft yellow hair, and she smiled at me as girls do. She would be going to church. Would I dare?

Yes, I was determined. I'd risk it. I'd take a chance.

I had gone from the room where I slept with two of my brothers and into my sister's room. There was a glass in there. My necktie must be just right. I was standing before the glass in my sister's room when she came in.

My sister went to sit on the bed.

"You are going to try to get a girl," she said and there was something, a certain tone in her voice, that made me turn to look at her.

Why what was this? Her cheeks were flushed and there was the suggestion of tears about to flow.

"Why I don't know. I was just going out. Why?"

My sister hesitated. Her head was bowed and she was looking at the floor.

"I had thought . . . ," she said. "It is going to be a fine night."

She had turned. She threw herself face down on the bed. She was crying and I had gone to her.

I felt curiously awkward and ashamed. Perhaps at the moment, for the first time, there had come to me a realization of what her life was like.

She was so young. She was beautiful. Our mother's death had thrown upon her young shoulders all of this responsibility.

There we were, a family of boys. There had been another girl child born shortly before mother's death but it had lived but a few weeks.[45] We could not afford a servant and our grandmother had been sent away.

My sister had won but she was now paying for her victory. She was cook. She was housekeeper. She was nurse for the younger boys.

45. Fern Anderson was born December 11, 1890. See *Tar* (1926), pp. 163–65.

She was a little upset now by her victory. She was there on the bed, her shoulders shaking. She was crying.

I stood over her. I was embarrassed. I wanted to take her in my arms, comfort her but she was my sister.

You did not do it in such families as ours. You did not hold your sister in your arms. Well, you teased her. You even occasionally wrestled with her. It was thus you expressed your affection.

My sister had stopped crying. She sat again on the edge of her bed. She wiped her eyes. We were alone together in the house, the other older boys having gone out into the town streets. Although I did not yet know it my sister had arranged with a neighbor woman who was to care for the two younger boys for the evening.

She had made certain plans but she had not consulted me. We two were to go off somewhere together.

"What is it, Stella? What do you want? What's the matter?"

She sat there before me, a little hesitant, suddenly shy.

"It isn't anything."

"Yes it is. Now you tell me."

It came out with a rush. It was the story of her loneliness.

"I wanted to get away, far away, somewhere, from this house. I wanted to go, with you, or someone, away from here."

It was growing dark outside the house and as I stood in the room, my sister's room in our house, she sitting before me on the bed, her face flushed, her eyes still red from weeping. . . . She was trying to smile now. There was a certain shyness. . . .

Can it be that I, at the moment, realized what my sister wanted?

She wanted me to pretend for the one summer evening that I was something I wasn't, that I was not her brother, that I was just a young male, any young male, come to court her.

She did not say this.

"Oh, I just wanted to be with you. I thought, perhaps, well I thought we might go off somewhere together, away from this house, away from this street.

"It is going to be a wonderful night," she said. "We could take a walk in the country. Do you mind?"

It was very strange. There I was, in the half darkness of the summer night with my sister. We had walked together, in silence, along a country road, we had climbed fences and crossed fields. We were in woodland paths, beside a creek. When we were in the woodland path where it was quite dark she had reached out and had taken my hand into hers and once, when we had stopped on a little hill, I had, for just a moment, held her in my arms and we had kissed.

It was all very strange. The whole evening with my sister, the only time during our life together in the same house where we were really close to each other, was passed in a strange silence. There was a game being played and I had, for the evening, given myself to it.

I had and I had not. I am quite sure now, as I think back on that strange evening with her, myself the young male, eager for the female, my sister eager for the young male, she being shut out from something she wanted, being as she was half young female poet. . . .

She was, for the evening, pretending that I was something I was not, that I was not her brother, and once as we walked along together, when we were in a little meadow beside a wheat field, the whole scene curiously vivid in my mind as I write of it after these years, she suddenly drew close to me.

We had stopped by a rail fence and as I stood, somewhat embarrassed, leaning against the fence, she came close. Her hand caressed my hair. She spoke in a soft whisper. There was a little breeze playing across the field of ripening wheat so that the wind seemed to be playing a game. The wheat field was like a little yellow lake with waves running across it.

"It's beautiful, isn't it, James?" my sister whispered but I was silent and for just a moment, a strange awkward shy moment, she put her arms about my neck and drew my face down to her face.

"Do you love me, James?" she whispered again and then she kissed me quickly on the cheek and drawing quickly away she laughed. It was an embarrassing nervous little laugh.

And that was the end of it. We came back across the fields and along a country road and to our house, my sister and I speaking now quite freely of things concerned with the family. She was talking rapidly now, speaking of certain plans she had for our younger brothers, plans that were never fulfilled. She had become again my sister, our sister. She had been playing a little game with the life she felt herself shut out from but now she had given up the game.

And so we came back to our house and I left her at the door and I went away, half hoping, I dare say, that I would still be in time to try for the new girl at the door of the church.

As to whether or not I was in time for that I can't remember, the memory of my sister and her mood on that evening crowding out all other memories, but I am quite sure that the feeling of strangeness and of a queer unreality that was to be the whole story of my sister's life must have stayed on me so that no doubt for the rest of that evening and before I returned to our house to crawl into bed with my brother Irve, that I must first have walked about alone trying to get some understanding of what had happened between me and my sister.

New World

I find I must hurry through my stories of childhood and boyhood. There is the temptation to go on and on. For the writer the impressions gained, say in the first twenty years of his life, impressions of events or of people so deeply impressed on the young mind, on the young imagination, are bound to be source material for him all his life. For example I am always being asked whether writing such and such a story, or novel, I had this or that town in mind and I find I cannot answer such a question. All his life the writer keeps gathering new impressions but nevertheless these boyhood impressions remain sharpest of all and I have found that often people met much later in life than the time of which I am now writing and when the temptation comes to use these persons in some tale I find myself, often unconsciously, placing them against a background known so well in those formative years of my own life.

Why how vividly the streets along which the boy walks or runs are remembered—the houses along streets, vacant lots between houses, fields at the edge of town, some small stream that flowed past the boy's town, the streets at night, say on a winter night, smoke creeping up out of the chimneys of houses.

A queer boyish sickness. It frightened me but for some reason I did not dare tell anyone of it. I thought I was about to die.

I remember a Sunday afternoon when I went off into the country alone. I went up along Coon Creek, climbed a little hill, sat down under a tree.

Was it all some queer boyish and half poetic illusion? It was at that period in a boy's life when the voice suddenly changes, when he becomes shy about his own body, when the body of the female begins to have a strange new significance to him.

I sat under the tree and it seemed to me that I held my own life in my hand. I became faint and weak. I had my own life in my hand and it slipped out of my grasp.

It became like a bird. This was on a clear day in the lovely fall and there were no clouds in the sky.

My life was flying away from me. It was going, going, going. It got very small, far out there in the clear blue sky. It was a very speck in the distance.

(Have I not, somewhere, written of this odd experience of young boyhood? Sure I have.[46] I never reread my own stories or books. I have the notion that it is bad luck to do so. I read once, when something I have written is printed, and never again.)

There was my own life, going away from me, far away. I had the definite feeling that, if it went quite out of sight, out there, I would be dead. My eyes clung, with desperate intensity, to the little dark spark against the blue out there.

Then it came back, slowly at first, and then, suddenly, with a rush. It flew back to me.

I was very weak for a time, after this experience, which I put down here, wondering if others have had a similar experience during boyhood or girlhood, and then I slept, a dreamless sleep. It was oddly like the sleep that comes later to a man when he has become satiated with love making with a beloved one and when I awoke I was well again.

Another hard winter for us. I was becoming too old to be a newsboy. After the incident of the girl, the daughter of the man of the stuffed whale, and when I was filled with shame, thinking the whole town would be laughing over this my failure as a lover and would be shouting at me as I went about town ("Lula, get your pants. Lula, get your pants," I imagined them calling to me.), I had, for a time, dreamed of suddenly disappearing from the town.

I was growing rapidly, at home we were again on the edge of actual want and so I took a job as groom of livery stable horses in Frank Harvy's livery stable.

And what a comedown for me. Here I had been dreaming of someday becoming a driver of fine race horses, another Ed Geers or Budd Doble,

46. See *Tar* (1926), pp. 104-5.

and instead now spent my days cleaning the mud off tired old livery stable horses, wheeling out manure, and washing buggies, and my nights with a man named Ed, both of us sleeping under horse blankets in a little office at the front of the long barn.

It was a time of adventure for me. My companion, a tall thin man with badly bowed legs, a big nose, red hair and a curious flaming scar from a knife wound on his right cheek, continually chewed tobacco and, as he was a light sleeper, talked often half through the night.

He was a great boaster and his boasts were all centered about women and his many conquests among the women of the town.

"Do you know Mrs. Black?" he would ask, naming some respectable married woman of the town.

"Well you are to keep your mouth shut, lad, but I have had her all right."

Having made such a start, Ed would launch forth on a tale of some secret night adventure, a husband gone from town for the night, a note received by Ed, telling him to come, the woman having suddenly become overcome with passion for Ed, all the details of such an imagined adventure told, the creeping through the midnight streets, his entrance into the respectable house, the woman's helpless passion and her remorse.

And then the bedroom scene, so elaborately described, the joy of the woman over having got Ed into her arms and later her tears of remorse.

It went on thus at times for hours, my own boy's imagination inflamed, knowing that all Ed told me was but a pack of lies and yet myself unavoidably inflamed by his talk so that I could not sleep and myself indulged in impossible dreams.

There was one night, not to be forgotten, when Ed was having a real adventure. He had disappeared from the barn late on a winter night and presently returned with a woman, a rather large red haired woman from the neighboring county seat. She was from a certain notorious house of our county seat and had been, I dare say, working the outlying territory.

She and Ed had been drinking together during the late evening and at midnight they came into the little office of the livery stable where Ed and I slept on two cots. It was dark in there and they fell into Ed's cot.

I heard then the beginnings of a crude manifestation of human lust that sickened me. I got up and dressed hurriedly in the darkness, Ed and the woman laughing at me.

"Ah what's the matter with you, kid? Wait. Maybe I'll share with you.

"What do you say, Kate?"

The woman laughed loudly, her drunken laughter ringing in my ears as I fled from the barn, something within me sickened as it had never been before. I kept thinking of how Ed's boastful lying about various women of the town had awakened a kind of lust in me and was ashamed. I was sick with shame and for an hour or two before going home to finish the night in bed with one of my brothers I walked in the silent winter streets. I had for the time the feeling that I was no better than Ed and the drunken prostitute, now no doubt sleeping peacefully enough in the livery stable office.

It was a sickness that drove me out of that place. It was late in February, a warm sunny day had come and we were storing hay, hauled from some farm, in the loft of the barn and I was in the loft helping to store it away.

The hay was being pitched up from the farmer's hay rack through an opening at the front of the barn facing a street and Ed, who was very strong, gathered up great forkfuls and running a few steps into the loft pitched it at my feet and it was my job to carry the great forkfuls to the rear of the loft.

Ed was too strong for me. He was too quick. He kept piling the hay at my feet and laughing at me.

"Hurry up, kid, hurry, hurry." Ed laughed and the farmer and his hired man put their heads in at the opening through which they had been pitching the hay and also laughed.

"Bushed eh? What's the matter with you, kid? Are you bushed?"

It was the old cry of the workman, proud of his strength, glorying in the weakness of a boy, and I became furiously angry. I ran under the great forkfuls of hay that kept coming faster and faster. I ran. I stumbled and fell. Tears came to my eyes.

"I'll show them. I'll show them."

I set my jaws and worked harder and harder. The sweat rolled from my body.

And then at last the hay rack was empty and in the darkness, at the rear of the barn, I drew my arms across my eyes to wipe away the angry tears and went to join the men.

"I'll not let them learn that I was angry because they laughed at me. They must not know that I have been crying," I thought.

And now the empty hayrack was being driven away from the front of the barn and another huge load was driven up to the barn door by the farmer's hired man.

However, the three men did not immediately go to work on the new load. They went off together, to a nearby saloon, while I sat waiting on the floor of the loft.

And then presently they returned and Ed had brought a glass of beer for me. He climbed with it into the barn loft while the farmer and his hired man climbed upon the second load of hay.

"Here, you drink this," Ed said handing the glass of beer to me. The farmer and his hired man came and put their heads in at the opening in the loft. They were all laughing. The farmer poked a finger into the ribs of his hired man and they both shouted with laughter.

So they thought I was just a kid who could not drink beer.

"I'll show them," I thought. How was I to know that a crude joke had been concocted in the saloon, that they had got the bar tender to fill the glass half full of raw whisky? Although I had never until that moment tasted beer I stood up and with a great gulp swallowed the mess.

It was a horrid sickness. It began almost at once. Ed had taken the glass from my hand and I had taken my place preparatory to doing my part in the storing away of the new load.

It began. The men kept laughing but now I did not mind. I carried one, two, three of the heavy forkfuls of hay to the rear of the loft. I began to stagger. Something down inside me seemed rolling and tumbling about. The dark hayloft began to whirl and dance before my eyes. I became suddenly faint and fell.

"I must not let them know. Now they are laughing again. If they can drink beer so also can I. I will not be overcome."

A kind of desperate inner struggle began. I grew faint and my legs would no longer hold me erect. The sweat poured from my body. I fell and arose, fell and arose. It seemed to me that, if I did not at once get out of the loft, I would choke.

"I cannot breathe in here," I thought. "I must have air."

And now, in a kind of drunken stupor, I ran, continually falling and arising, toward the opening at the front of the loft. I pitched through it, fortunately upon the load of hay. I could still hear the men laughing. Their crude working men's joke had proven a great success. I lay sprawled there upon the load of hay and then all consciousness left me and I was helpless in their hands.

When I awoke it was night and I was lying on straw in an empty horse stall, having been thrown in there by the men. I was there on a pile of litter, half manure, and in my unconscious state had been ill. I had thrown off the poisonous mess they had got into me and stood again on my feet. Fortunately I had been wearing overalls over my own clothes and these I took off and threw on the barn floor.

I staggered thus, weak and sick and with a great hatred for all men in me, out into the barn floor and there, dimly seen by the light of a lantern hung to a wooden peg, were the patient livery horses, each in his stall, the long suffering patient beasts seen in the dim light.

I had a queer impulse. It must have been late in the night when I came out of my stupor and a thousand little demons seemed lodged in my head and beating with little hammers on my brains but, following some obscure impulse, I went from one to another of the livery horses touching each gently with my hand.

And then I went out into the night, leaving Ed, no doubt by now soundly asleep on his cot in the little stable office. He it was, I was sure, who had concocted the joke on me.

"Well, I am not that low. I do not need to be with him any more. Even though I have no other job I do not need to be near him, hear more of his senseless boasting, sleep in the same room with him." Even on that night, as a boy, I had the conviction that the animals that are the servants of man are infinitely finer and better than many men a boy would have to deal with in living his life.

It was a conviction that was to stick with me through life. It was very strong in me that February night as I went out at the livery stable door determined not to return. It was even stronger in me for the time than the fact that my mother would, in some way, find out what had happened to me. It was a conviction that was to be of great help to me, strengthening a contempt that was later to become a part of my nature.

There was something going on in our town that must have been going on at the same time in towns all over the country. Now our family was breaking up. Our mother, after the long struggle to keep us all together, had at last been struck down by disease.

It came upon her suddenly. She had become as my memory now pictures her a tall gaunt woman continually at work. We were living in the little yellow house by the swamp land (now I believe drained) and there had been a hard cold winter during which she continued her duties as wash woman, running continually in and out of the house, her clothes wet with the warm wash water in the tub by the kitchen stove, her clothes often freezing to her body as she went to hang the wet clothes on the clothes line slung across the back yard, her bony hands growing thinner and thinner, her gaunt body continually more gaunt.

This must have been the winter when I was living in the livery stable with the man Ed, and as to where father was at the time I do not know. During all this period his figure becomes strangely vague and meaningless to me and it may be that he was as I myself am in this, that, seeing another, his wife, disintegrating under her hard lot and knowing himself a good deal to blame, he had simply run away.

There would have been enough places for him to go. He had made acquaintances far and wide through the surrounding country and was always welcome, for either long or short visits, at certain farm houses.

He would be paying his way by story telling and perhaps as at one such farm house where I once stayed with him for two or three days, he having taken me with him on one of his jaunts, there would be a woman (She might be a maiden woman in the house or perhaps a widow. He had it seemed a special preference for widows.) to whom he was secretly making love, creeping to her, as I was, on the occasion spoken of, conscious of his creeping along a hallway to the woman's room, he thinking me soundly asleep.[47]

At any rate I am quite without any memory of his presence in our house when mother was suddenly struck down. There was a cold that immediately ran into pneumonia (called at that time "galloping consumption") and in a few days she was dead.

But in *A Story Teller's Story* I have also written of that terrible time for all of us. I will not write now of it here. Mother was gone and my older brother Karl, having discovered in himself a natural talent for drawing (he had won a prize at our county fair for a drawing of our town high school building and had now made an oil painting from a photograph of our father's mother which stood on an easel in our little parlor), had gone away, first to the town of Mansfield, Ohio, where he had a job designing grave stones, and then to Cleveland, where he had become what was called a "spot knocker."

It was an occupation that, I dare say, needs an explanation. There were certain men who went through the middle western towns selling what were called "crayon portraits." You handed such a one a photograph, usually of some dead person in the family, and, for a certain price, ten, fifteen, perhaps twenty dollars, you were to receive what was spoken of as

47. In *A Story Teller's Story*, ed. White, the father is described as always faithful to his wife, but in *Tar* (1926), pp. 272–75, he is more believably described as unfaithful.

a "free hand life size crayon portrait in a gorgeous golden frame." You paid nothing for the free hand crayon drawing, only paying for the frame, but you could not have the drawing without the frame.

It was something to set up on an easel in your parlor. If it was a portrait of a dead child, or perhaps of a grandfather, you draped it in black cloth. The small photographs were taken away to the city and by some mysterious process, perfectly understood by photographers, were then run up into the desired life size.

There it was and it was the job of the spot knocker to make it look like a free hand portrait. He went over it with his stick of crayon, a line here, a dash of black there, shadows under the eyes, a kind of fixed stare given to the eyes, and there you were. A good spot knocker could turn you out some ten or twelve in a day and he got a dollar each.

It was a good job for our brother Karl and he could now send money home as well as put each week a little aside for the art education for which he longed and which he was presently to begin in the city of Chicago, where I was later to join him.

I have already spoken of something strange happening to our town, as it must, at about the same time, have been happening in towns everywhere over the country. It is a period in American life that I was later to try to cover in a novel I called *Poor White,* a sudden and almost universal turning of men from the old crafts toward our modern life of the machines.[48]

I was to see it happen. I was to be a part of it. It meant the end of the old craftsmen of the towns, the shoe makers, the harness, wagon, buggy, furniture, men's clothing makers. All the little shops scattered through the towns, in which men fashioned things with their hands, directly out of the raw materials furnished by nature, to go with amazing quickness. It was a strange time and as I now look back upon it seems to have happened with amazing rapidity.

It was a kind of fever, an excitement in the veins of the people, and later, when I tried to write of it, using no one individual but rather an American town as the central character of my story, it became to me strangely dramatic.

For this was a kind of blind faith that the machine would solve an old

48. For Anderson's philosophy of industrialism, see Thomas Reed West, *Flesh of Steel: Literature and the Machine in America* (Nashville: Vanderbilt University Press, 1967), pp. 21–34.

old problem for men, lifting the load of heavy brutal toil off men's bodies, making a new life of ease and comfort for all, this however always mingled with a feeling of doubt and fear.

It was in our little house. It was in every house along our street. It was in all of the houses in every street of our town. They proclaimed. They protested.

It was the end of the old workman.

It was all through the middle west. Here and there oil and gas began to spurt out of the ground. As I once said, in a novel that tried to cover this feverish period in middle western American life, "Old Mother Earth had indigestion." [49]

Now, in Cleveland, there was Mr. John Rockefeller busily at work. He was planning and scheming. His efforts reached down into our town. There was a certain E. M. Harkness there. He ran a little variety store, sold calico, thread, needles, pins. We called him Em. He was one of the Harknesses who put money in with Mr. Rockefeller and I remember years later, when I once went to Yale, when I spoke there, when I walked past the great Harkness Memorial Building there, thinking of Em, hurrying down to our main street in the early morning to open his little store.

What a wonder. What a place in which to have been boy and man, this America, in my time. Em to go off later, in his own youth, sailing over the world, to many far countries and cities. . . .

Harkness Memorial . . . well, I do not suppose that our Em built that. [50] It may have been a brother or a cousin.

Some brother or cousin no doubt writing a letter to our Em.

"You scratch up a thousand, or two thousand. You put it in with this Rockefeller. He's going to get there."

Stories of that sort sweeping over the middle west, huge fortunes to be made suddenly—a new idea abroad.

Money to make money for you, pile it up, while you stand aside, doing nothing.

"Why, here's a machine that will do the work of a hundred, of two, three hundred men."

All of this, I dare say, very puzzling to the old workmen, the men who

49. The Clyde Natural Gas Company began drilling in May, 1886, but within a year abandoned the effort. See Anderson's description of the drilling in *A Story Teller's Story,* ed. White, pp. 65–71; on p. 66, Anderson says: "Old Mother Earth to be given an emetic of a stirring sort. Forth would flow wealth, factories, the very New Age itself."

50. Em Harkness appears in *A Story Teller's Story,* ed. White, pp. 68–69.

worked with their hands, fashioning things for other men to use out of the raw materials of nature. Money was what you got by hand labor. It was a medium of exchange. You got so and so many dollars for building a chair, a table, a set of farm harness. You took the money to the grocer to get food, to the tailor who made you a suit of clothing or an overcoat against the cold of winter.

But, apparently, money was becoming more than a medium for the exchange of goods. It was power. It had a life of its own. You bought a thing called "stock." It was a bit of paper. Sometimes, away off somewhere, a mysterious thing happened. Some man, or group of men, you had never seen, never talked to, declared what was called a "stock dividend." You had ten shares of a stock and then, suddenly, you had twenty, thirty, a hundred shares.

Dividends began to pour in. Why, without lifting a hand, you were suddenly rich.

Or, as more commonly happened, disaster came. You put a mortgage on your house, your farm, your little business. John Jones was getting suddenly and mysteriously rich, why not you?

There were all sorts of scheming shrewd men who understood what you did not understand. In New York Jim Fisk, Jay Gould, that queer figure of the Erie Railroad, Daniel Drew,[51] many of these new men, jugglers, sleight-of-hand men pitching millions of dollars into the air, catching them between their legs, behind their backs, your hard earned dollars mixed in with all the others. Now you see it, now you don't, the hand is quicker than the eye, a kind of gigantic pin and thimble game going on in a big national way.

Little men puzzled, frightened, frustrated.

"John Jones made it. Now you look. He had a thousand dollars saved. He put it in. Now look at him. There he is, he and his family, now driving in a new carriage. Why, the man's got money to burn."

John worked down at the flour mill down by the Wheeling tracks. He got a dollar a day for twelve hours' work.

But John was a fellow who always managed to put a little aside, every day a little, every week a little.

He put it in, took a long breath and plunged. Now look at him. There he goes. Why he's suddenly a rich man.

51. Daniel Drew (1797–1879), treasurer of the Erie Railroad; Jason Gould (1836–92), owner of New York City elevated railroads and the *New York World;* Jim Fisk (1834–72), stock speculator.

Fancy schemes of sudden wealth, in the night, in the daytime, in small town hotel lobbies, on trains, in saloons, in bedrooms of houses where working men, store keepers, lawyers, doctors, farmers slept with their wives.

Gadgets and more gadgets. There was a sudden flood of new inventions.

"Why John, you can sell a million of that." "Look Jake, you make five cents on every one you sell. It will go like hotcakes."

"The thing to do, Jake, is to organize a company, sell stock."

In every town a little Jay Gould, a little Jim Fisk.

There was the old fashioned high wheeled bicycle. It was a strange dangerous thing. There was a huge front wheel on which you sat, high up, as on stilts, and a tiny little wheel behind.

You had to be mighty careful or you'd take a header from up there. A stone in the road or a bump to pass over and the little wheel at the rear reared up. It was a bucking bronco on wheels. It pitched you, shot you off, head first, into the air and, when you landed, you were lucky if you didn't get your back broken.

And then some fellow somewhere invented a new kind of bicycle. It was a crude form of the bicycle to be seen on the streets today. It was called a "safety." It was, at first, heavy and cumbersome, like the first of the automobiles always getting out of order, stalling you somewhere along some country road, but we all took to it.

We boys saved our pennies and nickels, went into debt, little bicycle shops set up in every town. We went on what were called "century runs," during which you tried to cover a hundred miles, often through the deep sand of country roads, up hill and down, between a summer daylight and dark.

It was something heroic. What pumping and puffing. What leg muscles we developed. It is true that I never achieved one of the centuries, usually performed on Sundays, of groups of ten or twelve young men and boys setting out at daylight but I tried often enough. I usually gave out somewhere around ten in the morning, my legs aching terribly, the sweat pouring from my body. I made some excuse. "My bike needs greasing," I said. "You others go on. I'll try to catch up with you."

I was thinking of the long voyage home, after the fifty mile point was reached, and so, when the others had gone on and were out of sight, I turned back.

There were excuses enough to be made as our bikes were always getting out of order but I was ashamed and often did not return to our small town until darkness came.

And how I envied the other stout fellows who had triumphantly completed the run. They had formed what was called a "Century Club." You got a silver chain, a new link added for each century run made, and there was one of our town boys (if my memory doesn't deceive me it was one Shorty Pengrin, a bold laughing fellow who was forever teasing and ragging our father when he was a bit the worse for drink) who had a chain as long as his arm.

And what a hero he was to us. How we envied him and how he strutted. He was a kind of town strong boy, the Ernest Hemingway of our town.

And then the machine would suddenly invade our town with a rush. We got a bicycle factory.[52]

It was set up in an old factory building along the Lake Shore Railroad tracks out near the town's edge, a factory that had been built for the manufacture of pianos but that had ended in failure.

It was revamped, new machinery shipped in, great lathes and other machine tools that were a town wonder shipped in and set up, crowds of us young there every day to hang about the factory doors and at the windows.

Here were machines with great iron legs, like the legs of elephants, delicate complicated looking machines all new to us. We gathered about and spoke in lowered voices.

"Why look at it. Gee, it will take some man to run a machine like that." There was something of the same reverence we had long felt for railroad locomotives and the men who understood and ran them.

And there was other exciting talk. Men were to be hired. Men were to get two dollars a day for only twelve hours' work. It seemed unbelievable. Why what a fortune.

And then the new men presently coming in, the trained machinists, kings among men to us, men who could guide great rods of steel across a lathe, cutting it to the hundredth, the thousandth fraction of an inch.

"Ah, it's all bunk I tell you. They can't do that."

"Yes they can. You'll see."

Dreams of a new era of prosperity. Money rolling into our town, house rents going suddenly up, the stores along our main street refurbished. Dreams of something happening to our town such as presently was to happen to the town of Akron, Youngstown and other Ohio towns.

52. A bicycle factory came to Clyde in 1894. See *A Story Teller's Story,* ed. White, pp. 148–49. In *Tar* (1926), pp. 275–76, Karl is described as working in the factory.

In Detroit Henry Ford, no doubt at this time in his own little Detroit bicycle shop and already experimenting with his "horseless carriage."

There were these new men, trained mechanics, now swaggering through our town streets. They seemed millionaires to us. It was even whispered that some of them got as much as three and even four dollars for a day's work.

And they did not have to work hard. It was what we called a "snap." Such a man was like a railroad engineer who merely sat up there in his engine, pulled certain levers and the engine did the work while he sat, like a lord, by his engine window and traveled from town to town surveying the country.

"I tell you what, knowledge is a good thing. Education's the thing."

We boys, now growing toward young manhood, gathered at night and sat on the express trucks by the railroad station. We walked down the dark railroad track to the factory. Who among us would get a job? There were plans made.

"No, I'm not going to work in any factory. I'm going to be a railroad mail clerk. I want to see the world."

A railroad mail clerk went to distant cities, went as far as Chicago, maybe even went east to New York. Once there had been such a railroad mail clerk came to our town. He was on a vacation from his job and was on a drunk. He had gone about our town talking of all the far places he had seen. His words had stirred longing in all of us.

There was a boy determined to be a jeweler. He was going away to a school where he would learn to repair watches and another who dreamed of becoming a dentist while my own dream, never to be realized, was clear enough. It was true I had been through the sad experience as a groom in the livery stable and had had the name "livery stable chambermaid" shouted at me but I still clung desperately to the hope of yet becoming a race horse driver and had even, during the summer before, gone off, my sister protesting, for some months with Tom Whitehead's string of trotting and pacing horses.

I had, it was true, been merely a groom, a "swipe," so called, a boy clad in an old pair of horsey smelling pants and a torn sweater, privileged however to lead one of the to me beautiful race horses out to the track before the grandstand at some county fairs and occasionally (ah, rare privilege) allowed one fall morning to climb into a sulky and jog my own particular horse, a bay gelding named Doctor Fritz, around and around some half mile county fair ground track, my heart swelling with pride, often when I was on the backstretch and out of sight and hearing of the other swipes allowing myself the joy of imagining Fritz and me engaged in a grueling race, talking to him as I had heard race drivers do, shouting encouragement to him, imagining some other horse and driver pressing me hard, indulging in the picturesque profanity almost all good drivers had at their command.

"Why, you son of a bitch, lay over or I'll cut you down."

This always however in the world of the imagination in which I was alas to live so much of my life, no other horse or driver near, Doctor Fritz, that gallant little gelding, who was down in front in almost every race in which he was entered that fall, merely jogging slowly along, to strengthen and keep tough and ready his legs, he seeming when I broke forth into some new outburst of profanity directed at some imaginary tough rough handed other driver whose goddamn head I was imagining myself punching at the end of the race, Doctor Fritz I say merely wagging his ears at me as though saying, "Go it boy, you're as big a race driver now as you'll ever be. You are too high strung, too easily excited to ever be a real race driver."

Something inbred wasn't in me, a certain coolness, a certain delicate but firm grip of the reins over a race horse, the horse I well understood.

A certain love no doubt between the gallant horse and me but something lacking too.

"I wouldn't want to trust you, boy, in a hard race. I really couldn't trust you, boy."

Oh sad, sad realization.

Well, never you mind, Doctor Fritz, I'll drive you in desperate grueling races in my dreams. Why I shall be doing it on paper one of these days, long after you, Doctor Fritz, are a dead horse. I will sit in an advertising office, in a sky scraper, high up in a Chicago advertising office, clerks and other advertising writers running up and down past my desk, before me an assignment to write certain advertisements of pills to cure people's bound up bowels, but instead of writing the advertisements I will be in imagination far away on some race track, the sound of the quick drum drum of each horse's hooves in my ear, crowds cheering me on as I drive some other even nobler and more beautiful Doctor Fritz through the home stretch, passing horse after horse, a string of such lovely profanity as men never heard flowing from my grim lips, my hands nevertheless steady, and sitting thus in that advertising office instead of writing the advertisements for the bowel difficulties of people I will be writing a story called "I'm a

Fool," [53] to be translated in languages all over the world, causing again in many breasts the love for the horse I once felt for you, Doctor Fritz.

But now I return to the factory gate when I was one of the fortunate ones and got a job, for fall had turned to winter and all the race horses were now on their winter farms.

I was doubly fortunate as my new job, as a factory hand, did not take me into the main factory building. In the morning I went in with the others and punched the time clock. The late fall days had come and, as we worked the twelve hour day, it was still dark as we factory hands hurried through the streets. I went on through the factory, through a rear door and along an elevated platform to a small brick building where bicycle frames were painted. However they were not painted but dipped in tanks of black enamel. We in the little building, some four or five of us, caught the frames on hooks and dipped them into the tanks. The black shining liquid in the tanks was said to be highly inflammable, it stunk horribly, making the nose sting and the eyes water, and there were signs everywhere forbidding smoking.

We stood over the tanks letting the frames drip and softly brushing away the enamel that tended to gather in lumps as it hardened. We ran with the frames into certain steel ovens where we hung them up to be baked. We worked earnestly, with a kind of desperate eagerness, until all the ovens were filled and then we rested.

I was again fortunate. My luck held. The boss in that place was one Rice, a short compact little man with broad shoulders, a dark leathery skin and a huge black mustache, a most delightfully charming man who sang all day long. He was an old time carriage painter and it was his particular job to supervise my work and to stripe the bicycle frames when they came shining and black from the oven.

He was very skillful and we all admired him. Grasping in his short stubby fingers a peculiar long bristled brush he made a quick sweeping stroke the whole length of one of the round steel tubes that made up the bicycle frame. He never missed. The line he drew with such amazing speed was perfect. There was the thin yellow or red line the whole length of the tube, of the same thickness from end to end.

We stood about admiring. Even when our boss had been off on one of his occasional sprees and the brush trembled in his hand the stripe drawn was nevertheless perfect.

53. "I'm a Fool," *Dial,* LXXII (February, 1922), 119–29; in *Horses and Men* (1923), pp. 3–8.

"Here you try it," he said, handing the brush to one of us, and one by
one we did try but in every case made but a struggling wavering line that
must at once be erased with a rag, a failure that always delighted our boss.

He crowed, he danced a jig on the floor.

"Why you do it like this. It's very simple," he said. He made another of
the long sweeping strokes with the brush and again the line was perfect.
He began to stroke his mustache. He strutted.

"Every man to his trade," he said. He began talking at length of his
years of work at the carriage making trade. He told of a carriage he had
once finished for a rich banker and of another job he did on a carriage
built for a governor of the state. "This dipping of bicycle frames in tanks
of enamel is all right for you boys but for a real workman like me. . . .
Bah," he shouted. He walked over and spat into one of the tanks.

"It doesn't take a real workman to do a job like you boys are doing."

He began to swear at the man who owned the bicycle factory, a round
fat little man whose name was James. The man who owned the factory
had come from a town where Rice had worked as a finisher of fine hand
built carriages. Our little boss began to recite to us the man's history.
"What does such a man know of real workmen?" he asked. The manufacturer of bicycles had been somewhere to a business college. He was a man
who, if you threw him into a rain, wouldn't get wet. He had a rich dad who
had given him his start. Everything the man touched simply turned at once
to gold. Such a man didn't have to have brains. His luck would always pull
him through. Our boss had heard that the bicycle manufacturer, already
making money hand over fist out of bicycles, was thinking of going into
the making of horseless carriages. He declared that the idea was a crazy
one but nevertheless would succeed. Everything Jim touched did succeed.

Except one thing. There was one thing Jim couldn't do. He couldn't
make our boss dip bicycle frames.

"Well, he stripes them." That was all right. He'd do the striping. It was
a job that took real skill. Boys like us couldn't do it. He had told Jim that.
The carriage making business was going to the devil all right, men were
crazy about bicycles and presently, no doubt, they would be equally crazy
about the startling horseless carriage everyone was now trying to build, the
carriage making business was getting shut and Jim had written him a
letter telling him to come to our town and he had come.

He had come and Jim, a man he had known when he was just a squirt
of a snotty nosed kid, had shown him into the shop where he was now
boss.

He had looked about there. He had seen the tanks filled with the black raw smelling enamel.

"For God's sake Jim, you don't expect me, a workman like me, to stand over one of these tanks, dipping bicycle frames into that stuff?

"If you do, Jim, you're barking up the wrong tree.

"I'd see you in hell, Jim, before I'd sink to a job like that."

Our boss had held the above conversation with the big boss Jim. He told us about it every day, repeated it word for word.

Well, after all Jim had known when he was up against a real man, a real workman. Jim was smart all right. He had at once assured our boss. He would get boys like us to do that sort of work. Our boss was to be a striper, nothing else. When there were no bicycle frames to stripe he could just boss.

There were the signs forbidding us to smoke in the enameling room and they tried to tell our boss. He placed one of us on guard by a paint spattered window facing the main factory—this against the possible coming of the big boss Jim, while the others hung out at windows at the back of the little shop. Pipes and cigarettes were lighted and a general good time was had by all except the one of us whose turn it was to stand on guard.

It was this dark and merry paint shop boss with the big mustache who gave me the notion for the figure of Sponge Martin, the old gaffer of the mythical town of Old Harbor on the Ohio River where the equally mythical character Bruce Dudley of the novel *Dark Laughter* had certain adventures.[54]

Not that my actual paint shop boss, in my first factory job, had any such a background as the one I gave my Sponge Martin. It is true that the man had a little wiry looking wife and that they seemed, when I saw them together, to be two people entirely capable of having a good time together but there was no daughter in a questionable house in Cincinnati and, as for their fondness for sawdust piles at night by the slow flowing Ohio, at least I was never there with them.

I do know that our actual paint shop boss in that place occasionally, on a Saturday night, sometimes invited some of us youngsters to have a few with him.

54. New York: Boni and Liveright, 1925. See Robert Crist, "Sherwood Anderson's *Dark Laughter:* Sources, Composition, and Reputation" (Ph.D. Thesis, University of Chicago, 1966).

"You boys meet me downtown tonight, at Body Adair's place. You come on. We'll lift a few."

He would have been dancing little jigs all Saturday afternoon as we finished up the week's work in the shop.

"Saturday night and supper on the table.

"It's the happiest time in a working man's life," he sang.

We did occasionally join him although I was, as yet, too young to be admitted to the fellowship of the men in Body's place and had to hang about in the street outside.

However I could hear our little boss singing in there and presently he emerged. There was something curious happened. When our boss had got a certain number of drinks under his belt he became suddenly silent. He had been singing and dancing but was, after several drinks, apparently overcome by sadness. He stood for a moment looking at the men he had invited to drink with him. Once when we were alone together in the paint shop on an evening when the others were gone he tried to explain to me his peculiar behavior on these occasions.

"I get proud," he said. "I am in there drinking with the others and then I get proud."

There was something on his mind he wanted to explain to me. He began to give me advice. I wasn't to stay long in the factory.

"Here we paint these bicycles," he said. "Well we do not paint them. We dip them in these goddamn tanks filled with this stinking black enamel.

"It is true I do not myself dip them into the tanks. I stripe the damn things. You see how it is, the thousands of these all striped just alike."

Sometimes, he declared, it drove him nearly crazy. He wanted to begin making flourishes on the frames of the bicycles with his striping brush. He spoke at length of his former occupation. He had been a partner in a small carriage building firm and in that place, he said, they made each carriage a little different than the one built just before it.

"We could keep planning and scheming how to make them better and better," he said. He spoke at length of what a carriage finishing job had meant to him, of a certain shining velvety finish to be got only after infinite labor, a coat of varnish to put on, that rubbed and rubbed, and then another and another coat with more patient rubbing.

And then the striping of such a job. He could let his fancy play a little. He didn't have to do hundreds of carriages all alike.

"As for you, boy, you get out of here as soon as you can. I am getting old now and I have to do what I can. I've got the old woman and my kids."

The boss had a son, a young boy who had lost a leg. He had been catching rides on freight trains, flipping on and off with other boys, and had slipped and fallen under a freight car wheel. The boss spoke of him. He had to be taken care of and there was a big doctor bill to be paid.

"They've got me trapped, boy, but you're young. Now, you see the carriage building business is going to hell. You've seen these horseless carriages on the street. Well, there'll be more and more of them. Jim, our big boss here, will be making them pretty soon now.

"And it will be the same as with these goddamn bicycles—all alike, all alike.

"You get into something, boy, where everything keeps changing, where you'll never be satisfied with what you do, always wanting to make it better and better."

He was trying to explain to me what sometimes happened to him when he was out on Saturday nights, lifting a few with the boys.

"I get proud," he said. "At first I'm proud and then I'm sad. I'm with the boys, there in Body's place, and somewhere else. I've been dancing and singing. You know how I do sometimes.

"And then a funny feeling comes. I go a little away from them. I stand there looking at them. I wonder if any of them know how I hate striping these damn bicycles, all alike, the same lines drawn on every one of them, day after day, week after week.

"I get to thinking about the big boss here, Jim. Hell, I knew him when he was a snotty nosed kid. Hell, I know he doesn't know a damn thing about how I feel. He thinks he pays me well and that settles it. He thinks I'm getting old now and for old times, when we were both young in the same town, he's taking care of me.

"As though that mattered a good goddamn.

"So, I'm thinking of him and all the others I'm with, there in Body's place, and how they don't any of them maybe give a damn and I grow a little loony.

"I know boy, I'm scared I'm going to cry or something so I run."

What happened to our boss, on these occasions (I was on our main street and near Body's place and saw it) was that he suddenly emerged from the saloon door. He got into the middle of the street and ran. He had lost his hat, his arms and legs were flying wildly and along the street men and boys were shouting at him.

"Go it boy," they shouted.

Some of the people along the street were curious.

"What's he running for?" they asked but as he had done the same thing on several other Saturday nights there was always some town wit who could explain.

"Ah he's going rabbit hunting," the wit explained. "He wants a rabbit for his Sunday dinner. He doesn't shoot rabbits. He runs them down."

Our boss had run through our town street and out of sight into the darkness. On the evening in the shop when he tried to explain to me he said he just kept running until he couldn't run any more.

"It's a kind of running fit I have, like dogs sometimes have," he said. "I run until I can't run any more and then I lie down. I cry a little like a kid. Then I get up and go home to the old woman. I start all over again.

"She's pretty good, at that, my old woman," he said.

Our little town was changing. Of a sudden life there began moving at a new pace. How isolated our lives had been, what an adventure to go off to another town, to Fremont, to the west, or to Bellevue, to the east, both some eight to ten miles away. We boys got aboard freight trains and stole rides to these towns and it was at Fremont I first saw a town all lighted by electric street lights. "But what a wonder. Do you mean to tell me that they just pull a switch and it lights all of these lights?"

So presently our street lamp lighter with his little two wheeled cart, hurrying through our street at dusk to light the kerosene street lamps, would be out of a job too.

A new wonder in the voices of men talking in groups all night on main street. When would all these new wonders cease?

Plenty of grown men and women in such a town who had never been out of the town, had never been on a railroad train. The great world outside the activities of our main street a vast unknown mystery.

A few men to be sure coming and going. There would be the traveling salesmen from Cleveland and Toledo or, occasionally, rarely, in from Chicago or New York, spending the night at one of our two hotels, these men looked upon almost as world travelers, gaping crowds of us standing about listening as such a one talked, in one of the stores or sitting on a summer evening, his chair tilted back against the wall at the front of the hotel, he speaking so freely of far away places and of strange events to come.

The bicycle was now an accepted fact. It was continually being improved and even the girls had begun to ride bicycles. Then soon a few more daring ones put on bloomers.

"Well now what do you think of that? Did you see that?"

"There's that daughter of Jim Grey's running right through main street with a pair of men's pants on."

"Great God, what next?" There was certainly to be plenty next. I had given up the place in the bicycle factory and getting on a freight train at night had beat my way east to Erie, Pennsylvania, and had for a time found work there.

It was because of a new restlessness that had come upon me and that was to keep coming upon me all my life. There was our house, with mother gone now. That and grandmother, the strange crafty old woman, had come and gone and there was the great world outside calling and calling.

And so I went suddenly, the impulse to be on the move, a hunger to see more of the world strong in me, climbing late one evening, with but a few dollars in my pocket, into an empty coal car, crouching there as the train rolled eastward.

I had planned to seek work in Cleveland but after two days there (my older brother Karl had moved on from Cleveland after mother's death) and walking the streets restlessly, in the company of another youth, applying for work at factory doors, I was discouraged, moved on with him to Erie. My new acquaintance said that Erie was his home town and he was sure we could find work there.

"Come on. You can stay at our house with my folks until you get a job," he said and so, going by street car to a suburb of Cleveland, we boarded another freight train at night and went on to Erie.

The fellow I had got in with, a tall bony youth of perhaps sixteen, met in a small working men's rooming house, was a cheerful talkative fellow. He declared that it was not inability to find work that had driven him from his home but that he had also a great hunger to see the world. He had been as far west as Denver and south to Atlanta. "I haven't worked a day since I left home," he declared, and as we got in an empty box car rolling eastward he told me of how he had managed.

He had simply panhandled his way along.

"You go from house to house," he said. "You have a good story made up. You tackle men and women on the street." He had, he declared, had his best success with women.

"They fall for me," he said. He declared that at several houses at which he had stopped to beg, during the month he had been on the road, when there were women alone in the houses, he had been invited inside the houses. Clothing and money had been given him and, in certain houses, he had, he said, nudging me in the ribs with a long bony finger, got something else.

He had invented a story he always told.

"I told them that I had run away from home, when I was just a young boy, because my father was dead and my mother had married again. I gave them, you see, a line of talk about a cruel stepfather and how I couldn't stand it and ran away. I said I had been working on a cattle ranch out in Wyoming but that a boyhood friend, with whom I was in correspondence, had written me saying my mother was dead.

"Then I told them that I had a little sister at home and I wanted to go home and take care of her. I gave them a line about how cruel our stepfather was and then, if I'd get one of them to listen that far and, if she was a woman, I began to cry."

His story sure knocked 'em, he said. He was full of craftiness and pride. He said that if he could get a woman to listen to him until he got his story really going he could nail her every time. They fed him, they gave him money, they gave him clothes and there were some of them who in their eagerness to comfort him even took him into their arms.

"And oh boy, what do you think, into their bedrooms too," he said.

So here was another tale of the livery stable but a milder one. There was more of Ed's vulgarity and he was no doubt merely practising as he told me of his adventures and I had already discovered that it was a common trait with many men to lie about their adventures with women. It was evident however that my new acquaintance did know his way about. He was in no way impressed and half frightened by the hugeness of the city of Cleveland as I had been.

"What, you think this is a big town? Wait until you see New York or Chicago." He was going home for a visit to his people in the town of Erie but did not intend to stay there. What was the use of sticking around one town? A fellow got a job. Well, he worked his head off, for what? He got clothes and food, a place to sleep.

But if a fellow had his wits about him he could get those things without work. He had but to think up a good story, tell it to women.

"What you've got to do is to make a woman feel she is your mother."

"But what about when you get older?" I asked.

"Ah, to hell with that. You got to think up a new story, that's all," he said scornfully.

My new friend had taken me about with him in the city streets during the two or three evenings we had spent in Cleveland and there I saw for the first time paved streets and the wonder of city crowds. It was all a little terrifying to me, the crowds pouring out of the factories and offices at the day's end, the street cars, run by electricity, the gayly lighted stores with the wealth of goods displayed in windows, the tall buildings. And there were the great crowds of people. How did they all manage to live? How could one in such a place ever get to know others, find friends and comrades? Already, after a few days away from my home town, I was growing hungry for the sight of familiar streets, houses and faces.

My stay in Erie was short. I had got a job wheeling goods on trucks to ships on the docks but found the work too heavy for me. After some two or three weeks of it I got aboard another freight train and crouched in a corner of an empty box car beat my way back home again.

I was filled with a new wonder, half fear. How strangely big and frightening the world was. In Erie I had stayed in the house of the family of the acquaintance I had picked up and there I saw a new and to me strange kind of life.

There were these girls in that family, two of them tall and strong looking, while the third was thin and looked ill, and the father, a little old man who seemed continually angry. He was a very profane little old man and was always storming into the house, a small frame one, on a street of working men's houses, and giving orders that were never obeyed.

"I am ruler in my own house. When I tell you you can't go out you obey me or I'll knock your head off," he would be shouting at one of the two tall girls. This in the evening, after the day's work, when the girls were dressing preparatory to leaving the house for adventures in the streets. The others would be sitting in the little kitchen of the house, having dined. (We always sat in complete silence at meals in that house and I would be sitting, with a newspaper in my hand, at the table while one of the girls, the younger of the three, who looked thin and ill, washed the dishes at a nearby sink and from where I sat could see, over my newspaper, into a bedroom, the door of which had been left open, where the two other daughters of the house were dressing for the evening's adventures.)

The two tall red haired girls worked during the day in some nearby factory and now they were half nude in there and kept going, one after the other, to stand before a glass over a small dresser in their bedroom.

The whole scene was very strange to me. There were the two daughters of the house, preparing to go out for the evening with new friends, and there was the little old father shouting, giving orders and swearing at them. He seemed often about to explode. He had been drinking but was not drunk although, as he sat quite near me, I could smell the heavy fumes of liquor on his breath.

"By God, you'll stay in this house tonight or I'll warm your behinds for you."

He kept jumping up and sitting down. He waved his arms about. He pounded on the table with his fist while his one son (the mother of the family was dead) occasionally looked up over his newspaper and winked at me.

"Ah, pay no attention to the old man. He's nuts," the son had said to me when I had first come to board at the house. I slept in a room upstairs in the house with the one son who had already declared his intention to "hit the road" again. I had been paying my board to the older of the three daughters, one of the ones now dressing to go out.

There was, the son told me, another daughter of the house who had disappeared from home. The father kept speaking of her. Her name was Sarah.

"God, don't you know what happened to Sarah?" he shouted. He declared that Sarah had become no better than a whore. She had disappeared from home and the son told me that she had gone off with a married man.

"And now you two go running about in the streets at night, just as Sarah did. Hell, I know what you do. You pick up men. You think you can get away with it, that you can fool me, but you can't."

The man kept scolding and screaming while the two red haired daughters of the house went calmly ahead with their preparation for departure. When they were dressed for the evening they came into the kitchen where we others sat, smiled at their brother and me, and pushed out into the night. It was a scene repeated over and over, evening after evening, while I stayed in that house. The father forever shouting and screaming, the son calmly reading the evening paper, the two older daughters preparing to depart for some unknown adventure in the streets of the town, and the younger of the three daughters, the thin sickly one (she couldn't have been more than sixteen) washing the dishes soiled during the evening meal, and myself sitting with the father and son and filled with a strange new fear at something, a kind of casual brutality that seemed to rule the people about me. It was a kind of brutality that appalled me. Here were these people, living together in the little working man's house. The father had some sort of job at the gate of a nearby factory. He sat all day in a little box-like office at the gate of the factory and checked the employees as they passed in and out. The son, as we lay in our bed in an upstairs room of the house, had told me the story of his father. He had been injured by a machine in the factory and had been given the place. "It is a cinch," the son said. He spoke of his father with a queer sort of impersonal indifference that I felt also in the two older girls. There was something in the house I was later to see and feel in other houses and in other families. There was a man, the father of the family, who had in some way lost his grip on life and on the people about him. There was in him a queer kind of spiritual impotence. Something had defeated him in life and he was continually protesting. He was there, in his own house, swearing at his two daughters, continually shouting orders to them to which they paid no attention. It had no doubt been going on for years. Was it then, or later, that I got the sharp impression that he, like all such men, was not really speaking to his daughters at all? They had ceased to exist for him as he had ceased to exist for them. There was, to me, a complete and horrid indifference, one to the other, of all the people in that house. There was no bond. Once the son, as we were lying in the bed upstairs, spoke to me of the sister who had left home, the one the father in his wrath was always speaking of as a whore.

"Even she went away with a man," the brother explained.

"Why not?" he asked. "The guy got stuck on her and he had plenty of dough.

"Sure he was married. He keeps his family here and he keeps Sis over in Buffalo.

"So he goes to see her about twice a week. Well, what the hell? She's got an apartment of her own. She's got plenty of dough to spend. She'd have been a damn fool, wouldn't she, not to take on a guy like that?"

There was this indifference, one toward another, of the people of that house. It was curiously like the feeling that was to become later a part of all life. It was to be, while I yet lived, in airmen flying over cities, dropping bombs on cities, unknown men and women killed on the earth down below the flying men, a strange new unbelief in life in others.

It was in the people of that house, in the young man with whom I slept, in all of them except perhaps the pale thin girl I was always to remember as standing by a kitchen sink and washing dishes.

She was to become fixed in my mind so.

It was a Sunday afternoon when I left that house to return for my last stay at home. I was in the room upstairs in the house where I slept with the young man who had been a hobo and who was planning to go off on another hoboing cruise. He had made no effort to get work since he had come home but the father rarely addressed a word to him. Now on the winter Sunday, a light snow falling in the street, he had left the house after the noon meal as had also the father and the two older daughters.

I stood by a window in the room upstairs. Before me was a little street of working men's houses. A man came into the street leading an old blind white horse that just seemed able to stumble along. The man with the horse, led by a rope, came slowly along the street and past the window at which I stood.

"There is a kind of indifference toward life in others that poisons all life."

Could I have had such a thought on that day? How do I know?

I only know that I was suddenly sick at the life there.

"I've got to leave here at once. I've got to. I've got to get out."

I kept whispering the word over to myself. Perhaps I was only homesick and wanting to see again my sister, my brothers, the people of my own town.

I packed quickly, putting my few belongings into a small bag, and hurried down the stairs and there was that pale thin girl still bent over the dishes left from our noon meal.

She turned and looked at me and for a moment I stood looking at her.

"Are you going away?"

"Yes," I said.

"Why?" she asked.

She was very pale and I have thought since was no doubt tubercular. Her thin hair was a dirty red and it hung in loose strands from her narrow bony head.

On an impulse I stepped over and stood beside her. She was leaning forward her hands in a pan of dirty dish water. She was looking up at me. There was [55]

55. The last page of this manuscript is missing, but this is Anderson's only description of his hobo experiences.

Since my mother's death my sister had become the head of the house while I was the oldest male at home. She had finished with high school. A prize student, she had graduated at fourteen and was ambitious. She wanted, as soon as she was old enough, to begin teaching school and there was, I am quite sure, another ambition. She wrote verses and dreamed of becoming a writer, perhaps even a poet.

There was about her a shining kind of beauty, at the time a young girl who was just coming into womanhood. She had a strong feeling of a moral obligation to carry on, hold the family together, and, as I can now realize, although at the time I did not, there were for her many other problems. Being as she was, so young and beautiful, she must have wanted pretty clothes, the attention of men, but as there were, besides myself, my brother Irve and my oldest brother Karl, now gone from home to begin his struggle as a painter, two other younger brothers in the house, she determined to be noble, to sacrifice herself.

We were living so, my sister more or less the female head of the house, myself playing the part of the dominant male, when an old woman, my mother's mother, descended upon us.

She was an old woman I later wrote much about. She is in a book of mine called *A Story Teller's Story*. It may be that, in that book, I have romanticized her a little, as we writers do, but not much. She was something terrific. One of her eyes had gone dead and she was in her late eighties, but she was as strong as a horse. Once I saw her in the top of a cherry tree picking and eating cherries. She had climbed up there. I have always attributed some of my own health to her strong old body.

She had come to our house without an invitation, having no doubt heard of our mother's death, knowing she would find in our house certain young males, wanting herself to be at the head of such a household of growing young men and, having come, she was determined to remain. As for father I do not remember where he was. He had gone off somewhere. He was always doing that when there was trouble brewing in our house.

As to just what really happened between my sister and my grandmother I have no way of knowing. My sister was a highly imaginative girl as she was later a woman. There was in her something that is in most writers of tales. Such a writer begins to tell a story, based perhaps upon some foundation of facts, and his imagination goes to work.

He becomes confused. Facts elude. He cannot himself tell where fact stops and invention begins.

There was the determined old woman in our house, and there was my sister, and a contest had begun between them. They were both, I fancy, determined to be the female head of the house. It was a women's war. In my sister, young as she was, there had already grown up a kind of pride. She had undertaken something. A sacrifice had been made. She, who had been so bright in school, who had stood always at the head of her class, who had planned a career for herself, had got, now, this mother feeling for us. There was our house to be managed, we three older boys in some way to find the money. It was understood that we would go on, that we would pull it off. She must have felt that it was a kind of sacred duty to be performed, herself to take the place of our dead mother. I am sure we had not asked her to do it.

"I have given up my own career. I have made this sacrifice. Life has wronged me so. You shall not take the wrong from me. Now I desire to be wronged."

All of this, I am sure, was quite unconsciously in her mind.

And there was this old woman. She so very strong, very determined. She would have gone about the house muttering words. She was always doing that. She was one who aroused fear.

One afternoon my sister took two of us, my brother Irve and myself, into a little shed that stood just by our kitchen door. She was very nervous and excited. She was dry-washing her hands and there were tears in her eyes when she spoke to us. The old woman was somewhere in the house. She was going about in there muttering words. Our house seemed haunted by her presence.

"It has to end. It cannot go on," my sister said. Her face was flushed and tears stood in her eyes. She swore that the old woman, who had come into our house, had threatened to kill her.

It had happened, she said, but a few hours before. She was standing in the kitchen, was at work in there, and the old woman had come in to her. There was a large kitchen knife lying on a table.[56]

In the woodshed my sister sat on a bench. She put her hands over her face. A shudder ran through her body. The old woman had been going

---

56. This is almost certainly an "invented memory," described also in *A Story Teller's Story,* ed. White, p. 78. Stella Anderson, who finished high school in 1891 as class valedictorian, did have to rear her young brothers after 1895. She taught school from 1892 to 1894.

about town. She had been making inquiries. My sister had wanted to be a school teacher. "Go and be one," the old woman had shouted to her. She had begun by trying to persuade my sister and then she had begun to threaten and it had ended, my sister declared, by her coming into the kitchen intent upon killing her.

The old woman had come into the kitchen. She had picked up the knife from the table. She had walked to where my sister stood. She had raised the knife to strike.

My sister got more and more dramatic as she told her tale. She arose from the bench. It developed that, for weeks, she had been saving money, a little at a time. She had it wrapped in a pocket handkerchief, and, as my brother and I stood listening to her tale, she unwrapped it and handed it to me. There was, she said, enough money to buy a railroad ticket for the grandmother.

"She can go back to the place from which she came. No one asked her to come here. It is that old woman or it is me," she declared. There was enough money saved to send the old woman back to our aunt, our mother's sister, who lived on a farm, somewhere in southern Ohio.

"She is in the house there. If she stays I cannot stay.

"It is now three and there is a train leaving at five," my sister said.

My sister got up from the bench. There was a determined look in her eyes. "You two will have to be men." She was no longer crying. She stood erect before us. "You will have to choose," she said. We were to go, the two of us, to the old woman, our grandmother. We were to explain to her, order her to pack and be gone. We were to tell her that, if she did not go, we would call the police. As she said all of this, giving us thus our instructions, my sister put the money into my hands. She stood, with her slender girlish figure very erect, and pointed toward the house. "Go," she said. There was in her at the moment a suggestion of the actress playing some tragic role. Years later when I saw the actress Ada Rehan [57] in some tragic role I thought of my sister Stella. She declared that she would never again enter our house while the old woman was there.

We did go. Accompanied by my brother Irve I marched into the house and delivered our ultimatum, my voice trembling. As my sister had suggested I spoke of the police and for a time, after I had made my speech, there was silence.

57. Ada Rehan (1860–1916), born in Ireland as "Ada Crehan," Shakespearean actress.

It was a silence that awoke fear. We stood and she sat and there was her one old eye looking at us. The other eye was always closed.

"She is not going to do it," I thought. The terror took possession of me and now, for the time, I believed the tale of the knife, told us by my sister. The one old eye of the old woman was, I thought, filled with hatred. I wanted to turn and run away, but presently, after staring at us for several minutes, the old woman arose.

She packed in silence and, in silence, marched to the station, my brother Irve and I marching in silence behind, and, at the station, I bought the railroad ticket and put it into her hand. There was nothing said, no good-byes, but, when at last the train came and she had got aboard and my brother and I stood on the station platform and she sat by an open window, her one old eye still staring at us, was it really hatred or sadness I saw in the old woman's eye? As the train pulled out I saw her thin old lips begin to move. She was saying words but, because of the sound made by the train, we could not hear. Was she muttering curses or was she pleading with us?

At any rate she had gone and, when we had seen the last of her, I became suddenly sad and, as my brother and I walked homeward, I remember that there was a sudden scepticism in us both.

"Do you really believe the story of the knife?" my brother asked. "You know," he added, "the threat to kill her, do you believe in it?"

I said I did not know.

My sister read a good deal and it must have been at about this time she began the writing of verses. The verses gave an impression of deep dissatisfaction with life and also of her feeling of loneliness, of her life having come to an end. I remember that our father had been very fond of quoting Poe and that had no doubt influenced my sister. There was a raven also croaking at her.

"Shall I see the lost Lenore?"

"Quoth the raven 'Nevermore.' "

Stella's lost Lenore would, at that time, have been a school teaching job.

For a time, later, things cleared a little for her. She had the college hunger. It had been eating at her for years and as we, her brothers, began a little to prosper, an arrangement was made. We all, that is to say Karl, Irve, and myself, chipped in what we could and the younger boys were for the time farmed out. They were put to live with a neighbor named Musgrave while Stella, at last free, got her wish.

She was entered as a student in the University of Chicago and, although now we did not live together, I occasionally saw her.

As for myself, I had become a young blade. I had got into the advertising agency and begun to prosper.

For me also there had been the education myth, that it was to be got at by certain years spent in college. You did that and then, emerging, you were prepared for life.

And now my sister was a student in the university. She became a kind of fixture there. The years passed and it went on and on. About every college and university there are such women. They stay until they become old women, they remain students for life.

It had happened so with my sister and at last, after several years, some of my brothers having already married, they also having a struggle, it was agreed between us that she would have to quit, go to work.

It was put up to me to tell her and I did. I remember the occasion. "I will have her down town," I said to myself. "I will buy her a dinner with wine."

And so she came and we were both embarrassed but at last, as we sat thus, at a table in one of the more fashionable restaurants of the city, I told her of our decision.

"Now I guess, Stella, it will have to end," I said.

I spoke of her former ambition to be a school teacher.

"Now you should be ready for that," I said. It was an embarrassing moment for me.

She began to abuse me. She felt then, as she later did, that, having stood by her younger brothers, as she said, sacrificed all of her young girlhood and womanhood, it was up to us, her older brothers, to stand by her.

"But you cannot always go to college. You have been there now, six, seven, perhaps eight years. It is not fair to the others."

She got up from her place at the table and I remember sharply my own embarrassment over the scene that followed. Could this be the sister of my childhood, Stella the dark eyed gentle one?

Many people in the restaurant had turned and were looking at us. She began to berate me bitterly, in a loud voice, and then, throwing up her head, she turned and with her open hand slapped me in the face.

It was, for me, a terrible moment. I was young and proud. She walked out of the restaurant and I stood there, staring at her retreating figure. A man, the head waiter in the place, had come up to me. "We cannot have such things going on here," he said.

I said nothing. Paying the bill I left. I was bitterly angry. "She can go to the devil. I am done with her," I thought but, after some weeks, when I had heard nothing from her, I got a letter.

She had asked my forgiveness. She had indeed become a school teacher and had taken a job in a town somewhere down in the state. In the letter she said that she had been through a great change. She had found God.

God, she said, had come to her in the form of his son.

"I have had a visitation from Jesus," she said. In her letter she described the scene. It was at night, and she was in her bed. She had been thinking of her brothers, blaming us, had been filled with a great bitterness against us but, while all of this was going on in her, as she lay in the darkness in her room in a boarding house in the town, there had come a great light into the room.

She said that it was Jesus himself and that he had taken her into his arms. He had caressed and comforted her but he had also told her of the wrong she had done to us. It was Jesus, she said, who had told her to write the letter, asking my forgiveness for the scene she had made in the restaurant.

My sister got married and became devoutly religious. She had returned to the city but I did not see her often and, when occasionally I did see her, she was profoundly changed. Sometimes, on such occasions, she spoke of her marriage, saying that it had been a mistake, that it wasn't the fault of her husband but that, after the visitation she had had, she should have devoted her life to religion.

"It is too bad I am not a Catholic. I should have been a nun," she said, and put her tiny face in her hands and wept. Without saying so she gave me to understand that not her husband, not any man, could ever understand how she felt.

"You are all carnal," she said, "while I, who have been touched by the hand of Jesus himself. . . ."

She could not go on and I, being on all such occasions deeply embarrassed, saw her less and less.

And then she died, and, with my several brothers, all now grown to manhood, I went to her funeral.[58]

It was held in a little Protestant church and when we, her brothers, all filed in (we sat in the front row of seats in the little church) the preacher began to speak.

58. Stella Anderson died in surgery in 1917. She appears in *Tar* as "Margaret."

He spoke, telling of what was, to us, her brothers, a strange enough story of my sister's life. He said that, having at an early age lost her father and mother and having, as all in the church could see, several brothers, she had devoted her life to them.

One by one the preacher began and told the story of our lives. There was my older brother, the painter. He had, by my sister's efforts, been sent to study painting in Europe. She had done it, he said, by patient toil, by saving money, by sacrificing herself. She had by bitter hard work, by such self-sacrifice, educated us all. This one had been sent to college, that one set up in business. The story went on and on, we her brothers turning occasionally to stare at each other, and I remember that one of my brothers, after we had got out of the church, turned and whispered to me.

"After this, we will go to your rooms." He felt we all needed a drink.

And so we buried my sister and I was curious. I went, after a time, to see the preacher.

"Where did you get the story?" I asked and he said that he had got it from a pamphlet.

It was, I gathered, a kind of tract. It had been printed and distributed by some tract society. It was called "The Story of a Christian Life." It was, he said, a pamphlet written by my sister herself.

II ❧

Work and War

In the warehouse I didn't have to work on Saturday afternoons. On Saturday nights John and I often walked together for hours.

The bond between us was an old one. We lived together when I first came to Chicago.[1]

His sister kept a rooming house there, on a street over in Chicago's vast West Side. We had known each other as boys and I had for him a rather intense boyish admiration. He seemed very talented. From the beginning, even as a boy, he was a good deal the actor, always took part in high school plays. In our little midwestern town the G.A.R. was a good deal what the American Legion was later to become. The G.A.R. like the later Legion was inclined to get into politics, keep the war feeling alive, make demands for increased pensions, etc. Grover Cleveland, when president, returned some captured Confederate flags to the capital of one of the southern states and what a furor arose from the G.A.R.

The G.A.R. was always giving "home talent" shows and my friend was always in them, really a star performer, although, as he later told me, his mother always objected.

"I'd lie to her," he said. "I'd tell her, No, I wasn't going to be in the show, then I'd sneak up there."

He had something of the same sort of talent that Robert Benchley[2] later developed. He'd begin a kind of hesitating explanation of something, assume a highly amusing nervousness, lose the trend of his discourse, fumble in his pockets, make little laughter creating side remarks. I used to laugh at him until my body ached, as later I was to laugh at Benchley.

He was never a strong boy or young man but had a quick shrewd mind. He always managed to get along. When there was something he wanted, a certain job, an advancement in the job he had, he would set about accomplishing his advancement with a cold, shrewd, patient determination that filled me with admiration.

There was a certain man, let us say, at the head of a company where he

1. Anderson went to Chicago late in 1896, where he and Karl lived with John Emerson's family. See "Chicago—A Feeling," *Vanity Fair,* XXVII (October, 1926), 53, 118. Karl Anderson remembers Sherwood in "My Brother, Sherwood Anderson," *Saturday Review of Literature,* XXXI (September 4, 1948), 6–7, 26–27; and in an unpublished autobiographical novel, "Knots in the Weaver's Loom," Newberry Library Manuscript. Karl died in 1956.

2. Robert Charles Benchley (1889–1945), actor, humorist, and drama critic, who reviewed *Poor White* in *Bookman,* LII (February, 1921), 559–60.

wanted a place. He would begin to study the man, search out his prejudices. When we were rooming in the same rooming house in Chicago (he worked as a clerk, myself as a laborer), he often came home ill at night.

However, he was up to something. There was a position, something of that sort he wanted. He threw himself on the bed in his room, had the faculty of going instantly to sleep, arose and went to work.

Let us say he was to have an interview with some man, regarding an advancement. He sat at a desk and wrote out what he planned to say, walked up and down the room, read it aloud to me, kept changing and improving it. He always ended by getting what he wanted.

He had a strange power over women. I have known two such men.[3] He was not handsome, was always thin and pale. We were both, as I presume most young men of a certain age are, intent upon sex.

Oh how I at that time wanted a woman, any woman. I grew restless, walked the streets, went occasionally to women of the town.

I remember sharply one such adventure. I had walked for hours through the night, too restless to go home and to bed. It is true that, at the time, I was doing hard laborious work all day but I was very strong.

I was in a street of drab little frame houses clustered about a factory. As I remember the night there was a huge bakery where bread was made. There was an elevated railroad going through the street.

A woman spoke to me and I followed her up a stairway into a small dismal room.

There were two small children on a bed in the room.

Was I to make love to her there, in that room, in the presence of the sleeping children?

I sat on a rickety chair in the room. It was in a little frame house just opposite the factory. There was only a dim light in the room. The factory was working at night. Through a window I could see men and women at work over there.

I began to ask her questions and she explained, saying she had been deserted by her man. She said she worked through the day getting a woman of the house to care for her children but could not make enough to feed and clothe them and herself, pay her rent, etc. And so, at night, she saw men.

"It is all right. I have it fixed with the woman here."

3. Maurice Long, discussed below; and George Daugherty, the "feeder."

There was a little alcove to the room and she put the sleeping children on the floor in there. She arranged a curtain across the face of the alcove.

"It is all right," she said. "Come on."

I told her I could not.

"It is all right. Here is your money."

She wouldn't take it.

"No," she said. "You have come up here, now you must go to bed with me.

"I'll not be an object of charity," she said.

I remember, later that night, walking about in the streets, filled with shame. I cried. An odd thing happened as I walked about so, overcome with shame, not necessarily of shame for myself or her but of all society, all mankind.

It seemed to me that I wanted to be something higher and nobler than my nature would let me be.

"Why was I ever born to be as I am?" I cried.

I was walking about thus when under a street lamp beside the sidewalk I saw something that, when I pondered upon it, turned out to be a woman's large purse.

There were five one dollar bills and some small change. There were some other small trinkets.

At that time I was still working as a laborer. I was making two dollars for a day of ten hours. My sister, older than myself, and two young brothers had come to live with me. I had moved away from the rooming house where I had lived with John and had taken on a small room in a tenement house. I had to save carefully to get money enough to be with a woman.

Money, money.

What a strange thing it is. It seemed to me that if I went back to that woman, gave her the money I had found, the act would in some small way remove a little of my own feeling of shame.

And so I did go back to her. I had some difficulty finding her house but at last did find it. Fortunately the door to the street was unlocked and I went in, lighted matches, found my way up a stairway to her room and knocked.

She seemed annoyed. "Well, what do you want?" she asked when she opened the door. I could see into the room as she had turned on an electric light. She had put the two children back into the bed and had been lying with them.

I put the purse into her hand.

"Here. I found this," I said and turning hurried away down the stairs.

I had at that time a dream. Certainly I was a very good looking young man. I was much handsomer than my friend John. Occasionally some woman looked at me, I thought, with something like an invitation in her eyes.

However I hadn't the courage to speak to her. With the prostitutes it was different. They spoke to me. I had the young man's dream of some mature wise woman, who had fallen deeply in love with me and knowing how I sometimes suffered from the persistent call of the life in me came to me, offered herself. Such things happened in fiction. They did not happen to me.

They happened however to John. Women were always attaching themselves to him. I knew it had happened at home, while we were boys, in our home town. It kept on happening.

I kept seeing him with attractive looking women.

"But do they give themselves to you?"

He laughed.

"Yes."

I knew it was true. There is something that, when you see a man and woman together, tells you the story.

We used to speak of it.

"You are too serious," he said.

"You want them to be in love with you. You are always falling in love. It means too much to you."

It was quite true. At the time I could see no future for myself. It seemed to me that I must go on forever being just a laborer.

I was continually falling in love. I saw a woman walking in the street, followed her at a distance. Had she noticed me, turned and spoken to me, I would have been frightened.

On the other hand John, for all his continual illness, was bold and successful.

"You are too serious. You want love. There is too much taking of responsibility involved in that. You frighten women by the intense way you look at them.

"As a matter of fact the women you see me with often like and respect you more than they do me."

It was apparent that, when John wanted to be with a woman, he simply asked her. If she refused that was that. He went on to another. There was something essentially vulgar in many women. They liked his casual way with them. It in some queer way left them free.

John was determined to get on in the world. We used to walk about and talk.

"I could make a success in business. I know that."

It was not however what he wanted. He wanted, he said, a career, to be a distinguished man. For a time he thought of giving himself to music. He had a marked ability for handling people. Near the rooming house his sister had set up in Chicago's West Side, there was a large church with a boys' choir and the choir master had resigned.

John set himself to get the place. In some way he had found out, weeks before it happened, that the choir master was about to quit. He began going to the church, made the acquaintance of the choir master and the minister. There was a carefully thought out campaign, people prominent in the church seen. For the time, when I was with him, he spoke of nothing else. He was like a general planning a war and when the choir master resigned he had pulled his strings so well, had so skillfully culti-vated just the right people, that he immediately got the place.

Once I went to see him at a choir practise. It was all wonderful to me. There was a large assembly of boy singers. He kept weeding them out, adding new ones. He walked up and down before them, intense, preoccu-pied. For some reason I could never understand the boys obeyed his commands instantly. I was convinced that, for the time, while they were in his presence, they were to him merely automatons. There was a way in which he could look at a particular boy inclined to be rowdy. He did not shout. He spoke always sharply but at the same time softly. He could make the boy feel that he was of no importance. He was nothing.

This faculty he had mystified me. Under his hand the choir constantly improved. It seemed to me that, under his hand, the individual boy in some way, for the time, lost sense of self. He was a part of the singing group of boys. Something in him was released. With a kind of new gusto he opened his mouth and sang. It may be the faculty great generals have, the faculty of command, that can make individuals, for the time, lose all sense of self and feel themselves only as a part of the powerful thing called the army. Once I spoke to John of all this.

"People like to be commanded," he said. "They want someone to tell them what to do, how to feel."

It seemed to me that there was, at bottom, a contempt for the individual.

It wasn't in me. As it was in my attitude toward women I wanted, so it was with all people. John spoke of that on several occasions. I kept wondering why he wanted to bother with me, why, apparently, he clung to my friendship.

Sometimes he spoke of that.

"I can see that you think I'll be a successful person in life while you probably will not," he said. We would be walking in the streets at night. He put an arm about my shoulder.

"It may be that you will always be the only man I'll ever love," he said. "To get along, get what you want, or think you want, from life, you have to be ruthless, have to use people, make them serve your purpose."

He said that he knew he would never be tempted to do that with me.

"There is in some way a different foundation to our lives. You believe in people, their good intentions, while I do not." These conversations between John and myself usually took place at night when we walked in Chicago's West Side streets. It was after we had both left our small town. In the place where I then worked, in a huge cold storage warehouse (All day I was handling barrels filled with apples and crates of eggs. We piled them high in great rooms kept at a low temperature. Most of the men who worked with me were heavy shouldered Swedes and Poles and Finns), in that place I did not have to work on Saturday afternoons and often on Saturday nights John and I walked together for hours.[4]

We were in the crowded business streets of Chicago's West Side. We were in West Halstead Street, in Madison Avenue. Often we walked along for blocks in silence. Sometimes we walked with John's arm about my shoulder and occasionally we passed men who turned to laugh at us.

I know now that they thought we were two fairies but, at that time, I had never heard of homosexuality. I was a little embarrassed when we walked thus, feeling perhaps something in the eyes of people we passed, something in their thoughts of us walking so, that made me uncomfortable. There was nothing of homosexuality in the feeling we had for each other. Of that I am sure.

4. See *A Story Teller's Story: A Critical Text,* edited by Ray Lewis White (Cleveland: Press of Case Western Reserve University, 1968), pp. 100–4, 139–40, 150–52. The warehouse days are fictionalized in *Marching Men* (New York: John Lane Company, 1917), pp. 67–74.

I was, however, peculiarly sensitive to the eyes of others, to something I felt in the men and women we passed. We were there, walking in the crowds. Sometimes we went into bars or into small restaurants. We ate and drank, John always paying the bill. Already he had begun to earn more money than I then thought I ever could earn. It embarrassed me his always paying the bills. I wanted to be with him. Vaguely I think I felt that he was something I wanted to be, a man who, in spite of physical handicaps, would get on, make his way, make people give him what he wanted from life.

I would go along on such occasions often absorbed in the people seen. There was a tired faced young woman, evidently half ill, going along with packages in her arms. There was a droop to the corners of her mouth, her eyes looked tired. I began to make a quick imagined picture of her life. She was, let us say, a stenographer working all day in an office.

Or a clerk who worked in a store. All day she had been standing and now she was very tired.

She had a sick mother at home and a brother who drank. As she passed us I had noticed a small scar, as from an old cut, just above one of her eyes.

One night her brother had come home drunk and quarrelsome and when she tried to quiet him, get him into bed, he threw something at her.

It was some hard object he had picked up in a room in their little cheap apartment.

This all passing quickly through my mind, pictures made thus.

Or there was a tired prostitute standing in a dark hallway. I got but a momentary glimpse of her face but about her also I made up a story.

These stories, often commonplace enough, of the imagined lives of people, passed thus swiftly through my mind as I walked with John.[5]

Or something, something more intense, a little hard to explain. Let us say we had gone into a little restaurant. John wanted a cup of tea. He could not drink coffee, beer or any hard liquor.

It upset his insides.

He was a little angry about it.

"If I only had your physique.

"I am always being ill. I get so tired sometimes."

There was a young woman came to wait on us and occasionally, when our eyes met, something happened between such a one and myself.

5. For Anderson's early extended fantasies, see *A Story Teller's Story*, ed. White, pp. 71–78, 81–90, 92–96; and *Tar* (1926), pp. xiii–xiv, 33–34, 150, 286–87.

I had again, as she came toward us, made a picture of her life but, this time, the thing had really happened. What I had imagined about her, the picture I had made of her life, so swiftly, was true.

This I knew and she knew. She knew when our eyes met.

It was almost as though the woman and myself had lived together in great intimacy for years. There was nothing about her I did not know.

But how shall I explain all of this? There is, sometimes, this sudden half mystic bond suddenly set up between people, deep knowledge of each other, something deeply felt, something known. All my life it has been happening to me.

There are times, to be sure, when I am for long periods shut off from people, something within me thus closed.

And then, again, it is happening suddenly, swiftly, sometimes even terribly. For the time being I know too much of too many people. Sometimes I have even had to walk along streets with my eyes on the sidewalk, not being able to bear any more of it, and once later I tried to write a book on the subject.

I called my book *Many Marriages*,[6] meaning to convey the feeling of contacts among people, of the flesh and not of the flesh—something deeply of the spirit that nevertheless has the flesh in it.

The book was not understood. When it was published I was widely cursed for it. There was a scene between a father and daughter that was taken for incest.

What stupidity. It hurt me deeply when it happened.

But I am with John when the thing has happened between a woman, a waitress, and myself. We do not speak to each other. Our eyes meet.

"Hello. You are here, brother."

"Yes, sister. I am here."

It is love. What else can it be called? It is another of the thousands of marriages I have made.

It is something that is always happening between people but they dare not or will not know it.

When men and women dare let themselves know it there will be a new life on this earth.

But I am with John and we have left the restaurant. We are walking in crowds of people.

"Look at them," he says. "For the most part they are merely cattle.

6. New York: B. W. Huebsch, 1923.

"They are that to me," he says.

He says it and becomes silent. He again puts his arm about my shoulder. We have turned out of the street of the crowds and are in a darker more silent street.

"I wish I could feel as sometimes I know you feel.

"You do not look upon people as I do."

"No, John. I don't."

He was half sick most of the time. He had the job of running the choir of boys in the large church. He held onto his clerkship.

"I think I shall become an actor," he said. It may be he remembered his boyhood successes in the home talent shows in our small middle western town. He had, I was quite sure, this indifference to the reality of people and yet, when we together met people, when he brought home women, he could be charming with them while, too often, I was awkward and silent.

Or I began saying things that seemed strange to me coming from my own lips, often quite coarse things, a kind of protest in me, against something I felt going on about me.

And all of this while, at the same time, I was deeply jealous of my friend, his quick way of getting on a footing with many people.

And something else. John spoke often of his determination to make and to have money.

"Someday we will both grow old.

"It is dreadful to be old and poor.

"I am afraid of poverty. It frightens me horribly."

Something hardening in the man when he said these things. You knew that he could be ruthless, determined. We would be walking in one of the poorer sections of Chicago's West Side. Broken down bums were drifting past. City panhandlers stopped us, begging for nickels.

"To get a cup of coffee," they muttered.

"If you don't get money you end by becoming like that.

"I hate them. I hate all poor people, all failures in life."

He spoke with a sort of intense bitterness, the more strange to me because I had always thought of his people, in our home town, as at most moderately well-to-do. As a young boy he had had so many of what are called "advantages" I could not have. He had had music lessons, had gone to college, had always, since I could remember, been well dressed, had lived, as a boy, in a rather big house on one of the more respectable streets of our town, his father a man much respected and looked up to in the community, as I remembered him a rather witty lovable man always being elected to some office of responsibility, while, as everyone in our town knew, my own father was a well known no-account, his family always shifting from house to house in the poorer sections of the town because he couldn't or wouldn't pay the rent.

This whole matter, my relations with my friend John, is something that has puzzled me all my life.

There was this obsession, always in him, about making money and having money. As I shall presently tell, it was in others also in his family.[7]

But where did it come from? At the time of which I am now speaking, when we were seeing a great deal of each other, some bond always between us, and when he spoke often of the necessity of making money, getting on in the world in which we would both have to live, I thought a great deal about his words.

Was it necessary to have money, to spend a life trying to grow rich?

What was to be gained?

Did a man not stand a chance of losing more than he gained? Often at night, in bed, in that little tenement in which I was living with my sister and the two younger brothers, both as yet children, I lay awake for hours thinking of the conversations had with John.

"Yes, he will get rich while I will not."

A hunger for things I was terribly afraid I could never get swept over me. Oh how I wanted fine clothes, a warm, comfortable house in which to live. Just before coming away from my home town to be a city man and being without employment I had taken a very lowly job.

I was, for a time, a groom in a livery stable in our town and that had led to something else. I had worked in the livery stable during the winter and during the following summer had gone about with a string of horses.

They were trotters and pacers, beautiful creatures, and I had loved them passionately. I still do. The old passion clings to me. Always I have hungered to have enough money to own such a string of horses, drive them in races.

It was a thing that could be accomplished with money.

So much to be accomplished. John was right. Occasionally, on Sunday afternoons, I went to walk on Michigan Boulevard in Chicago, then as now a noble and beautiful street, and there saw beautifully dressed women going along with faultlessly dressed men.

7. A subject that Anderson did not discuss further.

Myself perhaps clad in a cheap and half worn out suit bought on the installment plan.

I walked along behind some young and richly dressed woman and now it was not for the flesh of her I longed.

I hungered instead to touch her gown, feel the beautiful cloth with my fingers. I wanted to go with her into some expensive restaurant, buy champagne, myself elegantly dressed, expensive rings on my fingers.

Able to be careless about money, throw it back.

I would, in imagination, be living in one of the big hotels overlooking the lake, or in a great airy apartment.

"A man is a fool who does not get money.

"We who stay poor, always on the edge, deserve what life does to us.

"Or if not exactly poor one of the so-called 'middle class,' always grubbing along, counting pennies.

"Saving, saving.

"God knows for what."

Money becoming too important to us.

"Money. Money. God damn money," I cried.

Such thoughts racing through my head, the result of my talks with John. Why did I know that he would so surely accomplish what I would not? I did know.

There was a way in which I wanted passionately to be as he was, contemptuous of ordinary people.

"Why," I asked myself, "should I be sympathetic with such people?"

"Cattle," John called them.

"I have a good brain."

You must think of me on these occasions as sitting up in my narrow bed in our little Chicago apartment. In the winter the place was heated by small coal burning stoves. There was a stove pipe, a long one, fastened to the ceiling with wire that went across over my bed to its hole in a wall beyond my bed.

The joints of the pipe were always coming loose. Coal soot fell down on my bed and sometimes blackened my face. There were two beds in an adjoining room, my sister in one, the two children in the other.

"And why should I be saddled with them?"

A man wants freedom to go forth, to conquer.

It was true that I had never gone much to school but when I did go was always the top one in my class.

I had an older brother, also struggling to get up out of poverty, who every month sent me what he could to keep our little family going.

Mother dead now, killed by poverty. All the later years of her life, when we children were all small, had been spent being a wash woman, washing other people's dirty clothes to keep her little family alive.

Father, although oddly lovable, never having any sense of responsibility for the children he had helped bring into the world.

When he did make a little money spending it in a department store buying a new suit of clothes and going off to a convention of the G.A.R.

Or to buy a new horn to blow in the town band.

If, in later life, I was sometimes to be called a "red," even a communist, which, of course, I never was, it was because every working woman I saw reminded me of my mother, coming into our little frame house on a winter day, after hanging a wash out on the line, her clothes frozen to her body.

The look of patient suffering on her face.

Only to contract pneumonia and die suddenly.

Envy of the rich in me. Although I did not know it I was always, at bottom, the artist man, having the artist's hunger for luxuries.

"I will be like John, determined, contemptuous.

"Nothing shall stand in my way."

These determinations came to me and then doubt.

Did I have already, while so young, a sense of something that was later to grow in me?

"Get rich, get possessions and at the same time lose.

"Lose what?"

Just the thing that sometimes happened between me and the most ordinary people met in the street, as for example between that tired waitress in the restaurant and myself.

The thing that I knew did not happen between John and others, could not happen.

Penetration into other people's lives.

Understanding.

Could a man have the determination, faculty for using others, making them serve a man's own purpose and this other?

Doubt. Doubt.

Money. Money.

Eternal confusion.

I began at once to tell her lies. At the time I met her I was already, at least physically, a grown man. I had gone to the city of Chicago and had got work there. It was hard to get. For two or three weeks I tramped the streets and when I did get work it was as a laborer. I was employed in a warehouse where I rolled and lifted heavy barrels and boxes all day, working ten hours a day for a wage of two dollars.

My sister, a few years older than myself, came to Chicago bringing my two brothers, both too young to work, and we got two or three rooms in a tenement building, on Chicago's West Side.

My work was very heavy but I was strong. I lived on the West Side but my work was in a building on the city's North Side, just across the river from the "Loop." I used to "rat" all I could. We called it that. It meant that, when you were sent to some distant room in the warehouse, you stole ten minutes, fifteen, a half hour. I loved to rat in a certain room far up, in an upper floor, from where I could look out a window to the Chicago River. It seemed very beautiful to me. There were ships going up and down. I saw the sailors standing on the decks of the ships. I wanted to go with them, away, down through the Great Lakes, perhaps to sea.

To save money I walked back and forth from my work to the tenement where we lived and there were certain houses along the streets. Women spoke to me from the doors and windows of the houses, inviting me to come in and oh how I wanted to go to them.

I couldn't. I had no money. I think it must have been true that I realized, fully enough, what they were. I remember that I used to walk along the street, going a little blindly as the animal passions arose in me and, as I went, I argued with myself.

"They do not want you for yourself. What do they know of you? If you had money, if you could go to one of these women, it is very likely you would get a disease." I did something I am sure other men have done. I had discovered that it was entirely possible to get home from my work without going through any of the streets of the women but I nevertheless went. In this way I constantly let myself be aroused when there was no need of it.

I have said that I was strong. Soon however, as I went on in this way, working all day, at rather heavy work, walking to and from my work, going continually at evening through the streets of the women and later, in bed, lying awake, I would be having all sorts of imagined encounters with them. There would be one, very beautiful as I saw her in my dreams, who rushed out of one of the houses to me. "Save me. Save me," she cried, all of this going on and on in me in my bed at night, myself not sleeping, getting out of my bed tired in the morning, soon enough I was not strong. It is surprising I did not get fired from my job.

It was a fall night and I was walking in the rain. It was a Saturday night. I had gone abroad, out of our few rooms, having little or no money in my pocket. I remember how I felt. I was utterly discouraged. I remember other, often well dressed young men walking along. They were going to the theatre. They were with girls. They were going to dance halls. I went along with hands in my empty pockets. I was in a street of stores. I think it must have been in West Madison Street in Chicago. My clothes had become soaked, walking in the rain.

I had got far out, into the West Side, and there was a woman walked before me. She had come out of a store and carried packages.

There must have been a good many of them. They kept dropping from her arms. She would drop one and, leaning to pick it up, would drop others. I went to her. At the moment I did not think of her as, for some time, I had been thinking of women, always in the same way, the thing having become a kind of disease in me. I am quite sure I thought only of helping her.

"I am going in the same direction. May I carry some of your packages?" I asked and she said I could.

I walked along with her and at first we went in silence but presently, when we came to where there was a street light, the particular section of the street in which I had encountered her had been quite dark. I looked at her and she at me.

She was, at that time, when I first saw her, let us say a woman of thirty-four and I would have been, say nineteen. She smiled at me, said something about my kindness and I saw that she was very thin and, when I had got that first glance at her face, I thought her very homely. She had I remember a big nose, with a hook, her eyes were of a curious colorless grey and she had rather large upper teeth that protruded down over her lower lip.

All of this with, as I discovered later, thin, work worn hands and thin sandy grey hair.

But there is something here that has always interested me. For a long time I have had a certain theory. It is that, having encountered another person, this presupposing you to be a somewhat imaginative person yourself, having, as I say, encountered thus another and having come into some sort of relation to that other, you never see them again. This, I think, is so much true that, even now, after all of these years, as I write of this woman (For the sake of convenience I will call her Cora, although that was not her name. For some reason however the name Cora does seem to fit her.) she is one woman of whom I can say that, in these frank notes of my life, I do not wish to give away, even now, as I try to describe her, as I have her I am uncertain of the description.

As I have suggested here, I believe that, having, as I say, come into any kind of personal relations with another, it is impossible to see them again after the first glance.

I do not know what my wife looks like. I cannot remember the face of my one sister, my mother's face, the faces of any of my best known men friends and acquaintances.

And why?

It is because, upon all of them, my imagination has been at work. My own imagination has always, all of my life, been very active. It is constantly superimposing something on others, on my own eyes, on my ears. I am always building and rebuilding. I think it is something we all do. It is one of the things that makes any straight view of life, as we all live it, so difficult to get.

I was with this woman Cora before a small frame building, on a street just off West Madison Street, far out on the West Side. As I have said it was a Saturday night. I had looked at the woman and she had looked at me.

"You are very kind," she had said and I had protested. "It is nothing," I had said.

We had walked along in silence and there we were, before the building in which she lived. She lived as I did at that time, having two rooms on the second floor of the building. You went up by a stairway, on the outside. There was a bedroom and a tiny little sitting room.

Why how sharply and in spite of all I have said above, that place is etched in my mind. I have been using it ever since. There is a story of mine, in the book called *Horses and Men,* the tale itself called "The Man's Story," [8] in which I have used, as nearly as I could remember it, just the

8. "The Man's Story," *Dial,* LXXV (September, 1923), 247–64; in *Horses and Men* (1923), pp. 287–312.

setting of Cora's place. The house itself was of two stories, a frame house, unpainted and very ugly in design, with, as I have suggested, the outer stairway going up to the second floor, and I have the notion that, the house having been built as a residence, no doubt for some family, and, later, having been turned into a small tenement, the inner stairs had perhaps been taken away.

This may have been because the whole house had been split up, into the little two room holes. You could go up the outer stairway to a balcony and along the balcony to enter the separate apartments.

So we were there, Cora and myself, at the foot of the stairs. I gave her her packages and she thanked me. She started up the stairs. As I afterwards found out she was quite a shy person, much aware of her own physical unattractiveness, and, at that time, I was quite a handsome young fellow. She went part way up the stairs and stopped. We were in darkness. She spoke in a low voice out of the darkness.

"You are wet," she said.

"Don't you want to come up and get dry?" she asked.

So there it was. Why, I dare say, there are many men who, having, at the age of nineteen, had many adventures I had not had, having loved and been loved, will be amused at my description of my own excitement when I heard that voice coming out of the darkness. I do not think I answered at all. There was a curious thumping of the heart.

"What? Is it going to happen to me? Am I to go alone into this house with a woman?"

There must have been this sudden flare up of the animal side of my nature.

"Perhaps. Perhaps," I must have whispered to myself and I am sure that, at once, the woman Cora, who, when I had looked at her in the light of the street lamp, had seemed so strikingly unattractive and even ugly to me, must at once have begun to seem attractive.

"At least she is a woman. Perhaps. Perhaps," I must have told myself.

At any rate I went up to her, feeling my way in the darkness. There was a kind of hand rail and getting one hand on it I felt my way up while, with the other hand, I groped for her. Later, when I had become a well known writer and the critics, being often puzzled by my frank and original point of view and my way of telling a story, and wanting to describe me, they were forever speaking of me as "groping."[9] I was groping that night, all right.

And for what?

For a woman in the darkness, for warm life that I so wanted to come to me, for the breaking up of my own isolation in life.

Was it just to lie with a woman I hungered? I am sure it was not.

I was feeling my way upward in the darkness and my outstretched hand alighted upon her. It alighted softly upon her face. She must have turned to wait for me. My hand was on her face. It was on her neck, her shoulders. My hand caressed her breasts and her body and the packages she had been carrying and that I had helped her carry fell from her arms. I could feel them striking against my body. They were rolling down the stairs. As it turned out, she, the woman Cora, was as I was at that time. She was a worker, employed in some kind of shop where women's dresses are made. She was what is called a "forewoman" in the shop. She lived alone and, on the evening when I encountered her, had been to a store to buy food which she was to cook for herself.

There was this queer enough encounter, on a rickety stairway, a male and a female, but a few minutes before utterly unknown to each other. I was caressing her. She had asked me to go up into her place and I had not answered. I had, as described, groped my way to her. I had her in my arms. It was raining and when I presently kissed her cheeks and her lips they were wet from the rain.

And then she laughed. "Well, well," she said. In the darkness she took my arms from about her body and went on up the stairs, lighted a light in her room. She left me standing there and presently came down with a flashlight in her hand and we gathered together her packages. She held the flashlight to my face and laughed again.

"I guess you can still come up. Do you want to come?" she asked and I went. I began a life with her, a curiously concealed life. For some reason I cannot now explain to myself, on that first night and afterwards, when I went to her, continually I lied to her.

I think it was because I had some curious moral notion that, having

9. Studies of Anderson's critical reputation are William Robert Moses, "Sherwood Anderson: His Life, His Philosophy, His Books and What Has Been Said about Him" (M.A. Thesis, Vanderbilt University, 1933); and the Introduction to *The Achievement of Sherwood Anderson: Essays in Criticism,* edited by Ray Lewis White (Chapel Hill: The University of North Carolina Press, 1966), pp. 3–15.

taken her, having, through her and her continued kindness to me, solved a problem that had, for weeks, been keeping me in a kind of fever, having often, after that first evening, accepted from her food she had bought with the labor of her thin work worn hands, I felt it only fair that I should at least offer marriage to her.

"But I can't. I can't," I kept saying to myself. I became at once cautious and frightened and even on that first evening with her, when we had got up into the warmth of her little rooms and when, after our first embarrassment with each other and when, after I had partially dried my wet clothes before a small stove she had in her tiny living room, she having gone into her bedroom that was also a kitchen, and after we had dined together in half darkness were sitting together by the stove and began to talk I began at once to lie.

I must have told her some weird tale, of an early marriage, for I remember sitting there, the door to her bedroom having been closed, no light in the little room in which we sat except a dim light that came through cracks of her small coal burning stove (this must have happened in the late fall when the nights had begun to be cold) and of being carried away by my own lies. Although I do not now remember the details I am sure that I told her of a marriage that had turned out badly and of an invalid wife. I was being cautious, playing safe.

"I want to get you," I would have been thinking, "but do not want to get myself into a jam." I would have gone on like that, building my story, appealing to her sympathy while, as I would have thought necessary, protecting myself and then it would have begun.

It began and it went on, for perhaps a year. She had come to Chicago from a small town in Illinois and had a sister, still in the town, living as she said, with an aunt, who was tubercular. She had been saving money, wanting to take the sister to Colorado, in the hope of curing her and, after perhaps a year, she did go to the western state, taking the sister.[10]

And in the meantime she was my mistress, my first one. There was this meeting of two people, in darkness, the embrace on the stairs in darkness. It went on so to the end. I went to her only at night and, when I had arrived, always it was the same.

The lights were put out and we sat in darkness. We talked in the darkness, made love in the darkness. It was as though she wanted it so and I remember sharply that, on a certain night, being with her and after our

---

10. This episode is very similar to "I See Grace Again," below.

love making and when I had fallen into sleep and had awakened, I could not find her.

I called and she did not answer and so, as on the first evening, being sure she was in the room, presently quite sure, as I heard her voice, she did not speak but she was crying softly (this was just before she went away, taking the sister) as on that other evening on the rickety stairs in the rain I found myself groping for her in the darkness in her room.

I must have been on all fours.

"Where are you, Cora? Where are you?" I found her at last in a corner of the room. She was sitting on the floor and weeping and when I had got her into my arms I found she was not weeping because we were about to part. I kept questioning her and at last she told me. She was, she said, afraid that, when we had parted and when I remembered her, I would never be able to think of her as one who had been able to give me what I had really wanted of women.

There was another incident not so romantic that must have happened at about this time. It must have happened after my red haired woman had left me but while I was still employed as a laborer. Through the help of my older brother I had saved a little money, had got together twenty dollars which I had in one bill. I had brought with me to Chicago a pair of skates and it was Sunday afternoon. There was a small pond in one of the West Side parks and in the dark of a winter evening I went there to skate.

I was returning homeward along a poor little street when I heard a cry for help, coming from a house. It was a small and mean looking frame house and the door leading to the street was open. There was a low picket fence with a gate before the house and opening the gate I rushed through and through the door.

As I passed in the door was slammed at my back and I was in a lighted room with the curtain drawn. By the door stood a large and rough looking man and there was a woman sitting on a bed in a corner of the room. They were both laughing and as I stood puzzled and alarmed the man walked to me and grasped my two arms with his powerful hands. "Don't make any noise or it will be the worse for you," he said and I remained silent and trembling and the woman coming to me went through my pockets. She found my twenty dollar bill and with it in her hand walked back to the bed and the man released me. "You didn't find anything?" he said to the woman who was now sitting on the bed and smiling at me. I saw her hand which contained my twenty dollar bill pass with a quick movement under a dirty pillow on the bed. The woman was small and I thought before my arrival had perhaps been beaten by the man. One of her eyes was swollen and black. "No," she said, smiling. "The kid hadn't a cent. Let him go." And the man walked across the room and sat in a chair by a table. He filled and lighted a pipe. "Well, get out of here, kid," he said. "I ought to beat you up for coming in here and insulting my wife."

I was desperate. I had a passionate desire to own a bicycle and had been saving my money for that purpose. I walked across the room and sat beside the woman on the bed.

I began to plead. I told the woman a long story of my struggle against poverty. I spoke of my dear mother. Tears came to my eyes and I wept. I kept on and on and presently the man arose and began walking up and down the room. He came and stood before me and growled at me. "Oh, shut up," he said. "In another moment, I'll throw you out of here on your head." There was a door at the back of the room and he went through it leaving the door open. I took the room he had gone into to be a kind of kitchen. "I am going to have a drink," he said, addressing the woman, "and if you don't get that kid out of here I'll knock hell out of the both of you." I was in a desperate mood and determined to have my twenty dollars. With a sudden movement of my arm I knocked the woman who was sitting beside me flat on her back and thrust my hand under the dirty pillow. The woman screamed. "Ed, quick," she cried, and the man rushed through the door.

I was however a jump ahead of him and beat him to the outer door and in fact succeeded in swinging the door half closed behind me so that he rushed against it. He must have been half stunned as he did not follow me into the street.

However I did not look back. There was the low fence before the house that enclosed the little yard but I did not pass through the gate. I sailed over it like a bird. I had lost my skates but had the twenty dollar bill tightly clasped in my hand. I think I must have run ten blocks before I looked back. It was Sunday evening and the street in which I found myself was dark and silent. I returned home, my eyes red from weeping, a kind of nervous reaction from my adventure, but I did not tell the story to either my sister or to my friend John Emerson. I thought it made me look too much a fool and a green country boy.

Pick the Right War

I

I was in the city of Chicago, a young laborer, just come out of an Ohio small town. It was a time of depression. The World's Fair, of a few years before, had left the city flat.

What city man, come out of a small town, does not remember his first hours in the city, the tall buildings, the crowds, so strange and terrible to him?

I walked through the crowded streets with my brother. He was but a year or two older but, suddenly, what a gulf separated us. This was not his first city. He had been away from our small town for two or three years and in Chicago for at least a year. He seemed unimpressed by the hugeness of the place.

We were not, in our family, very demonstrative.

"Hello kid."

"Hello."

We walked in crowded streets, got aboard a street car. He was silent. He read a newspaper.

So, he had me on his hands. I had come to the city a raw boy. Work had been hard to find in our little town. I had taken the great step, separated from my brothers and my sister, my boyhood friend, familiar streets, fields, at the edge of town, where I went with other boys to hunt rabbits.

Familiar faces, walks with other boys through quiet streets at night.

Great plans made.

"I am going to be like my father, a lawyer."

"And I shall be a doctor."

"And me a merchant."

My own plans were vague. I was determined.

"You just give me a chance."

There had been a young girl, living not on our street, but on the one in which lived people far above us in the social scale. She had smiled on me and, on the night before leaving our town, I had gone to her.

It was a summer evening and I had found her sitting on the front porch of her father's house.

It is strange that now, after all these years, I have, in my mind, no picture of her. Was she blonde or brunette? I do not know.

I went to sit with her. Already, perhaps, I had the writer's impulse. I had written out the speech I wanted to make to her.

It was a declaration of love, a proposal of marriage.

"I am going out, away in the big world. I love you. I shall carry your dear image in my heart.

"It will be a fearful struggle but I shall win. I'll come back.

"Wait for me. Be faithful to me."

I think she must have been impressed. I must have written something of the sort set down above.

I have this memory, of sitting with her on steps before a house, of handing her what I had written, of her going indoors to read, of her coming back to me. I sat and held her hand. We kissed. The street before the house was lined with shade trees. I thought the night, the girl, my own thoughts and feelings all beautiful.

Later, when I had got work in the city, when I had there a little room of my own in a hall bedroom, I spent evening after evening writing to her.

I did not tell her of my fright, of the cramping fear of the city, of what seemed to me the hopelessness of any effort to get ahead in such a vast place, filled with so many people, but, later, a year later, when I went home to enlist in my war, to become, for a day, a town hero, one who, as our local newspaper said, had "left a lucrative city job to rush to his country's defense," I found she had become engaged to marry another.[11] He was, I think, a clerk, in a jewelry store. He had not enlisted for the war. The sufferings of the people of Cuba had not touched his heart. He had no soldiering uniform to put on and I had my moment of revenge. There came the day when we, of the local military company, were marching through our main street to the local railroad station.

There was a great crowd of people. Country people had come into town, and all the townspeople were out. The two or three small factories of the town had closed for the day. The schools had closed.

There were old men, of the Civil War, standing, I remember, on the sidewalks along main street. They were remembering their own war and their own youth. I remember in particular an old man, one Jim Lane. He had been in Andersonville prison. He had seen his brother die of hunger there. He was a tall old man and his lean face stood up above the heads of

11. Sherwood Anderson enlisted for five years in Company I of the Sixteenth Infantry Regiment of the Ohio National Guard in March, 1895. After the United States' declaration of war on April 21, 1898, Company I was called into service April 25, 1898.

weeping women. He also wept. I saw the tears running down his gaunt old cheeks.[12]

There was a woman who had been my school teacher. She was a stout, bravely built woman of forty. She ran out of the crowd. She embraced me.

"Oh boy, boy," she said.

I remember also that I tried to appear stern, to maintain an air of indifference. We, in our little company of local heroes, were, for the most part, boys. We kept whispering to each other as we marched.

"Well, what the hell?"

"I wish they'd quit it."

I think we were all relieved when we had got aboard a train, when it had left the town.

And then, in the crowd, seeing us off, standing at the creek, as we marched through the main street, she was with a party of other young girls.

There were tears running down her cheeks too. I remember that, as I marched past, she left the others and started toward me.

"Oh, oh," she cried. Perhaps she intended to embrace me.

"Forgive me my unfaithfulness. Forgive. Forgive."

I have no notion what she intended to say. She ran toward me and I turned from her.

I laughed the laugh of scorn.

"As for you—ha!

"Go to your jewelry clerk.

"You have been unfaithful to me and now I go to die for my country."

To be sure I said nothing of the sort. What I should have said I thought of, later, on the train. I, however, turned away from her, pretended I had not seen her eager face. I had my revenge.

We went, from our town, to the city of Toledo and stayed over night, in a great armory there, and there was a man of our company, the son of a saloon keeper of our town, who climbed up into a balcony and sang a song. I envied him.

"Oh we'll come back.

"Yes, we'll come back.

"From the isle in the sea.

"For the time will come

12. This old man appears in *Winesburg, Ohio* (New York: Viking Press, 1960), pp. 21–22.

"When the victory is won.

"And the island of Cuba is free," he sang and my heart leaped. I became suddenly patriotic. Can it be that it was not patriotism that brought me home from Chicago to enlist? I was like the others of our company, a middle western small town boy, and the island of Cuba was far away. We were what we were. We were farmers' sons, merchants' sons, sons of workers. There were among us young town roughs, gentle quiet boys, frightened ones and many, like myself, who wanted only to appear brave and indifferent. It is sure that our hearts did not ache for the suffering people of the island of Cuba. If they ached they ached for adventure. We wanted, most of all, to go see the world, to go into new strange places and, as the saloon keeper's son sang, I did not see in my imagination suffering people, released by us, by our bravery, from bondage but saw instead myself also standing up there, on a little balcony, in his stead. There was always a good deal of the showman in me, as there must be in all story tellers, and I wanted to make the hearts of others leap, as mine had leaped to the song.

We did not stay long, in Toledo, but were taken almost at once to Columbus, to the state capital, and there we were dismissed from the service of the state and became instead soldiers of the nation.[13] Something had been learned from the Civil War. There were to be no three months men, no hundred day men among us. We were to enlist for the duration of the war.

This was something not so gaudy. Most of us were sons of men who had fought in the Civil War and the Civil War had lasted for years. I think we were all a little frightened. My own father had been a soldier and I had heard many tales of battles and carnage. When it came time to re-enlist, this time not in a local military company, to get a uniform, to parade on summer evenings in village streets, all the town girls out looking at us, but for a real war, no bands playing, no women to embrace us and call us heroes, we all went a little into the great silence.

It was the evening of the day before we were to re-enlist and we boys were gathered in the company streets. We stood about, looking into each other's eyes. We had not been drafted. If we did not choose to go to the war there was nothing to compel us to go.

We camped in a large field and presently were gathering in little groups, in the company street, talking to each other in low tones. I walked

13. Anderson's company entered federal service at Camp Bushnell, Columbus, Ohio, May 12, 1898, when Anderson himself entered federal service as a private.

out, away from our camp and into an open place, under the stars. At home my father and my older sister had spoken, begging me not to enlist.

It did not seem to matter that father had also once been such a fool.

But there was something else. By going off to war I was dodging a certain responsibility. At home they needed the little money I had been able to send home from my job. My sister had pointed all of this out to me, looking at me with cold eyes as she talked.

This would have been at home, in a little yellow house, in a street of working men's houses. There were no bands playing there.

"And so, you have consulted none of us. You have chucked your job." Mother was dead, she was trying to get our two younger boys through the school and, just at that time, our father was out of work.

"There are so many others anxious to go. So why you? You know we need the little money you were sending us."

I had not answered her and had hurried out of her presence.

"But how can a woman know how I feel?" I asked myself. There was a fact to be faced that I did not want to face. When I had, on a sudden impulse, left my job in the city to hurry home, the local newspaper had spoken of the chucked job as a "lucrative position" and I had been singled out as a kind of special hero but what was the truth? The truth was that I had been glad to escape from the job. I had been working in a big cold storage warehouse, where barrels of apples were stored.

There were great rooms kept icy cold and I worked in one of them with three or four others, all laborers like myself, and the work was heavy. They were all heavy bodied strong quiet fellows and I was not. They were Poles and spoke a strange language and I had been, for weeks, half ill of overwork and loneliness.

We worked in that place ten hours a day and the work was too heavy for us.

I had kept going out of pride.

"I'm a man now and must do a man's work. I can't cave in," I had said to myself.

At night I went home to my little room in the house of a former citizen of my own town, a room taken because of city loneliness, and I had been compelled to walk miles to save street car fare.

I had been determined to rise in the world.

"What I need is education," I had told myself. In the neighborhood where I had got the room, on Chicago's West Side, there was a night school, in a place called The Lewis Institute, and I had begun going there.[14] I had seen clerks, white collar workers, sitting in the warehouse office and I wanted to be one of them. I had tried to study bookkeeping and accounting but it was no go. When I came home from my warehouse at night I put on my one suit of "Sunday clothes," brought from home, and went to the school.

It was warm there and all day I had been in the cold. I sat down at a desk and, at once, my head fell forward and I slept. The teacher, a young man, came and awakened me.

"You'd better go home and to bed," he said and smiled. He suggested that I try again on another evening. He perhaps thought I had been out late, on the evening before, on some gay party. "This is no place to sleep," he said and I stumbled out of the room, going with dragging steps to the house of my fellow townsman, now become a city man. I fell into bed. I lay in the bed and wept. "It is no use," I told myself. "I will never rise. I will go on, as I am going now, all my days and soon I will be bent and old." I got out of bed and seizing pen and paper wrote to the girl I had left. I poured out my sorrow to her but I did not mail the letter. "If she discovers the truth she will never wait for me," I thought and wept again.

There was however this other side to the picture. I had not played quite square with my sister, with those at home. I was perplexed. On the one side there was the dreadful risk of war, of being perhaps wounded, crippled or killed and I was young. I did not want to be wounded or killed. At the warehouse, in the city, my boss had said, as men do at such times, that when I returned from fighting my country's battles, my job would be there, waiting for me, and "That is not such a cheerful prospect," I had thought.

Of all of this I had said little or nothing to my sister. "How can a woman understand?" I had thought. It was true that my sister, an only girl in a family of boys, had also wanted to rise in the world. She had wanted to go to school, to become a school teacher, but had surrendered the dream. On the night, at Columbus, when I had walked out of the company street, away from the camp, and stood alone, under the stars, there was this terrible question to be answered.

"Shall I go or shall I not? To be or not to be?"

It seemed to me, on that night, that my whole life, its form and pattern, depended upon my decision. I came to a resolution. I went back into the

14. In the fall of 1897, Sherwood Anderson studied a business course at The Lewis Institute, now part of the Illinois Institute of Technology.

company street and presently cries arose and I found myself joining in the cries.

"I will not be a coward, a quitter, a shirker."

"Nor me."

"Nor me."

Now there was no longer sadness and fear. "Who cares? Sure we'll go," we cried. We began playing about, in the company street, under the stars. We slapped each other's backs.

"And you, and you, and you?"

"Yes me."

"Hurrah."

But presently it developed that there were, among us, some two or three who were not going to enlist and we became indignant.

"It is a disgrace to our town," we said and I am quite sure that, among them all, I was one of the loudest in denunciation. To denounce another had become a relief. I joined in the cries of anger.

And now those who were not going to re-enlist for the war were surrounded. We questioned them and they made excuses.

"I have a job at home. My folks need the money I earn."

There was one who was a farmer's son. He said his father was sick. He had been hurt, had been kicked by a horse.

"I got to go home and keep things going," he said.

And now we others formed ourselves into a mob. There were angry cries, in which I joined.

"Let's get 'em. The skunks."

They had retired into their tents but we dragged them forth into the company street. We beat them. There were four of us who grabbed one of the smaller of the men and ran him away to a place of trees. We took, each man, an arm or a leg. We beat his buttocks against the tree. He screamed with pain. It went on thus, for a time, none of the men who were going home resisting much, none of our officers interfering, their clothes torn and their bodies bruised and then we gave it up. Our victims had crawled back into their tents and again we others gathered in groups.

"Before I'd be such a skunk . . . ," we said. We felt that we had, each of us, asserted his manhood and, on the next day, we marched up and signed for the war.

Youth forgets quickly and quickly I forgot the shabby trick I had done to my younger brothers and to my sister by becoming a soldier. Now my sister, in going about in our town, would be hearing me praised, but she would be game. She would only smile and if, occasionally, she expressed her feelings she would do it only to father.

II

I had become a soldier and, as it turned out, I had picked the right war.[15] We, of the local military companies of the states, were, in our war, taken into the national service just as we were. Our local companies had been built up on the democratic plan and democratic we remained. We had elected our own officers, simply members of the company, selected sometimes for special ability and, more often, merely because they were liked. There was I remember a lieutenant, an Irishman, who at home ran a celery farm and who had a passion for the military life. After our war he stayed on in the service and, when the World War came, he got his chance. He became, I'm told, an efficient and outstanding officer in the national service. He stayed in the service.

He was the one of our officers who understood his work. He continually studied books of tactics. When he had got to the great camp, in Chickamauga fields, near the city of Chattanooga, to which place we were taken from our state capital, where we drilled and marched, sometimes all day long, he was the understanding one.[16]

He was quiet.

When he gave an order we instinctively obeyed.

There were two other officers, a captain and another lieutenant. Our own captain had been promoted, had become a major, and a new one had been appointed.

We did not vote for this one. He was a fat man, a German, with a thick neck. He had been, I think, a janitor in the armory in Toledo. He loved lying abed in his tent, late into the morning. He walked with a waddle.

Our previous captain, now that he had become a major, had to ride a horse. It was a new experience for him. He seemed always in danger of falling off.

We were at drill in a great field, this at Chickamauga Park, and he rode past. He had acquired a rather quiet animal that looked like an old livery

15. A parallel account of the war experience is *A Story Teller's Story,* ed. White, pp. 199–208.

16. On May 17, 1898, Company I left Ohio for Chickamauga Park, Georgia. The men arrived at Chattanooga, Tennessee, May 18, and moved to Rossville, Georgia, and then, on May 19, marched to Camp George H. Thomas, Chickamauga Park.

stable hack but his gait was uncertain. As he rode along the line someone always shouted at him. His name was, I believe, William, but we called him Bill.

"For God's sake, look out, Bill."

"There you go, Bill."

"Hold him, Bill, hold him," we shouted.

I dare say it was all wrong. The privates, corporals, and sergeants were old fashioned American democrats. We were at the age of rampant individualism.

Did we not know Bill? At home he owned a little shoe store. It was true we were soldiers now and there was a good deal said about discipline, but after all. . . .

The war we were in would someday be over. We would go back home. Bill would be wanting to sell us shoes. I am told that when the World War came this was all changed. Companies of soldiers were no longer commanded by men they had known at home. The smaller units, companies enlisted from the town, were split up. There was no more selection of officers by the men. You went, as a soldier, among strangers, had to make new friends.

And now we were in the south, in that very fabled land where so many of our fathers had fought and of which we had heard so much. What a trip it was, for me, crowded as we were in the day coach of a train, we boys from the low country, up about the northern lakes, places of bitter cold winter mornings, chores to be done on farms, stores to be swept out, fires to be built and for myself heavy barrels of apples to be rolled and piled in an icy cold warehouse. After that the long hours of drilling, of marching and counter-marching, with gun, knapsack and blanket roll, seemed as child's play to me.

There was the excitement of the journey south, to wipe out my guilty feeling at having deserted my brothers and sister to go help save my country. It did not look much as though it needed saving. Our trip south, from Columbus, our state capital (our governor having come into our camp there, to walk through our company streets, he kept saying the same words, over and over, "Fine boys," he said, "very fine boys") through towns of southern Ohio, our progress slow, great crowds of men, women and girls at every station, and then across the mythical Mason and Dixon line and on down to a place called Chickamauga Park, near the city of Chattanooga. Why, it was the very center and heart of something, to most of us. Here, on this very spot, stood grim Sherman. We saw, in fancy, Grant, clad in the uniform of a common soldier, a fine horseman, dashing across a field. And over there would have stood Thomas, "Rock of Chickamauga."

"But how, I ask you, did that governor know we were 'fine'?"

"I guess it's just some more of his bunk."

We were what we were. How far away the reality of battles seemed to us as we went, so triumphantly, south. There were the women and girls gathered at the stations, and not only in our own state but in the south itself. Why, how strange! These had been our fathers' enemies, with whom they had fought for four long terrible years. I think that most of us half expected that, when we had crossed the Ohio, we would plunge at once into a new and a strange land. There would be cotton fields, men and boys would dash out of houses to give the famed rebel yell. . . .

"They came tearing at us out of a wood. They gave a yell that made your blood curl. They were all tall lean hard looking men. We could not stand against them."

Remembrance of old words heard, some old soldier, come to sit for a time with my father on the steps before a frame house, in an Ohio village, on a summer evening.

Cotton fields in bloom, negroes sitting on the steps before their cabins, banjos in hands, singing their songs. . . .

"Oh, my darling Nelly Grey.

"They have taken you away."

"Why, they are just like us," my comrade Bert said to me.

"I thought . . . when we had crossed the Mason and Dixie line . . . why, I don't know what I thought."

He had expressed something for us both. Bert was a tall farmer lad and strong. What a pair of fists he had. But I will speak presently of him and of our going together into the banking business. He was a tall strong one and quiet, a kind of of Thomas Wolfe among us but without the restlessness and the terrific inner storm, always going on within, that was in the writer Thomas Wolfe I was long afterwards to know.[17]

My friend Bert had great fists that he never had to use. There was something commanding in him and I had been infinitely grateful when he

17. Thomas Wolfe (1900–38) wrote of Anderson in "A Letter from Thomas Wolfe," *Story,* XIX (September–October, 1941), 68–69. See *Letters of Sherwood Anderson,* edited by Howard Mumford Jones and Walter B. Rideout (Boston: Little, Brown and Company, 1953) and *Letters of Thomas Wolfe,* edited by Elizabeth Nowell (New York: Scribner's, 1956).

had taken to me. For some strange reason he had picked me out. In an army it is always so. There are two men, often altogether unlike, who, at the first sight of each other, become comrades. "Me for you and you for me." In the World War, I believe, they were called "buddies."

"So, my buddy and me, we went AWOL. We hiked into town at night and had some drinks. 'Let's see if we can get some skirts,' I said. And so we did."

Bert was puzzled, as I was. Together we saw, for the first time, the mountains. We were really in the fabled south and, it was very odd, the people of the towns, the women and girls, who came crowding to the stations in the towns, were much as were our own men, women and girls at home.

"Well now, will you look at that, that man over there. It might be Inky Tiffany, at home." Although Bert had lived all of his life on a farm near our town I had never seen him before we, together, went to war. He would have come into town, on Saturdays, with other farmer boys. He was from a family more prosperous than my own. Like me he was an eager reader of books. That may have been what brought us together.

"And what is it you read?"

"It is a novel by the Pole, Sienkiewicz.[18] I had, you see, in Chicago, a job among the Poles."

"Why, I never heard of him."

Two young men, talking eagerly.

"And have you read Dickens, and De Foe, his *Moll Flanders,* and *Tom Jones,* by Fielding?"

Before we, of our company, had left our own town, when I had come hurrying home from Chicago, to go to war with the others, I had been, one day, alone, in what we called our "armory." It was a dance hall above a store and there was a room in which military supplies were kept and, in there, I had found some several boxes of buttons. They were of brass and the state seal was stamped upon them and, being alone and unseen, I had filled my pockets. I dare say it was a theft, but, in any case, I did it, for, at that time, there was a passion for these buttons among the women. They were made into hat pins and I had thought, coming upon them in their boxes, in the military store room. . . .

18. Henryk Sienkiewicz (1846–1916), Polish historical novelist, author of *Quo Vadis?* (1895, tr. 1896).

"What a chance," I had thought. "What will these buttons not buy for me?"

It was a smart theft. I had divided with Bert and we were prepared for the women. What baskets of food we garnered. Oh, the fried chicken, the jellies, the pies! We fed until we could feed no more, collecting in each town as our train passed through. It was a slow procession, each town, of the north and the south, wanting to greet us. Why, was this war? To collect, as Bert and I were collecting, others had to tear buttons off from coats. There would be trouble for these men later but none for us. I had got a goodly supply, our pockets were stuffed, and when we could eat no more we occasionally collected kisses.

What woman would not kiss a young soldier, perhaps going off to be killed? Little did they know what a comic opera affair our part in our war was to be and, besides, there is, to most women, something almost irresistible in the young man in uniform. It may well be one of the reasons why wars go on, one of the reasons why men do not stand up and declare there shall be no more wars.

And I had got, for one of my buttons, something else. Now that girl at home, the one I had snubbed, or had wanted to snub, she who had preferred that jewelry clerk to me, now that I could no longer write letters to her, to whom was I to write? Writing, it seemed, was already a necessity of my nature and I would not write often to my sister. It would bring up a matter of which I did not want to think.

My problem was solved for me in one of the towns. I had traded one of my buttons for another basket of food, the button passed out of a car window and a heavy basket of food passed in, and I had caught a glimpse of her.

Oh, how fair she seemed. She was small and dark and had, I remember, a heavy mass of shining blue-black hair that fell about her face. This was in a Kentucky town and she stood with her hat in her hand.

I was speechless. When I passed the button to her I wanted to put it first to my lips, to make a speech, "See, I put my lips to it. It is the kiss of love," but the words would not come.

"But am I again in love?" I asked myself and oh, so quickly, the train moved on.

"Oh love, oh love." Was I to spend my life in love, always seeing new women desired, women, casually seen thus, to remain so sharply in my mind, wanting from them. . . .

What was it I wanted?

Later, when I had become a writer and had written and published books, I wrote and published a book of tales, called *Winesburg, Ohio,* and when it was published there was an outbreak of bitter denunciation. Letters kept coming to me, many letters, and they were all from women.

"You are unclean. You are one who has a filthy mind," they said and, for a time, there was so much of it that I began to distrust myself. I went about with head hanging in shame.

"It must be true. So many say it that it must be true."

But did I want what they were thinking about? I was puzzled and hurt.

"I do not," I cried to myself. Perhaps, after all, I wanted only someone to whom I could address myself. There was something warm in many women and I wanted warmth and, too often, men, seeing the adoration I had for many women, thought of me as the women of the letters had thought.

However it was not so with women known, and seen. That was a comfort to me.

I was on the train, sitting with Bert, and we were exploring the basket and in it there was a note. She had put down her name and address. "You may write to me," she had said, and, unseen by Bert, I had slipped the note into my pocket.

"Aha! And so!" Here was something for me. Here was someone to whom I could write.

I did write, almost at once, and when we had got to our camp, at Chickamauga Park, her answer came. Often since I have wondered. Where is she now? Has she married and has she children? Alas, I have forgotten her name and the name of her town.

I wrote many letters to her, often not waiting for her reply. I sent her picture postcards. I went into the city of Chattanooga and had my picture taken and sent it to her. I told her of my thoughts, of my life in camp and, when she had sent me a picture of herself, I had a leather case made for it.

I put it into my inside military coat pocket next to my heart. Had I not heard stories, were there not soldiers, of my father's Civil War, whose lives had been saved by something, carried thus, next to the heart?

In their case it was, almost always, a Bible but I had no Bible and, besides, Bibles are bulky and my leather case was thin.

When it came to the time of battles I would be fixed, I thought. There would be her picture, in its leather case, there next to my heart. There was this picture in my mind. Now we, of our company, were in a battle and I was there, one of the foremost, in the very front ranks. We were charging across a field, in the face of the enemy, waiting for us. I was reliving some old story, told no doubt by one of my father's cronies. I was in the front rank of our forces and there was the enemy, the hated Spaniard. (Just why I was to hate a Spaniard I did not know, did not stop to think. I had never seen a Spaniard. But they were there, the Spaniards, and they were crouched behind an embankment.) The picture had got very vivid to me.

We were advancing with shouts and with brave hearts and now the bullets were flying. This was something of which I knew. How often I had heard it described.

Was I afraid? I did not know. I ran forward with the others. The bullets came thicker and thicker. Now they were flying and singing about my head. Comrades were falling. In these thoughts, that came to me at this time, I was always killing, in battles, the men of our company I did not specially like.

"Why, there is Jim, fallen there.

"And now Sylvester goes down."

And there was that jewelry clerk, who had got my girl at home. He was safely at home, in his jewelry store, but, in fancy, I had put him in the front ranks in the battle. I saw him fall. I saw the blood gush from his heart.

But now I was myself struck. Down I went and on went my comrades. I lay stunned but presently consciousness came back to me.

I had been saved. The bullet had penetrated my coat but had lodged in the leather case I had carried at my breast. And now the sound of battle had moved away. I was alone, among the dead, and, looking up, I could see the sky. I took the leather case from my pocket and held it tighter to my lips. I had got this picture in my mind and it kept coming back. Almost always it came at night, when I was with Bert and others in our tent and, getting up, I got the leather case from my pocket and, creeping out of the tent, tried to see her face in the darkness.

I could not see it but it was better so. The better to imagine her dear face torn and mangled. I stood, holding it again to my lips, but, unfortunately, I did it also, sometimes, in the light of day.

I was doing it one day when alone in our tent when, suddenly, several other soldiers came in. They pounced upon me. They tore it from my hands.

"Why see, what he has got!"

"Why look, a dame."

They were passing it from hand to hand.

"And some baby too," they cried.

I had been lying on my cot and I turned my face from them. Well enough I knew that I should have jumped up, sprung at them, knocked them right and left but there were three of them and they were all larger and stronger than I was. They had seen me kissing it. As it turned out I, later, got it back but, that day, they went off laughing, taking it with them. After it happened a certain flair went out of my letters to her.

I continued to be uncomfortable because of what seemed my betrayal of those at home. There I was in the great camp with the soldiers and all day we were marching up and down. There was much complaining.

"Do they think we are horses?"

"What do they think we are?"

We were carrying guns. We had knapsacks on our shoulders. We became a part of a regiment, a battalion, an army corps. Our company officers marched beside us but they went light. The officer carried only a sword and, on some days, the marching and counter-marching went on all day long. We were being hardened for service.

But why should these fellows, the officers, be permitted to yell at us as they sometimes did?

"You get into line there. What do you think you are doing?"

"Huh!" We dared not answer. A low grumbling sound began to run up and down.

"Be silent there. Attention!"

"Why, what a fellow you have become, you captain, you lieutenant." There was our major, who had kept the shoe store at home. Now he rode a horse but he did not ride well and seemed always on the point of falling off. The fact made us a little charitable toward him. He was a little ridiculous. It made us feel better although, when he rode past, bouncing from side to side on his horse, shouting commands at us, we often wished he would fall.

There was this grumbling, always going on, among a few of us, but Bert and I did not grumble. In me there was the memory of the Chicago apple warehouse, the barrels of apples to be lifted up from the floor, the piles always growing higher and higher, my back always aching, and for Bert the memory of long days of following the plow on his father's farm.

There was something that I at once checked. I had been, earlier in life, at the races. I had had a job, helping to take care of trotters, and I had noticed something. In our stable of horses (we had four that went to the races) or in a neighboring stable, there was a vicious stallion or mare. Or it might be one merely sulky, and what a difference in the methods of handling them adopted by two trainers.

One went at the horse with a heavy whip. He had it out with him.

"I'll fix the bastard. He will do what I want or I will kill him." Such a one might have a fine courage and I had seen a man fight thus, with a vicious horse, fairly taking his life into his hands.

There was a great open barn floor, with box stalls along the side, and, in one of the stalls, a vicious stallion. He had just been brought to the stable and it was known that he had killed a man.

"Turn him loose," the trainer said to us. He was a small man with a mustache. We had closed the barn doors and now threw open the door to the stallion's box stall, ourselves dodging into an empty stall, and out he came. He was a great black and was in an ugly mood. The little man, with the walking stick, advanced upon him.

They had it out, there on the barn floor, blows rained upon the stallion, heels flying. Time and again, with teeth bared, the stallion rushed at him, only to receive a blow and, in the end, the stallion surrendered. Ever afterwards he trembled with fright when the man approached but he obeyed the man's commands.

There was one method and there was another. Vicious horses and grumbling men may also be conquered by quiet, soft spoken men. Here was a horse being driven in a race. In another driver's hands he wouldn't behave. He sulked. He would not extend himself.

"But look! See! There is one who has a hand." When certain men got into their sulkies, behind race horses, something happened to the horse. One of the great drivers I had seen, a man named Geers, had been called "Silent Ed." Such a one had the touch. When he picked up the reins it was as though something like an electric current ran along the reins to the horse's brain. The vicious or the sulky horse suddenly began to go true and it was so also with us. There was one of our officers who took us out to drill. All was to be done in unison. There was a command given. We were to wheel to the right or left. We had our guns slung over the right shoulder and were to shift to the left.

Or we were standing in a line. There was an evening ceremony, called "taps." Now the flag was coming down.

"Present arms!"

The command, coming from the lips of one officer, was executed raggedly. There was an ugly broken sound. Men shifted uneasily on their feet.

But now, see this other. What is it that makes his voice, giving a command, his very presence, so different from the other? When he is with us, in command of us, shoulders are straightened. Look, with what a swing we march, how perfectly we hold the line. When guns are to be shifted all is done in perfect time. And how strangely different we feel. Now we march without tiring. There is no more grumbling. When we come back to our tents, after this day of marching, we will look at each other with pride in our eyes.

"Hey, Jim, look, we were good today."

"Yes, we were good."

We were in the open fields. All day we marched, shoulder to shoulder. We were in the wind, in the sun and rain. How eagerly we ate, how soundly we slept. Now, if it were not for the secret fear of battles to come, a matter we never mentioned, it was a fear kept hidden away. . . .

We were soldiers now and, as privates, we got our monthly pay but it was small. There was a great hunger for money. Bert had an idea.

"Look here," he said, "we will buy up the time of the others." We did it on capital Bert got from his father, he, with a gesture, taking me into full partnership, and from the beginning we were quite heartless usurers. We loaned a man three dollars and when pay day came we made him return to us five.

It is our chance," said Bert. "We will make them pay. We will use the money as a starting point to our careers."

Bert was a farmer's son but he wanted to be an engineer. He wanted to go to college and so did I. There were stud poker games going on in some of the company tents.

"Look," said Bert, "they are throwing it away." We were a bit uncomfortable, holding our comrades up, but we consoled ourselves.

"If they do not lose it at stud poker it will go to some woman of the streets," we said. We had become, we told ourselves, a moral force.

"Why," said Bert, "see what we are saving them from."

We were raking in the cash and I could send money home. It seemed strange to us that our efforts, to steer the others out of the paths of evil, were so little appreciated. There was even a plot formed. It was at the end of our service and word was whispered about. Men went whispering up and down the company streets.

"Go in," they said. "Borrow up to the hilt." They would borrow all we had, our capital, and then, when the last pay day came, they would give us the laugh.

"Aha," they would say. "Usurers," they would cry. They would have this grand splash, at our expense, throwing our money about, but we fooled them all right. We put a sign up at the door of our tent.

"This bank has gone out of business," it said.

III

There is something fascinating in all this business of being a soldier. Man will have to find a substitute for it. It may be that something like the CCC will do the work.[19]

I have often wondered since what it was that induced most of us, in our company, to go into the army. We were not drafted. We volunteered.

To be sure there was a great fanfare. After the Spanish-American War something changed in American life. It was the beginning of American imperialism.

The ground work had already been done. We were all reading Kipling. There was much talk of the "White Man's Burden."

The newspapers, led by Hearst,[20] had been blasting away at Spain but I do not believe that most of us were newspaper readers.

We had been boys and we were at the edge of manhood. We wanted adventure. In the small interior towns, when I was a lad there, half the town went down to the railroad station to see the evening passenger train come and go.

It came out of the east and went into the west and we boys followed it with hungry eyes. There was something out there, beyond the horizon, we all wanted.

Then the war came. It was our chance. I do not believe we were thinking of the injustice done the Cubans by the Spanish. What did we know of the Cubans or the Spaniards? There were no Cubans in our town, no Spaniards there. A few years before the first sewers had been put down and foreign men did come in, were brought in by a contractor, but they were Italians.

19. The Civilian Conservation Corps, Franklin D. Roosevelt's program to employ and train jobless young men in the 1930's.

20. William Randolph Hearst (1863–1951), head of a vast chain of United States newspapers, partially responsible for guiding the country into the Spanish-American War.

We did not hate them. We did not love them. We were curious. We boys hung about. We watched them at work, tried to pick up words from their language.

In the evening we walked about discussing them. They did not seem to eat the same food we did. They had not brought their wives or families to town. Women and girls of the town were a little fearful. They were told to stay off the streets at night. Nothing ever happened.

What drew us I think was the hunger for distances, for strange places. There was no passion to kill.

There was however something very fine in the new kind of relationship, man to man. The continual drilling, in step, shoulder to shoulder, did something for us and to us. It became something like a dance. In a sense each of us, for the time, lost his identity. There was this feeling of self thrown away, and we, with society, can be too proud of self. I do not believe that, at the time, I thought much of all this but I have thought of it a great deal since.

There was loss of self and, at the same time, a new feeling of power. A man marching thus, with a great body of other men, attentive to the commands of his officers, the gun, now carried on the right shoulder, now, at a command, shifted to the left.

We marched across a field, all in step, and there was the need of presenting to the eyes of another man, our colonel, sitting on his horse, a straight front.

No one man to march an inch before the other.

Who has not seen it? There is a thrill in seeing, even to those not a part of it.

And there was a great difference in officers too. One of our lieutenants had been night policeman in our town. He was a very likable man, warm and friendly. Although he was much older, and when I was a boy at home I had many long talks with him. Like so many other American boys I had been a peddler of newspapers and often, in the winter, the evening train that brought my papers, to be delivered on door steps of the townspeople, was late.

Sometimes it was many hours late, did not arrive until after midnight, and I waited for it.

I sat in the station waiting room and there was a stove. The night telegraph operator came in and the night policeman came. They talked. There must have been, in the two men, something alive and sensitive to the needs of youth for, sometimes, they took me into their talk. The night policeman looked at me with grave eyes. There was a national election coming.

"You take the papers about. I guess you read them. You hear people talk. What do you think?" he asked and I swelled with inner pride. His question seemed to me to be a kind of salute to my coming manhood.

But he could not drill us as soldiers.

There was something wrong. Taken out for a morning's drill by him there was a queer slackness. I think it was because there were no tunes in him. He had no sense of timing. We drilled and we marched but presently there was, in all of us, an odd weariness.

It was not there when our other lieutenant, the ex-celery farmer, took us out. There was an instant tightening, a new erectness. Something new seemed to get into all of our bodies. Self got more and more lost.

And how well we worked, with what precision we slung our guns about. We were not weary when we came in from a long morning of drilling with him.

There is something to be learned here. There is something in men living together, using their bodies day after day in the same way. It explains, I think, why the individual who, in his own person, uninspired by this feeling of being a part of a mass of other men, the feeling after much marching and drilling got down into his very flesh, why such an individual who, without this feeling, would flee in terror, given it, will walk calmly up to death.

Hold it and you have an army of so-called "heroes." Lose it, let its grip slip, and you have a disorganized fleeing mob.

In the Civil War it was lost by the northern army at Bull Run but when Grant made the blunder at Cold Harbor, sending thousands of men to certain death, they had it.

They were just such fellows as we had, in our company, in our war. They were farmers' sons, sons of laborers, doctors, lawyers, merchants' sons. They knew they were going to death. The men pinned identification cards on their coats as they went in. This so that their bodies could be identified.

They went in.

There is here, in this little understood impulse that is in all men, to lose self in the mass, act with the mass, self for the time quite gone, a kind of relief in it, perhaps to the pain of living.

There is in it something strangely noble, strangely mean.

It can lead men to the committing of unbelievable cruel acts they could never do as individuals.

It can make common men act like heroes.

It explains lynching.

It is the strength of fascism.

It is labor's greatest weapon.

Someday it may be understood, and used.

As for example some organization, such as the CCC, every youth in the country compelled to serve, the tremendous power inherent in mass action turned, from a program of death and destruction, to one of building.

It seems to me sometimes that the whole land could thus be rebuilt, all men given a feeling of participation in building.

It will need a truly inspired leader.

I remember a certain hour, of a certain day. We were engaged in some sort of maneuvers. Let us say there were thirty or forty thousand of us. We had marched away to a certain place where the maneuvers were held and were returning to camp.

I remember that we marched along a road, down a hill, across a great valley. It might have been two or three miles across the valley. We ascended another low hill.

My own company must have been somewhere up near the head of the long procession. There was a little cluster of trees at the top of the hill.

With the permission of one of our lieutenants I had dropped out of the ranks. I had a stone in my shoe. The lieutenant was the one who had been a night policeman.

"Duck into the woods. Get out of sight," he said and I ducked. I dare say he did not want other officers to see one of his men leave the ranks.

I was in the wood. I went in far enough not to be seen. I took the stone out of my shoe. I sat down under a tree.

This strange feeling had taken possession of me. I was there, an individual, a young man, half boy, sitting on the ground under a tree, but I was at the same time something else.

We had been marching for hours, I was not weary. It seemed to me, that day, that into my legs had come the strength of the legs of thirty thousand men.

I had become a giant.

[185]

I was, in myself, something huge, terrible and at the same time noble. I remember that I sat, for a long time, while the army passed, opening and closing my eyes.

Tears were running down my cheeks.

"I am myself and I am something else too," I whispered to myself.

I remember that later, when I got back to camp, I did not want to speak to others. I went into my tent and threw myself down on my cot. I did not want to eat. I was a man in love. I was in love with the thought of the possibilities of myself combined with others.

It was a long time later. It was after the war. I was in Chicago and stood on the station of the elevated railroad. It was evening and people were pouring out of offices and stores. They came by thousands out of side streets and into the broad city street of faces. They were a broken mob. They did not keep step. There were thousands of individuals, lost like myself. As individuals they had no strength, no courage.

By that time I had become a writer. I had, after the war, been a factory man.

I conceived of a figure, a man, a kind of combination of Abraham Lincoln and that later American figure, John Lewis.[21]

I conceived of such a man really inspired, a poet.

He would be a poet of movement.

I tried to create such a figure. I wrote a book, a novel I called *Marching Men*.[22] What I wanted to do was to create a great epic poem of movement in masses. I had this notion of men, the employees of some great factory, going every morning to a common meeting place and falling into line.

They would march, a solid mass of men, each morning, to the factory and in the evening would again fall into companies and march away.

The possessors of the good of the world standing and watching.

There would be a new terror.

All men would suddenly feel strong.

In my novel I made the movement, thus started by an inspired man, go to pieces because of a fanatic.

There was a man crazed by the new feeling of strength who wanted

21. John Llewellyn Lewis (1880–   ), American labor leader.
22. See Earl Raymond Hilton, "Sherwood Anderson and Heroic Vitalism," *Northwest Ohio Quarterly*, XXIX (Spring, 1957), 97–107; and Rex Burbank, "The Populist Temper," *Sherwood Anderson* (New York: Twayne Publishers, 1964), pp. 48–60, reprinted in *The Achievement of Sherwood Anderson*, ed. White, pp. 32–43. See also *A Story Teller's Story*, ed. White, pp. 100, 107.

suddenly to use his strength to destroy. He began to blow up buildings. The movement fell apart. I do not think my novel quite came off. It should have been an epic poem, the thunderous march of a million men in its lines. I was not up to it and later when the fascist movement swept over Europe I began to see, more clearly, how such a movement, once started, may thus become identified with the state. When I saw the dream I had put into action I grew afraid of my dream.

Man, it seems, must still march alone. The impulse in man, here spoken of, can be too easily perverted. The democratic ideal is in the end safer for man than the ideal of my dream.

IV

The bands were playing. Men were marching. We were on dirt roads marching. We marched in fields.

There were sharp commands uttered.

"By the right flank."

"By the left flank."

I had become a corporal.[23]

Ha. Was not Napoleon once called "the little Corsican corporal"?

What about an Ohio corporal?

"Hold the line there men."

"You Jim, get into step."

There was muttering. Formerly, at home, I had borne the nickname of Jobby. I had got it by being forever on the look out for jobs.

"What the hell, Jobby? Don't get so goddamn biggety, you."

There was a reply on my lips for that. Perhaps I looked at Jim. He was a big one. He would knock my block off if I got too gay with him.

I kept my mouth shut.

"Hep. Hep."

You are in camp, with a hundred men. There are two rows of tents, down a company street. While we were at that camp at Chickamauga Park, in training there, I do not remember many days of rain.

The company street was of clay. There had been grass but it was all

23. Anderson was promoted to corporal July 1, 1898. For the war career, see William Alfred Sutton, "Sherwood Anderson: The Spanish-American War Year," *Northwest Ohio Quarterly*, XX (January, 1948), 20–36.

gone. Now and then some man of the company got drunk. He crept out of camp at night and, later, came staggering in.

He had been up before the captain. He was on "police" duty. He had to police the company streets.

He took a broom and swept it and we others, coming in from drill, laughed at him.

"Why hello, Maggie," we said.

"Come here, Maggie."

"Look. You have left a little dirt here."

"And will you go to hell?"

"Well you kiss my ass."

Or he is digging holes for latrines and we go down there. We stand about, give orders, make comments.

There were timid shy men who crept away into their tents. They had books in there.

There was a young man, a German, who read Goethe. He took me aside and spoke to me.

"You should read Goethe. You should read Howe." [24] He had come out of Germany to escape the army and then from some impulse he himself couldn't understand had suddenly volunteered to come into our army.

He had had a plan.

"I had a job. I was saving money. I intended to go to school.

"Would it not be strange if I was killed, here, in this war?"

He was one of the thoughtful ones.

"And what is it all about?"

"It is to free Cuba."

"Bah!" he said.

There was a heavy shouldered man who had been a farm hand. He was very awkward about handling his gun. He walked awkwardly. He was a silent one. He seldom spoke.

There were braggarts among us, profane ones, sensualists.

It was a Sunday afternoon and there were four men who had left the camp. They went to a distant town, and had some beer there. They were looking for women and inquired in the town.

"Is there any such house here?"

"No there is no such house."

24. Edgar Watson Howe (1853–1937), Kansas journalist and novelist, author of *The Story of a Country Town* (1883), which influenced later naturalistic fiction.

It was evening and they were returning to camp. There was a man of our company, a small man. He had been a clerk in a store at home.

He said there was a house, beside the road, and that the four men went in there. There was a woman, quite old, sitting on a little porch before the house. The woman was alone there.

The men came up to her and spoke to her and she got up and started to run into the house but they grabbed her.

The four men took her. The man who had been a clerk was coming along the road and saw it.

He said they saw him. They called to him.

"Do you want your turn?" they called.

They had put the woman on the low ground before the house. Two of the men held her. One of the men had his hand over her mouth.

The one who had been a clerk ran into a nearby wood and hid. He told me about it after. He said, "I was ashamed but I wanted to see."

Something held him there, he said.

He said she struggled for a time and then she appeared to submit.

"They all did it and then they went away."

"What happened then?"

"Nothing happened. She just lay there, for a time, and then she got up. She arranged her clothes. Before they went away the men had left some money on the porch. She went and got it."

He said there was a little dog.

It had kept barking at the men.

"Well?"

"I tell you she just sat there. She cried. She was quite old and thin. She made the dog quit barking. There was a stick lying on the ground and she picked it up and thrust it at the dog. The dog ran under the porch."

"Well?"

"I don't know. I came away. I went on through the wood and got into another road.

"The last time I looked she had begun crying again. I came on back to camp."

V

There was a certain looseness to our war. What we might have done, when it came to actual fighting, I don't know.

We were however reassured. There was a night, in Chickamauga Park, when suddenly, at perhaps ten o'clock, we were in our tents, there were card games going on, the drums began to beat.

Or rather, I should say, bugles began to sound off.

There was the cry of officers.

"Fall in. Fall in."

We were to strike camp at once.

"Hurry! Hurry!"

There was alarm among the men.

"What's wrong?"

"What's up?"

We rolled up our tents, loaded them on army wagons, packed our knapsacks. We fell into line.

There was a tense silence. Nearly all of us were sons of Civil War men. What stories we had heard, of night marches, sudden attacks.

"Stonewall Jackson, at Chancellorsville."

The grim all day fight, in the very fields, clumps of woodland along the very road in which we marched.

We marched in darkness.

As in all armies rumors ran from lip to lip. We spoke in whispers.

"They say. They say."

"They say that our troops are fighting desperately at Santiago, in Cuba."

"The Spaniards have cut them all to pieces."

"We are being rushed there."

There was this sudden feeling of dread. It kept on raining. We were marched through the darkness to a little railroad station. There was a long line of cars, some passenger cars, others freight cars. We got aboard.

Such a night. There were men praying. Others wrote letters, to wives, mothers or sweethearts. I was one of the scribblers.

"It may be I am going to my death. I do not know."

"They say. . . ."

There were two or three men reading Bibles and one man (he at least had his own kind of courage) knelt and prayed.

At that I think it likely that most of us would have been all right, if it had come to actual fighting.

The man who was praying (he had been a clerk in a store at home) had remembered a sentence. Afterwards we laughed at him a good deal but, on that night, we remained silent.

"Oh God, let this cup pass from me," he prayed.

There had been, as it was later explained, a protest from politicians. There were a great many thousand men in training at Chickamauga Park, near the city of Chattanooga. We soldiers were spending our money in Chattanooga. Knoxville wanted some of it. Our regiment and, I believe, another regiment were moved over there. We arrived, at Knoxville, in the early morning.[25] The trains stopped by a great field and the field was covered with tables. The women, of the city of Knoxville, had turned out, in force, to receive us. The sun was shining. The tables, standing in the field, were loaded with food. I got me a girl there. She waited on one of the tables. I thought she was very beautiful. She was the daughter of some prominent citizen of the town. She was someone I could later write to, telling of my adventures. She sent me later a photograph, which I afterwards carried in my pocket, next to my heart. I put her picture with the one I had got from another young woman seen at a railroad station. I have no doubt that, in my letters to them, I declared my undying love for both of them.

At any rate I meant it, while I was writing.

If we were reassured that morning at Knoxville there was more assurance when, at last, we were aboard ship. We sailed down along the shores of the island of Cuba.[26] We were off the mouth of the harbor at Santiago and there were the Spanish ships strung along a beach, a great string of them.

The power of Spain had been broken.

A new world power was coming, with a rush, into the world's consciousness.

The American white man had taken up the white man's burden.

Soon Hobson,[27] the hero of Santiago, would be traveling through America, being kissed by women admirers.

The Rough Riders (there was a rumor current in the army that a regiment of negro regulars had really done the job) had beat us to it.

I don't believe we were too sorry, although, aboard the ship, in our company, there were voices raised in protest.

25. On August 27 and 28, 1898, Anderson's company traveled by train from Rossville, Georgia, to Camp Poland, Knoxville, Tennessee.

26. On December 27–29, 1898, Company I traveled by rail from Knoxville, Tennessee, to Charleston, South Carolina; embarked on the *Minnewaska;* and arrived at Cienfuegas, Cuba, January 3, 1899. Armistice was declared August 13, 1898.

27. Richmond Pearson Hobson (1870–1937), American naval officer. The victory at Santiago Harbor was on July 3, 1898.

"Ah, now we won't get no chance."

"I just ached to get at them Spaniards."

There was a good deal of that kind of talk. It didn't last long. We laughed it down.

It may be that Dewey had already won his victory at Manilla Bay.[28]

Teddy had put himself in line for the presidency.

There were all sorts of stories going about. The ground work for the bitter Schley-Sampson controversy had been laid.[29]

There was a general named Shafter,[30] who had commanded the land forces at the battle of Santiago. A sergeant, who said he had been in the battle, later told us about him.

"He was very fat and it was very hot," the sergeant said.

"We put him in a hammock, under some trees. We left him there. We went on without him."

We had landed on the island of Cuba. We disembarked in a beautiful bay and were marched through the streets of a fine Cuban city. After the battle of Santiago there had been a truce signed. As we soldiers understood it a part of the agreement with Spain was that the Spanish soldiers, in Cuba, were to be sent back to Spain at America's expense. Many thousands of them, unarmed, had already been marched into the city of Cienfuegas.

"Place of a hundred fires."

We were to watch them, guard them.

We were marched straight through the city, the streets thronged.

There were Spanish soldiers, standing with hands in pockets. Our bands played. It is to be remembered that we were all middle western boys. Already we had seen mountains, we had been on a ship at sea, we had been in several American cities, in the south we had seen cotton growing, we had jumped off slow moving trains at the edges of fields and had plucked cotton balls to send home.

Thousands, perhaps near millions of picture post cards sent.

Negro life seen.

Before leaving home some of us had never seen a negro.

There had been warm friendships made.

28. George Dewey (1837–1917), American admiral, whose victory was on May 1, 1898.

29. Winfield Scott Schley (1839–1911), American admiral, and William Thomas Sampson (1840–1902), American general, argued over who deserved credit for the victory at Santiago.

30. William Rufus Shafter (1835–1906), American general.

The bellyachers, those who complained constantly of the army fare, those who, when there was a hard day of marching to be done, were always getting sick, were not known to us.

And now we were in this new strange semi-tropical place.

How strange the buildings of the city.

There were little balconies on which stood dark, and, to our eyes, very beautiful women.

"I wonder if I can get me a sweetheart here?"

"That would be something wonderful."

There were thousands of the Spanish soldiers along the street. At that time, apparently, the Cuban people all believed that we were saviors.

They cheered us madly.

The Spanish soldiers, all about us everywhere, now seemed to us harmless enough.

They were for the most part rather small dark men.

Their uniforms looked shabby. As we found out, later that night, they were glad enough to see us come.

I am sure that we looked very strong and valiant.

"Well, you see, after all, we do not need to fight.

"We do not need to kill or be killed."

There was gladness, in us.

We were marched out, some for miles, beyond the city limit. It was by this time late evening.

Tents had already been erected.

The mess tents were up.

Some rich American woman had provided for the soldiers who were to see service in Cuba a special kind of tent.

The tents were set up, well off the ground. We were not to contract malaria.

The tents were huge.

They were provided with tent floors.

There were rows of comfortable cots.

We were in camp, at the edge of the Cuban city, and were marched up before our colonel. He sat on his horse. There was a grim look on his face.

There was a speech made to us. We had been sent, some several thousands of us, to the Cuban city. We had guns but it had transpired that, for the guns, there was no ammunition.

It had not been sent.

It was true there were so and so many thousands of us but, in the Cuban city, there were three times as many Spanish soldiers.

There was a very solemn look on our colonel's face. The responsibility, resting, upon his shoulders, was great. It was a terrible load to bear.

There was a tense silence in the ranks.

"I have brought you safely here.

"Now I command you, every man of you, to stay in this camp.

"On the man who leaves this camp I will have no mercy.

"He will be court-martialed, at once."

It was night, it was early evening and we men were in our tents. I went outside. I made a motion with my hand to my comrade Bert.

"Bert," I said, "what do you say? Shall we try it?"

"Yes," he said.

When I had called him out there was no one else in our tent. All the other men, some six or eight of them, quartered in our tent, had mysteriously disappeared.

I thought I was being very brave.

I thought Bert was brave.

We were risking everything, disgrace, being court-martialed. I do not believe we knew what it meant.

It sounded bad.

We crept on our bellies along the ground. We saw the guard. There was a little railroad, running down, from our camp, into the city and it was black with men.

The whole regiment, except those unfortunate enough to be on guard, were on the railroad.

There was another regiment, made up of men from the West Virginia coal mines. Their colonel had also spoken to them.

They were there.

There was another regiment from another state. The men of that regiment were there.

We tramped down into the city.

The citizens were waiting for us.

The Spanish soldiers were waiting.

It was a wild night, a memorable night. It was like the first Armistice Day, in American cities, at the end of the World War.

The Spanish soldiers were going home.

Some of them had been in service, in Cuba, for years.

They were half drunk with joy.

There had been the long struggle, the hatred between the army and the citizens.

Now all of that was at an end.

They embraced us. They bought us drinks.

And more drinks.

And more and more.

We marched arm in arm with them through the streets.

We sang. We shouted. It must have been well on toward morning when Bert and I helped each other along the railroad to our camp.

There were no officers about. Whether or not any of them had also gone into the city I don't know.

We fell on our backs on our cots. We lay and laughed. We were not afraid.

After all, as Bert said, you can't court-martial a whole army.

"Now you look at it," he said.

"You see," he said, "it can't be done."

As it was in the camps so it remained all through our service in Cuba. There was the illusion.

We had come to free the Cuban people. We were invited to go about, dine in houses. Some of our men got Cuban sweethearts.

We remained to the end what we had been. Each company was a unit made up of men from one small town and from the farming country about the town.

Our officers were also men of the town. They expected to go back there to live. In the later World War all of this was changed. There were seldom two men of the same town in the same company. The men did not know their officers personally, had not gone to school with them, played ball with them.

I have seen a private of our company in a quarrel with our captain. The quarrel grew into a fight and the private knocked the captain down. This in our company street.

The private was not brought to trial.

By the regulations I believe he could have been sent to prison.

I remember later, a long time later, the telling of all this to an English army man I met in London.

He was amused.

"You Americans," he said. He declared that no army could be so run.

"But ours was," I said.

There was talk of what would have happened if there had been a real struggle, a real war, and I was of the opinion that, in such a test, we would have stood up to it as well as any army. I was of the opinion that had our captain been a man who had won the real rapport of his men the incident, in the company street, could never have happened. The angry private would have been worked over by his comrades.

It is true that, in our army, there was all of this looseness. We had got to Cuba.

Well, the war was already over.

Just why we were kept there I do not know.

We were presumed to see that certain Spanish soldiers embarked for Spain.

They were certainly glad enough to go.

We were to quiet certain advances, were sent out on expeditions.

I was on one such expedition. We went out to hunt bandits. We took a cow along.

There was, at the head of our detachment, a certain major. He was, I was told, the son of a rich man.

He had brought his wife to Cuba. He had brought his baby. He had brought the cow to furnish the baby's milk. We took it with us.

We marched slowly. We went with easy strides through a beautiful country. On some days we marched for two hours.

If we saw no bandits they perhaps saw us. We were a very peaceful, a very bucolic army. Sometimes we were in a new camp at ten in the morning and we boys had the afternoons to ourselves.

We went for long strolls through the country. Some of us had picked up a little Spanish. We went into houses. We talked to people. We hired little native ponies and rode through the country and into the hills.

I was for a time very ill.

There was an inadequate medical service and I was near death.

However I recovered. I got up from my bed with my comrades. Once, with two coal miners, of a West Virginia regiment, I went on expeditions.

I met the two miners in the streets of a certain town, near the coast. They had, they said, borrowed a boat.

They had got a file and had filed away a chain.

"We do not intend to steal the boat," they said. "We'll put it back."

"Do you know anything of sailing a boat?" they asked.

I did not know but I had a theory.

"I think we can work it out," I said. We took the boat and sailed away. We went for many miles down the coast. The boat was rather a heavy one, not easy to upset, and, gradually, we did learn, a little, how to handle the sails.

Fortunately the wind was fine and the sea calm. We had put provisions in the boat. Inasmuch as we had borrowed the boat we had set out at night.

We decided to capture a town.

"Why not?" we said.

Others had captured towns and besides we had sighted a town.

It was on the coast. It was a small place. It was inhabited by blacks. It had been, formerly, a plantation town, a workers' village. It had stood at the edge of a great sugar plantation.

The plantation house had been destroyed.

The Cuban army had done that and the owners had fled.

They hadn't yet come back.

We went ashore and one of the coal mining men, who knew a little Spanish, made a speech, a speech answered, with many gestures, by what we took to be the head man of the town. He was a gigantic black. He smiled and presently, rushing to us, he embraced us.

"*Americanos,*" he cried.

There was a great outcry of *vivas* from men and women. There was a kind of universal embracing.

It became later a dance.

We ordered that to be held.

We ordered rum brought.

It may be that the natives of the town, in the absence of their masters, had formed a soviet.

There was a street of thatched huts and our dance was held in the single village street. It lasted most of an afternoon and night. There were bonfires built. A woman, bent with age, a kind of leader among the women, was helped up on a table brought into the street. The table had perhaps been salvaged when the plantation house had been burned. I got up on the table with her. I put my arm about her. We danced. Glasses of wine were handed up to us. We held them aloft. We rent the air with *vivas.*

For America.

For Cuba.

For freedom.

For joy.

I tell you it was a real surrender. They had given us the town and the plantation and we gave it back.

"Take it. Keep it," we said. We declared that we were the messengers of a new day.

It would have been well had our country done, for the island of Cuba, what we did for the town that surrendered to us.[31]

On the Up and Up

I had been a laborer, a farm hand, a soldier, a factory hand. I had managed to get in a winter at college. This was in Springfield, Ohio. It was, at that time, a small Lutheran college. It was called Wittenberg.[32]

Later they called me back there. They gave me a doctor's degree.

It was at the end of the school year and I had to go to work. I was broke.

I had been chosen as the class orator. I delivered a speech on the Jews. I got it all out of books. I spent days in the library, cramming for it.

I made quite a speech. We story tellers are also, almost without exception, actors. I have always envied actors. Oh how I would like to strut the boards.

"Upon what meat does this our Caesar feed, that he has grown so great?"

There was a man who came to hear me speak. He was my brother's friend. He was the advertising manager of the *Woman's Home Companion*. At that time the editorial and business offices of the magazine were

31. On April 21, 1899, Anderson left Cuba on the *Sedgwick* and arrived at Savannah, Georgia, May 2, 1899. Company I left federal service May 24, 1899, and returned to Clyde, Ohio, May 26, 1899.

32. Karl and Stella Anderson were in Springfield, Ohio, when Sherwood returned from the war. He visited them and enrolled for one year in a high-school equivalency course sequence at Wittenberg College.

still in Springfield, Ohio. My brother worked there. Later he became a well known painter but, at that time, he was an illustrator, working for the magazine.

It may be that the advertising man had had a few drinks. The advertising man had a warm and an impulsive nature. I remember that he was a great admirer of the Emperor Napoleon.

He heard my speech and there was a good deal of applause. It came largely from my friends among the students but the advertising man rushed up to me. He embraced me.

"It was grand, magnificent," he said. On the spot he offered me a job. He said there was a vacancy in the western office of the magazine.

"I will send you there," he said. There was something Napoleonic about it all. I had been some of the things set down about. Now I would be a business man. I would have a desk in an office building in a city. I would ride about in trains, travel up and down. I would go into manufacturers' offices. I would wear good clothes. I would become a rising young man.

I did go to the city of Chicago [33] and did have a desk in an office in an office building. There was a woman, a stenographer, to whom I could dictate letters.

Of advertising I knew nothing and at once, when I had got to Chicago and had presented myself to the man, who was western advertising manager for the magazine, I could see and feel that I was not very welcome.

I had been employed off hand. It was a gesture. The man who was to be my new boss had not been consulted. Later, he told me frankly that he had had in mind another man for the job.

He was a man from a big eastern college and was enthusiastic about his college. He wanted a man who had graduated from his college. Perhaps he wanted to offer the job to some football hero. He had himself been a football player.

I was in an uncomfortable position but I did not stay long. Later the man and I had a little talk.

"You do not want me and I do not want to stay.

"Why not teach me the ropes, show me what you can?

---

33. In the summer of 1900, Anderson became a copywriter for the Frank B. White Company, which in 1903 became the Long-Critchfield Company. See *A Story Teller's Story*, ed. White, pp. 190, 214–15, 227, 236, 241–48, 257, 269–70, 285–86, 296. The standard study is William Alfred Sutton, "Sherwood Anderson: The Advertising Years, 1900–1906," *Northwest Ohio Quarterly*, XXII (Summer, 1950), 120–57.

"Why not help me get another job?"

There was a thing happened. It was amusing. I was sent to the office of a certain manufacturer. He had written a letter. Advertising in magazines, it seemed, was sold by what was called the "agate line." I knew very little of that.

I was afraid. I went by train to the town. The man had written saying that he wanted two hundred lines of space in the magazine and a mistake had been made by a stenographer. He wanted two thousand lines.

I was afraid and did not dare go into the office. I approached and went away. I came back and again went away.

I walked about. "Of what are you afraid?" I asked myself.

Formerly I had been employed, as workman, in just such a factory. I was in overalls then. I went in at the factory gate.

At last I did get up courage to enter. I walked timidly in. I can't remember what happened. I stood trembling before the man who had dictated the letter. He must have realized my fright, my confusion.

He was very kind, very good natured. He corrected the stenographic mistake. I did not have to talk. I had a rate card in my pocket and laid it, with trembling hand, on his desk.

He wrote the order and I went away. I breathed again. I went into a bar and bought myself a drink. Perhaps, later, I put it on my expense account. I had got an idea. I sent a wire, not to the company's western manager in Chicago, but to the man, his superior, in the Ohio town, who was an admirer of the Emperor Napoleon.

"I have called upon my first man," I said in the order. "The order was raised from two hundred lines to two thousand lines." I said nothing of the eloquence used in getting the order raised. As suggested I had used none.

I knew little enough of advertising but already, perhaps, my experience, in knocking about, had taught me something of men. I expected and what I expected came true. I returned to Chicago. There was a wire on my new boss' desk. I had got a sharp raise.

Naturally, I did not tell my boss, in the western office, how it had happened. He knew nothing of the wire I had sent. He stood before me with a blank puzzled air. He was temporarily my boss but the man who had sent the wire to him was superior.

"I think he has gone a little crazy," he said, but I only smiled. I thought that, after all, I might manage to make my way, even among the shrewd men of business.

I had become an advertising man. I wrote advertisements. They sent me to towns and cities where there were factories.

For a time it wasn't so bad. I went to a Kentucky town. There was a man who made a machine for digging ditches, for making terraces on hillside land.

I had his catalogue and there was a series of twelve or fifteen advertisements to be written. They were to go into papers read by farmers.

I was in the train going to that town and, as I sat in the train, I wrote the advertisements.

However I did not show them to the man in the Kentucky town. It was, I thought, a nice place to be. When I got to the town I went at once to the factory.

"Look here," I said to the man who made the machine to dig ditches and make terraces. "I cannot do this job off hand.

"This is a serious matter," I said.

He had shown me through his factory.

"A man needs time to think."

I suggested to him that the people in the Chicago office who had sent me to him might want to hurry me.

"You write them a letter. You tell them you want to keep me here for a week."

I was cheating. I was fighting for something. I wanted a little leisure. I wanted to walk about the streets of the Kentucky town, look at people, talk to people. I wanted to sit in the hotel room trying to put down my impressions.

"It is a war. I am fighting for a little time, to mature a little."

Every day I went to the factory, spending an hour there. I went into the office.

"I'm thinking. I want to get this thing just right," I said.

I had gained days and nights, away from the clatter, the eternal nervous rush of the Chicago advertising office. At the end of the week I showed the man the advertisements I had written on the train.

"They're wonderful," he said. He said it showed what could be done if you took your time to do it.

"You're the man for me. You don't just come here, spend an hour or two, rush away on the next train."

Oh, the precious days and nights gained, a chance to walk at night in the streets of an Ohio River town, go and stand on the river banks, talk to men met there.

I had begun to get on. The advertisements I wrote for the Kentucky manufacturer were very successful. I had other successes, got in the same way. My wages were constantly going up.

I began to strut, became for a time a dude. I bought a long black evening coat, such as congressmen wear, got striped trousers, patent leather shoes, a silk hat.

I had a leather case for the silk hat. I bought evening clothes. I carried a cane. I had one of the sort of tall hats that fold up flat.

You snap it and there you are. You can go to the theatre. People will think you are rich, a rich young blade.

On Sunday morning I went to church, to a fashionable preacher who preached in a Loop theatre. The preacher spoke of a settlement, on the West Side, in a poor district. It was a settlement maintained by the fashionable congregation. The preacher said they wanted workers, volunteers, who would go at night to the settlement. There were classes for tough young boys. They wanted teachers, he said.

"All right," I said to myself. "I'll go there, I'll volunteer."

I don't know now just what I had in mind. I wanted to be free. I did not want to work any more in the advertising place. It may be that I thought, "I'll get me a rich girl over there.

"I'm pretty good looking," I may have thought. "And now I've got all of these good clothes."

Anyway I did volunteer. I went there for a time at night, when I was in the city. I went two or three times a week.

And sure enough there the rich girl was.

They had a library and she sat at a desk and gave out books. "She's a pretty good looker," I thought.

She was small and dark. She had black hair and small black eyes. I might have been twenty-two or three and she would have been at least twenty-eight.

However her body still seemed young to me and I began to court her.

I had the class of boys and I was teaching them American history. It was all right. I had read a lot. I read to them.

However they were restless. They kept coming in and going out of the room, where I sat talking and reading aloud.

"What's the matter, kids? Why do you keep coming in and out?"

The kids explained. They wanted to smoke and so did I.

The kids liked me all right. They liked my clothes.

"Gee, you wear swell clothes," one of them said to me.

"I'll bet you're rich," he said.

We could not smoke in the room in the settlement house so I took them outside. This was in the summer and we went along the street, past dark factory buildings, to where there was a high foot bridge over some railroad tracks.

There was a street light up above and we stood on the foot bridge under the light.

I told them about Grant at Vicksburg. I told them about Lee and Stonewall Jackson. I told them about the Mexican War and how we gypped the Mexicans out of the whole southwest. I told them about how we got Texas and how big it was.

And then I got fired. There was an older woman, who ran the settlement house, and she told me I couldn't take the kids out of the house.

"You are encouraging the children in smoking," she said. She said it wasn't allowed.

"Oh, tell her to go to hell," the kids said, but I didn't do that. I quit.

I had, however, got in with my rich girl, had begun to court her hard. At night when the settlement closed I waited for her.

"I'll escort you home," I said.

"But I'm not afraid, I only go to the street car."

She said something that shocked me a little. She said that her father had wanted to send a car to the settlement house for her but that she wouldn't let him.

"It would seem too much like setting myself up above the people down here," she said. I didn't know why her saying that shocked me but it did. For a minute I thought, "Oh the hell with you," but I didn't say it.

I thought, "If I was rich I'd be rich and not pretend I wasn't."

"All right, I'll take you to the street car," I said. I rode home with her in the car. I held her hand. After a time, after a few nights, when we had got to the North Side where she lived, we began to get off the car before we got to her house.

It was a big house, with an iron fence. It was right where all of the richest people in Chicago lived at that time. It was near the lake.

So we walked along.

"Let's go over by the lake," I said.

"No, I must get home," she said but, after I had said it a few times, she went with me. We were there, by the lake and the park, on the hot summer nights. We were walking there. We were sitting on benches. We kissed. After a time we kissed a lot. She was one who when you made her any kind of proposal always said no.

She said no but she didn't mean it. She let me feel her a good deal. We were on a bench in the dark and there were other couples on other benches in the dark.

"It's common. They are just common people," she said.

"Yes, they're common," I said.

"Rich or poor," I said to her, "there are certain common things they do and we do.

"They kiss and we kiss," I said. I kissed her some more.

I decided we should become engaged. When I was with her it was all right but when I had left her I began to question myself.

"Do you want her or do you just think she's rich?" I asked myself.

I didn't know which it was. Her father was at the head of a big wholesale house in the city so I looked him up. There was a Dunn and Bradstreet book in the office where I worked and I went to that. He was rich all right.

She had already told me that there were only two children in her family, herself and a sister. "I'm twenty-three," she said, "and Sister is eighteen.

"When you see my sister you won't want me," she said. I thought she had clipped about five years off of her age. Her sister's name, she said, was Agnes.

I kept at her. I had got started and didn't stop and for a time she kept saying no and then, one night, she said she would.

"All right. I guess maybe I'll marry you, I'm not sure," she said. She had her head on my shoulder as we sat on a park fence and when she said it, in a kind of low frightened voice, she began to cry.

I thought, "I do love her. I do. I do."

She said she'd have to take me to her house. I'd have to come and live there. I'd have to meet her father and her sister. Her mother she said was dead.

"You'll have to get acquainted and then you'll have to ask father. It'll be up to him," she said.

So I dressed up in my evening clothes and I went to that house. I had a close shave. I had my hair cut. I was pretty near an hour picking out a necktie to wear.

I had bought a tuxedo.

"Shall I wear it?" I asked myself. First I decided I would and then that I wouldn't. I did wear it at last.

She had told me to get there at seven but I got there at six, so I took a walk. It had got to be late fall and it was already nearly dark.

I walked about, up and down. I looked at houses. I thought, "Maybe, someday, we'll live in one of these houses."

I remembered the little yellow house, by the swamp, where I had spent so much of my boyhood, in the town of Clyde in Ohio, the gravelly back yard where nothing would grow. I remembered my mother, grown so tall and thin, always at the wash tub, washing other people's dirty clothes to get the money to feed her children. I remembered her sudden death from exposure that had brought on pneumonia and how I had planned to someday get rich and buy a big house and a carriage for her. And then I remembered myself, working as a day laborer down by the river on that same Chicago North Side.

And now there I was, in evening clothes, all shaved and perfumed, and I was going to dine in a millionaire's house. I was going to ask him for his daughter's hand.

Someday, I'd be rich myself. I'd have a big house, like the houses along that street. I'd have servants to wait on me. I'd ride about in a big car with a chauffeur.

And then it was seven o'clock and I went to the door of the house and rang the bell.

A butler in a uniform let me in and I had to wait for quite a long time and then the rich man came.

He was a little man and kept tipping up on his toes. He was trying to make himself feel taller than he was. He had a little red face, a small nose and he had a bald patch over the top of his head. There were a few hairs growing above his ears and they had been carefully brushed over the bald place but they didn't cover it much.

He came and sat with me.

"Well, well, young man," he said.

"Let's see, did you come here to see Ruth or is it Agnes?

"Are you going to stay to dinner?"

He kept talking. He took a gold watch from his pocket.

"What's your prospects, young man, what's your prospects?" he asked but he didn't wait for an answer.

He held the gold watch in his hand and got up and came to me. He stood before me.

"It strikes," he said. He had moved the hands around to eight o'clock and a sharp little sound came from the watch. It struck eight times.

"My employees gave it to me on my birthday," he said. "It cost a lot of money. Do you want to hear it strike again?"

Ruth came into the room, dressed pretty swell, in a low necked dress, and then Agnes came and right away I began to have a hard time keeping my eyes from staring at her.

She wasn't specially dressed up as Ruth was. She was tall, strong looking and a blonde. She had bluish-grey eyes. I thought the moment she came into the room that she wasn't any more like Ruth than I was like her father.

"Ruth's been telling her about us," I thought and I had a feeling of resentment and fear. The moment I saw Agnes I knew she was the kind of woman I'd like a lot.

I'd been sitting there thinking about the two girls' father. He was a rich man, a millionaire.

"He must sure have inherited the business he's in," I had been thinking. I wondered who ran it for him. I was pretty young then but I had noticed something. I was working in that advertising place.

They sent me out, to some man, some manufacturer. There I was, hardly more than a kid. I went in to such a man.

I began telling him about his business, what he should do. If he had been advertising I told him that the way he was doing it was all wrong.

And some of them listened to me. They tried doing what I told them to do. Sometimes I used to think that if I were such a manufacturer and such a kid as I was then came in and talked as I had talked I'd have kicked him out.

So there was this man, in his rich man's house, with his trick watch. He was like an old child.

There was all kinds of expensive furniture in the room and there were oil paintings on the wall.

The little millionaire didn't pay any attention to his daughters. He concentrated on me. He began leading me around the room, explaining the oil paintings to me. He told me how much each one cost.

There was a big one of a nude woman. He winked at me when we came to that. "It cost thirty thousand dollars. Think of that, thirty thousand," he said.

I didn't know what to say. I looked at the two daughters. I could see that Ruth was annoyed but that Agnes was amused. There was laughter in her eyes.

"It's all right to have a nude like that in your house if it's by some famous painter," the millionaire was assuring me.

"Oh father, do come and sit," Ruth said.

"Quit talking," she said.

I could see that she was sore at him.

"She's got a temper," I thought. I liked Agnes for being amused. "I'll bet she wouldn't go to any settlement house or try to do good to people like Ruth's been doing," I thought. Once when I had been on my way home from the settlement house with Ruth she had begun talking about what a noble impulse it was in me that I had come to the settlement house to help teach the kids and I had wanted to laugh.

"Oh I guess I just did it for an adventure, to see what it would be like," I had said to her.

And then I had said something—a kind of half truth—about having gone over there hoping to find some woman like her.

"Maybe I'm just after a rich one, like you," I said and that had started her off.

She had got very serious about it. She scolded me. She said she didn't think I should deny my own noblest impulses.

She said something about devoting her own life to the working classes.

"But if I was rich I'd just be rich," I said. I said that if what she called the working classes ever got anywhere they'd have to do it themselves. I was going on like that and then, when I saw she was really getting sore, I let up on her.

This was on a street car when I was riding home from the settlement with Ruth and it was on a street car that I lost her and lost the chance to be the son-in-law of the millionaire.

Over at the house that night, during the dinner and afterwards, as we sat about and tried to talk, the little millionaire kept cutting up his capers. He kept making the watch strike for me. All evening he kept the watch in his hand and when the talk died down (Ruth was doing most of the talking. She was acting nervous. She was ashamed of her father. Agnes said hardly a word but her eyes kept laughing.), when the talk died down the father explained about the watch.

"They gave it to me. My employees gave it to me," he said. "It cost a lot of money, hundreds of dollars, but my employees gave it to me," he added. He kept saying it but afterwards I found out that he had little or nothing to do with running the business with which his name was connected. He had inherited the business from his father and it was run by other men. Someone told me. The man who told me said the others flattered the little millionaire, that they pretended to consult him. When I told the man about the watch he laughed.

"They did it to make him feel important," he said. He said he guessed that the men who ran the business made the employees chip in for the watch.

I was there that night to ask the man if I could marry his daughter Ruth but I didn't do it. She may have said something to him as I was sure she had to Agnes. Every once in a while, that evening, he would come over to me.

"What's your prospects, young man? What's your prospects?" he kept asking but I didn't answer him. I couldn't. Every time he asked it I could see that Agnes getting more and more amused and Ruth getting more annoyed and angry.

And so, after a time, I left. I was at the door and the little man was standing with the watch in his hand and there were Agnes and Ruth. I could feel that Ruth wanted to hit her father and that Agnes wanted to laugh at all of us.

I left. I was outside in the street. I began to laugh at myself.

"Great God," I thought. I tried to imagine myself married to Ruth and living in that big house with her father.

"If it was Agnes now," I thought. I thought that if I had got a start with Agnes before I met Ruth and, if I had the luck to have her take a fancy to me, we could have had a lot of fun. "She's one of that sort that can be onto herself and others," I thought. Agnes, I figured, was stuck with Ruth and her father. She could, I was pretty sure, be kind to them, but at the same time, I thought, she would be one who could get some fun out of it all.

I had asked Ruth to marry me so I thought I'd better see her again and I had her downtown to dine with me and it was a most uncomfortable dinner. "Shall I tell her it's all off?" I kept asking myself but I put it off and then, when it came time for her to go home, she wouldn't take a taxi.

It was some kind of an idea she had got into her head. She wanted to be one of the common people. She said something like that.

"No," she said. "You mustn't be spending your money on me." You see I had told her, on other evenings, of how, when I had first come to the city, I had to work as a laboring man. I had even pointed out places where I had worked.

"I had to live and try to keep my sister and two younger brothers on two dollars a day," I had said to her. I had rather spread it on, made it as thick as I could, and now I think that she, in allowing me to kiss her, in agreeing to the engagement between us, had thought that, by marrying me, she would herself become what she thought she longed to be—one of the people.

I may have got that thought that night when I was at her father's house or I may have got it later, on the night when she was dining with me. At any rate I had the thought and when I had it I began to think of Agnes.

"She would have known," I thought. In fancy I could hear Ruth telling her of our engagement and explaining why she wanted to marry me. It had been the reason Agnes was so amused when I came to the house.

I was in the street with Ruth and we were waiting for her street car and when it came, bound for the North Side, it was crowded with men. It had been raining while we dined but the rain had stopped. There was a crowd of men, working men I thought, on the platform at the rear of the car and we were being jostled about.

There was a man stepped on the toe of Ruth's shoe. It may be that I had made her angry. She wanted me and she knew she didn't. In the restaurant, when we were dining, she had said something about myself and Agnes.

"You liked her?" she asked, and "Yes, a lot," I had answered.

It had set me off. I had been thinking that I ought to tell her then that, after all, perhaps we had better not marry but I couldn't get up the courage.

So I had talked of Agnes.

"There is something about her that reminds me of my mother," I said. I had said that and had launched off, describing a kind of woman I thought Agnes might be, one, I said, who even if she had to lead a life of hardship, instead of being a millionaire's daughter, would be bound to have some fun out of life.

"You know," I had said, "the kind that knows something of what is going on among the people around, the kind that is onto you but you don't care if she is."

I had kept going like that and, as it gave me something to talk about, I had kept it up. I had been at it in the restaurant and I was still at it as we stood in the wet street waiting for the car.

It had been all about Agnes, all about what I thought Agnes' kind of woman to be, and she had grown more and more angry but I hadn't noticed. I was too absorbed with what I was saying.

And then we were on the rear platform of that car and there were a lot of working men, who have to wear the same clothes day after day, and they smelled pretty rank after the rain.

They stank. They were pushing and shoving.

"There you are, gal. Now you are one of the people. How do you like it?" I was thinking. I may even have given her a shove or two myself. And then the big man stepped on her foot.

He was big all right. He was in greasy overalls and he was standing on her foot and she grew suddenly furious. There was something in her that came out with a rush.

"You big brute," she cried. She began to swear. "She sure has become one of the people now," I thought. "Goddamn you, get off of my feet," she screamed. She kept on screaming and all the men on the platform began to laugh at her.

The big man who was standing on her foot was laughing and it made her so angry that she began to strike at him with her fists.

"Goddamn you. Goddamn you," she was screaming. "She must have learned to swear like that over at that settlement house," I thought. I had got into a kind of joyous ironic mood. I wished her sister Agnes was there.

"But Agnes wouldn't be enjoying this as I am doing. She'd be too decent," I thought.

What else I thought I don't know. It was the end of my chance to be the rich man's son-in-law. While she was standing there, on the crowded platform of the car, striking with her little fists at the big man, a worker, who was laughing at her, I had dropped off of the car and I never saw her again.

A Chance Missed

Whenever a new writer begins a little to come into prominence, at least in the literary world, the critics do strange things to him.

First of all they overpraise him. It is understandable enough. It is a boring job, this sitting at a desk, day after day, reading and passing judgment on other men's work.

Think, for example, of the man who becomes the literary critic for a daily newspaper. Some of them actually write of a new book every day.

To be sure it doesn't take long to pass on most books. You pick the book up, read a page, five pages, ten pages. It doesn't take much reading to find out whether or not a writer can write. A bit of originality, a flair for words—you are not asking too much. That curious inexplainable thing, the hidden music in prose, the overtone, the quality in real writing that sets your imagination flying off on a journey of its own, you'll not find that appearing very often.

The critic is fed up on commonplace books. A book comes that is a little alive. It is a good story telling.

You cannot blame the critic if he throws his hat into the air, begins to shout. Very likely he overdoes it. When my own first novel was published I was compared in the *New York Times* to Dostoevsky.[34]

"An American Dostoevsky," something of that sort.

To be sure I liked it but, at the same time, it made me secretly ashamed. The book, I felt, didn't come off. I felt that the book was, largely, a result of my reading of other novelists. I hadn't, as yet, turned directly to the life about me. It was an immature book, not completely felt, full of holes and bad spots. In a later edition of the same book I rewrote the whole latter part of it.

I had been a laboring man, then an advertising writer, then a manufacturer. I had not got the slant on business I got later. There was an upward and onward note in all the early pages of the book, a boy, coming out of an Iowa corn shipping town, to rise in the business world, that fitted into the American mood of the day.

The book sold well. It was praised by many critics. They did not like the ending but neither did I.

I had made my man, who had risen a little in the world of affairs, come to a place where he had begun to feel sharply the futility of his life.

I didn't know what to do with him.

A man, from the Curtis Publishing Company, came out to Chicago to see me.

Once, several years earlier, I had been visited by Mr. Curtis himself.

It was an exciting adventure. Mr. Curtis, with his *Saturday Evening Post, Ladies' Home Journal* and the newly founded *Country Gentleman,* was a gigantic figure in our Chicago world of advertising.

The advertising agency that was then employing me as a copy writer

---

34. See *The New York Times Book Review,* October 8, 1916, p. 423.

published a little house organ of its own and I had written a piece praising the life of the business man.[35]

It was quite sincere. But a few years earlier I had been a laborer, working at very heavy work in a cold storage warehouse over by the Chicago River.

And then I had got this place, in the advertising agency. To be sure I had got it through an accident but I had it. I had always a kind of flair for words and began to get on. I wore good clothes, dined in expensive restaurants, had begun to learn to drink wine and have women.

It seemed to me that business had done all this for me and I was grateful.

So I wrote, in our little company magazine, praising the business life, speaking highly of business men, and one day Mr. Curtis himself, in person, appeared at the door of our agency.

There was great excitement. Messages flew back and forth.

"It's Mr. Curtis himself."

There was a rumor in the office later that one of the women stenographers—she was the president's personal secretary—that she. . . .

But perhaps I had better not report the story. It may not be true. Perhaps someone just spilled a glass of water on the floor by the president's desk. She had been sitting there taking letters. She might have arisen suddenly, knocked over the glass of water.

Anyway there was Mr. Curtis himself, holding in his hand a copy of our little house organ. As he passed along the hallway heads popped out of offices.

"Hush. Be silent. It is Mr. Curtis."

The general opinion, later reported, was that he was angry. Someone had written something in our magazine that had offended him. He darted into our president's office and laid the magazine on the table before our president. It was open to the little article I had written.

35. Anderson's earliest writing was columns in advertising trade journals: *Agricultural Advertising* published "The Farmer Wears Clothes," IX (February, 1902), 6; "We Would Be Wise," X (January, 1903), 45–46; ten "Rot and Reason" items from February through December, 1903. In *The Reader,* Anderson published "A Business Man's Reading," III (October, 1903), 503–4; and "The Man and the Book," III (December, 1903), 71–73. From January to October, 1904, *Agricultural Advertising* carried ten "Business Types" items, followed by "The Fussy Man and the Trimmer," XI (December, 1904), 79, 81–82; "The Sales Master and the Selling Organization," XXII (April, 1905), 306–8; "Advertising a Nation," XXII (May, 1905), 389; and "Making It Clear," XXIV (February, 1913), 16. On the advertising years, see also Donald M. Wright, "A Mid-western Ad Man Remembers," *Advertising and Selling,* XXVIII (December 17, 1936), 35, 68.

"Who wrote that?" he demanded to know, pointing to the article. It was unsigned.

Our president, at that time a Mr. Long, did not know. He was a little frightened. It would not do for our agency to incur the wrath of the great Curtis Publishing Company.

"Why Mr. Curtis, I do not know. I'll find out. What is wrong with it, Mr. Curtis?"

"Why nothing is wrong with it. It's all right. It's fine. What I want is for you to find out who wrote it and send the man to me.

"I want that man."

Mr. Curtis had left our agency. He was gone but my own stock had gone up. For a time it soared. It all resulted in my taking a trip to Philadelphia, where I had a talk with Mr. Curtis and was offered a position as an editorial writer for the *Saturday Evening Post,* a position I did not accept.[36]

Just why I did not accept I did not at that time know. The Curtis Publishing Company was so big. It may have a little terrorized me.

Or perhaps already I had begun to be a little afraid of all bigness, didn't want to be a big shot.

Or I may have begun to look a little ahead. I had, I knew, a certain knack with words. Something may have told me that the life I was in, the booster's life, wasn't what I wanted.

I had that chance and lost it and then came another. I had published my first novel, the one spoken of above, and a man from the Curtis office came to see me.

It was a Sunday morning and I went to meet the man at the Blackstone Hotel. We were in a room in the hotel.

"We want novels, such as you started to write when you wrote *Windy McPherson's Son.*

"We can pay well for what we want.

"We felt that the last part of your novel wasn't what we wanted.

"In all the first part of your novel there is a fresh note. As for the later part, the ending. . . .

"In such novels that can of course be corrected.

"We feel you stumbled there."

"Yes," I said. "I guess I did."

It was what interested me, that "stumbling."

36. Cyrus H. K. Curtis (1850–1933), publisher of *The Saturday Evening Post,* 1891–1969.

I was trying to think and feel my way through a man's life. I wanted it to come to some satisfactory end for him as I would like my own life to come to some satisfactory end.

I think that, on that morning, in the hotel room, I tried to explain. Now that I think of it there were, I'm sure, two men present from the Curtis house. I had got into the writing of novels and stories in a curious way. I had not begun by thinking of myself as a writer. I do not yet think of myself so. There is something of the eternal amateur in me. I wanted if I could to clear up certain traits in myself. There was in me, there had always been in me, a certain slickness and foxiness. It is in me yet, has always been there.

I had been going about saying something to myself.

You see, there I was. I had come, from a small town, to the city. I had been a laborer, doing heavy manual labor for two dollars a day.

I had risen out of that. Now I was an advertising writer.

Even as a young boy I had always known, in the darkness of nights, that I was a bit too slick, too plausible.

Only a few days before the Curtis people came to see me that time a friend, Marco Morrow,[37] at the time working in the office with me, had said (no doubt I had put something over on him), "Sherwood, you are, now and then, just too damn slick, too plausible."

I had always been putting things over on my own brothers and sister. I knew it.

"All right. It may be a part of my nature but, if it is true of me, I'd like to face it.

"I wouldn't so much mind being a crook if I knew I was a crook.

"What is horrible is to be a crook and not know it.

"I would like, if I could, to at least develop in myself an honest mind."

I had been a laborer. Well, I did not like that. I wanted money and it cannot be got in that way.

There is no doubt that in all business, as in politics, a certain slickness is demanded. The advertising world into which I had got was full of it. In order to get money I had to give myself to that slickness.

And I wanted money because I wanted good clothes. I wanted to go to

---

37. Anderson met Marco Morrow (d. 1956) at Wittenberg College in 1899–1900. Morrow worked with Anderson in advertising in Chicago and finally became editor of Capper Publications. See *A Story Teller's Story*, ed. White, p. 267; and *Letters*, ed. Jones and Rideout, Items 148, 226, *passim*.

the theatre, sit in a good seat, drive a good car. I wanted to live in a comfortable, if possible a beautiful house, eat good food. I was the kind of man Mr. Bernard Shaw had described as "a simple soul, perfectly satisfied with the best of everything." [38]

But I had thought of my writing as a little outside all that. When I felt that I had dirtied the life about me, had made myself dirty with my slickness, I could not understand what made me feel dirty.

I had discovered something. I had discovered that I could, in writing, throw an imagined figure against a background of some of my own experiences—a thing all writers must do—and through the imagined figure get sometimes a kind of slant on some of my own questionable actions.

I doubt that it ever reformed me. It did give me a certain satisfaction.

I was there in the room with the two men from the house of Curtis. I tried to explain. No doubt I made a mess of it. I do not think I made them understand what I was driving at.

"But we can pay well. We pay for what we want."

It was true and how I wanted money.

"Do you play golf?"

The two men both said they did.

"You enjoy doing it just for the sake of doing it, not for money."

You see how confusing this is. I am always crabbing at my publishers because they do not make more money for me.

Dave: A Man Afraid

I have often wondered if there are many such business men. We were a small advertising agency and he came and made us a large one.

He seemed, at first, a rather sleepy, even stupid young man. He was in the bookkeeping department. He was always wanting to match pennies, nickels or quarters. He was a born trader. He traded jack knives and watches. He offered to trade neckties with you.

He was with our agency for a time and then went to another but, after a few years, he came back. I have no way of knowing how he did it. He had,

38. George Bernard Shaw (1856–1950), British dramatist mentioned in *A Story Teller's Story*, ed. White, p. 80; Anderson uses here *Pygmalion* (1913).

in the other place, learned something the head men of our agency did not know. Often I have thought that many of the big men of American finance must have been like Dave.

As he had once traded jack knives and watches, he now began to trade in shares of stock. He was a great talker. Once I heard one of the men he had victimized say of him that he could have talked birds down out of trees.

There was a sudden confusion in the office, whispered conferences always going on. He began hiring new men, filling the place with new men and presently, I never knew by what hook or crook, he had got into control.

It was a parade. Drums were being beaten. There was noise and shouting. Sometimes men, who had been in the place a long time and whose work had always seemed satisfactory enough, were suddenly fired.

"I do it to put the fear of God in them," Dave said. "Now and then you've got to fire a man, kick him out. You see, it keeps them on their toes."

Our agency grew and grew. It became, for a time, one of the big, the important advertising agencies of the west. Dave was driving a big car. He was flying about over the country. New and bigger accounts kept coming in.

"That is a good job you have done. Your salary is raised, a thousand a year."

Or.

"I told you to get that account. You didn't get it. You're fired."

There had been something quiet and peaceful about the place but now everyone was continually nervously alert. We were all frightened. We cursed him and feared him.

He was himself filled with odd fears. It may be that, in getting control of our agency, he had done something that was unlawful and was afraid of being found out. I wouldn't know about that. Rumors of something of the sort were constantly being whispered behind closed doors.

We were getting bigger and bigger. There must have been a good deal of money being made.

Once I was called into Dave's office. It was a large office, beautifully furnished. He sat behind a big flat top desk.

He had grown fat.

"You don't belong in this place," he said. "You have contempt for us.

"I ought to fire you," he said.

He took a revolver from a drawer of his desk.

"I ought to shoot you," he said.

He pointed the gun at me.

"Are you not afraid I might accidentally shoot you?" he said.

He put the gun away and laughed but there was something wrong with his laughter. I think it was then I realized how full of fear he was. He took a sudden trip to Europe but he did not stay long. Once I was with him and several others on a fishing trip into the northern woods. He knew I was not ambitious to be a big shot as an advertising man. We were out together in a boat and he spoke of it.

"You could get rich," he said. "I could make you rich."

"But I do not want to go to the trouble of getting rich," I said.

He began to swear at me.

"I've a notion to upset this boat," he said. We were far out from shore. "I could upset the boat and we would both drown," he declared.

"Shall I do it?" he asked, and "Yes," I said.

He began to row toward the shore. He kept swearing at me.

"Goddamn you, you want me to think you are not afraid but I know better," he said. I am sure I had nothing of the sort in mind.

He was at that camp for two days and then he suddenly left us. He rushed back to the office.

He started on an automobile trip to the Pacific Coast with a party of friends but left them at Kansas City. Again he took a fast train back to the office.

"He is afraid that, while he is away, someone will have our expert examine the books of the company," a man who was one of the stock holders said to me.

He knew I had been to Europe [39] and that time, when he went across, he again hurried back. He had a day in Paris, a day in London and then he took a fast boat back to America and the office.

Again he had me into his office.

"When you went to Europe were you afraid?" he asked.

I did not know what he meant.

"Afraid of what?"

"Of the water, so much water.

"I was sick with fear," he cried. "It was so with me all the way over and

39. Anderson first visited Europe in 1921 as the guest of Paul Rosenfeld, again in 1926, and finally in 1932. See *A Story Teller's Story*, ed. White, pp. 139, 286, 307–17.

back. It was terrible. I trembled. I shook. I was so ill with fear I thought I would die.

"And you are telling me you were not afraid?"

"No," I said. "I was not afraid.

"I did not think of it," I said and "Liar," he shouted.

He stood behind his desk shouting and cursing me.

"You are a goddamn liar. You were afraid. You were, you were."

He ordered me out of his office.

When Dave died he was still a young man. He died suddenly. He was taken with some minor illness and the fear of death fastened upon him. He died of fear.

We all went to his funeral. We came away. Life in the office went on. For a time we had seemed about to become one of the great, the powerful advertising agencies of the country but with Dave's death the spark was gone.

There was no one to put fear into us. We slumped. Presently we became what we had been before Dave came to us, a rather small agency.

We used to speak about it a good deal.

"Of what was he afraid?" we kept asking each other.

It was a problem we were never able to solve.

His Chest of Drawers

We worked in the same advertising office for several years, both being copy men, our desks being beside each other and, from time to time, he confided in me, telling me many little secrets of his life. He was a small, very slender and delicately built man, who couldn't have weighed over a hundred and twenty pounds, and he had very small hands and feet, a little black mustache, a mass of blue-black hair and a narrow chest.

That was one of his difficulties and he frequently spoke of it.

"Look at me," he said. "How can I ever get on in business? How can I ever rise?"

Saying this he arose and walked over to my desk. He slapped himself on the chest.

"I want space and spread there," he said. "The world is full of stuffed shirts and what chance have I? I have no place to wear a shirt front."

Although he was a son of Spanish descent, with much of the sensitivity and the pride of the Spaniard, my friend's name was Bill. When I first knew him, he had been married for several years and he was the father of four children, all girls. He spoke of this occasionally.

"It's a little tough," he said. He was a devout Catholic and once confided to me that it had been his ambition to be a priest. "I wanted to be a Jesuit priest," he said, "but I got married.

"Not," he added, "that I would have you think I have anything against my wife." He thought that we men should honor women.

"You look at me now. I know well enough that I am insignificant looking. A woman marries such a man as myself. She bestows her favors upon him. He would be an ungrateful man if he complained but you take the life of a priest now, he cannot marry, you see. He can be small or he can be large. He is respected by his people."

With Bill it was as it was with all of us who were writers of advertising copy.

There were other men, also employed by the advertising agency which employed us, who were called "solicitors." Nowdays I believe they are called "contact men." These men, having to bring in clients, keep them satisfied, convince them that we, who wrote their copy, were men of talent, quite extraordinary men, had, of course, to put up a front. They were provided with private offices, often expensively furnished, they arrived and departed, seemingly at will, did not have to ring time clocks, went off for long afternoons of golf with some client, while we copy men, herded together as we were in one room, away at the back, a room that looked out upon a lofty building, through the windows of which we could see rows of women sewing busily away, making men's pants, felt all the time that we were the ones who kept the whole institution going. We kept speaking of it to each other.

"We furnish the brains, don't we? If we don't who does?

"Surely it isn't these other guys, these stuffed shirts, out there in front," we said.

In our agency, as in all such institutions, there was an occasional flurry. One or another of us, in the copy department, had prepared, for some advertiser, a series of advertisements that were taken, by one of the salesmen, to the client. He dismissed them with a wave of his hand.

"They are no good," he said and, when this happened, we copy men burned with inner anger.

"I guess the guy's got indigestion," we said. As for our own work, or the work of others in our department, we never spoke ill of that. The man, the client, simply didn't know good work when he saw it.

Or it was the fault of the salesman, the contact man. It was his business to sell our work. If he couldn't do that, what good was he? Why was he provided with a private office, why permitted to lead a life of leisure, while we, poor slaves that we were, had to do all of the work?

We used to get ourselves all heated up over these things and, occasionally, when we thought that it had got too thick, one or another of us went off on a binge. It was a thing to be expected and, for the most part, it was overlooked but once, when it happened to Bill, at a time when a client, whose work he had long been doing, had suddenly appeared in the city and it was felt that he was badly needed, I was sent to look for him and, if possible, to straighten him out. It was understood that the client could be stalled overnight.

"You find him and sober him up. You get him in here," they said to me.

And so I went to find Bill and, knowing something of his habits, I did find him. He was in a certain saloon, run by a brother Spaniard, and when I found him he was leaning against a bar, a group of men, for whom he was buying drinks, gathered about, and he was delivering a talk on the position of small men in a civilization that, as he said, judged everything by size.

I had got Bill out of that place and we were in a Turkish bath and he was in a solemn mood.

"You think you know the reason why I got drunk but you don't," he said. He began to explain. He said that, this time, his getting drunk had nothing to do with affairs at the office.

"There is a greater tragedy in my life," he said. We were in the hot room in the bath and as the sweat ran in streams from our bodies he explained that, while his size, his inability, as he had often said, to wear a big shirt front, had, as I well knew, been a handicap to him in business, I had perhaps not known that the same handicap had operated against him in his home.

"It's true," he said, shaking his head solemnly. "You see, my house is overrun with females." He explained that, being unable, because of his handicaps, to make a big salary, he was compelled to live in a small house in a certain suburb.

"You know," he said, "that I have a wife and four daughters." His daughters were rapidly growing up. "I have given up having a son," he said and went into a long explanation of how, his house being small and the closet space therefore somewhat limited, he had been compelled (he had thought it the only decent thing to do) to cut down on his own wardrobe.

"What's the use of buying clothes to put on a little runt like me?" he asked and added that, as his daughters were growing up, he had needed all the money he could spare to buy clothes for them.

"I guess they've got to get husbands. I've got to give them a break."

He explained that in following out this policy he had gradually given up using any closet space in his house and that for two or three years had confined himself, in this matter of space in which to put his clothes, to a certain chest of drawers and, as he talked on, becoming all the time more earnest, I came to understand that the chest of drawers had become a kind of symbol to him.

It had come to the point where the chest of drawers had begun to mean everything in the world to him. He was sure I couldn't understand and said that no man, not put in the position he was in, living as he did in a house with five females, all of whom he declared he profoundly respected, could ever understand.

It had gone on so, in his house, for several years but, some several weeks before, his eldest daughter had become engaged. She had been getting a wardrobe together and one day, when he came home, he had found the top drawer to his chest of drawers gone.

He had stood for that. "I guess the girl has to have the clothes," he said. He hadn't even complained.

And then, two days before, his wife's mother had come on a visit and he had lost the second drawer in the chest.

"It was a hard dose to swallow but I swallowed it," he said.

His wife, whom he kept declaring was a good woman ("I don't want you to think I am criticizing her," he said), had been, he presumed, doing the best she could. She had taken his things, his shirts, underwear, etc., except what he needed from day to day, and had put them in a box. "She put it under the bed," he said and added that, on the evening when he had gone home and had found the second drawer to the chest gone, he hadn't said a word.

"I didn't say a word but, when we were at dinner that evening, and, when I was trying to take a boiled potato out of a dish, to put it on my wife's mother's plate, I was so wrought up and my hand trembled so that, when I had it nicely balanced on a fork and was just going to put it on her plate, it fell off and into a bowl of gravy."

He said it splashed gravy all over one of his eldest daughter's new dresses.

It made his wife sore because she thought he had been drinking when he hadn't at all.

And then it had come to the evening before. A sister of his wife had come. He thought the women had become excited because his eldest daughter had become engaged. They were gathering in. "I guess to look at the guy," he said.

He had gone home and to his chest of drawers, to the last drawer of his chest of drawers, and it was gone.

"But no," he said, "I want to be fair. It wasn't all gone." His wife had left him half of the last drawer. He thought his wife had done the best she could. She should, he thought, have married a salesman, not a little runt of a copy man, such as he was.

"I think we ought to treat our women with respect," he said.

"After all," he added, "they do bestow their favors upon us.

"I just looked at the drawer a moment and then I came away. I took a train back to town, I got drunk.

"Why not?" he asked. He thought that sometimes, when a man was drunk, he could get temporarily the illusion that he cut some figure in life.[40]

Pastoral

The most unforgettable man I think I have ever known was a country doctor, a little quiet seeming man going busily from house to house in his middle western town and through the nearby country. He had parked his car, an old Ford, beside a country road and had found a new variety of mushroom in a wood. There was a book on mushrooms in the car, another on birds, one on trees, and others on insects and wild flowers. I had a job as

40. Published (revised) in *Household Magazine*, XXXIX (August, 1939), 4–5; and in *The Sherwood Anderson Reader*, edited by Paul Rosenfeld (Boston: Houghton Mifflin Company, 1947), pp. 831–35.

an advertising writer and went often to his town. I wrote catalogues, booklets and pamphlets for a manufacturer of the town and often stayed for a week or two at a time.

I became ill and the doctor was sent for. He was a fat undersized man, of forty-five, a man with a big head, thin yellow hair that had begun to turn grey, and pale blue eyes. I was in the town's one hotel and the doctor had been sent to me by the manufacturer. I had been told that he was the best doctor in town, that he had an immense practise.

"But don't think you can get anything out of him. He won't talk much," the manufacturer had said.

The doctor came. There was a certain book, by an old and little read author, lying on a table by my bed.

The doctor had examined me. He had said little or nothing and his silence had begun to annoy me. I was about to break forth, demand that he tell me something definite concerning my illness when he suddenly picked up the book.

He became excited. An exclamation burst from his lips. He began walking up and down the room. The author of the book was the one author whose books he read. You occasionally met such a one. He was a one author man, and I had, by chance, hit upon his one venture into the field of imaginative literature. It created a bond between us. He said that he had never before met another man who read his author and that he thought the author must have been a very great man. "What things he did. Into how many strange places he went.

"And couldn't he talk to people. Right away they told him the strangest things."

The little doctor was one of the silent men you sometimes meet who, once they begin to talk, let out a flood of words. He said that in his opinion there never could have been such another author in the world.

He became embarrassed. "But how foolish of me to talk," he said. He explained that when he was a young man in college another had given him one of the author's books and that since he had become a doctor he had found little time for reading. "I go back to his books," he said. "On many nights I cannot sleep and I have one of his books with me by my bed.

"Or I am with a patient who is very ill. I can't go away. There is nothing I can do. I have one of the books in my car. I read it as I wait for death to come. It is foolish of me to say that he is one of the great authors of the world when I read no others."

My own illness amounted to nothing but the doctor and I became friends. I often drove with him. He had an office on the second floor of an old two storied brick building on the main street of his town, a place of some four thousand people, the office got to by climbing an outside stairway. During the hours he had set aside for his office practise, the large waiting room, poorly furnished, was always filled with people. There was the large waiting room and, facing the street, an inner office where he saw his patients.

The doctor had a large country practise and, except for the hours spent seeing people in his office, was seldom in town and I got the habit of riding about with him. It was a chance for him to speak of the adventures of his author. He had read the same man's books over and over. There was one of the books that was autobiographical and that was his favorite. It was evident that he had read it so often and with such absorption that the adventures of the writer, many of which I had thought rather unreal, no more than palatable lies, were as real to the doctor as though they had happened to himself.

I began seeing the doctor more and more, often when I visited his town doing my own work in my room at the hotel at night so that I could be free to ride with him during the day. He was one of the small outwardly quiet but inwardly intensely active men you sometimes meet who constantly amaze you by the amount of work they can do. He never seemed to tire. He was in his office, seeing people, one after another. He seemed always to go direct to the point. He was with all of his patients as he had been with me in the hotel room. He took the patient's pulse, his blood pressure, his temperature. He sat for a moment in silence looking at the patient. He had got, in the town and in all the country about, the reputation of being infinitely wise. There was the little stretch of time, often three or four minutes, when he sat thus, staring directly at the patient. If the patient spoke, began to ask questions, he did not answer. He could give, more than any other man I have ever known, the impression of being alone with his own thoughts in the presence of others. After staring thus, at the man or woman sitting before him, he smiled or frowned. If he was seeing a patient in the country he took some medicine from his medicine case or, if in town, wrote a prescription. In some way, the belief had spread that he was a wonderful diagnostician. "It is all nonsense," he once said to me. "All I know is that most people who are sick want to be sick. You humor them, take them seriously for a time. Why not? It helps." At times, without ever saying so, he gave the impression of being very contemptuous of people. He was going along the street and when people spoke to him he did not answer. He would look directly at the one addressing him as he looked at his patients, as though absorbed in his own thoughts, not answering the salutations, and when I first knew him I was surprised that he was not disliked.

He wasn't. He was admired. "He is a great student," people said. The town was full of stories of his wide reading in the literature of his profession. Whether or not he did such reading I never knew. The people knew also of his intense interest in nature. They seemed to have decided that this too was a part of the wide knowledge that enabled him at times to make what seemed to them quite marvelous cures. They looked admiringly at him going along the streets. "I wish I had that man's education," one man said to another.

Our talks, when on rare occasions we did talk, were always of the life of the author whose book he had found in my room. It seemed at times as though the only reason the man had for wanting my company was to speak of the life and adventures of the writer. He told me nothing of his own life and did not seem curious about mine. There was this one point of contact, the adventures of another written into a book. I kept trying to break into the doctor's long periods of silence, occasionally asking him questions about his work or his patients, but got no answers. Sometimes I was amused, and at times when I was with him, I grew impatient and irritated. "If he did not want me with him why did he come to my hotel for me?" I asked myself. We were driving on a country road when he suddenly stopped the car. He went into a wood, and did not ask me to go with him. I sat waiting in the car where he had left me thus, and, when he presently returned, he maintained his silence.

There were times he did talk, breaking into eager speech. He had discovered in the woods the nest of a bird he had long been seeking, or he had found a new kind of mushroom.

He got his bird or his mushroom book from the back of his car. The pages of the books were dirty with much handling. The doctor's clothes were shabby from long wear, and the car in which we rode seemed about to fall to pieces.

When he did talk thus I had always the feeling that he was not addressing me. He knew all of the long scientific names of the birds, the trees, the wild flowers, the insects. He had perhaps captured a tiny insect with delicately colored, almost transparent wings. He had identified it and spoke of it at length and with a kind of eager enthusiasm, but as he spoke thus, he did not look at me, did not seem to be addressing me. We were at the door of a farm house and, after seeing his patient, he had gone into the vegetable garden back of the house, while I had got out of the car and stood in the yard before the house.

A farm woman had come out of the house and had entered into conversation with me. When the doctor returned to where we stood he held a toad in his hand. He began speaking of the habits of the toad, but again did not seem to be addressing either me or the woman. He held the toad in the palm of one of his little fat hands and caressed it with the fingers of the other. He looked away from us and talked, and when the woman addressed a remark to him he was with her as he so often was with me.

He turned and stared at her. "So you are here?" his eyes seemed to be saying. "And why do you need to be bothering me?"

As he talked thus he stood looking off as though into some distant place and the farm woman, thus so obviously snubbed, looked over his head and smiled at me. "He has always been like that," one such woman once remarked to me. She said that people were used to him and that they did not mind. "We all know what a good doctor he is," she said.

There was a man plowing in a field near the road at a place where the doctor had stopped his car. He sat absorbed, apparently watching the farmer's team as they came toward us, the ground curling away from the plow, the heavy muscles playing across the horses' breasts.

The plowman also spoke to the doctor, but he got no answer, and, as he turned his horses and started back across the field, he winked at me. He did not seem offended. When he had gone back across the field the doctor sat for a time, still staring apparently at the man and his team, and then, before starting his car, he did begin to speak.

He never seemed to be speaking to me. For a moment he sat, looking directly into my eyes, as I had often seen him look into the eyes of his patients, and then he turned and spoke as though to another. I had sharply at such times the feeling of being in the presence of something like an invisible third. It was a little startling. There was this feeling of being pushed aside. At such times, when he spoke thus, there was an odd gentleness in his voice. There was never much said, some little comment made on the scene before us, on a bird that had just flown across the road, or on a flowering bush growing at the edge of a wood, and then again the silence. Sometimes when I had been with him for several hours he turned and looked at me as though surprised to discover my presence. "Oh, so you are still here," his eyes seemed to be saying.

The doctor had married, soon after setting up his practise in the town, and on two or three occasions I went to his house. I did not go there with the doctor. The manufacturer and his wife took me there.

There were two handsome daughters and a very handsome although somewhat overpowering wife. There was a big frame house of many rooms, beautifully furnished, on the best residence street of the town. My little doctor must have been making a good deal of money. He had built the big house with a wide and deep lawn, there was an expensive car the doctor never drove, and the older of the daughters was a student in one of the better known women's colleges of the east. As it turned out, after the doctor died, as he did suddenly of a disease of the heart, there was an insurance policy that enabled his family to go on living rather in affluence.

The wife, who was a large woman of striking appearance, was a leader in all the civic affairs of the town. She was everything the doctor wasn't, an organizer, a joiner, was the best woman golf player in the town, once having been runner up in a women's state tournament, was the president of a women's political club, a leader in the Parent-Teacher Association, a member of the local book club and the music club. It was a little difficult to figure out how and why she had married the doctor.

There was the doctor in his office that during the late morning hours was filled with waiting patients. He was in his old Ford, going from house to house in the town, or driving in the country. He was delivering babies, setting broken legs and arms, sitting in a farm house with a book on insects in his hand while he waited for some old man to die. He had come back into town after one of his country drives and it was early evening. Soon it would be dark. He parked his car on a street near his house and sat waiting, studying one of his nature books until darkness came. Many people of the town had seen him sitting thus. They smiled and spoke to him, but he did not answer. When darkness came he crept near and looked through a window of his house. If there was company for dinner or young men had come to call on his daughters, he went quietly away. Often he ate in a cheap restaurant in the lower end of the town. He went up into his inner office and closed and locked the door. He pulled the shades at the windows facing the street. At such times, if his telephone rang, he did not answer. When he was found dead, sitting in his car beside a country road, several specimens of wood mushrooms on the seat beside him, his big mushroom book fallen to the floor of the car at his feet, there was a lawyer of the town who took charge of his affairs.

He found, in a small locked safe in the doctor's office, a great batch of letters. The doctor must have been writing them for years. The lawyer took them to his office and as I happened to be in town he called me in. The letters were all addressed to a woman. There was a small and rather colorless seeming woman who worked as a clerk in a drug store on the main street of the town, a store just opposite the doctor's office, and the letters were all addressed to her. The man must have been sitting alone in his office, I always fancied, on a summer evening some years before I came to know him. He would long since have got himself married and he had the two daughters. I am very sure that, when he was newly married, he had tried for a time to interest his wife in his study of nature.

He had this passion for amateur research into the mysteries of nature, and would have been bringing the specimens he collected home to his wife and she, I am sure, would have tried to be interested in his interests, but there would have come a stalemate. She couldn't make it. All that was alive to him was dead to her. A mushroom was to her a toadstool, a bird was a bird. He hadn't blamed her for her lack of interest. "She is herself and I am myself," he would have thought. He had remained, all the rest of his life, what is called "loyal" to her, had worked hard to provide for the wife and the two daughters, both in character such like the mother, both having her interests, what he thought they wanted in life.

He was a man who, all his life, had found it difficult to make a direct contact with people. He must have been sitting alone in his office on a certain evening (I have always thought of him on that occasion as sitting in darkness and looking down into the lighted main street of his town) and he saw, coming along the street to go into the drug store, the little woman clerk.

He got up from his chair by the window. He pulled the shades and turned on the lights. He began a letter to her. The lawyer thought the letters had not been destroyed because he thought the doctor was like many men making a will. He would always have intended to do it tomorrow. He had begun writing the letters and immediately had found for himself a way to pour himself out. After an investigation carefully made by the lawyer after his death, it was quite sure that the woman to whom the letters were addressed had known nothing of his passion. On the few occasions when, having to go to the drug store, he had been fairly compelled to speak to her he had been rude and once had made her cry. He spoke of that in one of the letters. After it happened he returned to his office and also cried.

The letters written by the little doctor were very tender. As they have all been destroyed I will not try to quote from them. There were many little stories of his discoveries in nature. For all his seeming indifference the letters revealed that he had been a close observer of others. There were tales of people and how they acted at the moment of death, of men and women among his patients and their relations to each other. Although in all the letters he addressed his woman clerk as his "darling" there were never any direct mentions of love, nor did he ever, in any way, criticize his wife, but there was this continued going out of himself into what he saw and felt in nature and in people. There was even a kind of hidden poetry and the lawyer and myself, as we sat in his office at night reading the letters, were both deeply moved.

There was this man and his life, as I and all the others who had known him had seen it, as it was understood by his wife and daughters, and there was this other and secret life he had led. The lawyer, a dignified looking man with greying hair, read the letters. There must have been at least two hundred of them. We had begun reading in the late afternoon and finished quite late at night. We went to the lawyer's house and into the cellar. We burned the letters in a furnace. We went then for a walk together and presently, as though pulled by some force outside ourselves, found ourselves in the drug store.

Although it was late the little woman clerk was still there and busy at her job. The store was one of the modern drug stores that is also half a restaurant and a place of soft drinks. It was filled with people, for the most part young, and there were booths in which they sat, and many little tables. The lawyer and I seated ourselves at one of the tables at the back of the store.

The doctor's woman clerk was running about. On that particular night she must have been very tired, but she kept trying to smile. She made gay little remarks. The lawyer explained to me that she was the daughter of a workman in a factory of the town and that her father had died some years before. He said that there was a half invalid mother that she no doubt supported. As the lawyer and I sat at the table at the back of the store, I saw her go behind a counter piled high with goods and stand a moment hidden from the customers of the store.

As she stood thus her shoulders seemed to droop and she put her hand to her head. For just a moment she was a figure expressing infinite weariness, and then she began again running back and forth, delivering drinks. Again she smiled. Again she made gay little remarks.

The lawyer and I went out of the store and, for a moment, stood in the empty street of the town looking into each other's eyes. There was nothing to be said. I remember to have thought that we looked at each other as my little doctor had always looked at people. We said good night to each other.[41]

White Spot

I am quite sure that some of the women I had during this period never became real to me. I do not remember the names. They exist for me as a kind of fragrance as Ruth, Prudence, Genevieve, Holly, etc., etc. There was the very brutal looking very sensual woman seen one night in a low dive in Chicago. I would have been with certain business men on a spree. The business men were better when drunk. The shrewdness was gone. They became sometimes terrible, sometimes rather sweet children.

For example there was Albert, short, fat, baby faced. He was the president of a certain manufacturing concern for which I wrote advertisements. We got drunk together.

He had a wife who was rather literary and already I had published a few stories. Albert had bragged to her about me and once he took me to his house, in an Illinois town, to dine.

She would have talked only of books, as such women do talk. They can never by any chance be right about anything in the world of the arts. Better if they would keep still. They never do.

Albert being much pleased. "The little wife. You see, Sherwood, in our house also we have a highbrow." He was proud of her, wanted to be loyal. As woman, in bed with her man, she wouldn't have been much.

Albert knowing that and wanting in the flesh. He had got himself a little warm thing, bought her fur coats, sent her money. He could never go to her except when he had been drinking.

He explained to me, when we were drunk together. "I am faithful to my wife, Sherwood." He had his code. "To be sure I sleep with my Mable but I have been faithful. I never kissed her on the lips." His reserving that as his own rock on which to stand. I thought it as good as most rocks upon which men stand.

But I was speaking of women, certain women, who touched me vitally in the flesh, left something with me, it all very strange sometimes. I have

41. Published (revised) in *Redbook*, LXXIV (January, 1940), 38–39, 59.

just thought of that rather big, thick lipped woman seen in a cheap restaurant, half dive in South State Street. There was a little burlesque show a few doors up the street.

Business men, perhaps clients of the firm for which I worked, explaining to me. The president of our company would have been deacon in some suburban church. "Take these men out and entertain them. You do not need to make an itemized account of expenses.

"I would not want company money spent for anything evil."

Oh thou fraud.

I would have been blowing money. The burlesque women came down along a dirty alleyway from the stage door of the cheap show and into the restaurant, half dive. They may have got a percentage on the cost of the drinks bought for them.

And there was that big one, with the thick lips, sitting and staring at me. "I want you," and myself wanting her.

Now! Now!

The evil smell of the terrible little place, street women's pimps sitting about, the business men with me. One of them made a remark. "God, look at that one." She had one eye gone, torn out perhaps in a fight with some other woman over some man, and there was the scar from a cut on her low forehead.

Above the cut her shining blue-black hair, very thick, very beautiful. I wanted my hands in it.

She knew. She felt as I felt but I was ashamed. I didn't want the business men with me to know.

What?

That I was a brute. That I was also gentle, modest, that I possessed also a subtle mind.

The women would have been going and coming in at a back door of the place, as the act they did, a kind of weird almost naked dance before yokels, was due to be repeated. I went out into the alleyway and waited and she came.

There were no preliminaries. Now or never. There were some boxes piled up and we got in behind them. What evil smells back in there. I got my two hands buried deep in her beautiful hair.

And afterwards, her saying when I asked her the question, "Do you want money?" "A little," she said. Her voice was soft. There were drunken men going up and down. There was the loud rasping sound from a phonograph, playing over and over some dance tune in the burlesque place.

Can a man retain something? I had no feeling of anything unclean. She laughed softly. "Give me something, fifty cents. I don't like the foolish feeling of giving it away."

"O.K."

Myself hurrying back to the business men, not wanting them to suspect. "You were a long time."

"Yes." I would have made up some quick lie.

That other one, met on a train, when the train was delayed because something went wrong with the engine. Is there a sense in which the natural man loves all women? The train stopping by a wood and that woman and I giving into the mood to gather flowers.

Again. "Now. Now. You will be gone. We may never meet again."

And then our coming back to the train. She going to sit with an older woman, perhaps her mother, taking her the flowers we had got.

It was Sally, the quiet one, who saw the white spot. It was in a room in a hotel in Chicago, one of that sort. You go in without luggage. You register. "Mr. and Mrs. John James, Buffalo, New York." I remember a friend, who was a women's man, telling me that he always used my name.

We were lying in there in the dark at night, in that rabbit warren of a place. For all I knew the place was full of other such couples. We were in the half sleep that follows, lying in black darkness, a moment ago so close, now so far apart.

Sound of trains rattling along a nearby elevated railroad. This may have been on an election night. There was the sound of men cheering and a band played.

We are human, a male and a female. How lonely we are.

It may be that we only come close in art.

No. Wait.

There is something grown evil in men's minds about contacts.

How we want, want, want. How little we dare take.

It is very silent, here in the darkness. The sounds of the city, of life going on, city life, out there in the street.

A woman cry of animal gratification from a neighboring room.

We exist in infinite dirt, in infinite cleanliness.

Waters of life wash us.

The mind and fancy reaching out.

Now, for an hour, two, three hours, the puzzling lust of the flesh is gone. The mind, the fancy, is free.

It may have been that fancy, the always busy imagination of the artist man she wanted.

She began to talk softly of the white spot. "It floats in the darkness," she said softly and I think I did understand, almost at once, her need.

After the flesh the spirit. Minds, fancy, draw close now.

It was a wavering white spot, like a tiny snow white cloud in the darkness of a close little room in a Chicago bad house.

"You not wanting what our civilization has made of us.

"It is you men, males, always making the world ugly.

"You have made the dirt. It is you. It is you."

"Yes. I understand."

"But do you see the white spot?"

"Yes. It floats there, under the ceiling. Now it descends and floats along the floor.

"It is the thing lost. It eludes us.

"It belongs to us. It is our whiteness."

A moment of real closeness, with that strange thing to the male, a woman.

I had a thought I remember. It was a game played with my brother Earl when I was a lad and he not much more than a babe. We slept together for a time and I invented a game. With our minds we stripped the walls of a room in a little yellow house quite away. We swept the ceiling of our room and the floors away. Our bed floated in space. Perhaps I had picked up a line from some poem. "We are between worlds. Earth is far far beneath us. We float over earth."

All this on a hot August night but we could feel the coolness of outer space. I explained the game to the woman in the room and we played it, following on our floating bed the white drifting spot her fancy had found in that space.

How strange afterwards, going down into the street. It might have been midnight but the street was still crowded with people.

"And so we did float. We did see and follow the white spot and we are here. You make your living writing advertisements and I have a job in an office where they sell patent medicine.

"I am a woman of twenty-eight and unmarried. I live with my sister who is married."

The cheap little hotel room for such couples as we were had its office on the second floor. There was a little desk with a hotel register. What rows of Jones, Smiths, and, yes, Andersons. That friend of mine might have been in that place. He might have put my real name down there.

I would have gone down the stairs first, looked up and down the street. "O.K." The pair of us dodging out. "You'd better take a taxi home. Let me pay."

"But can you? It is such a long way out. It will cost so much."

"Yes. Here."

Who was it invented money? There it lies, the dirty green bill in her hand. The taxi man looking, perhaps listening.

"But, but, does anything of beauty cling to me? Is it to be remembered?"

"Yes. You are very beautiful. Good night." A lie. There was no beauty. The night, the street, the city was the night, the street, the city.[42]

42. Published (revised) in *The Sherwood Anderson Reader,* ed. Rosenfeld, pp. 708–12.

III ❧

Business

O Youth! It is the great fertile time for the taking in and for the storing of impressions. There are these towns, fields, hills, cities, days and nights, men and women, seen and felt when seeing and feeling, often dumbly, an aching hurting thing. How passionately the youth wants an outlet for all of his pent up feelings and how difficult it is to find the outlet.

There is the mind. There are these senses, at the finger ends. How slowly life unfolds. How am I to learn to taste, smell, hear, see to the limit? At its best the practise of an art is so little concerned with the actual work done, pictures hung in galleries in cities, books on book shelves, monuments standing behind shrubbery in parks. Art also is a way of life. It is a doorway into . . . what?

Too often into a new capacity for being hurt.

But away with all this. There are moments. Shall I ever forget a certain night in a rooming house in Chicago? It was a soft damp night in winter and a heavy snow was falling. I had come into my room that night in a blue funk but after I had been in the room for an hour a change came. I walked nervously up and down the room and a fellow lodger came and wanted to sit with me. "No. Go away," I said to him rudely and then, suddenly, sitting, at a desk in the room, the wet snow pelting against the nearby window, I wrote my first authentic tale and having written it (the story is called "Hands" and it is in my book called *Winesburg, Ohio*), having completed it cleanly at one sitting, I jumped up and again walked but I walked now with a new gladness.[1] I think now, remembering that moment, that I laughed and I am sure I cried and that, pushing up the window, I shouted.

"Aha. Aho," I shouted and it seemed to me that a voice answered out of the wet Chicago night.

"Aha. Aho."

"They may go to hell."

"Who?"

"Well, never mind who.

---

1. A remarkable study of the *Winesburg, Ohio* manuscript is William Louis Phillips, "Sherwood Anderson's *Winesburg, Ohio*: Its Origins, Composition, Technique, and Reception" (Ph.D. Thesis, University of Chicago, 1950); summarized in "How Sherwood Anderson Wrote *Winesburg, Ohio*," *American Literature*, XXIII (March, 1951), 7–30, reprinted in *The Achievement of Sherwood Anderson: Essays in Criticism*, edited by Ray Lewis White (Chapel Hill: The University of North Carolina Press, 1966), pp. 62–84.

"All who say that this tale is not authentic, that it is not solid, having structure, beauty, strength.

"And it did not come out of reality," I said to myself, "but out of that strange, more real life into which I have so long been trying to penetrate and that is the only real reality."

I

I had, some two or three years before, run away from my earlier life as a young American go-getter, young business man, young manufacturer. I have already told the story of these adventures in another book—*A Story Teller's Story,* a book more or less, if not entirely, authentic. It has I think the true authenticity of a thing felt. What fun it was writing it.[2]

I had come back to Chicago, from where I had gone on my Ohio adventures and had got a room on the South Side. I had money. Let me say, at a guess, that I had already been scribbling for perhaps seven or eight years and it may have been my scribbling, during those years as a coming man in the business world (I was less and less a coming man the more and more I gave my time to scribbling) that had killed the go-getter in me.

And why did I scribble? I think I know now. I think that during all of my earlier years I had been cursed by a kind of cleverness with other people, that I wanted passionately to escape. If I could write truly and with understanding of the life of any other American, rich or poor, high or low, I could, by that road, perhaps get a little at self. To tell the truth I was pretty slick. I could bend people to my will. I was plausible, thought faster than most people about me, was always putting others in the wrong. I have spoken of myself as a manufacturer but really I wasn't a manufacturer. I was a salesman who got control of a factory.[3]

2. This famous but complicated episode took place November 28, 1912, when Anderson walked dramatically from the office of his products-distribution company in Elyria, Ohio, and wandered for three days, a victim of amnesia. After brief hospital treatment in Cleveland, Anderson ended his business and family affairs and, in February, 1913, returned to Chicago. See *A Story Teller's Story: A Critical Text,* edited by Ray Lewis White (Cleveland: Press of Case Western Reserve University, 1968), pp. 96–99, 215–36; and William Alfred Sutton, *Exit to Elsinore* (Muncie, Indiana: Ball State University, 1967).

3. In the late summer of 1906, Anderson moved to Cleveland, Ohio, as head of The United Factories Company, a mail-order outlet. In the summer of 1907, he went into business for himself in Elyria, Ohio, with a paint-distribution company, The Anderson Manufacturing Company. See William Alfred Sutton, "Sherwood Anderson: The Cleveland Year, 1906–1907," *Northwest Ohio Quarterly,* XXII (Winter, 1949–50), 39–44.

You readers must know what that means in America, this being a plausible ready salesman. In America no one buys anything. In America everything, even art, is sold to people.

And so, as a salesman, I was beginning to get on. I had picked up ideas about selling goods by mail by my earlier experience as an advertising writer and at first, when I first launched out for myself, I did very well.

Presently money came rolling in. Why I do not mean to say that I was rich or even on the borderline of anything like great riches but I had learned how men get rich. There is something you do. You strike upon an idea.

Or there is some man you have stumbled across quite accidentally—it may not be an accident. The hunger for money begets schemes for getting money. Some mechanic has invented some mechanical contrivance or another man has invented a process for refining oil. There are always men working in the mechanical world making inventions, discovering secrets they do not know how to sell.

You hop aboard. O individualism! O survival of the fittest! O rugged individualism!

And here your word fellow comes in. This new thing you have got your hands on must be rammed down people's throats. Up and at 'em, boy!

I will admit that to the clever man there is a kind of temporary excitement in all this. You get money and money brings possessions. Now for the fine house on the principal street of your town. You have become a solid middle class citizen of your town.

But where do we go from here?

Wait. There are places to go. You have got a talent now, the talent for getting money. Cultivate it. Go on. You have found a method. Expand it. You may well land among the great ones.

But are these great ones of America's past, that is to say the past here that a man in middle life may look back upon, are they really great?

There is that annoying question.

It is amusing to me now to look back upon the struggle going on within me at a certain time in my own life, a time when it seemed to me, and I have reasons to know to others, I had learned the trick of borrowing other people's money from banks. It is a trick, and I take it for granted that I would not have been allowed possession of the money to play with if the bankers, those astute ones, had not begun to think of me as a coming man.

And so, hell! You have found this golden vein that may be worked. I know a man who got rich because some advertising writer, writing of a soap he manufactured, had chanced upon the suggestion that the use of that particular soap would make the skin of even middle aged ordinary women like the skin of a young girl and very desirable to touch. You have got your vein. Go on working it. In she rolls.

There was my own vein and it was promising. I had returned to Ohio where my youth had been spent. As a boy in a neighboring Ohio town I had been half a young hustler. Because of my eager hunger for jobs I had been called "Jobby Anderson." I had been half the young hustler and half the young dreamer who wanted to sit forever looking at people, listening, wondering about people. In the town it was the dreamer that was remembered and only last year I saw and talked with a man who had been my boyhood companion.

"What was I like then? What was your impression?" I asked and he told me that he remembered me only as a lazy fellow, sitting on the curb on the main street or before the little frame hotel at evening, listening to the tales told by a traveling man. Or I sat with my back against a barn wall listening to men talking within a barn or to women gossiping in the kitchen of a nearby house.

"But whose barn? We had no barn to our house."

"No. It was our barn. You would be listening to my sisters and to mother talking in our kitchen."

"Ah! And so I was at it even then?"

"I would come out of the house. I wanted you to go play ball with me or to go with me to bring home the cows.

"I remember you sitting there, your eyes glassy, and that I walked over and stood before you. I shouted but you did not hear. I had to lean over and hit you to get your attention.

"With a book in your hand you were ten times worse."

"But," I protested, "I was called 'Jobby' in the town and it seems to me that would indicate a hustler."

"You were both a hustler and bone lazy," he said. "I do, now that you speak of it, remember periods of intense activity, when you worked feverishly at any job you could get. You used to go about at such times declaring your determination to be a rich man, the most powerful man in the state, and when we others laughed you wanted to fight."

And so, if the two things had been in me at the beginning it was evident that later the hustler had won and I remember now that after I had become a manufacturer I once visited my home town and that people spoke of the change in me. There was an old carriage builder who stopped me on the street. I was about to hurry past. "Stop," he cried. "There isn't any fire." I stopped and we talked, I speaking of my fine prospects in life, and he said to me, stepping a little away and looking. . . .

"Why you have changed," he said. "When you were here, a kid here, you used to pull your words and now you speak crisply. And you look so like a hustler and when you were here you were always sitting lost in your dreams."

I had got into the position described, the money beginning to roll in, my house on a good enough street. I would have a bigger and a finer house in a few years. Someone had organized a golf club in the town where I had my factory and I had begun to go there in the afternoon. A business man needs his exercise. No man likes to get fat.

"I tell you what . . . I sit too many hours a day at my desk.

"We men who have responsibility. . . ."

It may have been the golf playing, chasing the little white ball over the Ohio fields, just such fields as I had once worked in, planting cabbage in fields, cutting and husking corn in fields. I must have begun looking at the other men about me, my companions in the new sport, a good stiff drink at the nineteenth hole. "I tell you what, let's you and me skip off to Cleveland some night next week. My wife is out of town. I know a pair of cute little blondes."

There was evidence enough in the men about me of what my friend Paul Rosenfeld afterwards called "the American mouth." [4] There is a queer tired droop to the mouth. What's wrong? It should be remembered that at that time, when I was a boy, there was a great and glowing faith in Americans. It has weakened since. That is the obvious reason for the puzzled uncertainty about life here in America at the present but at that time no man much doubted the great destiny of America. We Americans had got into that great empire, the middle west, mid-America, the real

4. Paul Rosenfeld (1889–1946), music critic and literary critic and editor, member of the New York literati from 1916. In "Sherwood Anderson," *Dial,* LXXII (January, 1922), 35, Rosenfeld wrote: "Anderson has to face himself where Freud and Lawrence, Stieglitz and Picasso, and every other great artist of the time, have faced themselves: has had to add a 'phallic Chekov' to the group of men who have been forced by something in an age to remind an age that it is in the nucleus of sex that all the lights and the confusions have their center, and that to the nucleus of sex they all return to further illuminate or further tangle."—a comment that fascinated Anderson. Rosenfeld also wrote of Anderson in his Introduction to *The Sherwood Anderson Reader* (Boston: Houghton Mifflin Company, 1947), pp. viii–xxviii. See *A Story Teller's Story,* ed. White, pp. 251, 272–74, 286, 300, 305–6, 318; and Anderson's correspondence with Rosenfeld in *Letters of Sherwood Anderson,* edited by Howard Mumford Jones and Walter B. Rideout (Boston: Little, Brown and Company, 1953).

body of America, the great fat land stretching from the Appalachian Mountains to the Rockies, and had built our towns and cities. The land had opened slowly at first and then had come what we now call the "industrial revolution." The pace of life had been set by the horse, the ox, and the plow and now it was being set by the locomotive. Great trains roaring through the Ohio towns. On to the west! New towns and cities still to be made, to the west. Thomas Jefferson had died thinking it would take two hundred years to settle America and he had been dead but little more than a hundred years. Look at us go, boy!

The bicycle had come, followed by the motor car. An automobile plant came to the town of my childhood, moving into what had been a piano factory, and my first experience as a factory hand had been in the shop there.

But there was something in our family. It may have been the influence of my mother. She died at thirty-five, having borne seven children, and on her death bed told us frightened youngsters, gathered in, that we were made of a special clay. "I do not fear to leave you. You are of the stuff of which kings are made."

What nonsense! The poor woman couldn't have said that but she did say something that fixed a certain impression in our minds, of that I am quite sure. We had all been stung by something and knew in our hearts that we were not to remain as we were, really of the very poor laboring class.

And why not? What was wrong with labor? Obviously there was something wrong with labor in the forests and fields of early America. Oh, the heavy brutality of it! I myself had been rather a slight boy and had been compelled to work the long twelve hour day of that time, in the corn cutting, the cabbage planting, at the digging of ditches and the shoveling of coal and earth until my bones ached and in the morning, in some cheap rooming house or in a farm house at dawn, I had been compelled to fairly pry myself out of bed and walk about the room naked, slowly lifting one aching leg after the other to get the stiffened joints to working again.

That must have been the tone of life in early America, say in my father's youth. The south had escaped it by bringing in slave labor and in New England and the east. . . . Well, I have always thought, since I saw the play one night in New York, that the figures of the two sons who went off to California in Mr. Eugene O'Neill's *Desire Under the Elms,*[5] those

5. Eugene Gladstone O'Neill (1888–1953) produced and published *Desire Under the Elms* in 1924. Anderson and O'Neill were acquainted but not intimate. See *Letters,* ed. Jones and Rideout, Item 258, *passim.*

dumb creatures, tied to the soil and brow beaten by the arrogant old father, that grim hard European peasant life transferred to America, I have always thought that the true note of early New England.

Then had come the machine and oh the faith in it! It must be true that a nation, the tone of a nation, is made by the necessity of the land and that America was so big, the middle west so wide spread, that the mechanical flair that came into its people and became a part of its people was inevitable. But for slavery the south would also have developed it.

The machines had come with a rush. Everyone was inventing but my own impulse did not run to mechanical invention.

What then?

Why not be a salesman? If you cannot make the new age try to help sell it. There is your place for your word fellow in such a time. This slick plausibility in you. Here is where it may be used.

I had got into it and there was something wrong. Go with me now dear readers to my factory in Ohio. Most of the factories were already being run and controlled, not by the mechanically minded men, who had invented the things being made in the factories, but by the slicker men who could sell what was being made, just as later they were to be controlled by financiers, and I was one of the slick ones.

Was that what was the matter with me? I was on the road to prosperity and, if I held on, to riches, but already I was sick. Was the sickness that was in me general among men of my sort?

It is to be borne in mind that all of this attempt to think out my own situation at that time, and the only justification for this book, for all of this word slinging here, is that I believe myself and have always thought of myself as a very typical American.

My point is that, although I had developed into this plausible thing, this slick one who could by words sell people what were often inferior goods, I wasn't yet onto myself. I had got into this certain position I have described, was more or less looked up to in the town to which I had come to be a manufacturer, was, at least for the time, in good standing at the banks. Money came and went. I was married and already had children.[6] If I went on, doing over and over the tricks I had learned, developing the native

6. Cornelia Platt Lane (1877–1967) and Sherwood Anderson were married May 16, 1904. Daughter of a rich Toledo manufacturer, Cornelia was graduated from Western Reserve University in 1896 and had been in Europe, 1901–2. There were three children from this marriage: Robert Lane Anderson (1907–1951), John Sherwood Anderson (1908–   ), and Marion Anderson (1911–   ). Cornelia divorced Anderson at his request July 26, 1916.

plausibility in myself, there was no special reason why I should not establish a family of my own. We Andersons had been down long enough. I could, when the time came, send all my children off to some fashionable eastern university, make young Yale, Harvard or Princeton men of them. We business men used often to speak of such things, sitting with drinks before us on the porch of an Ohio golf club house.

It was all a bit queer. If my mother on her death bed had not got that off about kings (and I have the grace to doubt it, the imagination is a tricky thing) but if she had surely I was on the way to being at least one of the smaller American kings. I was in house paint. Why not the American house paint king?

And so I played golf, to ease my tired brain that wasn't really tired, and presently I was unfaithful to my wife. Most of the bright young business men I knew were. Why not?

There was so apparently a hole somewhere in our lives and our wives . . . I dare say most of them were thinking of their children, not of us.

And there was something else in the air. I have represented myself, here, as a young American business man, trying thus to make a kind of background for another story I would like to try to tell, as a good deal of a Babbitt,[7] but I dare say I was never very completely that and the truth is that it is the most natural thing in the world for such men as I am here trying to describe, knowing without ever quite knowing what they are up to, it is so easy to lie to oneself, I dare say I never did make any first rate house paint. There were always traveling men coming to my office to show me some substitute for the more expensive ingredients I had been using and I usually bought. I had, all the time, I dare say, a kind of pride in my ability as a word slinger and most people who buy house paint are like the people who buy anything, at bottom probably yaps. I have, I say, represented myself as a good deal of a Babbitt but I wasn't one.

No man is really one. Look at President Harding. Poor old dear.

I had not been made physically for physical labor but I am sure that I was in my own way quite strong. I never did need much sleep and was never bothered much by the matter of heat and cold. Even at the time I am now describing, when I worked rather long hours in a factory office, surrounded constantly by a cloud of young women stenographers, dictating letters for hours at a stretch, getting up very plausible sounding form

7. George Follansbee Babbitt, zealously middle-class realtor in Sinclair Lewis' satirical *Babbitt* (1922).

letters that went out in their thousands, going to the golf club to play golf, running to the bank to arrange about a note coming due that I did not want to pay. . . . I put my arm about the grey haired banker's shoulder and looked into his eyes. I swear he was a sweet man. Bankers are caught in the muddle of life just as are we others. Oh, if the communists would only dare realize that. I put my arms about his shoulders and said, "Look here, Will," I said. "I can't and won't pay the damn note. I need the money for other things. You know us, Will. The destiny of America lies in our hands."

To be sure he liked the laughter in my eyes when I said that. He knew what I knew. No man, in his heart, can really believe in rugged individualism, this superman stuff. It was fun, being in common at least a little onto ourselves. As I have already perhaps suggested, most business is done under the table.

All of this going on. I think of it as the average life of the average more or less successful American. All of this going on but even then, in the midst of it all, I did find a good deal of time to read.

My reading was done at night. I went home. After all the town I was in and where I had my factory was not yet a city. The night life was to say the least meager. "Why not to bed and a book?" I said to myself. The wife I had got (I never knew her. How could I? What chance had I?), she was, I dare say, absorbed in her children, our children, American children. Was there ever such a people as the Americans for always looking to the children, vaguely hoping they may live, may get something out of life we living Americans do not quite dare let ourselves take?

Whoa. I may have struck upon something here. Do you suppose, dear American readers, if I write this book as I should I am quite sure no one but an American will ever quite understand it. Do you suppose that we, Americans, human beings dropped down as we were in such a glorious continent, have always been rather buffaloed by the land itself? That is at least an idea. We do all seem to have a dreadful inferiority complex, thanks to Mr. Freud,[8] but I swear we do not, as a people, feel so damn superior to any other people, even the English. But do you suppose the land itself has got us that way?

It is such a goddamn grand land.

8. Anderson's knowledge of Freudian psychology is a confusing subject. See Frederick J. Hoffman, *Freudianism and the Literary Mind* (Baton Rouge: Louisiana State University Press, 1957), pp. 229–50, reprinted in *The Achievement of Sherwood Anderson,* ed. White, pp. 174–92.

Say, do you know what? Perhaps God, when he let Christopher Columbus discover us, should have been considerate enough to have invented a new people to occupy the land he let Christopher stumble onto. It's an idea, as we old advertising men love to say.

I had, as suggested, got to this place, with other men, some of my own age and many older, and I had begun to look around. There was a queer kind of stoppage of something in myself. At that time such organizations as the Kiwanis Clubs and the Rotarians had not come to the towns but we business men frequently got together. We were the men, or we thought we were, who were doing what was being done to America.

Were we not making the towns bigger, bringing people in? At one time I myself had a hand in as many as five different ventures in one town. Some of them turned out, made money, while others went on the rocks.

It was fun, in a way. There was the gamble. You got an idea, and at that time I was full of ideas, or some fellow came along. I remember the coming of one man, a slender yellow haired young man who had been a bar tender in the Ohio town of my childhood.

"Why hello, Sherwood. I heard you had settled down here. I hear you are making plenty of dough.

"You see, Sherwood, I've got a scheme."

The scheme, as I now remember it, was crooked enough. It was really a plan to blackmail money out of women who belonged to church organizations, Ladies' Aid Societies, etc., and what the scheme needed was just what I had.

As for the money to back it, I didn't need that. Already there were men about who had faith in me, men who had money and no ideas.

"All right, Harry. I can get the money. The scheme sounds all right to me. What do you want for your cut?"

It was another venture to be started in the town, people employed, mostly young stenographers, getting out slick letters I could concoct. The churches also were to get a cut. I am quite sure the scheme worked and for that matter would work today. What was the matter with all of this? It puts people to work. The more people you get to work the bigger your town grows.

I used to go out to the golf club in the afternoon and I remember things that happened there. I was playing with three other bright young business men of the town and suddenly, at the fourth or fifth hole, I had sliced my ball and had driven it far off the course into a neighboring corn field and I went after it.

Was I sick of my companions and of their talk? There is no use my being upstage about them. I was what they were.

And here again comes in something that has always puzzled me. There are these moments come in all of our lives. There are certain moments in any life instensely remembered ever afterwards. Does a man's life then consist of hundreds of little revolutions?

At any rate I remember very vividly climbing over a barb-wire fence and into that corn field and one of my companions shouting at me.

"Ah let it go, Anderson," he called and suddenly something cracked in me.

I stood there in that corn field, having walked perhaps a hundred paces from the fence. The corn was already knee high. Another plowing and it would be ready to lay by. There was a wood beyond the corn field and I walked toward it muttering. "You go to hell, you bastard," I found myself muttering to myself.

At whom were the words addressed? The man who had called to me was a young Jew. He was one of the bright young business men of the town and I think owned a department store there. He had walked down to the fence that separated the golf course from the corn field and stood looking over. "You go to hell, you bastard," I muttered, being careful that he did not hear and pretending to look on the ground under the corn for my ball, putting the corn aside with the golf club held in my hand and then, gaining temporary control of myself, I spoke, telling him to go on. "Hell," I said, "I've got a splitting headache. I hate to break up our foursome but I've got to go back to the club house." I walked obliquely across the field pretending I was going toward the club house but in reality making toward the woods and after a moment's hesitation he went back to join the others.

It had begun. What?

I went on my way that day, walking across the corn field, looking back at the others, at the men of that foursome, men who were my friends in that town. One or two of them were in deals with me. They had money in ventures of mine.

I kept watching them furtively. There was talk among them, a foursome spoiled. "Hell, what do you suppose is the matter with him?"

"If he had a headache why the hell didn't he say so before we got up this foursome?" The Jew who was in our foursome was struggling hard to cut down his score and always kept strict account of the score on each hole by any member of a foursome in which he played. There was something to be achieved, even if you lost the foursome, a low score achieved, to make the course in what we then called "bogey." "Bogey" indeed!

There must have been something, perhaps a kind of warm male comradeship in life sought. I had already read Whitman.[9] There were no books in our house at home when I was a child but as I grew prosperous I accumulated books rapidly. The night was my reading time and I had fixed up a room in my house to which I fled. There was a cot in that room, a table and books. I had got a passion for history and spent long evenings reading the story of men's efforts. "Why am I not a soldier?" I asked myself. I have an idea that more men than will admit it play such games as I was then playing with myself. It is an old story. After all, the amount of real energy put into work by the average man of business must be small. I knew about that because, after my earlier life, making my way by physical labor, I had got into business. This before I became a manufacturer. This when I was a Chicago advertising writer. I knew about the men who got the most money from advertising, the solicitors, salesmen, contact men. These men going to the Chicago Athletic Club, going off to play golf with clients. Coming back to hurry into the office. "I am so busy."

Busy hell!

We others doing the work. Now, for the time, I had others to do the work. I had others to keep my books, write my letters, direct the men in my factory. Schemes for getting more money, by one slick dodge or another, kept flashing into my head, the inventive passion in me thus kept alive, it constantly being corrupted just the same, a curious feeling of dirt following the success of each of my schemes.

I went home at night and after eating, looking at my children, myself often in a silent sullen mood, I fled upstairs to my room.

"But what's the matter, dear?" This perhaps from my wife.

Matter? How was I to know? I went upstairs to my room and shutting the door locked it. "I have to work," I called down to my wife.

"But I also have a life to live. All day I stay here attending to these children and then in the evening you go off by yourself."

9. Anderson wrote of Whitman in his Introduction to *Leaves of Grass* (New York: Crowell, 1933), pp. v–vii; and in *A Story Teller's Story*, ed. White, pp. 106–7, 117. See Viva Elizabeth Haught, "The Influence of Walt Whitman on Sherwood Anderson and Carl Sandburg" (M.A. Thesis, Duke University, 1936).

I have put down the above as the probable thoughts of the woman. In reality I do not know what she thought. I had got a certain feeling about my house and my room and I think I had better try to speak of that here.

"There must be a place, some place," I had said to myself. I had selected this room in a wing of the house, upstairs, a room to which the noises of the house did not penetrate often, and had furnished it myself, after my own fashion, keeping it very plain, a plain flat topped desk, unpainted, two chairs, a cot to sleep on, my books. I had got a special lock put on the door and kept the key in my pocket.

"But how will it be cleaned?" my wife asked and "Never mind. I'll clean it myself," I answered. I did. Well, there was no use unnecessarily hurting her feelings. I became canny. "Wait until she has taken the children out for a walk," I said to myself and when she had left the house I ran down into the kitchen and got a pail and cloths. There was a huge negro woman in the kitchen and it was from her and her attitude toward me that I got the impulse for a book written long afterwards, a book called *Dark Laughter*. The laughter of the negro women in that book, house servants in another house, in a town down on the Ohio River, was the same laughter I had heard coming from the lips of the negro woman servant in my own house. I ran down the stairs and spoke to her. "Quick, Kate, a pail of warm water, some soap and cloths." She stood looking at me, the laugh beginning to form about her lips.

"And some soap please."

The laughter came and she went to get me what I wanted. She was hired to do certain work in our house but if I wanted to do it what did she care? I took the pail of water, the soap and cloths and ran up the stairs and she came to the foot of the stairs to see me go. She put her hands on her hips. How huge, how thick she was! A little game had begun between us. Sometimes I stopped at the head of the stairs and stood looking down at her. The wife and the children had gone out of the house. There was just this big black woman and myself. She was laughing at me, her laughter ringing through the house and, as I stood looking down at her, I also laughed.

"Oh thou worried, neurotic whites, always trying to solve things. So you think it important that you do something with your lives."

I stood looking down at her. Were these her thoughts?

Certainly not.

She wasn't thinking at all. She was amused.

"But oh," I thought, "if some white woman, who might conceivably love me, who would be willing to live with me, would but be willing to take the attitude toward me this negro woman now took.

"There's a thought. There's an idea to play with," I told myself, going on up into my room and closing the door. I took off my clothes hurriedly and threw them on the cot and getting down naked on my hands and knees washed the floor and the woodwork of my room.

"Now for clean sheets on my bed." I had brought clean sheets from below. "No. I'll go and bathe first." I ran to the bath room at the end of a little hall and after bathing myself returned to my room and set the pail of dirty water on the landing at the head of the stairs. "Kate. Come and take the dirty water away.

"I am clean now, Kate. My room is clean."

How close that big black Kate had come to me. I went into my room and closing and locking the door stood to listen. Kate was a great hulking black woman with huge shoulders and like most older negro women, who spend their lives being servants, she had bad feet. It came from always wearing someone else's shoes. Kate came slowly and laboriously up the stairs to get the pail of dirty water, the soap and the soiled cloths and I stood naked behind the closed and locked door to listen to her slow chuckle of amusement, a chuckle interposed with groans of pain because of her aching feet.

Something to amuse.

"Quick now. Put on your clothes. This is your room. You are lost, far away from everyone here. Kate laughs but she does not know."

But perhaps Kate did know.

"What difference would that make?"

In the room I could be what I pleased. I had already read Carlyle's book *Sartor Resartus* [10] and at home, when I was a lad, my father in his rare gay moments had often sung a ballad.

"Fair words can make fair songs, me lads,

"But it's the clothes that make the man."

That might be. The room into which I had got was then but another suit of clothes to cover my nakedness. "Uncover not thy father's nakedness." There was my own nakedness, the naked fact of myself, my own figure in the little world of men and women about me, a subtle kind of cheating I was always practising. I couldn't face it yet. "I will not be

10. Thomas Carlyle (1795–1881), Scots essayist; *Sartor Resartus* ("the tailor re-tailored") appeared serially 1833–34.

myself. I will not admit to myself that what I am I am," I cried in my closed room.

I escaped out of myself.

And here let me explain what the artist is.[11] Why not add my own explanation to the thousands of others that have been given? It will be as good as any of them.

The artist, any man born artist as I was, and caught as I was and, I dare say, as all such men are caught, has this hunger always to remake, to recreate. There is this shapeless thing all about him everywhere and the fingers ache to reshape it.

"What, a whole civilization?"

"No. Leave that to the statesmen."

"This thing, your own life?"

"Well now, go easy on that too.

"You are a tangle of God knows what influences coming down into you out of the past and now, at the present moment, playing over you. Even Shakespeare had said that the world was but a stage and that men and women were merely players."

The above put down as though there had been a conversation going on in a room, say as between two men, and perhaps there was. Often I walked about the room talking to myself, arguing with myself. I am only trying here, as anyone who has gone this far with me will readily see, to make a picture of what must go on constantly in a million rooms of houses when men and women are in rooms alone. There is this restless questioning spirit in all of us and I have probably been a bit too pretentious in thinking of myself, at this stage of my life, as a more or less thwarted artist and thus a little set aside from the others.

At any rate there I was and in the business world of which I was then a part there was a saying that kept ringing in my ears. There was always talk in our world of what was called "playing the game." Such and such a one does or does not "play the game."

To play the game was the thing and men who did play the game were looked up to with respect. Well, we all wanted that, the respect of others. I know I did.

I did at any rate when I was in the office of my factory, in the bank,

11. See Anderson's "Man and His Imagination," *The Intent of the Artist,* edited by Augusto Centeno (Princeton: Princeton University Press, 1941), pp. 39–79; and Robert Charles Hart, "Writers on Writing: The Opinions of Six Modern American Novelists on the Craft of Fiction" (Ph.D. Thesis, Northwestern University, 1954).

where I was arranging for the extension of a loan, at some public meeting, or even when walking alone in the streets. In the street I looked about to see that I was unobserved. I think it was my dream, even then, to be a man easy in life and in the presence of others and later I did see and meet men and women who had the thing I wanted, a kind of easy swing at life. "No hurry now. Take this in your stride." By all that I meant a kind of loitering grandeur of living, looking, watching, absorbing.

"Now do not always be thinking, 'Am I a deserving man in the world? Am I proving myself a man of worth?'" I think any man, thoroughly American, will know what I mean. I do not mean the punishing self-consciousness of a Sinclair Lewis but rather the ease in life say of a Clarence Darrow or of that sweet flowing man, my friend Lincoln Steffens.[12]

My point is, the picture I am trying to give here, is of a man not easy flowing, in fact terribly self-conscious. I was that and hated it in myself. I was doing the thing millions of Americans do, trying to make my life and my work at that time, that was of no importance, seem important. Having been a slow moving dreamy boy I had made myself into this crisp thing that hurried to an office, sat at a big desk, rang bells, got suddenly and sometimes nastily executive. "Do this and that," I cried to others, but now, alone in my room, sometimes a change began to come over me.

It is true that I had enough of my father in me to be often quite silly. I had been reading let us say a life of Napoleon, he being the hero of more than one young American business man, and I had got, in a store in Cleveland, some little lead toys which I had brought home and carried to my room. I had told myself, when I bought the toys, that I had got them as playthings for my children but the children never saw them. You will understand that I had got, at the moment of the purchase, the nice feeling of being thoughtful of others in remembering my children, had absorbed that nice feeling, had wrung it dry like a sponge, and then, when I had got

12. Harry Sinclair Lewis (1885–1951), midwestern author of *Main Street* (1920) and *Arrowsmith* (1925), discussed by Anderson in "Four American Impressions," *New Republic*, XXXII (October 11, 1922), 171–73; *A Story Teller's Story*, ed. White, pp. 280, 300; *Letters*, ed. Jones and Rideout, *passim*. Lewis reviewed *A Story Teller's Story* in *New York Herald Tribune Books*, November 9, 1924, pp. 1–2. Anderson and Lewis are discussed in Theodore Johnson, "Realism in Contemporary American Literature: Notes on Dreiser, Anderson, Lewis," *Southwestern Bulletin*, N.S. 16, No. 4 (September, 1929), 3–16; Carl Van Doren, "Sinclair Lewis and Sherwood Anderson: A Study of Two Moralists," *Century*, CX (July, 1925), 362–69; and Alfred Kazin, *On Native Grounds* (New York: Reynal and Hitchcock, 1942), pp. 205–26.

Clarence Seward Darrow (1857–1938), Chicago lawyer who helped Anderson divorce Tennessee Mitchell in 1924, discussed in *A Story Teller's Story*, ed. White, pp. 280–81, 282. Joseph Lincoln Steffens (1866–1936), leader of the "muckraking" journalism of *Maclure's* and *Everybody's* magazines.

home, I had taken the toys to my room, to which the children were never allowed to come.

They were on a shelf in my room, little red soldiers in red coats, some on black prancing horses and others in blue coats and mounted on white horses. There were foot soldiers in red coats and with tiny guns on their shoulders and all of these I arranged in rows, an absurd picture, all of this, I realize, but a quite true one. I got a walking stick out of a closet and walked up and down. "What the hell, after all, this Napoleon?" I cried. I stood before the little lead soldiers and shouted at them, imagining myself at the moment some great figure, little Corsican corporal, little Ohio paint maker too.

The outbreaks of this sort couldn't last long, although the tendency in me to pretend, to be always trying to make myself out something I wasn't, went on and on.

There would be these times of such pretense, not always so obviously absurd as the little game with the lead soldiers but also not often so harmless, and then came the reaction. Let us say that I was naked, strutting up and down in my room so. There was a kind of sickening fear also that someone would catch me at one of these absurd moments. My being naked and in particular barefooted was not without reason. I was no admirer of the beauty of my own body. The being barefooted prevented my being heard about the house as I tramped restlessly, often at this time in my life for hours, up and down in the room.

I got my clothes and put them on and going to my desk sat down. The desk was by a window and I looked out into the back yards of neighboring houses.

Bear in mind, dear reader, that you are to think of me as a man nearing thirty. I am living in this Ohio town and I am one of the respectables there. I have a wife and children. Why, you may ask, did I not go with my troubles to them?

That I do not know. I was too confused.

So that, in its implications as regards the Ohio of say twenty-five years ago, me in my room, my wife having gone out for her walk. In the end she would conclude I was a bit insane as perhaps I was. Furtive and often half desperate efforts to draw close to each other, efforts that never succeeded.

II

It must have been that at that particular time in my life I wanted more than anything in the world to draw close to someone and the scenes that took place in my room, when I was alone in my room, had, at least not all of them, the silliness of that walking naked up and down before lead toy soldiers, wanting to command them.

Could it not be, is it not possible that, in the world as it is now organized, the great, the bitter contest is ahead and that it was in the air even then, percolating down even to the comparatively small town where I then lived? Shall I put it broadly as a contest between individualism and socialism, Christianity and paganism, the idea being that man must continue to struggle toward a world ruled by something like love, at least awareness of others, or that he must go utterly the other way—as apparently Germany is trying to go at this moment?

"Reach out to someone. Find someone in this muddle. Lose self." Actually these words sometimes shouted aloud to myself in a room in an Ohio house. I went and sat by a window, where I had a desk, and putting my face in the crook of my arm wept.

Not, however, willing to face myself as yet.

I remember an incident. There was a man, an Italian, who had come to that town and he had prospered. He was in some business in the town as I was. I remember now, thinking back to that time, that he had opened a restaurant there and I had been in his place, a great shining room, filled with cheap shiny American furniture, scenes painted on the walls, a place of soapy looking red, pink and yellow soft drinks, young blades coming with their girls to eat and drink, American girls in pink and blue uniforms to wait on them, on the wall scenes painted, towering, snow clad mountains overlooking dark little lakes. On one of the lakes, in the far distance, a military man in a row boat. A bird mounting into the distant sky. No Ohioian of that town had ever painted such scenes. It must have been done by some visiting Italian.

The Italian, who was my neighbor, in my so respectable part of that town, owned several such restaurants in Ohio towns, had built up a chain of such places, and had selected our town and our neighborhood to live in.

There must have been, were I'm sure, comments among the neighbors. "Such a fellow as that coming in. This part of town is going down." There was resentment. "What the hell are you talking about? Who are we that we should be so high and mighty about him?" I had been walking back and forth from my house to my factory with some neighbor doctor, lawyer or merchant, and hearing his comments on our new neighbor had wanted to rebuke him but hadn't.

Other thoughts coming. "We Americans, with God knows what ancestry, my own was surely vague enough, busy as we are, some of us, trying to climb up out of the working class into the middle class, hoping to climb up beyond that, grow rich, be of the new American ruling class. I was an Ohioian born and had returned to Ohio and already, in nearby Cleveland, a man named Rockefeller had pushed himself up, apparently quite free from the mass, so that he could now live and act quite regardless of the law, defying blandly all of the carefully built up older American idea of things, Jeffersonian democracy, equality of all men before the law, etc. There were others. Hanna getting McKinley[13] elected just at that time, himself later to the senate from Ohio, by heaven knows what chicanery, the rest of us blinking it, our turn may come next. There was this new movement going on, society reshaping itself after the Spanish-American War. McKinley to be followed by Roosevelt and the big stick, myself, at least a part of the time, feeling myself of the stuff of which rulers are made, often when I was alone in my room telling myself that. I had got a glass in there and went to stand before it. "Look at the size and shape of your head. There is something of the stuff of which the old Romans were made and the old Romans learned how to rule the world," such hours of vainglory always to be followed by other hours of extreme humbleness, even weeping, but always returning. . . .

Talk with other men. "Hanna is the kind of man we want. We ought to make him president." This perhaps to my banker or to the men with whom I had begun to play golf.

These words from my own lips, talking to some neighbor, we walking together, under trees, along our respectable street, going each to his own scramble.

I think however, always, even then, another kind of reaction in me. I would have left my neighbor at some corner and was alone. "Whoa," I cried to myself, "don't be some damned biggity." I would remember a certain Italian grandmother of my own, Italian peasant with big hips. I dare say she couldn't even read and write. Often, after such a talk regarding our new neighbor, the Italian restaurant keeper, I came home later to my house. Let us say that my wife had someone in to dinner. It would be some quite respectable person of the town, perhaps the local superintendent of schools.

Or some of the professors from a nearby college town. My wife was a college woman and had a degree while I . . . .

I remember now that the college in the nearby town had a rule against

13. Marcus Alonzo Hanna (1837–1904), Ohio businessman and politician, responsible for electing William McKinley president (1897–1901) and himself senator (1897–1904).

smoking and that the men and women who came to us liked to smoke so that, after dining, we would draw all of the house curtains and have cigarettes, with beer.

Oh choice wickedness! Damn! I got habitually nasty. There were stories I had begun to pick up. I had begun going furtively, through back alleyways, to the town saloons, spending secret hours there when I should have been attending to the building up of my paint dynasty, none of this sort of waste of time and energy in The Rockefeller. I was already sure of that.

I had got stories that would curl the guts of college professors, in for an evening with their wives and other men's wives, and I wanted to tell them and sometimes did. Painful moments of silence. Quick talk of other things, literature preferably. Oh literature! Hast thou got respectable too? Names mentioned, Thomas Hardy with held breath . . . *Tess of the d'Urbervilles, Jude the Obscure.* . . .

"Such vulgarity creeping into books."

"Now there is W. D. Howells, an Ohioian." I got him and read him.

All of this was, at that time, a comparatively new world to me. If I had always been rather a vociferous reader my reading had been largely confined to men's lives, histories of people, etc. It still is. I however got Howells and went through him and found him flat. "What the hell's he so afraid of? He is like me in his fear," I thought.

I think, am quite sure, that it was on some such evening that I first heard the name of a later friend, Theodore Dreiser. There would have been a college professor at the house, from the English department of the college, and he would already have written a book on English literature. For a college professor in any field to get anywhere at all it is almost necessary for him to have written a book. I didn't know that then but found it out later.

The women and men, gathered at our house, listening to the college professor. I remember now that Arnold Bennett had just come to America [14] and, as he got off the ship, had been asked by some reporter what, in America, he was most interested in and "Why, Theodore Dreiser," he had replied, shocking, I dare say, innumerable college professors in America as he had shocked the one who came to us.

"Why Bennett . . . Bennett says. . . . I can't understand it.

"Yes. I got the book. His *Sister Carrie.* It is so crude."

14. Arnold Bennett (1867–1931) toured America in 1911–12.

[256]

But this Bennett. He had already written his marvelous first books, *Old Wives' Tale, Clay Hanger* and others, was being proclaimed in London and, as usual, with a reverberating echo in New York.

A real writer that Bennett, laughing in his sleeve at our Howells and others of his type, dear to the professorial mind at that time, long chain of respectables.

In painting, in America, the Chases and Alexanders [15] on top of the heap, forgotten kings now.

At any rate a certain reverberation through me. The name—Dreiser. Although at that time I had read nothing of Dreiser and oddly did not until much later, when I had myself begun to write and publish books and stories and the critics had begun to say that I had got my stuff from him, myself in vainglorious moments also often saying it, although I knew nothing of Dreiser, when I first heard his name so mentioned, in a rather stuffy room, during what must have been an exceedingly stuffy conversation, I can say, I think truly, that the name of the man did, at that moment, reverberate through me like a bell hit by a hammer and also that something else happened. I wonder if I am now romanticizing. It seems to me now that, at that first moment, when I first heard Dreiser's name mentioned, I saw the man standing in that room, behind the closed curtains, the curtains closed so that none of the neighbors could see certain college professors drink beer and smoke cigarettes, and that I hated him.

He being, if my present imagining of the incident is at all correct, just the Dreiser physically I later knew.

My hatred of him at that moment not however being personal and not at all the hatred of such a disturbing figure in the life of the college professor at that moment discussing him, but a deeper and more pregnant hatred.

Was there in the very name, heard thus in that company, a challenge? That I do not know now and it may well be that what I think happened immediately after is but a myth too, for it seems to me that, having heard the name, I jumped up, crying, "What 'Dreiser,' the heavy Germanic son of a bitch?" shocking everyone in the room and having cried out so that I tramped out of the room where the others were sitting and, going up to my own room above, slammed and locked the door and that then, going to my desk, I sat down with my head in my hands and became for the rest of the night sleepless and utterly miserable.

15. William Merritt Chase (1849–1916), European-trained American painter; Francis Alexander (1800–81), conservative Connecticut painter.

Myth or no myth, let it stand and let us now return to my Italian neighbor. I could not see the house he had bought, in our so respectable neighborhood, from the window of my own room, but I could see his garden. The house stood alongside ours and was one of those pretentious huge frame affairs, great square boxes, often with a kind of chicken coop stuck on top, the chicken coop having little windows, a place to which you could climb to view your enemies, that is to say your neighbors, and the front of the house, that I saw daily as I walked to my factory office, was always closed and the blinds were drawn.

The Italian man, a short heavy set fellow, with such great hips as my own Italian grandmother and with a black shiny mustache, did not live his life at home at the front of the house or on a porch built on in front, as did we Americans, his neighbors, but lived in the back yard and in his garden.

It was the garden that first attracted me and, now that I think of it, I realize that this period of questioning everything in the period of my life through which I was then passing must have begun in the winter.

There were a good many sleepless nights but at that time I was very strong and did not feel the want of sleep. It may be most people make too much fuss about sleep. I do not know but for myself I rather hate it. Life is too short at best. It does seem a waste to spend so much time in unconsciousness.

It must have been winter when the thing began with me, eternal questioning of self, effort to lose myself in books, the lamp burning in my room often until three or four in the morning, toys brought in there to play with. I have an idea that my wife spent a good deal of time crying at that time as I seem to remember her, for a long period, as a person whose eyes always looked as though she had just wiped tears away. "Well, never mind her now," I said to myself, "never mind anyone." It must be that I am a genius as it is only the genius who can be as cruel as I was then. You see I take the genius to be a man who has something to settle with himself and I presume that I did at that time feel that there was something in me trying to arm itself against the enemy—society—and I remember often thinking thoughts like these. "Hell," I thought, "there is this woman I have happened to take as wife. It must be an accident that I have taken her rather than some other woman. It is quite sure I do not love. How can such a man as myself love?

"There must be," I did at times think, "such a thing as love." Men in the books I read were always speaking of it, and I think that faintly I did begin, perhaps during that winter when all of this began in me, to conceive of love as a kind of flow, the sort of thing that D. H. Lawrence was always afterwards speaking about, consciousness of others, self lost. Well, I can't yet define it. What's the use trying?

Cruelty then. The woman I had got as wife and the children I had got by her simply did not exist for me. "Why as for these people," my wife and children, brothers and sister, some of whom I might have been helping and wasn't helping (I at that time never wrote to my brothers and sister) already scattered about America, "to hell with them. They are after all but people and in what way do a few more or less people matter?" By some accident of life I had got married. It was a thing a man did. Perhaps like old Ben Franklin I had thought it would be more economical. "If you have to be eternally chasing after some woman it takes a lot of time and costs too much money." There had been some daintiness in me that would never let me run to prostitutes. "What the hell, I am making them a living," I must have thought. We Andersons had been a ruined family and if my father had stayed in the southern country, from which he said he came, we would have sunk into the hopeless class of the poor whites.

But I, Sherwood Anderson, was going to be something different. I was going to be a rich man, establish a family. We were in this respectable house now, the biggest and best that I, at least up to that time, had ever lived in, but I told myself that it was nothing. "Wait and see," I often said to myself as I walked along the street toward my house at evening. "Next year a bigger house and after that, presently, a country estate." I had no idea that we would stay in the town we were then in. The stopping in that town, perhaps for a few years, was but an incident. I had to find out how things were done in the American business world. "Talk a good deal about honesty but keep your eyes open and when the chance comes, slip it over on them," I often at that time said to myself, laughing as I said it. Of course this may all be somewhat twisted but I am trying to put down what went on in me at that time. I think I did realize that I had a good mind and I remember that often, even then, I said to myself that it wasn't the stealing, robbing others, cheating others, that ruined a man but that what did ruin him was getting to the place where he did not know he was stealing. You see what I mean, a man trying to make himself a success in the American business world of that day and at that time to keep an honest mind. An impossibility to be sure.

As for the family, those close to me, "I'll compensate to them later," I thought. Sons in some small college in the east, none of the western and middle western stuff for my sons and daughters, Yale or Harvard at least for my sons and some place like Smith or Bryn Mawr for my daughter. Oh gorgeous future! My wife in swell gowns all day long and with a cloud of servants to wait on her.

You will see that it was all to be, in the end, a kind of decoration of self, the woman who happened to be my wife not at all considered, my children never considered, the fallacy that you could succeed in the American business world, or in any individualistic world, and at the same time have in you awareness of what you were doing. Success doesn't come in that way. If you are to succeed ever, in any individualistic world, you must never let your right hand know what your left hand is doing. You must be slick with yourself too. Cal Coolidge, who was president later, and the older Rockefeller are true types of the successful man in any individualistic world but, as you will see, I did, all the time, want passionately an honest mind.

That was perhaps my difficulty. I wanted to have my cake and eat it too. Was there a way? "Yes," I cried to myself, thinking of Napoleon. I was always reading about him at that time. *"L'audace, l'audace* and yet more *l'audace,* I cried to myself, mixing men I was trying to quote as I did my scraps of French and English, but having cried out thus, perhaps before the toy soldiers in my room, I almost always immediately became ashamed of myself.

And I think that I did, even during that dreadful period of my life, have moments when I saw my wife and children but, if I did, I saw them as from a great distance. There were moments. I had begun, being strong and often sleepless, and tiring of the eternal sitting alone in my room I crept out at night. I waited until the house was, as I thought, asleep and got into the back yard. This might have been at two or three in the morning. I got out into the street and, putting on my shoes, walked, often for hours in the silent empty streets of that town, and sometimes into the country, and little revealing moments did come. There was a night when I came back to my house just before dawn and was about to creep back to my room but as I came about the corner of the house I saw the figure of my wife doing the same thing I was doing. Why I did not go to her and try to establish some sort of real relationship with her at that moment I do not know. It must be that I confused her with something I had begun to hate. She had come out of a middle class family and I credited her with having impulses she may never have had. I thought that she also wanted me to go on in the individualistic business world into which I had got, that she believed in it and that, if she was unhappy, it was because she felt the resistance to it arising in me and wanted to put it down.

At any rate there she was, in the back yard of our house that night there in the darkness, walking nervously up and down. There was a lawn and a hedge at the back and across the side of the yard and getting to my hands and knees I crept to the hedge at the side and got under. I stayed under there watching her and she walked from the house to the hedge at the back, back and forth, making little movements with her hands. Occasionally there was something very like a little cry from her lips, but I was unmoved. "No you don't," I said to myself. This must have been in one of the periods when the abhorrence of the thing I was in was strongest in me and I must have thought that her unhappiness was all predicated on the thought that I might break loose at any time. It is hard to get a clear sequence of events in such a history as this I am trying to write and now it seems to me that this incident happened after I had begun trying to be a writer. You see the woman I had married had been to college and had a degree. She had traveled in Europe while I, to tell the truth, I could at that time just spell the simplest words. I was a man just out of the laboring class and to the American middle class that was then, and is perhaps yet, a disgrace.

I do not believe the woman felt that, am in fact now sure she did not but she did perhaps think, quite naturally, that a man as ignorant of the world of words as I was could never be a writer and she had already spoken to me of the matter. Her speaking to me on the subject must surely have happened before the night I saw her walking in the yard. She had said to me, intending only, I am sure, to be kind, that I was not at all the sort of man that could ever become a man of letters, trying, as I thought unfairly, to shut a door that might be a way out for me and perhaps, just because I may have been more than half afraid she was quite right in her pronouncement, I hated her for making it.

But no. I did not hate her personally. I must rather have hated something I had the illusion she represented and so I could lie under the hedge watching her quite coldly that night. "No you don't, goddamn you. You don't get at me in that way," I must have said to myself that night and I remember that I did lie quite indifferently under the hedge, watching her moving figure, but half seen, and hearing the little cries from her until she returned into the house.

And I remember also that I did not on that night return to my house at all but going down into the town ate at a downtown restaurant and went from there to my office and to work, getting new form letters that I hoped would sell more and more of my particular brand of paint to the American people.

It was the Italian neighbor that got me and I think now that he got me just because he was in no way close to me. If there was something wrong with me and with my whole attitude toward life he was in no way to blame. By no stretch of the imagination could I blame him as I was inclined, at that time, to blame the woman who chanced to be my wife, the children whose coming had, I thought, cramped my style, throwing on my shoulders obligations I didn't want to take, and the society in which I lived, that had set up certain moral codes, laws, axioms, etc., that also, I thought, cramped me and held me bound.

In the early spring of that year the Italian, my next door neighbor that I had never made a neighbor, began working in the garden back of his house and I sat often in the window of my room above and watching.

There was something stirring back there, in that Italian man's back yard. Spring was coming.

But there. I will not try to describe here the wonders of the coming of a middle western American spring, ice beginning to break up in little creeks, water running along the gutters in main streets, flurries of snow coming, to melt quickly, little ugly heaps of ashes in yards back of houses, the appearance of the first robin, men bragging, "I saw a robin today," and the answering brag, "Ah, I saw one. There was one in my yard mor'n a week ago."

That and something new in people, even in us business men. I presume that, at that time, I was a great egoist and thought that what I felt then, the sense always of struggle in me, feverish times of activity in business followed by times of depression, I felt I must conceal from the other young business men I knew, all of this I must have felt then as something peculiar to myself.

At any rate there was that Italian man, my neighbor, beginning his work in his garden that spring and I was watching. I myself had no garden and "What's the use?" I said to people in explaining. "You fuss with a garden endlessly, get your hands dirty, fight bugs, and raise a few tomatoes and then along comes a man in a wagon who will sell you a whole basket of better tomatoes than you can ever raise for twenty-five cents."

And so that pronouncement from me, wiping earth away, man's relations with earth quite gone. It didn't pay such a one as myself.

With the first faint coming of spring that year the Italian appeared at the back door of his house. He had a paper in his hand and came out followed by his wife. The wife was round and growing fat and had dark skin and large dark eyes and the husband was the short dark squat man with big shoulders and a mustache.

As for myself I had been in Cleveland on the afternoon before, having gone there in a car with three other young business men of the town, and we had been drinking.

But never mind that. The night in the city is now mixed in my mind with a good many other nights, all of us a bit ashamed, a big dinner and then drinks. "What about some women?" The women had been managed. They always can be. As I remember that particular evening and night one of our party had called up some Cleveland business man, a long argument over the phone, "Ah, Ed, come on down. I've got three other live ones here. We want to cut a watermellon." Something of that sort. Young business men in the pagan mood. Wives safely at home. There might have been a meeting of the wives on that evening, say a literary evening, some American or English writer got in for a lecture, or it might well have been a musical evening, God save us all!

Then Ed's appearance. Oh, how many Eds have I not known! He would have been a big heavy set fellow with big hands, red hairs sticking up from the back of his hands, a big cigar. He sold something to someone in our crowd and had felt it expedient to come to our call.

"Sure boys. Let's have a shot or two. I can see that you boys are several shots to the good." God, why did we always have to call each other "boys"?

More phoning now to certain Lillians, Kates, Sues, and then into our car, Ed at the wheel, and off to some apartment where there would be an older woman, she making her living out of just such fellows as we were, keeping a place where gentlemen could meet the . . . ladies.

Lillian, Kate, Sue . . . Jesus Maria! I was to meet them again, over and over, with advertising men, in Chicago and New York, in Denver, Rochester, Des Moines, in the apartments of publishers, out with successful writers too. They hang queerly in my memory, at the edge of consciousness, the Kates, Lillians, and Sues.

Mary, Mable, Agnes.

Tall ones, blonde ones, little things with black hair and eyes, big red haired ones, loud ones, too obviously shy ones.

"Give 'em the works, Kate, Lillian, Mary."

Mable, Agnes, Sue!

Little lusts awakened, not really awakened. Who was it that said that our American movie lovers were the worst any stage has ever known? The same thing in the Cleveland apartment, the women already showing wear, although they would have been young. The woman of that place getting them on the phone. Ed had told her, "Now we want live ones," and she telling the Mables and Sues that we were men of importance. "Put on your best. Show 'em a good time. They'll pay for it."

I presume Ed paid and my most vivid memory of that evening now is of Ed, getting rather gayly rough with some Mable, grabbing her, his big hand, with the red hairs upstanding, hands on her bare shoulders, a look in her eyes she thought no one saw, intense hatred.

"You boys come on. We'll have a hot time tonight."

But why were we "boys"? Too many oldish boys in America and I must suppose I was tired of them, tired of myself, filled also with hatred of myself, as I was of my companions, and, now that I speak of it, I must say that I have hated every method by which I have ever been able to get money in America and, although I was an advertising writer for years and, as an advertising writer, was compelled to attend many of the meetings called "conferences," sitting often in them for hours, individuals remembered as I now remember the eyes of that Mable in a Cleveland apartment, Ed's hand hurting her shoulder, he would have pulled her down onto his lap and she would have smilingly let him kiss her, doing her poor job of the moment the best she could, as later I was to try to do my job, throwing words onto paper, to try to help sell some man's damn soap or toothpaste, some man who had already too much money.

Sitting in conferences, men in such conferences afterwards to be remembered, say like one might remember seeing a dog tear at the flesh of a long dead horse beside a desert road.

Words. Words. Words, I apologize to you.

Words. Dear little words.

A man in an advertising conference who had a bald head. There was a queer furrow straight across the middle of it. He was one of these fellows who pick up words. "Psychology." "What is the psychology of this situation we confront?"

Myself sitting there, near a big inkwell, fingering it. Hatred, as in the eyes of that Mable later pawed by the Ed. Hello, little sister whore! We are all whores, sunk in our whoredom. Ah, freedom.

That sort of thing not for us, Mable, little sister whore.

Just the same there must have been something of the same sort of hatred in all of us bright young men that night in the Cleveland apartment, for I remember now, quite clearly, the ride homeward afterwards. We might have arrived in our own town at three in the morning. Automobile tires were still uncertain experiments. Read Dreiser's delightful *Hoosier Holiday*.[16] On the way home a fight broke out between two of the men of the party. God knows what it was all about, and as I sat in the car, a fourth man trying to quiet the two, profane names roared in an empty road, blows struck.

Then afterwards the two in tears in each other's arms. "I'm sorry, Joe." "Fred, you know I love you."

The next day the men meeting. "Jesus, Joe, what'd you say to your wife? Mine was sore as a boil."

At least I said nothing to my wife. "Well, I went to Cleveland. What the hell of it?" So that was that.

And then myself in the window at dawn the next morning, and that Italian man coming out of his house. He held a piece of paper in his hand and walked down a little path to where the garden was to be, stopped, stood a moment and then ran back to the door of his house to call his wife.

The two people had come out of their house into the dawn and I was at the window of my room, behind a curtain, watching. I was absorbed. There was this shame in me, memory of a hot over furnished city apartment, shall I say smell of the Mables, Lillians and Sues still on me? I have always had a passion for dancing and there was one Mable with whom I had danced up and down the rooms, her body held close to mine, a phonograph playing jazz.

An incident. I bit her on the shoulder. Why? God knows there was nothing inviting to me in the flesh on her bones. It was a vicious bite. "Goddamn you and myself and all men and all women." Something like that.

Anyway she turned and struck me, a vicious blow on the cheek. All right. Now we're even. We have expressed what we feel for each other," I said to her and she laughed a little and we were a bit closer to each other after that.

Oh vice! What a sellout you are!

Staleness of all this on me in a dawn as I watched two people preparing

16. *A Hoosier Holiday* (New York: John Lane Company, 1916).

[265]

to make a garden. The paper the man held in his hand was evidently a plan. He held it before the woman and the two talked, in Italian.

The man went to the house and got a ball of string and when he came out again several children followed.

And now the whole family were in the garden, the people in all the other houses of the neighborhood still sleeping, the curious dawn quiet that lies over cities and towns, little sounds heard, the chattering of the Italian's children. They began running about the little bit of ground back of his house like birds. They were pulling old weeds and carrying them to a place the father had designated. The father, having got the string, was busy, with his wife at the other end of the string. Stakes were put into the ground and strings run from stake to stake. One of the children, a boy of nine or ten, suddenly began to dance. He threw his arms up and began whirling about the pile of dead weeds and vegetable stalks left from another year, the other children, some three or four of them, one a babe that could just totter about, the boy the oldest of the children, the others all laughing as he danced there in the dawn, the father and mother also stopping work of laying out plots from a plan drawn to also laugh with the children.

Myself above, in that room I had set aside for myself in my house, myself stale and dry mouthed from my night of so-called "fun," American business men's fun.

Myself and my own attitude toward my children at that time, self-absorption, ambition, self, self, self.

III

Dance of life but no use my going on with that particular Italian family in America, the other dawns of watching that followed that particular spring of my life, sense caught in both the man and woman of earth love, their fingers seen putting out plants, the man making rows and the wife or one of the children dropping seeds, the children later taking turns in driving early birds away, the father and mother coming out of their house often to greet each particular plant as it emerged from the ground, cries of greeting, the children coming running, the broad hips of the woman and the man, working side by side, bending over to pull weeds, something horse-like in that man, cow-like in the woman.

I had got in me a great curiosity and although the man and I never became friends (I was still too stuffy to go toward him as I should have done) I went sometimes during that spring into his restaurant.

To note the change in him away from his garden and in his so gaudy place of business. He was so polite there, so withdrawn. Was he, when he was in that place, full of the American notion, get every year a bigger and bigger restaurant, a chain of restaurants? Already he had a chain, four restaurants, all alike, in four Ohio towns. I had asked my banker and he had told me. "A good shrewd fellow," the banker had said. Had he got an idea fixed as I had? "Pretty soon I'll be rich. My kids will be Americans, maybe go to Harvard, Yale or Princeton, play football maybe, big American me. Ah!"

I used to go into his place and sit, drinking a cup of coffee I didn't want and wanting to shout at him.

"Come here. You tell me. Is the whole racket worth a damn? What the hell do you think you are up to? Hello brother! What the hell do you suppose I am up to?"

And again digression. Oh again sweet digression.

For I have had experiences as to what the typical American critic will say to my having made so much of the simple incident of having seen from my window an Italian man at work, with his wife and children, in his garden, and only last week I read an article on myself, by one of our more brilliant younger American critics. Someone had taken me to lunch in a speakeasy with the man and another young critic,[17] both afterwards to patronize me with the curious viciousness of the critic, and, not wanting to talk letters with the men, myself having real love of letters, I began telling anecdotes and told one of a Virginia mountaineer, met on a country road, and of the conversation that went on between us, the critic afterward using the anecdote, trying to retell it and failing miserably. Damn a bad story teller who will still try to tell stories, spoiling my good yarns for example, damn them, they all eventually turn critics or economists!

But at that I would like to meet the fool critic on his own ground and to rest our meeting upon his own statement, "All of Anderson is in that, in the telling of some little incident, in a curiously illuminating way." God help them, I wish they would let my sketches alone after I have made them and not add their own clumsy fingered touches!

All right then for the meeting, it being my contention that the illuminating touch is all of painting, music, sculpture, dancing, poetry, prose,

---

17. John R. Chamberlain (1903–   ), journalist for the *New York Times, Fortune,* and *Life.* He reviewed *Beyond Desire* in the *New York Times Book Review,* September 25, 1932, p. 6; *Death in the Woods* in *Saturday Review of Literature,* IX (April 29, 1933), 561; and *Memoirs* in *New York Times,* April 9, 1942, p. 17.

what have you. How silly this demand that life be thought out clearly. Who can do that?

I will admit that there is an underflow, a current, but God man, you cannot get at it by statement.

Who has not had an experience I have often had? You are walking, let us say, on a country road. Let us suppose a day in summer, in the late afternoon. You walk over a hill and out a strip of woodland and there is open country stretched out before you.

There is a man plowing. It is late summer and this is late fall plowing he is doing. It happens that the furrow he is running runs diagonal to the road in which you are walking and so you sit on a grassy bank to watch.

And to think.

And to dream.

And to wish.

What?

It is unlikely any man ever makes a wish not related to himself.

The nice thing in the play of muscles over the breasts of work horses plowing, as nice as the same play of muscles over the breast of a Man of War running through the stretch, that forward reaching thing, or over the breast of a pacing JIC of another generation, noble horse I once saw at the full stride, land curling up under a marching plow, man moving back of a plow. Why have painters always loved painting the reaper or the plow-man, poets singing of these?

But the wish, the dream.

I have already said that no man makes a wish not connected with self, and so, wishing this unison in men, horses, field, sky overhead, old passion-ate wish in man for flowing accord with the materials of his life. . . .

What I am trying to say is that if you, being by the roadside and seeing the plowman, have this wish to know in him this unison with nature it is because you so passionately also wish it in yourself and also that in transferring it to him, for the moment, you also become for the moment not yourself but a part of him.

Does it seem complex? It is really very simple and that is why nothing matters but the illuminating moment.

For example again myself in that window after the night of debauch and the man in the garden below. I had of course been reading books. Books also have their values. And I had, from my father, been hearing a good deal about the Civil War and the south.

Back of me then was the fact. There had been, before I was born, this thing done to the land in which I was to live. It had been done in the north and worse in the south. Here was a people given a land too big, too sweeping, too magnificent for them. Afterwards I was to see, with my own eyes, by observing men, how the wealth men were always trying to get and that I was myself at that time eager to get, how it destroyed.

A man sought security and having got it something stopped and having stopped began to rot. On all sides of me, among the men I then associated with, the young go-getters of an Ohio industrial town, I thought I saw this slow rot going on. We were together fingering and fiddling about a golf course, going about in automobiles, taking the damn little cheating and robbing we were all doing so seriously, going off on such parties as the one I had been on during the very night before all of these things came to me, insulting womanhood at such parties, the women there insulting us.

"It is all a sort of universal whoredom," I said to myself, sitting there in that window on that early morning in the early spring and through a window watching an Italian man and his family in their garden.

My own throat dry from my debauch, my head aching.

Still the thoughts kept coming. I do not believe I looked any more at my neighbor in his garden. There was a bathroom near and I kept going there for glasses of water. There was a kind of semi-nudeness. Having come home from my party in a rotten physical condition I had started to undress but then, realizing I could not sleep, that I did not want to sleep, I went to sit in my underwear bare-legged by the window. Not a nice picture but nothing of this present picture is nice or intended to be nice.

What the hell we humans, Americans? For all of us there must surely come these moments when the land we live in, this broad sweet rich place on which we have got a foothold, calling it our land, when its significance must a little come home to us.

Think of it this way. There is no need taking a great stretch of country as an example. There is, for example, this vacant lot on a street in any American town. Let us say it becomes mine by ownership. (*Ownership* eh? A queer word. Even as I sit here writing and stopping to try to say the word aloud it sticks in my throat, rasping my throat.) There is a vacant lot in a town. It is mine and I may do what I please with it.

I am what I was at the time of which I am now writing.

And now I recall something. On the night before, at the party in the apartment in Cleveland, during the process of our debauch, one of my comrades had spoken to me.

It was during our drinking and in the midst of the false laughter that always goes on at such affairs. Let us say that Ed, our pilot on the party, had got his Mable or his Lillian on his lap. In a doorway over behind him stands the woman who has taken the apartment and who makes her living by getting women and girls for us young business men.

And so, at that moment, another man of the party approaches me. I am sitting in a somewhat sullen mood at the side of the room and he pulls a chair over to me. I am quite sure that I can see his figure, even yet, at this moment, although it may well be confused with a hundred other such figures remembered in the mood he was then in.

You will see how it was. There we were, we men, in that place, helping certain women and girls along their road to whoredom, and he had gone momentarily sick of it, as I had, and a thought had occurred to him. He would be a sandy youngish man with sandy hair and eyebrows and so he comes to me.

"Sherwood," he says, "I've got something about which I have intended to speak to you."

"Yes," I say sullenly and our conversation is interrupted by one of the Mables.

"Go away, we're talking business," Sandy-hair says gruffly and then he begins.

He has got, he says, an option on a certain piece of land. There is to be a new factory come to town. It is to be a big concern that makes iron pipe. They are moving out from Pittsburgh and he explains that labor has got a bit high handed in Pittsburgh and that they are coming to our town where labor can be handled.

And so they are to put up this big plant in a place out near the edge of our town, by a river and near the railroad tracks, and a certain fellow in the company, high up in the company (the man who is talking to me knows him well, went in fact to college with him, the two roomed together) the fellow has tipped him off. "Of course he is in on it," my companion says to me.

"And so I have got this option on this certain piece of land, a large piece. The banker will let me have any money needed. He also is to be in on it.

"We are going to stick up a lot of little working men's dwellings, cheap affairs. They should make easily fifteen or twenty percent."

He had looked up suddenly and had seen me sitting there at the side of the room. Self-disgust in me as perhaps in him at the moment. "Here, we have wallowed long enough. Hello, there's Sherwood, sitting over there! Divine Sherwood! This women's world we have got into tonight. Damn women."

Some such thoughts in him as he moved over to me. Man's return to his man's world.

"Out of the dawn of a sudden came the sea
"And the man looked over the mountain's rim,
"And straight was a path of gold for him
"And the need of a world of men for me."

And so, the rest of that can safely be left to the imagination of the average American reader, the house built, profits taken, growth of industrial towns, any American industrial town, mill villages in the north and south, tenant houses of farm hands, both white and black, on southern plantations, the rows of terrible little frame houses, stuck up on stilts and blackened by coal dust about mining shafts, endless miles of long Chicago West Side streets, afterwards to be so well known by me, long nights of restless wandering there, bathed, soaked in ugliness, the great ugly prison-like streets of upper Manhattan.

Mankind, as it is in America in the year of this writing, 1933, crying out that there is no work to do here and the great mass of mankind in America still living as suggested above.

Man thus making the equipment for a framework surrounding the lives of other men.

Ruthless profit taking going on meanwhile.

"Does it pay?"

"Does it pay?"

Memory in me as I sit writing of a night long after my morning when I sat in the window of an Ohio house and saw an Italian-American making his garden, streets of working men's houses, in that old French city, as ugly as any in an American city, profit taking going on there too.

There was, on that night, an American man, Ralph Church,[18] then a student at Oxford, who had come over to Paris to meet me and we walked and talked of this, of my own American experiences in business, of Ralph's father and the money he had made.

Profit taking. Money. Business. Business.

Ralph and I, on that later night, must have used the word "business" a

18. Ralph Church, Oxford student and later professor of aesthetics at Cornell University, who was recipient of many of the items in Anderson's *Letters*.

good deal, the influence of the business world on American education, American thinking, American politicians, words running, we walking absorbed in our talk through street after street, stopping now and then to look about. "God I didn't know there were streets like this in Paris." Wanderings into little bistros to drink, dark little holes, very like the pubs in Eastside London, ghastly enough specimens of humanity all about, we nevertheless absorbed in our talk, coming out of some such hole to walk again in more dark ugly little streets.

All of this old in its ugliness, the festering going on a long time.

America rapidly coming to it.

Just the same, between us two, at the moment, one of those rare fine moments of comradeship that come occasionally to men. If Ralph ever reads this he will remember the night.

The talk jumping about as such talks will. First American business, the American universities, from that to Synge in Ireland and George Moore[19] in London, then back again to American business.

As I have already suggested the word "business" must have floated up time and again, out of our conversation, for suddenly, in a dark little Paris street, we found ourselves surrounded by a mob of French people. They might well have been Paris Apaches. At any rate, there they were, a street full of them, they having surrounded us in our absorbed conversation, thinking no doubt that we were a pair of American men, in Paris on a bust.

Saying in an American of an older generation that when he died the good American went to heaven while the rich American went to Paris.

Hatred of America and its success at money accumulation having begun to grow before the World War, intensified during the war, more and more intense later, that very America that was once the hope of Europe, one of humanity's greatest dreams betrayed. "Land of the free and home of the brave."

Plenty of misunderstanding too.

How?

Why?

Damn little realization in Europe of the nameless masses down below in America, as in all European countries, real quality of the nameless masses down below in America as yet unknown.

19. John Millington Synge (1871–1909), Irish dramatist and poet; George Moore (1852–1933), Irish author of escapist Bohemian tales. See *A Story Teller's Story*, ed. White, p. 288.

The masses in America as yet being shaped, educated only by advertising billboards, newspapers run for profits, educational institutions as yet all being controlled from up above, by business.

"Presto Sherwood! Don't preach like a soap-box orator! Tell your story."

"But don't you see, man, this is also a story of thoughts."

That night in Paris Ralph Church and I surrounded suddenly by that strange mob. How vivid the scene yet, the dark little street with the tip of an old moon just looking over the corner of an old building, little passages running out of the street we were in, ragged men and boys, a few women and girls, gaunt faces, vice touched faces, these confronting America as represented at the moment by us two, there, in that place, on that night, they all suddenly dancing, throwing gaunt arms upward, dancing, jeering, derisive laughter. They had got a little refrain out of some Frenchman's meager knowledge of our language and suddenly they all took it up, dancing about us as they sang. I remember two French working men (they might well have been bums, criminals, how do I know?) they suddenly separating from the others and walking up and down before us, imitating the earnest mood we had been in, looking at each other, making gestures to each other, each saying over to the other with profound earnestness, "Business is business. Business is business."

The crowd surrounding them and us taking up the refrain, more dancing, more and more derisive laughter, the cry running through streets, echoing through streets.

"Business is business. Business is business."

Then Ralph Church and I, two stout hearted American figures, hurrying through street after street, followed by that dancing, singing, laughing mob, we wanting both to laugh and cry.

Afraid too. At any moment stones might be hurled.

"Business is business."

"Business is business."

"Business is business."

Thus Europe to America. Who now dare say there is not everything, all history, all thought, in such illuminating moments in life?

In such a book as this things happening and thoughts have to be scattered and often without true sequence of time and place. I wish it were possible for me to write without hurt to anyone. We are all, in America, in this day, caught in something. We are, in a queer way, sold out.

I remember early impressions caught. They were not definite impressions. It might have been just the feeling of wonder and strangeness in life that has never left me. I must presume that life, in the village of my boyhood, in our house for example, was pretty crude and who wants or likes crudeness? My mother must always have been tired. Life had run out early for her and her man, my father, hadn't made good. To tell the truth he must have been to many people rather a joke.

I mean his continual big talk, pretence, etc. This sort of thing must grate horribly on a wife, who must, after all, live a great deal of her life in her man.

And I dare say it isn't just failure that counts most with a woman and I can imagine a kind of failure, a man unable to meet life as it is, such failure as my own brother Earl knew, he falling dead in the streets of Brooklyn after fifteen years of painting and never once getting what he wanted, unsuccessful paintings piled like cordwood under a bed in a miserable Brooklyn rooming house, he working as a baker in one of the great city bakeries, failure faced, such a failure might make an appeal to a woman. But what a really horrible lot depends upon ability to make money, buy nice clothes for your woman, put her in a good house on a good street, a room with pictures on the wall. Good taste grows slowly but it cannot grow at all when there is nothing for it to feed upon. For, after all, good taste has nothing to do with nature. A field or a tree cannot be in either good or bad taste. It is what you do with the things about you that gives you away.

I am thinking now of my father's continual talk of the good family he came from and of mother's silence when such talk was going on. There she was, you see, the daughter of that old Italian peasant woman, who, after mother's death, came to our house. I have often wondered what my grandfather, on my mother's side, must have been like. He had died, a young woodsman in the forests of southern Ohio, shortly after marrying my grandmother. She had four husbands all told, and mother had been bound out to a neighboring farmer.

And so I remember our house, the meals always being served in the kitchen, how I hate this kitchen eating, lack of formality, smell of soapy water, food cooking on the stove nearby, the continual sameness of the food, the shabby neighborhood, mother at the stove cooking, frying, frying, frying.

Smell of hot grease.

Now my father is out of work again and is always coming home with the smell of liquor on his breath.

Or he has become a house painter for a time. Formerly he had been the owner of a harness shop of his own. I know what would have become of that. He could never count pennies as a man must do in a small business, be shrewd and careful of small sums.

"Come on boys." Half the hangers-on of the town, the no-accounts, would have been continually loafing in his shop. I know the qualities in him that would have destroyed him in a small middle class world because they are also in me.

"Come on. What's a dollar? What's five dollars?"

Fool. That is not the way you get rich or well-to-do, get the respect of others. You have to get a sense of money in a money civilization. Money makes more money. You save and save, being always careful of small sums, until you have a stake and then you invest it shrewdly. A thousand dollars saved and put out at six percent will make you sixty dollars a year. Now look, there is some money you do not have to earn.

Let it alone, add to it, get a sense of money. You get three thousand, then five, then ten thousand dollars.

Dollar sign already on your soul.

Sure, but never mind that.

Let's say you invest in real estate. There was a man in our town who worked in a flour mill for a dollar a day and that man, in the course of years, by God knows what carefulness, saved pennies, never spending a cent for pleasure, putting by a few pennies today, a dime tomorrow, watching, thinking, that man, in the course of a life got, owned, a dozen houses. Look at that!

Some man who owns a house is always getting into trouble, drink, a woman, God knows what. He owned a house but now it has to be sold at sheriff's sale.

You go down there, to the sale. Watch out now. Make your bid but be careful. The house will rent for six, eight, ten dollars a month.

If you get two or three houses, working men's houses are the best, your working man with a large family, his job a bit precarious, isn't going to be always asking for improvements.

If you get two or three houses, paying pretty well, you can go to the local banker. "Hello, Mr. Wells."

"Why, hello."

"I've got a chance. I want eight hundred dollars."

The banker thinking. "Tom's a good steady fellow. He's a good risk."

"All right, Tom. What collateral you got?"

He knows Tom has got it all right.

"But Jesus, what a life!"

"Whoa now. Don't be like your father!"

If you are in a certain kind of civilization what good are you if you can't fit in?

On the other hand there would be the wife and the children of that man, Tom the miller of our town. I remember, when I read Dreiser's *Sister Carrie,* sitting for a long time, after reading, and thinking, not of his Carrie, or of that Hurstwood ("Goddamn him," I said of him, "let him go, suck in his gas in his New York lodging house, what do I care?") but of Carrie's father, working in the mill at Columbus, Indiana, or wherever it was, and of the curiously dirty, unforgivable thing he must have done. You see, I am presuming that he was rather like the hand in a flour mill of our town, a careful saving man, a dime saved here, a nickel there.

It is just possible that there was also memory in me of Tom's family. Now wait. Let's see. There would have been the wife and two children, both girls.

Why the hell didn't he have more, a dozen say? He would have known nothing of contraception.

Well, that would be easy enough. You get a wife, a country girl, let's say. The woman Carrie, in Dreiser's book, is a good enough sample. Don't think for a moment that Carrie couldn't have been tamed. Nothing tames a woman like the slow determined putting her nose to it, characteristic of any good steady honest citizen who plans to get somewhere in our civilization.

Make her like it. That's the ticket. Get her on the tobog and keep her there. A woman loses it fast. Pretty soon no other man will want her at any price. If you get a woman where no other man wants her you've got her. O.K.?

And then too, this sex thing. It isn't so important. Is sex necessary?

Surely not.

You can get the duplicate of that, or something near enough like it, in warm sense of security. Imagine Tom, the flour mill hand of my town, walking away from his talk with the banker, eight hundred dollars to buy another house. If he manages well the rent of the house will pay him out in ten, twelve, say fifteen years. "He sure knew I was all right." Don't think for a moment that Tom couldn't get enough from that to make it O.K. with him about missing, say, the deliciousness of sex, moonlight nights, pretty women, nice clothes, all of that.

Besides, as you know, all of that outwardly making life delicious is immoral. It's the way of death, hell, burning brimstone, what you got in the churches of Ohio towns at that time. Tom, the miller, who got security out of his dollar a day at the flour mill would have been a staunch church member.

Easy enough to see how the puritanism that came out into our section of Ohio, edge of the Western Reserve, how it ran naturally into a kind of tightness in money matters. God and the dollars. Methodism and Presbyterianism. The communists are obviously right in attacking religion as it is in the American Protestant churches. God and property are so closely bound together in the American notion of goodness and respectability.

And then there is always lust in the background to take your mind away from the Protestant God and it isn't only the lust of the flesh. There are other lusts. My father, when he had any money, went to the saloon. For fifty cents he could get drunk and when drunk what dreams of greatness realized. Now he is a great general, winning battles, receiving the acclaim of the people, he is a solid citizen of the town. It is only an accident that he is not rich. I remember a night in the winter. He was drunk and perhaps mother had said something sharp to him. We were at supper in our poor little kitchen, warmed by the kitchen stove, one coal oil lamp to light the scene, and it was snowing outside. "So I am not respected in my own house," said father, lurching up from the table. He looked at us children, sitting in the lamp light, white faced. "You may be like your mother," he said. "You may think I'm a poor stick."

"I'll show you," he said, staggering into the front room and returning presently with some sheets of white paper. Mother stood over by the stove and I am sure there were tears in her eyes. Well, when we artists are at work, women must weep. Father stood before us children with the papers in his hands. "These," he said, "are deeds to some fifteen acres of land in the very heart of the city of Cincinnati.

"The land belonged to my ancestors and I have a perfect right to it," he said, not looking toward mother.

"And now you see. . . . Only today there was a man here from Cincinnati to see me. The city wants to settle with me for three million dollars. 'No,' I said. I intended to leave it all when I died to you my children, but now. . . .

"I intend to burn these deeds," he said, staggering out at the door, and we children went and huddled by the window to watch. He went down into the back yard, to a place near the outdoors privy, and burned the papers and I can still, in fancy, see him bending over, lighting the match, just the way his half kneeling figure was outlined in the little flare of light, the little flame and the darkness. When years later the scene gave me the idea for one of the finest short stories I or any other man ever wrote, "The Man's Story," in the book *Horses and Men,*[20] the woman in the room with the absorbed man, the poet (and if father was not a poet, at that moment, what was he?), the flare of light from a fireplace filled with papers, the woman shot by a rejected lover, not wanting to disturb the poet, lighting the papers in the room and walking across the room to fall dead at his feet, it is a story that will someday be counted one of the very great and beautiful short stories of the world and father gave me the key for it.

Oh golden key.

Thou dear one!

And all of that for fifty cents spent on liquor, the miller in our town, who got security, would have saved, not lighting flames to imagined Cincinnati millions but lighting real flames in his children too.

That, let us say, with all my mother's suffering. I dare say she didn't suffer so horribly. That compared with what life must have been in the house of the miller who owned say twelve houses in town, the meanness of it, the gaunt wife and the starved girl children.

IV

And see how things click.

Let us go back now to me as a coming young man in an Ohio town.

I had got in with a certain man of the town, a man a little, by the way, a fellow of letters. He had a little business in the town, a little print shop on a side street, and occasionally he did printings of form letters and circulars for me.

The fellow used to come into the office of my factory.

"Well, Anderson," he said coming into my private office and closing the door. He did not come more than two or three times before he began calling me Sherwood.

He would come into the office with one of my paint circulars in his hand, having brought it for me to read, and would stand at the door looking about. One of the girl stenographers sat by my desk. "Could I see you alone?" he said mysteriously and when the girl had gone out of the

20. See *A Story Teller's Story,* ed. White, p. 67, for the same incident.

room and had closed the door he drew a chair up close to my desk and whispered. He was a small man of perhaps thirty with dry leathery skin and was unmarried.

"Sherwood," he said, when the girl had gone out of the room. He looked at me with curiously weary eyes. "Do you mind," he said, "if I talk personally and intimately with you?"

"Of what?" I said and he began to explain.

"I have got this circular here," he said, holding up the sheaf of proofs.

"Well," I said.

"Well, it is like this. You see me sitting here at your desk. I am a man in a small business. It is my business, as a commercial printer, to print what is given me to print."

I remember the first time he said something of this sort to me because I was angry. Afterward I was always amused by him but the first time he said it I grew angry.

"Well, what's wrong with it?" I said, taking the circular from his hand, and he laughed and winked at me.

"It is so eloquent and so full of bunk," he said and got up from his chair and walked about the room.

It was perhaps this man who first suggested to my mind the idea of being a writer. At first, when he first tried to tell me of what was on his mind, he was somewhat hesitant. "You are sure you will not get angry with me?" he kept asking and when I assured him he began trying to tell me that I wrote well and I remember now that this little Ohio printer, with his shop on a side street, told me something that was afterwards told me by Gertrude Stein in Paris.[21] "You sometimes write what is the most important thing of all to be able to write, passionate and innocent sentences," Gertrude Stein said and the little printer, in trying to tell me what was on his mind, said something of the same sort.

At any rate the man interested me and I am not sure but that he became the first friend I ever had.

We began going about together. The man did not dress well, going about the streets of the town, going into little saloons and drinking

21. Gertrude Stein (1874–1946), expatriate author whom Anderson met in Paris in 1921. Miss Stein wrote of Anderson in "Idem the Same—A Valentine to Sherwood Anderson," *Little Review*, IX (Spring, 1923), 5–9; *The Autobiography of Alice B. Toklas* (New York: Harcourt, Brace and Company, 1933), pp. 241–42, *passim;* "Sherwood's Sweetness," *Story*, XIX (September–October, 1941), 63. See also her review of *A Story Teller's Story* in *Ex Libris*, II (March, 1925), 177; and of *Puzzled America* in *Chicago Daily Tribune*, May 4, 1935, p. 14.

together. The man always drank sloe gin, saying that he thought the drink increased his vitality. "It puts me on edge," he said, "makes me want women.

"And women," he said, "are among the few things in life it is worth a man's while to desire."

It was this man, whose name was Luther Pawsey (he is dead now so I may write of him with ease, and besides Luther Pawsey was not his name), with whom I began spending a good many hours together and going off with on secret trips. "We will go to Cleveland tomorrow, what eh?" he would suggest suddenly, coming into my office and closing the door, or perhaps it would be a visit to the Ohio town of Ashtabula or to Sandusky that had taken his fancy. "Come on now. You must go home and get your bag. We will have three or four days."

"But what will we do there?"

He said frankly that he did not know. "It is another place. It is not this place," he said. In a fresh town, where we were unknown, there would be more chance for adventure. "Who can tell what will happen? We will go there, not to a big central hotel but to some little hotel where there is small chance of seeing anyone we know."

"And then?" I asked. At first, when he first made these proposals to me, I was puzzled. "There is the matter of time wasted," I said and he smiled.

"Time? And what are you doing that makes time so important?" At that time, like most Americans, I was always being in rather a hurry, often about nothing.

"Well, and then," he added, "you see. . . ." He was himself puzzled. "A town is like a suit of clothes," he said once, in trying to explain.

He had difficulty in making an explanation, stuttering and walking about in my office. "Well, you see, I am not exactly like you. I am a small man in a small business. Unlike you I have not married. That is because I cannot make up my mind about any one woman.

"Oh I do not mean to be immodest," he said quickly. "I have never asked any woman to marry me and so the matter, my attractiveness to a particular woman for a prolonged period, as in marriage, you see it has never been put to the test but as for women in general. . . ."

He laughed. Always when he got upon the subject of women a curious change came over the person of my friend. There would be a sudden glistening of the eyes, a new aliveness in his body. "Look at her," he would cry suddenly, when we had got off together to some town and were walking in the street. There was a woman walking on a sidewalk before us. With him curiously it was not often the sort of woman who usually attracts men. "Such women do not attract me," he would say, pointing out some quite richly dressed woman we had passed, some woman with what is called a good form, plenty of IT, such a woman as most men turn the head to look at. "As for that one," he would say, "I have nothing she needs. Such a woman is like one walking in an orchard where there is plenty of ripe fruit. Every tree is loaded with it. She has but to put out her hand to pluck and eat the apple.

"But this one," he would cry, pointing out another woman we had passed or were, at the moment, following. The women so pointed out were always of a particular sort and, after I had gone with the man on several such trips I myself began to see a good many of the type.

They were always women, not too obviously attractive and, when you looked at them sharply, always with a kind of sweetness. "You see, they are the starved ones," Luther explained to me and on this subject he would go on for a long time, talking in little rushes, a bit I must say like the figure of the man Joe Welling, in the story called "The Man of Ideas" in my book *Winesburg, Ohio.*[22] It may be that I got the figure of Joe from Luther.

Luther would go on talking for hours, sometimes coming to the office of my factory in the evening or sometimes I would go to his print shop where we would sit talking or we would go for a walk on the back streets of the town at night or off on one of our seemingly meaningless trips. Sometimes, on such occasions, he would get onto the subject of women and again on the subject of himself.

"As to the matter of words," he said. We would be sitting in his shop in the evening. It was a dark messy little place and he would run and get one of my paint circulars. As we grew to be better and better friends I gave him more and more of my printing to do, not asking him to bid. "Now, you see, here is a sentence you have written," he began, reading aloud a sentence from the circular. When he began in this matter he always looked at me a bit doubtfully. "You are sure you will not be angry because of what I may say?" I reassured him, filled with curiosity, and he read one of my sentences aloud. "Of what were you thinking when you wrote that?" he asked.

He did not wait for me to answer. "Ah," he cried, "I will tell you. You

22. "A Man of Ideas," *Winesburg, Ohio* (New York: Viking Press, 1960), pp. 103–11.

see it is a sentence, purporting to describe a certain paint you are making and that you want to sell, but when you wrote it you were not thinking of paint.

"As to your paint, that you make down there in that factory of yours. . . . well, as to that I say nothing and when it comes to that you yourself do not make it. Your own hands never touch it.

"When it comes to that you are not interested in the making of paint. In what are you interested?"

When he was talking in this vein Luther always jumped out of his chair. Let us say that the two of us were in his little Ohio print shop at night. It is a night of the early fall and it is raining outside. The street on which Luther had his shop was just off the main street and it was dark at night. There were several wholesale houses down that way and at night they were all dark.

So Luther had jumped out of his chair and was walking up and down in his shop. There was a gas light burning. The office of the place was not partitioned off from the shop. There were two desks, two typewriter stands and three or four chairs. When Luther walked thus, up and down in his shop, expounding on the subject of words, man's curious obligation to words, there was a curious effect.

The shop had a cement floor and there were printing cases and flat topped tables, each with its printer's stone, these making shapeless masses in the darkness at the back. All of this is rather queer, as so much of life is queer, if we but dare feel its queerness. There was Luther, with his rather small and dried-up looking face and his slender alert body. He walked quickly but there was a peculiar dragging of the feet. There were always papers lying about on the floor of the shop. "We do not sweep until morning, a boy does it, he is a stupid boy and never sweeps clean but I only pay him two dollars a week, he cheats me by not sweeping clean and I cheat him by paying him such a small sum," he had explained to me several times. There were these papers on the floor and as Luther walked and talked, going sometimes into the darkness at the back of the shop so that his figure was lost among the cases back there and then suddenly emerging, as he did this his feet made a queer shuffling noise among the papers. It was like a man walking in a wood in the fall among dead dry leaves.

"And so there you are, a man sitting and writing," cried Luther, holding one of my paint circulars in his hand and walking up and down in his shop in the way described above. He had a peculiar gleam in his eyes now as he sometimes had when he saw a woman on the street. "You sit and write and the ostensible purpose of your writing is to sell paint.

"But what has happened? You do not know but I do. I myself am not a writer. I can talk but I cannot write. When I sit down and get a pen or a pencil in my hand I become paralyzed. But for the fact I might have become one of the great writers of the ages.

"But never mind that. Let us talk of you," Luther said. "You sit and write. I know well enough what happens to you. Someone told me that, before you came here, to our town, to set up as a manufacturer here, you were an advertising man in Chicago. Is that a fact?"

I told him it was. I was curious as to what he was trying to say and besides I was flattered by his interest in me and in my paint circulars.

He began to scold me about my writing. "Suppose you were a woman with some beauty of person and went and threw yourself away, going into any kind of dive, lying with any kind of man. How long would you be thought of as any kind of woman at all? You'd be a slut, a whore, wouldn't you?"

He began then to talk of words as no one had ever spoken of them to me before.

And now there it is. I speak of this man Luther, found in a little print shop in an Ohio town, and people and the critics will be saying that I am romanticizing. "No such fellow ever existed," they will say. "It is a romantic conception."

But why should I care? The man Luther did exist and we spent more and more of our time together. He would take a sentence out of one of my paint circulars. "Now tell me the truth," he would say, "when you wrote that you were not thinking of paint.

"The truth is," he went on, "that, as you wrote that, you were thinking of someone else. I know how it was. You imagined some man getting the paint circular in the mail. He is a man you never saw and never will see. Now you tell me this. At bottom you are not so proud of the business you are in. You are a word man. I can tell that from reading these circulars you give me to print and you are not interested really in making paint.

"And you are not interested in getting rich either. If you were you would not be wasting your time with me."

He began to explain, as though he thought some explanation necessary, why he had taken up with me. It was because he was lonely. "I go after women a good deal," he said, "being careful not to get caught in marriage by one of them because I am a man whose fancy, in the way of women, constantly changes, but women cannot satisfy something in me.

"There is something that should be built up between men," he said.

He thought also that I was selling out my life. "Suppose you should begin to respect words and ideas," he said. "You can't continue to use them, really, to deceive people, as you are doing here." He pointed again to my paint circular. There was something he was trying to say and that I was trying hard to understand. He thought that when I wrote my paint circulars, striving as I thought to make them as slick as possible, to attract people so that they would buy the products of my factory, I was really doing nothing of the sort.

I was confused he thought and I did not know what I wanted. In reality, according to this fellow, as I sat writing, I thought nothing at all of my paint or of my money getting but rather thought of some mysterious man, away off somewhere in the distance, to whom I wanted to get close.

"I was attracted to you," said Luther, "because, one day in setting up one of your circulars I suddenly realized the truth about you."

I laughed but was at the same time embarrassed and I remember going homeward one night, after one of our first talks of this sort, and that there came one of those odd moments that again I contend are of such infinite importance in a life. There was the going away from Luther, after a lot more of the same sort of talk with him. I never went to a psychoanalyst but I have often thought of what must have happened, at least at the first, some other man attempting to thrust in and in, to search out your very soul, resentment, all kind of resistance. "Whatever I am you let me alone." The psychologist Trigant Burrow [23] will remember an experience once had with me, at Lake Chateaugay, in northern New York, he trying to get at me, my resistance, the half comic situation that developed between us.

I would have walked away from Luther's print shop on a fall night, thinking, trying to understand what he was driving at with me. "If he is so hot on this thing," a certain respect for words seemed to be at the bottom of what he had said to me, "if that's it, why doesn't he become a writer himself?"

---

23. Trigant Burrow (1875–1950), psychologist whom Anderson met in 1916. See Burrow's "Psychological Improvisations and the Personal Equation," *Psychoanalytic Review*, XIII (April, 1926), 173–86; and the Anderson *Letters*, ed. Jones and Rideout, Items 38, 41, 42, 61, *passim*.

Why I dare say what I had thought of the art of writing, when I had thought of it at all, was that, at bottom, it was very much like paint making, or like running an advertising agency. You did it to make money.

To be sure, to do it at all you had to have, born in you perhaps, a certain kind of talent.

For example to be a real story teller. I rather think I always was one. You see this experience with the man Luther must be thought of as also a growing thing, my being more and more with the man, sensing things in him. Let us think of it as a kind of love making on his part.

And I do not mean physical love making. Luther was no fairy. I shall prove that by going further with him a bit later.

But he had got hold of something in me. When we were together we did not always talk seriously. Sometimes he spoke of nothing but the art of printing. He had a passion for certain papers and for certain fonts of type he thought beautiful, and would sometimes run clear across town to my office to show me a page he had printed. "Look. Isn't it beautiful?"

It may have been. I did not know. This matter of the surface of things in life, the shape of an apple or a pear hanging on a tree, the tree, the bed you sleep in, the chair you sit in.

The effect of a room on an inner thing in yourself. All of this was, I think, at that time, rather Greek to me.

And here let me say something to those who are beginners in the arts. It is a slow painful process, this training the senses toward the more subtle things of life, toward something of getting, or at least beginning to get, some sense of the real beauty of life in its physical aspects. Why I, who now have rather trained faculties in this direction, when I began I thought many things beautiful that I now think ugly. I think it must have been under Luther's influence that I began, in the matter of pictures for example. I got a scrap book and kept it in my room. "This man has something I am going to get," I said with determination and so I kept the scrap book and began cutting drawings out of magazines. I pasted the drawings in the book and sat thumbing it. Occasionally I took it to Luther.

He was polite. I can see his eyes yet, looking at my book, and I can hear his polite words. "Very nice. Some of them are quite nice." It was like a man speaking to a child.

"What the hell is it?" I said. It was the old cry, "What is art? What is beauty?

"Oh, beauty, truth, where are you?"

V

The slow painful effort of a man to arise out of something. It is quite true that, at that time, I had no connection at all with the world of art or letters. Is it any wonder that all of my reactions to those immediately about me at that time, my own family for example, were often so brutal?

I was walking home from Luther's shop on a night in the fall. I remember several such walks. "It is curious," I said to myself, "but this man is doing something to me. There were moments of doubt. I have never been a man to whom homosexual men are attracted, the sort of thing that happens to men, leg grabbing, sudden caresses bestowed, the sort of thing that other men are always telling me of having had to go through, but already I knew of such things.

"Is it something of that sort he is after?" I asked myself. The idea that love could grow as between man and man, a thing outside sex, a feeling perhaps founded upon brotherhood, realization of self in another man, your own curious loneliness in life in him too, understanding of self a little got at perhaps through understanding of another, all of this was, at the time of which I am now speaking, new to me. "Bunk," I would have said had anyone suggested such an idea to me and would have gone on defending my scorn of any such notion by pointing out that life was but a game. "You are cast down here," I would have said. "Well you came out of something, out of a woman of course. The chances are that you really know little enough of the woman who gave you birth.

"A seed from some man starting all of that in her.

"Back of it all, to be sure, some sort of mystery.

"What have you to do with all of that?

"You can't fathom it so you do what you can."

Men talking, in the churches and in other places, of love, as between man and man, but all the time you knew or thought you knew, from your own experience, that what you got, in the way of joy, pleasure in life, you got really by watching your chance and then grabbing as other men all about you were grabbing.

"Well, what do you get?"

I had begun asking myself that question. I must presume Luther had rather started all this in me.

The question asked and then thoughts coming and I remember sharply a night, going homeward to my own house from Luther's. There was no doubt that something he said to me about my paint circular was true enough. Already for several years I had been doing what I was doing when I wrote the circular.

And what was that?

I had been using the words of our human speech, really, to deceive men.

I was making and selling paint and there was no doubt that houses needed painting and if all of this reasoning of a quite ordinary man as he walks along the streets of an Ohio town alone, say on a moonlight night, having just come from the shop of his friend, an obscure little printer, seems somewhat primitive and simple it at least should be of interest as revealing what must go on in many such men.

The questions asked, defenses made. The real implications of what Luther was that time saying to me were that I was sinning in some odd way in my paint circulars rather well. A great deal of the business that at that time came to me was done by mail and to create confidence in the breast of some man at a distance, who had never seen you, knew nothing of you personally, it was of course necessary to write well.

Luther, you see, had said to me, "You are not thinking of paint as you write. I know of what you are thinking."

Did he know?

Myself groping and trying to find his meaning and also the meaning of his interest in me and in my affairs.

It was quite true that in writing anything, for example a paint circular, the object sought was some sort of entrance into the confidence of the other man and so, even in such a crude approach to the art of writing, you thought, not of the thing of which you were presumed to be talking, but of the man addressed. "How can I win his confidence?" you thought and this led inevitably to the secret watching of men.

So you went about in life, always a bit on the alert, listening, watching. In modern society you were like a little animal in a jungle. It was a question then of survival. Some men were strong. They fought and bullied others.

Others were shrewd and sharp. They could think faster than other men, take advantage quicker.

And you?

Perhaps you had none of these qualities so you developed another. You became quick and plausible with words because you had found out that words could throw men off their guard and so you began, more and more, to use words to serve your own private ends.

[287]

And all the time also using them to keep up the illusion in others that you were really naïve, quite innocent, had nothing but their good, rather than your own good, in mind.

This never however done too obviously. You watched yourself always to grow more and more skillful.

It is to be borne in mind that I had already been at this thing, this advertising writing, for several years. Some accident of life had led me into being an advertising man.

But was it an accident? I had begun life as a laborer but had found the sort of labor I had to do too heavy for me.

You must now think of me now as going along a street in an Ohio town and arguing with myself, much as I am doing here.

Thinking.

"If what this man Luther implies, by the things he had begun saying to me, be true, who is to blame?"

It had so obviously begun with me, even in childhood. "My father didn't provide for us, did not look into the future and mother couldn't," I said to myself. I had got sunk down into the ranks of common labor, working on farms, in factories, digging ditches, etc.

And at night, after such a day of work, I was too tired. My back ached and my hands were blistered.

"This won't do," I had said to myself and, walking home from Luther's place, I remembered nights in Chicago, when I was a laborer, working as it happened in a cold storage warehouse for two dollars a day, ten long hours, and all the time crying out to myself.

"You've got to get out of this."

How? How?

"You've got to get out of this."

How? How?

Going at night, at this time, to a night school, provided for just such cases, to The Lewis Institute, on Chicago's West Side, unable to work there, to get the education I thought might get me out. I went to my desk in a room and letting my head fall into my arms slept through the lessons.

"I can't. I can't.

"I am too tired and sleepy."

Then at the warehouse finding out that I could slowly and with gradually growing subtlety talk men into a certain frame of mind.

A word here. A word dropped there.

The foreman in the room in the warehouse where I worked. What were his particular passions, what his prejudices?

He was a German and hated the Irish. It turned out he had an Irish wife.

Very well. Think up mean but entertaining little stories about the Irish. Get him. Get him on your side. Get a slightly better and easier place.

Onward and upward.

And then the chance that led into advertising writing.

Now there is more leisure. You can read books, think more, watch men more closely. Why you have got a gift, God knows where it came from. Many of the more successful advertisements are written, not primarily to sell more of the goods advertised, but rather to flatter, in some subtle way, the maker of the goods.

Find that out among other things. Get on.

Very well. But why should I be doing all of this for some other man? Why not do it for myself?

All of this in some queer way twisting you too.

"Is that what he means?" Myself asking myself as I walked home from the shop of my friend the printer.

"Very well. You are a whore then." These words said aloud to myself as I walked alone in the streets of my Ohio town at night. My mind groping to find an answer to that. Was there a kind of male whoredom, brought about by a certain sort of civilization, inevitable perhaps? I remember that when I was in Chicago, after getting into advertising, how very glad I was to get in, how I worked to impress others about me with my talent, my enthusiasm, this before I went to Ohio to become a manufacturer.

Even then I had my moments of doubt. I went sometimes to the office in the morning and passed in. It was a big office with many men sitting at great flat topped desks, all of these advertising men, word writers, word sellers. "We sell here the words that will make men and women want the goods you have to sell. Come to us and we will give you the word that will make you rich."

Manufacturers of goods coming in there. They were usually big, important acting men. This world of ours was a bit strange to them. The bigger ones, that is to say the ones with the most money, had however always a certain arrogance.

And why not? We men and women in that place, how we bowed down. There would be the word running through the office. "Mr. Jones is coming in today." Mr. Jones was spending a million dollars a year to say words about certain goods in newspapers, on billboards and in magazines. "Jones' Soap for the Toilet." The agency that employed me got a fifteen percent cut on the million spent yearly by Mr. Jones. There's a hundred and fifty thousand dollars for you. This hundred and fifty thousand dollars to be split up, in the way of commissions, salaries, etc., among the men and sometimes women working in that place, the word writers, word sellers. Myself one of them.

The sudden coming of Jones into that office of tremendous importance. There were plenty of other advertising agencies, like our own, in Chicago. Others in Detroit, Cleveland, New York and St. Louis. Other little or large groups of word writers, word sellers, eager for the hundred and fifty thousand we made from Jones.

He suddenly wiring, "I will be at your office tomorrow morning at ten."

Tenseness in the office in the morning when I went in. There were quick little conferences being held. "What's the matter with Jones?" All of us knowing, well enough, that a whim might throw him away from us and into some other office of the town. There were word writers, word sellers, out of other little hunting packs, always dropping in on Jones.

You have to get hold of such a man, hold him, hold him, but how?

Watch him as a man might watch some woman for whom his loins ache. What does Jones like when he is off duty? Is he coming to Chicago today because he has suddenly become dissatisfied with the word machine we have concocted for him, has begun to flirt with some other agency, or is he merely coming because he is momentarily bored with life in Peoria, Louisville or Dayton, Ohio, and wants recreation? If that is the case you'd better know what he likes, a big dinner, wine, women. Does the fellow like blondes or brunettes? "For God's sake get busy men. Hurry! Hurry! It's half past nine now. He'll be here by ten."

All sorts of men and women employed in that place with me, nice middle class men living in suburbs with their wives and children, going regularly to Methodist, Presbyterian, Baptist churches.

Catholics, Free Masons, Rounders.

Billy Holden. He is the fellow best of all of us in our office for the clients who have a fancy for women. Billy can show them the town. He knows wine. He knows places. He can get them regular women, who make a business of it, or he can get them amateurs.

You know, the kind that hold a man off a little, act girlish, brash and bold, but moments of weakness come. We copy writers, word makers, phrase makers do not have big separate offices as do the word slingers, a cause of infinite, ill concealed jealousy on our part. "The bastards. Who do they think is holding Jones?" etc. But occasionally Billy having me into his office. "Jesus, Sherwood, I was at it again last night.

"That man Miller, from St. Louis. Old Holdbrook shuffled him off on me."

Holdbrook is one of our bigger word sellers, a vice president and a very respectable man. He thinks that Miller, one of his more profitable clients and a man who likes to cut loose a bit when he gets away from his own town, should be taken care of but doesn't want to do it himself. Billy says Holdbrook is a big Presbyterian out in his North Side suburb. He says to Billy, "You take care of him. Never mind expenses," he says.

Billy talking to me. "I had to do it. I guess that's what they hire me for.

"So I took him to the theatre and to dinner. I got the champagne corks to show old Holdbrook if he wants to see them but he won't. My little boy's got typhoid. Did I tell you? I wanted to be at home.

"What the old bastard likes is to get one on his knees. I say to them, 'Tell him the story of your life, how you happened to be wrong.' A lot of them ain't got no imagination so I give 'em a story.

" 'Look here, Lil,' I say, 'he'll be asking you, as he fingers you, so you tell him.

" 'You tell him it was in a barn. You were a country girl and didn't know a thing and it was a farm hand. He forced you but your mother was terribly strict and found it out and drove you away from home.'

"He don't do nothing but put his hands around on them and ask for their stories. I don't know, maybe so he can tell it to a Sunday school class or something later, back home, in his own St. Louis suburb, or wherever he lives and goes to church when he is at home."

Nice people.

Dull people.

Smart ones.

Brash ones.

Plenty of heartaches, headaches.

That's an advertising agency. That's any office. That's your broker's office, your jobber's office, your manufacturer's office. All of them have customers. Customers have to be taken care of.

So me, like any of them walking into that office of a morning, going back to the copy department.

Jake. Lewis. Hallie, who did women's stuff.

John, Fred and Harry.

"Hello girls," I said, coming in of a morning, trying to put as brave a front on it as I could, as were all the others. I guess they all knew what I meant. I wonder sometimes what girls in a parlor house talk about when there are no customers about. Afterwards, as I found out, it not so different in publishing houses. The racket going on there too. People do not buy books. Books are sold to people. When things are sold to people there will always be a racket.

Had I known all of this when I fled from the advertising agency to go back to Ohio and become a manufacturer, setting up a racket of my own? Walking at night through the night streets of an Ohio town, after one of my talks with Luther, he having put his finger on something in me, love of words. "You have a kind of talent in the use of simple words. Occasionally, when you try, you can make a sentence. It's rather a shame, really, Sherwood, for you to be in the racket you are in."

These little knives stuck into me by Luther, left sticking in me. I walked uncomfortably, coming from his shop. Sometimes, even though it was raining and my clothes were wet, I didn't go home. I think I must have made, over and over to myself, the kind of protest most men make.

I think it is not unlikely that had I been able to go into my house and sit down, call my wife and children to me, and had I been able to say to them, "Here you. Listen to me. I am a man born with a certain sort of talent that I have just discovered in myself and it is being perverted. I have been dreaming a dream, a childish sort of dream, but I am beginning to awaken. As for you, my wife and children, if you have got off on the wrong track in life, it is not your fault, but now we must right about-face." Had I been able to explain to them all might have been well.

I felt myself unable to explain. Oh land of the free, what is freedom? I think that my notion of the life of the writer, a possibility a little opened up to me by Luther's words . . . "I might be able to do it," I found myself saying to myself. Afterwards when I did become a writer and began telling tales it was said of me by critics that all of my tales were of one sort, they were stories of escape.

It must have seemed to me then, as for that matter it does yet, that the real tale of American lives is as yet just that.

Eternal fleeing from something.

"I will. I won't. I will. I won't."

"It is the fault of this woman. I will flee from her."

"I can do nothing in this town."

"City life may save me."

"No. It is not that. I will flee from the city to the town, from the town to the country."

It must have been that upon me, as upon all men, rested a responsibility. How loath we are to take it. Upon me, an obscure and scheming little paint maker, dreaming my dream of riches to be acquired, great houses to be lived in, myself clamoring up to all of this over the shoulders of others, dragging after me my wife and children, a penny lifted out of the pocket of this man, a dime out of the pocket of that man, slow accumulation at first, then faster. Now you have more elbow room. Now you may begin to play with thousands, not hundreds.

Really big men playing with railroads, whole railroad systems, chains of newspapers, great oil companies, steel companies, chains of retail stores.

Bigger and bigger you grow. Now there are gigantic children playing with gigantic toys and you are one of them.

As I have suggested, having started home from Luther's shop, after one of my talks with him (how much of the starting of all this in me he intended I'll never know), having, as suggested, started homeward I did not go home.

I began wandering in the streets at night. Schemes began coming into my head and I think it was at this time, under the influence of Luther, who never spoke of politics, that I became a socialist.

The writing of words can lead to all sorts of absurdities. I had the factory, I manufactured goods that were sold in stores. The business world was forever talking of "service."

"All right, let us be of service," I said to myself.

I had at that time just come upon the idea of socialism, of the cooperative commonwealth.

"Why not start to really do it?" I thought.

I began going about to merchants, talking to them, I for a time wrote and published a magazine. I wrote a long book called "Why I Am A Socialist." (Afterwards I burned it. I do not think there are any copies of my magazine in existence. I am lucky if there are none.) [24]

I sent out thousands of copies of my magazine. I went all over Ohio talking to merchants.

"I will," I said, "run the factory on a very small salary. All I want is enough for food and clothing. I will do away with all the cost of selling, of advertising.

"And then you, in turn, will sell the goods for a very small profit, let us say a profit of ten percent."

24. There are, apparently, no copies extant of Anderson's manuscript "Why I Am a Socialist" or of his magazine *Commercial Democracy*. Of course, neither may have existed.

I was manufacturing house paint.

"We will make the paint better and better. All unpainted houses will be painted. We will be doing a great service to mankind."

I was in stores, talking to merchants. I think now that, for the most part, they thought I was insane. No one responded.

"Very well," I said to myself, "I will call a great convention of merchants." I dare say I had, at the time, a picture of myself as a kind of William Jennings Bryan [25] of business. I went about secretly practising a great speech, I sent out thousands of copies of my magazine.

I rented a great hall, I engaged hundreds of folding chairs. It all seems absurd now. It is all true.

The great day came and I went to the railroad station in my town to meet the arriving crowd.

But one man come.

He was an old man who had been a merchant but had failed in business. He had nothing else to do so he came. He was staying with a son in a nearby town and he had brought a grandchild.

He brought also a paper bag filled with bananas. They were ripe and, no doubt, he had bought them at a low price. I can, as I write, still smell them. He was the only passenger who got off the train.

"I've come to the meeting," he said. "This is my grandchild. I brought him along.

"Have a banana," he said.

I took the old man and the child to my house. They stayed with me for three weeks. He was a pleasant old man, if a little weak in the head.

"Well," I thought, "if his head is weak it is no weaker than my own."

When I had got him and the child that morning to my house I went up into my own room and closed the door. I wept a little and then I laughed. My laughter rang through my house.

I See Grace Again

I had come to the city to lecture and was at the hotel in the afternoon. The lecture agent had told me at what hotel to stop but I had gone to

25. William Jennings Bryan (1860–1925), reform Democratic presidential candidate in 1896, 1900, and 1908.

another. This was when I was building my house.[26] I had gone broke when the house was half finished and to get the money to finish it had gone on the grand tour.

I had been at it for weeks, going from city to city, from town to town, and I was oh so tired of it.

I was doing colleges. I was doing universities.

I was doing girls' schools.

I was doing women's clubs.

In the colleges they did something to you. They got two for one. Well, you delivered your lecture. I had prepared four lectures, giving them each some large spongy title so that I could deliver any one of them under any one of the four titles. I worked one until I couldn't stand it any more and then I worked another. I began to understand how the actor must feel who works a thousand nights in the same role.

"The Younger Generation."

"America—A Storehouse of Vitality."

That's the sort of titles I gave my lectures. They went big for that one about vitality. Perhaps they thought I might say something that would make them feel vital.

I spoke of the colleges. So you lecture. You are all in but a professor of the English department comes up to you.

"I have got together a few choice spirits. There are a few members of the faculty and some of the brighter students, those who are particularly interested in your work."

You are led off somewhere. They set you down, question you. You are often made to feel a good deal like a witness in a murder trial, a kind of accessory before the fact.

"What do you think of the work of Ernest Hemingway?"

They pick out other writers who are personal friends, others who are not friends.

How are you going to answer such questions? All your reactions to the work of other men, in your own art, are complicated. You can admire another man's work and dislike the man. You can love another man and dislike his work. You don't much like spilling your likes and dislikes about. You are tired. You want to shout at them.

"Go to hell, all of you."

But then you think, "I may be broke again. This lecturing is, after all, a way to get some money."

26. Anderson refers to his 1926 lecture tour. See below, "I Build My House."

Sometimes something nice happens. I was up at Dartmouth. They had got me into a kind of hall, after my lecture in the big hall.

"I'm sunk," I thought.

There was a platform with a table, a chair, a glass of water.

"Good God. It's going to be a second lecture.

"Or a grilling." They were coming into the room, the members of the faculty, the brighter pupils.

"They've sure got a lot of bright ones up here," I thought.

I was standing by a door, up there on the platform, the second platform I'd been on that night.

And on the next night I'd have to be on another platform.

There was a sudden row started in the hallway outside. It was beyond the door through which this my second audience for that night was coming. It sounded like a fight.

The crowd that had come to grill me surged back through the door.

For a moment I was alone, there in that hall, and then it happened.

I was standing by that door at the rear of the platform and it opened. Someone pulled at my coat.

"Come on, Sherwood," a voice said and in a moment I was through the door and in another hallway.

I was in the company of four or five young men and, later, we were joined by the two who had started the row in the other hallway.

We hurried along a hallway. We were out of the building. We were running across the campus.

And presently we were in a room with whisky and sodas. We could relax. The lads who had kidnapped me hadn't any perplexing questions to ask. They wanted simply to drink the highballs with me while we told stories, and later they took me to my train.

It made me strong for Dartmouth. I've never been there since but I have always remembered with gratitude the Dartmouth lads and when, in the sports columns of some newspaper, I read that Dartmouth is in a football or baseball game with some other college I go about silently rooting for Dartmouth.

But to return to Grace, whose name I have put at the head of this section of my book.

I was in another city, during the same lecture tour. I hadn't gone to the hotel that had been recommended to me by my agent but to another and more obscure one.

"The lecture agent will have told them that I will be at the other hotel and they will go there seeking me," I thought.

I thought, "I'll relax awhile, maybe walk about, forget for a few hours that I am a lecturer. At the last moment I'll show up."

I thought, "They'll feel they should entertain me and just now, this afternoon, for the next few hours, I don't want to be entertained."

So I was walking around the town and I found Grace. She was coming along the street and spoke to me.

"Hello Sherwood."

"Why hello."

I did not know her. She had always been thin but had grown thinner. She saw my confusion.

"It's Grace."

So there it was, after the long years. We went to my hotel, to the mezzanine floor. We found a quiet corner.

There was a bell boy, going through the lobby below calling my name. They had located me. Some committee from the organization that had engaged me as lecturer was after me. They intended to get me into a car, perhaps with several ladies, and take me for a drive, show me the sights of the town.

Then I might be taken to an afternoon tea, or a cocktail party. No men.

"Oh, Mr. Anderson, I have so enjoyed your books."

"Well, that's nice."

"Which of your own books is your own favorite?"

I would have an answer to that one. I had thought one up.

"Are you a mother?"

"Why yes."

"Which of your own children is your favorite?"

There would be a woman who would come up to me saying that she thought my *Winesburg* the best thing I'd ever done. It is so tactful telling a man of fifty-five that a book done when he was thirty-five contained his best work.

I would get a little sore when that one was sprung on me.

"What other and later books of mine have you read? Name them. I dare you."

I wouldn't say it of course.

"Yes? You do? Well, that's interesting."

I'd get off something like that, wanting to say, "Oh, the hell with you and what you think."

I didn't answer the bell boy's call. I sat in a chair facing Grace in a quiet corner on the mezzanine floor of the hotel.

We were silent for a time. Memories crowded in on me as no doubt they did on her. I hadn't known she was living in that city. For years I had not heard from her. When the last letter had come from her she was in the west, in the city of Denver. She had gone out there with her sister Susan who had tuberculosis.

In order to break the silence between us I asked about Susan.

"She died," Grace said.

"And you, now?"

"I'm married. I have two children."

She explained about her husband. He was a good man. He was a mechanic and worked in a garage.

"He has a night job. He works nights. He is a good man. He doesn't drink.

"I didn't think I'd see you," she said.

It was evident enough from her dress, the shoes she wore, the stockings on her thin legs, her hat, that she was still poor.

"I saw in the newspaper that you were coming to town, to lecture here. I went and bought a ticket. I didn't tell Ed."

Ed, I gathered, was her husband, her man.

"If I told Ed that once you and I. . . . You are such a big man now. He'd laugh I guess."

She certainly wasn't making me feel big. I had begun to feel very small there before her.

"I thought I'd just go, see you again, hear your lecture."

There was no rancor in what she was saying to me. We had met, that night, so many years before. I certainly needing her then, she giving herself so freely.

That would have been twenty, twenty-five years before our accidental meeting that day in the street.

"I mustn't keep you. They were calling your name from down there. Your friends, your admirers here will be wanting to see you."

She got up to go and again, for a long minute, we stood in silence, looking at each other. I did not protest her going so soon. It was quite hopeless. It was one of the things that happen to a man and woman in life.

We were quite alone, at the moment, there on the mezzanine floor of that hotel.

"Shall I take her in my arms, hold her again for a moment?"

When I had seen her last we were still lovers. She had simply gone off, to the west, with her sister Susan. She had a little money saved, a few hundred dollars. She was going to spend it trying to save Susan's life.

We had certainly clung to each other then, at that parting.

"It will be the last of it," she had said.

"Anyway, it had to come to an end, sometime."

She had what I had thought, at the time, a rather childish faith in me. Just at that time I was so desperately discouraged and she had, in her queer awkward way, given me so much new courage.

"It won't be very long with you as it is now."

She knew nothing of writing, read no books. At that time she was in a factory, was some kind of floor woman in the factory.

She had charge of a floor in the factory, that was it. It was the same factory her younger sister Susan worked in. It was a dusty place. It was that place had made Susan ill.

Then she, Grace, was quite young. She might have been three years younger than I was. She had red hair, not a shining red but a rather dull brownish red. I remembered that Perry, my friend, who was with me on the night when I picked her up, at the shabby little resort, had laughed at me.

"Well, you're some picker. My God!" he had exclaimed when I saw him the next morning, after I had walked away from the resort with Grace.

She had brown freckles all over her thin face. She still had them as she stood before me on the mezzanine floor of the hotel. They were on her thin hands, too, on her thin legs and her thin body.

I wondered, standing there before her, whether or not I should again take her into my arms, hold her close again.

"But she is married to this Ed. She has children now. She has got a good man. That's good.

"I don't think she expects it. She wouldn't. She was always so timid and shy, with so much feeling of inferiority about what she had to give.

"And she really gave so much.

"But she never knew how much she gave."

I was remembering the night when I took her to that small town where there was but the one hotel. It was crowded. There was some sort of church convention in the little town and the rooms in the hotel were all filled.

The clerk had told me of the German woman, in the little white house, surrounded by flower beds, who occasionally took overnight guests and we had gone there.

She had stood, frightened, by the white picket fence outside while I had gone to the door of the house.

Something had got into me that night. I was in a play boy mood.

"We have just been married. We are a bride and groom. We came here and the hotel was full," I lied to the woman.

She was a little bustling soul, one of the extraordinarily neat German housewives you sometimes see, and she was at once full of German sentimentality.

It was growing dark but she could still see Grace, standing out there by the fence.

"Is that her?"

"Yes. You know how it is, with a woman who has just been married. She's shy."

"Yes, yes, I know. You come in here."

She was explaining that her own man was dead. She took me into the parlor of her little house.

"It was my parlor but I have made a bedroom of it. I take guests sometimes. It brings me in a little money.

"But I've never had a bride and groom."

She was obviously excited.

"Do you think it will do?"

I expressed my satisfaction with the room and she asked me to take my bride away.

"You two go take a walk, say for an hour. I want to fix it up for you.

"I want it to be so nice. I remember the night when I was a bride," she said.

So Grace and I did and then we came back to the little house and there were flowers everywhere in our room.

It was on that night that Grace cried. I had awakened in the night and she was not there, in the bed with me, and when I called she did not answer so I lit matches.

And there she was, on the floor, in a corner of the room, by a window that looked out on the German woman's little flower garden, and she was crying softly.

Because, she said, it couldn't be like that night always.

Because she had so little, she thought, to give.

"I'm so thin. I haven't much vitality. You know that.

"If we could go on as we have been I wouldn't let you," she cried.

"It isn't for you or for me either.

"It is just something that has happened and I'm glad it has but, oh I wish I were a beautiful woman."

She had cried, for a long time, in my arms that night, and then there I was, with her again, after the years, in that hotel. Time is like that. It mixes you up.

I was wondering whether or not I should again take her into my arms, hold her for a moment again, when she put out her thin hand.

She gave my hand a little quick shake.

"Good-bye."

She had gone quickly away. Downstairs, in the hotel lobby, the bellboy was again calling my name.

Perry was my friend. He ran a newspaper in the town. At night we walked about together. He was a young old man. There was something in him very warm and friendly. He also had, vaguely, some notion of some-day being a writer. He was a great admirer of O'Henry.[27]

We continually quarreled about that.

"No, that is not what I want."

I couldn't explain what I wanted. We went on sprees together. I lied to my wife.

"I am going away on business."

Why I could not explain to her I can't say.

We were at the resort when I first saw Grace. We had been on a three days' debauch. How we got to that place I don't know.

There was a little dance hall, by a lake. There were small cottages along the shore of the lake.

Everything was cheap. There was an open air dance hall, many people, men and women, half drunk, dancing on a kind of raised platform, out under the summer night sky. While we were there, that night, there was a man stabbed.

It was over a woman. Some half drunken man had put his hand under the dress of another man's wife.

He was stabbed. They took him bleeding away. Whether or not he died I do not know.

---

27. William Sydney Porter (1862–1916), known as "O. Henry," prolific author of "trick-ending plot" stories that Anderson hated. See *A Story Teller's Story,* ed. White, p. 292. "Perry" and "Luther" may be the same unidentifiable man.

The dance went on. Perry danced. He went from one woman to another dancing.

I was in one of my worst moods. I was, at that time, becoming a manic-depressive. The disease of living had got me down.

I had been trying to cure myself with liquor but the liquor was dying in me.

There was a kind of park with trees and benches and I wandered about, in the half darkness, getting as far away as I could from the dancers.

I had found Grace, sitting alone on one of the benches, and went up and spoke to her.

She was then, as she always was, while I knew her, thin and tired looking.

I sat near her on a bench and began to talk to her. Something happened. I had been unable to talk to my wife, to my best man friend, Perry. To Grace, from the first moment, I could talk.

I was there with her on the bench, in the half darkness. It was then I saw in the distance the taking away of the man stabbed. Perry later told me the details of that.

At the moment I paid it no attention. I was absorbed in Grace. I had begun telling her of how I had gone off on a drunk hoping thus, for a time, to escape from myself and of how it had not worked.

"Something has happened to me. I have found you. You are one to whom I can talk.

"I want to talk to you. I want to know you. I want to be with you," I said to her.

She was on a vacation from her factory job and had come to that place. She had brought her sister who was, already, half ill.

"It doesn't cost much here," she said.

She was direct and simple. She was like someone out of my boyhood. I had been, all evening, filled with contempt for people and she restored my faith. Already she was making plans. She wanted to take her sister out of the factory.

"She ought to be outdoors. I am saving money for that."

We sat talking on the bench for a time and then we went to her cottage and she made coffee for me. It was then, when we were walking past the dance pavilion, that Perry saw me with her.

He saw her thin figure and her thin, always rather sad face.

"You are a bum picker," he said later but I did not answer him.

For how could I explain to him? She was one to whom I could talk. In her presence thoughts I had never been able to get into words, got into words. To talk with her was like sitting at a desk writing but it was not quite like that.

It was infinitely better. For all her thinness and her essential tiredness there was something very alive in her.

But aliveness is not the word. She received me into herself. As for our physical intercourse, that came later. It was strangely not important.

There were times, it is true, when it was important to her. As on that night in the German woman's house.

It assumed importance in her mind because she over-estimated its importance to me.

Later I was with her on many nights. I was with her on afternoons. She was in a Cleveland factory and on Saturday afternoons she was free.

She took a train and went to some town and I joined her there.

We walked in woodlands. We were beside small streams, in Ohio called "creeks." We were on our backs lying. Once, in a wood, we found a solitary old man, living alone.

We went hunting bees together during the afternoon and then I walked to a nearby town and got food that Grace cooked for us. There was but one small bed in the old man's hut and Grace and I lay in it while the old man slept on the floor.

He insisted.

"I would not let your wife sleep on the floor," he said.

When I was with her I was at peace. I knew a new peace. I talked and talked. It was like writing but it was not like that.

I do not think we ever spoke of marriage. She knew I was married but we never spoke of my wife. We both knew that what we had could not last.

There was a kind of peace—something that cannot be described. I had been bitterly discouraged, at times near suicide, and she gave me new courage.

"I cannot write letters to you," she said. She had wept, sitting that night on the floor by the window in the German woman's house, because she was afraid she could not give me what I needed physically. She had the feeling that she was not passionate enough for me but she must always have known of what she did give.

We were in that hotel and I was, more or less, a famous man. I was, in a small way, what is called a "celebrity." People were waiting for me. In the town, where she had come to live with her husband who was a mechanic in a garage, so-called "fashionable" women were waiting to take me about in a car and show me the town.

They would take me to a tea or to a cocktail party. A woman, the wife of a merchant, a lawyer or a politician, would come up to me.

"Oh I think it is so wonderful. To be a writer must be very wonderful."

Grace was there with me, on the mezzanine floor of that hotel. Bell boys were calling my name. We had said nothing to each other of the past. I had a half impulse to again, for a moment, take her into my arms but I did not do it.

"Well, I must go. Good-bye."

She went thus awkwardly away. She was still, as when she had meant so much to me, thin and tired looking. I just stood there and she went away down a flight of stairs.

I was engaged to deliver a lecture and it was time to show up.

"Well, I will have to show up. Damn it, now I will have to show up," I was thinking.

Brother Earl

My brother Earl's last days taught me something. His was indeed a strange life and death. Like all of us in our family Earl had perhaps at birth been bitten by a strange bug. Without exception each of us (there were five boys and two girls) in some way tried his hand at some one of the arts.

But wait. Earl was the next to the last born and the last, a girl (she was named Fern) lived but a few weeks.[28]

I remember Earl, when he was little more than a babe (he might have been three or four), sitting on the sidewalk before our house at Clyde, Ohio. How the mind and the memory play tricks. It seems to me that my older brother Karl would have been perhaps thirteen or fourteen and I might have been eight. There was the little house, of brick. It was not

28. The records are confusing, but Fern Anderson may have died December 9, 1892, when she was almost two years old. Her death is described in *Tar: A Midwest Childhood* (New York: Boni and Liveright, 1926), pp. 163–65.

larger than a good sized chicken coop. I went back there once, at night. It was at night and at that time I was in love with Prudence.

Poor Prudence. She was certainly not prudent. I had been courting her for months in an eastern city and she had fled. She went west, to her people, somewhere in Iowa, and for months she was silent.

Well I did not want marriage. I had tried that and had failed. Letters began to come from her. "It is very very dull here." It was a hot dry summer and she spoke of the hot still nights on her father's huge farm. She had been wanting marriage, saying she was not afraid. She had inherited money from an aunt and once she had held out the bait to me. "We will marry and I'll leave you altogether free. With the money I have you can have your life of leisure. No more writing of advertisements. You may let your fancy run free. Perhaps, as you are always hoping, you will someday become a real artist."

Why, Prudence? Why do I speak of you here, in connection with my brother Earl? You never saw him.

But now I remember why. What a curious mixture life is. There was this temporary passionate love for you, Prudence, and the life long love I have had for my strange brother.

I remember that Prudence wrote me finally, throwing open the door. This also would have happened while I lived in Chicago but I had not met Prudence then. I met her while traveling. There was an eastern city to which I had been sent to write advertisements for a manufacturer.

He took me home to his house, to dine, one evening, and there I met Prudence.

There was one of life's quick strange contacts made, sex crying out in me and in her.

"I do not want it. It is not as I have planned my life." She was studying to be a physician. "Once we begin God only knows where we will end.

"I have kept myself a virgin.

"This I know, that for any woman the man who first takes her, to whom she really gives herself. . . .

"There may be others later but she will always love that one.

"And you do not want marriage?"

"No."

She had relented. "Very well. I will sin with you." I had got a little money ahead and had bought a second hand car. "I do not want to meet you in Chicago. I am going back to school." The school was in an eastern city. She must have put her hand on a railroad map. I fancy her in an Iowa farm house on a hot dry afternoon in August. She was an only daughter but there were three brothers, all, like her father, farmers. I never saw them but always in fancy pictured them as great tall broad shouldered brown handed fellows. They would speak always slowly and quietly.

So different all of them from the younger sister. She blonde, with yellow hair and blue eyes. She was my only blonde woman.

She was tall, slender, intelligent, excitable.

She is in that farm house, on the summer evening, and has the railroad folder spread out before her. A hot wind, blowing dust, comes in at the window. She runs a slender finger down a column of names of towns and it stops. It was the town of Sandusky. "You will meet me there. The through train stops there in the early evening." The town was but a few miles from my own boyhood town of Clyde.

She would not have thought of that. "I remember your saying you were born and were a boy in Ohio. I do not remember your speaking of any town.

"For the time I am going to give myself to this love, this passion, I would like to go to some town where you were a boy.

"If what we are about to do is sin then I accept sin.

"We will have a week, ten days. I enclose money. You will drive alone from Chicago to Sandusky. I will be there on such and such a day."

After all I have repaid your sweet graciousness, Prudence. You are married now and a mother of sons. You did not after all stick to your profession, stay simple. Wherever you are and if you read this, Prudence, read also my *Winesburg, Ohio*. There is a little prose poem, the woman strong to be loved. I called it "Tandy." [29] It was written for you.

It must have been after eleven or twelve when we got that night to Clyde, where I had not been for many years. We had loitered along, talking.

But perhaps I did the talking. She, I have a feeling, remained silent. She would have been a woman of say twenty-eight.

"But I am very cold."

The night would have been hot.

"Now that I am face to face with it there is something very cold inside.

"It is so strange to think about. I did not sleep on the train.

29. "Tandy," *Winesburg, Ohio* (1960), pp. 143–46. This is Anderson's only acceptable explanation for the most confusing story in *Winesburg*.

"There is this strange intimacy to think about, flesh to flesh. We in our family have never practised that kind of intimacy. At home we do not kiss. Our bodies do not touch. I think I never saw my father kiss my mother. I have never kissed one of my brothers."

There had been the tenderness, when she had written me from out there, but it was all gone. It is likely that I began brutally. "Well, if it has never happened to you it is time it began." My own theories of the value of intercourse, love, the final intimacy, spun out. Everything must have remained very mental between us. The car I had got was a little roadster and we drove slowly, stopping for long periods to sit beside the road. There is something very brutal in life too. Now, you see I have got that Prudence mixed also in my mind with other women.

Myself wanting, lustfully wanting. How long it took to find a woman who satisfied all sides of me.

I would have gone off on some fool's track with her for I have seldom been a wholehearted lover of women. I could never really believe in women dentists and cannot to this day. Perhaps in some essential part of me (never in the flesh) I have, all my life, loved men more than I have ever loved women.

I can in fancy hear myself now, talking to Prudence on that night. Instead of taking her into my arms, caressing her, coaxing thus the warm life in her down out of her mind and into her body, I would have sat beside her, talking and talking, she pale, grown more and more silent.

It may have been there was again something said of marriage, she quietly, in a low cold voice. "Nowdays, when divorces are so easily got. . . .

"Surely you know that I will never try to hold you.

"At least I should have that much sense. If the feeling you have for me is not strong enough to resist then there should nothing happen between us.'

"And besides, I am terribly afraid."

"Afraid?" I would have said. Perhaps on that night I got started, began to spin out a long theory as to the artist's relations with women. "What matters it, Prudence, that I am not yet an artist? I am of the type.

"We are so and so." I would have remembered a certain very compact, very dark little woman named Clara with whom I had had an affair of the flesh.

Myself suddenly wanting no more of her. Something said or done that offended something in me.

Myself afraid to tell Clara. I would have shilly shallied, lied to her.

She would have got onto me. There was a night. We were on the stairs in the house where she, Clara, was living with certain relatives. They had all gone off to the theatre.

It was the sort of opportunity for which, formerly, we were always planning and scheming and I was running away from her.

Some lame excuse made. "I must go. I am very sorry. It is imperative."

Clara getting me told. "You! You! I have never been anything but dust under your feet.

"You are not just a coward. You are so altogether absorbed in yourself.

"You do not need to think that I shall regret when you finally go. This moment may in fact be final. I am telling you. I doubt if you can stand being told."

There were words thrown at me. A few times Clara and I had had nights together. "When it has been so after our moments."

She had spoken of nights when we had been together. "I was striving, striving," she, Clara, had said. There was something she had wanted, the excitement of love making, to utterly shatter something in her, so that she no longer existed. I had got it that it had failed and that the failure was mine.

"You have only been using me." She had got it, I gathered, that if I also, through the medium of physical love with her, had wanted also to lose self it was only that I wanted to be set free of self.

That I might leave her and all women, going far out and away from her.

"Afterward, with you, it has been like lying with a stone, or a Buddha.

"You become like something I do not and cannot understand. You are an old, an ancient thing." I remembered, on the night with Prudence, the blonde, all Clara, the dark one, had said.

"It was the last time I ever saw Clara."

"And you think what she said, you think it was true?"

"Yes."

I do not think I loved anyone, man or woman, with the possible exception of my mother, who had died years before and, perhaps, in a way all such fellows as myself have, I had made a purely romantic figure of her. Of this also I cannot be too sure and it may well be that I had only the hunger down inside me to love someone. To love the figure of a mother, long since dead, was not difficult. I could constantly recreate her figure in my own mind. I was not yet a writer but she had become to me, no doubt, like a figure in some written romance.

Did I say there was no one I loved? There is a possible exception. There was a younger brother named Earl who came to live with me. In our family there had been from the beginning a kind of instinctive feeling for the arts. An older brother had become a magazine illustrator and was on his way to becoming a painter.

And there was this younger brother, Earl, who came to live with me at that time.

He was a tall gaunt boy with narrow hips and broad shoulders and large rather strange eyes and was markedly unsuccessful.

Having, like all of us, his living to make, he could not do it. Since he was a lad of fifteen, he had been drifting from place to place. He got jobs and immediately lost them. He was absent-minded and likely to do strange things. Once he arose in the morning and came down to my factory clad in a bath robe, having walked thus through the streets of the Ohio city. It was a cold day and he had put on the bath robe thinking it was his overcoat. I gave him a job as shipping clerk in my factory and he sent every other shipment to the wrong destination. It cost more to employ him than it would have cost to keep him in luxury unemployed but he was sensitive and the situation was embarrassing. He did not want to be dependent upon his brothers. He was the youngest of all the sons in our family and when he was born the family was passing through one of its worst periods of poverty. He had got the idea that he was an unwanted child, a fixed idea that always stayed with him. Among my other enterprises I had taken a contract for painting a whole group of buildings belonging to a steel company in southern Ohio, having taken the contract to do the work in order to sell the paint, and my brother asked to be allowed to go there and work on the job.

He did go there and one day absent-mindedly walked off the roof of a building, falling some forty feet and injuring his head so that he was for a time insane. A blood clot formed on his brain, which was afterward absorbed although in the end it killed him.

Earl had come to me from the city of Chicago, where he had a position as cashier in a cheap restaurant in South State Street. The restaurant did its big business at night and was patronized chiefly by women of the town and their pimps. He had come to know these people intimately and afterward when he came to me and when he walked about with me at night, myself at that time still a good deal the bright young business man, the young American go-getter, he talked to me at length of these people. He had left the place and come to me at my invitation and because the terrible food he had been eating had brought on an illness.

I think now that it was this brother who had a great deal to do with my becoming a writer and understanding a little the impulses and purposes of the artist man. I think I must have clung to him a good deal—this was before the day of the automobile but I got a horse and buggy and we drove into the country on summer nights. Tying the horse to a tree beside the road we went walking over moonlit fields. My brother Earl was ordinarily no talker but on these nights, walking across fields or standing by a fence at some wood's edge, trees casting long shadows over fields washed by moonlight, he began to talk.

Why here was talk such as I had never heard before. It was always of people, of things in people felt, and of the wonders and glories of nature. Sometimes he talked thus passionately for hours. He knew that he would never become the painter he dreamed of being. "I cannot finish things," he said and I understood that there was a kind of passionate eagerness in him that constantly dejected him. He wanted too much. "I cannot finish one thing because I am always driven to beginning another. I cannot get into life, steady myself."

I remember his telling me on one of these nights of his experience with women.

The story was a little terrible. He saw some woman and fell in love with her beauty but could not talk to her, could not approach her. "I have to run away," he said. "If I stayed near I would assault her. I would have to do it. It would be the only way I knew of trying to get some of her beauty for myself." My brother left one day, going to another brother, a manufacturer in New Orleans, staying with him a short time and then disappearing entirely. When he disappeared he wrote a letter to the family addressed to the wife of one of my brothers with whom he must have set up some sort of accord. He said in the letter that he would have to disappear, could not go on living dependent upon his brothers. "I have to learn to stand alone on my own feet first," he said.

For thirteen years he disappeared entirely and one day when I was returning from Europe and was stepping off the boat a telegram was handed to me. My brother had been picked up suffering from a stroke on the streets of Brooklyn.[30] He had fought in the World War and had taken a position as a laborer working at night in a big bakery in Brooklyn and had lived alone all these years in a Brooklyn rooming house, painting during the day. Under his bed in the room there was found a great pile of unfinished paintings. What he had said of himself was true. He could not finish anything, never become a complete workman. It may be that his inner nature was too rich. He lived for a few months, unable to talk and just able to scribble an occasional sentence, but told me once by this method that he had once followed me for several blocks along Fifth Avenue in New York. He had walked so close to me that he could have put out his hand and touched me. "I didn't," he said. "I couldn't. I had first to learn to stand on my own feet.

"I had not learned to do it yet," he said.

I think it must have been after my brother left me in the Ohio city and after our walks and talks together that I began to write and I am trying to think now what impulse led me to it.

30. Earl Anderson suffered a paralytic stroke February 16, 1926, and died in March, 1927. For Sherwood's feelings before Earl "returned," see *A Story Teller's Story*, ed. White, pp. 5, 9–10; and *Tar* (1926), pp. 115–21. See also *Letters*, ed. Jones and Rideout, Items 126, 133, and 256.

The Mother

Emma Smith Anderson as a Girl

The Father

Irwin McLain Anderson as a Young Man

The Children

Left to right: (standing) Stella, Karl (seated) Irwin, Ray, Earl, Sherwood

The Boy

"Jobby" Anderson

The Home

Anderson's Boyhood Home in Clyde, Ohio

The Workman

The Bicycle Factory (Sherwood Anderson third from left)

Courtesy of The Newberry Library

The Soldier

Anderson in the Spanish-American War

The Family

Left to right: Karl, Ray, Sherwood, Stella, Irwin, Earl

The Rake

Anderson in Chicago, about 1900

Business Types
SHERWOOD ANDERSON

The Undeveloped Man.

THE advertising man sat upon his upturned grip at a railroad junction. It was midnight, a drizzle of rain was in the air and close about him lay the unbroken blackness of a cloudy night.

Down the tracks in the railroad yards a freight engine was making up a train. The banging of the cars, the rumbling of the wheels, the swinging lanterns and the voices of the trainmen lent interest to a long, dull wait. Suddenly up the track there came a rippling string of oaths, and for the next ten minutes the air was filled with them. In the words of Mark Twain, there was "swearing in that railroad yard, swearing that just laid over any swearing ever heard before."

The engineer swore and he wasn't half bad; the conductor deftly caught up the refrain and embellished it, and then from far down in the yards the voice of a brakeman cut into the game.

It was all about a box car and a coupling pin that wouldn't catch, and it was nothing less than genius the way that brakeman handled his subject. He swore scientifically. He worked over the ground already covered by the engineer and conductor and from it harvested another crop, and then he caught his breath, waved his lantern and started into the dense forest of untried oaths. The best part of it all was the way he clung to that box car, he went far enough afield for words but when he used them they were pat, they were all descriptive of the car and its peculiar and general uselessness.

"He is a sort of genius in his way, ain't he?" said a weak, piping little voice at the advertising man's elbow.

SHERWOOD ANDERSON.

Courtesy of The Newberry Library

The Copywriter

From Agricultural Advertising, *May, 1904*

My Word to You

"I promise as a decent man trying to be square that every man, rich or poor, small or large, shall have a square deal from my Company.

Every word of this book is written under my personal supervision, and for it I am responsible 'to you.

As you and I may never meet face to face I give you my word now that what is written in this book is true in spirit and in fact.

I stand ready to do what is right by you, the buyer, and if you at any time buy anything of the factories whose goods are sold through our catalogues, and if you are not satisfied, you can feel free about taking the matter up with me personally, and I promise you that I will not delegate the matter to a clerk or pile up words to confuse you, but will satisfy you with what you have bought or return every penny of your money no matter what we lose by it."

SHERWOOD ANDERSON,

President.

"STRAIGHT FROM OUR FACTORIES TO YOU"

Courtesy of The Newberry Library

The Businessman

From the Catalogue of Anderson's Company, about 1906

The Husband

Anderson with Two of His Children, John (left) and Marion (right)

The Author

Photograph by Edward Steichen, 1926

The House

"Ripshin," the Country House in Southwest Virginia

The Manuscript

Last Page of "White Spot"

The Memoirist

Anderson in 1941 at "Ripshin"

The Last Picture

Sherwood and Eleanor Boarding The Santa Lucia, *February 28, 1941*

The Grave

*Anderson's Grave in Marion, Virginia: "Life Not Death Is the Great
Adventure"*

IV ❧

Chicago

Any American who has traveled much over the country comes finally to fix upon one city as his home city. He may have been born in a small town or on a farm but that particular city is his big town.

And that's what Chicago is to me. I went there, from a small Ohio town, as a very young boy, saw my first play there, felt all of the terror and loneliness a small town boy must feel pitched down alone in a great city. I was a laborer there, went from there to join the army, gradually made friends, walked restlessly Chicago streets at night, became in love with Chicago women, wrote many of my best stories there, hung over the old wooden bridges that formerly crossed the Chicago River, watching the gulls float over the river, got out of the ranks of labor and became a business man, began to scribble and was less and less good at my job, chucked the job and wandered away, came back to try again.

It was in Chicago that I first knew other writers and was interested in literature.[1] It was in Chicago newspapers that my own work was first both damned and praised.

Any how many notable men known there, friends made. Justin Smith, Ferdinand Schevill, Robert Lovett, Burton Rascoe, Lloyd Lewis, Ben Hecht, Floyd Dell, Arthur Ficke, Murray Hauser, Carl Sandburg, Lewis Galantière, Ernest Hemingway.[2]

1. The two standard histories of the Chicago Renaissance are Bernard Duffey, *The Chicago Renaissance in American Letters: A Critical History* (Lansing: Michigan State University Press, 1954) and Dale Kramer, *Chicago Renaissance: The Literary Life in the Midwest, 1900–1930* (New York: Appleton-Century, 1966). See especially the essay by Duffey in *The Achievement of Sherwood Anderson: Essays in Criticism,* edited by Ray Lewis White (Chapel Hill: The University of North Carolina Press, 1966), pp. 46–59.

2. Henry Justin Smith (1875–1936), journalist for the *Chicago Daily News.* Ferdinand Schevill (1868–1954), history teacher at the University of Chicago; see *Letters of Sherwood Anderson,* edited by Howard Mumford Jones and Walter B. Rideout (Boston: Little, Brown and Company, 1953), Items 86, 92, 160, 165, 168, 179, 183, 186, 214, 228, 233, *passim.* Robert Morss Lovett (1870–1956), literary historian and teacher at the University of Chicago, 1892–1936, who wrote of Anderson in "The Promise of Sherwood Anderson," *Dial,* LXXII (January, 1922), 79–83; "Sherwood Anderson," *English Journal,* XIII (October, 1924), 531–39; "Sherwood Anderson," *New Republic,* LXXXIX (November 25, 1936), 103–5; "Sherwood Anderson, American," *Virginia Quarterly Review,* XVII (Summer, 1941), 379–88. Arthur Burton Rascoe (1892–1957), columnist, editor, and critic, literary editor for the *Chicago Tribune,* 1912–20; wrote of Anderson in *Arts and Decoration,* XXI (August, 1924), 66–67, and in *Before I Forget* (Garden City: Doubleday, Doran, 1937), p. 368, *passim.*

Lloyd Lewis (1891–1949), drama and sports columnist and editor for Chicago newspapers. Arthur Ficke (1883–1945), sonneteer, satirist, and enthusiast of Japanese

With these men and others I sat about in restaurants, talked of books, had the work of old writers brought to my attention, discovered new writers.

With Ben Hecht in particular I often went while he covered news stories. We quarreled and fought, made up, remained friends.

Other men, not to become literary figures, made life long friends, the big Irishman George Daugherty, Roger Sergel, now at the head of the Dramatic Publishing Company. Talking also with these men of books and writers, drinking with them, sometimes spending most of the night walking and talking.

And there was that fascinating figure Margaret Anderson. I knew her when she burst forth with her *Little Review,* wrote for her first number,[3] wrote for the old *Dial* when it was published in Chicago,[4] became a part of what was, for a time, called "The Chicago School" of writers.

How many men known, women known during the years there. They come flocking into my mind, men of the advertising office where I was for long years employed as copy writer, men infinitely patient with me and my idiosyncrasies.

And there was that rather glamorous fellow, the Italian poet Carnevali,[5] who came from the east to help Harriet Monroe on *Poetry Magazine,*[6] he sometimes raging about my rooms at night.

art. Murray Hauser, unidentified. Carl Sandburg (1878–1967), poet whom Anderson met in 1917 and discussed in "Carl Sandburg," *Bookman,* LIV (December, 1921), 360–61, and in *Letters,* ed. Jones and Rideout, *passim.* Lewis Galantière (1895–   ), literary sophisticate who wrote of Anderson in "French Reminiscence," *Story,* XIX (September–October, 1941), 64–67; see *Letters,* ed. Jones and Rideout, Item 65, *passim.* Ernest Hemingway (1899–1961) met Anderson in the fall of 1920 at the Chicago home of Y. K. Smith.

3. Margaret Anderson (1893–   ) and Jane Heap (–1964) published *The Little Review* from March, 1914, through May, 1929, in Chicago, New York, and then Paris. The first issue carried Anderson's "The New Note," I (March, 1914), 23. Miss Anderson wrote of Sherwood Anderson in *My Thirty Years' War* (New York: Covici, Friede, 1930), pp. 38–39, *passim;* reviewed by Sherwood Anderson in "Real-Unreal," *New Republic,* LXIII (June 11, 1930), 103–4. Jane Heap reviewed *Windy McPherson's Son* in *Little Review,* III (November, 1916), 6–7.

4. *The Dial,* founded in Chicago in 1880, moved to New York in 1916 and failed in 1929. Scofield Thayer, editor from 1919 to 1925, published many of Anderson's works.

5. Little is known of Carnevali except the material in *The Autobiography of Emanuel Carnevali,* edited by Kay Boyle (New York: Horizon Press, 1967).

6. Harriet Monroe (1860–1936), founded *Poetry: A Magazine of Verse* in Chicago in 1912. See her autobiography, *A Poet's Life* (New York: Macmillan, 1938).

And Bodenheim,[7] with his corn cob pipe and the broken arm he carried in a sling, although it was but an imagined break.

It was a time of a kind of renaissance, in the arts, in literature, a Robin's Egg Renaissance I have called it in my mind since. It fell out of the nest. It may be that we should all have stayed in Chicago.

So many of us began there, got our early impressions of life there, made friends there. Had we stayed in the home nest, in Chicago, when it all began for so many of us, the Robin's Egg might have hatched.

Then we would all have been chirping away and picking at worms up and down Michigan Boulevard until this very day.

We Little Children of the Arts

I was living in Chicago, let us say that this would be about 1912 or 1913, and there were certain people with whom I was intimate.[8] There might have been a dozen, perhaps even two dozen, of these men and women. We were all following, or we hoped we were following, the same path. We were devotees of the arts. Oh what talks we had, what walks in city streets at night, what gatherings in rooms, what attempts to find, in the huge undisciplined city, little nooks, quiet places, little restaurants where the food was cheap and unusual, where we could sit, as we imagined it might be in some old world city, hearing some strange language spoken by dark heavily built men with beards or huge mustaches who sat over their food and drink.

We were all in the same boat. None of us had any money and we were all working at jobs. We wrote advertisements, we worked on newspapers, clerked in stores or offices, all of us determined that what we were doing, to earn a little money for room rent, for laundry bills, for food, to buy, in the fall, an overcoat, socks, neckties, suits of clothes, etc.—this, we hoped, but a temporary matter.

"Oh, for freedom," we kept saying to one another.

7. Maxwell Bodenheim (1893–1954), poet and dramatist, wrote of Anderson in "Psychoanalysis and American Fiction," *Nation,* CXIV (June 7, 1922), 683–84; and "The Pagan Meditates," *Oracle,* II, No. 2 (July, 1926), 12–13, 22–23.

8. "Little Children of the Arts" is Anderson's name for the boarding house group at 735 Cass Street, where Anderson was living by the spring of 1915.

"I shall manage, somehow, to get me a little piece of land. I'll build a little shack. I'll settle down there. I'll till the earth."

There were story writers among us, young musicians, who dreamed of becoming great composers, young painters and sculptors, young poets.

They hoped they were poets.

They wrote verses.

Pictures were painted, heads modeled in clay, rented pianos thumped. We were all living about in rooms, in cheap rooming houses. We had formed a rather loose unorganized group, partly to comfort each other, to have, each of us, others to whom we could talk of our plans and of our hopes.

In any such group (And they are always being formed, in towns and cities, all over America, by young intellectuals. It is hard to find any other word that fits. Those who make up the groups are government clerks, in Washington. They are living in San Francisco, New Orleans, Bangor, Maine, Springfield, Missouri. There must be dozens of such groups in New York City.) . . . in all such groups women are to be found.

And that is confusing.

You are a young painter, a poet, a sculptor. You are a young man at work on a novel. Sometimes you sit in your room and write for hours. How splendid it seems.

You have been working all day, let us say in an office where you have a position. You are in charge of a room where letters are filed.

You are working for a big firm. It is a mail order house, and there are several women who are employed in the filing room. You are in charge. You direct their work. If it is not done correctly, and an important letter filed away cannot be found, you are called into an office. You are on the carpet.

"A few more such mistakes and out you go. You understand that?"

"And what is it all about? Suppose they never find the letter?

"Will the stars fall down out of the sky? Will the planets cease swinging through space? Will not the corn ripen in the fall?"

You ask yourself such questions but you do not ask them aloud, not in the presence of others, in the place where you work.

You go home, at night, to your room. It is in a big house, of brick, that was, formerly, the residence of some rich or well-to-do family. The particular street, the neighborhood, has become a little shabby. The rich people —successful men, men at the heads of businesses such as the one who employed you, men who have got up in the world and have established fortunes and families—have all now moved out of your street. It is no longer fashionable to live there. There is some new part of your city that has become what is called "desirable."

And so there you are. You are one of the little children of the arts. How many there are of us! How many thousands. We are going to write world shaking novels, become intellectual leaders of a nation, paint a picture that will be at once recognized as a masterpiece, sing a song that will reverberate through the hearts of all men.

"Oh, if I only had a little leisure. If I had money. If I had even a small income."

Some of us, after a time, give it up. We settle down, as the saying goes, into life, get married and have children. Others of us take to drink while still others keep on. There are little children of the arts who are just sixty. "I will do it yet," they keep saying. You will find such old men climbing, with trembling legs, the stairs to rooming houses. They sit at little desks in the rooms and write. Let us say that such a one writes plays. Once, some ten or twelve years ago, he had a letter, from a play reader at the Theatre Guild.

"Your play has undoubted merit but it does not fit into our program," the letter said.

Or he is a man at work on a novel. He thought he had finished it and sent it to a New York publisher.

He got a letter which he keeps always in his desk. It is getting a little yellow and dirty now but he takes it out from time to time and reads. How was the publisher to know that, when he sent the novel, he was already an old man?

"Your novel, in its present form, does not fit into our program," the letter says.

There are other phrases. There is some man, perhaps a young fellow employed in the publisher's office dictating a letter to a stenographer. He wants to be kind. He is thinking that the stenographer is rather good looking. He is wondering if he dare ask her to go out to dine with him.

"I might get myself into a jam," he thinks.

"We are of the opinion that your novel needs more work.

"Keep it by you for a time.

"We do not think the end quite a fitting one.

"It may be well to rewrite the whole novel and then let us see it again."

That for the older children of the arts. For the most part however we were young.

There was a constant danger. A man, such a one as is mentioned above, the one in the filing department in the mail order house, comes home to his room at night.

With all of us it was the same. A man can never tell when what is called "inspiration" will come.

So the young man comes into his room and drops into a chair by a window. He sits with his head in his hands. He is tired and discouraged.

"I will never make it," he says. It has been a particularly bad day for him, all sorts of annoyances. He raises his head and looks out into the street.

It has begun to rain and people are going along. Some have umbrellas, or raincoats, while others dodge along, hopping from doorway to doorway.

It is at such times, when a man is altogether discouraged, when, to use a Carl Sandburg figure, the bottom has dropped out of his bucket of dreams, that inspiration sometimes floods in.

Suddenly the young man begins to write. He writes away, hour after hour, forgetting that he has not dined, forgetting the shabbiness of his room, in a shabby house, forgetting that he has no money, that his prospects in life are not very brilliant.

He writes and writes. Aha! Now something must happen. There is a story of the Russian Dostoevsky. He was just such a young man as the one described here. He wrote a book called *Poor Folks*. He sent it to an older and more experienced writer.

And what excitement. Now an older writer is driving furiously through the streets of Moscow. Or is it St. Petersburg, this before the revolution? He is arousing other writers, dragging them out of their houses.

"Ha! A feast. A feast!

"Another great one is born.

"Let us go to him, surround him, feast him."

This sort of thing perhaps in Russia. But we are speaking of Chicago.

We have there this young man. He has just finished what seems to him, at the moment, a masterpiece. Now he must, at once, have someone with whom to share it, to whom to read it. It is late at night. It is raining outside.

He stands in his room, trying to think.

"To whom shall I go?

"If I go to Fred he will begin talking of his painting.

"As for Joe he will interrupt me in the midst of my story. He will begin speaking of his socialism."

The young man stands thus in his room thinking and then rushes out into the night. He has thought of a woman to whom he can go. In any group of young devotees there are nearly always women.

Some of them write verses.

There is one who takes photographs.

Another models in clay. She models the heads of children.

So our young man rushes to a telephone. He calls one who takes photographs.

Yes. She is at home. She has, with another woman, a small apartment but the other woman is not in. She has gone to the theatre.

So our young man rushes there, to her. He has his manuscript in his pocket. He reads to her. They sit close together, under a shaded lamp, and as he reads—let us say the more emotional parts of his story—he steals furtive glances at her.

He sees that her hands are moving restlessly. She is sitting quite close to him and she breathes heavily. He sees her bosom rise and fall. Occasionally an involuntary sigh comes from her lips.

"Ah! Ah!

"How wonderful."

But look out, boy.

It is thus they put their hooks into you.

If you are not careful, young man, you will, before you know what is happening, be married.

You will have responsibilities. There will be children.

Now you are dreaming of finding new leisure. You want to escape from the job in the mail order house.

You are dreaming of a little shack in the country.

Ah freedom, freedom.

Look out, young man.

There was a big man named Ben. He was rough in speech and often profane but he had a tender heart. Although he was much older than most of us, there in Chicago, he had got into our group. We would be sitting in a room. There we were, young men and women, devoted to the art of writing, of singing, of painting, of sculpture. We were always gathering in rooms in rooming houses.

"Let's have some beer."

"And what about some sandwiches?"

"Let's pass the hat and get a bottle of gin."

There was talk, of the arts, sometimes of revolution, a new society to be built. That talk grew more intense in such groups later, after the World War. There we were, young men and, always, women. The women were going to be actresses or singers. Now and then one of us got hooked. The light of love came into our eyes. Such a one, for the time, quit talking and sat near his lady love. There was a mist over his eyes. He and his lady love sat with us for a time and then they got up and left. They were going to sit together somewhere on a park bench. Now lips would be meeting. For a time art would be forgotten.

There we were and there was the man Ben. He looked at such a pair of lovers and laughed. He was much older than the rest of us. He might have been forty.

"He is a man who has lived," we sometimes said to each other.

"He knows life."

He had been brought to us by one of the young painters and was himself a painter.

"He has been everywhere, has been a soldier, a laborer."

"He is married and has children," said the painter who had brought him. When Ben was not present the young painter who had introduced him sat talking. He made of Ben an epic figure.

"He has been a lumberman, in the lumber camps of the north west. One summer, when he was a young man, he was with the wheat harvesters of the Dakotas. With other men, rough strong men like Ben himself, he followed the wheat harvest, down across the Dakotas, into Nebraska, into Kansas.

"He has lived a rough life with rough men. For two years he was a sailor. He was on a freighter and went to Europe. He went to China."

It seemed strange to us that this Ben, who had seen so much of life, who had lived among rough ones, should seem willing to become one of us.

But, like the rest of us, it seemed, he could not make his living by his painting. He was with us in the room of one of our group, another young painter. As always happened the man's painting had to be shown.

There we were, sitting about. On such occasions it is always necessary to have something to say.

There are twelve, fifteen, twenty canvases being shown. You sit waiting. There are voices of young men and women, exclaiming.

"Oh, oh!" they cry.

"Isn't that beautiful?"

"Oh, I do like that one."

"It is your brush work that pleases me," says another one presently. You also cry out. You feel it is your time. You do not want to appear dumb.

And there was Ben. How bold he was, how honest.

"I do not like it," he says and there is a sickly smile on the face of the painter. Ben gets up before us and walks about the room. He is a huge figure of a man.

"We are all of us like lice crawling," he says.

There had been a bottle of gin brought in and he goes to it. He pours himself a whole drinking glass of the stuff and tosses it off. He begins a harangue, pounding with his fist on a table in the room.

"This Art we are pursuing, what is it?" he thunders.

"Art is a bitch female," he cried. He makes for us a picture of Art as a bedraggled female of the streets. There are young women in the room and they look at him, half shocked and half admiring.

"There is this passion comes upon a man. What does it mean?

"We have, all of us, at times, been overcome by quite another passion.

"We are young men and we are in a street of prostitutes at night.

"So we see one. We walk up and down. She is inviting us.

"We want to go to her but we are ashamed. Sometimes we do go and sometimes we run away.

"And what does it all come to, in the end?"

Ben went off into a string of profanity. Sometimes after such an outburst he leaves us abruptly. He thumps noisily out of the room and down a stairs.

"This pursuit of Art is like that.

"I am going to get drunk," he shouts.

When this had happened to our Chicago group we sat, a little amazed, a little frightened. The man who had been showing his pictures put them away.

"I don't think he really looked at them at all," he said.

We were thinking of Ben as more virile, more manly, stronger than the rest of us, but once, when I was walking with him, he began suddenly to speak.

And this time he did not swear. I remember that it was evening and we were walking by the lake. "I got married. I got hooked," he suddenly said.

He began to tell some intimate details of his life.

Since he had been a young man, he said, he had wanted to be a painter. "But I thought that, first, I should live."

He had knocked about in life in the way already suggested by the man who had brought him to us for a time and then he had come to Chicago.

He had got a room somewhere, on Chicago's West Side. He began working as a laborer in a warehouse.

"So I was in this place. I had begun a little to try to paint. I was unmarried. I was free.

"It is true I was working as a common laborer and making little enough money but I was strong. The work did not tire me.

"I was in a cold storage warehouse, where barrels of apples are stored. I piled them in the rooms."

He began describing to me the life in the place where he had the room. There were, he said, two women, a mother and a daughter, and the mother was ill.

"She pretended she was ill. She still keeps it up. She should be jerked out of her bed. I would do it but it would hurt the feelings of my wife," he said. There was a little flat and they had taken Ben in, had given him the only large room.

The daughter, he said, was working in the city. She worked, he said, as a stenographer. He said she was a little thing. We were walking. It was a summer evening and he stopped. He stood in silence for a minute.

"She is no taller than that," he said and put out his hand.

He had come to live in that place. The daughter, he thought, was killing herself with work. There had been a man, the husband and father, who was a bookkeeper in a small factory but he had embezzled money and had run away.

The daughter, Ben said, was very brave. When he came to live in the apartment she gave up her own room to sleep in the room with her mother.

The mother was bed-ridden.

And so the daughter was out of bed at five in the morning. She did the work in the house, made the breakfast.

She swept the house. She prepared a lunch for the mother. She put it on a table by the bed.

Ben said there was something queer about the mother. She rarely spoke. He declared she was cheating.

She was always in her bed when the daughter was in the house but, sometimes, on a day when Ben was not working, when he was in his own room, busy at his painting, the mother got out of her bed and walked about.

"She is a damned fraud," he cried and laughed but the laughter wasn't very pleasant to hear.

He was there, living in that place, in that way.

It was, he said, a gloomy room. "It is still gloomy," he said.

He began talking, not loudly, as was his custom, but softly. He spoke of something.

"When you are in a house, with such a one as my wife," he said, "so patient, so good. . . ." He was speaking of the daughter.

"It is as though something came to you through the walls.

"You want to be of help."

He said that for a time, after he went to the apartment to live, he rarely saw the daughter.

"I just felt her about, in the early morning and at night. I could hear her footsteps, clicking, clicking. Sometimes she worked late and I sat in the room waiting for the sound. When she was busy, getting the evening meal for her mother, running up and down a little hallway, the sharp sound of her heels hitting seemed to cut into my flesh."

He said that he had thought of moving out of the house to avoid the sound but that he couldn't.

"It was because of her, that little one, the daughter."

It went on for a year, his living like that.

"I knew she needed the little money I gave her for my room."

He began speaking of his former life. He had, he said, known a good many women.

"I used to go, with other men, you know, of a Saturday night. We went to certain houses. I paid for it."

"I was there but I seldom saw the woman. Had I begun to love her? How do I know?

"On a Sunday morning I paid the rent for my room.

"I went into a little hall and called. I did not even know her name.

" 'Hey,' I called and she came.

"I stood and made her come to me. She did not come up to my shoulder.

"She had grey eyes," he said. "Her eyes always looked tired."

And so, he said, it went on and on, for months, and then. . . .

"It was a Saturday night," he said. He explained that formerly, before he came to live in that place, he occasionally went on a spree.

"I'd paint and paint and then I'd realize that what I had done was N.G.

"I don't know why I wanted to keep it up. I can't explain. I'd go and get a little drunk."

He had come home to his room, he said.

"I was not very drunk.

"I had to climb up a stair. I had to go along a hall and there she was.

"She was in the hallway, standing.

"She was near the door of my room. What she was doing there I don't know.

"You see, I stumbled into her.

"And then, because I was a little drunk (It wasn't because I didn't respect her. I knew she was good, you see.) I took her into my arm and I dragged her into my room."

He said she didn't cry out. He thought it was because of her mother in the bed in the nearby room.

And it may be she wanted a man, wanted his help in her life.

"She was very pale. She was small, a little thing," he said.

He stopped talking and we walked along but "We're married and now have three children," he presently said.

He explained that it was because of the children and the sick mother that he had stopped being a laborer. He had found that he could sell his drawings. People put them in catalogues. He said that he did not have to go about selling the drawings.

"My wife does that," he said.

"She takes the orders for work," he added. He laughed.

"There is a drawing of a man reclining in a chair. He is reading a book. There is a lamp on a table by the chair. They want to sell either the lamp or the chair.

"If it is a lamp they send the lamp to my house. I must make an exact drawing."

He laughed again. He acted a little crazy.

"Peter the Hermit has been reborn. Didn't you know that? He is teaching in the schools. He is directing the footsteps of the young.

"I am myself the father of a son and two daughters. I am replenishing the earth. I am another Abraham. My wife is good. She thinks I am quite happy making the drawings she sells."

It was a Sunday and I was in the country. I had gone into the country with Ben and Joe and Ed—all painters. We went on a train and got off at a small station. It was a day in the spring and we went across fields and along a path by a small sluggish river, the painters all carrying their traps.

I had brought a book.

We had our lunch out there, beer and sandwiches, and afterwards the painters set up their easels and began to paint.

I was by the stream. I was lying on my back on the bank of the stream, on the grass, and there were big white clouds in the sky. Sometimes I read and sometimes I looked about. I remember that, across the stream, in the distance, there was a farm house. There was a woman, neither young nor old, who kept coming out at the kitchen door to go to a pump. She pumped pails of water and took them into the house.

How many pails of water. "And what does she do with them?" I asked myself.

All afternoon I saw no one else moving about the yard of the farm house. I counted the pails of water. I quit counting. I looked at the clouds and I read my book. I counted again.

Evening was coming when Ben, who had been painting a field at my back, came to where I was lying. He did not look at me or speak. He carried a canvas in his hand and threw it into the distance.

He walked away from me and sat with his back to a tree. His easel was sitting nearby and he went presently and smashed it against the tree. He gathered up the fragments and threw them away, into the grass.

Again he went to sit by the tree and there was silence but, after a time, the others, Joe and Ed, came along the path.

"Where is your canvas?" they said to Ben but he did not answer them. There was his palette and a tin box filled with tubes of paint on the ground, near where his easel had been sitting.

"Go to hell," he presently said to the others. He had begun wiping the paint off his palette. He rubbed it over the grass, leaving streaks of color on the grass. He wrapped the palette in a newspaper.

"Come on," he said.

"And you too."

He was addressing me. He walked over to where I was sitting.

"You'd better throw your book away into the stream," he said. He had begun to feel a little better and even smiled.

And so, after a time, we walked together along the path by the river. The others, Joe and Ed, had gone ahead. We could see them walking and talking. They were laughing. They were loaded down, each holding a freshly painted canvas in the one hand and clinging to his trap with the other. Ben had only the box of paints and the palette in one of his hands and in the other he held his brushes. We walked in silence until we came to where the path left the stream and went across fields, to the distant railroad station. There was long grass growing in the field by the path and suddenly, putting down his paint box and dropping the palette, he hurled the brushes away. They fell into the long grass.

"I won't. I won't. You go to hell. I won't," he called.

He did not look at me but, leaving the palette and the bag of paints in the path, he walked away.

And presently I followed. I had picked up the palette and the box of paint. I could see Ben striding along ahead.

He went thus half way across a broad field and then he stopped. Now the sun was going down. It was late summer and soon it would be dark. Ben stood for a moment, his back to me. When he had stopped I also stopped and, after a few moments, he turned and hurried back.

He went silently past me and began running about in the field gathering up the brushes and when he had got them all back again went down to the edge of the stream and I followed. His usually ruddy face was white and ashen, bent over the stream. He had begun to wash his brushes. I saw his shoulders shaking.

"Can it be that he is weeping?" I asked myself. I was embarrassed and walked away.

"You will have to hurry or we will miss our train," I called but as he did not answer, I started away across the field.

I did not go very far. There was a shout and there was Ben standing by the stream. He had begun to laugh. He stood, a huge figure in the evening light, and was waving the brushes over his head.

"All right. Wait. I'm coming," he called.[9]

In Fifty-Seventh Street

It was an exciting time for me. I had come back to the city of Chicago after my adventure as a manufacturer. There was a great bag, full of

9. Published (revised) as "A Robin's Egg Renaissance," *Story*, XIX (September–October, 1941), 11–28.

manuscripts, with some of which I was satisfied. There were, if my memory does not now play me tricks, four long novels and any number of attempts at short stories, poems, essays.[10] I had got a room in 57th Street on Chicago's South Side and, after some hesitation, the advertising agency that had formerly employed me had taken me back.

"I do hope you'll go straight now."

This would have been Bayard Barton, who had now become president of the agency, talking to me. Bayard was too gentle a man to be really gruff.

"And what do you mean by 'going straight'?"

The conversation would have taken place in his office.

"Well, Bayard, you have certainly risen in the world." He had been a copy writer as I had been. We got together in the same little hole of a room, writing of cough cures, fertilizers for farms, rouge for women's cheeks.

I had something on Bayard. Did he not formerly show me verses he had written?

And now he was lecturing me. It was an old story. From my own wife I had got just such lectures.

"It is about this scribbling of yours. You cannot have such divided interest. Either you are an advertising man or you are a writer."

"Yes, I know," I said. "You are about to speak now of my lack of education. Such men as myself, who are not college men, whose minds have not been disciplined, cannot become real writers.

"I have heard all of that, have heard it to weariness, but I do not see that what I do after hours, when I am not employed here in this office, can matter to you."

He would have called my attention to my failure as a manufacturer.

"It was because your real interest was not in the business.

"And then besides I know that, in coming back here, you are only coming because you are broke.

"You have no interest in advertising writing. In a month you will be swaggering before us, your tongue in your cheek."

"And writing damn good copy for you," I said, laughing at him.

For well I knew he would not turn me down. There was something between us, a kind of affection.

10. Besides *Windy McPherson's Son* and *Marching Men,* Anderson probably had written on at least two other novels while in Ohio, "Mary Cochran" and "Talbot Whittingham."

And had he not also once said to me that, when he had made his pile. . . .

That is an old dream. No man or woman among us doing what he wanted to do. We were waiting, dreaming, hoping.

"When I make my pile."

Among us writers the dream of writing for the popular magazines or the so-called "pulps," or if more lucky getting a script job in Hollywood. Big money to be made and put aside. Then some real work done.

It didn't seem to work out.

I sat looking at Bayard who was looking at me. There was a silence between us. We were both thinking of friendships, when we had both been copy writers together, walks taken in the evening, talks we had.

"There is so much whoredom. I wonder if it is possible to escape it. All of this spending our lives struggling to get a little ahead of the other fellow, make more money. It a disease of our civilization.

Bayard, as copy writer, had been sent down to write copy for Firestone tires and Mr. Firestone had taken a fancy to him. He had a quality I did not have. He had felt a real obligation to Mr. Firestone and his huge organization. For the time the goal of more and more Firestone tires had become all important to him and no doubt Mr. Firestone had appreciated what he had in the man Barton.

He had turned the account over to him, a huge one, and Bayard had been lifted up to his new position of power.

He could force his way up.

"Give me what I want or I will take the account somewhere else."

He had been made president of the company. Well, he was on his way to making his pile now. Poor man, he did not live long to enjoy it. You get into some such a position, in the world of business, and where are you?

It is true some men can stand it. They go on and on accumulating and accumulating. To them the risk, at times seemingly insane struggle, is a kind of game at which they play.

But my friend Barton had other dreams. I saw the tired look in his eyes. Given the same opportunity he had had with Mr. Firestone I would, inevitably, have made some sarcastic remark.

Then out I would have gone.

We sat looking at each other, sitting there in his big luxurious office. We were both remembering vows we had taken to each other.

"I am going to keep something of myself and of this.

"It's true we advertising writers have to write a lot of bunk.

"The great thing is to know when we are writing bunk.

"We mustn't begin to believe in the bunk we write. We must keep honest minds."

"Ah, what the hell. You have chucked the attempt to be a manufacturer. You're broke and don't know where to turn.

"All right. Go to work. I'll give you a job for old times' sake."

Poor man, he was himself caught. He was a sensitive man caught in the wheel. In two, three, four years he would be dead.

"Look here," he said. "You know how I got to where I am. I stole an account, a big one. I was proud and glad when I did it.

"And now I have ahold of something and I can't let go. I don't know why but I can't. My pride is someway involved.

"So let me tell you something. If you ever have a chance to steal an account, take it away from me as I have taken the Firestone account from the others here, do not do as I did. Steal a little account, steal two or three little accounts. Do not get into the big time. Stay under the guns."

He laughed and turned away and oddly enough I did later steal two or three small accounts from him and when I did it he laughed again.

There wasn't, however, on each occasion, much joy in his laughter. He was no longer the old Bayard Barton with whom, when we were both younger, I had worked and talked on many a summer evening while we told each other of our dreams.

I had taken rooms in 57th Street and there I was, back in the old grind. However I did have my evenings and there were the week ends. I began again at my stories, the piles of manuscript, all I had written in the room at the top of the house in the Ohio town where, for five years, I had been struggling to be what nature did not intend me to be, a man of business.

They were there before me, the attempt at short stories, the long novels, the piles of verse, piled high on a long table I had bought at a second hand store.

And what peace and quiet in the room. I wonder now how much I thought then of the matter of publication, of becoming a real author. It seems to me that I did not take all that too seriously. For years I had been going about, observing, making notes in my mind. My own life, the living of my own life, had seemed most unsatisfactory to me. In the Ohio town I had been, for a time, seemingly on the road to success.

And then had come a sudden sickening. I had been married. I had children. I had been unfaithful to my wife. Always I had been doing things that shocked and hurt some inner part of me but I kept on doing them. I had begun drinking and, for a time, had been on the way to becoming a drunkard. I left my home town and went to Cleveland. I went from saloon to saloon, picking up some companions. I became drunk with them, went with them to houses of prostitution.

There had been one tall rather handsome prostitute who had taken a fancy to me.

"You be my man," she said.

I had been sitting about in the parlor of such a house, with companions picked up. Men were drinking with the women of the place and now and then one of them disappeared up a stairway with one of the women.

So it had come to that, the relationship between men and women, of which I had dreamed such dreams in my boyhood, come to that.

"And why am I here?"

I kept asking myself that question. I kept drinking. I became drunk and fell off the chair in which I had been sitting.

I had spent the night in that place. The tall woman had taken care of me. I awoke there in the morning.

I was on a couch, in a little alcove off what was called the parlor of the house, and presently there was that tall woman sitting beside me and we began to talk.

It was a strange conversation. When I had become drunken on the night before some of the other women of the place along with the men with whom I had come there had wanted to undress me. The idea had been to expose me to the view of all who came into the place. They had planned to paint my body, decorate certain very private parts of my body, make a kind of vulgar spectacle of me, but the tall woman had stopped it. She told me of that. She had, she said, a brother, at home, who was much like me.

"Did you come here to get a woman?" she asked and I told her that I had not come with that in mind.

I had come to that place, as I got drunk, in an effort to escape from myself.

"There is something about myself I do not like."

There is, I realize, a danger of sentimentalizing all this. Men are always doing it in regard to prostitutes. All I can be sure of is that, on that morning, I had left that place, filled with shame, my eyes taking in the street, as I emerged from the door and hurried away, the shame that came when, on a nearby street, I passed some children playing on the sidewalk, but later on two or three occasions I did see the tall prostitute again. In a kind of spirit of defiance I phoned to her. I invited her to dine with me at one of the big Cleveland hotels, took her on a certain fall afternoon to the trotting meeting, walked in streets with her, was seen in her presence by men from my town where I was a respectable manufacturer.

And all of this out of a spirit of defiance, wanting in some way to defy the respectable, money making, scheming money prosperous life of which I had been a part.

"And so you want to be my man?" The tall woman was puzzled.

"It would be a little like sleeping with my own brother. You and he look so alike."

There was of course her own story told to me. Whether it was a true story or not I cannot say. It was all connected with the brother, whom it seemed I resembled. He did not know what she was doing. He was, she declared, a student in a college in the west, was at the University of the State of Wisconsin.

"We are Italians," she said. She was going to get her brother started in life. He had no idea of what she was doing. When she had seen him through college, had got him established, she would no longer be a prostitute.

"Man, there are women who have been a whore and have afterwards turned out to be a good wife to some man," she said.

"Do you want to be my man, my special man?

"Well I do not want you to be. It would be too much like being with my own brother."

Such happenings in my life. Obviously that tall woman wanting something outside the life she was living, a kind of grasping at a friendship, or so it had seemed to me.

Myself struggling to get at something outside the life of buying and selling, finding it in the writing.

So there it was, more and more of it accumulating on my desk, great piles of it.

And then my older brother Karl, now an established painter, came to the city. He was having an exhibition of his paintings there and while he was in the city came to stay in my rooms with me.

"And what is this? So you are writing now." Picking up one of the novels I had written, he took it away with him. He took me into a new world. It began with his visit.

[333]

He had taken one of my novels, the one later published under the title *Windy McPherson's Son,* to Mr. Floyd Dell with whom he had become acquainted and who was then the editor of the special Friday book section of the *Chicago Post.*

So there was Dell reading my novel and presently, in the columns of the Friday *Post,* writing of me.

I was, it seemed, the great unknown.

Why, how exciting. There I was, as Dell was saying, in print, in a newspaper read, as I presumed, by thousands, an unknown man (I do not now remember whether or not he mentioned my name) doing, in obscurity, this wonderful thing.

And with what eagerness I read. If he had not printed my name at least he had given an outline of my novel. There could be no mistake.

"It's me. It's me."

I would have pranced excitedly up and down in my room.

"I must know this man."

It seemed to me that I had of a sudden been chosen, elected as it were, given a kind of passport into some strange new and exclusive world.

It was true that I had already published a story. It had appeared in *Harper's Magazine* and had been called "The Rabbit Pen," but I had not taken the story very seriously and had not been much excited by its publication.[11]

The story, in fact, had been written in answer to a kind of challenge. An old friend, Miss Trilena White, a school teacher with whom I had become acquainted when I was, for a brief time, a student at Wittenberg College at Springfield, Ohio, had come to visit at my house and there had been much talk of William Dean Howells, a man she much admired.

At the time Howells was editing what was called "The Easy Chair" section of *Harper's.*

I had made some sharp criticism of Howells and my friend had challenged me.

"They are all of them, Howells, Twain, Hawthorne, too much afraid," I had declared. "In all their writing there is too much of life left out."

There was, for example, the matter of sex. My own experience in living had already taught me that sex was a tremendous force in life. It twisted people, beat upon them, often distorted and destroyed their lives.

---

11. "The Rabbit Pen," *Harper's,* CXXIX (July, 1914), 207–10; reprinted with a critical note by Ray Lewis White in *Readers and Writers,* April, 1968, pp. 32–37. See Anderson's "On Being Published," *Colophon,* February, 1930, pp. 1–4; and "Why Men Write," *Story,* VIII (January, 1936), 2, 4, 103, 105.

"It must be that these men know what an influence it is on lives but they are afraid of it. Twain, for example, had written and published privately (or at least it had been published, I had seen it) a thing he called *Conversations in the Court of Queen Elizabeth.*[12]

"But what about conversation in everyday American life, in saloons, in the backs of stores, in factories, workshops and streets?

"And I dare say often enough among American women too?

"Why hesitate to put down whatever is in men and women's lives, making the picture whole?

"I tell you that someday, soon now, men will come. . . ."

My criticism of Howells and others had a little offended my friend.

"Why I myself can write a story that *Harper's* will print."

I had made the boast. The story I wrote and that was published was not the kind of story I was already feeling my way toward. Its publication had merely been a sort of triumph over my friend.

But here I was now in Chicago and here was Dell writing in a newspaper of an unpublished novel of mine. I had got a letter from Margery Currey, Floyd Dell's wife, asking me to come.

I went, filled with excitement. Now I was to go into a new world, men and women whose interests would be my interest, the curious feeling of loneliness and uncertainty broken up. I thought of the nights when I could not work, the hours spent walking the city streets, great projects forming in my mind, these coming to nothing.

I went to the address, at the corner of 57th and Stony Island Avenue, and found there a row of low one storey buildings. The buildings had been, I was later told, hurriedly thrown up at the time of the Chicago World's Fair. They had been stores then but now they had become the houses of men and women of Chicago's intellectual and artistic set. On that first night I walked back and forth before the store fronts. Curtains had been put up and they were now drawn and behind the curtains in the rooms I could hear voices. Shouts of laughter went up and a voice began to sing.

I had my hand on the door knob of the Dell house (It was indeed a single large room that had once been a retail store. A partition had been thrown up at the back and a kind of kitchenette made.) but I lost courage.

"Why these must be indeed quite wonderful people but would they really receive me?"

How many times had I been told that, by spending my time scribbling

12. Secretly printed in Clemens' lifetime as *1601; Or, Conversation as It Was by the Fireside in the Time of the Tudors.*

away at stories, I was but wasting my time and energy. That, it had been pointed out to me, was a field for educated men and I was not educated. I spelled badly. It was a curse that was to cling to me all my life. I knew nothing of punctuation, to save my life could not have parsed a sentence. It was true that I had read eagerly, since childhood, but, for most of my life, I had associated with working men, had been, for a time, a hanger-on of race horse men. To associate with advertising writers was one thing but to be in the actual company of men who had perhaps actually written books that had been published, who wrote reverently of books in newspapers and magazines. . . .

All of this is I know a little absurd but there I was. I was at the door of Dell's little one room house and went away. I went to walk in Jackson Park.

"This is absurd. You are being cowardly. They may indeed be kind to you. They may help you," I told myself. I remembered how Dell had written of my own unpublished book and returned again to the door but again I left without daring to enter.

And then, on a day, perhaps a week later, I did enter. I had come home early from the office and went to stand in the park until I saw little Margery Currey enter alone.

A new life began for me. As has been the case with me time and again Margery Currey, like other women I have known, was infinitely kind to me. At once she made me feel at home.

"Come," she said at once, "we will go for a walk in the park."

We did walk and she told me of her friends. It was through Margery that I met Ben Hecht, Arthur Ficke, her husband Floyd Dell, who became for a time a kind of literary father to me. Their marriage was at the time breaking up as my own had broken up and this fact may have drawn me closer to Margery. In her company I saw the poet Eunice Tietjens. Lucian Cary came to her house.[13] I went with her and Ben Hecht to a town down state where Ben, then a star reporter on the *Daily News,* covered a murder trial and a hanging. Summer came and we went off, often a great crowd of us, to some little town on the lake. It was during that summer that I met Carl Sandburg, Michael Carmichael Carr, that infinitely charming man, with the red beard and the endless flow of talk, came from the University

13. Eunice Strong Tietjens (1884–1944), poet and novelist, wife of Cloyd Head and assistant editor for *Poetry,* 1913–44; Lucian Cary edited the *Friday Literary Review* after Floyd Dell left it in October, 1913.

of Missouri. Alexander Kaun, a Russian Jew, short and squat of frame, came to tell stories of life in Russia, of the persecution of the poor there, of life in little Russian villages. Ernestine Evans, that strange world traveler, later always turning up in some unexpected place, in Europe or the far east. I was to see her later in several European cities but was to have occasional notes from her from all over the world. She was then newly graduated from the University of Chicago and had taken, for living quarters, one of the vacant store rooms near Margery. She brought Robert Lovett to her rooms. Llewellyn Jones came through Ben Hecht. I met Justin Smith of the *News,* Burton Rascoe, then doing books for the *Tribune,* and Lewis Galantière who was to become a life long friend.[14]

It was a time of something flowering in Chicago and the middle west. At the very moment Edgar Lee Masters must have been writing his *Spoon River Anthology* and in Springfield, down the state, Vachel Lindsay was shouting forth his stirring verses, Dreiser, from Terre Haute in Indiana, had written and published his *Sister Carrie*[15] and Margaret Anderson still working as editor of some church paper was soon to break loose and start her *Little Review.*

It was a time of excitement, something seemingly new and fresh in the air we breathed, and there was little Margery, who had rather taken me under the wing, who was then employed as a reporter on the *Daily News* and who knew so well all of these to me seemingly so wonderful people.

And what cannot such a woman do for such a man as I was then? I have spoken a good deal here of my fears but I do not believe that my fears were based on lack of faith in my own talent. I was then as I have always been not a proud but an infinitely vain man. At bottom I was an egotist, as Ben Hecht once said of me, so much the egotist that nothing ever really touched the central core of my egotism.

"Why I can write as well as any man alive. I have not come to it yet but

---

14. Ernestine Evans, hostess at an early Chicago-period party for Anderson, before he became famous, organized by Floyd Dell; Michael Carmichael Carr, eccentric original for the installment collector in Dreiser's *The Titan* (1914); Alexander Kaun, friend of Margaret Anderson and a political exile from Russia; Llewellyn Jones, editor of the *Friday Literary Review* from May, 1914.

15. Edgar Lee Masters (1868–1950), published *Spoon River Anthology* in 1915. See William Louis Phillips, "Sherwood Anderson's *Winesburg, Ohio:* Its Origins, Composition, Technique, and Reception" (Ph.D. Thesis, University of Chicago, 1950) for the relationship between Masters' and Anderson's work. Nicholas Vachel Lindsay (1879–1931), Illinois vaudeville poet; see Anderson's "Lindsay and Masters," *New Republic,* LXXXV (December 25, 1935), 194–95. Dreiser's *Sister Carrie* was published in 1900 but was not really circulated then.

I will come to it," I was always secretly saying to myself. Among the men at all interested in books and writing I had known, until that summer, O. Henry had been time and again pointed out to me as the great American story teller.

But I did not think he was great. "He has learned too many tricks," I thought. I thought that Mark Twain, in his *Huckleberry Finn,* and Melville, in his *Moby Dick,* had been our great tale tellers. I was myself a man outside the schools. At the time, and not until years later, I had not come to Chekhov or Turgenev in his *Annals of a Sportsman* but I had found the delightful and swaggering George Borrow.[16] I was, I knew, in a curious position. Although I had been a passionate reader my reading had never had any fixed direction. There were, I knew, whole continents of literature that I had never visited. My own vocabulary was small. I had no Latin and no Greek, no French. When I wanted to arrive at anything like delicate shades of meaning in my writing I had to do it with my own very limited vocabulary.

And even my reading had not much increased my vocabulary. Oh how many words I knew in books that I could not pronounce.

But should I use in my writing words that were not a part of my own everyday speech or my everyday thought?

I did not think so.

"No," I had long been telling myself. "You will have to stay where you have put yourself." There was the language of the streets of American towns and cities, the language of the factories and warehouses where I had worked, of laborers' rooming houses, the saloons, the farms.

"It is my own language, limited as it is. I will have to learn to work with it." There was a kind of painting I was seeking in my prose, word to be laid against word in just a certain way, a kind of word color, an arch of words and sentences, the color to be squeezed out of simple words, simple sentence construction. Just how much of all of this had been thought out, as I have spoken of it here, I do not now know. What I do know is the fact of the limitations I had to face.

And then too there was something else. I felt then as I am sure most of the men of the time did feel that writing, the telling of tales, had got too far away from life as we men of the time were living and what was so wonderful to me, in the new associates I had found, was a certain boldness of speech.

16. George Borrow (1803–81), English author.

We were in fact wallowing in boldness. At the time Freud had just been discovered and all the young intellectuals were busy analyzing each other and everyone they met. Floyd Dell was hot at it. We had gathered in the evening in one of the rooms. Well, I hadn't read Freud, in fact wouldn't read him, and was rather ashamed of my ignorance. Floyd walked up and down before us. He was at that time wearing a stock and looked I thought like pictures I had seen of Poe. When he was on the subject of literature he talked I thought brilliantly. I had never before heard such talk. How it flowed from him. What vast fields of literature he covered. He became excited. He shouted. The intense little figure became more and more erect.

And now he had begun "psyching" us. Not Floyd alone but others in the group did it. They psyched us. They psyched men passing in the street. It was a time when it was well for a man to be somewhat guarded in the remarks he made, what he did with his hands. On a certain evening, when there were several of us gathered together in a room, and, in an unfortunate moment, I brought up the subject of homosexuality.

I was puzzled. Some years before, when I was newly come to Chicago, when I was employed as a laborer in a North Side warehouse, I had for the first time seen homosexuality that was unashamed.

It had happened that in that place I worked a part of the time on an unloading platform at the warehouse door. The warehouse was on a street on the near North Side and in a house farther down the street several men lived together.

I was a small town man newly come to the great city. At home, in our town, there had been, to be sure, certain men and boys who were somewhat feminine as there were women and girls who seemed somewhat on the masculine side.

We others had called such boys "sissies." They were no good at baseball, or at the football (1 imagine that it would have been somewhat the so-called "Rugby" sort. We did not carry the ball. We kicked it up and down the field, often enough kicking one another rather than the ball.), they walked with mincing steps, often outdid us all in the classes, they spoke with soft feminine voices.

But these others, these of the city house on the street of the warehouse. They came by our platform sometimes in groups, they had painted cheeks and lips. The others, the workmen and truckmen on the platform with me, shouted at them.

"Ah, you Mable."

"Why, if that isn't Sweet Little Sugar."

The men passing, who were so much like women, giggled at us. There was a tall German who worked beside me. He began to swear.

"If one of them made a pass at me I'd knock his goddamn block off," he declared. Once when I was alone on the platform (it was late fall and darkness had come) one of them stopped and spoke to me. He approached and whispered to me.

"Don't you want to come and see me some night?"

I didn't answer, was a little shocked and even frightened.

"I have had my eyes on you. You do not shout insults at us as the others do. You know where I live. Do come some night. There is so much I could teach you."

He went off along the street, turning to throw a kiss at me, and I stood dumbly staring at him.

What did it all mean? I felt a strange unhealth within myself. I was not angry and am quite sure that, when this happened, I felt even a kind of pity. There was a kind of door opened, as though I looked down through the door into a kind of dark pit, a place of monstrous shapes, a world of strange unhealth.

It is difficult now, as I write, after the years, to remember just all I did feel on that occasion when first I came face to face with a fact in many other human lives and in the years since several such men have come to me and have talked to me of their terrible problem, some few stories of my own, the story "Hands" in the volume *Winesburg* and the story I called "The Man Who Became a Woman" in the other volume, *Horses and Men*,[17] having had time to think I could sympathize with them in their plight, but at the same time, during the summer when I first found comrades in the little place in 57th Street in Chicago, I was, on the whole, only puzzled.

So I asked the question.

"What makes men like that?"

I went further. Perhaps I expressed a kind of fear of something in life I couldn't understand and the fear in me was pounced upon.

Why, I was myself, unconsciously, one of them. The thing was in me too and the fear I had expressed was a sure sign of its presence.

On another occasion when I had been walking in the park on a Sunday afternoon with one of my new acquaintances we sat on a bench and as we talked of books and life, I leaned over and picking up a twig from the path

17. *Horses and Men* (New York: B. W. Huebsch, 1923), pp. 185–231.

before us began to break it between my fingers and "Ah," he exclaimed.

It seemed he had found me out. I was breaking the twig between my fingers and obviously, he explained to me, the twig was a phallic symbol. I was wanting to destroy the phallic in myself. I had secretly a desire to be a woman.

But it was not all like that. What nights we had, what excursions at the week ends. There was in us, I am sure, something of the fervor that must have taken hold of those earlier Americans who had attempted to found communistic communities. We were in our own mind a little band of soldiers who were going to free life (first of all to be sure in our own lives) from certain bonds.

Why it wasn't exactly free love we wanted. I doubt that there was with us any more giving way to the simple urge of sex than among the advertising and business men among whom I worked for certain hours each day. Indeed sex was to bring a new dignity and, as for marriage, well it was obvious that on all sides of us there were men and women living the lives of married men and women without love, without tenderness.

I think we wanted to reveal something. Later my own observation of life in small middle western towns, as boy and young man, was to lead to the writing of my *Winesburg, Ohio* and it has been said of the *Winesburg* stories that they did give story telling among us a new tone.

We had been brought up on English literature, sifted down to us through New England, on walls of houses all over America pictures of Longfellow, Whittier, Emerson. The New Englanders had lived in a cold stony land. There were the little fields, surrounded by the stone walls, through a large part of the year the skies cold and forbidding overhead.

Puritans, eh? Well, I dare say they were no more pure than we of the middle west.

The sons of the New Englanders had come into the middle west. They were in Ohio, Indiana, Illinois, southern Michigan, Iowa. Their blood had been mixed with that of those pushing up from the south, with those who had pushed down through Pennsylvania into the Valley of Virginia and even the mountains, and through Cumberland Gap into Kentucky and on into the middle western states bordering on the Ohio River.

These joined also by men of North Carolina, Scotch-Irish many of them. They would have come also seeking the warm deep soil of the middle western states.

There was an empire there, Chicago its capital, to become the breadbasket of the nation. My own father would have come up that way, from the North Carolina country. By his own story, or rather by one of his stories, he would have been of Scotch-Irish blood but in another book of my own, *A Story Teller's Story,* I have told of how he, when he was in the company of Germans, became a German, when with Italians an Italian, when with the Irish an Irishman.[18]

And I dare say, the North Carolina soil was rather thin and sandy too, a place of small farms, a few slaves, more poverty. My friend Paul Green,[19] one of the great story tellers I have known, has told me enough rare, often Rabelaisian tales of the North Carolinians.

Anyway there we were, intellectually dominated by New England. We wanted to escape from it. If European literature had not much come into our middle west the Europeans had come. We had got the Irish, the Germans, the Swedes, Danes and Norwegians. There was a new race being made.

And we had seen, in the towns and villages over the middle west, a kind of life going on that was not reflected by our story tellers. We had all read our *Huckleberry Finn,* that amazingly beautiful book, something of the whole vast valley of the Mississippi in it, but it was after all a tale of childhood.

But what about the real life on the Mississippi, on the river boats, in Natchez under the hill, in the tenderloin districts of St. Louis and New Orleans? What stories really told in the pilot houses of river boats? Abe Lincoln,[20] telling his stories in little taverns in Illinois, stories told in the back rooms of saloons in the towns in which we had lived, our own experience of thwarted lives, often sex bottled up as it was in women, twisted lives in New England, to become so furious a world, so many of the men striking out into the richer middle west, leaving their women behind.

Howells shushing Twain, so many of the stronger words of our everyday speech absolutely barred in our writing.

I do not think that any of us, at that time, wanted to over play sex. We

18. Hence the title of *Tar.* Irwin McLain Anderson was born in West Union, Ohio, August 7, 1845.

19. Paul Eliot Green (1894–   ), North Carolina teacher and dramatist. See below, "Tobacco Boy."

20. See Anderson's "Father Abraham," *The Sherwood Anderson Reader,* edited by Paul Rosenfeld (Boston: Houghton Mifflin Company, 1947), pp. 530–602; and David D. Anderson, "Sherwood Anderson's Use of the Lincoln Theme," *Lincoln Herald,* LXIV (Spring, 1962), 28–32.

wanted in our stories and novels to bring it back into its real relation to the life we lived and saw others living.

I remembered an experience of my own. I had for a time, when I was newly come to the city—this when I was still working as a laborer—been at a certain house. They were people to whom I had been given a note of introduction and I went to call.

There were a great many books in that house and I was buying few books and seeing there a volume of Walt Whitman I borrowed it but when I got home to my own room, in a working men's rooming house, I found certain pages torn from the book.

I was curious. I managed to get ahold of an unmutilated volume and discovered the reason. Old Walt had simply expressed, in certain verses, his healthy animalism and they couldn't take it.

The idea being that it would be terribly corrupting to read, in the printed pages of a book, what was so much in all our minds.

Or another experience, this out of my own life in a country town before I came to the city.

I had gone to the home of a certain girl at night, on a Sunday night. I had, in fact, got with her as she walked from church.

We had walked about. It was a summer evening and we were both young. We began to kiss.

We went to her house and sat on a porch at the back of the house. It was dark there.

And now she was lying on the floor of the porch.

"I am sleepy," she said. She pretended to go to sleep.

"Take me if you please. Do take me. Do it while I sleep.

"I must pretend to you that I do not know what is going on."

It ended so and later she could pretend to me, and even perhaps herself, that she did not know what had happened, that it had happened in her sleep.

All of this in relation to something new in my own life that I found among new people in the little crowded retail store room at 57th and Stony Island Avenue in Chicago. Mike Carr, Floyd Dell, Arthur Ficke, Lawrence Langner coming now and then from New York to blow us out, give us perhaps a bust with drinks. Ben Hecht, Alexander Kaun, occasional young professors from the University, talk and more talk.

A kind of healthy new frankness was in the talk between men and women, at least an admission that we were all at times torn and harried by the same lusts.

Our own lusts a little faced. It meant everything to me. And then excursions at the week end, to the country, often to the low country, then quite wild, south of Chicago.

Ben Hecht, having just read Flaubert, walking up and down declaiming. Ben then, as he remained, full of strange oaths, adjectives falling over adjectives, Mike Carr, with his little red beard and tight fitting red bathing trunks (for hours he would recite the verse of Swinburne), Alexander Kaun, telling tales of life in Russian villages, myself, for the first time hearing of Russian writers, Tolstoy, Dostoevsky, Chekhov, Turgenev, a new world of writers to be opened up to me later.

Was I not later to be called, by one of our American critics, "The Phallic Chekhov"?

I am trying to give here an impression of what was to me a gay happy time, the gayest and happiest I have ever known, a feeling of brotherhood and sisterhood with men and women whose interests were my own. As yet I had not begun to face what every practitioner of any art must face, the terrible times of depression, of bitter dissatisfaction with the work done, often the difficulty of making a living at your chosen work, the facing of the petty jealousies that pop up among fellow craftsmen, the temptation, always present, to try to get into the big money by attempting to give them what you think they want, the times when the ink will not flow, when you have worked, perhaps for weeks and months, on some project only to have to face the fact, on some sad morning, that it is all N.G., that what you have attempted hasn't come off and must be thrown away.

All of this still ahead of me during that summer in 57th Street with my newly found friends.

And then the women. How we do need them. There were two Margeries, Margery Currey, who had been Floyd Dell's wife, and Margery Jones. It is to such women that a man takes his first work.

"Now you tell me frankly what you think."

To be sure a man doesn't mean that. What he wants is praise, to be reassured, and it is this that women understand.

For often enough, for the young worker, it is only praise that helps.

"Yes. You have real talent. Do not be afraid."

Such a woman will often remember for years some sentence you have written and how it stirs and flatters a man to have such a sentence remembered and repeated. It is a special gift some women have, due perhaps to a lack of the competitive feeling in them, they wanting to make you happy and being not too scrupulous about it, thank heavens for that.

For the road is very long, to accomplish anything in any of the arts worth remembering through a winter day is so difficult.

So there was that summer, to be always remembered, the days got through in the advertising place and then the summer evenings, the walks in the park, the gatherings in one of the little rooms, Arthur Ficke, then a young lawyer at Davenport, Iowa, but already itching to throw all of that over and devote himself to poetry, coming to town to give us a blow out. Wine, whisky and beer brought in. Songs sung. Ben Hecht trying out a play in a tiny theatre arranged in one of the rooms, Lawrence Langner, a New York patent attorney, interested in the theatre, come to Chicago, perhaps on business but devoting his evenings to us.

Then the week ends at some little town on the lake shore, six or eight of us men and women sleeping perhaps, or at least trying to sleep, under our blanket by a bonfire built on the shore of the lake, even perhaps going off in the darkness to a secluded spot to bathe, all of us in the nude, it all quite innocent enough, but such a wonderful feeling in us of leading a new free bold life, defying what seemed to us the terribly stodgy life out of which we had all come.

And then perhaps a walk during the evening alone with one of the women. For me it would have been with little Margery Currey, her hand on my arm.

I would have given her an attempt at a story to read.

"Do not be afraid, Sherwood. You have real talent.

"You will do it. You will do it."

Oh wonderful words.

Songs being sung by a fire on the beach at night.

"Have you read Stephen Crane's *Maggie, A Girl of the Streets?*" [21] Men and women, far more widely read than I was, talking and talking. Poetry recited. Myself taking notes.

"I'll read that. I'll get it tomorrow."

It was all I dare say, in the great dreams we had, the vows of comradeship taken, a little childish, an interlude, for most of us the difficulty of what we wanted to do, dreamed of doing not yet faced, some of us to fail

21. Stephen Crane (1871–1900), novelist and journalist. See Anderson's Introduction to *The Works of Stephen Crane*, XI (New York: Knopf, 1926), xi–xv; and *A Story Teller's Story: A Critical Text*, edited by Ray Lewis White (Cleveland: Press of Case Western Reserve University, 1968), pp. 117, 203.

dismally enough, all of us to have to go through years of disappointment to accomplish little enough but, for that summer, a gay time, for me at least a happy time.

Comradeship. How life and the living of lives here in America tears us apart.

Random Notes

We were discussing what must be in the mind of the average man seen walking along a city street. There were several ideas put forth and then Ben Hecht said that it was a mistake to think of the man as thinking. He was dreaming. He had just come from a tilt with his wife. He had got the worst of it and now, as he walked along the street before the bar where we sat drinking, he was reconstructing the scene. In the new dramatization he was building he was giving himself the best of it. Ben went on with his theme. He thought most men spent their lives so. Such a man had been to a ball game and was now pretending to himself that he was a Christy Mathewson or a Babe Ruth.[22] He got into imagined fights with other men and always won, was always making brilliant remarks, performing heroic feats. As Ben talked, describing what we were calling "the average man," I was quite sure he must be right in his analysis. At any rate he convinced me that I was the thing called "the average man."

When I wrote the stories in the book called *Winesburg, Ohio* I was living in a cheap room in a Chicago rooming house. I dare say that all of the tales in the book came out of some memory or impression got from my boyhood in a small town but, as I had lived in several such towns, I had no one town in mind.

The house in which I had the room was on Chicago's North Side and was occupied by a group of people new to me. They were all either actively in the arts or they aspired to a place in some one of the arts. They were young musicians, young writers, painters, actors, and I found them delightful.

They were always coming into my room and I had many talks with

22. George Herman Ruth, famous baseball outfielder; Christy Mathewson, famous pitcher.

them. For the most part they were what I came afterwards to think of as "Little Children of the Arts." There was a great delicacy in them. They seemed to me to live, most of them, in a little closed-in world of their own. I felt in them little or no lust and it was a strange enough experience to me, coming as I did into that house, out of the world in which my own life was lived and feeling the amazing separation of their lives from the other lives I knew.

I came to them at evening out of an advertising office. A few years before I had been a laborer. I was myself, at that time, filled with all sorts of strange lusts.

I had been sitting with other men at a poker game in a hotel room.

I had been with a woman of the town.

I had become discouraged with life and had been on a drunk.

How strange the house seemed. There was something new to me. It happened that I had come into the house in the later afternoon and there was a young woman crying on the stairs. She had come into the house and had put on men's clothes and as she had rather huge breasts the clothes made her look somewhat absurd.

It may be that I had got into talk with that one and that she came with me into my room. She explained to me. She was in love with another young woman in the house and said that the young woman did not love her.

There were these somewhat strange relations going on about me and, coming out of the sort of life I had known, it was all new to me. Whether there was actually any of what is commonly called "perversion" in the house I don't know. I doubt that there was.

The people about me were intent on poetry, on music, on the art of acting. They took all of the arts with a kind of terrible seriousness new to me. They seemed to me always curiously gentle with each other and above all tremendously in earnest.

At the time I lived in this house I had already written and published two or three books.[23] I am quite sure that, up to that time, any writing I had done had been largely influenced by the writings of others. However the critics, suspecting that I had been set off by this or that older writer, never picked the right ones. They were always accusing me of imitating some man I had never read.

I was in this house and it was winter. I began suddenly to write short

23. Anderson's chronology is confused. He had not published any books when he lived on Cass Street.

tales. The tales were all written in a few months, one following the other, a kind of joyous time for me, the words and ideas flowing freely, very little revision to be done. I had set upon an idea and am quite sure the idea had come out of a certain rather fine feeling, toward myself, by the people about me. These rather strange little people (I cannot avoid thinking of them so), so gentle, kindly, so intent upon the arts, seemed always to be paying me a kind of respect that was certainly new to me.

It may be that I had been too much with business men, advertising men, laboring men, men who felt the practise of the arts as in some way unmanly. These new people, in some way a bit hard to explain, emphasized in me, shall I say, my maleness. At least they gave me a new confidence.

The idea I had was to take them, just as they were, as I felt them, and transfer them from the city rooming house to an imagined small town, the physical aspects of the town having, let us say, been picked up from my living in several such towns.

There was a young man, living in the house, who was an actor. He aspired to be an actor. It may be that he was really working in some store, as a clerk. I tried to put him, as I felt him, some inner truth of him, into another.

The other might be say the lonely figure of some queer man who lived upstairs over a drug store in a small town.

I changed, you see, every physical fact of my young clerk's life. Had I got him?

As suggested the stories were written, one following rapidly on the heels of another, and, in the house to which I had come, we played a game. I got them all into a room. I read my story aloud.

"Can it be one of you?" I asked.

They looked about, from one to another. They smiled. The test never failed.

"Yes. It is Alfred, or Clara, or James." Not once did they miss.

And so the stories came, in this rather strange way, into existence. I had, in relation to them, a somewhat new feeling. It was as though I had little or nothing to do with the writing. It was as though the people of that house, all of them wanting so much, none of them really equipped to wrestle with life as it was, had, in this odd way, used me as an instrument. They had got, I felt, through me, their stories told, and not in their own persons but, in a much more real and satisfactory way, through the lives of these queer small town people of the book.

So there the book was. It has made for itself a place in the world of books. How much I myself had to do with it I don't know. When it was at last published, having been for a long time peddled about, from publisher to publisher, a few of the stories having got into print in some of the small literary magazines of the times,[24] there was not a single critic who had a good word to say for it.

There was indeed a quite horrible time for us. For weeks, after the book appeared, it was almost universally condemned by those who wrote of it, generally recognized as in some way a powerful book, for weeks my mails were flooded with letters.[25]

Why, I do not mean to say there were not men who recognized the quality of the book. A few did, Mr. Van Wyck Brooks[26] and others. They wrote me letters but did not come to my defense in public.

And these other letters kept coming, for the most part from women. What names I was called. They spat upon me, shouted at me, used the most filthy of words and I remember one letter, in particular, from the wife of a man who had been my friend. She said she had once been seated beside me at a dinner table. "I do not believe that, having been that close to you, I shall ever again feel clean," she wrote.

And so it went on. How strange to think of it now, when the same book is being used as a text book in colleges, a book that was burned on the public square of one New England town, that such critics as Floyd Dell and Henry Mencken[27] had condemned, not publicly and not, with these men, on moral grounds, but, as they said, because the stories were not stories.

I think that later, a good many years later, both men made claims to having been, more or less, the fathers of the stories. I think that by the time they came to make the claim they had both convinced themselves it was true. I think that it is now generally recognized that the little book did something of importance. It broke the O. Henry grip, de Maupassant grip.

---

24. For a chronological list of Anderson's magazine publications, see Raymond Dante Gozzi, "A Bibliography of Sherwood Anderson's Contributions to Periodicals, 1914–1946," *Newberry Library Bulletin*, Series II, No. 2 (December, 1948), 71–82.

25. For some early reviews of *Winesburg, Ohio,* see the students' edition of the book, edited by John Ferres (New York: Viking Press, 1966).

26. Van Wyck Brooks (1886–1963), American literary historian, who wrote of Anderson in *The Confident Years, 1885–1915* (New York: Dutton, 1952), *passim;* and who reviewed *Sherwood Anderson's Notebook* in *Forum*, LXXVI (October, 1926), 637. See Anderson's "Letters to Van Wyck Brooks," *Story*, XIX (September–October, 1941), 42–62.

27. Mencken reviewed *Winesburg, Ohio* in *Smart Set*, LIX (August, 1919), 140, 142.

It brought the short story in America into a new relation with life.[28] I myself think that the real fathers and if you please the mothers of the *Winesburg* stories were the people who once lived with me in a Chicago rooming house, the unsuccessful Little Children of the Arts.

The Finding

It is the most difficult moment of all to write of. You are in a room. The particular room in which I sat was in an old house, old as Chicago houses go. Once it had been the house of some fashionable family.

The family had moved into some other, some newly fashionable section of the city. There had been one of those sudden shifts of the rich and fashionable, from one section of the city to another, so characteristic of our American cities. There had been a bath room on the third floor of the house but now, that whole section of the city having fallen into a place of cheap rooming houses, thin partitions had been put up.

There were many little rooms separated by thin partitions and they were all occupied.

The occupants were all young. They were young musicians, painters, young women who aspired to be actresses. I have always wanted to write of the people of that house. They were, for the time, so close to me.

I was no longer young. I was the oldest in that house. At the time the room in which I lived seemed large and later, in my thought, it kept growing larger.

I often described it to my wife.

"There was a great desk," I said, "as long as this room in which we now stand." I described for her my bed, the shelves built into the wall. I have always, when at work, loved to walk up and down. I am sure I gave her the impression of myself striding up and down a long room, grown in my imagination into something like a great hall. The council room of a king. Something of that sort.

28. There is still no adequate discussion of Anderson's influence on the short story form. See Russell H. Barker, "The Storyteller Role," *College English,* III (February, 1942), 433–42; and Ralph Elwood McIntyre, "The Short Stories of Sherwood Anderson" (M.A. Thesis, Columbia University, 1949). The best study to date is William V. Miller, "The Technique of Sherwood Anderson's Short Stories" (Ph.D. Thesis, University of Illinois, 1969).

CHICAGO

And then once, years after I had lived there, I made the mistake of taking her to the house.[29]

It was still a cheap rooming house. We drove up in a cab.

Why how shabby it had grown. There were dirty torn lace curtains at the windows, and, as we went into the little hallway, on the ground floor, the door being open, we came upon a young couple engaged in a quarrel.

They stood facing us, paying no attention to our entrance. The woman was young. Her hair was in disorder and a cigarette burned between her fingers.

The quarrel was over money. He was accusing her of taking money from his pockets.

"Liar. Liar," she screamed at him.

She ran suddenly up a flight of stairs, the man following, and we heard a door slam.

The landlady appeared. She was a short fat woman of fifty clad in a torn dirty dress.

I wanted to run away. I didn't.

"We are looking for a room," I said and followed her silently up first one and then another flight of stairs. In a room on the second floor, behind a closed door, there was the sound of a woman crying.

"That would be the woman we just saw, quarreling with her man down below," I thought.

We had got to the door of the room. How heavy I felt. My feet were heavy.

"This room is unoccupied," the landlady said. Her hand was on the doorknob.

"Don't," I wanted to scream. "Don't open that door.

"Leave me my dream of the room, what it was."

The door opened.

Why what a shabby little hole. It was all tawdry, the room so small, the wallpaper so dirty.

"We will go there. If the room is unoccupied we will spend a day, a week there." I had dreamed of sitting with her at the window that looked down toward the Chicago Loop in the evening, as the day faded, as the lights flashed on in the great buildings of the Loop.

People passing along the street below the window, passing under the street light at a nearby corner, shabbily dressed old men, smartly dressed

29. This visit took place in 1933. Cass Street is now Wabash, and the old house no longer stands.

young women. The house had stood just at the edge of the once fashionable section of the city and then, to the west, began the streets where the
poor lived.

"It was in this room it happened."

What dreams, hopes, ambitions. Sometimes it has seemed to me, when,
as a young man, I sat at the window of that room, that each person who
passed along the street below, under the light, shouted his secret up to me.

I was myself and still I fled out of myself. It seemed to me that I went
into the others.

What dreams. What egotism. I had thought then, on such evenings,
that I could tell all of the stories of all the people of America. I would get
them all, understand them, get their stories told.

And then came the night when it happened.

But what happened?

It is the thing so hard to explain. It is however the thing every young
man and woman in the world will understand.

I had been working so long, so long. Oh how many thousand, hundreds
of thousands of words put down.

Trying for something.

To escape out of old minds, old thoughts, put into my head by others,
into my own thoughts, my own feelings. Out of the others, the many many
others, who had worked in words, to have got so much I wanted, but to be
freed from them.

To at last go out of myself truly into those others, the others I met
constantly in the streets of the city, in the office where I then worked, the
others remembered out of my childhood in an American small town.

To be myself and get, at the same time, the others.

And then, on a day, late in the afternoon of a day, I had come home to
that room. I sat at a desk in a corner of the room. I wrote.

There was a story of another human, quite outside myself, truly told.

The story was one called "Hands." It was about a poor little man
beaten, pounded, frightened by the world in which he lived into something oddly beautiful.

The story was written that night in one sitting. No word of it ever
changed. I wrote the story and got up. I walked up and down in that little
narrow room. Tears flowed from my eyes.

"It is solid," I said to myself. "It is like a rock. It is there. It is put
down."

There was, I'm sure, an upsurge of pride.

"See, at last I have done it.

"It is true. There it is."

"In those words, scrawled on these sheets of paper, it is accomplished."

I am quite sure that on that night, when it happened in that room, when for the first time I dared whisper to myself, perhaps sobbing, that I had found it, my vocation, I knelt in the darkness and muttered words of gratitude to God.

That I had been on the right track, that I dared hope.

Pride, exaltation, all mixed with a new and great humbleness.

"It happened in that room.

"There I found my vocation.

"It is what we all want.

"All of this frantic search for wealth, fun, fame, position in life. It is all nothing.

"What we want, everyone of us, is our own vocation.

"It is the world hunger."

The above words going through my mind as I stood at the door of a shabby room in a shabby rooming house years later with my wife.

Remembering all my failures that night when I alone there in that room found, for the first time, my own vocation.

Getting for the first time true belief in self.

I must have muttered words to the landlady, taken my wife's arm, hurried out of that house, feeling deeply the shame of my many failures since that, the greatest moment of my life.

When I found my vocation.

What every man and woman in the world wants.

A vocation.

Ann and Jack

I had gone off, escaping from the advertising place, as I sometimes did. I had saved a little money. I wanted the south. It was winter in Chicago and there was the dreary round of advertisements to write, day after day.

"I will have to quit this. I am using here the words that are the tools of my real trade. I am soiling my tools."

I went to Mobile, in Alabama.[30] I had never been there. I had just put my finger on the map.

Perhaps I remembered how Grant, after he had taken Vicksburg, kept wanting to go to Mobile.

They wouldn't let him. They called him east to meet Lee, made him the head of all the armies.

But there was no danger of anyone's making me head of anything. I was glad of that.

I was in Mobile, on a winter day, had found a room in an old house, not far from the bay. It was a rooming house in which dock workers lived.

It was night and I went to walk. It was one of my memorable nights.

I thought the city very beautiful. It had begun to rain, a soft slow rain, and I walked through a little park, where, even on the winter night, there was a scent of flowers and had got into a dirty poorly lighted street when my foot struck something on the pavement.

It was a pocketbook and I picked it up. It was filled with bills. I hurried back to my room.

There was a billfold and in it was a hundred and forty dollars.

What luck. I sat in my room counting the money over and over. I do not think it occurred to me that night that the money belonged to someone else. It seemed sent to me by God.

A hundred and forty dollars. Why it meant to me two or even three months more of freedom. There was a novel I wanted to write, the novel I did begin and carry along all that winter.

It was the novel *Poor White*,[31] later put into the Modern Library series of books. I wanted to tell the story of a town, what happened to it when the factories came, how life in the town changed, old patterns of life broken up, how the lives of people of the town were all affected by the coming of the factories. The book has since become a sort of historic document of that change. It is used nowadays by a good many historians to give present day students a sense of the so-called "industrial revolution," brought down into a single American town.

I was in the southern city and had suddenly grown rich. Although I did look in the newspapers for the next several days I never saw any demand

---

30. Anderson spent the winter and spring of 1920 at Fairhope, Alabama. See *Letters,* ed. Jones and Rideout, Items 46 and 47.

31. See Walter B. Rideout's Introduction to *Poor White* (New York: Viking Press, 1966), pp. ix–xx.

for the return of the money. I wondered what I would do if there came any such a demand.

I went again out of my room, into the rain of night, having hidden the money in my room. I walked. I was so excited I couldn't sleep. I was free. Now, for weeks, perhaps for several months, I would not have to write advertisements. I had got into a negro section of the city.

It was late, after midnight, and the streets in which I now walked were unpaved. There were long rows of little shacks and although it was so late I could hear voices in the houses. There was something found, a new advantage for me. It was in the voices I heard in the night, in the dark muddy little streets. There was something, not tense, not full of the false excitement and nerve-tension of the advertising place, and, for that matter, of all Chicago. I heard soft voices. I heard laughter. There was a negro woman's voice, perhaps speaking to her man.

"Now honey, you be quiet. We got to sleep now."

It wasn't what the woman in the house said. It was the timbre of her voice, something I felt that night in the negro street, something I wanted. It seemed to break something in me.

There was that money found in the street and hidden now in my room. There was the soft black southern night, the gentle rain, the voices of negroes in the darkness, something in me released. I had been thinking. . . .

"Now I have these few free weeks and months. I must work hard, constantly. If I am ever to do this novel I so want to do I must be at it at once. I must work on it day and night."

The feeling of tenseness still in me, the rushing, pushing Chicago streets still in me, Illinois Central train to be caught, to be at the office at just a certain hour, a time clock to be rung.

Or, when I had moved to the North Side and come down into the Chicago Loop afoot in the morning, no time to lean over the rails of the old wooden bridges then spanning the Chicago River, to watch the gulls floating so beautifully over the chrysophrase water of the river.

Freedom. Soft voices. Laughter.

"Be quiet honey. We got to sleep now."

I found myself, on that night, my first night of freedom in the far south, going along in the negro streets saying over and over the words of the negro woman to her lover.

"Be quiet now.

"No hurry.

"Let your book come if it will."

A great sense of relief, of tension taken off, something I have always got in the south. It made me very happy that night. I must have walked for hours in the rain. I talked to myself, reassuring myself, an old fear that had long been growing in me, that I would never succeed in escaping the advertising place, that I would never get to the work I wanted, quite gone.

"Why I could sleep here in the street. A few cents a day would buy me food here."

Earlier, in my walking that night, I had gone to the docks and there was a banana boat being unloaded. Ripe bananas were lying about and I had picked up and eaten two or three.

"I could feed thus, as a bird or a beast feeds."

It was all absurd enough, I dare say, the feeling the southern night, the negro voices gave me, but it was all wonderful to me and I remember that later, as I walked in the rain that night, I doubled my fist into a hard knot.

"The north, from which I have come, is like this," I said, speaking alone to myself.

"And the south, I have found, like this."

I opened my fist, let it lie open and relaxed before me.

I had crossed the bay in a little steamboat. Jack Jones, who at that time was running a place called The Dill Pickle in Chicago,[32] had written me, asking me to go to the little town of Fairhope across the bay. There was a woman named Ann Mitchell who had come down there.

"She wants to talk with you. You go see her. She has something on her mind."

The town of Fairhope had been established by the followers of Henry George.[33] There was some scheme, in regard to the ownership of real estate. I never did understand that.

As for Jack Jones and Ann Mitchell, I shall have to tell their story against two backgrounds. For Ann it is a tragic story but the tragic part of it came later. It belongs to another place and another setting.

There was a rumor that, earlier in his life, Jack Jones had been one of a

32. The Dill Pickle, opened in 1916 in Tooker's Alley, published *The Dill Pickler* irregularly. See Kramer, *Chicago Renaissance,* pp. 310, 334. Anderson wrote of the club in "Jack Jones—The Pickler," *Chicago Daily News,* June 18, 1919, p. 12. See *Letters,* ed. Jones and Rideout, Item 336.

33. Henry George (1839–97), economic theorist, famous for his land-tax theories in *Progress and Poverty* (1879).

band of safe robbers. He had been, it was said, a "soap maker," meaning that it was his job to handle the nitro-glycerine used in blowing safes. He had several fingers missing.

He had reformed. Once he talked to me of his impulse in establishing his Dill Pickle.

"I had cut it out but they were always bothering me," he said. "Whenever there was a job done in Chicago they raked me in. I had to explain every movement to the police."

Jack had decided to organize a club.

"If you have some sort of a club, with an enrolled membership, they think you control votes. They let you alone. They think you can swing some votes for them."

If it were true that Jack had been what he pretended he had been, always in the wrong pew, he was a born showman. He had let his hair grow long and wore a black flowing tie.

He had gone in heavy for the arts. Having got an old building, on Chicago's North Side, he established a little theatre. Poets came there to read their verses. There were plays given and lectures delivered.

It had all worked out quite splendidly for Jack. There was a touch of the bizarre, the strange. You went there in the evening and there was Maxwell Bodenheim or some other poet, reading his verses. Many of the respectables of the rather well-to-do neighborhood had come. They whispered to each other, pointing to Jack.

"They say he's been a safe blower." It was a little like being in the actual presence of say Jesse James.[34] Whether or not Jack had ever been the desperate character he represented himself as having been I have no way of knowing.

"I give them the high brow stuff until the crowd begins to grow thin and then I turn on the sex," he once said to me. I had gone there to hear a woman speak. "Men Who Have Made Love to Me" was the subject of her talk. Jack knew his public. He was raking in money.

I remember her as a small and rather thin woman of forty. She walked nervously up and down.

Such and such a man had come to her room. He knocked on the door.

"At first I decided I wouldn't let him and then I did."

She had a job at the time. She was a stenographer and lived in a certain

---

34. Jesse Woodson James (1847–82), leader of the most notorious band of robbers in the Midwest. See *A Story Teller's Story*, ed. White, p. 61.

rooming house. She had been married and divorced. It was because her husband drank.

"He never offered to make love to me except when he was drunk. I couldn't stand his breath."

She returned to the man who had come to her room, in the rooming house. She was excited. There was something unpleasant. Her being there, standing thus before a crowd of men and women in Jack's place (It was down an alleyway off a street of houses, a very respectable street. The place had been a stable.). . . . She stood before us excited, her thin face flushed. It was exhibitionism.

Jack had paid her nothing. She had wanted to do it.

There were voices from the floor.

"You didn't know the man who came to your door?"

"No. I just wanted a man."

She began to cry.

There wasn't much of this sort of thing. It happened sometimes. Men and women sat looking furtively at each other. There was something happened to all of us. We felt degraded.

Still we went. The sex evenings did bring crowds to Jack's place.

He was a new kind of man to me, very vain, shrewd, with something brutal under a sensitive exterior. I was very cautious. I went about with him. We took walks together. He seemed very proud of his past, had got, because of his past, a certain standing among us intellectuals.

"He is a man of action," we thought. He made great claims to being an expert mechanic.

"You see," he said, "I have been what you know.

"And now . . . here I am.

"I am providing a place for poets to recite their verses. I shall presently open a theatre. We will do fine things.

"The plays of Synge and Chekhov."

We, of the Chicago Intelligentsia, had, already, some of the passion that was later to sweep over and well nigh engulf our world—the passion for the proletariat. Jack spoke with biting contempt of the bourgeoisie. He called them "bourjoices."

He took me, with three other men, into the country. We took food. We took beer. We went far up north, to a beach. We swam in the lake. I was given to understand that the men were members of a gang of robbers. I was excited, being with such men. Now I am not quite sure. It may be they were spoofing me. I remember that I spent the day in a kind of fever of excitement. They said nothing of their occupation and, although I was afire with curiosity, I asked no questions. They were men who might have been machinists in some factory, where I had formerly worked. We had driven to the place in a car.

"It is perhaps a stolen car," I thought.

I had pictures of the police, suddenly descending upon us.

So I would be in a hell of a fix. How would I explain my presence with the gang? Jack had whispered to me, this after we had got into the car. He had said the men were house breakers.

They were big-time men. They were leaders in their profession. We had our swim, ate food, drank our beer and returned to the city. I had got a thrill.

I had become the friend of such men, could cultivate their friendship, occasionally go about with them and then, later, when I was with my own set. . . .

I would be spending an evening with a woman. She was one who wrote verses.

She was a married woman but her husband was out of town.

He was, let us say, a business man. He supported her, provided her a home. She lived in an expensive apartment, in an expensive street.

It is not to be understood that I went to her to betray her husband. Nothing of that sort happened. I had gone to her because we were both, in a way of speaking, living on the same plane.

We sat together. She perhaps showed me some of her verses. She was a woman whose husband did not and could not understand a certain side of her nature. She told me about that, making it quite clear that, much the same, she was very fond of him.

"He is just a great boy," she said.

And then my own chance came. I could speak to her, quite casually to be sure, of my new acquaintances. I could let my fancy loose. She would be given to understand that I did not lead my own life in any world of thin aesthetics. I was one who knew all sorts of men, touched, with my own life, all sorts of strange other lives. There would be a kind of wonder in the woman's eyes. I would have myself a swell evening.

Things did happen. I was asked, by one of my new acquaintances, to come to his apartment for dinner. It was to be a Thanksgiving dinner. His wife, I had been told, was a famous cook.

I did go. I got another thrill. The reader is to understand that I myself did not, at any time, take part in any of the activities of the gang.

However Jack had explained. The wife of the robber, if he was a robber (she was a smiling cheerful soul, a fat woman), went as cook into the houses of the rich.

She went to work in such a house. She could make a map of the house. Keys could be made. She stayed until all was arranged, and then she quit. She got another place.

The gang did not descend upon the house at once. They waited. Suspicion must not be thrown upon the cook.

I had dined at the house of the robber. It was a good dinner. It was something more for me to speak about. We story tellers are avid for such material. We are always looking for new color in our own lives. There are these long hours spent in our imaginative worlds. We grow weary of our own imaginings.

"Give us life, life," we cry.

I went to dine at the house of a friend. She was a very charming woman and was married to a friend. We were seated at a table and suddenly a door, at the side of the room, was opened.

There was an animated conversation going on. There were several people at the table and some man was telling a story. All at the table were absorbed.

I looked up. A shiver ran through my body. A door at the side of the room had opened and there was a fat face looking at me. It was the face of the wife of the man at whose house I had dined. I was in a sweat. I squirmed. On the next day I went to the house of the robber. I explained to him and he shrugged his shoulders.

"It will be all right," he said.

"If they, in that house, are your friends I'll call it off," he said.

I was very proud. As already suggested the whole thing may have been but a spoof. I can't be sure. Later however I went back to the house where I had seen a woman's face in a doorway. I sat in talk with the woman of the house.

"I had a wonderful cook," she said.

She said she couldn't understand. The cook had suddenly left.

I was living, at that time, in an apartment on the ground floor of a North Side building. It was a small apartment with but one bedroom. While I lived in that place there was a race riot in Chicago. Gangs of young roughs rode through the streets in cars, shooting at negroes. They did not come into my neighborhood but there were several negro men, working about a nearby building, I knew.

I gave them the key to my apartment and they slept in there and I remember a night when there were six or eight of them lying asleep on the floor in my little living room. I had come in late. I unlocked the door and went in. There was a little hallway and a negro man stood in the darkness with a club in his hand.

I had a distinguished visitor. The French theatre man, Mr. Jacques Copeau, had brought his company of players to New York. He had, I understood, been sent by Clemenceau.[35] It was for the purpose of French propaganda. The World War was on but we had not yet gone in. The French and the English were hard at it, trying to get us in.

Copeau had come with his company of players. He was a tall distinguished looking man and I thought a good actor and trainer of actors. He was also a maker of plays.

He had been selected to bring the company of French players for a season in New York. The venture was being backed by Mr. Otto Kahn [36] and, during the first season, Copeau had what he and I, later when he spoke of it to me, thought a magnificent salary.

He with his company had the season in New York. I dare say Mr. Kahn got his red ribbon. At any rate, after the first season, the support of Mr. Kahn was withdrawn and Copeau, with the money got from the first season's work, carried the venture on for another year. I was at the theatre once. I saw Molière's *Doctor in Spite of Himself*. I thought it beautiful.

I had got a letter from Copeau. He had read some of my books. He was very kind. He said that some of my stories gave him a new feeling for American life. He proposed that he come to see me.

"My work here, in New York, is at an end," he said. "I want to see and talk with you and I want to see Chicago."

He came. He stayed with me in my apartment. I had but the one bedroom, a small one, facing an alleyway, and I put him in there. I myself slept on a couch.

There was a week of close and, for me, very exciting companionship. I for the time gave up my job. Although I had already written and published several books I could not yet make my living by writing.

35. Jacques Copeau (1878–1949) was in New York with his Vieux Columbier Theatre players, 1917–19. Georges Clemenceau (1841–1929), French publisher and World War I premier. See *Letters,* ed. Jones and Rideout, Items 85 and 123.
36. Otto Kahn (1867–1934), German-born banker and patron of the arts. See *Letters,* ed. Jones and Rideout, Item 155, *passim.*

It did not matter. If I had been feeling that life was unjust to me the feeling passed. I had been selected by this man as friend. He was a distinguished one. As you went about with him people stopped to look.

"Who is that man?" they were asking. There are men like that. Clarence Darrow was one. When such a man comes into a room everything in the room changes. The very air of the place seems to change. People in the room begin to come alive in a new way. The man Copeau had brought this feeling to me and there was something else.

He was, at that time, particularly interested in a book of tales I had written and that I had called *Winesburg, Ohio*. He said the tales had excited him.

"It is because of them I came to see you."

We walked about. We talked. We went into little saloons. We went into factory districts, went to baseball games.

He insisted on being, for the time, very American and I remember that he smoked a corn cob pipe. He insisted on smoking it in street cars and when a street car conductor protested he didn't understand.

"He's a Frenchman," I said. "He doesn't speak English. He doesn't know any better."

I explained that, in France, all men smoked corn cob pipes in street cars and the conductors, for the most part, grinned and went away.

My friend had it in mind that he would make a dramatization of my *Winesburg* tales. We talked of it at length, made plans, even drew up outlines of scenes. The dramatization, at his hands, never came off and, later, I did it myself. I made a play that was produced by Mr. Jasper Deeter in his Hedgerow Theatre in Pennsylvania but that, although I did sell it to various New York producers, was never performed in New York. Later I put it in a book.[37]

We were there, the distinguished Frenchman and myself, in my apartment at night and Mr. Carl Sandburg was there. He was singing songs for us.

And perhaps I had better explain. Copeau, like most artists I have known, was a great lover of clothes. He loved to array himself. He had had this chance, in New York. He had been financed by Mr. Kahn.

He had gone in for clothes.

Such trousers, shoes, ties, overcoats, pigskin bags. There was a closet, in the bedroom, filled with them.

37. Jasper Deeter produced the dramatic version of *Winesburg, Ohio* on June 30, 1934. See *Letters*, ed. Jones and Rideout, Item 251, *passim*. Anderson refers to his *Plays, Winesburg and Others* (New York: Scribner's, 1937).

"I shall go, so, back to Paris," he said.

The clothes were all he had left from his venture here.

"I shall walk so arrayed through the streets."

He got the clothes out of the closet and spread them on the bed. He called to me.

"Come look, Sherwoodio," he said.

He let me feel the cloth of the coat.

"Ah! Feel! How soft, how warm.

"And my striped trousers, and these shoes, and these ties and socks."

He went into an ecstasy.

"It is something new in my life," he said. He had been poor as I had.

"Now I am again poor. I must begin again. I must struggle."

He had certain ideas about the theatre. It would take a long time and much patience to work them out.

"But with these clothes, these pigskin bags. . . .

"When I arrive in Paris. . . .

"They will think me a rich American," he said.

We were, on the night, in the apartment. Carl Sandburg had come. He had sung for us. He had gone. He put his arms about me and we walked to the door of his bedroom.

There was a cry out of his soul. The window of the bedroom, that looked into the alleyway, was open. There had been three new overcoats, several suits, dozens of pairs of socks, dozens of gaudy neckties, the striped trousers, the shoes.

They were all gone. It was a moment never to be forgotten.

"I was rich and now, you see, again I am poor.

"I am returning to France. I must work.

"I shall never again have money to buy such clothes, such shoes, such overcoats.

"Oh, Sherwoodio, Sherwoodio.

"I was beginning to love your Chicago, your America, and now. . . ."

It was a desperate situation and I ran to my friend Jack. The police had already come. They stood in the little bedroom and spat out the window. They had us make a list, myself at the typewriter, Copeau walking up and down.

The two policemen stood and watched. They spat out the window. They looked in wonder at Copeau. He was walking up and down. He was nearly bald but he ran his hands over his head. He turned occasionally to smile at me, a sad sad smile.

"If I had any hair I'd tear it out," he said.

"Oh, Sherwoodio, Sherwoodio. My striped pants, my overcoats."

I ran to Jack and he failed me.

"Sure," he said. He made one of his Napoleonic gestures.

"I'll have them back in twenty-four hours," he said.

"I'll go see some of my old pals. They'll know. I'll fix it for you," he said.

He had already heard of Copeau.

"There is something at stake here," he said. He said something about the honor of Chicago, its treatment of a distinguished man. He filled me with hope but later the hope faded away. His influence, in the underground of Chicago, was not as strong as it was fancied to be.

He had sent little Ann Mitchell down to see me.

"I want you to talk with her. You tell her just what you think."

There had been a lot more to Jack's letter. Ann had come one day to The Dill Pickle and had, at once, become in love with Jack. She was a small woman and a painter. She had, I gathered from Jack's letter, had a hard rough life but she was, he declared, a woman of talent. "She is the real thing. She's got it," his letter declared.

Jack had proposed marriage to her but she was undecided.

"Well, you go away. You go off down south. You think it over."

It was evident that Jack was really touched. He had given her money. He was also in love.

"I don't want her to do anything that isn't the right thing for her. I want her to have her chance as a painter," he declared.

But this was not the Jack Jones I had known. I had seen him on the street just before I had left Chicago and had told him of my proposed trip to Mobile and he had, through the office in which I had worked, got his letter through to me.

I had gone across the bay to Fairhope and had found Ann. She was small. She was far from a beauty. She had about her something you couldn't mistake.

She was an aristocrat, that was it. There was, evident from the moment you first saw her, a quality, a fineness of spirit, that could not be mistaken. It was that had got Jack. It had cut through to him and, as for Ann, I knew, after the first hour with her, that she had also found in Jack something none of us others who knew him had ever seen.

She was troubled however. Was a marriage with her the best thing for Jack? "I'll never be much of a housekeeper," she said. Jack had, she said, a new plan in his head. He was planning to turn his Dill Pickle into a real playhouse, do only high class plays. I gathered that what he had in mind was something of the sort Jasper Deeter was later to do with his Hedge-row Theatre in the little town of Media near Philadelphia. It was Ann's notion that he needed, as wife, a woman skilled in the theatre. She was afraid, she said, that she would only be in the way and I wanted to protest to her.

"He is what he is. He will always be the same. He will always be making these grand plans but they will come to nothing," I wanted to say but I kept silence. It was so evident that Ann was in love with Jack.

"It is none of my business," I told myself.

I had a day with Ann at the little town of Fairhope on Mobile Bay and decided to go there to live. I could get a little house, facing the bay, at a low price. I would do my own cooking. The bay was full of fish. I could get clams and crabs. I talked it over with Ann who helped me find a house. There was a table, a kitchen stove, chairs and a few dishes. There was a small iron cot and Ann thought that the getting of enough bedding to keep me warm would not cost me much.

So there I was, with a house of my own, a view of the bay, with steamers going up and down. The bay was fed by three great rivers coming down from the north and, as all the country above was a red clay country, the red had washed down into the bay after the heavy winter rains and, as the sun went down in the west, over the city, just to be seen on clear evenings, its lights shining at night, the bay became a warm blood red.

It was blue. It was green. It was pale green and there were miles of open beach on which to walk. Living there would cost me little or nothing. There were people with whom I could play about. There were the pincy woods, stretching away behind the town, the bay with its changing colors and the long stretches of deserted beach on which to walk. Storms of the past had cast up strange fantastically shaped tree stumps swept down into the bay from the rivers. Some of them had been lying for years in the southern sun. They had been washed by waves and rain. In the night, on moonlight nights, as a man walked on the beach, their shapes constantly changed.

It was a fantastic world and there was Wharton Esherick [38] who at once became my friend, and Ann, both painters. There was Wharton's wife Letty, very dark, very beautiful, and presently another, Florence King (we

38. Wharton Esherick (1887–   ), American sculptor and designer.

called her The Kinglet), the wife of Carl Zigrosser. As I wrote she would do my typing for me. She was an expert at that.

It was all something wonderful. It was the out of doors in a strange and beautiful land. It was good companionship and freedom.

And so a new life began, a winter not to be forgotten. I wrote and wrote. I swam in the bay, my little hoard of money made me seem, to myself, suddenly rich. I loafed with Wharton, quarreled with him, as one dares with a friend.

I even did some painting and a curious thing happened. When I had returned to Chicago, after the free winter, broke again, again in the advertising place, there was an exhibition of my paintings.

They were crude enough. I had merely been experimenting with color, its effect on the forms of things I saw. When it was suggested that I show the paintings I had an exciting evening.[39]

How does a man put a price on painting? I was in a room with my own crude attempts. "All right, I'll put prices on them. Two hundred, three hundred, two hundred and fifty," I thought.

It was all to be sure quite meaningless. I had my stories I could not sell. I was no painter. I put the prices on my canvases thinking, as I wrote down the figures, of stories I would like to sell and then, at the showing of my paintings, a strange woman, from Denver, appeared. I never saw her. She sent me a check for seven hundred dollars and walked off with two of my paintings. There was a note from her.

"They make me feel as I would like to feel," she said and I danced about in the little coop where I sat with the other advertising writers and waved the check under their noses. I was a slave suddenly freed.

It meant freedom again, more freedom for me.

As for the story of little Ann Mitchell, unlike myself a real painter, she married Jack Jones. She was in love with him and he believed in her talent but over and above his belief in himself. It was that belief that led to her death.

She had been living with Jack for perhaps two years when I saw her again. It was summer and I had been given a house up near the town of Ephraim on Green Bay and was at work again. The house had been given me, for the summer, by my friend, Doctor Charles Millspaugh, curator of the department of botany at the Field Museum, and I was very happy there. The house was built of logs, a replica of the one the doctor had seen

39. Anderson's painting was displayed at the Radical Book Shop in 1920 and later at the Arts Club. See *Letters,* ed. Jones and Rideout, Item 53.

in Norway, there was a large stone fireplace and there were rooms for guests.

The guests kept coming. Waldo Frank came with his wife, my friend George Daugherty came from Chicago and others followed.

And then Jack Jones came with Ann.

It was a summer night and there was a storm. The wind blew a half hurricane and the rain beat against the walls of the house.

It was a night to be indoors, to sit with friends before a fire, to drink, to tell stories. A little party of friends, men and women, had come from Chicago.

The house was in a wood and on the shore of the bay. It was a mile or more from the town of Ephraim.

There was a knock on the door and I went and threw it open and there they were. They had come up, the whole length of Lake Michigan, in a little open boat with an outboard motor, and had just got into the bay before the coming of the storm. They were wet to the skin and Ann was pale. When I had got them into the house I saw the terror in her eyes. There was no terror in Jack's eyes and at once he began to boast. He had beat the storm. The boat was one he had built with his own hands. People had warned him of the dangers of the lake in such a boat but he had laughed at them.

"It is my boat. I built it with my own hands. I wasn't afraid of the storm. I would have ridden it out," he boasted. He went with me into the kitchen of the house. There were others there, my friends, who had come for a visit.

"It is all right," he said.

He took a marriage certificate from an inside pocket and water dripped from it onto the floor.

"Take a look," he said. "It is all right. We are legally married," he said, and so Jack and Ann stayed with me for several days. The weather cleared and we fished and Ann got out her equipment and painted. It was then she painted the charming little water color I have here now on the wall of the room in which I sit writing of her.

"But Ann, you will not venture back with him, not in that boat?"

The question was being put to her.

"Yes, if he says so, I will.

"He is my man. I will do what he says."

There was a little fishing along the shore and Ann was painting there. The fishermen, who knew the lake, took me aside.

"That woman," they said, "she will not go back with him in that boat."

They talked to me and they talked to Jack.

"It is my boat. I built it with my own hands. It will ride out any storm that can come."

As the fishermen talked, Ann stood a little aside. She grew a little pale. I could feel the terror in her.

"He is my man. What he says I will do."

There was something she had always wanted. There was her Jack. He made a living for her. She was free. She could paint.

"I'll do what he says. Anything he wants me to do I will do."

I pled with her and the fishermen pled. They grew angry with Jack.

"It is by sheer luck the man has got here in that boat.

"If he had arrived here an hour later when he came the boat would have been swamped."

The fishermen went about swearing at Jack.

"Let the damn fool go in his boat he has built with his own hands but do not let the woman go with him," they urged.

However he did set off and he insisted upon taking Ann. The sun was shining as I stood on a little dock before the house pleading with Jack but he only laughed at me.

"What? It is my boat. I built it. You have been listening to the fool fishermen's talk. I tell you I myself built the boat."

Ann was smiling. I could see the terror in her eyes but they set off and I watched until the boat disappeared down the bay into the lake. It was the last of her.

It was off Racine that the storm struck the boat and they were there, floating on the upturned boat for thirty-six hours before they were found, and Jack was still alive but Ann was dead. When the boat had overturned he had managed to tie himself and Ann to the upturned boat with a rope but the waves kept washing over them. Ann was drowned but Jack survived.

"He is my man. I'll do what he says." She had gone to her death for him, I have always thought, to save his pride.

There was a curious finale to the story. The Art Institute of Chicago had offered a prize for young painters and Ann had won the prize. It would have meant much to her. She who had never won any recognition as a painter would have got thus the recognition for which she had hungered so long. The prize however was for living artists and she was dead, so they did not announce her name as the winner. The prize was given to some other painter.

"It is for him to say. He is my man. I will do what he says."

It was the final word for her. The artist in her had surrendered to the egotism of the male, the craftsman, and I never went to see him again.

Ben and Burton

When we were all in Chicago, Ben Hecht, Burton Rascoe, Lewis Galantière, Justin Smith, Carl Sandburg, Harry Hansen and a half dozen others, we used to dine often at a place called Schlogl's on Fifth Avenue. Later I believe the name of the street was changed. It became Wells Street. The *Daily News* was in a ramshackled old building near there under the elevated railroad.

We all gathered around a big table and indulged in literary talk. At that time Henry Mencken was our great hero. We all read the old *Smart Set* and later Mencken and Nathan's *Mercury*.[40] Many of us had got letters from Mencken. He was the great letter writer. At that time he must have been in correspondence with all of the young writers in the country. It must have paid the *Mercury* well. A man was in great luck who got more than twenty-five dollars for a story from that pair.

Still we got the letters and the letters made us proud.

"Well, I had a letter from Henry Mencken today."

You said it casually off-hand but, in your heart, you felt that it was like being knighted by a king.

You knew darn well the others felt the same. Henry made a great mistake. He should, at just that time, have made a grand tour as Gertrude Stein did later, picking as Gertrude did just the right moment.[41] In Chicago we would have delivered the town over to him.

A few years before Francis Hackett and Floyd Dell had been the literary band masters in Chicago but they had both departed for New

40. Mencken and Nathan, who had founded *The American Mercury* in 1924, withdrew from it in 1933. In *The American Mercury,* Anderson published "Caught," I (February, 1924), 165–76; "Death in the Woods," IX (September, 1926), 7–13; "Five Poems," XI (May, 1927), 26–27; "A Jury Case," XII (December, 1927), 431–34; and "They Come Bearing Gifts," XXI (October, 1930), 129–37.

41. Miss Stein toured America in 1934. Anderson wrote of her in "Four American Impressions," *New Republic,* XXXII (October 11, 1922), 171–73; Introduction to her *Geography and Plays* (Boston: Four Seas, 1922), pp. 5–8; "Gertrude Stein's Kitchen," *Wings,* VII, No. 9 (September, 1933), 12–13, 26; "Gertrude Stein," *American Spectator,* II, No. 18 (April, 1934), 3; *A Story Teller's Story,* ed. White, pp. 260–61, 263, 272, 286, 305–6; and *Letters,* ed. Jones and Rideout, Items 67, 69, 75–76, 109, 240, 257, 334, *passim.*

York, Hackett to the *New Republic* and Floyd to the old *Masses*. Floyd published a novel that Hackett reviewed and the review was a masterpiece. He took Floyd's skin off inch by inch. It was the best job of literary skinning I ever read.[42]

They were both however now gone from Chicago and Burton Rascoe on the *Tribune* and Ben Hecht on the *Daily News* were doing books for the town.

We were all at lunch and an agreement was made. I think it must have been Ben Hecht who proposed it.

"Look here, Burton, we'll take up some writer. You go big for him and I'll go against him. We'll keep it up. You blow your horn and I'll put on the Bronx cheer."

I think something of that sort must have been said. At any rate the agreement was made and, as usual, Ben had got himself into an advantageous position.

Abuse was meat and drink to him. He loved it. He was a genius at it. Later, I am told, he used the talent with wonderful effect on the movie magnates of Hollywood. I am told that the more he abused them, the more they paid him. He could do it with a smile on his face.

The point is that it was all fun to Ben, in reality a very smart man, full of kindness, but it was temporarily poison to Burton.

For Burton was then, as he always was, a highly nervous sensitive man. He was easily hurt.

The two men had decided upon James Branch Cabell [43] as the man to be praised and abused. They began and I have no doubt that Burton, although Ben had proposed the plan, had proposed the man. He was sincere in his admiration of Cabell while Ben was out to be vehemently insincere.

It began. It was carried on for weeks. Columns in the newspapers were filled with it and the Chicago book stores were, for the time, loaded up with Cabell's books.

For the book dealers it didn't, I was told, turn out so well. Too many people, induced to buy by all the clamor being raised, brought the books back.

They said they didn't understand the books.

They were too sophisticated, they said.

At that time, among us in Chicago who were literarily inclined, there

42. Anderson refers to Hackett's review of Dell's *Moon-Calf* in *New Republic*, XXV (December 8, 1921), 49.
43. James Branch Cabell (1879–1958), Virginia novelist.

was a great passion to be sophisticated but our ranks were small in numbers. Ben and Burton were overselling the possible Cabell market.

It had all begun by the praise and abuse of Cabell but presently the war became more personal. Ben began to call his opponent "the sophomore Rascoe" and Rascoe attempted to meet Ben half way in the matter of personal abuse.

It was for him a hopeless struggle, although, naturally, he had made of Cabell a lifelong friend and you can understand that Cabell later dedicated a book to Burton.[44] Under the circumstances I would have done the same.

It had all been begun as a stunt but it had grown serious. Now Ben and Burton, when they met, did not speak. Ben growled and Burton fumed. Two men who had been and later were to become again real friends were for the time bitter enemies.

I decided to give a dinner and invited ten or twelve men. I invited Ben without telling Burton and when I invited Burton did not tell him that Ben was coming.

The dinner came off and we all sat at a long table, Burton and Ben opposite each other, and Ben was in fine feather. He talked. He made insidious remarks, for the most part directed at Cabell. He did not look at Burton but kept addressing his remarks to the others at the table and Burton kept hopping up and down in his chair.

He could not eat. He kept opening and closing his mouth. He stuttered. There was a bottle of whisky on the table and he kept filling a glass and drinking it off. I am quite sure that, at the moment, he was so excited that he did not realize that he was not drinking water.

And then at last he spoke. Burton, as all his friends know, always was, to the last inch, a literary man. He pointed a trembling finger at Ben.

"You talk," he shouted.

"You think you know something about life, about literature."

"But what do you know of life? You tell me. You answer me. What do you know of life?"

Burton turned from Ben to the rest of us. He spoke of Ben with infinite scorn.

"You look at him. What does he know of life?"

Then the really temendous statement that set the table roaring and in the end patched up the broken friendship came from Burton's lips.

"This Ben Hecht," he said, "he knows nothing of life.

44. Cabell dedicated to Rascoe his *Jurgen: A Comedy of Justice* (New York: R. M. McBride, 1919).

"Why the man has never had but one mistress and she was a charwoman."

It was the final literary thought. It broke something. It was all of England's literature come to our modest little dinner table. When he had said it even Burton had to laugh. It patched everything up, made Burton and Ben what they had been before the great Cabell war began, again warm and intimate friends.

All Will Be Free

I was always a little sore at Ben Hecht that he first told the story. When last I saw him in New York he was at work making it into a movie.

However I cannot resist the temptation to tell my impression of the man. He was so cheerful, seemingly so full of life.

We had gone, Ben and I, with some four or five others, to lunch at the German restaurant. It was a cold rainy day in the late fall, let us say in November, and we were all in a cheerless mood.

For one thing it was during the time of prohibition and, on such a Chicago day, in the mood we were in, we all wanted drinks. But drinks were expensive.

Yes, they could be had in the place, at say fifty cents a drink, that is to say for a second rate stuff.

So we sat there growling at each other. Except myself, all the others were newspaper men. Although, at bottom, Ben Hecht is one of the kindest men I have ever known he has always had a talent for insult.

We had begun insulting each other, insults thrown back and forth, each man trying to get some other fellow's dander up.

We were interrupted by the waiter.

"That man over there, that little dark man sitting in the corner, wants to buy you all a drink."

"Listen man, don't attempt to torture us.

"Is this some crude and cruel attempt at a joke?"

We were all staring at the little strange foreign looking man who smiled blandly at us.

"No, he means it. What will you have?" the waiter was asking us. There was no one else in the place except ourselves and the man at the table in a corner at the back of the room.

"Sure. Sure. Hell yes."

"He wants you to have the best stuff."

Ben half arose from his chair.

"I've a notion to go and kiss him," he said.

The drinks were brought and we raised our glasses to the man and, in a few minutes, there the waiter was again.

"He wants you to have another drink."

It was too much. We were all so filled with gratitude that we were struggling to keep the tears of gratitude from running down our cheeks.

"What a man. What a man. Bring him over here."

Two of us arose to escort him to our table. This wasn't a fellow to miss. Why, the drinks we had been having were costing seventy-five cents each.

The man came. It is something shameful in me that I have forgotten his name.

He was so cheerful, so generous, so happy seeming.

We began to question him and he talked. More drinks flowed. Ben later told the story in a book he called *A Thousand and One Afternoons*.[45] At this point in the story he made me begin singing a song. Ben couldn't remember the words of the song he put into his story. He invented words. He made me responsible for his misquoting of the words of the song I didn't sing. He was, I dare say, too lazy to look them up. Or he was just taking a good natured shot at me.

"This is the song as Sherwood sang it." He said something of that sort.

Anyway there we were at the table in that place and a gloomy cheerless day had become bright and shining. More and more drinks kept coming.

The man we had thus found was a little dark Russian Jew. He was in a mood for talk. He told us his history.

He had been born a poor Russian Jew boy in a ghetto. He was drafted into the Russian army. He went to serve in the Caucasus.

He spoke at length of that, describing his life in the army under the Tzar, the mountain villages seen, the herds of cattle on the great hills, the rushing rivers, the beautiful village girls.

"They were Tartar maidens," he said.

"Oh they were so strong, so straight, so full bosomed." He went into a

45. Hecht's story is in *A Thousand and One Afternoons in Chicago* (Chicago: Covici-McGee, 1922), pp. 31–34.

kind of ecstasy as he described the mountain maidens seen while he was a Russian soldier.

And then he was in America, had escaped from the army life and had come here. He was in New York, working there, having hard enough times.

"But, oh, the beautiful country, America. Life so free here." Here, in America, and here only, on all the earth's surface, such a poor Russian Jew as himself has his chance.

Words kept flowing from the man's lips and the liquor, at seventy-five cents the drink, also kept flowing.

"You are all newspaper men, are you not?"

Except myself, all were. The others put me in among themselves.

"Yes, yes. We are all newspaper men."

"I knew it. I could tell by looking at you. You all have such intelligent faces."

"You must have been looking at me," Ben Hecht said.

He had, he said, come to Chicago and had become a manufacturer.

"I make boxes in which other manufacturers ship their goods. It is a box factory."

He explained that his factory was in the northwest section of the city. He had begun in a small way but his business had grown large. There had come the necessity of building a larger factory and he had done that. The factory was almost completed.

"It is now November but by Christmas time it will be completed. Or let us say by the first of the year, on New Year's Day.

"Here is the point," he cried. He had become more and more excited. His eyes were shining.

On that very morning he had gone to have a look at his new factory.

"Oh, it is so beautiful. It is such a beautiful factory."

He had walked about on the floor of the new factory. There was, he said, a great room, as large as a hall. He had been standing in the great room and looking about.

And then a thought had come. It had come upon him suddenly. He had gone pale. It was, he said, as he stood in the new factory (this he explained was in the very early morning before the workmen who were building the factory had come) as though there were voices coming out of the walls and calling to him.

"It is like this," he said. "I cannot manufacture boxes in that factory. It is too beautiful. I can't do it. I can't. I can't."

He explained that he had suddenly realized what America had meant to him. He had come here so poor. He was a Russian Jew but America had opened her arms to him.

"I can go on with my old factory. What do I care? I have money enough. I am prosperous enough."

He had decided that he would make of the new factory, when it was completed, a place of joy. That was it. It would be a place for dances and plays. Everyone could come. It would cost the people nothing. He would build a stage, would hire musicians to play music.

"It is to be free, like America itself, a place of joy.

"There is more joy wanted, more places of joy!"

The little man got up from the table at which we had all been sitting, listening and drinking his drinks. At that time in Chicago there was an intense struggle for control of the streets going on between the Yellow and the Checker taxicabs. Battles between them were being fought in the streets.

He was proposing that we all write of his plans in our newspapers. We were to invite the whole city to come. Everything would be free. He kept saying the word over and over.

"Everything is to be free. A place of joy. It will all be free."

He had taken a little notebook from his pocket. He took each of our names and addresses. We were to bring our friends. All would be refined. It was to be a place of refined joy. As he wrote our names and addresses, saying that the great opening would be on the day of the beginning of the new year and that he would send a taxicab for each of us, he asked us a question.

"Do you prefer a Yellow or a Checker taxicab?" he asked.

He had got up to leave. It was growing dark outside in the street. It was still raining a cold drizzle of rain. At the bar he stopped and bought for us another expensive bottle of whisky.

He bought a quart. He bought us a box of expensive cigars. He stood at the door smiling his joyous smile.

Would we all come? Would we write it all up? Would we promise him?

"Yes, yes," we cried.

"By the gods we'll give you a send-off."

"We'll be there."

"We'll be there."

The man had gone and we sat stunned. The men with me were all so-called "hard-boiled" newspaper men but they had believed. There had been something so very convincing about the man.

"He means it."

"Yes, he does."

"Sure, he means it. What are you talking about?"

We separated, each going his way, all convinced. It may be that the impulse in the man was something we all secretly wanted in ourselves.

We also wanted freedom. We wanted more places of joy in our city.

It wasn't until the next morning that I found out the truth. Ben phoned me and he was excited.

"You come over here at once," he said.

It was true that the little man we had met in the restaurant was a box manufacturer. He had been.

He had owned a little box factory over on the northwest side of the city but it had failed.

On the morning of the day when we had met him he had found himself on the edge of bankruptcy. He had gone to his bank and there was a little money left, perhaps a hundred dollars, and he had drawn it out.

He had come down into the city and to the German restaurant and he had found us there. He had had the afternoon with us, had built for us his new factory, that was to be his place of joy.

The place where all would be free.

He had left us and had walked alone in the cold rain washed streets. He had come to a bridge over the Chicago River and had thrown himself in.

Ben told me that when they hauled out his body they found ten cents in his pocket.

How could I help hoping that he had found his place of joy, the place where all is free?

It is Ben's story but it is also mine. I was there. I was a part of it. Such stories will bear telling over and over, from many angles. It should become, by someone's telling, one of the classic stories of American life.

The Feeders

I have a letter from him this morning.[46] So he is still there. He is one of the sweetest men I have known.

46. Anderson is again writing of George Daugherty.

He is one of the thousands who aspire to be writers. He has written two or three long novels.

They never quite came off and I do not believe he has ever submitted them to a publisher. He decides they are too intimate. Well, I dare say people very close to him, his wife perhaps, others who live in the same house with him, have been brought into the novels. He has got a certain satisfaction in writing them. Something is got off his chest, things he wants to say have been put down.

He was for years a newspaper man and his writing is filled with newspaper clichés. He is what Miss Petulengro, in George Borrow's *Romany Rye,* called "a newspaper Ned."

I set great value on my friend. He has been one of my own best feeders. When you are with him you are always a little amused. He is a big man and very awkward. He stumbles over chairs, stumbles, knocks against you.

At one time he made a good deal of money, let us say some six thousand a year. He has always been very fond of women and has had several intense affairs during the time I have known him. When he is in love he is in it with his whole being. It is a kind of insanity of love.

That also gives him the impulse to write. He is not very successful or fortunate in love. He relieves himself by writing.

That, however, also stands in the way of his sending his novels to a publisher. He has none of the real writer's abandon. He has written of his love for some woman, perhaps employed in the office where he is employed, has let himself go in writing of her. He describes her, the way she walks, the clothes she wears, the color of her hair and eyes, the shape of her nose and mouth. Alas, he has never been permitted to kiss that mouth. He kisses it in his books.

But, if the book were published, his wife would read it.

"There would be hell then. I couldn't stand it. As it is she is always suspicious," he says.

"Now and then she comes to the office. She looks about. Let us say that, on the occasion of such a visit, I am dictating letters. There is a woman, not bad looking, taking my letters.

"I am not in love with her. She is one of the employees of the office, that is all, but, immediately, when I arrive home in the evening, she begins making accusations.

" 'Well, I saw the way you looked at her. You can't tell me.'

"That sort of thing, carried on endlessly."

My friend decided that, for a time, he would escape his home. His work compelled him to do a certain amount of traveling. He had however apportioned all his money. His wife controlled the money bags of the family, so much for the children's clothes, so much for this and that. It was all apportioned.

He handed over his monthly pay check to his wife and each morning, when he left home, she handed him his lunch money.

He came to see me. At the time I was not working. I had saved a little money and was living in a cheap room, engaged in writing a book, making my money go as far as it could.

"Could you get me a small room, very cheap?" He had managed to save a little out of his lunch money. There were certain books he wanted to read. "I cannot read at home," he said. "There are too many children underfoot."

If his wife knew that he had taken a room in the city she would be suspicious. She would think he was living with some woman. He however did get the room, a very small one at a low price. To save money he cooked his own meals. He bought himself some kind of small tin outfit and cooked with canned heat. His diet, for the most part, was fried eggs.

"I've eaten so many eggs that I awaken in the night by clucking like a hen," he said.

He sat in the room at a small desk writing away at a novel. That was twenty years ago and I am quite sure he is still at it. He writes the same novel over and over. Once I read one of his novels.

"Let me try my hand at it," I said.

I was quite sure that with some editing, a touch here and there, some of the characters of his book more developed, I could make it at least publishable. I thought, "Now he has been at this for a long time. It will do him good to see all of his efforts in print."

He was indignant. He was hurt. He took my suggestion as a sort of insult.

Or it may be that he was afraid the book might be published. There was in every book he wrote a certain woman. I had never seen his wife but was quite sure she was the woman of the book. He was getting even with her, that was it. Sometimes he made her tall, with red hair, again a small black haired woman, but there she was. She was fat and lean, tall and short, but always the same woman.

He had made up his mind that, whatever happened, he would stick to her. He had several children. I was sure he didn't hate her. It was marriage that irked him. He wanted to be a free bold man having many women but he was, at the same time, a man of certain rigid principles to which he was determined to stick.

In conversation he was wonderful. He came into my room and sat. He spoke of his youth, told stories of his childhood, of his young manhood, of his courting of his wife. There was in all his talk a curious naïve honesty and I listened filled with joy. He had, in conversation, a way of suddenly dropping a sentence that illuminated perfectly the scene or person he was describing and as he talked thus my own fingers itched to get a pen in my hand. It may be that my affection for him was largely due to this. He was a feeder. He fed me. Often, after an hour with him in my room, I put aside the story I was working at to put down his story just as he told it. Some of the best stories I ever wrote I got from him thus, using often his very language. Once or twice, when he had told me one of his stories, I sent him off to his own room.

It never came off. With the pen in his hand he became again the "newspaper Ned."

What clichés, what flatness. I grew unscrupulous. I let him feed me. I used him. In my life I have known several such people, feeders to others. Their talk is wonderful. There are sentences dropped into their talk that make you want to shout with joy. With pen in hand they become self-conscious.

"Now I am writing."

It may be they are conscious of a possible audience for what they write. What is in them will not flow down their arms and into their fingers. The pen in their hands kills for them all spontaneity, all free expression.

Annoying things were always happening to my friend and how well he told of them.

He had an affair, with a woman somewhat older than himself. She was living with her father and mother in a house on Chicago's South Side. This was when he had a room near my own.

He used to go to her perhaps twice a month. Her father and mother, he told me, were quite old.

"So I go there. If they have gone to bed the window shade of her room is fixed in just a certain way.

"The front door of the house has been left unlocked. She has crept down and unlocked it.

"So I go up. I have taken off my shoes. I go up softly and there I am, in her arms."

It was hard to imagine my friend in a woman's arms. He was so big and awkward, so like a huge bear, but there he was. He had loved the woman for a long time and there was something sad about the story. From all he told me she must have been a very gentle one, a contrast no doubt to his wife. She believed in his writing.

"She thinks I am a genius," he once said to me, smiling sadly. For all his continuing to write he was always sharply aware of his own deficiencies.

"I'll never make it but what do I care? It gives me great satisfaction," he once said to me.

It was a winter night and snowing and being restless in his little cramped room he had gone to his love. He had already told me that she had a weak heart.

He had gone there at perhaps two in the morning. He crept up to her. In the ecstasy of love she died in his arms.

He must have been horribly frightened.

"So I arranged everything in the room and then I crept out," he said.

He was on the stairs of the house and the stairs creaked. He did not know whether, in creeping away thus, he was trying to protect himself or her. She had always, he said, been what is called a "good" woman. No breath of scandal had ever touched her.

"I wanted her old father and mother to find her there, thinking her innocent as they had always thought of her," he said.

He got out of the house and into the street. It was snowing and there was a heavy fall of snow on the ground. With his shoes in his hand he ran. He ran through street after street. There was a kind of wild ecstasy of running. He stumbled and fell. He got up and ran again. In some way he got through the business section of Chicago and to the North Side unnoticed.

Once he was noticed, he later told me. Some men shouted at him but he dodged about a corner and kept running.

He arrived in my room (it might have been at three in the morning) with his shoes still clutched in his hand. He lay on the floor and sobbed. It was one of the strange sort of things that were always happening to him.

His whole life, as I knew it and as he told it to me, was filled with strange, sometimes terrible, sometimes amusing adventures but he could not write of them.

I had a letter from him this morning. No doubt as I write this he is sitting somewhere in a room writing. He has started another novel. He has read a novel, let us say by H. G. Wells.[47] He tries his hand at one rather

47. H. G. Wells (1866–1946), British novelist and social critic.

like that. His writing will still be flat and rather meaningless. It will be full of newspaper clichés. Strange, amusing and sometimes terrible things will still be happening to him but he cannot really tell of them except in talk.

It is his fate. He is not a writer. He is one who feeds writers. There are a good many such in the world.

I Believe in Purity

Oh how sincerely I now believed in purity, in virginity, in holy innocence.[48] There was something happened that had happened to me before, a sudden and abject humility taking possession of me. I did all sorts of absurd things.

She had been in my room, had come in there with another man who wrote novels. I remember it all very distinctly. "I will show that I am indifferent." On the evening before I had been seated at my desk for hours, composing a letter to her.

"Very well, I will see now whether or not I am a writer." This was the real test. Could I make her love me with written words? Oh how many writers have tried that and how seldom they have succeeded. I have often wondered since whether or not the woman kept that letter. I dare say she did. Alas women seem always to keep such letters. It may be they use them to check up on men. "Did I make a mistake not marrying that one?" An old letter, yellow with age, is pulled out and reread. See the knowing smile that so distracts men on the woman's lips.

"No, it was not a mistake."

My letter had been a plea for purity, for innocence in love. This from one who but a short time before had been in the bedroom of the woman of that cracker factory.

But this one is different. The truth is that I had no doubt taken up the virginity plea, the innocence plea, fearing she would surrender to some other man before I had won her.

She was very lovely and, like Lillian Whitworth [49] of the dark people, was of a well-to-do family. The truth is that I am now a bit confused concerning her. Later I was to meet a great many women of the so-called

48. Title of this section supplied by editor. Contiguous material is not extant.
49. Lillian Whitworth, unidentified.

"Better Class," women with rich husbands or rich fathers who became suddenly devoted to the art. Nowdays such women would take to socialism or communism. Art is, at least temporarily, in a very very secondary place and radical and labor leaders have suddenly become social lions.

But at the time of which I write, the revolutions had not come. Art was still on top. It may be she had decided to be a painter, or an actress.

Or a woman writer of poetry, or a sculptor.

I can't remember.

I only remember her sitting in my room, very slender, wearing a beautiful gown, that man, the young poet (or was he a musician?) sitting beside her, his silence. He was not rich. He was shabbily dressed. He had not wanted to come with her to my room. His eyes looked resentfully at me.

Had she talked to him of me, shown him the letter I had sent? I am quite sure now she had.

She had me playing with her, as women do, letting me take her occasionally to the theatre. In the theatre, in the darkness, while the action was going on, she had even let me hold her hands. "It is safe here. I can keep him in hand here."

Odd that I remember so sharply mother's hands and even the hands of the Polish woman of the restaurant, just written about, but do not remember the hands of this lovely one.

But I must give her a name. Caroline.

I do not remember her real name and if I did would not use it. Now she is perhaps married. For some reason I imagine her living in a big house in Des Moines, Iowa. Why Des Moines? I don't know. She is married to a railroad official and has a son in Harvard and a daughter in Bryn Mawr. She belongs to a women's literary society and speaks sometimes of her own former life among the artists. When a new book of mine appears she gets out the letter I once wrote her. She reads it and smiles.

But now she is in my room and to my eyes, at the moment, very lovely.

Did I say that I now remember her sharply as she sat there that evening? She had come in, bringing the other man, the young poet. "I wanted you to meet him." What a lie. She wanted to use me against him, him against me. The man nodded his head. "I am very glad."

"Fool, you are not glad.

"She will make a fool of you too."

The man went to sit on a couch in a corner of the room, and she went to sit beside him.

"I hope we don't interrupt. Were you at work? Were you writing?" Oh for the courage to have cried out at her. "Yes you do interrupt. Get out."

The truth is that, although I denied it, protesting, I had been writing. It may be I was at work on another letter to win her, or I had been trying to compose a poem. The sheets were lying before me on the desk, at which I sat.

I had been writing words. "You are a young tree that has been blown out of the ground by a strong wind.

"It is a hot dry time. Your roots were drying. You were dying, your roots in barren ground. There was a strong wind come to blow you down to me. I am a little river running through a hot dry place. The wind has blown you down to me. Your roots have reached down to run into the blood of me."

There would have been more of the same. The love of a writer, beware of it, woman.

I would have been in my bed on the night before, her lovely figure floating through my mind, and then, words coming, would have jumped out of bed to put them down.

The words on the paper, in the night. How lovely they seemed. Sentences marching, figure of speech, forest. . . .

Where are you now, woman?

Recently, in an old pile of verses, stored away in a box, I came across these attempts at verses and at once I concluded they must be the verses I was trying to write to Caroline that spring evening when she came with the poet to my house.

I am very sure the letter I wrote her must have been something like the verses.

She would have shown my letter to the poet. "It is too bad. I cannot love him but he is very wonderful.

"He will someday be a great writer.

"I want you to know him."

There would have been in me some sense of the betrayal but I would not have directed it toward her. Not at that time. I would have looked at her escort, wanting to go over to him, plunge a knife into his breast, choke him with my fingers. There was a paper knife on my desk and I fingered it nervously. She would have him building me up thus to make her own conquest the more complete, more full of meaning.

By this time I would already have begun to publish articles and stories in the little magazines, *The Little Review* and others. I may even have printed verses in *The Poetry Magazine,* run by Miss Harriet Monroe in Chicago.[50] She would have told him.

He perhaps not yet having been published. She was rubbing it in.

She was having a good time, bringing him in there, sitting beside him on my bed, smiling across at me, sitting at my desk by a window, turning to smile at him.

"See, there he is. I have got him. I can so easily make a fool of him.

"You have seen the letter he wrote me."

She was sitting there smiling at us and I remember her, I must say rather vaguely now, as having a cloud of soft blonde hair, blue eyes, something soft, always inviting in her smile.

Her lips would be a little heavy, even sensual.

Was she wanting some man to break through her apparent withholding?

Why how had I got this notion of purity, virginity connected with her figure? I was always, in my thoughts, connecting her with fresh green things. She was a young tree, just putting out delicate little spring leaves. She was a field planted to winter wheat and the first flush of spring had come to the land. There was just a suspicion, a blush, of green, of a new and virgin forest, brown and black winter earth.

All of which I had no doubt put down, in the letter I had written her, going along, as such fellows as myself do, writing a sentence and then stopping to look at it, read it over.

"Pretty good, eh?"

Working myself up, in this matter of love. "It is time now to be sincerely in love."

A good deal afraid too. "She wears such beautiful clothes." Now she has some sort of silken gown, drawn rather tightly across her slender hips.

For what did she come away from her home, to live in the city? Let us say she has been at the Art Institute, has got among the young artists there. The house in which I am now living is full of young artists.

She has got tired of her own house, the young men met in her own circle, in an inland American city.

What is her father? Is he a successful lawyer or has he a factory in the city?

50. In *Poetry,* Anderson published "Mid-American Songs," X (September, 1917), 281–91; and A. C. Henderson reviewed *Mid-American Chants* for *Poetry,* XII (June, 1918), 55–58.

She is tired of the young business men met at the country club in her town, has, let's say, a little talent for drawing.

I remember that she told me once about her father. "We are very close. We are almost like lovers."

She was an only child.

"My father is a very sensitive, a very fine man. He also should have been an artist.

"If I were not his daughter I would be in love with him."

"Ha! So she has worked him too."

Once, in a fit of anger, walking with her in the street at night, I suddenly seized her, pressed her body to my own body, ran my hands down over her hips, kissed her eyes, her neck, her lips. We were in a dark street and for a moment she submitted. I felt the yielding of her body and then she cried out.

"There is someone coming." It was true. There were footsteps in the street behind us. I let her go.

"Don't you ever do that again." She began to cry and ran away from me and later, in one of my most sappy fits of humility, I wrote her a letter she no doubt also kept, blaming myself, speaking of my own crassness.

"How crude of me to have thought that I was fit to even touch such an angel.

"You are my star, shining for me in the dark night." That sort of thing.

But enough of her. I had my time of being what I called "in love." She would have gone off with the other man to the theatre. When she was alone with him she would have spoken of me with respect.

"He, in many ways, makes me think of my father. If I could love I might love him but I cannot love." She might even have spoken to the young poet of her own devotion to her art while I, filled with rage, weeping and then cursing, would have gone out of my room to walk in the streets.

It may be I got drunk.

I remember one such occasion, concerned with her. Something, such as I have described above, had happened. She had been encouraging me, using her woman's talents on me in the presence of others, and then, when we were alone, pretending to become frightened.

"You are such a crass one. You frighten me.

"Do not touch me.

"I cannot bear it."

I had fled from her full of rage, cursing her as I walked in the streets. "Why do I bother with her? Why do I not free myself?" It is strange, now that I sit down here to write in this rather intimate way of the life of a young American man, I am myself amazed to find how much it is all concerned with women, with sex.

"Have I been an exception in this?" I quit writing and ask myself the question. As for the woman Caroline who once gave me sleepless nights, awoke in me the impulse to write verses about young trees dancing at the edges of forests, stars dancing in the sky on winter evenings, she does not matter.

It doesn't matter if today, in her house in Des Moines and after an afternoon or evening of say some literary lecture, she gets out my old letters, to gloat over them.

It does not matter if I am too much concerned with women and sex.

Again as a thousand times before in my life I sit pondering this matter. "There is no use writing if your own experiences do not have a kind of universality," I tell myself and begin to think back over my experiences with other American men.

I think of men in factories where I have worked, of soldiers with whom I have slept in tents, of business men on trains and in offices and suddenly thousands of such men seem to crowd into this room.

They are all talking. There is a roar of voices. Of what do they all speak?

Of sex. Of their experiences with women, of their hungers, their desires. All. All.

"But wait, men, wait. Be silent for a moment. Go away. For a moment leave me in peace."

I am alone now thinking, not of women but of American men. Why do we talk so much of women? I remember suddenly that with the men I knew when I was a boy, the men of the small shops, it was not so. I see myself again a boy in an American town. There is the shop of a carriage maker on our street and beyond, in an alleyway, between two streets, a blacksmith shop, and I remember how as a boy I loved to hang about these places.

From such places going to work, to be myself a laborer in a factory, at first in a bicycle factory, then later in one of the new automobile factories. Something strange in the difference in the men working in the new places and the old places.

In the new places, the factories, when already the work is divided in the new way, each man doing the same minor operation, over and over, day after day and week after week, the men never having sense of completion of self in work, in these places always, all day long, talk of women.

Men forever declaring their potency. I remember it so well, in the factories where I worked, a kind of perpetual boasting of potency, myself presently coming to feel that it had its bases in fear.

There was fear that it was going, going, going.

Why?

I thought then and still think that it is because man has his source of strength, of quiet, of life itself always coming into him through his hands.

He touches. His hands hold tools. They hold the plow handles, the saw, the hammer, the scythe, the painter's brush, the pen, the hoe.

Man is a doer. It is his nature to find strength in doing. It is what he does through things in nature, through tools and materials, that feeds his manhood and it is this manhood that was being lost.

The death of manhood went on everywhere about me when I was a young man. As young advertising man I was sometimes taken to the haunts of the great ones.

Some great one took me to lunch at the Union League Club in Chicago or to the Chicago Athletic Club and for a time I sat listening. In the factories the men were asserting against fear.

"Good morning, Jim. How's the old cock this morning?"

"She's standing up, Harry."

"Ah, the hell she is."

"She sure is, and after a big night too."

"Big night, eh?"

"Sure, I sure gave the old lady hell."

This endlessly among the factory men. In the advertising office something the same but a bit more withdrawn. There was the continual telling of off-colored stories, often without point, without wit.

Stories of the hired girl and the mule, the soldier and the saw, the stories remaining in my mind as a sort of strange and unhealthy wallowing.

Why? Why?

Long afterward, when the time of the wise-crackers came, life often taking a new kind of brittle hardness, new tone in popular magazines, effort to drag down, always to drag down, even life itself.

What was hurting everyone, making everyone want to hurt?

At the Union League Club the men were nearly all old. They had got position in American life. There was a certain stiff formality among these bankers and manufacturers but there was one of them, a man of prominence in American life, who spoke to me.

He asked me to dine with him and I went. It came out. He had heard I was a coming writer. I had certain acquaintances. He spoke continually. His wife had gone off to Europe for the summer and he had an apartment, on the North Side.

It must be that I knew a good deal of a certain kind of people. There were women, young actresses, beautiful young women of what he called "Bohemia." He had read about them in books.

Love among the artists, eh?

We were in an expensive restaurant and he had leaned across the table, smiling at me. He presumed that a man in his position had to be careful. He didn't want to be held up.

At the same time he was tired of getting women only by paying for them.

There could be a dinner at his apartment with champagne. He looked hopefully into my eyes.

"I'll see what I can do." I wanted to send my fist smashing across the table and into his face.

Why?

A kind of eternal childishness in him as well as in me, lack of true manhood, maleness.

At the Athletic Club there was continual talk. This was the younger sporting rich crowd, young men on their way up.

"I'd like to, Charlie, but how can I fix it with the little woman?

"She is already onto me. I'm being watched like a hawk.

"Even if I stay in the office to work at night she checks up on me."

A tale told by a young man who had forgotten and left his "stud book" in his coat at home. His wife had found it. A stud book was a book of addresses. The young man talking was in insurance. He had been a big football player in college. He had many clients among the rich.

He had to take them out occasionally. A man collected addresses of places where it was safe to go. Girls were brought in. You could call up certain numbers and order what you wanted.

There was an apartment, perhaps in a quite respectable residential street. You took your friend there. What did he like, blondes or brunettes? There were drinks provided. No one spoke of money. That was all settled later.

There were many little girls, working in offices or in stores, who needed terribly a little extra money. Such girls wanted silk stockings and fur coats.

You could, if you were good looking and young, get yourself registered in several such places. You worked all week for ten dollars but in such a place, a quiet high class place, for a few hours spent with older men you could make as much in an evening. Sometimes one of the men got sentimental. He slipped you an extra twenty.

What difference does it make? What all this talk of God and sin? Did God make the modern department store?

What chance did a girl have if she had no decent clothes to wear?

The young man, in the Chicago Athletic Club, whose wife had found his stud book, got a detective to look up the addresses in the book. He had a hell of a time with her. She left him and went to her father's home. He had to confess that he knew many such places, swear that it was a necessary part of his business to sometimes entertain clients.

"But I never myself have anything to do with the girls."

The men, his fellows in the club, laughing at this thrust.

"Well what the hell? I had to knuckle down, crawl before her, make promises. We've got two kids. If it hadn't been that we had the kids I don't believe she would ever have come back."

The man talking was from downstate, in Illinois. Once later I was on a train with him and we talked. He was the son of a farmer, not too prosperous, but his father had managed to send him to college.

He had become a famous football player, his name for a time always in the newspapers, and he had managed to marry a rich girl.

He had to knuckle under to her. He spoke of his father-in-law. "He has to knuckle under too. We all do. The damn women have got something on us."

He also had heard that I was interested in writing. The conversation on the train took place after I had published my *Winesburg, Ohio*. He had read a review in the newspapers.

"I understand it is pretty sexy," he said. "I wouldn't want my wife or my kids to read such stuff.

"I guess you do it for dough. I like clean books myself," he said.

There it was on all sides. I had found it so in the modern factories, men there robbed of any creative impulse in work. I had found it so, everywhere, in business.

This combined with a curious new fear of women. Women, in all sorts of life in America, becoming more dominant. They were controlling American life. Life in America was becoming a matriarchy.

Could it go on? Could the American passion for success, possessions, more and more of the material of man's life gathered about him, other men crushed, could all of this go on without ultimate loss of manhood?

Carping dread of loss of manhood in the air everywhere. It never brought out and faced. It was to lead eventually to the rise of fascism, the upthrusting of the dictator, a glorification of the state, the attempt to get back feeling of manhood by identification with the state.

Harry.

I'll call him that. I knew him. He was a commercial artist although he did not work in the place in which I worked. I was drinking with him and he told me.

He had wanted to try his hand at being a painter but couldn't make it. "Why?" he said, "I'll tell you why."

He was already a man of forty and he had two children.

"I got married young, when I was nineteen, and right away she had two kids, both girls.

"The first one was all right but when the second one was born I guess the doctor we had bungled things.

"Anyway my wife has been no good ever since and our second kid hasn't ever been right."

He described to me the difficulties he had had with his second child, the doctors seen, the bills paid. There was I gathered some muscular difficulty. The child, now almost a woman, couldn't walk. She had to be wheeled about in a chair.

And there was the other girl. She was now a woman. She got a job as a stenographer but because of the invalid mother and the other daughter it took every cent Harry could make and that the girl, whose name was Mildred, could make to keep the family afloat.

Harry was telling me all this. As he talked he drank and I drank. "Have all you want, Harry. I'll pay for it."

His older girl had got a kid, out of marriage.

"Wasn't that hell?" Harry said. He said she did it, fell for a man in the place where she worked. "A married son of a bitch," said Harry, "for money.

"She wanted money for her sister, to help me out, to get a few more things for herself.

"And what the hell do you think? She'd never tell me who the man was. We've got her kid now, a boy, and she is back at work, in another place, but she has never told me a thing.

"I put it to her and put it to her strong," Harry said, "but she wouldn't peep. Said she'd taken the chance herself.

"Said she had known what she was doing and that the man had little or nothing to do with it. I'd told her I was going to go and kill the son of a bitch and so she tightened up on me.

"Said she wouldn't have it, that it was none of my business, that it was her own affair.

"She offered to get out, if I was ashamed of her kid, but of course neither I or her mother could stand for that.

"After all, she is a pretty swell kid. What do you think?" Harry said.

Rehearsal

I was living in a little ground floor apartment in Chicago, the same one in which Jacques Copeau got robbed while Carl Sandburg sang for us. I was having some friends in to dine and had got a woman to cook the dinner.

I came home from my job at five and went into the bathroom. The apartment was small, a little sitting room, a dining room, bedroom and kitchen. The bathroom was between the sitting and dining rooms. The walls of the bathroom were rather thin.

I was in a gay mood. I shaved and bathed. I sang.

"These people are coming to dine. I must be entertaining," I thought.

I began to practise the telling of certain stories. There was a fellow in the office who always spoke very slowly. He was very solemn about everything he said. He qualified, elaborated every statement.

"Now I am not one to set himself up. I may be right and I may be wrong. I know my opinion doesn't amount to much. You fellows may have your own opinions. I don't like a man who is too cocksure. I'm not that kind of man myself but I'll say this, not intending to set myself up, you understand, but, before the day is over—I'm not naming any particular hour—but sometime between now and night I think maybe it may rain."

I began practising some such long absurd qualified statement like the above. I laid it on thick. I imitated the man's slow hesitating speech.

Then I got out my bag of parlor tricks, practised the telling of certain stories. I imagined conversations, speaking the part for some other man and thinking up witty rejoinders.

Oh I was going good. I was in fine form. It was a dress rehearsal.

When I had bathed and shaved and had gone through the long rehearsal, I went through the dining room and into my bedroom to dress. The woman I had employed to prepare the dinner was in the kitchen at work. The table was set for the dinner.

How was I to know that, while the water was running in my bathtub, while I was making the speeches, expressing all sorts of wise opinions, telling stories, being witty in them, the woman now at work in the kitchen had admitted my guests?

They had been sitting in there, in my little living room, highly amused, listening to me.

I got dressed. I went in to them.

"Oh, you have arrived. You are early, you must be hungry."

No. They were not early. Watches were pulled out. They sat there with a queer expectant look in their eyes.

"When is he going to begin?

"We have heard the rehearsal. Now let's see if the performance is up to it."

That is what they were thinking.

I began. I launched forth. I must have been in the bathroom a long time. I had used up my entire repertory. All evening, whenever I opened my lips, a shout went up.

"Do you think he is better now than he was in the bathroom?" one of them asked another.

"No. He is not half as good."

"Say, Sherwood. Give us that one about the man predicting rain. Let us hear that."

They got me confused. When I tried to ad-lib, get away from the part I had played in the bathroom, they wouldn't let me get away with it. If I tried to tell a story they pretended I had already told it to them through the bathroom wall.

They certainly destroyed my evening. They were friends but, all through the dinner, I sat there hoping that, one after another, they would choke on the food.

I had got a job as copy writer in a Chicago advertising agency. How that came about I shall explain in another place. It is a little difficult in such a book as this to get everything in its proper place. The time sense becomes confused.

Now I am thinking of my years as an advertising writer. It went on, I thought, endlessly. As my books did not sell well for a long time I had to keep at the advertising writing for years after I had begun to get some literary fame.

Now that I think back over the years in that place I realize how decent, how kind and patient the men in control of the agency were with me.

I was there working in that place. I got a little money ahead and then quit. I went away, often to the south, to Mobile or New Orleans. I got a room in a cheap rooming house in one of these cities.

I had my days. I had my nights. I did not have to ring a clock in an office. I could go about among people. Sit in my room thinking.

And then, suddenly, I was broke again. I had to go back to that place.

They always took me back but, sometimes, they made me wait for a time.

"So you are back here, eh?

"One day you walked in on us.

" 'I'm quitting,' you said. You did not ask us whether or not we needed you at that time.

"And now we do not specially need you. We are getting on very well. Suppose you wait until we really need you again."

It was a way of punishing me because I had been too defiant.

"Well, never mind. Soon they will need me again."

I had come back from the south nearly broke. I had but a few dollars. I found a room in an old building on the South Side. It was near the end of a street car line and street car conductors and motormen lived in the building.

They had little apartments there and one of them rented me a room at two dollars a week.

I was on the street car conductor's car and as I stood with him on the back platform had asked him about a room.

"I am looking for a cheap room. I am promised a job soon but may have to wait for a time.

"I have a little money but must make it go as far as I can."

This was in the early fall, after a summer of freedom, and the street car conductor asked me to meet him at the street car barn that night.

I went there and he took me with him to his apartment.

"I'll have to explain," he said. He said his wife had tuberculosis.

"She is going to die, one of these days.

"We are up against it for money," he said.

I remember that as we walked along a street, from the end of the street car line to the apartment building, he was embarrassed.

"It may seem a little queer to you that I am willing to let a young man come to live in my apartment," he said. He explained that he had no children.

"I will be going away every day and leaving you alone there with her.

"But it does not matter," he said. "She is a sick woman. Nothing can happen."

I was there for some three or four weeks in a small room in that place and there was the sick wife, lying in the bed in which she slept with her husband or sitting in a rocking chair by a window.

While I was there the street car conductor and I did the house work. We made the beds, we swept, we cooked our own breakfast. I had found a place where I could get a great stack of wheat cakes and a cup of coffee for fifteen cents. When the street car conductor came home from his work at night I cooked his dinner.

"No, I do not want to eat. I have had my dinner," I said. I went to the advertising agency perhaps twice a week to inquire for my mail but did not again speak of a job.

"If I seem anxious they will want to cut my pay," I thought.

"There will come an emergency," I thought. Emergencies are always arising in advertising agencies.

What an uproar now arises. Men are running up and down. Conferences are being held.

"Where is Smith? Where is Jones? Where is Albright?"

"We must have something absolutely original now."

"Where is that Anderson? Where is he?"

I had begun to strut. I had got my job back. Perhaps I had even got an advance in pay. For three or four weeks I had been sitting through long fall afternoons with a sick woman far out in Chicago's South Side. In the evening I had been cooking her husband's dinner.

She was a woman who had been a girl in an Illinois small town as once I had been a boy in an Ohio small town. We spoke of that.

"It seems so queer to have a strange man like you in the house," she says.

"Yes, it is strange as all of life is strange.

"It is strange that we did not live, as boy and girl, in the same town."

I tried to describe to her the main street of my own town. She coughed violently. Once she had a hemorrhage and I had to hold a bowl for her.

"You would not think, to look at me now, that I was a fat little girl.

"If I had been a girl in the town where you were a boy you would not have looked at me. I was too fat," she said.

I was again at my job in the advertising agency and had left the apartment of the street car conductor. The conductor had told me that he would have to give up the apartment.

"I will have to send her home to her mother."

The street car conductor and his dying wife never spoke of each other by their names. She did not say, "Frank thinks" or "Frank says." She said, "He thinks" or "he says."

It is odd to think that I never knew that woman's name.

"I cannot keep the apartment. The doctor's bills are eating me up. I will have to send her home to her mother."

They began to "stage" me in the advertising place and I fell in with it. There was my love of clothes. When I began to write and long before anything of mine was published I had begun to strut before the others.

It all may have been a kind of defiance. I had presently begun to hate what I was doing. On more than one morning when I came to the door of the Chicago office building, I turned away. There was a sickness in me.

"Good God, it may be that I am really a word man.

"So I go in there. I write words."

I had begun to write in my room at night.

"With words I try to put down things I feel. I try to penetrate into others with words.

"Then in the daytime I come here. I use the same words to describe some diarrhea cure, some patent medicine for loose bowels."

It was a making dirty the tools of my trade, of my at that time secret trade, practised at night, in rooms in rooming houses. There, in the room, often a cheap one in a cheap rooming house, I felt curiously clean. In the advertising agency, at work in the copy department, I felt dirty.

I began to drink. Sometimes, after a day in that office, I stopped at several saloons. It was a rainy night in the summer or a cold snowy night in the winter.

"Tonight I am not fit to go to my room to try to write.

"All day I have been dirtying words. How now can I make them clean?"

To many all of this may seem absurd but it was all terribly important to me. It seemed to me that only in the advertising place could I make enough to buy a little leisure. It was a curious, a silly world. It took so little actual time to write an advertisement.

Italian Poet in America

He did everything with a quick rush.[51] He was like an old man, full of cynicism, and then, in the next moment, childishly young. He stayed quiet, talked quietly for a time, sitting in the Chicago apartment on Division Street where I then lived with Tennessee. He spoke of his childhood and boyhood in Italy, of fields remembered, the Italian skies, the olive groves, the vineyards on hillsides, the wine making. I do not remember that he ever mentioned his mother. He said nothing of brothers or sisters but when he spoke of his father he grew excited. He had been sitting quietly, a well built, handsome young man, dark skinned, with thick black hair, the sort of man, you'd say, many women would fall in love with, although he had told me it didn't happen. He had said that was the great problem, the sorrow of his life.

"I need a woman, terribly, but I frighten them," he said.

He would be sitting thus in the apartment, talking softly, Tennessee not very attentive.[52] Tennessee liked young men always half in love with her. She had a following of such young men, young minor poets, men with half finished novels they never would finish. They came to read and discuss

---

51. Anderson is again describing Emanuel Carnevali.

52. Anderson married Tennessee Mitchell (1874–1929) July 31, 1916, and divorced her in April, 1924. See William Alfred Sutton, "Sherwood Anderson's Second Wife," *Ball State University Forum,* VII (Spring, 1966), 39–46.

with her, as years before I had done, and often in the later afternoon or early evening when I came home to the apartment I found her sitting in the half darkness with some such young man.

I did not care, had got beyond caring. There was that feeling in the air, half love, worship at a safe distance, so many women enjoy feeding upon. She could not get it from my Italian friend.

He hated that sort of thing as he hated his father. When, in his tales of his early life in Italy, he came to his father he became violent. He jumped to his feet, strode up and down in the room.

"I should have killed him before I left.

"He was a brute. He understood nothing.

"You do not understand, a peasant, brutal and ignorant."

One who had, however, made his way in the world, doing it by sheer brutality.

"That his blood should be in my veins, that ignorant brute, that animal."

My Italian poet had strong white teeth. There was a bowl filled with oranges on a table in the room. He took them, one by one, bit them in two, the juice squirting in all directions, threw the half oranges on the floor. Tennessee had bought some new and expensive rugs. She was so angry at him she couldn't speak. She got up and ran out of the room, into her own bedroom, slamming the door.

"You see," he cried, sitting again in his chair and smiling.

"You see what I do to women. It is my violence. It frightens them.

"It angers them. It is too much for them. It is the poet in me. I am all hatred or all love.

"These half women, in America," he said, "they want it all softened, made half meaningless. The strong wine of life frightens and sickens them.

"They are not really women. A woman, who is all woman, is something glorious. She is not afraid. She meets the strong man, fights with him, is conquered. She loves.

"It is what I seek. When at last I find her, if I ever do, I shall be quiet. Love will flow from me. I will be all love.

"Then I shall be a really great poet."

In spite of Tennessee's protest, often angry, I kept having him at the apartment. Summer came and I went with him to swim in the lake. We swam far out, until I lost courage and returned, but he kept on until I thought he had really gone into the unknown—to his death out there. I stood on the shore and trembled. Later I wrote a poem to him, of his coming at last out of the sea.

I called my verses "A Dying Poet." [53] I spoke of a man who had dirtied himself, besmeared himself and plunged into the sea.

He came out of the sea something new and strange. He was a soldier, a ragged old man, one going on a journey, a white clean youth.

He ran. He crept through bushes. He was seeking a goddess who walked by the seashore in silence. She wore heavy gold wristlets and in her hair was a chain of finely wrought silver. I never showed him my verses.

There was beyond a doubt something befouled. He said it was the commercialism of our land, that he had come to America to find here a new life, a life free, rich and glorious. There had been a dream, of meeting, knowing and loving understanding men and women. He grew angry and cursed the land and then suddenly he again grew gentle. As we walked he told me little stories of his life.

He had fled, he said, from his father and as, at that time, men could come quite freely into America from all countries, he had come here, landing at the port of New York. He had a little money.

"I stole it from my father and ran away from him," he said. "I should have stayed until I had killed him." I gathered that his father had become a merchant. He also owned farms.

"He could not understand that I was a poet. He wanted me to be like himself, lying, cheating, grubbing for money."

In New York he had walked the streets seeking work. He knew no one.

He had got a room in a crowded tenement house with an Italian family. He was quick at learning our language. There was a daughter of the Italian family who worked in a factory.

"I crawled into her bed at night," he said. She was, he said, a coarse but kindly woman. The family, discovering him in bed with the daughter of the house, demanded that he marry her and he did.

"And why should I not have married her? There are many kinds of marriages, marriages of thoughts, of bodies. To lie with her was a relief to me as it was to her. Sometimes," he said, "in the darkness of her little room, to which I had crept, the sounds of the streets coming up to us as we lay close together in the silence and darkness, I could in imagination make her into the real woman of my desires."

But it was not, to him, he said, the real, the ultimate marriage. He

53. In *A New Testament* (New York: Boni and Liveright, 1927), pp. 98–100.

sought, he said, a marriage of the very soul, of the very mind. There was, to be sure, the flesh but it must be beautified by the mind, the soul. He spoke at length of the woman of his dreams. She was like a slender young tree, he said, at the edge of a forest.

"Thoughts flow through her as a soft wind blows over a field of ripe wheat." He said he was always with her in his thoughts. "I walk with her in a snow covered field. I am with her in a rain storm in a forest. I am living with her, now in a humble house, now in a palace."

In New York he had got a place to work, in a restaurant, where he washed dishes.

"It was horrible," he said. "It was disgusting, terrible." He described the place, the dirty dish water into which he was compelled to thrust his hands. "Food had fallen on the floor and had been trampled underfoot by waiters hurrying in and out.

"I stood in it. It was on my shoes, the smell of it in my clothes.

"All day I stood silently working while inwardly I cursed."

He had run away from his wife, had taken a room in a house over the East River, in New York City.

"At night I went to the river," he said. "I swam. I was always a strong swimmer. In the night when it rained, when the summer rain fell on the surface of the river where I swam in the darkness, vessels sometimes going up and down, I was happy. Then I saw the woman of my dreams. She swam with me.

"I made verses then, oh such beautiful verses."

He had gone to a place (I understood it to be some sort of mission) where he was taking lessons in our language.

"I thought I had found her there," he said.

There was a young woman came to the mission to teach. She was a rich young woman. He said she had come to work in the mission wanting to help such poor young men as himself. A cynical smile played about the corners of his mouth as he spoke of her. He began to go about with her, even with her to her house. He wrote poems to her.

"She began to give me money," he said. "She bought me clothes. Now I did not have to work in the restaurant. I walked about, went into parks. I listened to the voices of your American people speaking your language. I was learning fast."

"It was all false," he said. To the woman, the daughter of the house, he was a young genius. She had become his patron.

"And still, in her own way, she tried to love me," he said.

[399]

"She was like the woman you have there in your house," he said. She thought he might someday be a man of note. She liked his writing verses to her eyes, her hair, her lips, her hands. He said she had very beautiful hands.

"I wanted them to touch my body, heal the unquiet thing in me," he said.

"It was because of the verses I wrote to her that she had taken me up.

"She did not understand my inner self, how I am so often wretched. She could not understand that I am the smallest of all the small things God has made, how I am both infinitely small and at the same time infinitely great.

"However I worked on her. Mine is a passionate nature. I wanted to lie with her, to possess her."

He said he thought that, in possessing her, he might have awakened her.

"I would have merged her thus into myself," he said, "made her a real part of my smallness, my meanness, my greatness."

He declared that she was very beautiful, that she dressed beautifully.

"When I walked with her I loved touching the cloth of which her dresses were made."

He kept making verses to her, kept declaring his love, but she would not surrender herself to him.

"She gave me her lips. I held her in my arms. My hands crept over her body but she would not let her hands creep over mine."

He became angry with her. He began to hate her. He plotted and one day, late in the day, when he knew the Italian peasant woman he had married would be at home with her family in the Italian section of the city, he took her there.

"I told her I wanted her to see my own people. We got into a cab and we went there, to that place. She left the cab at a corner and went with me to the apartment house in which my wife's parents lived," he said. She did not know he was taking her to his wife, did not know that he had a wife.

"I knew my Italian women," he said. "I took her there, into that apartment house, in a street where only Italians lived. We climbed the stairs. My wife's family lived on the fifth floor of the house.

"She went up with me, the fool, and I began to shout.

"Look what I have got, an American woman. She loves me, she is my mistress," I cried.

He said that Italian women came crowding out of many apartments in the building. His wife and his wife's mother ran out to a landing at the head of the stairs and the young Italian woman he had married began to scream and curse.

"The women began to beat her," he said. He said they surrounded her, tore her beautiful clothes. She was running down the stairs pursued by the women and he followed. He stood in the street and laughed. It was thus, he said, that he got even with her.

"For daring to think herself above me, my patron, me, a poet," he said.

I have written of my friend's brutality, of which he was no doubt proud.

"You must be brutal. Sometimes nothing else is understood. If you are a poet they will trample you. They will destroy you. You must destroy them first. It is the only way," he said. A harshness came into his voice.

"It is for every artist, every poet to defend himself. There is something precious he carries within himself. He must be strong to fight for it, to defend it," he declared.

He had come to Chicago, attracted, he said, by what he felt was, at that time, going on in the western city. It was at a time when the poets Vachel Lindsay, Edgar Lee Masters, Carl Sandburg and others were just coming into the public notice. All over the middle western country, for a time, there was an upflowing of interest in verse. Poets went about reading their verses in public. Carl Sandburg had written his *Chicago Poems*, Vachel Lindsay was working heroically to make the public sing with him and Masters' *Spoon River* was selling like a popular novel.

"Alas, it will all fade. It will come to nothing," my Italian poet said.

He had, however, been taken up by Miss Harriet Monroe, who had begun to give him money. She, that strange little maiden lady, so gentle seeming, so lady-like, had a flair for such men as my friend.

"You go to her. You walk in upon her. You begin to curse. The stronger you make your language the better for you," he said and laughed.

"If you are profane enough, rough enough, she will buy and print your verses," he declared. I have spoken a good deal of my friend's brutality. He could be very gentle.

"I am gone, done for," he said to me. We had gone to walk together by the lake and he confessed to me that he had become a victim of syphilis. He spoke of having gone about at night after he had left his wife, after he had come to Chicago, in the night streets of the city. There were, he said, prostitutes also walking the night streets of the city and lurking as he sometimes lurked. He said that, at the time, he had wanted to become a robber, a hold-up man. "It was only the dread of being caught, of being sent to prison, that kept me from it.

"I began," he explained, "to feel very close to the fallen women of the streets." They were outcasts as he was. As he talked, speaking of the strange beauty he declared he had begun to find in outcast women, he became very gentle.

"I began to think," he said, "that if I was ever to find the woman who could quiet me, make me live quietly with others, I would find her among these women."

He had begun to talk with the women found thus at night in the city streets, to go about with them. When one of them had an unsuccessful night she sometimes took him to her room in some house. The women began to feed him. They bought him clothes.

"I made love to them. They were as I am, always wanting love and never finding it," he said. He was always very gentle when he spoke of the women outcasts, one of whom had given him the dreadful disease. "What they give to men for money is nothing. It is but an empty gesture," he said.

"There is however something reserved that they hope to give.

"Few enough of them have the opportunity to give it to a poet."

He had become diseased and when, later, a group of Chicago men became interested in him, believing in his genius, and tried to have him cured (they put him in a sanatorium) he would not stay.

He had been taken by a rich man to his country estate. It was an estate on which the rich man lived but a few months during the year. The rich man was a fancier of song birds. He employed a man to feed them, to protect them, but my poet friend, having gone into one of his strange fits of anger, got a shot gun and began killing the birds.

Afterwards he came to try to explain to me. "It is something dreadful I have done. It is the disease eating away at me.

"I did not want them to sing for him," he said. "I went with the gun. I began to shoot them, kill them but, each time, as I fired the gun, as I saw the bird that was also a singer fall down dead, I wept.

"But I went on killing until they ran me off. I began and, although it hurt me, I could not stop.

"They wanted to cure me of my syphilis but it may be because of the syphilis that, before I die, and because for an hour I gave my love to some poor woman, an outcast as I am, I shall yet sing one pure and beautiful song."

He came at last on a winter night to my house. He was very pale and I thought a queer light shone in his eyes.

"It is such a night. Come with me," he said. He was living he told me with another woman of the streets.

"She is at work tonight and I am lonely," he said. I had not seen him for several months and his sickness had grown in him. He was very thin and was thinly clad, having no overcoat. The night was bitter cold and there was a heavy fall of snow.

He stayed with me, on that night, for a half hour, talking at first quietly, urging me to go out into the night with him.

"I have taken up with this woman," he explained. "She is in a house of prostitution. She has gone. She is at work there.

"She has provided me with a room and in the afternoons she comes and sits with me."

He said that he knew that he was near to death, that the beautiful poetry he had hoped to write would never be written and that the woman prostitute who was supporting him had declared that when he died she would die.

"I have found the thing I have been seeking in her and she has found it in me," he declared.

He began to shout.

"She has. She has. I declare she has," he shouted.

"It is the one thing I have been able to do.

"I have given her love. I have. I have."

He stood there shouting before me and then, before I could interfere or stop him, he ran out of my apartment. I heard his footsteps on the stairs and ran to call him back, wanting at least to give him a warm coat to wear, but when I got down a flight of stairs and into the street he had disappeared into the storm.

He must have run wildly about, for hours, that night in the storm. When he was in my apartment and before he grew excited and ran away he had spoken of the beauty of the storm, saying that he had been abroad in it because he wanted to feel himself a part of it. "I want its beauty in me," he had said.

And so he ran from me into the storm and later in the night they found him. He was kneeling in the snow before the house of prostitution in which the woman who was supporting him was at her work. There would have been, I am sure, some man, a customer of the place, no doubt some outwardly very respectable man, come out at the door. He would have looked cautiously up and down the street and then he saw my friend, the poet, kneeling before the door of the house in the snow.

He was there, kneeling in the snow before the house of prostitution and shouting.

He was shouting to God, to save his soul and the soul of a woman at work at her trade in the house, one of the women in taking up with whom he had got the disease that he must have known was killing him.

The whole thing, his adventure of that night, was, I am quite sure, a way of suicide. It was the end for him. They got him into that house, telephoned to some hospital and took him away. I lost all track of him. What was his final end I never knew, having always the feeling that his real end came that night, kneeling there before the house of the fallen women, in the snow. At least I am quite sure that what we humans call our "mind" was gone from him after that night.[54]

54. In his *Autobiography*, p. 177, Carnevali dramatically describes Sherwood Anderson's chasing him out of his house. This discussion by Anderson was published (revised) as "Italian Poet in America," *Decision*, II (August, 1941), 8–15.

V &

The Twenties

An Explanation

Again I was in New York and, upon one of my visits there, my friend John Emerson secured for me a sinecure.[1] He did not say that there was no need to work at the job he got for me, that of being a publicity man for one of the big movie companies, at some seventy-five dollars a week, but I am quite sure he knew well enough how it would turn out. It was, you see, during the first flush days of the movies. Money was being flung about. Why not cut in on it a little? I did. I never did write any publicity, or at least none worth printing, but it must have been several months before some clerk found a name, that of a stranger who never did any work, in the payroll and cut it off.

It was O.K. with me. By that time I had finished my novel.

I got a cheap room, somewhere over on the West Side, in the twenties, between Ninth and Tenth avenues, and there I worked. The World War was on and I had been opposed to the war and had narrowly escaped arrest. Some of the political radicals, Jim Larsen, the English Labor leader, and John Reed,[2] had been my friends. It was a relief to be in New York where I was comparatively unknown.

It was a good room. There was the hoarse cry of steamers in the river at night. I was at the back of the house, upstairs, and looked across little city back yards into many other people's rooms. At night I could turn off my lights and sit by my window. There were people making love, dining, quarreling. I saw a good deal of the inside lives of young married couples, old married pairs, bachelors and old maids, all, I dare say, of the working class.

"Perhaps it would be well for you to at least be seen, now and then, at the studio." It must have been some man met about the theatre who gave me that tip. I did go, for a time, quite often, in the afternoon. The studio was at a place called Ft. Lee.

Why how very like the factories to which I had been going, as advertising writer. There was immediately something sensed. "It is not the actors

1. Anderson worked for John Emerson in New York in the fall of 1918. See *A Story Teller's Story: A Critical Text*, edited by Ray Lewis White (Cleveland: Press of Case Western Reserve University, 1968), pp. 22–23; and "Listen, Hollywood," *Photoplay*, LII (March, 1938), 28–29.

2. Jim Larsen, unidentified; John Reed (1887–1920), journalist and propagandist for the Russian Revolution. See *Letters of Sherwood Anderson*, edited by Howard Mumford Jones and Walter B. Rideout (Boston: Little, Brown and Company, 1953), Items 224, 332, and 368.

or the makers of plays, those who write for the theatre, who are in command here," I told myself. There was immediate disillusionment. As it was in the factories, the workers every year less and less having anything at all to say about the work they did (this discovered earlier when I was a young factory hand), as it was in politics (this made clear to me by friends among Chicago newspaper men), so here also, in this new art of the theatre, the movies, there was a force, certain men, up above all writers, all actors.

"Business is business."

"It's money makes the mare go."

The movies were new then. The disillusionment that came did not come at once. When I first began going to the studios I was for a time excited. There was this great new field for actors and for play makers opening out. For a long time I had held to the notion that every real story teller was in part at least also an actor. At that time I knew few actors, was just beginning to know them, but I felt close. "There is a great door opening here," I told myself, "a door through which the actor and the play maker may go out into a new wide world.

"What is stopping it, what is closing the door just opened?"

Was it money again, business? It is true that, while I was hanging about the movie studios, I did not try to write any movies. For a time the whole thing seemed too wonderful to me. I went about in a kind of daze. "Now," I said to myself, "if the impulse to write for the theatre comes I will not need to confine my imaginings within the arch. I can let my fancy roam over the wide world. Short stories may be done in pictures. It is even possible to do novels in pictures.

"Some man's life, here in America, can be taken, put on the screen. It will be possible to show, in pictures, that everyone can understand how accidental life is, how men are blown about like dry leaves before a wind, some called 'good,' others 'bad.' It will be possible to tear down, before everyone's eyes, some of the little lies by which we all live."

A time of inner excitement. It didn't last.

In Chicago I had been an advertising man. I worked in one of the larger advertising agencies. The agency was often visited by representatives of the magazines. I had found out that the magazines were, first of all and always, business institutions. Occasionally a representative of one of the larger magazines came to us. We were got into a room. "This is what we are going to have our writers do during the coming year." At that time there was, among artists in America, a struggle going on. There was, in writing, what was called a "middle western movement." It was an effort to escape from an English domination of American thought, brought to us, in the middle west, through New England.

We had been for a long time under this domination. Many of the early settlers in the country had come from England. They were puritans. They settled in a cold hard stony land. It may be that, if you live thus, in a cold stony land, you are compelled, in fancy, to leave the land. You escape from the cold ground up into the thin air of transcendentalism, always away and away and away from earth, the flesh of people, the warm human passions of people.

But we, of the middle west, were not in that kind of land. We were in a rich land where the corn grew like forest trees. The English had quit coming to us and instead we were getting the imaginative Irish, the beer drinking, food loving Germans, Italians, great new hordes of people from the southwest of Europe.

And all the time our minds were being dominated by English puritan thought, the dreadful hypocrisy of English puritan thought.

There was an effort to escape. Most of us, who were writing at that time, became what was called "sex-obsessed." We had, some of us, discovered a profound truth, that not every woman who went to lie with some man, out of wedlock, driven only by her own passions, passions very old in all people, that not every woman who did that ended by having an illegitimate child.

She often, in fact, came out quite splendidly, had a fine time, didn't get caught, held her head up, slept well at night. We said so, told the story as we saw it.

The representative of some magazine came into the advertising agency. "We are going to have our writers cut that stuff out this year. It offends too many people." I had myself written, in my *Winesburg* tales, the story of a woman who seemed to me a rather fine mother. It happened that she had been with two or three other men before she took one in marriage. I called my story "Mother," and one of the editors of *The Seven Arts* magazine, they having published the story,[3] told me that when it was printed the advertising manager of the magazine came in and resigned. "I wouldn't have minded your printing the story," he said. "It's giving it that title." Had the magazine been one of the big fellows, run for profits, not

---

3. "Mother," *Seven Arts,* I (March, 1917), 452–61; *Winesburg, Ohio* (New York: Viking Press, 1960), pp. 39–48.

subsidized, it might well have been a big advertiser so offended. Then where would I have been?

There was a place for me but not in the theatre or in the movies, I told myself. I had got this notion fixed in my head. "You can make it all right if you will only be satisfied to remain small," I told myself. I had to keep saying it over and over to myself. "Be little. Don't try to be big. Work under the guns. Be a little worm in the fair apple of life." I got all of these sayings at my tongue's end and used to go through the streets of Chicago, muttering them to myself. I remember a talk I once had with a banker. I did have, although my intimate friends never would believe it, a head for affairs. I remember Theodore Dreiser once laughing at the idea. "If you have a head for business then I have one for breeding sheep," he said, but he was wrong. I was, had always been, more on the inside, understood more clearly the impulses and the machinery of business than he ever did. I had given the banker a suggestion about a certain business in which he had money and it had worked.

"Why, what the hell man, why haven't you money?"

He declared he would put me in.

He had heard I was a writer. He had a son in the University of Chicago who had told him. "He tells me you are pretty good." There was a professor in one of the son's classes who had spoken favorably of a book of mine. The banker had a friend in New York who had large holdings in one of the movie companies. "Why not let me speak to him about getting you on? I understand there's money in it."

The banker had an idea. The son had told him that I was something of a highbrow. "I know it isn't true," he said, "but let them think so." He tried to explain something to me. He was himself interested in art. He bought paintings. He had married a woman who was something of a high brow. He had read things about painters and poets who starved all their lives.

It was all nonsense. He could see, by the suggestion I had made to him, that I had a head for business but if, for example, I wanted to write books that wouldn't sell why not wait?

I could get into the movies, write the stuff they wanted, for a time, get myself some dough. Then I could cut it out. I remember that when I had this conversation with the banker we were dining. He had taken me to an expensive restaurant. The suggestion he was making had been made to me by many others. The banker was a fine physical specimen of a man. He had a passion I also had, for race horses. I knew what he wanted. He wanted to give up his life as a banker, be a horseman, live about horses. We had had many conversations about horses. "They are such clean fine creatures, not tricky as we are. A good one will give you all he's got. He likes to."

The conversation drifting back to my own situation. "There you are, working in that place, in that advertising agency, in a minor place, holding down a piker job."

"Yes. They do not pay me much. For them my salary is a small matter. Because my salary is comparatively small I can occasionally go off, waste time in some town. They do not much mind."

"But have you no ambition? Don't you want to be something big? You could take on this job I am suggesting for a time, get some money. Then you could get out."

"Like you," I said and he stared at me.

"I see," he said, "you mean. . . ."

He had got it all right. I did not want to be as he was, spending my life working at something I did not care about. He owned a string of race horses and hired a man to train them. I had been with him to his stables.

There was the fellow at the stables, the trainer, a man of the banker's own age, a solid looking quiet man. He had his feet on the ground, was a man of parts I thought. "Why not?" I thought. The man was taking the beautiful graceful young creatures, the thoroughbreds, training them, watching them from day to day, picking the good ones, the ones that had it.

The banker standing there. He owned the horses. For this one he paid so and so many dollars, for that one over there some other amount. "Like hell you own them," I thought that day. It was as though the trainer had read my thoughts. We walked over to a two-year-old, a young stallion, a tall tawny-yellow fellow, and the trainer turned and looked hard at me. It was as though he had spoken. "Keep your thoughts to yourself."

A minor man, eh, in a minor place? As we stood that day by the young stallion I had seen something in the banker's eyes, envy of that other fellow, the trainer of his horses, his servant, eh? I couldn't help smiling.

"But you want money, don't you?" It was the banker speaking, that day in the restaurant.

"God yes." How I did want it. I just didn't want to earn it. I didn't even want to deserve it.

I wanted everything money could mean, escape from the advertising agency, from all buying and selling. I looked about the restaurant. There were beautifully dressed women sitting at the tables. I was perhaps in love at that time. I always was in love with some woman.

How wonderful to take some woman loved into an expensive shop, buy her beautiful clothes, expensive furs, elegant shoes, to buy also such things for myself. When I saw beautiful fabrics my fingers ached to go and touch them.

"Yes. Sure I want money. Why don't you give it to me?"

The banker laughed. "Not me," he said. I understood how he felt. He was spending his life doing something he didn't want to do for the sake of money, really to get, someday, an imagined freedom he never would get. He wanted me also to pay for my freedom.

"No," I said. "You won't, you couldn't set me free while you remain in prison." We sat staring at each other. There are moments when men who instinctively like each other can also hate. "Be careful. Do not get too near the truth when you talk with the rich," I was whispering to myself.

"But what do you get out of it?" He was switching the conversation. "All right. I'll tell you." I tried.

I tried to describe a certain day of my own life, a certain evening. All writers, painters, actors, all men of the arts have had such days and such evenings.

It is something also understood by workmen. It is a feeling good farmers know.

There is a piece of land, neglected, overcropped for too many years, gone to pot, scraggly weeds growing, and it comes into the hand of the good farmer.

He goes to work, is patient, a land lover. He feeds the field, begins slowly to enrich it, gets at last a stand of clover, plows it under. Patience. Wait now. At last a day comes.

"Look." You are standing with him at the field's edge. "Look," he says. His figure straightens. He is even a little embarrassed, boasting to you. "The finest stand of corn in all this section.

"You should have seen this field, some five years ago, when I got it." Just that, man's old inheritance, your own sudden swift love of him, respect for him. "Here's a man." Something workmen sometimes know, writers, painters, actors, builders of all sorts sometimes know.

Myself, sitting in one expensive restaurant with a certain banker and trying to tell him of a certain day and of a certain night, following the day, a night in a cheap Chicago rooming house.

I would have begun with the day. There I was. All day I had been sitting at my desk by a window in the advertising agency.

There would have been a little room, quite crowded, and the other offices of the advertising agency would have occupied the whole floor of the building. There were big offices out there, men sitting in them, one man in each office.

They were the business men. They brought advertisers, "clients" they were called, into the agency. They went forth, traveled up and down in fast trains, played golf with manufacturers. There is a man out there, growing rich now. Once I was traveling with him on a train. He was taking me to see a client, a certain large manufacturer. He boasted to me, told me how he got the client for our house.

"I got him with my little old stud book," he said, taking a little notebook out of his pocket. It was filled with the names and addresses of women. He had got the manufacturer a little drunk, had introduced him to one of his women.

"And after that?"

There had been what was obviously a case of blackmail, the one business man coming into a hotel room, the other business man in bed there with a woman, the click of a camera. "I told him I destroyed the negative but he doesn't believe it.

"And why shouldn't his account be in our house? We have got some smart advertising writers. You know that."

The man who had told me the tale, who had shown me his stud book, was in one of the big offices at the front of the building. There would be an expensive rug on the floor. He sits at a big mahogany desk.

But now. It is March. It is cold and rainy. He has gone off with a manufacturer to play golf somewhere in Florida.

I am at my desk by the window in my little room at the back of the great general offices. There are several other men, also advertising writers. Now look, what a puzzle life is. The same business man, who had showed me his stud book, who had boasted to me of his slickness in getting a new big client for our house only two weeks ago, had me in his office. "You come home some night with me," he said. "You bring a notebook. I will tell you the story of my life. It is a wonderful story.

"I have often wished I was a writer," he said and began to tell me of his wife, what a pure and wonderful woman she was.

He had also a daughter and a son. What plans he had for them. "I have had to wade through much," he said, "but I have done it to give them a finer way of life." He declared to me that he loved his wife and that he had been true to her. "Of course," he said, "sometimes when I have been out with a client, you understand. . . ." He wanted a woman. We perhaps a little drunk.

"I never kissed one of them on the lips," he said.

But I would have been trying to tell my acquaintance the banker of that day in the office. I had been given an assignment. I was to write that day a series of advertisements for the daily newspapers, a new cathartic.

And so, I was to spend the day delving in people's bowels. I had come in through the wet streets, some of the others already there. "Hello girls." We, in the so-called "copy department," were making a struggle. Sometimes, at lunch, in some little saloon, we talked it over among ourselves. "For God's sake let us keep trying. It may be we can hold on." There would have been two or three of us who dreamed of someday becoming real writers. This fellow was, in secret, working on a play, that fellow on a novel.

"We are little male whores. We lie with these business men. Let us at least try to keep our minds a little clean. Let us not fall for this dope that we are doing something worth doing."

"Hello girls."

"Good morning, Mable." There was a fat man who always addressed me as "Mable." He had already heard of my assignment for the day. "Mable, they have got you a new man."

"Yes. He deals in excretion." The fat man has worked out a theory on life. He believes in heaven and hell. "It's as plain as the nose on your face," he says. All the people in this life have lived before. They have been sinners in another life and are being punished. We might as well face the facts," he says, "we are in the advertising department of hell."

I am trying to describe my feeling of that day to my acquaintance the banker. I launched off into talk and he sat listening. My desk in the room was by a window. I told him how several others who worked in that room with me ended by committing suicide, and of how others became drunkards. As I sat by the window in the little back room I could look across a street and see into a shop where cheap women's dresses were made. There was a woman sat over there, by another window, and all day she never looked up. How her fingers flew. There was a kind of insanity of speed in the woman's fingers. Sometimes, at night, in my dreams, I could see them flying, flying, flying thus.

There were many women's fingers, flying, flying, flying. They were perhaps making some man rich. "If I can write good persuasive advertisements for this man's cathartic I may help to make another rich man," I thought.

Thoughts also, sometimes, of my own mother, that her life had been much like that of the woman over there, by the window in the building across the city street. Her fingers were also never quiet. They were flying, flying, flying. They were trying to earn food to raise her five strong sons.

Myself, you see, trying to give a picture of all this to the man with me in the fashionable restaurant, the little happenings of a particular day, thoughts in a man's mind.

It would have been one of the days when I rebelled. That was always happening in the advertising place where I worked. Our bosses had to allow for it. I worked at the writing of the series of advertisements for perhaps an hour or even two hours and then I spoke to the "hell" man.

"Come on, Eva. Let's go get a drink." I habitually called the fat man "Little Eva" and he called me "Mable." It was a kind of mutual recognition of our common whoredom. He was a man who might have weighed two hundred and fifty. Formerly he had been a newspaper writer but he had come into advertising because there was more money in it. He explained that he had a growing family, several sons and daughters. "I want to give them an education, give them at least a chance at a more cultured life."

"So that, in the end, they may be ashamed of their father," I said.

"Yes," he said.

We would have started out, going from bar to bar, making our way, not into the busy part of town but into side streets. Some instinct seemed to lead us into tough streets and tough saloons.

"Have another, Mable."

"No, Eva. This one's on me."

There would be down-and-outs hanging about. They leared at us. "What have we here, a pair of fairies, eh?" All of this a kind of satisfaction to us. We were getting a little drunk. "Shall we go back to the office? It may be that now, while I am drunk, I can get through that series of advertisements."

"No. We will not go back today. Hell is there but it is also here. We are destined to live out our lives in hell. It may be it is not hell. It may be purgatory. Let us spend the day going about, seeing how other people live in this purgatory."

[415]

I would have got home finally that day to my room, did not take off my wet clothes. When you are sunk the imagination sometimes plays rather madly. At that time I had already written several long novels but none of them had been printed. I lay on my bed in my room, my head whirling. I could look through a window into the rainy streets. As often happened with me at that time, figures began to appear before my eyes. It may be that I slept and then awakened. My bed was by the window and I could look out into a rainy Chicago street. Now the lights were lighted. I sat up.

Does all of this seem trivial? I am trying to tell it as once I tried to tell it all to that banker.

I was there, sitting there, at the edge of the bed in that room, no light in the room. There was darkness but there was a spot on the wall where the reflected light from a street light came through.

"So, this is my life? This is what I am?"

"But never mind what you are. It is unimportant. It is the disease of the world, that question as to what you are or are not." It was as though there was a voice in the room speaking to me.

There was the dim light spot on the wall before me and the faces of people kept passing in and out of the light. I speak of this incident because, a long time afterwards, I tried to make a one act play of just that scene, a man, some other part of himself, and the figures of many others, all dim shadows of some reality, all whirling and dancing in that room that night. I had, during my experience as business man, known two or three people who afterwards committed suicide. There was one woman, an advertising writer, who went one afternoon to a department store and bought a revolver. She had it sent with cartridges to a little hotel where she stayed.

This at the noon lunch hour. She went back to her desk and worked during the afternoon. She was, I thought, a rather keen intelligent woman and that day, as she was leaving the office, she spoke to me.

"Come on," she said, "walk a little with me." We went along in the city street. I missed her. There was something I should have sensed but I didn't. It must have been one of the days when I was soaked with self-pity. We went along, she talking, seemingly very brightly, very cheerfully. She kept making sarcastic remarks about herself. "I'll tell you of an experience I had," she said and told a tale of going one night out into the street to pick up a man. She said she had seen prostitutes doing it and wanted to know what it would be like to be a physical prostitute. "I'd been another kind so long and wanted to see what it would be like to go the whole hog," was what she said. She said she had tried to do the thing physically but couldn't. She had to give it up. "I spoke to two or three men but when I looked at them they hurried away," she said. She thought that they had thought she was a detective. She thought the failure was due to the fact that the whole thing was too much just up in her head.

"That's the trouble with me. All of life is too much up in my head," she said to me that evening when I left her and immediately she went home and up to her room and with the revolver blew her head out of the picture.

"And so, it is so also with you." This myself speaking to myself that night in my room. I got up and lit a light. I was suddenly quite sober. I had been writing but, in all my writing, I had been using only my head. I had never let other people with their lives come into me. "That is what this is all about," I said to myself. There was one face that had appeared to me, in the light place on the wall that night, the whole thing no doubt partly just a drunken dream.

But it also mixed up with something else, the passionate desire in all people to be understood, their stories also told.

Something perhaps in some way done to break the terrible isolation of all lives.

Among the figures on the wall there had been one of a little frightened man. He perhaps came out of some memory of my own, a face seen sometime on the street, a half told story told by some man in a bar room, the experience of that day, the fat man calling me "Mable," me calling him "Eva," the suspicion of us in the eyes of other men, hangers-on of cheap bar rooms.

I went to the desk and began to write. I wrote a story called "Hands." It is in the book *Winesburg, Ohio* but not in the play. It was the first real story I ever wrote. I tried to tell the banker of the experience, the story written, the sudden almost terrible joy in me, of my afterwards walking up and down in my room, the tears streaming from my eyes.

"It's there. It's solid. It does not matter if anyone else ever understands all of the implications of my story, it is nevertheless sound." It seemed to me, that night, that it didn't much matter what happened to me personally during the rest of my life. (I admit that was a passing thought. It didn't last.) "I have anyway, once in my life, had my feet on the real path," I told myself.

I remember trying to tell all of this to the banker. "Yes indeed, I want money. I do not want to have to earn it, to do what you would call 'deserve' it. Will you give it to me?"

"No," he said. He laughed. It wasn't a very pleasant laugh. "I see," he said. "You think you have got, now and then, a thing I can't get."

"No," I said. "I do not mean that. I do not mean you can't get it. I mean you won't.

"You had better keep your money," I said and "You go to hell," he replied. He paid the bill and we went out of the restaurant. I never saw him again but later I heard that he did sell his string of race horses.

I Steal the Accounts

I had got into a certain position.[4] I was a little known as a writer. There had been a story of mine in *Harper's*. Word had been whispered about.

I had begun to let my hair grow a little long. Upon such a trifle as the necktie you wear a reputation may a little be built. I got strips of gayly colored cloth and passed the ends through a finger ring. I had bought, for the purpose, an old and heavy silver ring, seen in a shop window. Now I did not wear such neckties as other men wore. I wore the strips of brightly colored cloth, passed through the ring. I was a little noticed. We, of the American business world, were (it was at least true at the time), in our dress, all of a pattern. Any little variation in our garb was at once noticed. I began, a little, to attract attention. I wore my hair long and did not comb it. When I was engaged, on these occasions, in one of these grim wrestling matches with advertising ideas, I continually passed my hand through my hair. It would not work now. My hair has grown thin.

I had begun to get a little ahead. After all the solicitors, the salesmen, had to depend upon us. We were the writers. They were compelled to send us to the factories, where the goods we were to advertise were made. Sometimes we stayed at such a factory, in some town, for days. Acquaintances and sometimes something like friendships were made.

There were two men, in Kentucky towns, another in an Ohio town, a fourth and fifth in Illinois towns. I had selected these men from among all those whose accounts I was sent to write. I made it my business to cultivate them. All of them were men who had a certain flair. They or perhaps their wives or daughters were after culture. It is an American passion. I got

4. Editor's title for this section.

invited to their houses. I spoke of books. Some of my stories had begun to appear, for the most part, it is true, in the smaller literary magazines, of which they had never heard, but I saw to it that they did hear of them.

And then there was my older brother, a painter. I spoke of him. There was an exhibition of his work in one of the Chicago galleries and I saw that they got a catalogue. All of the men, thus worked upon, were manufacturers of goods sold to farmers. None were big advertisers. In the aggregate the commissions, from all of the accounts, if I captured them, might be five thousand a year.

I worked steadily on all of them for a year or two, went to see them as often as possible and then, when I thought my position quite comfortably safe, I made my move to "steal" the accounts.

I succeeded. I made a bluff. I went to such men with my story.

"I am dissatisfied," I said. "It may be that I shall resign from my job and go instead with another outfit." I put it on grounds they could not fail to understand. I was not getting enough pay for what I did. As for the morality of what I was doing I do not believe that I thought much of that.

"It is a matter of survival," I told myself. "Can I escape from this trap, in which I am caught, before my nerves are gone?" If I was to do anything of any account, in the field in which I wanted to work, it would be a long pull. If I could capture thus some accounts of my own there would be no more time clocks for me.

I could come and go, wander about in streets, sit in little bars, spend days and even weeks consorting with all sorts of men.

I would be picking up stories. I would be finding out more and more about the lives of other men.

"If I do go to another place may I depend upon you?"

One by one I got them and, when I thought all was secure, I made my play. Was it plain stealing? I am sure I do not know.

"I am going to resign, quit," I said.

"But what's wrong?" I was asked and I explained.

I did not like being compelled to ring a clock. There were certain accounts on which I was willing to work. On others I was not.

"Now I have got some accounts of my own," I said.

I frankly explained what I had done and there was talk.

I had been disloyal, in fact a scamp. This talk would have been held with a man who had but recently become the head of our agency. He had also been a copy man.

"It is to laugh," I said. Did I not know by what road he had got to where he was? I remember that, for an hour, we sat in talk. It was understood that, first of all, he would make an effort to shake the accounts loose from my grip.

"And, if you do not succeed?"

"Yes. In that case we will deal," he said and "I should have watched you more closely," he added.

So there was Bayard and there was Mary. I found Mary sitting on the porch of a little house, on a country road that was half a street, at the edge of an Illinois town. The town might have been some forty or fifty miles out of Chicago and I had come there on one of my week end trips.

I was searching for a house, a place of my own.

"I will get a little one," I had said to myself. It would be a small house, perhaps at the edge of a wood.

Or there would be a stream and open fields.

Now I would begin to live, more or less, the life of a monk.

Old Mary, the Dogs, and Theda Bara

There were two of them, sisters, Mary and Kate, but I did not know Kate well. When I got the little house, at Palos Park (it had been Kate's house), she came to see me once.[5]

She was, as I remember her, a tall woman, and at fifty-five still handsome while Old Mary was growing fat.

I had been strolling about, taking trains out of Chicago to nearby towns. I was looking for just such a little house as the one I found when I found Old Mary. It was Sunday and I had taken a Wabash train.

Palos Park.

I remembered some verses Mike Carr had once recited to me.

"When out of Palos came the gold."

I thought of Columbus' ships sailing out of the little Spanish port.

"Perhaps I will find my own gold there."

The little town (I hear it has grown since, that there are paved roads leading to it) was perhaps a mile from the station.

5. Sherwood Anderson was living in Palos Park by the fall of 1920 and apparently lived there until 1922, when he moved to New Orleans and then New York.

It was a strange little place at the edge of a state forest, a little town occupied, for the most part, by old people. They had come out there. They had little money. Many of them were widow women. They raised chickens, tended little gardens.

I was walking in a dirt road at the edge of town where the forest began when I first saw Old Mary. She was sitting on the front steps of her house and there was a cigar box beside her and in the cigar box was tobacco.

She was fat. She might have been sixty. She was rolling a cigarette.

At that time women did not smoke cigarettes.

"She is one of my own sort, a rebel. I'll bet she is a grand old girl," I thought. Her dress was clean and the yard before her little frame house had been neatly trimmed. The porch on the steps of which she sat was banked with flowers.

There was a plot of ground, surrounded by a low fence, and on it stood two small frame houses. I opened a gate and went in.

So there I was, having my first talk with Old Mary.

"I am a writer. I am looking for a small house. I would like it if the house were furnished.

"I cannot live much in the house. I want a place to which I can come, be alone. Perhaps occasionally a friend, man or woman, will come to spend the day with me."

"Or a night," Old Mary said and laughed.

"No, that is not my object," I explained. "I am employed in the city. Although I am a writer I cannot live by my writing. Occasionally however I have a week end or even, now and then, a whole week free. I want the house as a place in which to work, where I won't be interrupted."

There were two sisters, Kate and Old Mary. They had been in burlesque. They had done the vaudeville circuits. They did a song and dance act. They were in the far west, in the little boom mining towns, had been in Goldfield, Rawhide, Virginia City.

"Out there," Old Mary told me, "we made our best money getting a cut in on the drinks. We'd do our act, then we'd go sit at the table with the miners. The waiters would serve us tea in a whisky glass. We worked 'em. We kept them buying. 'My God, women, but you can sure store it away,' they would say to me and Kate. We got a good cut on every drink they bought."

I had got Kate's house. The two women had retired. They had saved some money and planned to live together in the country but, as Old Mary explained, Kate couldn't stand it.

"She isn't like me," Old Mary explained. Old Mary liked to dig in the ground. She didn't mind the loneliness. It was true that most of the others, in Palos Park, had little to do with her.

It was her past, she said. It was because she smoked and swore. She said she couldn't help swearing.

"I always did swear like I do now. Goddamn it, I can't say ten words without swearing."

It was because of the people with whom she had always associated. She had got used to it. It meant nothing to her.

Kate was different, she always had been. Kate could swear too, when she wanted to turn it on. There was that time when Kate and Old Mary were doing their time in New Orleans. There was another team, two women who were also doing a song and dance act, on the same bill.

"They were jealous of us. You see we wore tights in our act.

"So one night we came to the theatre to do our act and what do you think the two goddamn bitches had done? They had thrown our tights down in the privy hole, that's what they had done.

"And you should have heard Kate then. Goddamn, I was proud of her. The way she cut the ground out from under those two goddamn bitches with her tongue was something to hear."

The cellar of Old Mary's house was a museum. It was filled with the sort of apparatus vaudeville actors use for their acts. It all belonged, Old Mary explained, to old timers like herself and Kate.

She explained how it was with them. They had got too old to do their acts but wouldn't or couldn't believe they were through.

"They bring their junk to me. 'Keep it for me, Mary,' they say. They are always looking to get good billing again but they won't get it.

"So their junk stays here in my cellar and now and then they come to see me. Jesus, they are all through, washed up, but they can't admit it to themselves so I just keep their junk for them."

She told me of how, sometimes, when such an old actor came to see her, he went down into her cellar and got his equipment out. He might be an old trapeze performer. His equipment for his act was silver-plated and he got it out and polished it.

"Christ, it makes me want to cry to see him but I don't let on," Old Mary said.

I was in Old Mary's house, had come, for the first time, on a Saturday morning in the spring. There was a little sitting room, a kitchen, a bedroom. It was neatly enough furnished.

But where and how was I to eat?

"I'll consult Old Mary," I thought. I went to her. It was a mistake.
"Could you, Mary?"

I was wondering if she might be persuaded to cook my dinner. My breakfasts when I stayed over night I thought I could manage.

"Well, I'll be goddamned. Of all the goddamn nerve. What the hell do you think I am? I'll have you to understand, young man, that I'm no servant to any goddamn man."

It may have been on that occasion that she explained to me, her explanations richly larded with profanity, how she had always differed with her sister Kate.

They had had their troubles and it had always been because of men.

Old Mary had always liked men all right. Occasionally she had been, she said, stuck on some man.

"So I gave him what he wanted—what the hell—but I would not marry one of them."

And then Kate had gone and got married and Old Mary had been furiously angry. She said that she and Kate had fought with their fists. They had torn each other's clothes, scratched each other's faces. She laughed telling of it. For over two years, she said, she and Kate had stayed at the same hotels or boarding houses, had traveled on the same trains, done their act, sometimes twice nightly, had even, often, occupied the same room, but during the two years they had not spoken to each other.

Old Mary would make no arrangement to cook my dinner. She had rented me Kate's house. Kate, being unable to stand living in the country, had moved into Chicago. She had bought a movie house there and was doing all right. She was still in the show business and the show business was meat and drink to Kate. She had rented me Kate's house but wanted me to understand that she had not rented me herself.

And that evening she brought my dinner to me on a tray, a wonderful dinner, beautifully cooked. She brought it to the front door of my little house, set it on the step by the door, knocked and went away and later, as long as I stayed in the house, she did the same nightly. She simply wanted me to understand that she was not to be my servant.

Yes, I could bring her presents from town. I could not buy food for her but I could buy her hats or dresses. I could buy her a dressing gown to keep her warm on cold mornings when she got out of bed, could buy her bedroom slippers or, in the winter, flowers to put in a vase in her bedroom. My gifts would show my admiration for her and we became devoted friends.

I was there in my little house and there was an occasional visit from

Kate, who came in a big car with a chauffeur. Old Mary, she said, was an old stick-in-the-mud. She liked it, grubbing in the ground.

"But I don't," said Kate. Kate was even a little on the literary side. I had brought out books from the city and had arranged them on a shelf by my typewriter desk and she went to look at them. There was even a novel of my own, my first published one, *Windy McPherson's Son.*

"And did you really write it yourself?" She seemed full of admiration for the feat. She was very sorry, she said, that because of a busy life, she had never had time to do much reading.

"I suppose Mary has told you what we did for years, ever since we were young girls?"

Yes, Mary had told me.

"She would," Kate said and smiled. She was very handsome standing in the room in the little house and fingering my books. She borrowed *Windy McPherson's Son* and read it but was a little shocked because of the way I had treated my father.

"I guess it was your father?"

"Yes," I said.

She thought I was a shade too rough on him. She did not remember her own father.

"But I always terribly wanted a father," she said.

It was a winter and I was walking in the forest. All summer and through the fall I had been coming to the little house, had been working there, and a curious thing had happened. I came to the house, I worked there, I ate Mary's dinners and in the evening, often, sat on the steps before my house talking with her and hearing always new tales of her adventures.

The town was full of dogs, belonging for the most part to old women, and Mary had one. It was a great shepherd dog and in the afternoon and often in the evening, when I went for a walk in the forest, her dog accompanied me.

I left her house for my afternoon's stroll usually at three o'clock and when I opened the door to go out there the dog was, lying by the steps to my front door and waiting for me. It made Old Mary a little jealous.

"He is growing fonder of you than of me," she said with a laugh of regret in her voice. She swore about it.

There was Mary's dog waiting for me by the door and presently there were other dogs. They kept increasing in numbers until the yard was full of them. I was the only one in the village in the habit of walking thus in the forests and they wanted to go along. When they were not there when I took my stroll at odd hours I whistled for Mary's dog and he came barking with joy and his voice brought the others.

It was a winter night and there was snow on the ground. It had snowed all afternoon but now the sky had cleared and the moon had come out. I set out followed by the troop of dogs.

Something that seemed to me very strange happened during my walk. The dogs, big and little, ran in a troop before me. They seemed excited by the night, the moonlight and the white world in which we walked. They ran in circles, they snapped at each other, they rolled and tumbled in snow. It was on that night I got the impulse for one of my best stories, the title story for the volume *Death in the Woods*.[6]

I did not succeed in writing it at once. It was one of the stories I wrote, threw away and rewrote many times.

I came that night to an open place in the forest. Someone had evidently intended building a house there. Trees had been cut and the ground cleared of underbrush. No doubt the building project had been stopped because the state had taken over the forest.

A large tree, at the edge of the open place, had been cut and in the falling had lodged against another tree so that I could walk up the trunk. I did walk up the trunk and stretched myself on the log.

I was halfway to the top of neighboring trees. The one on which I lay had been a giant among them. In the afternoon the falling snow had been soft and had clung to the limbs of trees but now it had turned cold.

There was the moon floating in the sky. White clouds drifted across its face. I looked up through the bare branches of neighboring trees and little clumps of snow, freed from the leaves, kept falling.

The little clusters of snow crystals in falling thus softly touched my upturned face. It was as though soft cold fingers were caressing me. I lay very still, something of the mystery of the night, the white world and the frost having come into me. How long I lay there that night I'll never know. I was warmly clad. It is possible that I slept and dreamed although I do not think so.

The dogs had become silent and then suddenly there was one of them, a large German police dog with his bare leg on my chest. He was standing,

6. "Death in the Woods" appeared as a sketch in *A Story Teller's Story,* ed. White, p. 92; and as autobiography in *Tar: A Midwest Childhood* (New York: Boni and Liveright, 1926), pp. 199–222. It was also published in *American Mercury,* IX (September, 1926), 7–13; and in *Death in the Woods* (New York: Liveright, Inc., 1933), pp. 3–24.

his hind legs on my legs, his forelegs on my chest and his face close to my face. In the moonlight I could look directly into his eyes.

I thought there was a strange light in his eyes.

Was I frightened?

Well, I can't remember. The dog stayed there, his eyes staring thus into my eyes for two or three minutes, and then he turned and ran down the log.

I turned to look and there the dogs were. They were running in a circle in the open place in the forest. There may have been twelve, fifteen, even twenty of them. Each dog ran with his head at the tail of the dog before him. They ran in silence. They had made a path in the snow in the forest. At least I did not dream that. I went on the next day and saw the circular path they had made in the snow.

They kept running, thus, silently in their circle, and I lay still on the log. There was this strange feeling of having been transported suddenly to a primitive world. It was a feeling I once, years later, had at a place called Grande Isle on the Gulf of Mexico south of New Orleans. Once I went fishing there at night in the moonlight. I had waded out into a channel that separated an inner bay from the gulf and stood, almost shoulder deep, in the sea.

I was alone that night and suddenly again I had the feeling of being in a primitive world. That night porpoises came and played about me. They were close and I could almost reach out my hand and touch them.

In the forest on the winter night dogs kept leaving the mysterious circle in which they ran and coming to me. Other dogs ran up the log to put their forelegs on my chest and stare into my face. It seemed to me, that night, that they were caught by something. They had become a wolf pack but there I was, that night that the dogs, in breaking thus out of the running circle to come to me, one after another, wanting to be reassured.

That there was such a thing as man, that they were the servants of man, that they were really dogs not wolves in a primitive world. That night I stood the strange performance as long as I could and then I arose and ran down the log. I shouted. I had picked up a stick and ran among the dogs, hitting out at them. The running circle was broken and, as I walked home along a woodland path, the dogs again played about me. They got up a rabbit and with a glad outcry gave chase. They were village dogs again.

I kept the little house beside Old Mary's house for several years and we became fast friends. I got several stories from her. On summer nights when I was alone she came often to sit with me. She was growing old and spoke often of death.

There was a summer night of stars.

"Look," she said, "do you know what all of those stars are?

"They are each a separate heaven," she declared. She said that, in her opinion, God was far from the damn fool a lot of people think he was.

"Just imagine," she said. "The goddamn fool people think everyone is going to the same heaven. What a lousy mess. As though God would do us dirt like that.

"No," she said. "He is not that kind of a damn fool. He has all these heavens. You go with your own kind of people, with your own gang, with people you like to be with.

"Just imagine," she said, "having to stay in a heaven forever with a lot of goddamn swine you meet while you are here, on the earth."

I had been for a summer in Europe. It was a trip I had taken with Paul and I will speak of that in another place. I had kept my little house at Palos Park and for the summer had given it to two friends, both young painters. They were like me, compelled to work at jobs. They used the little house during the week ends.

I had met in London a woman actress who had been the wife of the English poet and dramatist John Drinkwater [7] and during the following winter she came to Chicago and I, on several occasions, dined with her.

She was in the company of the American actress Theda Bara. Theda had been the first Greta Garbo [8] of her day. She had been the American glamor girl of the movies, America's vamp, but she had quit the movies—or the movies had quit her—and had gone on the stage.

She was in a play called *The Blue Flame* and my friend, the English actress, was in her company. I had been to see the play with Ben Hecht and Mr. W. L. George, who was in Chicago on a lecture tour and that is a story too. However I'll not try to tell it here.

I had been dining with my friend the English actress and had told her of my little house, in Palos Park, and of Old Mary.

"You should come to see me out there." I wanted her to meet Old Mary and I kept urging her until she said she would come. She would drive out

7. John Drinkwater (1882–1937), English poet and dramatist.
8. Greta Garbo (1905–   ), Swedish-born actress, in American films first in 1926; Theda Bara (1890–1955), queen of silent movies, who visited Anderson in Palos Park on November 12, 1920. See *Letters,* ed. Jones and Rideout, Item 53.

bringing Theda with her and an appointment was made. They were to come for the afternoon, driving out and having tea, or cocktails, with me and Old Mary.

I told Mary and she was excited. She hurried off to town and bought herself a new dress. To her Theda was one of the great ones of the world. She was an actress who had reached heights of which Old Mary had never even dreamed for herself.

She was afraid that, in Theda's presence, she might inadvertently begin to swear. That would be awful, she thought. For days she had been busy, cooking all sorts of delicacies. What was to have been but a modest tea party had become a feast. She kept trying on her new dress and running over to me.

"Is it all right? Do I look all right?"

Although it was winter she had been at work in the ground and her hands were rough.

"Do you think I should wear gloves?"

She kept swearing.

"Now you stop me if I do it when she is here. You wink at me if you hear me swearing, you remember to do that and I'll be watching your face."

The great day came and Old Mary told me she had been unable to sleep on the night before.

"Think of it," she said. "Theda Bara coming to see us."

All morning she kept running in and out of my house, interrupting me in my work. She had washed and ironed my window curtains, had brought table napkins and linen of all sorts from her own house, had brought her silver.

And then Theda arrived and she snubbed poor Old Mary. It was a brutal snubbing and we all felt it. I kept explaining that Old Mary had also been an actress and my English woman friend, sensing the situation, fought to help but it came to nothing.

I could not understand it but later I thought that perhaps Theda thought we were playing a joke on her. Later my English woman friend said she thought that might have happened.

"The critics have recently been rather rough on her," she said.

We kept trying and trying to take Old Mary in on the conversation that afternoon but it was no go. With a kind of pleading hopeful light in her eyes, Old Mary kept addressing remarks to Theda. She tried to tell her of some of her own experiences as an actress but she got no response. Theda did not even look at her. She did not answer her questions and presently Old Mary fled.

She had been deeply hurt. She had behaved herself and hadn't indulged in any profanity. She came to see me after Theda had left. We had all been through an awkward two hours and I was furious.

And then Old Mary came and sat with me and she cried. She cried for a time and then she swore. She let loose. She did some of the most illuminating swearing I had ever heard from her and then she cried again. My little party which I had arranged thinking of the joy it would give my Old Mary had turned out to be a sad failure indeed.

I suppose I could go on here for hours telling you stories of Mary the old actress. She had lived a rough life. She was good. She was very profane. She told me hundreds of stories of her adventures, as a small time actress, in vaudeville and burlesque.

However that is not the point. I spoke of the criticism that was poured over some of us when we first began writing. For one thing we had a notion that sex had something to do with people's lives. In American writing it had been barely mentioned before our time. No one ever used a profane word. When we brought sex back, to take what seemed to us a normal place in life, we were called "sex-obsessed."

I had this little place in the country and went there for week ends. Occasionally, on Sunday afternoons, friends from the city, men and women, drove out from the city to see me. A certain young man, a friend, liking the country, took a place near me.

And now I must tell you the story of this man. He was the son of a college professor. As a young man he was threatened with tuberculosis and went to Saranac, in upper New York, to take the cure.

He met a woman there. It seems that this woman had been through an unfortunate experience. She had been a stenographer in New York City and had fallen in love with her employer. She became his mistress. Something happened and she had been compelled to have an operation. She was ill after that and her employer sent her to Saranac to be cured.

She and my friend met there. They became friends and presently found themselves in love. They talked it over. They decided that, because he was threatened with tuberculosis and as she had been through a very sad experience, they would marry but that they would live in continence. They did that.

It went on so for a year, for two years, and then she fell in love with another man, my friend's friend. The three talked it over. Having lived with my friend for the three years in continence she wanted to continue living so with him. She could not think of him in a more intimate position with herself. She told him so.

However they decided to go on living together. He was in love with her. He felt that he was himself responsible for the situation. He decided to take his friend into his house, to live there. The friend became his wife's lover. Later I had all this from the lover.

Now I think you can all see what a healthy situation this created. It was this man who, with the wife and lover, took the house near me in the country. At first I knew nothing of the story but, as anyone must have done who was at all sensitive to other people, I felt something was wrong. I think they must have been three of about the most unhappy people I had ever known.

But they were trying to keep up an air of cheerfulness. They came in the evening to see me. We talked. We told stories. When a story was told we laughed together.

But there was something hysterical, a bit unhealthy, about the laughter. I wondered. I kept wondering.

It went on so for a time and then the husband no longer came out to the country place. Only the wife and lover came. I used to meet them on summer nights walking in country roads. They no longer came to see me.

And then came the tragedy. I presume to console himself the husband, although still married to his wife, took up with another woman. She was I believe a Russian girl. I dare say he told her his story and, as a woman will, when she is in love with a man, she put all the blame for the quite terrible situation on the wife.

She decided to kill her. She got a gun and came out to their country place. The wife had employed a gardener and was working with her in her flower garden.

The Russian woman came there. She saw the two people working in the garden, fired at the wife, missed her and killed the gardener.

She fled. She managed to get back into the city. She took a train to another city. She went to a hotel and engaged a room. She went up into the room and shot and killed herself.

Two or three years passed and one day I was walking with my friend, the husband. I had begun to publish stories and he was a man much interested in literature. He began to scold me. He said, "Anderson, I have no doubt that, as a story teller, you have some ability but there is something wrong." He said that I wrote too much of queer people. He said he thought it was unhealthy. It gave the wrong impression of life, of people. "Most of us, after all," he said, "lead quite uneventful lives. Nothing unusual," he said, "ever really happens to us."

What Time Is It?

"First the infant, mewling and puking in its mother's arms."

"The lean and slippery pantaloons."

What a short stretch of years.
What a long stretch of years.
I cannot do my book in that way, checking off the days, months, years by the calendar. They do not come into my mind so.

Time is slippery. The days months and years slip and slide down a smooth, sometimes jagged incline. Sometimes the incline is set thick with nails and huge fishhooks that tear and lacerate.

Was I a boy of ten when that little neighbor girl got me to crawl with her under the porch of the house? How hot still and strange it was, lying so close to her under there, tasting, for the first time, of the fruit of the tree. We were merely nibbling at it. Was I ten then or was I fifteen?

When Perry and I went that time to the resort where I first saw Grace was I twenty-five or thirty-five? When I first saw Dreiser plain was it in a street of Chicago or in New York?

There are days that stand forth shining in a man's life. Sometimes nothing in particular happens on such days. You merely walk about. You are in the garden before your house and suddenly you are all alone.

There is an opening between two hills and a great bank of snow white clouds floats across the opening. Off to the south, as you look down a long valley, the horizon seems to run from you. It runs away and comes back.

On such days you look, for a moment, into the world of the painter.

There has been a week of rain and now the sun has come out. There is a little wind blowing. The leaves of the trees, the branches of the trees are flirting with the sun.

There is love making going on. The sun, that old goat of a male, is abed with mother earth.

How good to be alive.

How glorious to be alive.

I am a sensualist. I am filled with lust. I walk in a hill cemetery. Now all the hills take on the forms of giant women.

How good to be alive.

Or I am an advertising man. I am employed in an office, high up in a city sky scraper. I go and lean out at a window.

Far down below me in the city streets there are people hurrying along. They are city dwellers hurrying about their city offices.

But I do not belong to this. It is not mine.

I belong in little towns, in paths through forests, I belong beside a stream, flowing through a meadow. As I lean thus out at the window of the city sky scraper, something happens to me.

It is one of my days, one of my moments. At that moment the hand of God reaches down to me from the sky above. I do not look up but I feel God touching me with the fingers of his hand.

But why did it happen at just that moment? In what year did it happen, what month of what year?

How am I to know? Why should I care?

I was in the advertising office and had been given an assignment. There is a manufacturer of commercial fertilizer who decided to advertise his wares in papers read by farmers.

"Write ten advertisements, to run in a series. They are to be ten inches, double columns. Here is the manufacturer's literature."

"Yes sir. O.K."

Literature is dead.

How carelessly words are used.

I am at a desk in a long narrow room. Crowded brother and sister advertising copy writers. George is there, and Jake and Miss Strahn and that woman (I have forgotten her name) who shot herself.

I was in that place ten, twelve, fifteen years. I had written books of short stories and novels but they did not sell much. They were praised by some of the more discriminating critics but they did not sell. I was given the assignment to write the advertisements for the manufacturer of commercial fertilizer.

I began to write. Men came into the room and went out. Some of them spoke to me.

Another copy writer came to my desk.

"You have written copy for this account. What slant did you take?"

I told him.

When interrupted I was writing rapidly. With one section of my brain I answered questions, took part in conversations but another section of my brain was removed from it all.

It was that section of my brain that guided my hand as I wrote.

I wrote a story called "I'm a Fool." It is a grand story, one of the great stories of our literature.

What did it matter that when the story was written I could not, for a long time, get it published? It in the end made its way into many anthologies of great short stories. It is one of the stories that never had to be retouched, no word, comma, period ever changed.

But why did it come at that moment and in that place? In what year or month did it come?

How does it matter?

You are a man and you are sitting with friends in a fashionable restaurant. You sit by a window. Conversation is going on about you but, at that moment, a man or woman passes in the street. There is a beautiful woman or a beautiful man.

Once, I went to a wedding, walked into a room and there was Maurice Long[9] of Washington.

What a moment.

I felt it in my whole body, in my toes, a friend found.

What a noble fellow. How alive. I had found another man I could love, not as fairies love but as men love.

But to return to the window in the restaurant. There is a beautiful woman passing in the street outside and you are again in love.

Once, in the city of Paris, I followed a man and woman for two hours as they strolled. There was a beautiful old man with a beautiful young woman.

They were aristocrats of life. They were both successful.

Was it the man's daughter?

Was he an old roué with his mistress?

It did not matter to me. For an hour I followed them through streets, through the Luxembourg, drinking of their beauty.

---

9. Anderson met Maurice Long in March, 1930; and Long died in 1931. See *Letters,* ed. Jones and Rideout, Item 175, *passim.*

But when did all of these things happen? Is there any such thing as time sequence?

I am at breakfast in my house. The laughing Alice is there.[10] She has come to visit us. My wife Eleanor is there.

We are talking and I am telling stories. I am like Abraham Lincoln in this, that I cannot carry on a conversation two minutes before I begin telling stories. When I wish to make a point I must tell a story to illustrate it.

I come from the breakfast table to my desk.

Why, I have told a story that should go into my book. I write it as I told it at the breakfast table.

How am I to place it in time? I cannot.

There is that story of Lincoln's about the man's age.

The man was in court and was asked his age.

"I am sixty."

The judge knew he was much older.

"But man, I know you are older."

"Well, there was that fifteen years when I lived on the eastern shore of Maryland. I do not count that."

The man was right. So many years, days, months that do not count.

There was that day in the city of New York. I had been restless all night, could not sleep and arose at dawn. It was raining and I was wandering in the city streets when I came to Stark Young's house.[11]

Stark lived then on Vesey Street. It might have been eight o'clock in the morning when I came to his door and he was coming down a flight of steps.

It was at that moment I knew why I had been restless all night.

"Stark, is there anyone in your apartment?"

"No. Why?"

"May I borrow it for a few hours?"

He laughed and let me in. I found paper. I began to write. I wrote a

10. Anderson refers to Alice Armfield, a member of his group of friends at Olivet College.

11. Stark Young (1881–1963), dramatist and drama critic for *The New Republic* and the *New York Times*. See Young, "The Prompt Book: New Mine for Dramatists," *New York Times*, November 16, 1924, VIII, p. 1; and "A Marginal Note," in *Paul Rosenfeld, Voyager in the Arts*, edited by Jerome Mellquist and Lucile Wiese (New York: Creative Age Press, 1948), pp. 195–97. For Anderson's comments on Young, see *A Story Teller's Story*, ed. White, pp. 277, 305–6; and *Letters*, ed. Jones and Rideout, Item 145, *passim*.

story I called "The Man's Story." It is in the book of short stories called *Horses and Men.*

I wrote furiously all day, didn't stop. As I wrote I numbered the pages and threw them on the floor. There was an open window and a breeze blew in and scattered the sheets.

I had begun writing at eight in the morning and I wrote until five in the evening. In a closet I found a bottle of whisky and when I began to grow weary I drank.

The drink had no effect on me.

I was in a timeless space. I was at a desk writing and could not have told whether I had been sitting there one hour or ten. I emptied the quart bottle of whisky, finished the story and staggered into Stark's bedroom.

In the evening he found me there, very drunk, on his bed. I was sprawled across the bed. The sheets of my story were blown through the house. When, at last, he aroused me and I sat up in bed I proclaimed myself.

"Stark, I am drunk now but, before I got drunk, I wrote oh such a beautiful story."

Time is a slippery thing. Time sequence is meaningless. I have to tell my stories of the people and events of my life as they come into my head.

The Walks in New York

The walks in New York were always puzzling to me. Why was the city so different from the western cities I had known? Already I knew Cleveland, Toledo, Cincinnati, Chicago, Denver, Salt Lake City, St. Louis, New Orleans, Mobile. In a story of mine called "In a Strange Town," [12] written much later, I tried to tell what wandering in some new and strange town did to me. There was a bath of new impressions, of people seen. Always, at certain times, usually when I am physically tired and when I am in a depressed mood, almost ready to drop, I have even thought of suicide at such times, and then something happens.

It is as though the person called Sherwood Anderson went suddenly

12. "In a Strange Town," *Scribner's Magazine,* LXXXVII (January, 1930), 20–25. Anderson wrote of New York in *A Story Teller's Story,* ed. White, pp. 249 *ff.;* and "New York," *Vanity Fair,* XXVIII (July, 1927), 33, 94.

away. I remember that, as a small boy, I was often ill and the illness was of the same sort that came later. It was a kind of life illness, a war going on between myself and myself. The house that was myself was in some way dirty and I wanted it cleaned. Myself worked to make it clean and myself dirtied it. Why not kill myself? There must be thousands of people who have this feeling. Americans are restless wanderers and what American more so than myself?

In a strange place, often, I got entirely rid of self. Something, in me, seemed to go away, freeing me. I spoke just now of boyish illness and I can remember sitting as a boy against a barn wall. I was employed there as a helper with a threshing crew and it was the noon rest hour. The men of our crew were in the barn talking and laughing with the farmer for whom we were threshing. There were neighbor men in to help and they were in the barn. I sat against the barn wall trembling. Something came out of me, a dark floating mass. It went away into the sky, growing smaller and smaller. Now it was a small speck in the distant sky. Was it the corrupt mass of self?

There was an obsession. The dark mass that had floated out of me had become a tiny speck in the clear blue distant sky. I felt that I could let it go on, that I could draw it back.

I sat against the barn wall trembling with fear. I am quite sure my eyes were fixed and glassy as might have been the eyes of one having a fit.

The point is that had I let the darkness go I should have died. It is perhaps all foolishness, all of this. Even as a child it seems to me that I knew myself. There was a kind of selfishness and slickness in me. I could use people, bend them to my will. In the world of men I could grow rich, get power, control and use men and women.

All of this was darkness. It was the dark mass I tried to throw out of myself but if I threw it out I would no longer live. I write all of this down full of curiosity as to whether or not it will interest others. I am passionately interested to know whether or not others will say, "Ah, he is like me."

Or will they have a remedy, write me letters, as people have done, recommend that I become a Lutheran, a Methodist?

"Go join the Catholic Church," as did T. S. Eliot and Ernest Hemingway.

"Come to the feet of Jesus."

"But to me Jesus is but an artistic creation. Some artists created him as I have created people," I say to myself.

"The whole story of Christ has too much form to be a truth.

"But art may be the ultimate truth. God may be but the supreme artist.

"You yourself," I say to myself, "should be something you are not. You should either be all artist, letting everything else go, or you should be simply man, living passionately in the world of flesh and reality."

"But is there reality even in flesh?"

"Stop, Sherwood Anderson."

This experience I have described I realize largely came often as a boy and young man and less frequently later.

As a young man I went for a time to work about race tracks. Something drew me there. It was the beauty and wonder of the race horses.

I could not become a driver of fast trotters and pacers, a thing I supremely wanted to be, for just the reason that I was too temperamental. Good drivers were calm quiet men, quiet inside. I knew and the horses knew. I was allowed sometimes to jog horses for exercise, round and round the race tracks, the horses' legs being hardened so.

And there also I had the experience described above. That I did not fall out of the racing cart or that the horse I was driving, a great fiery fellow, a stallion, did not bolt with me is a wonder.

When I had the experience always a great weakness came over me and it did that day. How long the fit lasted that time I don't know. I was on a country race track and it was early morning. I sat rigid in the sulky, my arms and hands lifeless, and at last at the back of the track near some sheds the horse stopped. He stood patiently until my fit passed. Did he know? As I have said he was a great fiery fellow and even dangerous black, a pacer. After that day I left the tracks, taking with me the passion for beautiful thoroughbred horses I could however never master. Later, in the introduction of a book,[13] I described Theodore Dreiser as a horse, thinking of him and of a certain supreme and beautiful horse, with the honesty of a horse, coming into a banquet room where other men were dining and drinking, and there was talk Dreiser did not like what I had written.

I think he should have.

13. See Anderson's Introduction to Dreiser's *Free and Other Stories* (New York: Modern Library, [1924]), pp. v–x.

I was with Frank Swinnerton and Arnold Bennett at a club in London.[14] I had met Swinnerton on the boat and had found him charming company. Swinnerton was a great admirer of Bennett and I thought Bennett's *Old Wives' Tale* one of the richest novels I had ever read.

At the club I was rude. I thought the later Bennett had gone too obviously into cheap romancing. Someone had told me that Bennett was hungry for money and position. He wanted to become Sir Arnold Bennett.

The club to which we went seemed to me also a heavy ponderous place, and I thought that Bennett had become ponderous. I got a little nasty and could not resist the impulse to remind Bennett of what we were.

"You know," I said, "what we are. We are all little whores."

Perhaps Bennett was not as shocked as I hoped. Later Bennett wrote his autobiography (We all do it. We are doing it all our lives.) and in it he spoke kindly enough of the meeting.

I was on the boat with Swinnerton and there were two American writers on the boat. Swinnerton spoke of them.

"They would like to meet you but they are afraid of you."

At first I didn't understand.

"Afraid? I do not understand."

It was explained that they were afraid I would have contempt for them.

They both wrote detective stories. They were men who made twenty, thirty thousand a year by their trade.

"But Frank, that is something, twenty, thirty thousand. . . . How wonderful."

I was thinking of all the things I could do with all of that money. All my life I had had a secret passionate desire.

With that much money coming in I would buy a stable of race horses.

I would not buy any runners. I would buy trotters and racers.

In the winter I would go, say to the Old Grassy sale of colts. At that time the sale was held every winter in an armory in New York City. Whenever the sale was on and I was in New York I went there.

14. Frank Arthur Swinnerton (1884–   ), English editor and novelist. Anderson refers to his 1926 trip to Europe. For the meeting with Bennett, December 15, 1926, see James Schevill, *Sherwood Anderson: His Life and Work* (Denver: University of Denver Press, 1951), p. 237.

But I had no money to buy colts and what glorious crackers they were. They were being bid off at four, five, six hundred, two, three, four thousand dollars each.

I had to sit down among the buyers.

Oh what fortunte men. How passionately I wanted to buy four, five, six, a dozen of the beautiful creatures. And then to train them, patiently, sitting day after day on one of the little carts, some such highly bent colt between my legs.

The stroke of the colt to be perfected, the perfect balance caught. The man, the driver himself, to become more and more a part of the horse.

Oh what had man sacrificed when he had given up the horse, as duty companion, for the automobile.

The trotter or the pacer so different from the runner. Here was discipline. I would train the colts to hold and perfect the stroke of the trotter, pacer. I was always trying to train my hand to march across the pages on my desk.

The sentences to march, to be disciplined, to hold a balance and get to go at speed.

More and more speed. There are so many stories to be told.

But never mind the sentences, the sheets of paper, the books.

I would be just a horseman, nothing more. I would take my colt off, in the winter, to some little southern town where there was a race track. There would be negro grooms, one for each colt, and all day they would train the colts, living in that world of delicately adjusted horse flesh.

At night sitting over a little stove, with the negro men.

Perhaps we would sing songs, tell stories. That would be a life.

And then, later, when the colts were trained, to go at speed, not to lose their stride, to go off to the races, to go to country towns, all over America, the common folks, farmers and small towners, gathered in, men who still understood the delicacy and balance of the finely tuned racer or trotter.

Myself drifting daringly, taking my life in my hands, darting my colt through narrow openings where the wheels of racing carts just touched on either side of me.

The other drivers, such hearty fellows, swearing at me, cursing me.

It all in the game. Later, when I had won the race, the same men coming to slap me on the back.

"Boy, that was glove hand driving you did."

No puny artist men here—artists instead in horse flesh.

Ernest Hemingway might shoot his elephants and tigers, fight his bull fights, catch his big fish. Given twenty, thirty thousand a year, for one or two years, I would disappear into the ranks of the horse's horse drivers.

An old dream, coming back one day as I sat on the deck of an ocean steamer with Frank Swinnerton, hearing him tell me that two other writers aboard the ship were afraid to meet me, because they were making twenty to thirty thousand a year by writing romances and detective stories.

Really a kind of envy in me.

So much money coming in. So much to be done with it.

I sat staring at Swinnerton. I was puzzled.

"If I could write detective stories, make that much money, surely I would do it."

This thought in my head.

It was, surely, a gift, this fabricating detective stories. It was a special talent. You worked it out like a mathematical problem.

I had myself no talent for solving problems. It happened my mind did not work that way.

My own stories were picked up from observing people, from my own experiences of life, my own feelings.

Often my stories shocked people, challenged them.

Did I want to do that?

I certainly did not.

It was true that I had, always, a shrewd streak in me. I managed to get along, ate well, wore good clothes. Once I had been in business and might, had I stuck to it, have become rich.

I had chucked it because I was bored.

There was no reformer in me. Often I had said to myself that, if the power were suddenly given me, as Omar said, to break life into bits and then remould it, nearer to the heart's desire, if the power were given me to smash and remould all society by the turning over of my hand, that no power on earth could induce me to turn it.

I had wanted to tell the story of things seen, felt, tasted, heard, nothing more.

It had been on the whole rather fun but I had got no riches by it.

And it was impossible, I had often thought, that the thing I was always trying to do—to bring the smell, the taste, the sound, the feel of life into my tales—was really immoral.

After all, life, as I had known it, in myself and others, wasn't so sweet and these others, the romancers, the writers of detective stories, novels, etc., do at least, for a time, take people away from the often pain of living.

I had quite worked myself up, that day in the boat with Swinnerton, was ready to cry "All hail" to the successful writers of detective stories. Earlier in my life I had, for several years and because I could not live by selling my stories, been a writer of advertisements in an advertising agency and once later I happened to pick up a detective story by the English woman Dorothy Sayers [15] and what joy it had given me.

Oh how perfectly she had got the place, the English advertising agency. So perfectly like its American counterpart.

I had run about giving the book to everyone.

"Read it. Read it. It is wonderful."

I had begun to urge upon Swinnerton that he bring one of the two successful detective story writers to me.

"Please do. I want to talk with him."

And then I met one of the men and together we walked about the deck of the boat.

How strange. Why was this thing always happening?

Man with a Book

I was in Reno, had gone there to get a divorce. I was getting the divorce from the sculptress and musician, Tennessee Mitchell.[16] It seemed to both of us the best thing to do but we did not dare let it be known that we agreed. There was some queer twist to the law. If the man and woman both wanted the divorce they could not get it.

And there was a point of disagreement. We had no children and I felt her as well able to support herself as I was. I had the three children from my first marriage and, when we had married, I had told Tennessee Mitchell frankly what my situation was. It turned out that, after I had got established in Reno, she wanted me to sign certain papers, committing me to the payment of a large sum, at some future time, in case I ever became

15. Dorothy Leigh Sayers (1893–1957), English story writer. Anderson refers to her *Murder Must Advertise*.

16. Anderson was in Reno from February, 1923, to April, 1924, because Tennessee Mitchell hesitated to grant him a divorce without demanding future alimony payments. See *A Story Teller's Story,* ed. White, pp. xii–xiv.

prosperous, a thing I refused to do. I had gone to Reno expecting to be clear within a few months but, because of the struggle between us, was compelled to stay more than a year. I did not too much mind. I began writing vigorously. It was at Reno that I wrote one of my best books, *A Story Teller's Story.*

We had been married but not really married and had been persistently unhappy together. Once, having saved a little money, I ran away from her. I went to Mobile, Alabama, and, crossing the bay, got a little house near a place called Fairhope, in Alabama.

She followed me. I think that, while she did not want me, she also did not want to let me go and, when she appeared there, at the retreat I had found for myself, I was annoyed. It was then she became a sculptor. I taught her. I got clay for her.

"If you are to stay about here you will have to have something in which to absorb yourself," I said. I put the clay down before her. There was a great mass of it.

"You do not have to think of being a sculptor. Let that go," I said. I explained to her that, somewhere, within the mass of clay, there was a figure buried. "All you need to do is to release it.

"Sit down before the clay." I had made for her a few simple wooden tools. "If necessary, just sit, for two or three days. Do not think of what you are to do. Think only of the figure buried away, inside the clay. When your fingers begin to itch to cut away the superfluous clay you may begin."

It worked and afterwards I used to sit with her, telling her stories of people about whom I planned to write or about whom I had written. I kept talking of these people, planting them thus in her imagination, and presently, after I had kept it up for a time, she did cut the superfluous clay away from certain heads. Some of these I later used, as illustrations in the book *The Triumph of the Egg.*[17]

But our marriage had been a mistake. We were both too much on the artist side and it is a mistake for two such people to marry. Our marriage, that was not a marriage, had been brought about by a curious stream of circumstances.

In the first place, my first wife, the mother of my children, had been unable to believe in me as an artist and I could not blame her. She was a woman who, having married one sort of man, had awakened to find she had got another. She had married a bright young business man, one who might, had he remained as he seemed to be when she had married him, a

17. New York: B. W. Huebsch, 1921. Anderson refers to May, 1920. See *Letters,* ed. Jones and Rideout, Item 46.

good father, a good provider, one who would have seen to it that her children were brought up in the classic American style (that is to say the classic style for the well-to-do), who would have provided them with automobiles, sent them to the best colleges, etc. She had herself been through college, had traveled in Europe and, when she married me, I had just emerged from the ranks of labor.

As for my becoming a writer, it was, to her mind, not in the books. The writer was an educated man and I, from her point of view, was completely uneducated.

However I was determined, would not be turned aside, and there had been a long silent struggle, ending in a divorce, that she had got.

And then, feeling as I did at the time, more or less disgraced, a man who had gone back on his own children, avoiding, for the time, old friends, constantly saying to himself that he was completely rotten, at the same time curiously and persistently determined, feeling, even from the beginning, that there was in himself a something that, developed, might be of value, being in this mood I had met and married the woman Tennessee Mitchell.

For she had been the first to encourage me.

"Do not let them turn you aside," she had said.

As I knew that, if I went along the road that seemed to me the right one, I could not make money by my writing and as it sometimes seemed that my determination to go this road, rather than to attempt to do a kind of trick writing that might bring quick success, was a kind of perversion in me, so that I continually questioned myself, the words of the woman who told me to go on, were, to me, at the time, golden words.

And so we had married, it being agreed that we would have one of the kind of marriages being a good deal talked of at that time. She had been a strong woman suffragist and, having been named for an early suffragist, one Tennessee Claflin,[18] was very proud of her name. We were each to lead the free life, to come and go as we pleased, to live together when in the mood and apart when in another mood. She was above all to retain her own name which, ironically enough, she did, persistently, until after our divorce, when she took mine.

So there I was in Reno, a strange enough city. However, there was the desert and, as suggested, I had got to work on a book that I very much loved doing.

18. Tennessee Claflin (1846–1923), American social reformer, feminist, and spiritualist.

And there was something else. At that time we who got divorced, and particularly one, like myself, who was getting a second divorce, were more or less outcasts. We felt ourselves that but, in Reno, we were all in one boat. There was a kind of comradeship. A man went about making new friends.

I had been at the public library and had got several books. I came out into the street and, in the street, was hailed by a friend. It was a New York doctor, sitting in his car, and he asked me to get in and ride with him. He was in Reno for the same purpose that had brought me there.

We rode and talked and presently, as it was a topic being much discussed in Reno, at the time, we got on the subject of public prostitution. The subject had become a political issue. There was, in the town, at the edge of town, a place into which the prostitutes had been herded. It was called "the bull pen," a great enclosure, something, as I had been told (I had not been to the place) in the style of county fair grounds, at the edges of small towns in the middle west. There was this place, a circular enclosure, with a high board fence, a row of little one room houses along the fence and a circular sidewalk that went before the houses.

It was a place openly and frankly devoted to the one trade and, to many of the citizens of the town, many of whom were there for the same purpose that had brought the doctor and myself, it was too frank. They did not, they said, object to the institution of prostitution, it being perhaps a necessary evil in our civilization, etc., but this openness, this brutal frankness, they could not take it. They were protesting loudly.

There was this party, struggling for political control in the town, and there was another.

"If," said the second party, the so brutally frank one, "we do away with our bull pen we will lose trade. No, we are dependent upon the people who come here to seek divorces. It is an uncertain business." There was, already, competition springing up. There was the possibility of getting Mexican divorces. There were other states seeking the business, while, on the other hand, there were certain men, sheep herders and cattle men.

"If we do away with our bull pen the sheep herders and the cattle men will go to other towns. They will spend their money in other places."

There was this struggle that had become a political dog fight.

"Have you ever been to the bull pen?" asked my friend, the doctor. I said I had not and that I would like to go.

We drove there and having parked the car we went in. This might have been at nine o'clock at night. I had the books, some five or six of them, under my arm.

And there the place was. It was as it had been described to me. There was the high board fence and the little one roomed houses, each with its bed, its wash basin, wash stand and a chair. I had been told that the women did not live in the place. It was, for them, a place of business. It was their Wall Street, their sky scraper.

"They live in the town," the doctor said to me, "and come here in the evening." The evening, it seemed, was the time for business.

There were men walking about. They went along the sidewalk, before the doors of the houses, a woman standing at each door, some of them speaking to the men as they passed, others remaining silent, the men, as befitting the mission that had brought them, all appearing strangely isolated from each other, going along, some of them silently, in little groups, more often single, all with a queer and significant separateness from each other.

It was a strangely depressing place and there were the doctor and myself, also walking. We did not go far.

There was a sudden outcry. It was startling. It was begun by one of the women who stood at the door of one of the houses near the gate and was immediately taken up by the others. It grew in volume and, presently, the women had come out of the houses and into the street. They ran to us. They surrounded the doctor and myself. The other men, who had come to the place and had been walking silently along the circular sidewalk, had stopped walking and now stood staring. The women continued the cry they had taken up, following the doctor and myself as we hurried out through a gate and to our car. Although they did not touch us it was an assault, an assault of voices, directed, not at the doctor, but at myself.

"Look! Look! A man with a book," they cried, shouting with laughter. They kept it up until we had got into the car and had driven away.

"Look! Look! A man with a book!"

We could hear the voices of the women, still going on with the cry as we drove through dark little streets and toward the gay seeming lights of the town.

Waldo Frank

I was filled with admiration for Waldo Frank. I was also very grateful to him but in the end something came between us.

It is a thing that may be very old in the world. To my mind (the realization came to me slowly) it is about the most destructive thing in life.

As to Waldo Frank, he seemed to me, when we met, to be very warm and alive. He had so much that I wanted for myself. Waldo Frank was a college man. He had, as a young man and after college, gone to live in Europe. He had acquired languages, spoke French, German, Spanish, Italian. He was one of several men who, when I had begun to write, was struggling to get something within myself out to others, put out a hand to me.

I had written some stories, about people I had seen.

But no, they were not that. They were people who had come to life in a special world of my own.

These people had become very real to me. Had I actually plucked them out of life? I never knew.

They were in me for a long time. I felt with them, had their thoughts, passions, fears, lusts, moments of hope and of despair.

In my stories I had tried to let them be born out of myself and when the stories were at last printed I was terribly shocked and hurt to find that the stories offended others.

There was, for me, a bad time, a horrid time. I began getting letters from people who had read my stories. It is true that, at the time, I was rather immature. Having felt, while at work writing the stories, very pure and clean (the time of writing had been, for me, a joyous time) I could not understand when people, the critics, those who wrote me letters, called me filthy minded.

It is true that the people of my stories had almost all been twisted, torn and hurt by the workings of the sex impulse, but I did not feel that the stories were primarily concerned with sex.

A French critic wrote of the stories. He spoke of my people as terrible.

"These terrible people."

That also shocked me.

"If they are terrible then I am also terrible.

"They are only people going along as I am. What happens to them in the stories happens to everyone."

For a time the criticism of my stories affected me rather profoundly. I began to feel hatred about me. I got a letter from a woman at whose house I had once dined. "Having been seated beside you at table I feel I shall never again be clean."

A young man wrote me a letter filled with filthy words.

There was a woman who spoke to one of my men friends.

"When I am in Sherwood's presence it always seems to me that his eyes are tearing off my clothes, making me naked," she said.

That made me smile.

"It's quite true. I do want to see people naked," I thought. "I want to see all of them. It is the way I am."

I however became for a time afraid of people. I went and hid myself, did not open letters that came to me.

I was in an Indiana town and at a railroad station saw my name on the cover of a magazine. It was the first time such a thing had ever happened and as I paid the newsdealer for the magazine my hand trembled so that the money fell to the floor of the railroad station.

I had been about to take a train but didn't. I walked out of the town into the country holding the magazine in my hand. I left the road in which I walked and went across a field, through a wood, and came to the bank of a creek.

I sat down there to read and tears came into my eyes.

"At last. At last."

Here was one who knew what I had done, that I had written my stories out of a true and honest impulse, wanting only to share with others what out of life I had found for myself.

There was that gratitude in me, that exaltation, and then the shadow came.

It was Waldo Frank writing of my stories but in writing he had used a curious phrase. He had spoken of me as "a great man."

"A great man is being born into the world," eh?

There was a shock. Something ugly had happened again. There had been in what Waldo Frank had written this warmth, enthusiasm, fine generosity.

"But why that about 'greatness'?"

It was sometime later that Waldo Frank and I became friends and for a time we were much together and my admiration for Waldo Frank for a time kept growing.

"Oh that I could know so much, could speak languages, have this man's familiarity with the literature and thought of the world." It was, for a time, something wonderful for me that I could have, as friend, such a man as Waldo Frank. I went to my friend's house, went to dine with him, went with him into the country. For hours often I sat, filled with wonder and admiration, while Waldo Frank talked.

There was this seeming ocean of knowledge. Waldo Frank had read all of the great masters in their own languages. He had traveled over the world, had talked intimately with men who had written notable books. He was the son of a rich man and knew the cities of the world, how to order wines, how to live richly and well.

Waldo Frank was also a writer. He wrote books and stories. His talk began to take on a new tone. There was again the talk of "greatness."

"Will our names go down to posterity?"

There were pictures made for me of statues to be built for us when we were dead. Once we were walking on a bridge that crossed a river and later I remembered gulls flying in the air over the river.

I remembered the color of the water of the river. In the distance there was a ship tied to a dock and I began to think it was like a gull alighted there in the distance on the water but at that moment Waldo Frank spoke to me of something.

He spoke of what a tragedy it would be to literature if the bridge on which we two walked should go down.

It is true he said it with laughter but nevertheless it hurt me.

It was as though a black cloud had descended, hiding the ship in the distance, the gulls flying, the river flowing.

So I began to see less and less of Waldo Frank but one day I got a letter. The letter again spoke of "greatness."

"Do you not think, Sherwood, that you and I and (he named a third) that we are the great men of our times?"

I did not answer the letter but one day Waldo Frank came to my room. I was living at that time in New York. It was when the World War was on and I had hidden myself away.

I had got here a room in a working men's quarter of the city. I was hiding there.

It was a time of too much "greatness."

Great generals.

Great statesmen.

Great hatreds sweeping up through the world.

Great writers glorifying war.

Great diplomats at work.

It was a flood. It was to me terrible, unbearable. I had hidden myself away. More and more I had retreated into an old life I had known before the war came. I wanted passionately now to think not of great soldiers, statesmen, writers, but of being first of all little.

I wanted again the little life, in streets, on farms, in towns, in little frame houses in towns and cities. I was fighting to live in that life, in spite of the great roar and hubbub going on everywhere about me to keep that old life alive in myself.

I was there, in that place, when one day Waldo Frank came to me.

He came into my room. He sat in a chair. He was as he had always been. There was warmth in him.

This was after my first marriage. I did not live with my wife but I had become the father of children as had Waldo Frank. For the time we had both escaped the draft. In the end we did escape.

The man was sitting in my room and I was angry. I got up from my chair and walked to a window. I did not face my friend. I talked.

I was very bitter. I spoke of the letter I had received. "It was vile," I said. I asked Waldo Frank to leave my room and not to return.

"There is this talk of 'greatness.' It is your disease and you are trying to give it to all." I declared that no such thing as a great man could exist. I said, "I am trying here in this room to hang onto something and you come to destroy it.

"It is hard enough," I said, "for me to keep myself, occasionally, out from between myself and what I am trying to do.

"The struggle is hard enough without you and your goddamn 'greatness.' "

I had begun to shout. I wanted to run to Waldo Frank, strike him in the face, knock him down, kick him down the flight of stairs that led to the street, but when I turned from the window there was Waldo Frank in tears.

Waldo Frank had gone very pale. He had moved from his chair. He was on my bed. He was lying on the bed, his face buried in a pillow, his shoulders shaking, and when he had a little recovered he began to thank me for all I had said.

He said that what I had said was like a door opened for him into life. He sat up on the bed and talked. He wiped away his tears and coming across the room took my hand.

"You are the only friend I have ever had. You have spoken truth to me. Your words have been like knives. They entered my heart.

"What I have been I shall never be again."

There was this moment between us. We stood holding each other's hands. The warmth in Waldo Frank seemed to flow over me. I also felt like crying.

[449]

We two left my room and went for a walk. We were walking just as darkness came in a city street.

It was a poor section of the city and children were laughing and playing in the street. There was for me on that evening as I walked with Waldo Frank, for a time, for five minutes, ten, perhaps even twenty minutes, something very wonderful in the city street, in the sight of wives of workers going in at the doors of little stores, in the shouts of children.

The war seemed for the moment very far away. We were walking in silence.

"I have got my friend back," I thought. I was thinking that, just at that time, more than anything else in the world, I was wanting such friends.

"I have been mistaken in him. He is not what I had begun to think and fear. This talk of 'greatness,' himself great, me great, or to become great, is only something superficial in him.

It has passed now. There will be no more of it.

"It may begin now.

"Two men friends.

"Then four.

"Then more and more.

"Man to man.

"No more 'greatness' or talk of 'greatness.' "

A beginning. A new passion loose in the world, to want to be little, not to be big.

I had got into a kind of exaltation. I was walking thus with Waldo Frank, thinking these thoughts, when Waldo Frank spoke. He spoke of the fact that he had money.

"You have never been to Europe, have you, Sherwood?

"You see this war will not always go on.

"Peace will come and we will go there.

"We might go together but not yet.

"Not yet," he said. "We must wait.

"We must wait until our names have rung through Europe, until we are known, appreciated, until all Europe is standing with open arms waiting for us."

Waldo Frank had said this to me. We were walking together. When I had got the letter from Waldo Frank and when Waldo Frank had come that day to my room, I had been very angry. I had wanted to strike Waldo Frank, to choke him, hurt him, but now I only smiled. We had come to a street corner and I put out my hand. I took Waldo Frank's hand. I smiled. "Well good-bye, Waldo Frank," I said and smiling went back to my room.

Dreiser

I

For a long time I had been an admirer of Theodore Dreiser. For a time, after I began to publish, some of the critics kept saying that I had got my impulse from him.

It aroused my curiosity and I began to read him.

I was filled with admiration for his courage. Here was a man doing something that I also wanted to do. He was actually writing about the life about him frankly and boldly as he had seen and felt it.

Before I came to Dreiser I had already written several novels, none of which were ever published. Then I had written two novels that were published. I think now that my best stories, put down, had been largely the result of my reading.

I had been for some time under the spell of H. G. Wells and Arnold Bennett. Later some of the critics, a good many of them, said I had soaked myself in the Russians.

I hadn't. It was a good deal later that I began to read the Russians, Tolstoy, Chekhov, Dostoevsky, Turgenev.

I think that then, when I came to them, that I did feel a kinship. Is it egotistical of me to say so? I felt a brotherhood with Chekhov and, in particular, with Turgenev in his *Annals of a Sportsman.* I remember that Paul Rosenfeld soon called me "The Phallic Chekhov."

I think it may well be, however, that it was the reading of Dreiser, his *Sister Carrie* and his *Jennie Gerhardt,* that started me on a new track.

The books jolted me. "Look homeward, angel," they shouted at me. They did, I felt, turn me away from books, from other writers, to the life about me, as I had myself seen and felt it.

I was profoundly grateful to Dreiser. I dedicated a book to him. I wrote to him a prose poem, using it as the foreword to a book of stories I called *Horses and Men.*

I had never seen Dreiser and did not know, until years later, when we became friends, that it was his word, given to the publisher John Lane, that got my first three books published.

I was in New York City. At that time I was still working in the Chicago advertising agency. Already I had got some literary recognition but little or no money had come in.

I used to work in the advertising place for several months, saving what money I could and, when I had got a few hundred ahead, I ran away.

I had been offered the use of an apartment in St. Luke's Place in New York. Whether or not I paid anything for it I can't remember. It was a cellar apartment. You went down a flight of stairs. It was very comfortable. This was in the summer and the apartment belonged to two young men, professors at Columbia. They had both gone away for the summer. If I paid for the apartment I paid little enough.

I decided I would go and call upon Dreiser. His apartment, unlike my own, was above the street level. You went up a flight of stairs to the front door.

I went up the stairs and there was his name, on a little white card, and there was a bell to punch.

My fingers trembled above the bell but I did not ring it. I turned and hurried away.

"But how do I know he will want to see me?" I asked myself. To me he was and has always remained a great man, one of the few really great ones of America.

"He may be at work on a book," I said to myself. On several occasions I climbed the several steps to his door, my finger hovered over his bell but I did not ring it.

And then, one morning, I did. I rang the bell and waited. I dare say I trembled a little.

"Well, you sure have a nerve. You've got a nerve bothering the man," I said to myself.

And then the door opened and there he was.

Once before I had seen him. He was walking in a street in Chicago, and I was walking with Ben Hecht. He had a woman with him. He was dressed, I remember, on that occasion, very gaudily.

There was a mauve overcoat, a mauve tie, a mauve shirt. He was all pastel colors. We, in Chicago, had all been making him our hero. This must have been after his *Sister Carrie* had been got out of hock to a puritan publisher and after Arnold Bennett had come to America to proclaim him.

And I was walking that time with Ben Hecht and he pointed.

"Look. Theodore Dreiser."

There was, in Ben's voice, a sure sign that he was tremendously impressed. It took a lot to impress Ben Hecht.

So there I was on Dreiser's doorstep facing him. I am quite sure my voice trembled.

"I am Sherwood Anderson. I thought I would come to see you."

"Oh, hello," he said. He shut the door in my face.[19]

So there I was on The Dreiser's doorstep, facing the blank door. I was shocked. Then I was furious.

"The beast," I said. "The son of a bitch." I went to walk. I swore. I cursed him. In that prose poem I had written to him I had spoken of him as an old man.

But I had been careful to say that I did not mean old in years.

"He is old in spirit and does not know what to do with life, so he tells about it as he sees it, simply and honestly."

I had only been speaking of his great tenderness that had so attracted me to his books.

"The old bastard. I'll bet he's after a new girl, some young thing no doubt. He's sore because I said he was old. He's a fool. He hasn't sense enough to comprehend what I was really saying of him."

I went along a street, muttering thus against The Dreiser. I went into a saloon and had drinks. I got half drunk.

And then, later in the day, I went home to my apartment and there was a note from him. The man had simply been embarrassed, as I was, when we stood facing each other. He knew that I was newly come to the city and he thought there were many interesting men in the city I should meet.

So he had arranged a party for me. It was all very characteristic of The Dreiser, the awkwardness that is in his prose, the thoughtfulness for others, the kindness always covered by a gruff manner.

The note from him made my heart jump with gladness. There it was. He was as I had thought he would be.

I was at the party in the evening in Dreiser's apartment and there were a dozen other men present. They were all men of some note in the city. They were men of whom I had heard. I was excited and a good deal scared.

19. Anderson is writing of the winter of 1922–23. See W. A. Swanberg, *Dreiser* (New York: Bantam Books, 1967), p. 324.

We were in a large room with pictures on the wall and at an end of the room there was a large flat top desk at which no doubt The Dreiser sat every day at work on his stories. Along the walls of the room were bottles of liquor of various kinds and there was also beer and wine.

We sat in little groups talking. An hour, perhaps two hours, passed and at last Henry Mencken, one of the party, said what we were all thinking.

"Dreiser," he said. "I see you have got this liquor here. You have beer and wine.

"What's the idea?" he said. "Are you keeping it? Do you plan to drink it all yourself or what the hell?"

The Dreiser laughed.

"Go to hell, Mencken," he said. "If you fellows haven't sense enough to help yourself you can go without."

There was a thing happened at The Dreiser's party I have never forgotten. Scott Fitzgerald was in New York at that time. His glowingly alive books had just begun to appear. I have no doubt that Scott, at least at that time, felt toward The Dreiser as we, in Chicago, had been feeling. He must have felt as I had felt and as I had written in the foreword of the book dedicated to him that Dreiser, the heavy footed, had tramped through the real wilderness of puritan lies making a pathway for all of us.

Fitzgerald had in some way heard of the party being given at The Dreiser's and had wanted to come. He had wanted to pay his respects to the man.

So he had bought some bottles of expensive champagne. He came to Dreiser's door as I had come. He rang the bell as I had done.

And then it happened to him as it had happened to me. He was there, standing at the door and holding the bottles of champagne, and there was The Dreiser standing and facing him.

The Dreiser would have stared. He would have said nothing.

"I am Scott Fitzgerald. I have brought you this champagne."

It is true that, on that night, sitting in the room with the others, I did not hear what was said at the door.

"I am Scott Fitzgerald. I have brought you this champagne."

The Dreiser would have reached out and taken the bottles. He could not have failed to know of the man who stood there before him. At the moment the whole literary world was filled with the name of Fitzgerald.

"Here is this champagne."

"Hello.

"Thanks."

The Dreiser had closed the door in Fitzgerald's face as he had done in mine. He came back into the room holding the bottles. Already he would have realized what he had done. He would have known how eager we all were to meet Fitzgerald.

He had simply been unable at the moment to do what he had wanted to do, invite the man in.

"Hello.

"Thanks."

He had shut the door in the man's face.[20]

"What the hell, Dreiser?" someone said. We were all, as he was, deeply embarrassed.

He sat in a chair and had put the bottles of champagne on the floor.

"Oh, you go to hell," was all, at the moment, he was able to say to the one of us who, by the tone of his voice, had rebuked him for not having Fitzgerald in to be one of the party.

Whether or not Fitzgerald ever knew why that happened that night when he came to pay his tribute to The Dreiser, I have no way of knowing.

II

He is a gruff man, very tender at bottom. He is heavy handed, heavy footed. He is the most honest man I have ever known, is honest with the honesty of a fine animal. Often when I have been with him, I have in my own mind compared him with one of the race horses in a stable of race horses for which I once worked as groom.

There was a particular young stallion named Doctor Fritz, for a time in my charge, and sometimes when I entered his stall and he was feeling fit he let fly with his heels but, before doing so, always turned his head to be sure he missed me. He just felt like kicking up his heels. That was all.

There are innumerable touching stories going about concerning Dreiser. His friends call him "Teddy." The poet Arthur Ficke told me one.

He said, "Teddy came to my house. There was something on his mind. He wanted me to take a walk with him.

20. For this party, see Swanberg, *Dreiser*, p. 327. Apparently, Fitzgerald was invited in to join the party. Anderson and Scott Fitzgerald (1896–1940) were not close friends. See G. Thomas Tanselle, "Fitzgerald Letters at Newberry," *Fitzgerald Newsletter*, No. 15 (Fall, 1961), p. 6; and *The Letters of F. Scott Fitzgerald*, edited by Andrew Turnbull (New York: Scribner's, 1963).

"I was living in the country and it was winter so we walked in frozen fields. He wouldn't talk so I talked. I went chattering along. I don't know what was on my mind but all of a sudden I made a remark at which Dreiser stopped, and stood staring at me.

"We were in a frozen meadow, in a wide flat place.

"A man must learn to forgive himself for what he does to others," I said. "He does something, hurts someone. If he could not forgive himself, he would go insane."

Ficke had made the remark. He said that Dreiser stopped walking and stood staring at him. He went a little pale. He walked away from Ficke. Tears were in his eyes.

"It is wonderful," he said. "It is what I had forgotten. It is what had been troubling me. A man is a man. He is like other men. He does someone else a wrong. He must learn to forgive himself. He must. He must."

It was the sort of remark that Theodore Dreiser would treasure forever, some chance remark, made by a friend, that helped him a little in the difficult business of living. He would be forever grateful to the friend. I can imagine him later speaking of Ficke. "That Ficke. He is a wonderful man. What a mind he had. It is wonderful, wonderful."

There was a woman who taught a class of children in an orphan asylum. She said, "I got Dreiser to come visit my class." She spoke of a habit he has. When Dreiser is absorbed or moved, he takes a handkerchief from his pocket, lays it on his knees, begins folding and refolding it.

She said, "My children were reciting their lessons and he sat looking at them. I'll never forget his figure, that great hulk of a man, sitting there, folding and refolding the handkerchief, the tears running down his cheeks.

"Just because—well I don't know—because," she said.

"It was pity, not for one of the children, for all children.

"Life, what it does to people."

Dreiser will call a friend on the telephone.

"I think you had better go see Fred."

"Why?"

"Well, I saw him on the street. There was something I felt. I am quite sure he is a little below, a little discouraged. You had better go to see him. Go at once."

Dreiser is a great writer. No more awkward writer ever lived. He can write sentences that fairly jar the teeth out of your head. They flatten out. In his hands words go sick and lame. They get rheumatism. They have pernicious anemia. Many of his sentences have broken backs. They can't walk, can't even crawl.

He is a great novelist. He builds and builds, slowly, patiently. Something arises, huge, significant, real. He does not play cheap scurvy tricks on life. Many another, honest enough in what we call the "real" world, is a crook in the world of the imagination. It is the world of real significance, where men get shown up for what they are. The arts are very dangerous institutions to fool with and how casually many people go into them. Look out. They give you away. They show you up for what you are.

Theodore Dreiser is a great figure. He is something out beyond his books. He will remain a significant figure to other American men working in the arts long after men have quit reading his books.

I was at the house of a friend in Pennsylvania. A play I had written and for which I had at the time a good deal of hope had been produced the night before. It had been produced at the Hedgerow Theatre, directed by Mr. Jasper Deeter.

A good many of my friends had come to see the play and, after the performance, many of us went to the house of my friend who lived but a few miles away from the theatre. It was a Sunday morning in the summer. There must have been at least twenty people who had slept the night in my friend's house. Others drove there in the morning. With me, when I arrived, was a certain southern woman of sixty, a very old and very dear friend, one of the extraordinary keen, alive, witty and gentle women often found in the south.

We were at my friend's house, on the lawn, some fifteen or twenty of us, drinking our morning coffee out there, when Dreiser appeared. He was quite naked. He had spent the night in the house, had wanted a bath when he awakened and perhaps all the bathrooms in the house were occupied. He had got a young son of our host, a mere boy, to come out on the lawn and turn the hose on him.

He stood there before us all. He quite unconsciously took his morning bath and returned to the house and there were murmurs of indignation.

"For me it doesn't matter but there is Mrs. Blank."

The Mrs. Blank would be my southern woman of the grey hair, of the intelligent eyes. I sat beside her.

The whispers must have come to her ears for she turned to me and smiled.

"He didn't," she declared.

She explained. "While he was taking his bath I did not look at his body. I looked at his face. I was curious. I am too old to be concerned about men's bodies. I only wanted to be sure that he was quite unconscious that he was doing anything startling and he was.

"He is an innocent man," she said.[21]

Dreiser is a man who, not knowing what to do about some situation in which he may have become involved, may do anything. I am sure most of my readers, who know their Dreiser, will remember the toothpick story. He is a man about whom amazing stories are always being told. He went, with several other writers, down into Harlan, Kentucky, to protest the treatment of the coal miners. I knew about it at the time because, on the way down into the Kentucky coal mining district, where there had been a good deal of shooting and killing, some of the protesters had stopped at my house in Virginia to get me to go with them.

I didn't go. I was indignant enough about the treatment the miners had been receiving but I preferred to express my own indignation on paper. Frankly I was afraid to go. I think it quite possible that when it came to facing death, say from a bullet, I might be able to stand up to it all right.

But to be beaten.

The thought appalled me.

So there was Dreiser at Harlan and the mine owners, through their hirelings, wanted to get something on him.

He was staying in a room in a hotel in the town and had brought with him his secretary. She was in his room, working with him, and they crept up and stuck toothpicks against the door.

Their idea was that if the woman secretary came out of the room the toothpicks would be knocked down. They declared they were not knocked down, that they were still standing upright on the next morning and Dreiser's answer to them was magnificent.

"But I am finally and irrevocably impotent," he said.[22]

Would any other man in America have thought of saying that?

21. This happened in June, 1934; but, according to Swanberg, *Dreiser,* p. 505, the woman, Mrs. B. E. Copenhaver, fled embarrassed.

22. For Dreiser's visit to Harlan, see Swanberg, *Dreiser,* pp. 461–69. The date was September, 1931; and Dreiser's remark was that he was "completely and finally impotent." On Harlan, see Anderson's "I Want to be Counted," *Harlan Miners Speak* [National Committee for the Defense of Political Prisoners] (New York: Harcourt, Brace, 1932), pp. 298–312. For the correspondence, see *Letters of Theodore Dreiser,* edited by Robert H. Elias, *et al.,* 3 vols. (Philadelphia: University of Pennsylvania Press, 1959); and the Anderson *Letters,* ed. Jones and Rideout, Items 8, 11, 95, 208, 261, 272, 277, 283, *passim.*

There was a woman who for a time lived with Dreiser. She told me the story of her experience.

"He got tired of me," she said.

"One day I came home to the apartment where I lived with him and there were all of my belongings on the steps of the apartment building."

"And what did you do?"

"I got a cab and took my belongings away."

"But were you angry?"

"Yes. I was heart broken. You see, I loved him. I still think him the finest man I have ever known. You see, he is very tender hearted. He could not tell me to go away. He knew it would hurt me and that would be more than he could stand.

"So he did it in his own way. Afterwards, when I had recovered from my anger, I thought after all it was the best way."

Dreiser published a little book of verse privately circulated, in which there was one verse he called "The Beautiful." It was a reproduction almost word for word, sentence for sentence, of a prose poem of my own. My own piece, published several years earlier, was in the book *Winesburg, Ohio.* It is called "Tandy." Frank Adams published the two things in parallel columns in the old *New York World* [23] and I, living at the time in the country, began to get telegrams from other New York newspapers.

The whole thing made, at the time, a mild literary scandal. I didn't answer the telegrams. When it happened I was puzzled, knowing Dreiser as I did, but later figured out what had happened.

What I am sure had happened was that Dreiser had tried putting my "Tandy" into blank verse.

He liked it better so. He forgot where he had found it. It became his own.

The whole matter was never mentioned between us but later, some years later, I saw a line in an eastern literary magazine.

By that time I had lifted my piece from Dreiser's verse. So what does it matter? This thing is sure, when Dreiser is gone, we shall not see his like again.

23. Franklin P. Adams (1881–1960), columnist and humorist. For background and reprinting of the parallel passages, see Swanberg, *Dreiser,* pp. 377–78. Adams is quoted in the *New York Herald Tribune,* September 7, 1926.

His aunt (he called her "Tante") came puffing and groaning up the stairs to my apartment, this in the old Pentalba building in New Orleans.[24] I had just come south and had taken the apartment on the third floor of the old building. It was furnished. At that time there were a good many men, of the so-called "upper classes," the well-to-do, who kept such apartments in the French Quarter.

After all the city was French and do not all Frenchmen keep mistresses? If not we have been much deceived by French literature.

It may be that the man who had rented me the apartment had lost his mistress or that he had grown tired of her.

Or perhaps there had been financial reverses.

At any rate there I was and there on the stairs was Tante. My apartment was on the third floor and, as the ceilings were high, so were the stairways long. I could hear her puffing and groaning. She arrived. She sank into a chair.

She was heavily corseted, a woman of fifty, very fat, with high heeled shoes, much bepowdered, much befrilled. When she had got her breath she explained her mission.

She said I was to go to a certain town. She had a nephew living there. He had a beautiful house, surrounded by beautiful grounds. He was an artist, a painter, more than that, he was one of the greatest possible distinction among all of a certain class of which I, a northern man, had heard much. He was an aristocrat of the aristocrats, one of the real, the notable ones.

He had begun life, as a young painter, when he was poor. She told me the story of the family fortunes. There had been this family, a great slave owning one. They had lived on land, charter to which had come to them directly from the French kings.

Upon this land they had lived and prospered and then. . . . Her voice broke.

"You are of the north," she said.

I said I was but tried to explain. I understood that my own father, a solider it was true in the Civil War, had not been in the far south.

She said that she had been quite sure that my ancestors had had nothing to do with what had happened to her people.

24. Sherwood and Elizabeth Prall Anderson went to New Orleans in the summer of 1924, after which Anderson met Weeks Hall, a painter mentioned by Anderson in *Letters,* ed. Jones and Rideout, Item 110, written March 5, 1925.

There had been a descent of northern soldiery upon the south, and in particular upon the country about New Orleans. She grew excited. They were great brutes. They invaded houses. She did not mention the word "rape." She told a tale of her own mother. There was again a story I had often heard. It concerned spoons. "Aha, the spoons again," I thought.

There was a certain northern general, in charge of troops, that came into her parish.

"He stole my mother's spoons."

I said that I thought it was too bad.

I gathered that the family, a very notable one, a rich and cultured family, had, by the coming of the Yanks, been quite destroyed. From being rich they had become very poor and their possessions, in land, from being vast had shrunk to practically nothing. There had been left to them only certain acres of swamp land and a few islands.

And there was her nephew, a young man of talent, the only male descendant of a long and aristocratic line. He was a young, a struggling painter. She spoke at length of his talent.

"It broke our hearts to think of him so," she said. She took a small handkerchief from her hand bag and dabbed at her eyes. She said he had been such a beautiful boy.

"And the last of the line," she said again.

They (and by "they," I gathered, she meant the surviving females of the family) had been quite in despair and then, suddenly, on one of the islands, left them out of their former great estates, a salt mine had been discovered.

It had been sold for a huge price and, as I got it, the other females having died, Tante and the nephew had divided the money.

The nephew, being, as Tante said, a true artist, therefore anxious to restore to its former dignity the family name, had returned to the old estate. He had rebuilt the family house. He was living there, she said, had not married.

He had heard of my coming to the city and had sent her to me. I was to go there, by train, to a certain town, to be his guest. There was, in Tante, something magnificent. She had come to me, had climbed the stairs to my apartment, to bring in person the invitation. It was a thing she said that she had rarely done. I gathered that her bringing the invitation thus, in person, made the matter of my going something like a command.

She did not ask me whether or not I would go.

"You are to go to him," she said. She handed me a slip of paper.

"How nice," I said and she arose. There was in her no doubt that, having received the invitation, having had it brought to me thus, there was no question of choice. As she had come to me so she sailed forth. I could hear her as she went, groaning heavily, down the stairs and, as I went back to my desk and to my work, I thought of how, often when coming up or going down my stairs (they were always dark) I was in the habit of meeting certain rats. They were quite huge fellows and, as I descended, they sometimes ran before me and as I ascended ran between my legs. "After all, she is a southern lady and no doubt one of the real ones," I thought. I did hope that the rats, to which I had become somewhat accustomed, would realize with whom they had to deal and would remain respectfully quiet until she had got down again to the street and to her car.

Faulkner and Hemingway

I was in a southern town, sitting with him, one evening, before the cathedral, in New Orleans, while he contended, with entire seriousness, that the cross between the white man and the negro woman always resulted, after the first crossing, in sterility.[25] He spoke of the cross between the jack and the mare that produced the mule and said that, as between the white man and the negro woman, it was like that.

However there was never any doubt in my mind about Faulkner. He was, from the first, a real writer. He had the touch and there was always in him something finer and certainly more generous than, for example, in Hemingway.

I speak of the two men together because it happened that I knew both men before either had published and it was through my efforts that both first got published.

It was a thing Hemingway couldn't stand. When he began to write he began with the short story and I had already published my *Winesburg, Ohio.* I had published also my *Horses and Men* and my *Triumph of the Egg,* and I dare say more than one critic, in speaking of his work, attributed his impulse to me. They had even perhaps intimated that I was his master.

It is a thing that happens to every writer when he begins. My own

25. Anderson met William Faulkner (1897–1962) in New Orleans in 1925. See Anderson's "A Meeting South," *Dial,* LXXVIII (April, 1925), 269–79.

impulse had been attributed to Dreiser, to the Russians, whom I had, at that time, never read. Anyway it is sure that, if others had said that I had shown Hemingway the way, I had not said so. I thought, as I did in the case of Faulkner, that he had his own gift that had nothing particularly to do with me. What man doesn't look to others? I am sure I constantly do.

In the case of Hemingway there may have been something else. Having a very great talent, there are men who say that he is incapable of friendship.

At any rate I had taken it for granted that we were friends when he went off to Paris and later, I am told, he attributed what happened to the influence of Scott Fitzgerald, and there is even a story, born in the brain of Hemy, that, wanting to leave the firm of Boni and Liveright, and that, figuring that they would not stand for an attack upon me, I being a special little pet of that firm, etc., he wrote the book to break his connection with the firm.

If I had ever been a special pet of the Liveright firm I wish someone had let me know of it. I might have got more money from them.

I got a letter from Hemy. This after he had written and published the book called *The Torrents of Spring,* and I thought it the most completely patronizing letter I had ever received.[26]

In the letter he spoke of what had happened as something fatal to me. He had, he said, written the book on an impulse, having only six weeks to do it. It was intended to bring to an end, once and for all, the notion that there was any worth in my own work. This, he said, was a thing he had hated doing, because of his personal regard for me, etc., but that he had done it in the interest of literature. Literature, I was to understand, was bigger than both of us.

There was something in the letter that was gigantic. It was a kind of funeral oration delivered over my grave. It was so raw, so pretentious, so patronizing, that it was amusing but I was filled with wonder. Just what I said to him, in return, I don't remember. It was something to the effect that I thought it foolish that, while there was so much to be done in writing, we writers should devote our time to the attempt to kill each other off. In the letter he had used a prize fighting term, speaking of the

---

26. *The Torrents of Spring* (New York: Scribner's, 1926). Hemingway's letters are digested in Ray Lewis White, "Hemingway's Private Explanation of *The Torrents of Spring,*" *Modern Fiction Studies,* XIII (Summer, 1967), 261–63. See also Richard B. Hovey, "*The Torrents of Spring:* Prefigurations in the Early Hemingway," *College English,* XXVI (March, 1965), 460–64.

knockout blow he had given me, and in my answer I think I did say that I had always thought of myself as a pretty good middle weight and that I doubted his ever being able to make the heavy weight class.

However I can't be sure. I kept no copy of my letter. I find that I am often inclined to think of what I consider rather clever replies I make long after the event.

I did not see Hemingway for a long time after the above incident. When he had gone to Paris I had given him a note to my friend Gertrude Stein, with whom he was also, for several years, friends. Later she told me, in regard to the above incident, that Hemingway's difficulty was that I had written two stories, "I'm a Fool" and "I Want to Know Why," and that he could not bear the thought of my having written them. She suggested that he had, in his own mind, staked out the whole field of sports for himself. He could not bear, she said, having anyone else write of sports.[27]

When he had gone to Paris I had given Hemingway several letters to friends there and among others one to Mr. Ralph Church, who was, at that time, a student at Oxford (he was specializing in philosophy), who ran over to Paris and, for a year or two, he and Hemingway were much together.

And then, after several years, I came to Paris and there was Church and there was also Hemingway and Church was amused. He used to go to Hemingway saying, "Sherwood is in town. Why don't you go to see him?" and, when he had said it, he told me that Hemingway always declared his real friendship for me.

"I am going to see him today," he said, each time when the matter was brought up, but he did not come.

27. For Anderson's letter of introduction, see *Letters*, ed. Jones and Rideout, Item 67. Miss Stein discusses the quarrel in *The Autobiography of Alice B. Toklas*, pp. 241–42. For Hemingway's version, see *A Moveable Feast* (New York: Scribner's, 1964), pp. 25–31.

The Anderson-Hemingway literary problem is discussed by Charles A. Fenton, *The Apprenticeship of Ernest Hemingway* (New York: Farrar, Straus and Young, 1954), pp. 116–20, 145–50, *passim;* John T. Flanagan, "Hemingway's Debt to Sherwood Anderson," *Journal of English and Germanic Philology,* LIV (October, 1955), 507–20; and William L. Phillips, "Sherwood Anderson's Two Prize Pupils," *University of Chicago Magazine,* XLVII (January, 1955), 9–12, reprinted in *The Achievement of Sherwood Anderson: Essays in Criticism,* edited by Ray Lewis White (Chapel Hill: The University of North Carolina Press, 1966), pp. 202–10. Anderson further refers to the matter in "They Come Bearing Gifts," *American Mercury,* XXI (October, 1930), 129–37. See especially Hemingway's review of *A Story Teller's Story, Ex Libris,* II (March, 1925), 176–77.

It came to my last day in Paris and I was sitting in my room, having packed. Church had told him of my plan to depart and there was a sudden knock on the door of my hotel room and there he was.

He stood in the doorway.

"How about a drink?" he asked and I followed him down a stairway and across a street.

We went into a small bar.

"What will you have?"

"Beer.

"And you?"

"Beer."

"Well, here's how."

"Here's how."

He turned and walked rapidly away. It was the sum of what happened between us after our having known each other well in Chicago, after what I had thought of as an old friendship, and, in fancy, I can still see the man, after the "here's how" and after the beer had been gulped, as he hurried away.

And so it was with Hemingway but what of Faulkner? After the New Orleans days and after I had made a fight to get his first book published, as I had with Hemingway, going personally to Horace Liveright, who was then alive, to plead for the books, as, with Hemingway, I did not, for years, see him again.[28]

It is true that Bill had dedicated a book to me [29] and he had written me no patronizing letters speaking of knockout blows, of his sorrow over my

28. Anderson discusses Faulkner in "They Come Bearing Gifts" and in *Letters,* ed. Jones and Rideout, Item 138, *passim*. Whereas Hemingway never acknowledged a debt to Anderson, Faulkner wrote thankfully of Anderson in "Sherwood Anderson: An Appreciation," *Atlantic,* CXCI (June, 1953), 27–29, reprinted in *The Achievement of Sherwood Anderson,* ed. White, pp. 194–99. The influence of Anderson on Faulkner is studied in H. Edward Richardson, "Faulkner, Anderson, and Their Tall Tale," *American Literature,* XXXIV (May, 1962), 287–91; Walter B. Rideout and James B. Meriwether, "On the Collaboration of Faulkner and Anderson," *American Literature,* XXXV (March, 1963), 85–87; and, finally, H. Edward Richardson, "Anderson and Faulkner," *American Literature,* XXXVI (November, 1964), 298–314.

29. Faulkner dedicated *Sartoris* (New York: Harcourt, Brace and Company, 1929) "To Sherwood Anderson through whose kindness I was first published." He also parodied Anderson and his style in William Philip Spratling, *Sherwood Anderson & Other Famous Creoles* (New Orleans: Pelican Bookshop Press, 1926; Austin: University of Texas Press, 1967).

death as a writer, etc., but there is an old story a man remembers. It is the story of the politician who, finding a certain man fighting him, speaks to a friend.

"What is the matter with Bill?" he asks. "Why is he so against me? I can't understand his hatred of me. I never did anything for him."

Not that my going to bat for either of the two men, mentioned here, was personal. They were both men of ability. I went to bat for that ability.

But I remember the story of the politician and, when, after a good many years, I was, one day, in New York, at a cocktail party and saw Faulkner there, I avoided him.

"It will be better," I thought, but presently, as I did not approach the man, he came to me. He took hold of my coat sleeve and pulled me aside. He grinned.

"Sherwood, what the hell is the matter with you? Do you think that I am also a Hemy?" he asked.

The Sandburg

I got into a quarrel with Carl Sandburg, the poet. It was at Roger Sergel's house. Roger had invited some men in to meet me and there were some women present. There was Lloyd Lewis, who wrote the beautiful book on Sherman,[30] and, among others, a young newspaper man, Percy Wood, of the *Tribune*.

And there was Carl. He was in one of his more elephantic moods. The women had gathered about him and he was making pronouncements. "President Roosevelt was so and so," "the farmers of the west were in such and such a mood," etc., etc. There was a sort of heavy finality to his remarks and as he talked I began to think of what he was.

"He is a kind of gorgeous phrase maker, nothing else," I told myself. The man did to me a trick he had done before. He spoke of some movie he had seen. It was a "western." He said there was a character in it that made him think of me. "He was one of your people, Anderson," he said.

I let that pass but presently I spoke, not addressing Sandburg but

30. Roger Sergel was head of the Dramatic Publishing Company in Chicago. Eleanor Anderson confirms the facts of this story. Anderson refers to Lewis' *Sherman, Fighting Prophet* (New York; Harcourt, Brace and Company, 1932). *Letters,* ed. Jones and Rideout, contains many items to and about Sergel.

someone else in the room. I spoke of a book I had been reading. It was the life story of the poet Vachel Lindsay and it had been written by another poet, Edgar Lee Masters.[31] I thought it a very fine book. It was the story of the suffering and the terrible death of one poet told by another but it was evident at once that Sandburg did not like my tone, in speaking of the two men. He began to make deprecating remarks and I grew angry.

It is an old story. Here, in the poet Sandburg, was, I thought, a man who had collected more, in respect and admiration, while giving less than any poet of my time. He began writing, came into his fame at about the time I did. He was presumed to be a part of a certain movement that sprang up. At the time there were certain men, Theodore Dreiser, in his own way Sinclair Lewis, in the theatre Eugene O'Neill, myself, I could easily name others, who were making a fight. We were all, I think, striving to bring life back into writing. To do it we had to tackle the problem of sex. We were called sexy men, condemned, some of our books censored out of existence. I remember that I had myself, upon the publication of my *Winesburg, Ohio,* been held, almost universally, in the public prints, as a filthy minded man and that after the book was published, for weeks and months, my mail was loaded with letters calling me "filthy," "an opener up of sewers," etc.

Which was all right. We men of that time had a certain pioneering job to do and we tried honestly to do it. It wasn't that we wanted particularly to speak of sex, but knowing, from our own experiences of living, what a vital role sex played in lives and, being honest workmen, we could not avoid doing what we did.

It seems silly to speak of it now but no man, who lived through what some of us did at that time, can ever quite forget it.

And here was Sandburg, counted so often as one of us and yet forever playing safe. It had always seemed strange to me that no critic had ever pointed out that the man never wrote anything that couldn't, when written, have been published in the *Ladies' Home Journal.*

He was a man who had never made a fight for any other first rate poet of his time, although it was true that he had occasionally had something to say for some minor and totally unimportant man and that night, at Sergel's, the women gathered about, he making his rather heavy pronouncements, I thought of a time when one of the Chicago dailies got several of the more outstanding American poets to pick, from the work of

31. See above, Chapter IV, note 15.

another poet, a verse they admired and how Ben Hecht made me a bet as to what Carl would do.

"He will pick a verse by some absolutely unknown and unimportant man, probably from Oklahoma," said Ben and he did.

And I thought it so also of his *Lincoln.* It was too full of horse collars for me. There is a kind of too earthy earthiness that makes you tired. I remember speaking to Carl of what I thought a curiously tender Lincoln written by Stephenson,[32] of South Carolina, and of how Carl had turned up his nose.

At any rate, that night at the Sergels, I left Sandburg with the women and went into the kitchen and was followed by Wood, the newspaper man. He had come to that place wanting especially to meet Sandburg. We poured ourselves a drink.

"I thought he was a great man, a poet," he said.

"And have you changed your mind, and why?" I asked.

"Oh, I don't know," he said. "He is so goddamned pontifical," he added.

We had a quarrel later and I do not now remember on what it was founded. It was probably my own doing. I wanted to quarrel with him and have no doubt I picked away at him until the quarrel broke out. Bitter words were said and I went to bed.

I was in an upstairs room in the house and I could hear his voice downstairs. He was speaking to Sergel.

"What's the matter with Sherwood?" he was asking and afterwards I heard him arranging to stay the night. He wanted to make it up.

"But I'll fool him," I said to myself and determined that, if necessary, I would spend the day in bed.

"I don't want to make it up with him," I was telling myself. Why, I dare say I was pretty petulant, pretty small. I thought that I would just stay in bed in my room until I wore him out and he had gone away.

And so I did stay until noon the next day. I went down the stairs and there he was patiently waiting.

"Why, what's the matter with you, Sherwood?" he asked. I had never seen him more pontifical.

"Why, you don't need to worry. They can't dismiss you with a phrase," he said and for a time I was puzzled.

32. Nathaniel Wright Stephenson, *Lincoln: An Account of His Personal Life* . . . (Indianapolis: Bobbs-Merrill Company, 1924); reviewed by Anderson in "Betrayed," *Golden Book,* I (May, 1925), 743–44.

"And what is the old bastard talking of now?" I asked myself and then I knew. He had concluded that I was upset because, in the evening before, he had not given his attention to me instead of the women. He had stayed over the night to reassure me. After all, as I had to admit to myself, the man was something magnificent.

Tobacco Boy

The play writer, Paul Green,[33] told me a story. He was raised, as a boy, on a farm in eastern North Carolina. It was in the great coastal plain.

He was ambitious, eager, strong. He wanted to go to college.

His father gave him a chance. There was a certain field.

"It's yours. You take it. Raise yourself a crop of tobacco."

Paul Green, as a young boy, must have been very much alive. He is still that way. Life bubbles and boils in him.

So he went at it. He did raise himself a crop of tobacco. It is a job.

First you must make your seed bed. The best plan is to go find yourself a bit of new ground. You go perhaps to the edge of a wood. For a long time leaves have been falling and decaying. The ground is rich.

You put some litter on it. You burn it over. This is to kill the insect life in the ground.

You prepare the ground. You put in the seed. You go to town and get a thin kind of cloth. It is called "mosquito netting." You stretch it over your seed bed.

The plants come up.

You have prepared your field, plowed it, harrowed it. You set out your plants.

But, for its strength, the tobacco plants are delicate. You must cultivate the ground. There is a certain worm. Look out for him. Every day you must go, lift the leaves, look.

"Ah, there you are."

33. Anderson apparently first met Green in 1931 and visited him in North Carolina in 1936. See *Letters,* ed. Jones and Rideout, Items, 205, 303, *passim.* See Paul and Elizabeth Green, *Contemporary American Literature: A Study of Fourteen Outstanding American Writers* . . . (Chapel Hill: The University of North Carolina Press, 1925), pp. 27–29. Anderson discusses tobacco growing in " 'Sold!' To the Tobacco Company," *Globe,* II (July, 1938), 30–35.

You keep after the worms, you cultivate, you pinch out the buds that will grow into blossoms.

You are not raising seed tobacco. You are raising tobacco to sell.

The tobacco grows. It puts out broad leaves. The tobacco plant is a magnificent plant. In all nature there is nothing more gorgeous than a field of tobacco.

So it grows strong and big. You cut it. There are some who cure the tobacco on racks, in the field. Others take it to a barn.

You must have a special barn. You must let the breezes blow through. You must not let too much dampness in.

Your tobacco must be cured properly. It may become spotty. Look out. You must know how to do it.

You make it into bundles. They are called "hands."

You pile it on a truck.

Now you are going to the tobacco market. Your tobacco is to be auctioned off.

Paul told the story of his experience. He went through it all. All summer he worked. He had no truck and his father had none.

He had to hire a truck. He went off with the truck and his tobacco to the tobacco market. The owner and driver of the truck was a neighbor.

He was at the market. Farmers had gathered in. Paul's tobacco, with that of many others, had been put in great baskets. It was on the floor. The floor was huge. There were long rows of tobacco.

There were farmers walking up and down. They were experienced men. The sale was going on. A group of farmers came to Paul's baskets.

Paul said he was leaning against a wall. He said his heart was thumping. Soon the auctioneer would come to his baskets.

There was a group of farmers idly walking. Paul said they came to his baskets. They stopped. They inspected his tobacco. They looked at it. They pulled out hands.

They laughed.

"Well, for God's sake, look at that trash."

Paul said he sat down on the floor, near the wall.

"I wasn't thinking of the money. I was ashamed," he said. "I was so ashamed I wanted to cry."

He said the auctioneer came and sold his tobacco.

"I didn't listen much," he said. He said he got, for his whole summer's work, just enough to pay for the truck.

He said he rode home with the man who owned the truck.

"We rode a long way and he didn't say a word nor did I.

"Night was coming on," he said.

He said that he and the man who owned the truck had got almost home before the man spoke.

"And what did he say?"

"He said that life was hell all right and I agreed that it was.

"And then," said Paul, "we both laughed.

"What else was there to do?" he said.

We Whites and the Negroes

When Frank Crowninshield was running *Vanity Fair* I often wrote pieces for him. I did one on the south [34] that he later published in a little paper bound booklet. The hope was that it would arouse the south's anger, that southern newspapers would flare up, write pieces about my article, for, in what I had written, I had more than hinted at a thing that in such a civilization must inevitably happen.

There are now the two races, the whites and the browns, the browns in a subservient position, young men and women growing up together, young brown girls servants in the houses of the whites.

A young white man speaking to me. "Sure a good many of us lose our cherry in that way."

I had spoken to several colored women of this matter.

"Yes, it happens. It happens less than it did in the old days.

"How do you suppose our race gets constantly lighter? It sure doesn't come through white women and brown men."

The south had seen to that. It made any such mating practically impossible in most southern states. To be sure there were a few such marriages, or at least white women and brown men living together in New Orleans, but the cases were rare and after all New Orleans was an essentially Latin city.

I had written the article for *Vanity Fair,* putting into it my own

34. Besides several small-town notes and stories that later appeared in *Death in the Woods,* Anderson published the following articles on the South in *Vanity Fair:* "The South," XXVII (September, 1926), 49–50, 138; "A Great Factory," XXVII (November, 1926), 51–52; and "A Mountain Dance," XXIX (December, 1927), 59, 110.

observations, things that had been told me by southern men and by negro women. It didn't matter too much if the south got angry. There might be a good deal of free newspaper publicity for *Vanity Fair* and anyway the magazine had little or no circulation in the south.

The scheme, in which I had no part, didn't work out, that is to say if the editors of the magazine really had in mind what I have hinted at here. The southern press didn't arise and spout. Several southern newspaper editors did in fact take the matter up and discuss it but they all remained quite sure.

Yes, the thing did happen. In the past there was a lot of it. However it was happening less often. The negro women were getting constantly more and more self-respect. There was a race pride growing in them.

That was about the tone of the newspaper editorials sent to me as a result of my piece.

However I got a good many letters, both from southern negroes and whites, and some of them were a bit startling. There were two in particular from young southern white women. They both said about the same thing.

"Yes. It's true. The brown girls have been getting away with that but some of us southern white girls are out to put a stop to that."

Both of the letters, one from South Carolina, one from a town in Alabama, spoke of an attitude of many southern white men in regard to southern white women. There had been too much talk of purity, the spotless white purity of southern white women.

"We are tired of being spotless or of being thought spotless. We are first women. We sure have had to stand a lot from some of our southern white men.

"They are running off to the brown girls.

"Well, some of us are loosening up. We aren't going to go on letting the brown girls have all the fun."

The two letters, in this tone, I received as a result of my article in *Vanity Fair* may have been fakes. I have no way of knowing. I do know that the south wasn't at all startled by my piece. If Crowninshield and *Vanity Fair* had in mind what I suspected the shot missed fire.

I was in the house of two southern white women on a big plantation some miles from the city of Baton Rouge. I was a guest in the house and it was a charming place to stay.

There were those two women running the place, of some five thousand acres, and there may have been a hundred employees, all negroes. One of the women was tall and strong of body. She might have been fifty and she had the frame of a strong man, a strong and kindly face, while the other was small, very feminine and gentle.

It was such a pair of women as you sometimes see, going through life together. There is between them such love as might be between a man and woman but, being with them, knowing them, you sense that it is not a Lesbian love. It is often a love based on natural loneliness, the desire for at least one close companion in life. I think the thing happens often between two men as it does between two women. There is among us, in the modern world, with all our new literature and sex perversions, the great Sigmund Freud passion that swept through the American intellectual world in my time, everyone trying to psychoanalyze everyone else, too much inclination to suspect all such relationships as I am speaking of here.

I have myself suffered from all of this. When some of my own earlier stories were first published a good many critics declared that I had soaked myself in Freud but it was not true. I had, at the time, never read Freud, had scarcely heard of him.

However a man, frankly out of the half world, once spoke to me of this matter. There was a story of mine called "Hands." It is in the book *Winesburg, Ohio.*

"We fairies," he said to me, "have a great fear of growing old. We are always after young and to us beautiful men. I myself often read your story 'Hands' aloud to young men among us. We are as we are. It is an effort to bring a little nobility into our relationships.

"I do not mean to suggest anything about the school master of your story. I am only trying to tell you that real love does sometimes enter into our relationships."

But I was speaking of negroes and whites, in the south and in the north. I was in this southern town, was a guest there and there were the two southern women.

They were I believe cousins. They had inherited the property and were running it. The house was huge. It was very alive. There were negroes everywhere, negro men coming in and out of the house, negro women, often negro babies crawling about on the floor of the house.

It was a house squirming with life. It was, I dare say, as close a place to what life may have been on a big slave holding plantation before the Civil War as could have been found in the whole south. There were the negroes, men, women and children always about, hens wandered in and out, against a wall in the dining room there was I remember a row of bushel baskets filled with eggs (the women went in for chickens in rather a huge way), there was a hen on a setting of eggs on an old unused piano in the darkened parlor, there was food, food everywhere, at each meal the long table loaded with it, sense of abundance.

The two women raised cotton, they raised corn, they had thousands of chickens, sold eggs, kept perhaps a hundred dairy cows, sold cream, milk and butter to distributors.

And in some way, in spite of a vast seeming disorder, the place was well run. The women made it pay. There were negroes in the place that had never been off the place. They had their own little village of huts. In the evening you could hear their singing and sometimes, when the stronger of the two women (I heard later that she occasionally whipped a negro man who got out of hand. She was the one who ran everything, managed everything.), when she was in the mood she sometimes had the negroes come into the yard of the house in the evenings, after dark was come, and sing for us as we sat in the darkness on the porch listening.

She went out to the porch of the house and shouted. Her voice was strong and commanding.

"Jim, Jake, Mose, Tom, Sally, Kate, Agnes, you old Lizzy, all of you singers come up here into the yard. We want you to give us some songs."

They came. They seemed to love coming. They sang beautifully. I had never before heard such singing.

I was with this woman, the strong one, and we were driving in her car through the streets of a nearby town and I spoke to her of something I kept noticing there as I had noticed it in many towns and cities of the south.

There were the negroes on the street, men and women, young and old, and they were of every shade of brown. Brown became a pale yellow, high rich mahogany became walnut brown, black, blue-black. The lighter shades however seemed to predominate and I spoke to her of it.

She flared up.

"Yes, it is true," she said.

"It's terrible," she said, "but there is one thing I would like you to understand.

"It is none of our boys," she declared. "It's just these northern traveling men, that's what does it."

It was I thought the whole south speaking in her.

[474]

When I was in Ohio, running the factory there, I met a certain highly educated negro girl. Her father was a political force in a mainly industrial town where there were a good many negroes employed. She had been sent off to some eastern college, was interested in political science. She told me some interesting things about her life, really impressions of life. Her father was a prosperous man.

"We lived in a quite large house. There were servants to take care of me. For a long time it never occurred to me that I was different from other children along the street.

"You see I am quite light in color but my father's color was a deep brown and my mother almost white. I dare say, back there somewhere, some white man. . . . It may have happened when mother's people were slaves.

"Anyway I thought nothing about it and then one day (I may have been five years old) I was riding with my father and saw a very black child.

"The child, you see, was playing in the street and there were white children about. I asked my father about it.

" 'What is that? What makes her like that?'

"It is strange but it hadn't occurred to me that father was different from many of the men who came to our house to see him. He more or less, you see, swung the negro vote in our town. White men, in politics, came to see him.

"They came as you came to see me. You are curious as to how I feel being a negro."

We were sitting on the porch of her house when she said this to me. She turned and laughed at me. She might have been twenty-five then. She had been through college, had got her doctor's degree in some eastern college. At that time the women's suffrage was just getting under way. She was working in the cause among the negro voters of the town. She was far from being a pretty woman. Her color was rather bad, a pasty sort of yellow, but she was all alive, witty, intelligent.

She told me how, as a small child, she had noticed, for the first time, that there were people, separated from the others about by color, of how her father had tried to explain to her. He had, she said, been very gentle. She thought it might have been later, when she had grown somewhat older, that he told her of all the difficulties she would have to meet in life, how she would be called "nigger" by other children, the difficulties she would meet with in travel, hotels that would not admit her. She said that when he finally talked to her of all these things she went up into her own room and cried.

"And I wasn't crying about the difficulties my father had told me I would have to meet in life. There was something else. I had got suddenly a picture of what my father's life had been. I saw him in a new way, was touched by what I thought must have been his patience, his gentleness. Why he hadn't gone about killing people who insulted him, as I could now see how, many times in his life, he must have been insulted, I couldn't understand. You see I loved him very much. I was his only child and he had always been so gentle and kind with me. I cried and then I grew angry. I was in my room, lying on the bed and crying, and then I got up. I suddenly hated all whites. I pounded on the wall of my room with my fists. However, later, I found I had to cultivate some of my father's patience. There was nothing else I could do. I did pummel and scratch some white children in the school yard and in our street who shouted 'nigger' at me but I wasn't very strong. Sometimes three or four of them went at me. They beat me and scratched my face. I had to learn to be silent, walk away. It was all I could do.

"And when these things happened to me I tried not to let father know. Mother had died and I was living alone with him. I thought he must have been hurt enough. I didn't want to tell him of my hurt."

I was in London. I was no longer a manufacturer. I had become a recognized American literary figure and had gone on a visit to England. Something a little odd had happened. Before I had left America I had got a letter from Mr. Van Wyck Brooks. The letter was about a man, from a city in upstate New York.

The man had been, as I had, a manufacturer but, unlike myself, had grown rich at it. He had become an American millionaire.

And then a thing had happened to him. It had happened to other rich Americans. He became ashamed of his wealth. For a long time he studied and brooded over the matter and more and more he became convinced that he had lived a life of sin.

He wanted to clean the slate, get rid of his money. He began to give it away. He had one sister and, before starting to dispose of his money, had bought her an annuity.

He had gone on from there, had thrown all of his money away, become a poor man, penniless, and then he died.

But he had kept a daily diary, had from day to day, as the notion that having wealth in a land where there were so many who were destitute was a living in sin, put down all of his thoughts.

The diary was in the hands of his sister and she had written or had spoken of it to Van Wyck Brooks. She thought it should be given to some writer.

"Who shall I give it to?" she had asked Van Wyck and he had recommended that it be given to me.

I had written to the woman and had got her answer. Yes, I could have the diary but she was in London.

"Shall I send it to you?"

This had happened just as I was about to set out for London and I had written telling her so. I was afraid the diary might be lost. I would see her there. I gave her the address of my English publisher.

"You write me there. Tell me where you are and I will come to see you." The English publisher would hold the letter for me.

I was in London and had got her letter. She was in the country but on a certain Sunday afternoon would be in London at a certain address. I was to come to the address for tea.

I got a cab and I went there. It was a long ride. It had turned out that the address she had given was far out. There was a row of rather comfortable looking frame houses each with a name.

I was to find a house called "Wildwood."

"Why, how very American," I thought. I thought of thousands of American houses called "Wildwood," or "Homewood," or "Hillcrest."

"They must have got it from over here," I thought. It was evident that, in the naming of their houses, the English were no more imaginative than we were.

"We, in America, must have got it from the Virginians and the Virginians got it from the English," I thought.

But "Wildwood" was an empty house. There was no one there. I had dismissed my cab and stood on the little lawn before the house, its curtained windows staring at me.

"So I have again made a blunder."

I took the woman's letter from my pocket. Yes, there it was. I was on the right street. The house was called "Wildwood."

As I stood thus, perplexed, before what was so obviously a vacant house a man, evidently some kind of caretaker, came around the corner of the house and I submitted the mystery to him.

"But there is no such person here. The house is empty as you can see."

"But there is this letter." I gave it to him to read. He scratched his head.

"Strange, strange," he said.

And then a light came into his eyes. There was, he said, a group, they were some kind of fanatics. They had rented a room on the second floor of the empty house. They came on Sundays.

"You go on up there. Open the door and go up the stairway."

He turned away with a gesture of his hand.

"You are another of the same sort? I can't be bothered with you," his gesture seemed to say.

I opened the door of the vacant house, found the stairway and went up. I had never seen the woman of the diary. I heard voices. I pushed open a door on a long room and there she was.

She was a very tall woman. As I remember her now she had very large feet and hands. I thought of Abraham Lincoln. Her legs were bare and she had some sort of barefoot sandals on her feet. She wore an artists' smock.

She came toward me, a look of joy in her eyes. There were some four or five people sitting solemnly on benches along the wall of the room and among them was my negro woman of the Ohio industrial town. She told me later that her father had died and that she had come to London to study political science. When I came into the room she smiled, a rather knowing smile I thought, as though to say, "Here's something. Oh boy you have got upon a hot spot now."

The room was bare. There were no chairs. There were some long wooden benches along a wall. There was a table in the center of the room and upon the table was a large cardboard box and over it had been spread some white cloth mosquito netting.

The tall Abraham Lincoln looking woman was coming toward me. (Forgive me, Abe.) There was a glad joyous light in her eyes.

"You have come. Oh how I have longed to see you."

She had her hands on my shoulders. She drew me close, looked down into my face.

"Oh but this is a great moment. It is historic. You are the man. You are the one we have most wanted. You so understand human nature. You are a genius. Now the work needs that most of all. It needs a towering genius to carry our message to the American world."

I had squirmed a little away from the woman. The others in the room, except only the negro woman by the wall, sat stiffly and with solemn faces on the benches by the wall. The negro woman was indulging in silent laughter. She squirmed and wriggled with it, fighting to keep it from breaking forth, breaking the silence of the room.

"The message?" I asked, turning to face the tall woman. "What message?"

"The message of love," she said.

She burst into a flow of words. She had come she said to England hoping to find there some great truth that would solve the riddle of human life. She had found it. In a certain village in England a group had been formed.

"Oh it is so wonderful, the life there. It is full, full.

"We are men and women but there are no men and women. We love freely in love."

I was interested. I became absorbed.

"And what do you mean by 'full,' dear? Tell me all," I said.

She took my arm and began leading me about the room.

"These," she said, "are city people who have become interested in our new life.

"Love is everything," she said again.

She spoke of marriage. Men and women had both known always that it was an absurd institution, she said. She declared that now that a group had been formed all men and women would soon begin living in a new way.

"You cannot really love just one person, you must love many." It was the only way.

For example, you had suddenly, being a woman, a secret longing to sleep with some man, or you were a man and had the longing toward some woman. It might well be that you had never, until the moment when longing struck you, seen the particular man or woman.

And what was the right thing to do? What did nature, in all its ramifications, in the animal world, in the vegetable world, in trees, in grasses, in fishes in the sea, prompt you to do?

"Why it prompts you to go at once to the other, get into bed with the other."

"And in your group you do that?"

"Yes. Yes. Oh it is wonderful. It solves all. It takes sin away.

"And you, you are the one. You might take our message to America."

"But your brother's diary? You know I came for that. I am interested in that."

She dismissed her brother's diary with a wave of her hand.

"Oh that!"

I was not, I gathered, to divert my mind with that.

"But you will give it to me?"

"Oh yes, sometime perhaps. It is of no importance now. Now," she said casually, "you must keep your mind clear for the great work."

We had got to where the cardboard box, covered by the thin white cloth mosquito netting, stood on the table and I raised a corner of the cloth and looked in. There were some caterpillars crawling about on the floor of the box.

"And what are these?"

She explained.

"We will be persecuted," she said. "All great new truths, when they were brought into the world, had to meet with persecution." She declared that they, her group, were ready to meet what would come. They would be persecuted. The time might come when they would be deprived of food and clothing.

"And these?" I said, pointing to the caterpillars in the box.

"Why," she said, "they are silk worms. I am cultivating them. We may have to weave our own clothes. They are, you see, a part of nature. There will be free love there in that box too," she declared.

And so I left, accompanied by the negro woman. I did not get the diary of the man, who, tortured by the feeling of sin because he had accumulated wealth, had day by day written down his thoughts. The diary was dismissed. It was a matter of no importance. The great thing was the message I was to take from that room in the vacant London suburban house to the American world.

I was outside the house in the street. I was with the American negro woman, who could now laugh freely. She had, she said, come to the place because she had been told that I would be there.

"I was even under the impression that you had agreed to become the business representative of the group.

"And besides," she said, still laughing, "I wanted to see if they were really so broad-minded as they pretend, if they intended to include my race also in this great revolution they are bent on bringing into the world."

I was in Mobile, Alabama, was living on the bay down there and, being new at that time to the south, was absorbed in the mixed life of the south.

At that time there were still river steamers, running up the river from Mobile to Selma in Alabama, and I often went for the round trip. The position of the negroes in southern life fascinated me. I was across the bay from Mobile, at a place called Fairhope, that winter, but before going there had lived, for some weeks, in a workmen's rooming house in Mobile.

The docks were, at the time, extremely busy. The World War was on and shipping was very heavy. Ships were being built in a nearby ship yard and I saw one ship launched then that was made of cement. I dare say it was an experiment. I never heard it failed. The idea was to build ships fast. I dare say a good many useless ones were built.

On the docks and about the shipping both negroes and whites were at work. The work was portioned off, a certain part of the work for the negroes, another part for the whites. The one job seemed about as hard as the other.

There was a thing I felt, that the negroes, when they were grouped, no whites about, were one thing but when a white man appeared I believed a change took place. I wanted to prove this to myself and so on several mornings I went, very early, and concealed myself in some piles of lumber near where a group of negroes would be, I knew, at work.

I felt that the thing I had anticipated did take place. When the negroes were away from the whites at their work there was a tone of sadness. The songs they sang were in a low key. They spoke to each other quietly and it was only when laughter broke forth that there was a change. To me the laughter was a bit too hearty. It shook their bodies. It was as though they were shaking a load off their backs.

And then a white man came among them and they became, I thought, self-conscious. They seemed to be performing for the white man, being for his benefit what they thought of him as wanting them to be. The slave and cook had not gone out of these negroes of the southern city. In the presence of the white man the negroes spoke of other negroes in the group as "niggers." They didn't do that when there were no whites present. Then it was Mr. James, or Mr. Smith, or Mr. Grey. In the presence of the white man there was no mistering.

"Hey you nigger. Mr. Johnson done spoke to you. Didn't you hear him nigger?"

A kind of human dignity gone, self-respect gone.

The men who loaded the river boat, the *Peerless,* on which I often took the trip up to Selma and back, employed for the trip a squad of deck hands. They loaded and unloaded cargo on the way up and down the river but did not load or unload at Mobile. For that job another group of negroes were hired.

So there I was on the river boat, just such a boat as Mark Twain might have been on, first as a cub and then as a full fledged pilot. I kept traveling up and down, the fare for the trip being very low and I having brought with me on each trip a basket of fruit to lighten somewhat the heavy and greasy diet.

I was walking up and down on the deck of the boat. I was in the pilot house, talking to the pilot. One of the pilots was a young rather handsome mustached fellow and a great braggart, always telling of great feats of piloting he had done, crews saved from disaster, etc., a great liar I thought, and the other a quiet and rather small grey haired man of fifty.

And there were the negro deck hands. They had a reputation of being a tough lot. They sang constantly. They had no beds or bunks but slept about, on bags of fertilizer, on the bare deck, and when feeding time came the food was dished out to them in tin pans.

They had no knives or forks. They ate with their fingers.

And they were called to duty at any time day or night.

It was a warm light spring night in that southern cabin and I was sitting in darkness on an upper deck of the boat. There was flood water in the river and great logs were floating down and now and then one of them struck the boat making a heavy booming thud.

And then, down below in the boat, bells began to ring. We were to make a landing and presently there we were, the gang plank out on a huge muddy bank at the edge of a deep wood.

There was a dirt road going away into the darkness of the wood and on the river bank stood a solitary white man with a lantern in his hand.

He was a small pale, or rather, yellow skinned man in shabby clothes. The flood light from the boat was turned on him. He shouted something to the mate, a tall gaunt man, and the mate began to swear.

He kept swearing, a string of profane words flowing from his lips.

And now the negro deck hands were at work. They ran up and down the gang plank at a strangely rhythmic lope. It was a curiously sprawling lope, all the muscles of the body relaxed.

They were running thus up and down the gang plank and along the dirt road into the forest. There was perhaps some trick of the light. Their heads, as they loped up and down, carrying cargo, seemed huge to me. They were carrying roughly hewn staves for the making of wine barrels from the forest to the boat. They sang as they pranced thus up and down. Their bodies as well as their faces seemed to be carrying the song. The song was a dance in their bodies.

There was that tall, sullen faced mate standing below. He swore. He cursed the workers. He was striving to hurry them but his swearing and shouting seemed to have no effect. The rhythm of the movement of the workers did not change and suddenly it seemed to me that the white mate down there was like a man standing and swearing at the skies or the spring moon because they did not move at his command faster across the southern sky.

I was on the lower deck of the boat (this must have been on another trip, perhaps in another year) and there had been low water and that day as I stood on the deck looking down at the slow moving water of the river a negro deck hand came and also looked down.

He looked and turning to another deck hand made a remark. "I see dey's working de road," he said and another negro came to look. Several came to look.

"Dey sure is workin' de road," they said.

I was puzzled. What had they meant? I went to the captain. I described the scene to him, reported the remark of the negroes.

"What did they mean by saying someone had been working the road?"

He said he didn't know.

"Very well, I'll ask one of them."

"But you must not do that. I don't want those niggers to think that sometimes, when they talk, I do not know what they are talking about."

The captain was a fat, rather jolly man and we had been friends.

"But look here. I am curious. I want to know what these men meant when, after looking at the river, they began talking of someone working some road. If you do not find out I'll go and ask one of them."

Again the captain begged me not to do that.

"I'll work it out. You give me a little time," he said. He explained to me that the negroes sometimes did seem to have almost a language of their own. I am not able to quote his exact words but what he said was that the negroes of the south had developed among themselves a kind of figurative language. He thought it might have come down from slavery days, the negroes, working as they did in gangs under a white driver, often wanted to say things to each other they didn't want the slave driver to understand.

"They make up these figures of speech.

"And now I've got it about this road work," he added.

He explained that most of the negro deck hands were country bred negroes. They were adventurous fellows, often what he called "bad niggers." They wanted to get out and see the world. So they became "river niggers."

"And up in that back country, where they were bred, the roads all during the winter are horrible and, in the spring, often the planters up there cannot get their crops out until the roads are worked for them."

He explained that, during the last trip up river, the water had at certain places been so low that in several places the boat had got stuck on sand bars. It had made a lot of hard work for the deck hands. They had to run ropes ashore, help haul the boat over sand bars.

"You see," he said, "there has been rain up river. The river is rising a little. That's what they were telling each other."

We were at the dock in Mobile. It was a hot day in May and we had come down river with a heavy cargo of fertilizer in bags. When the negro deck hands had loaded the boat at Selma there had been much low voiced cursing and groaning for the acids in the fertilizer, mixed with the sweat of bodies, had made festering sores on the shoulders of the men.

However, at the dock in Mobile the deck hands did not have to unload the boat. They had hired out for the trip only and their work was done. It was the custom aboard that boat to pay off at the last stop up-river above Mobile keeping back but one dollar of each man's pay.

That the captain had explained to me was what he called "tie-up money." It was held back so that the negro deck hands would not, the moment the boat touched the dock, jump ashore without waiting to tie up the boat.

So the deck hands had been paid off. Their work was done and they had been warned by the captain and the mates to say nothing to the negroes who would unload the boat about the nature of the cargo.

The negro deck hands had been marched silently off the boat, watched by the captain and mate, and had disappeared up a street into the city, the cargo of fertilizer in bags had been concealed under tarpaulins and we were ready to hire negro stevedores to begin unloading.

They were gathered together in a group on the dock. They had seen the deck hands march silently away. They were suspicious.

And there was the mate, shouting at them, swearing at them.

"You goddamn niggers, are you going to come aboard, sign up, or aren't you?" He kept swearing at them, pleading with them but no man moved.

They must have stood there, in silence, for a half hour and then one negro man did come aboard.

He went up into the captain's quarters and came down. No doubt he had been told by the captain to go and get the other men to come aboard. When he had gone down a stairway and along the lower deck of the boat, heavily loaded with its concealed cargo, he had perhaps lifted a corner of one of the tarpaulins. It was a scorching hot day and he would have known what the unloading of the boat, the carrying of the heavy bags of fertilizer on shoulders in that heat, would mean in festering sores. He went ashore and stood before the silent group of negroes. He looked up at the boat. The name *Peerless* was pencilled in big letters along the side.

He sighed. He shook his head. He spoke in a long voice.

"*Peerless, Peerless,* why that not the *Peerless.* It's the *Titanic,*" he said and immediately all the negro stevedores walked away leaving him standing alone while the long gaunt mate poured a whole river of profanity down on his head.[35]

I Build a House

I was in New Orleans and had been there through a summer and winter. I had very little money. Having lived through one New Orleans summer, with its oppressive heat, I wanted, if possible, to avoid another.

I began to write letters to men I knew.

"Tell me, if you can, of some place to which I can go, where it is cool and where it doesn't cost much to live."

The letters brought me several suggestions, among others one from Julian Harris. Julian was at that time running the newspaper at Columbus, Georgia. He had made a fine and courageous fight against the Ku Klux Klan and I was full of admiration for him. In his letter he spoke of a Mrs. Greear, at Troutdale, Virginia, and I have the impression that he said that Troutdale was a place to which his father, Joel Chandler Harris,[36] had often gone fishing. I wrote to Mrs. Greear and received an answer. I could, she said, come to live in her family for a dollar a day.

"That will be for a room," I thought. I found, in fact, that it meant a room, my meals, my washing and mending. It meant living in a delightful family.

So I was here, where I am now, in the Southwest Virginia hill country. I had come, by train, to the town of Marion, where I later ran two newspa-

35. For comparable tales see "Old Mississippi River Men," *Return to Winesburg: Selections from Four Years of Writing for a Country Newspaper,* edited by Ray Lewis White (Chapel Hill: The University of North Carolina Press, 1967), pp. 173–78.

36. Joel Chandler Harris (1848–1908), Georgia humorist and journalist, publisher of the *Atlanta Constitution.*

pers, one Democratic and the other Republican,[37] and from there went on to Troutdale by a lumber railroad.

The train, pulled by an engine geared to climb steep hills, with the drive wheels apparently flying at a furious rate, sparks flying out, often setting afire the neighboring woods, really crawled along at about ten miles an hour.

It was a strange, a new sort of country to me. On all sides were the magnificent hills, in the Greear family a troop of boys. They all bore biblical names, John, Joshua, David, Philip, Solomon. There was a corn field beyond a hillside apple orchard in a little hollow in the hills and in the corn field a small one room cabin that had not been occupied for years.

The cabin stood in the tall corn. It had no windows. For years the dust had blown in through the openings where the windows had been and through the open door. It was a foot thick on the floor.

The boys came with shovels and brooms. They cleared it out. They built me a rude table at which I could sit. They brought a chair from the house.

It was a long summer without rain in the hills and the daily train, from down in the rich Holston Valley, down in the place of paved roads and prosperous farms, sent sparks into the dry woods. The engine of the train, built for hauling long trains of cars loaded with heavy logs, went slowly. It crawled painfully up wooded mountainsides, throwing off the stream of sparks. The little lumber town of Troutdale was in decay. Now all the best of the timber had been cut out.

The town, in the hills, had tried valiantly to go on being a town. When the lumber was cut off and the army of lumber men had gone, the men of the town, the merchants, men who had saved money working in the lumber camp, tried to establish an industry. There had been a little bank and my host John Greear had been the cashier.

So all of the money of the community was put into the building of a factory and it had failed, impoverishing the little mountain community. From the Greear house I could see the remnants of the factory. It had all but a tall brick chimney been torn away and beside the chimney lay a huge old iron boiler to leer at you as you went past it on the dirt road that led over the mountains to the prosperous land beyond.

I was in the corn field at work. I wrote a book there, a book of childhood I called *Tar*. Often enough I had said to myself that a book should be so written that it could be read aloud in a corn field.

37. For a history and bibliography of Anderson's career in country journalism, see *Return to Winesburg,* ed. White, pp. 3–23, 207–11, 217–23.

I even tried it. I was alone there, often all morning at my desk. It was cool up there in the hills, or at least it seemed cool after New Orleans, and the sunlight came through in to me through the tall corn.

The corn had begun to wither in the long drought. When there was a breeze blowing there was a sharp rustling sound. My feet, as I sat writing, were on the warm earth floor of the little floorless cabin. The corn seemed talking to me.

"What an ideal place for an American writer," I thought. I grew poetic.

"The corn, the corn, how significant in all American life," I thought. I thought of all the great corn fields of the middle west, of how, when I was a small boy, I had often crept into the corn fields at the edge of my Ohio town.

I used to crawl in there and lie under the corn. It was warm and close in there. On the ground, under the tall corn, pumpkins grew. There was the singing of the insects. Little insects flew about my head or crawled along the warm ground. Then also the corn fields had talked to me. Like Henry Wallace,[38] whom I was to know later, I became, for the time, a kind of corn field mystic.

I even tried what I had often thought of trying. When I had written a chapter of my book I went outside my cabin and read it aloud to the corn. It was all a little ridiculous but I thought, "No one knows."

And the corn did seem to talk back to me.

"Sure, you are all right. Go ahead," it seemed to say.

I had rented an old horse and buggy and, in the afternoon, drove by many dirt roads over the mountains.

The old horse went slowly. I had a book with me and, putting the reins on the dash board, let the old beast take its own way. I might well have had with me a volume of George Borrow, *Lavengro* or the *Romany Rye*. They were books I loved and always carried in my bags.

I kept meeting mountain men and women, who turned to stare at me. The mountaineers are like the gypsies, described by Borrow. They look directly at you with a strange fixed, somewhat disconcerting stare. For a long time, after you begin to know them, they say little. They are watching you.

"What sort of fellow is this?"

38. Henry Agard Wallace (1888–   ), agriculturist in the government of Franklin D. Roosevelt and vice-president from 1941 to 1945. See *Letters,* ed. Jones and Rideout, Item 225; and "No Swank," *Today,* I (November 11, 1933), 4–5, 23–24, reprinted in *No Swank* (Philadelphia: Centaur Press, 1934), pp. 59–76.

Sometimes, as I rode thus, often in forest roads, some mountain man appeared suddenly out of a path that led away into the deep bushes. There was an old bearded man sitting on a log with a rifle on his knees. It was not until I had lived in the mountains for several years that Dave, one of the Greear boys, told me of how I was all that summer under suspicion.

"They were watching you, quite sure you were a revenuer," he said. He explained how people came to the Greear house asking. All of this was during the time of prohibition and the business of making moon was flourishing.

The mountain man was poor. He lived far from the railroad. His little patch of corn, often but three or four acres, would not support his family.

The mountain families were prolific. One of my neighbors, Will Pruitt, who became a friend after I built my own house in the hills, had nineteen children by one wife. He was still vigorous, still strong. He went out on horse trading expeditions. The farm I later bought had on it a little frame tenant house and after I had built my own house the American sculptress Lucile Blum once came to live in the tenant house.

She was young and beautiful. She bought and rode a great black horse and once Will stopped in the road.

"That woman," he said. "It's a good thing my old woman hasn't died yet.

"I'd never let that woman get out of this country," he said.

But that came later. I was there in that corn field writing. Some of the mountain men had gone to the Greears to inquire.

"Why, he's a writer. He's writing a book."

It seemed like nonsense to them. One of the mountain men later told me about it.

"You didn't look like that to us," he said.

He told me of how they had sent men through the corn, creeping toward my cabin. It may be that they heard me, spouting there in the corn field. It may have saved me. They perhaps thought I was crazy.

"Well, it's a good thing you didn't get out of that old buggy and walk about much in the woods. We'd have plunked you," the man said to me.

"We thought dead sure you were a revenuer but we couldn't be sure. There were two or three men drew a bead on you but didn't shoot.

"You came out mighty lucky," he said.

In my wanderings, with my old horse that summer, I went often along a particular road out of the lumber town. It was a little winding road that followed the windings of a branch. It kept crossing and recrossing the brook by fords. I got into a little valley between the hills.

It was a sweet little valley in which there was one small farm, owned, I was told, by a widow woman. She had lost her man. He had gone off to the West Virginia mountains, to the coal mines, and had been killed there. There were two small brooks passing through the valley and beside one of the streams, crossed by a long bridge, was a mountain cabin in which the widow lived with her children.

She was a sturdy woman and was farming her own farm and doing the work of a man.

Once I stopped at the house and, the widow being absent, I spoke to the children. They had come down to the bridge to stare at me.

"Does your mother want to sell this farm?" I asked.

It was a senseless question. I had no money with which to buy a farm. I was but indulging in a dream.

"If I had some money I'd buy this farm. I'd live here in these hills. The hunger may have come down into me from my father, who had, as a boy, been a North Carolina hill boy.

"If I could just buy this farm, I could live, comfortably enough, in that little cabin, over there."

My dream ran far ahead. Sometime I might write a book that would really sell. All of that country was full of beautiful building stone. I might someday build such a stone house as I had seen in England or France.

The children, frightened by my inquiry, had run away to hide but presently one of them, a young girl, came timidly back. She stood across the creek from me and shouted in a shrill voice.

Yes, her mother wanted to sell.

"She wants to move to West Virginia," she screamed and ran away. It seemed a curious desire to me.

Fall came and I still lingered in the hills that were now covered by color. An old desire to be a painter came back to me but I did not surrender to it. I had finished my book and had written and sent off several short stories.

And then luck came my way. Two of the short stories sold and I had some money and one day, when I was again driving through my little valley, a book in my hand, the old horse meandering along, the hills surrounding the valley covered with flowing color as though beautiful oriental carpets had been laid over them, I met a woman in the road.

Was it a woman or was it some kind of monster? I reined in the horse and sat staring. The thing was coming down the hill toward me. It was a woman with a great brass kettle, for making apple butter, on her head. I hailed the woman and she came out from under the kettle.

She was the coal miner's widow who owned the little farm in the valley below.

"Do you want to sell your farm?"

"Yes, I want to move to West Virginia."

Again that strange desire. I bought the farm there in the road.

A number of things happened. I went south again, to spend another winter in New Orleans. I wrote there the novel *Dark Laughter.* It is the only novel of mine that ever sold in a big way, that became what is called a "best seller."

And that is a story too.

Meeting Horace Liveright

It was a time when Horace Liveright [39] was the outstanding figure in the American publishing world. He was tall and very handsome. Having come to New York from Philadelphia he had got a job on the stock exchange and once, when I was lunching with him, he told me of how he had, by a quick succession of speculations, run a few hundred dollars into a hundred thousand dollars.

The man was a born gambler. At the time I was being published by Ben Huebsch who had taken my *Winesburg* stories after they had been kicked about in several publishing houses. I had been grateful to Ben and had stuck to him in the face of a good deal of courtship on the part of other publishers. I had been getting a good deal of literary kudos but little or no money on which to live and again a return to advertising writing in the advertising agency threatened.

When *Winesburg* was published Ben had taken a two inch advertisement in two magazines, *The New Republic* and *The Nation,* and it had advised people to get the book at the public library.

Ben had but one book salesman, a little cockney Englishman, and a

39. Horace Liveright (1886–1933), of the firm of Boni and Liveright, Anderson's major publisher from 1925 to 1933.

friend who ran a book store told me of how the little Englishman would open the door of a book store, stick his head in and say, "You don't want any tosh books, do you?"

Evidently they nearly all said they didn't.

There had been a book, *A Story Teller's Story,* from which I had hoped much. The book had been written with great joy. I had thought it might possibly remove the danger of the return to advertising writing. It hadn't and I was in a mood to try another publisher.

"My loyalty to Ben has gone far enough," I was telling myself. There was a whole row of books written and printed—*Winesburg, Poor White, The Triumph of the Egg, Many Marriages* (and how that book was cursed by the critics), *Horses and Men, A Story Teller's Story*—and there was I, always in the same situation, always being sucked in and out of the advertising agency.

So one day I was walking in one of the streets of New Orleans and there was Horace Liveright. He had come down there. He was striding along with a beautiful woman clinging to his arm. Horace was famous for his women, that I knew. I had already, on many occasions, seen him with many woman and they were always beautiful.

He stopped and introduced me to the woman he had brought with him to New Orleans.

"Meet Mrs. Liveright," he said and I laughed.

"But why does he need to do this to me?" I thought.

"I'll not let him get away with it," I thought.

"Mrs. Liveright, oh yeah?" I said.

Well, it was Mrs. Liveright and I was sunk and so was Horace. There was an uncomfortable moment.

"It may have been an uncomfortable moment for you but it was a lot more than that for me," Horace later told me.

However he forgave me. He came to see me later in the same afternoon and we went to drink together and, when he inquired, I told him that I was looking for a new publisher.

"It isn't that I am not fond of Ben," I said and "Yes, I understand. We are all fond of Ben," he said.

He made me a proposal that took my breath away. I had spoken to him of the advertising agency. "I'll have to go back there, begin again to write of tooth paste, of kidney pills, of how to keep your hair from falling out." There must have been a note of desperation in my voice and Horace, on that occasion, as always with me, was very gentle. We were at a table in the little New Orleans café and were drinking absinthes. He reached across the table and put his hand on my hand.

"So you are discouraged, eh? You think your books cannot be sold? What nonsense. You come with me." He made me a proposal.

"For five years I'll send you a hundred dollars a week. I'll not bother you. I'll take what you write. I'll sell your books."

And so a new and a strange life began for me. I gave Horace the novel *Dark Laughter* and he did sell it. The sales climbed up and up. I went on a visit to New York and saw my own face staring at me from the advertising pages of newspapers, on the walls of buses and subways.

I saw men and women sitting in buses and subways with my book in their hands. They were stenographers taking it with them to the office.

"Have you read *Dark Laughter?*"

That question being shouted at them from the pages of newspapers and magazines. I was there shouting it at them from the walls of the subway.

It was all very strange. I was as excited as a young girl about to go to her first dance. I wanted to go speak to the men and women holding my book in their hands. I was in the subway and got up and clinging to a strap stood over one such woman. She was at page 181 of my book. That would be where I told of the orgies at the Quat'z Arts Ball in Paris in the year after the ending of the First World War. I remembered the American newspaper woman who had, as an adventure, gone to the ball and was telling of it.

She had told much that I hadn't dared put in the book. I stood in the New York subway looking down at the woman whose eyes were fixed on the pages of my book. She was reading rapidly, turning rapidly the pages.

Why she was such a respectable looking woman. She was well dressed.

"She will be the wife of a lawyer, or a doctor or perhaps a merchant," I thought. She would live somewhere in a respectable suburb. She went to church on Sunday, belonged to a women's book club.

I was reconstructing the life of the woman reading my book. A few years before I had written a sort of fantasy of the flesh in a book I had called *Many Marriages* and there had been a storm of criticism. Again, as when I wrote my *Winesburg* stories, I was being called vile and unclean in the pages of newspapers and magazines.

I had been putting down feelings and impulses that had often come to me. Everything I had written in the book I had observed in the men and women about me. The very details of the story I had put into my book had been told me by a man, not, as in the book, a manufacturer of washing machines in a Wisconsin town, but rather a manufacturer of agricultural implements in my Ohio town.

That the adventures, told of in the book, could have happened to a respectable seeming American had seemed terrible to American readers.

"That was my mistake," I told myself as I stood over the respectable woman reading my book in the subway. In the book she was reading the adventures in sex were taking place in Paris and that made it all right. That, I thought, had had much to do with the success of the later book.

I returned to my Virginia farm in the mountains. Already, during the winter, the cabin, by Ripshin Creek, had been torn down and a log cabin, in which to work, had been built on a nearby hill top. It was to be a place in which I could work while the building of a new house went on.

For now I had formed rather grand plans. Money was, for the first time, rolling in to me. I was what is called in the south "nigger rich." I had determined to have a house of stone to stand at the recess where Ripshin joined Laurel Creek. There was a fine old apple orchard at that spot and my house, when built, would be protected from storms by the surrounding hills.

There was plenty of stone everywhere about but, in all the mountain country, there were no workmen who had ever built a stone house.

However, they were all ready to try. I had got an old man named Ball to be my builder and he was full of confidence. Bill Spratling, who was then teaching architecture at Tulane University, in New Orleans (He went afterward to Taxco in Mexico and set up as a silversmith. He prospered there.) drew some plans for me.

However, we could not use the plans much as neither the builder Ball or myself could understand the blueprints.

"But never mind," Ball said. "We'll get along."

Ball was a huge old man of near seventy who had been a builder of saw mills and it was said also that, as a younger man, he had been a famous moonshiner in the hills. I had been told that he was somewhat dangerous when crossed but he was always gentle with me.

He went about boasting of his new position. He engaged to have lumber sawed in the hills. He employed neighboring hill farmers. He set men to hauling huge stones. He stood before the store at Troutdale boasting.

[493]

"I'm something now," he declared. "I've got into a new position in life. I'm secretary to that millionaire who has moved in here."

But I was no millionaire. I had got a few thousand as royalties on my book *Dark Laughter* and there was the hundred dollars that came every Monday from Horace Liveright.

I was intensely bothered by that. There I was. I was presumed to be a writer.

"But a writer should be writing," I told myself.

And now Ball had engaged many of the neighboring hill farmers to work for me. I had built a small frame house in the valley below the hill on which my log cabin stood. It had been thrown hastily up. I thought, "When my stone house is built I'll use it as a garage."

I slept and ate down there but in the morning I arose and climbed faithfully up to my cabin on the hill. I sat at a desk by an open window and before me stretched away were the tops of other hills.

The hills running away into the distance were a soft blue in color. They were covered by forests and the trees were just coming into leaf. Here and there, on distant hillsides, were small cleared fields and men were plowing. A mountain road climbed a distant hill and a man on horseback went slowly up the road.

It was all too grand. I sat in the cabin and there were the blank sheets on the desk before me and down below, on Ripshin Creek, the materials for my house were being brought in.

Men were at work down there. My house was being planned. It had been determined that although the main part of the house was to be of stone it would have to have two log wings.

And now trees were being cut in the forest on nearby hills. We had got a small saw mill, a planer and other machinery, rented for the time. Men were at work down there and there was I up there on that hill, my pen poised in my hand, no word coming to me.

I sprang up and went outside my cabin to look out.

"Why I cannot write. It is too exciting down there. This is the great time in a man's life. We are all, at heart, builders. It is the dream of every man to, at some time in his life, build his own house.

"And so my house is to be built and I am to stay up here, writing words on paper. How silly."

But there was that hundred dollar check. It came every Monday morning.

Horace had said, "I will send it to you every week for five years. I'll take what you write.

"I'll not bother you," he had said.

But oh the power of money. It was all something new to me. Each week the arrival of the check was a reminder that I was not and perhaps could not be a writer while my house was building.

"But I am under this obligation to Horace." I went again into my hilltop cabin. What really happened was that I never did write a word in that cabin. Even after I got clear of Horace's weekly payments I could not work up there. It may be that the view from the hilltop was too magnificent. It made everything I wrote seem too trivial. I had, in the end, and after my house was built, to move the cabin down the hill, tuck it in away under trees by the creek.

But I was still up there and down below the work on my house was under way. I had to give it up. I took a train to New York.

"Please, Horace. Quit it."

"Quit what?" he asked.

"Quit sending me that money."

I tried to explain how it affected me.

"But," he said, "I have made enough on the one book. I am in the clear. Why should you worry?"

I had a hard time convincing him. He even became suspicious.

"Are you not satisfied with me as your publisher? Is that it?"

It seemed, as he said, impossible to him that a writer should refuse money.

And so I was released. It is true that, when my house was half finished, I had to go lecturing. It was bad enough but it was better than having the checks come every Monday to remind me that I was a writer, not a builder.

And this suggested something to my mind. Do you the reader belong to some literary circle in your town or city? Do you attend lectures by novelists and poets? Would you like to know something of the financial standing of these men and women? If so, you do not need to go to Dunn's or Bradstreet's. If they are lecturing it is a hundred to one they are broke.

We were hauling stones up from the creek for the walls of my house. We were taking stone from neighboring hillsides. Mountain men from all the surrounding hills and hollows were working for me. We sawed lumber, cut shingles, dug and laid stone walls. We built a dry kiln to dry our green lumber. Mr. Ball, that gigantic old mountaineer, ex-liquor maker, now past seventy, climbed like a squirrel over the rafters of the house. My brother Karl came and made a painting of the half completed structure and a drawing of Ball.

Ball had his own way of life. He built heavily the stone walls eighteen inches thick, all the lumber seasoned oak.

"I'm going to build you a house that will stand here until Gabriel blows that trumpet," he said. I had been told he was a somewhat dangerous old man when crossed so I rarely crossed him.

Most of the men working on the house were small hill farmers. They proved to be wonderfully efficient workmen. When there was work to do on their own farms, wood to cut for the wives, corn to be cut or cultivated, or even perhaps a run of moon to be made for the West Virginia trade, they did not come.

Well, it was all right. While the money, made from the sale of *Dark Laughter,* held out, I did not mind. Perhaps once a month old man Ball came to me. He had been, I had noticed, for several days, growing a bit irritable. I thought of shooting and knifings among the hill men. There was his son Ezra working on the job. He had killed one man.

"I'm afraid," said the old man, "that I will have to lay the men off for a few days.

"I'm not feeling so very well."

A slow grin spread over his old face.

"All right," I said. I knew what was coming. Marion Ball would hire a man who owned an old open faced Ford to drive him about over the hills. He would load the car with a few gallons of local white moon, would sit sprawled on the back seat. He would drive from farm house to farm house stopping to invite men to drink with him. He would make his driver stop while he slept for an hour beside some hillside road. It was his great bragging time.

"I'm going to build that millionaire down there the finest house was ever built in this country. They said I couldn't do it, that I was just a saw mill builder. Why that fellow down there, that writer, he trusts me like a brother. I'm his secretary, that's what I am."

Ball's vacation would last for perhaps three or four days and then he would reappear. He looked as fresh as a young boy.

"It rests me up to go on a bender now and then," he explained.

All sorts of annoying things kept happening. Old man Ball had his own notion of me. I was more or less a child who had to be taken care of. There was a fireplace upstairs in the house for which a stone arch had to be cut.

All of the mountain men, I had found out, were natural craftsmen. They loved stone laying. They had pride in the job they were doing.

An old man came down out of the mountains. He was driving a mule and sat in a broken down wagon. Later I learned that his wife was dead and that his children had all moved out of the country. They had perhaps, as so many sons of mountain men did, gone off to the West Virginia coal mines. The old man lived alone in a mountain cabin somewhere back in the hills.

He stopped before my house and came to where Ball and I were standing in the yard. He was nearly bent double with disease. In truth the old man was slowly dying of cancer of the stomach.

"Do you need any stone cutting here?" he asked. I thought of Tom Wolfe's father, in *Look Homeward, Angel*. This man was also a gigantic old fellow.

"And are you a stone cutter?"

"Why I have been a stone cutter for twenty-five years," he declared.

I looked at old man Ball. I had never heard of any stone cutters in the hills.

"Do you know this man?" I asked Ball. "Is he a stone cutter?"

Ball looked over my head at the sky.

"Why, I'll tell you, man and boy I have lived in this country for fifty years and some of the best men I've ever known in this country have been liars," he said.

Ball laughed and the strange old man laughed with him.

"Well I've heard of this building going on down here," he said. "You know, Marion, I ain't got long to live. I got cancer but I want a hand in building this house."

And so he got a hand. Ball took him upstairs to where the fireplace was building.

"We want an arch over that fireplace.

"So you claim to be a stone cutter. All right, you cut the stones for the arch.

"If they are all right, if they fit and look all right, I'll give you five dollars. Otherwise you don't get a cent."

Ball went about his affairs and I went up to where the old man was puttering about. He had got some pieces of string and was taking measurements. He kept tying knots in the string. He muttered.

"I'll show him, damn him. I'll show him," he kept declaring.

He put the pieces of string in his pocket, went painfully down the temporary stairway we had rigged up and getting into his broken down wagon went away.

"So that," I thought, "is the last of him. He will be dead soon now."

Very soon, after three or four weeks, he did die and we built a coffin for him. We built several rude coffins for hill men and women while my house was building. We took a day off and all went up to the old man's cabin to bury him.

And then, after several more weeks, it was time to lay up the arch over the fireplace and old man Ball came to me. We drove up to that other old man's empty cabin. Ball had had a hunch.

"We might as well go up there and see," he said. He had known well the old man who had died.

"You can't tell, that old fool may have cut them stone."

So we drove up a mountain road to the empty cabin and there the stones were. They were in a little shed back of the cabin and when we brought them down they made a perfect little arch for my fireplace. The old mountain man, with the cancer eating at him, had sat up there, slowly and painfully cutting the stones. He had managed to get a chisel and a hammer. He must have worked slowly, no doubt having to rest for long periods. He had wanted a hand in building my house. He had wanted to show old man Ball. He had done a fine job.

Many interesting and often revealing things happened. There I was in the mountains building my house of stone. It must have seemed a very magnificent house to all the neighborhood. Men from all the hillsides and hollows about came to work for me. Their own houses were, for the most part, small unfurnished shacks, often of one two or three rooms.

The civilization about me was not a money civilization. There was little money coming in. Moon liquor was about the only cash crop. When a man needed a new pair of shoes for his wife, a new pair of overalls, he sold a calf. Many of the people would have nothing to do with liquor making. Often they were Primitive Baptist and devoutly religious men. For the most part I found them trustworthy good workmen and honest. If they were suspicious of strangers, slow to establish friendships, they were also, when once they had accepted you, very loyal.

One of the mountain men explained it all to me.

"We wait until we are sure we can fellowship with a man," he said.

The Primitive Baptists (sometimes called in derision "Hardshell Baptists") were also foot washers. They had several big meetings during the summer, meetings called the "Big June," "Big July," etc. They were really great folk gatherings, often several hundred people coming out of the hills and hollows, to gather about some creek.

Whole families came, the young girls in their best dresses, the men shaved and bathed. They gathered in the road before the church and in nearby fields. All had brought food and everyone was invited to eat. In the church preaching went on all day long and among the young men the moon bottle was passed back and forth.

It was a folk movement in which all joined. People came in wagons and on horseback. They came in Ford cars and afoot. It was a great day for courting, girl meeting boy. If there was some drunkenness it did not amount to much.

In the church preaching went on all day long. The Primitive Baptists had no paid preachers. Their preachers, like the members of the congregation, were farmers. Abe Lincoln once said that he liked a preacher who preached like a man fighting bees. He should have been there.

There was another folk meeting that was very curious. Once all of our country had been covered with magnificent forests. The forests had been cut away and my neighboring town, Troutdale, that had been a prosperous lumbering town, was now half empty, small empty store buildings along the little main street, the buildings just falling into decay.

There were no negroes in our section. For years, before I came there, to build my house, there had been a tradition that no negro was to come to live in that neighborhood. It was all right for a negro to come for a few hours but he was warned.

"Get out before dark. Do not let the sun go down on you in the neighborhood."

I was told that the prejudice against the negro had sprung up because of labor trouble. When lumbering in that district was at its height there had been a strike and negroes had been brought in to break it.

The mountain men had run them off with guns. It had set up a tradition.

And then besides my neighbors had before the Civil War never been slave holders. Like the men of east Tennessee they had been Union men. Perhaps they felt that the negro was in some way to blame for all the trouble and hardship brought on by the war. Some of the older men had been forced into a war they didn't understand. Government had long been to them a thing far off. They got no benefit from it. Roads were paved and there were always government men interfering. They sent in men to stop their liquor making. They wanted to collect taxes.

"For what?"

What had government ever done for them?

There was this feeling about the negro but there was a summer Sunday every year when it was set aside.

It was "Nigger Meeting Sunday." On that day the negroes from all the far valley country to the north and south came to a neighboring high mountain top. They held services there. They preached and sang all day long.

And the negro congregations came. They were on the mountain top with the white mountain men, women and children. All sang together. All together walked up and down in the road. They became neighbors for the day. On that day negroes and whites fellowshiped together.

Life in the hills was changing. In a few years after I came into the hills to live a paved road was built over the hills. It passed through Troutdale. Big cars began running over the mountains. A garage was built and there were two or three bright shining gas filling stations. The people of the hills had long been snuff dippers but the younger generation stopped dipping. They went down into the valley town to the movies. A few radios were bought. In the road I saw a woman of twenty-five. She had been reading some women's magazine, had bought a cheap model of a dress of the latest New York style. Her lips, her cheeks and even her fingernails were painted but she still had a snuff stick protruding from a corner of her mouth.

It was a new world come into the hills and I was a part of it. To my neighbors I was a rich man. The few thousands of dollars I had got from the sale of my novel had made me, in their eyes, a millionaire.

There was an old woman lived on a side road near my house. She had a little farm, her man was dead and she with her young daughter worked the farm.

She was something special to me and often I went to visit her, to sit with her in the evening on the porch of the little unpainted mountain cabin. She was one who proved something to me. In the south I had been hearing much talk of aristocracy. I had not heard it among the mountain people but, when I went down into the now prosperous valley town, where later I ran the local newspaper, I heard much of it.

It seemed to me to be always connected with the former ownership of slaves, with the ownership of rich valley land and money in the bank.

To tell the truth I had grown a little weary of the talk of southern aristocracy and had been asking myself a question.

"But what is an aristocrat?"

I thought I had found one in the hills. It was my little old woman neighbor. She had pride. She seemed to feel no one below her, no one above her. She was very poor. She worked hard. Her little thin bent old body was all hardened by toil. When I had first come into her neighborhood, she had come to see me and what poise she had.

She had heard I was a writer of books. She came to sit with me.

"Mr. Anderson," she said, "I guess we are glad enough to have you come in here and build your house. You do not seem to us an uppity man but I thought I had better come and warn you.

"They tell me you are a writer of books but, Mr. Anderson, we cannot buy any books. We are too poor and besides, Mr. Anderson, there are a lot of us who cannot read and write."

It was a summer day and my neighbor, the little old woman, was going to mill. She was going to have corn ground for flour and went along the road past my new house half bent double with the load on her thin old shoulders.

I called her in.

"You are tired," I said. "Come and sit with me for a spell."

Now my house was half completed. Workers were scrambling up walls of stone.

We sat on a bench and I made a gesture with my hand.

"Tell me what you think of it," I said.

"Do you not think it is going to be a beautiful house?"

"Yes," she said. Her old eyes were looking steadily at me and again she said she did not think I was an uppity man.

"I guess we are glad enough to have you come in here and build your house," she said. She mentioned the fact that I was giving men work. They earned cash money working for me.

"But there is something else," she said. "We were all poor together in this neighborhood before you came."

So I had set up a new standard of life, had changed things, perhaps I was profoundly disturbing a way of life that had had its own values. I could not answer to the old woman. I sat looking at the ground by my own feet. What she had said had sent a queer wave of shame down through my body.

There was a great arch of stone to be built in my house.[40] It was a puzzle to us. However we laid it out in the yard in the apple orchard behind the uncompleted house and built a wooden frame for it.

We had no tools and there were no stone cutters so my neighbors began bringing stones and trying to fit them into the arch. A man, at work on the house, would keep his eyes open as he came over the hills from his own cabin. If he saw a stone he thought might fit into the arch he hoisted it to his shoulder and brought it along. We gradually got the arch quite complete, lying there on the ground in the orchard, and then the question as to which one of the men was to lay it up.

There was a good deal of controversy. Nearly all the men wanted the job but, after a good deal of discussion, it was given to a man named Cornett.

He did a good job and we all laid off work to watch him. The arch went up perfectly and when it was quite completed I went away to lunch.

Something happened. Why I dare say the man Cornett was proud of his accomplishment. He got ahold of a chisel, may have gone off to the valley town to buy it. He carved his name in large crude letters across the face of the keystone of the arch. He did it while I and all the others were at lunch and when I returned I was furious.

I began swearing in a loud voice. I shouted. Here was something, I thought, that we had all had a hand in doing and this one man has slapped his name on it. The keystone had been specially selected. It had a beautiful face. It was ruined.

I kept on ranting and raving and all the other workmen gathered about. There were shy grins on their faces.

As for Cornett he said nothing. He went out of the room into the yard and when I came out he stood with his coat on and his lunch pail in his hand.

"I want to talk with you. Come on down the road with me," he said.

"He is going to give me a beating," I thought. We walked in silence along the road until we came to a bridge. I had begun to be ashamed of some of the things I had said to him. When he spoke he spoke quietly enough.

40. As there is only one stone arch in "Ripshin," Anderson is giving here a variant version of the earlier tale.

"I'll have to quit you," he said. "I can't work on your house any more."

He explained that it was because all of the others would have had the laugh on him.

"I'll tell you what you should have done. All right, I made a mistake. Next Sunday, when none of the others are here, I'll come back and cut my name off the stone. But, if you felt you had to bawl me out you shouldn't have done it before the others. You should have taken me aside. Then I could have stayed on here."

The man Cornett stood on the bridge looking at me. After all he had done a fine job in laying up the arch.

"Let's see, you write books, don't you?" he asked. I said I did.

"Well, when you have written a book you sign it, you put your name on it, don't you?" he asked.

He had me there. I had nothing to say and with a slow grin on his face he walked away.

We had got near to the end of our job. The walls were up and the roof was on my house but there was the question of getting it plastered.

And then a man came, from some distant town, who was a professional plasterer.

He was quite frank.

"I'll tell you," he said. "I am a good man at my job but I get drunk and when I get drunk I stay that way.

"You'd better keep liquor away from me," he said and so I called the men together.

It was agreed that no one would give him a drink.

"We'll wait until the job is done and then we'll give the fellow a real send-off."

So the plastering was started and presently all was done except one room. I went away to town.

It was late afternoon when I came back and there was a scene I'll not forget. Ball later explained that they had all thought they could get a start on the celebration while they were doing the last room but the moon liquor they had secretly brought for the occasion must have been very potent.

The craftsman instinct in all the men had taken control of them. There was a scaffold in the room and one by one they had all climbed up on it. As they did this they had kept taking drinks of the moon and the plaster was already, when I returned, a foot deep on the floor.

It was in their clothes, in their hair, in their eyes but they did not mind. One by one they kept climbing to the scaffold.

"Now you let me try it, Frank."

"Now you get down, Luther. You've had your turn."

Several of the men had fallen from the scaffold and when I got there two of them were lying in the soft mess on the floor. They were shouting and singing. They were boasting of their skill.

"Come on, Anderson. You try your hand at it," they shouted when they saw me standing at the door of the room.

And so I went away. There was nothing else to do. I left them at their game and, on the next day, nothing being said, they all came back to clean up the mess they had made.

My house was my house. It is true that I had to go on a lecture tour to pay for having it finished and, when it was finished, I had to close it for two years, being unable to support living in it, but there it was.

It was a place for my books. It was a place to come and to bring my friends. It was, I thought, a beautiful house and in building it I had got into a new relationship with my neighbors. They were John and Will and Pete and Frank to me and I was Sherwood to them. I was no longer a man, a poet, a writer, something strange to them. I was just a man, like themselves. I had a farm. I planted corn and kept cows and, in the end, they found that I was far enough from the millionaire they had at first taken me to be.

Truly's Little House

It was built out over the creek on stilts and there was a board walk running out to it. I saw it standing there, very erect and proud when I went up past Truly's house to see if the creek was all clear of such houses.

It was illegal, having it there. The law demanded that all such proud little houses be so and so many feet from any running stream but we did not think too much of the law in the hills.

What had the law done for us? It interfered when we wanted to make a little moon from our corn, raised on our own land. It collected taxes, wanted to regulate our trout fishing in mountain streams, at that time paid no attention to our roads. The law was a given, rather determined thing, far off, that occasionally lit down on us. It even wanted to decide, if you shot another man, whether you were in the right or in the wrong.

Truly was a rather small athletic looking man with a red beard. He had cold blue eyes. He hadn't joined the others in helping to build my house. He was a man who asked no odds of any man. He was a good farmer and it was whispered about that he had money.

"If he ever made any he's got it," old man Ball once said of him.

I remember well that occasion. There was a wide spreading old apple tree, full of little hard round apples near the front door of my house and I had been fussing about it. The men were hauling stones for the wall of my house.

"Do be careful and don't bark that tree," I kept saying. I wanted the tree for its beauty, not for its apples.

It may be that I had fussed too much about the tree. Perhaps old man Ball was tired of it. I suddenly asked him what kind of apples grew on the tree.

"It's an apple we call 'the farmer's friend,' " he said and that slow grin again spread over his face.

"You take that apple now. You can keep it for years and years and years.

"It ain't worth a damn when you do eat it," he said.

It was then Truly came along the road. He didn't speak to us, or look at us.

"There are men who could make and save money in hell and there's one of them," old man Ball said.

It was after that I discovered the little house.

"I'll have to have it out with him," I thought. Our spring, from which we were to get our drinking water, was on a hillside above the house and by laying a pipe we could bring our drinking water to the house readily enough. It would obey we thought the law of gravity.

The creek, near the house, that murmured and talked to you at night as you lay awake in bed was another matter. It was fed by other mountain springs and was cold and clear. Such mountain streams do not come from a long distance and I had followed it to its source.

But there was Truly's little house.

"I'll have to have it out with him," I thought so I went up the road to his house.

He was in a field by the creek bottom. He was cutting corn.

[505]

I began to talk and no doubt, at the very beginning, made a mistake. I mentioned the law.

"The law says so and so." I had looked it up, and even consulted a lawyer.

"The law says. . . ."

I could feel him harden.

"There, there, I've made a mistake," I thought. I changed my approach. I offered to pay him for moving the house.

"You put it so and so many yards back from the creek. I'll pay the cost."

"All right," he said. He didn't look at me but turned and again began cutting corn.

"He is not going to do it," I thought. I was embarrassed by his silence and not knowing what else to say went away.

And then Truly began to talk. He went from one man to another.

"That fellow. He has come in here. He is building this house. He thinks he can tell us how to live.

"As for that little house, it is my house. I built it. The creek runs through my land. Does he think he can tell me what I shall do on my own farm?"

I had explained to Truly that I planned to use water from the creek for baths. I had built a tank, set in the ground on a neighboring hill, had put a hydraulic ram in the creek.

"So he wants to bathe, eh? He wants me to move my little house so he can bathe, huh?"

I was up against it. If I had the law on him I'd be in trouble. In our mountain country we do not think too much of men who appeal to the law. Formerly, when old man Andy Pierce was alive we said to go to him. We all thought old Andy a fair and square man. We both told our side of the case and put it up to Andy, let him decide.

But all of this happened before I knew of Andy and the power he had over neighboring opinion.

Should I go to law with Truly or should I not? I was puzzled and upset.

And then one day I saw Truly in the road. I had an inspiration. I stopped him in the road.

"Truly," I began, "I am hearing from all the neighbors that you are saying you aren't going to move the little house."

I could see the hard look coming into his eyes.

However I hurried on with my speech.

"They are saying that, they are all saying it, but they lie," I added.

"I've been telling them, I've told them, that Truly is as good a neighbor as they are," I said.

I had hit the mark. At once I knew it. For the first time Truly smiled at me.

"You're damned right I am," he said and walked away and on that same afternoon the little house was moved. It was put well back from the creek.

A year, two years, three years passed and, again, one day, I met Truly in the road. There was a field, half way up the mountain, owned by him, that was overgrown with beautiful wild azaleas and I had got a wagon load of them to put on the bank of the creek near my house.

I had sent a man to Truly and, "Yes, sure," he had said. "Go and get them."

He had said that he wanted the field cleared, was planning to plant it.

"Get all you want," he said.

I was there with Truly in the road.

"The azaleas I got on your land are very beautiful. I think I should pay you for them," I said but Truly scoffed at the idea.

"Why I couldn't charge you for things like that," he said.

"What kind of a neighbor would that make of me?" he added.

He started to walk away along the road and then he stopped. A grin spread over his face. After all, Truly is a careful man. He likes to get along.

"I guess you might pay me for moving that little house," he said and when I had passed the money to him he went away with a look of keen satisfaction spread over his face.

The Negro Woman

I was in a rich man's house. I was a guest there and they were being very nice to me.

There was a great house in the country.

This was in the south and there were many negro servants.

It was all beautifully arranged, very formal. The people of the house did not meet at breakfast. There were several other guests and everyone breakfasted in his room.

They met later in the day. They walked, they rode horses, played games, drank together.

In the evening, often, there was music.

The master of the house arranged to have some of the negroes come in the evening to sing.

They did not come into the house. There was a wide veranda on which the whites sat while the negroes, men and women, stayed at some distance half hidden among trees. The man who had bought the southern house with some thousands of acres of land was from a distant city. He had made a fortune in the city and was spending it on the land.

He was a collector of first editions of books. He bought painting. After he had made his fortune he, with his wife, had traveled abroad in many lands. Their southern house was filled with art objects from many lands. There were so many art objects that they had become meaningless. They meant nothing.

The negro people were indistinct, in the darkness. They sang negro spirituals. They sang negro work songs.

The singing was very beautiful. The voices seemed to run away into the dark distance, under the trees, across distant fields. The voices ran away and came back. The voices were along the ground, in the grass. They were in the tree tops.

Voices called to each other. I had never before heard such singing. There was one high color negro woman's voice that seemed to go up to the stars in the blue-black southern sky.

It did something to me. It seemed to me that, for the first time, I saw something clearly. I sat among the other guests in the rich man's house thinking what were, to me, new thoughts. My thoughts concerned the land on which stood the great house in which I was a guest.

The house was in the so-called "Sugar Bowl" in the lower delta country of the Mississippi.

There were many flat acres of sugar cane fields stretched away from the river and the levee. In the distance there were forests, in a low swamp land, forests of cypress and gum trees.

It was a dark land, a strange rich land. The negroes had been there a long time. Negroes singing that night, standing in the darkness in a grove of live oaks hung with ghostly moss, had been born on the land.

From childhood they had worked in the fields. Their ancestors had been slaves on the land. It was under their fingernails, in the creases of their flesh, in their crinkly hair, in their eyebrows.

As I sat that night listening to the singing negroes something came clear to me. It concerned ownership.

[508]

How could a man really own land, own trees, own flowing water of rivers? The land had been there so long.

There was a rich man who had made money and what a strange thing money. The man had been shrewd. He had, no doubt, a certain talent, the talent of acquisitiveness. There had been in him an instinct that had enabled him to see certain opportunities. At a certain critical moment he had bought certain stocks.

Then, at just the right moment, he had sold them and bought other stocks.

Stocks were like money itself. There were certain pieces of paper with words printed upon them.

In the case of money, the picture of some man, a president.

Oh the power of words.

"I promise to pay . . . ," etc.

You could burn the pieces of paper and they were gone.

The land remained. The trees, the grass, the flowing brown water of the river remained.

Burn the trees and they would grow again.

The land was there before man came. It would be there when there were no men left.

But there were certain people, the poor whites of the south, the negroes, slaves and free, farmers of the middle west, who worked their own fields, who were related to the land.

There had been a marriage, man and the land.

Sometimes also woman and the land.

The land was in them as a lover is in his sweetheart in the embrace of love.

So, as far as ownership, it is their land as a man's wife is his wife.

The thought set down above coming to me as it did, in a certain house in the south on a certain night, was no doubt not a new thought in the world but such thoughts mean nothing to a man when set down in books, when expounded by some speaker, some political revolutionist. The thought was in the throat of the negro singers, it was in the trees under which they stood in the southern night sky. It explained so much of the south, the land distinction of the predatory whites, the secret hatreds, the insistence upon white supremacy, the secret jealousy of something the negroes had, of something that had come into them from the land as it sifted through their black fingers. I was suddenly quite sure that the man sitting beside me that night, my host, the rich man, deep down within himself would have given all his wealth to have been, not as he was, the overlord, but one of the brown men, a man close to the land, living simply, as an animal lives.

He had gone about seeking something he did not have. What did all of his buying of pictures, his collecting of objects of art, of first editions, mean?

It meant obviously an attempt to buy his way out of one world into another, to, at any rate, get a little close.

He had even said something of the sort to me.

A few months earlier he had come to me. He had wanted very much to buy the manuscript of my *Winesburg, Ohio*.

Did it exist?

Yes. It existed.

The book had been written on the pages of a cheap tablet. It had been written in a Chicago rooming house. The manuscript existed only because a certain woman, at the moment in love with me, had collected the scrawled sheets, thrown carelessly aside, and had saved them.

She was, at the moment, in love with me but was I in love with her?

Probably not.

I had valued her because she had kept saying to me, "You are good. These little stories you are writing are wonderful."

Her words had been sweet music to my ears. I had, for the moment, thought her very wonderful.

So the manuscript had been saved and later, when it began to have some value, I had managed, because the woman who had saved it had died, by lying to her sister, by telling her sister that the dead woman had only been keeping it for me, by such crookedness I had got it back.

So there it was, in my possession, and did I value it?

I did not.

I had been told that, someday, it would bring me money.

Well I wanted money, was always hungry for money. I was no fool. Well enough I knew that, without money, the artist man is helpless enough.

So there had been this rich man who had come to me, wanting to buy my manuscript, and I had been shrewd.[41]

41. The major collector of Anderson's manuscripts was Burton Emmett (1871–1935), a New York advertising executive. See *Letters,* ed. Jones and Rideout, Items 174, 209, 233, *passim;* and "Burt Emmett," *Colophon,* N.S. I, No. 1 (Summer, 1935), 7–9.

Was I shrewd or had a moment of honesty come to me?

I had not yet sold the rich man the manuscript.

I had laughed at the man.

"But why do you want them, these sheets of cheap paper upon which certain words have been scrawled?"

I had told the rich man that his wanting the sheets upon which certain stories had been scribbled was like wanting an old dress, discarded by a woman, rather than the woman herself.

However the rich man had been patient with me. He had invited me to be his guest. This was in the winter and I was hungry for the south and the sun. I had been given a separate house, at the foot of a path lined with bushes. It was by a little quiet bayou.

I slept there and, as it was winter, there were no mosquitoes.

In the early morning an old negro woman, very black, a huge old woman with big hips, came to me. The door and windows of my little one room house were open and there was a sharp tinge of frost in the air.

The old woman had brought me a pot of hot black coffee. She built a warm fire in my fire place.

I was in bed, drinking my coffee. I began a conversation with the old woman. She had lived as a child in the West Indies. A kind of friendship sprang up between her and me. I lied to her, told her I had negro blood in my veins. It was a trick I had got from my father.

If you are with a Catholic become, for the time, a Catholic, if with a Swede a Swede, if with an Irishman Irish. There was, I had told the old black woman, a grandfather who having much white blood had gone north and had gone white. The old woman was not to tell my secret.

"You can see I am here, a guest. You come here and wait on me. I can go up to the big house, can live there. By law, by all the social customs of the south, I am, really, like you, a negro."

There was something established between me and the negro servants about the rich white man's house. The servants were always coming secretly to my little house. I was presumed to be at work there, creating masterpieces. The rich man and his other guests were impressed. I must not be disturbed.

I was getting many stories out of the lives of the negroes on the place. It pleased them that I was, as they thought, cheating the whites. I was gathering up all of the servant's gossip.

There was one young negro woman, very straight and strong of body, who came often, secretly, to my cabin. She had stolen a bottle of champagne which she brought to me. Sometimes she came late at night when I was in bed. She had brought some delicacy from the kitchen.

She came in and sat on the edge of my bed. She had heard the white guests speaking of me and my work.

She was impressed.

"So you are really one of us? They look up to you. You should be telling the story of our lives."

There was one of the guests, a young white man who had married a rich woman much older than himself. He was after the young negro woman.

He was giving her money.

He had given her a ten dollar bill. When she went into the room where he slept with his wife he came in there.

She had gone in the late morning to make up the bed, to arrange the room, and he had been watching for her coming.

He was somewhere about the house or he was sitting with the other guests on a terrace before the house and when she went upstairs, to arrange the rooms, she made a point of letting him see her.

She said he always sat, in the late morning, where he could see her going up the stairway. He was a great horseman. He had on riding britches. There was always something he had left in his room so he followed her up.

She said, "I let him kiss me. I let him hold me in his arms. I keep promising him I will meet him outdoors at night.

"I am not married but I tell him I am. I tell him my husband is watching me.

"I pretend I am crazy about him. When he is holding me in his arms I cry a little and when I do he always gives me money.

"He has given me several presents. He thinks he is going to get me but I am only fooling with him."

The young negro woman was sitting on the edge of my bed. She laughed, the laugh of the negro woman. I was smoking cigarettes and she asked for one. She sat smoking with me. She told me little human stories of the rich man, his wife, the other white guests. One night she came at two in the morning. It was the woman's time. She had become the daughter of the moon. She explained that it was always a terrible time for her.

She was in great pain. She said that the great pain lasted but a few hours but that, at such times, she could not bear to be alone.

"I want someone to be with me and hold my hand and I do not want a woman. I want a man."

I put her into my bed and, having put on my bath robe, sat beside her holding her hand.

She kept groaning. Tears ran down her cheeks. It was a cold clear moonlight night and the moonlight came in through the open door. I could feel with her the spasms of pain. When they came her hand gripped my hand so that my fingers ached. It was like a childbirth. When it had passed she got up and I returned to my bed. She had gone out of my little house but presently returned. She had been with me nearly three hours and soon day would come. I felt curiously close to her.

She came running back into the cabin and kissed me on the cheek. I was smoking a cigarette.

"I guess it is better for you to stay white. If you took one of us, me for example, it would spoil it all.

"It is better for you to stay white. You get all the best of it by being white."

For a moment she stood thus beside my bed, in the moonlight. She was of a light brown color and the moonlight, coming through the door, made highlights on her brown skin. She stood thus, in silence, for a time, looking down at me. To her it was inconceivable that a white man, a real white, could tell a lie, claiming negro blood. She believed my lie. She wanted me to go on fooling the whites.

She went slowly out of my cabin and while I remained a guest in that place she did not return to me again.

VI

The Thirties

I have already told of how, after years of waiting for the publisher Ben Huebsch to make me a living, feeling very loyal to him because he did publish my *Winesburg* after I had almost given up finding a publisher for the book, I went with Liveright's.

And what a place. Here in this publishing house was none of the dignity, the formality of the older publishing houses, the Scribner's, Harper's, Century, Macmillan's, etc.[1] The place was a sort of mad house and I remember that when I told Ben Huebsch that I would at last have to quit him and that I was going to Horace Liveright he was shocked.

For Horace was in and out of the stock exchange. He was in the theatre. When you went to see him in his publishing house often enough the whole outer office was filled with chorus girls.

Horace it seemed was figuring on putting on a musical comedy and there they were. It wouldn't have surprised me when I went there to have had one of the women jump up and taking a practise swing kicked my hat off.

And there was Horace in the midst of it all. Men and women were rushing in and out, phones were ringing. Horace was talking on the phone to casting agencies in regard to players for some show he was producing, he was buying or selling shows through some broker, authors were coming and going. It was a bedlam, a mad house, and yet a man felt something very gratifying in it all.

"At least this man is not going to tell me how to write my book," you thought.

The man had a way of trusting his authors. If at that time you went to him with a new man, and during the days of his splendor I did take both Hemingway and Faulkner to Horace with their first printed books, he took your word for it.

"Do you think they are all right, men of real talent?

"All right. I'll take them on. You send them to me."

And there was his check book, always at hand, often with a bottle of whisky on the desk beside it. You knew some young author who needed a little lift. You thought he had talent.

1. On Horace Liveright, see *Letters of Sherwood Anderson,* edited by Howard Mumford Jones and Walter B. Rideout (Boston: Little, Brown and Company, 1953), Items 106, 114, 115, 119, 128, 164, 167, 172, *passim.* For a comparable impression of Liveright, see L. Kronenberger, "Gambler in Publishing: Horace Liveright," *Atlantic,* CCXV (January, 1965), 94–104.

"If he had five hundred, a thousand dollars. . . ."

"All right. If you think he has the stuff send him in. I'll fix him up."

It was all rather crazy, rather splendid. Horace was a gambler and, if he believed in you, would gamble on you and I have always thought, since the man's death, that too much emphasis has been put on the reckless splendor of the man rather than his never failing generosity and his real belief in men of talent. I dedicated one of my books to him and I have always been glad I did.[2] In a way I loved the man.

As he lived he died. Certainly it was not his generosity to authors that broke him. The stock exchange did that and I shall always remember the last sight I had of him.

His publishing house had failed, being dragged down by his plunges in the stock exchange, and after an attempt to find for himself a place in Hollywood he had returned to New York.

On the street I saw Tommy Smith who had been his editor-in-chief.

"Horace," he said, "is at such and such an address. He is in bad shape. Do go and see him."

And so I went to the address given and there he was. It was summer and some friend had given him the use of his apartment. He was there, surrounded, as always, by people. It was morning but there had evidently been a night of carousal and Horace was in black pajamas.

As for the people about him they were of a sort you would only find in New York. They were failures in the theatre, men and women who hadn't made it but were desperately keeping up a bluff. There was much loud talk, much boasting.

Horace was sitting on a couch and the morning sun was streaming through a window. He was very pale, very thin and one of his long arms had almost withered away.

I was told later that the withered arm was the result of a struggle with a woman. It was said that she had bitten him and that the arm had become infected.

And so I stood in that place, in that motley crew. There were drinks going about. I had seen a few weeks before the picture called *The Cabinet of Dr. Caligari* and Horace had become that.

He was I think a little ashamed of his surroundings. He arose and went with me into a hallway. He put his good arm about my shoulder.

"Well, what the hell, Sherwood. I've sunk," he said.

---

2. Anderson dedicated *A New Testament* to Horace Liveright.

He said that and then braced. His shoulders straightened a little. I said something about his having lost control of his publishing house. As he knew and I knew the house had been sold by the receivers at a low price. Its glory was quite gone. It had been something no other publishing house in America had ever been. It had put me on my feet.

"Why I am not out of the publishing house," Horace said proudly.

"It is to be reorganized on a big scale," he said.

He said that he did not think that, with all the other interests he had, in the theatre, in Hollywood, on the stock exchange, he would be able to take any very active part in the new and bigger Liveright's.

"I'll just be chairman of the board," he said and then with a bitter little laugh and knowing that I knew what I knew he turned and walked away.

As for myself I took the elevator down out of that apartment building and walked in the street below with tears blinding my eyes.

A Man

I

A woman friend had invited me to the christening of her child. She stayed with me, promised me that, if I would come to the christening, she would name the child for me. I went and she didn't.

This was in the city of Washington. I went in my car.

I was sitting in the room where the christening had taken place and we were drinking champagne. I was a little high. I felt gay. I was happy. I was in a room with many well dressed people. I did not know many of them. Probably they were rich.

I liked being there. I liked the feel of the people gathered about. They had christened the child and had taken it away. I remember little of that. All babies look alike to me.

I have always liked women beautifully dressed. There is something in the touch of fine fabrics that sends a thrill through my body. I love to feel, touch, see.

I remember when I was a boy standing on a winter day by a pond where people were skating. I was of a very poor family and had no skates. There were holes in my shoes.

I was with some other boys, standing about, and we had got wood from a nearby place of trees and had built a fire. There was a young man, the son of the rich man of our town, who skated up to us. He wanted someone to hold his overcoat. He was a young man who had come back to our town from some eastern college for the Christmas holidays. He was an only son. He lived with his father and mother at the upper end of our town.

He skated up to me.

"Here, kid. You hold my overcoat," he said.

Afterwards he gave me twenty-five cents.

He was accompanied by a young woman, one I had never before seen, and who was, I thought, beautifully clothed. I do not know how long I stood there by the fire, holding his coat.

I only remember the feel of it in my hands. There was some sort of soft fur at the collar of the coat. It was lined with silk. The fabric of which the coat was made was good to the touch.

Oh, how good the coat felt in my arms. There may have been in me some sense of the good workmanship employed in making the coat. A man remembers such moments in a somewhat barren childhood.[3]

I was at this other place with the fortunate ones. A child had been christened. I had been told that it was to bear my name. It hadn't happened.

Perhaps the woman who had said that had forgotten. It didn't matter.

I was a little high, full of champagne. There were many voices in the room. What seemed to me, at the moment, very beautiful women kept coming up to me. I drank with them. We touched glasses.

And then suddenly Maurice came into the room. He was a big man, an Irishman with a big head. He was a proud man, an adventurer in life.

He was, at that time, rich but he had been poor.

He had come to America as a young lad. He was poor then, a young lad off some poor Irish farm. There was a curiously alive gay quality, such as I have known in other Irishmen, George Daugherty, I knew in Chicago, Paddy Walsh, of Tucson, in Arizona, the Irish poet Padriac Colum.[4] Later Maurice and I had many long talks of his childhood and my own. We told each other stories, some of them perhaps true, many of them, I am sure, pure inventions. He had come to America on money lent him by an uncle, who was in politics here.

3. See *Tar: A Midwest Childhood* (New York: Boni and Liveright, 1926), p. 278. This essay concerns Maurice Long, owner of a laundry in Washington, D.C.

4. Padraic Colum (1881–), Irish-born dramatist and poet.

He came, a green Irish boy, to a certain American city and, right away, he got a political job, landed a job.

He was in politics and then in business. He arose and fell. He was a big laughing man. He had a big head, covered, when I saw him first, with a mass of iron-grey hair. He was a woman lover, a life lover. Later he died suddenly, just as he and I together were about to set off on a journey.

We had made plans. We were always making plans.

"I am rich now," he said to me. "I have all my life been looking for a comrade. We will go look at the world."

We had planned to go together in a car. We would see America first. We planned to spend a year, two years, five years just drifting about.

"None of us know anything about people," he said to me that first time we met at the christening of the babe.

"We'll go look," he said. "And look. And listen."

It was understood there was enough money, nothing financial to worry us.

It was all arranged. And then he suddenly died. I thought it was unfair. After he died he kept coming back into my dreams. Sometimes, when I was in a half sleep, I saw him in my room.

"You are a cheat, for dying," I cried.

There was however a period of two or three years. He came often to see me and I went to him. When we were together, with other people, we both became wonderful.

He was a man who set me off.

I set him off.

He was a story teller and sometimes I was also good.

We knew how to feed up to each other. We made openings. There have been, during my life, some three, four, perhaps six or eight men I have truly loved. I loved Maurice.

I remember how it came over me, a kind of gladness, that first time I saw the man. It was like being in the surf, at the ocean's edge, on a hot day.

A great wave came and you plunged into it. You let it carry you along. It tumbled you about, played with you. What did it matter?

Why is it that men, as males, constantly deny their inheritance, the love of the male for the male? The love of man for woman is a different matter. The two passions are not alike. The whole thing has nothing to do with a man's being, or not being, a fairy.

I have always been afraid of fairies. They sell you out. They are in some queer way outside the life stream. They know it. The male lover of the male is something else. It is something that must, someday, come back into the world.

It must be proclaimed. Walt Whitman proclaimed it. It must be understood. Upon the understanding of it, the acceptance of it with pride, may hang the chance we males have of again getting, a little again, on top of our lives.

Maurice was a man I loved. We were comrades. He had always been muddled about women, as I had been, both of us loving them, both of us wanting permanently some precious things we thought they might give. How many talks we had of it. These talks were had often in a car, long after midnight, in both of us a deep sense, I think, of the mystery of existence.

Often Maurice or myself sinking into vulgarity, as men do.

Not wanting that.

The fact that he was rich and I was not not mattering. He used, sometimes, to laugh at me.

"I used to think of you, a good deal, before we met," he said.

"There are a few tales you have told in print that get down close. And now to find you confused as I am confused."

It made a kind of open thing between us, the man my friend, with a life so different from my own. He was so much more physically handsome than myself. Wherever we went, the women, like flocks of birds, were always flying about and after he died I got many letters from women.

I saw some of them, talked to some of them and they all said the same thing.

"If he had only let me I could have given him what he wanted, what he needed," they said.

Oh the vanity of women.

Thinking that they can fulfill a man without, for him, men comrades.

A man, walking across the life of another man for such a brief period, taking him in, not afraid with him of the love of the male for the male.

That so frightens most of us.

Because of some filth in life, man-created, woman-created.

Having nothing to do with the reality of living.

Maurice died, too soon, after we became comrades.[5] It was the only thing he ever did to me that wasn't O.K. After he died women kept

5. Maurice Long died in 1931. Anderson thus knew him only briefly. Eleanor Anderson confirms the many telephone calls that came to her husband about Long.

coming to me, to explain that if he hadn't been confused, if he had only accepted what the woman (it was always the one talking), what she had to offer.

But what was wrong with him?

To me he was O.K.

What of his confusion?

Who is not confused?

He understood something.

He understood that I loved him.

I understood that he loved me.

There were a dozen, a hundred little adventures.

We were sitting on the porch of my house and there was a man walking in the road.

Maurice was rich. He was Irish. I have no way of knowing how rich he was.

It didn't matter. We were sitting on the porch of my house. It was morning and there was a man, a poor farmer, walking in the road.

He was a man with a huge family. He was in debt. He went slowly, laboriously, along the road.

"That man, there," said Maurice.

"Yes," I said. I began to lie.

"He is Irish," I said.

He wasn't.

"He is from your country."

I was fabricating a lie.

"He's a Galway man," I said.

I knew little or nothing of the farmer, just that he was broke, his farm mortgaged.

"A Galway man," cried Maurice. He sprang to his feet.

"How did you know I was a Galway man?" he asked. I hadn't known. There are moments when a man is inspired.

He got up from the porch and ran down to the man. He wrote a check. He lifted the mortgage on the man's little farm and the man was stunned. He couldn't understand. He went away, holding the check in his hand, and Maurice came back to me. He sat beside me and laughed.

"He wasn't Irish at all," he said.

He went away. It was arranged that we go together to see the world. He was one who never did me dirt.

[523]

The only thing he ever did, not on the square, was to die.
He had no right to do that.

II

I would like to be able to write of him. I can't. The words will not march. The words describing him, his great head, with the mass of greying hair, with his great body, should walk as he walked.

He came often to see me in the town where I lived, this after I had myself begun to grow grey.

The hair on his head was thick and mine was thin. He was handsome. The eyes of women followed him along streets in the town. The town clerk, the man who ran the drug store, a lawyer, the men who worked in my print shop (this was when I published and edited two county weeklies) —all of them spoke of him.

I had got a farm, back in the hills, and there was a man who worked there. He was a quiet man who seldom spoke, but he spoke of Maurice.

"When will he come again?"

"When will he come again?"

The question became a refrain. Men asked the question, women, old and young, asked it.

I see him often in my dreams. It is seldom in life this feeling comes to a man, to love wholly and without reservation another man. I am asleep and he comes into my room. It was thus, in dreams, that, after her death, my mother came to me. She has not come for a long, long time.

My friend comes into the room, walking, as he always walked, with his free easy stride, and he sits in the room.

He is as he was in life. He is a somewhat swaggering man. Look, how well he is dressed. He wears loose fitting tweeds. He loves colors. He has on a bright necktie. He wears gayly colored socks.

Sometimes he sits talking to me and sometimes he sits in silence. We make plans as we were always doing when he was in life. He is a rich man, rich in many ways.

How many women have loved him?

How many men have loved him?

"There are too many," he used to say. "I love too many.

"I want them all."

The women flocked about him. There were tall women, short ones, dark ones, light ones, beautiful women and plain ones. When he died there was an item in the newspapers. The Associated Press sent out a story. It said that he and I were friends.

I remember sharply the day he died. It was around the time we were to meet. I had packed my bags. We were going together on a journey.

I was at the door of my house when the telephone rang. It was his son speaking.

"Father is dead. He fell down in a field."

He had been walking in a field. He was accompanied by an old horse and a dog. The dog was a little thing. It ran whining to his house.

There was an old horse, an old gelding.

I had been with him in the country. We were riding in his car and had stopped before a farm house.

There was a sale of horses going on. There were old horses and young horses. There was an old gelding.

The gelding was old and worn out. In his youth he had been denatured. His legs were all bunged up and he had sad eyes.

The bidding was going on.

"Three dollars."

"Four dollars."

"Five dollars."

"I'll give ten," said Maurice. He got the gelding.

"I will walk home. I'll lead him home," said Maurice. He spoke of him at length.

For years and years he, the gelding, had served man. He had plowed fields. He had gone up and down over roads. Men had beaten him. They had half starved him.

In his youth they had taken his horsehood away.

"Now he shall have a home," said Maurice. "He shall eat rich grass. He shall have oats."

He was fond of walking alone in the fields. He had been a poor boy in Ireland. He had been poor and had become rich. In his life he had made and lost three or four fortunes. Men friends crowded about him. Women wanted his love.

He walked alone in his fields. It was a Sunday morning, in the state of Maryland, and the sun was shining. He had sent a wire to me. "Come and we will go on a journey."

He went alone upon his journey. He walked in a field and fell down dead. The little dog whined and ran to his house. His son came and found him lying there. The old gelding, that worn out old farm horse, that, since he had come to live with Maurice, had on all such walks accompanied him, followed at his heels, stood over him. The son told me.

"The old horse just stood there," he said. "He was looking down with his sad patient old eyes into my father's face."

"He was a man. Take him all and all, I shall not see his likes again."

He was a king, a lord among men. As a young man he had been married but his wife had left him. He did not blame her. "I have loved too many women," he said.

He said he could not help it.

He was one of the men who can give and give again. When he died and, in the newspapers, it was mentioned that I was among his friends, and as I was more well known than he was, the women turned to me.

For days my telephone rang. There were calls from Chicago, from San Francisco, New York, St. Louis. There were calls from country towns. Old women called me. Young and beautiful women called me.

"You were his friend. Let me come to you. Let me talk of him."

I did see some of them.

"Yes," they said. "It is true. He did love many women.

"There were many others but there was a way in which. . . .

"I was closer to him than any other woman can ever be."

They all said it.

They kept saying it. For a long time I was determined that I would write his life. He had been one of the great adventurers I have known. He was one of the rich men of my life. He was rich in money, rich in friends, in the love of women. He was rich in giving.

He was a story teller and, when I have been in his house, the room filled with men drinking, going about, and when he began to tell a story all became hushed.

He could touch the heart with his stories. He could make tears come to the eyes. He could make the room ring with laughter.

His life had been one of many strange adventures, and more than once, after his death, I sat down to my desk. This might have happened after one of the nights when he had come into my dreams.

He had come into the room as he used to come in life. There was the same proud half swagger. There was the half sad look that sometimes came into his eyes. In the dream he sat in the room in silence.

"It may be," I thought when I awoke, "that he wants something from me.

"He may be like all other men, all wanting their stories told."

I tried and tried. I could not do it. The words would not come. There were no words with which I could tell his power over others.

I Become a Protester

They had got me again. There was another protest to be made. The Bonus soldiers had marched on Washington and were driven out by guns and gas. When I was asked to go with other writers to protest to President Hoover I went.[6]

I thought it was all a sad mistake, that had the president had the courage and more understanding of the everyday man he would have gone to the Bonus soldiers and spoken directly to them. It seemed shameful to me to drive them away with guns and gas.

I was told that there would be a crowd of writers going down from New York. We were to meet at the Pennsylvania Station. "There will be newspaper men and photographers."

When I got to the station there were but three of us—Waldo Frank, Elliot Cohen [7] and myself.

"However I'll stick it out," I thought.

Had notice been sent to the president? Had he been asked if he would see us?

Yes, a telegram had been sent and a reply received. He would not see us.

"But why then go?"

It was for the sake of publicity, that was it. Our going would call attention again to the injustice done to the Bonus soldiers.

6. In the summer of 1932, President Herbert Hoover refused to accede to the demands of dissatisfied veterans and had them evicted from Washington. Anderson tried to talk with Hoover August 10, but Theodore Joslin talked with him instead. See *Letters,* ed. Jones and Rideout, Items 213, 238; and "When Are Authors Insulted?" *Bookman,* LXXV (October, 1932), 564.

7. Elliot E. Cohen was a secretary of commerce in Mobile, Alabama. Also accompanying Anderson and Frank were William Jones, a Negro editor from Baltimore; and James Rorty, a poet from Westport, Connecticut.

I had my doubts. I had been given to understand that reporters would crowd about us at the railroad station in New York, that we would be interviewed and photographed. A man gets himself worked up on such occasions. He thinks up snappy things to say. He begins to feel that what he has to say is of importance to the nation.

But there were no reporters in sight, no photographers. We got on the train. We were joined in Philadelphia by a negro writer.

So there we were. We got to Washington and went to the president's office. There were newspaper men and others sitting about.

There was a man very drunk. Did it happen on that occasion, or on another? I can't be sure. Anyway on one occasion when I was waiting in the president's office building a drunken man came up and embraced me. He began kissing me on the cheek. He clung to me and there was a roar of laughter in the room.

"So you are Sherwood Anderson. Well, you understand, I'm no fairy but I've often said to my wife, 'If I ever meet that man I'm going to kiss him,' I've said."

As suggested this may have happened on another occasion.

Anyway there we were, we four American writers, in that place to make our protest. It was, we were told, the president's birthday. Newspaper men, who were evidently not fond of Mr. Hoover, kept coming to whisper to us. They said he was getting birthday presents. They were from big corporations, they said. Whether the tales were true or not I never knew. They kept naming the corporations that had sent presents.

We were in a long room with chairs down each side and, at the end, a desk back of which sat a grey haired dignified looking man.

On the train we had selected Waldo as our spokesman. He seemed to be willing. We others were all a little shy. It may have been an old feeling, come down from childhood.

"Well, the president."

I am sure I would have stammered. He would have seemed so high up there.

We were kept waiting in the room. An hour, perhaps two hours passed. Waldo kept going to the grey haired man at the desk. The president would not see him but we would presently be seen by one of his secretaries.

I had my own reason for being embarrassed. Once before I had gone to see Mr. Hoover. That was when he was in Mr. Coolidge's cabinet.

I had been sent there by one of the popular magazines. All had been arranged. I was to be well paid.

"Go to the president's office. You will receive there a wire, telling you what questions to ask."

I had gone.

"All right," I had thought. I had never talked to a man who was likely to become president.

"It will, at any rate, be an experience," I thought.

I had gone to Washington on that occasion and had received my instructions.

"So you sat in President Harding's cabinet. You sat cheek by jowl with Fall of Texas.[8]

"Do you mean to tell me you did not know that there was stealing going on?"

There were a dozen such questions and I could not ask them. I had however been escorted into Mr. Hoover's office. There had been, at that time, great floods in the valley of the Mississippi and he had been sent down there.

"There are these questions I am instructed to ask you but I do not ask. The questions are too impertinent. I cannot ask them."

Mr. Hoover seemed to be pleased. "We will talk then of the Mississippi River," he said.

I said that would be nice.

And so we did talk and I thought him a little too cocksure about the river. He said that control of the Mississippi was all very simple but when I had lived in New Orleans I had talked to many river men, had traveled up and down the river with them.

I thought Mr. Hoover a shy and rather sensitive man. We did not talk long. I thought him the soul of respectability. I did not write the piece for the magazine. I told them I couldn't ask the questions they had sent me.

So that time I was free, for the day, there in Washington. I went about the city. I visited the Freer Galleries. I wrote a piece about my day that was later published. It was republished in several large newspapers and in the *London Times*. In the Freer Galleries I had seen the Whistlers, collected by the rich man Mr. Freer, and I saw also some old Chinese paintings.

There was one that had particularly taken my eye. It was a painting of a Chinese emperor walking in the evening in a garden with his concubines

8. Albert Bacon Fall (1861–1944), President Harding's Secretary of the Interior, convicted in 1929 of bribery and sentenced to prison, 1931–33. See "In Washington," *Return to Winesburg: Selections from Four Years of Writing for a Country Newspaper*, edited by Ray Lewis White (Chapel Hill: The University of North Carolina Press, 1967), pp. 60–68.

and in the piece I wrote I tried to assure people that if Mr. Hoover were elected president he would never walk in the evening in the garden of the White House with his concubines.

I was remembering that on this other occasion as I sat waiting with the others in the president's office. Mr. Hoover was president now. I had laughed at him for taking the Mississippi River so lightly. I had made that crack about his solid respectability. If, by chance, he did see us I would be embarrassed.

However he did not see us. We were seen finally by one of his secretaries. He lectured us. He said we had no business there, bothering the president. He said, "I do not speak to you for the president nor as the president's secretary but as a fellow craftsman," but what he meant by that I did not know.

"I wonder if he also writes books," I was thinking. I was wondering if a man could do that and be also the secretary to a president.

We were there in the office of the secretary. We were not asked to sit. We had filed in and stood with our backs against a wall. When we had come in the president's secretary had not, for what seemed a long time, paid any attention to us. He sat writing by a desk. He sat there writing.

And then, at last, after what seemed to me at least a half hour, he arose and delivered his lecture.

I was embarrassed and wanted to leave.

"We are getting nowhere," I thought.

However Waldo had something to say. He began to say that we were there as representatives of the writers and artists of America but I did not think that was true. He was suggesting that we exerted a wide influence on the public mind and I did not believe that we did. I thought it made no difference who we were.

"If we had been four laboring men or clerks in stores it would have been the same," I thought.

An injustice had been done.

"Any Americans should have the right to come here and protest an injustice," I thought.

"What does it matter that we happen to be scribblers?" I thought.

We were, at that time, in the midst of the Depression. Mr. Hoover had come into his presidency during the Coolidge boom days and then had come the crash. I was a little sorry for the man. I was remembering that other time when I had come to interview him and the impression of a rather sensitive and puzzled man I had carried away.

So I went, after the attempt to protest the wrong done the Bonus marchers, to a hotel. I had said good-bye to the others. They were taking a train back to New York. I sat in the hotel writing room and wrote a letter to Mr. Hoover, an open letter that was later published in the *Nation*.[9]

In my letter I called attention to something that was on my mind. I had, at that time and for several months, been going about. I had visited many towns, many cities. I myself had known what it meant to be stranded, out of work, to have no money, to know the desperation of hunger. In my travels I had seen men, with hopeless desperate faces, hanging about closed factory gates, I had seen them eating out of garbage cans in alleyways.

Mr. Hoover and I had come out of the same sort of background. We had both known something of poverty, had both been small town boys.

Now he was a big man, in power, and I was not. He had grown rich. No doubt he was surrounded by all kinds of "yes" men. I spoke of how sorry I was that he could not come away with me, for a week or two, get into my car, be, for a time, not the president, with all the power of a president, but just a man going about looking and listening. I had, you see, a kind of faith that if he could do that (he was, I was quite sure, a sensitive man) in some way things might be changed.

And so I wrote my piece. I had it published. I have sometimes thought since that the expedition of protest by us writers was got up by the communists. If it was I didn't know it then.

At any rate, later, when I was in New York, I was asked, by some of the leaders of the Communist Party, to come have a talk with them and I went.[10]

I went to a building in Thirteenth Street in New York and I was told then that my open letter to the president was a mistake.

"You should not have done it," they told me.

"And why?" I asked.

"It may arouse some sympathy for the president."

9. "Listen, Mr. President," *Nation*, CXXXV (August 31, 1932), 191–93.

10. See Anderson's "How I Came to Communism," *New Masses*, VIII (September, 1932), 8–9. On Anderson's adoption and later rejection of communism, see James Schevill, "The Glitter of Communism," *Sherwood Anderson: His Life and Work* (Denver: University of Denver Press, 1951), pp. 275–94; reprinted in *The Achievement of Sherwood Anderson: Essays in Criticism*, edited by Ray Lewis White (Chapel Hill: The University of North Carolina Press, 1966), pp. 140–54.

"Yes," I said.

They thought that shouldn't be done.

"But I am sympathetic. I understand what power does to a man, what he is up against."

They declared that it was all money. They scolded me but I only laughed.

"Fortunately, I was expressing my own point of view, not yours," I said and so walked out of their presence.

Bertrand Russell and the Negro Women

I used to see Bertrand Russell at Horace Liveright's apartment in New York, this before he became Lord Russell, and I found him a very friendly and charming man. He sat amid all of the hullabaloo going on in the Liveright apartment smoking his pipe and with a dry smile on his face.

Some man had an idea. He engaged Russell and myself to debate on the subject of the care of children. We were to have five hundred each but, in the end, had to settle for something like three hundred each. It seemed that the populace wasn't sufficiently interested. The man who gambled upon our drawing a great crowd was disappointed.

We were to debate the question as to whether it was better for the children to be raised by the state or by the parents of the children and I was on the parents' side.[11]

My daughter made an amusing remark. She had come to see me. "I hear you are to debate with Bertrand Russell."

I admitted that there was some such plan afoot.

"And what is the subject of the debate?"

I told her.

"And on what side are you?"

I told her that too.

"What? You?" she said.

I rather think I did Russell dirt. I went through his books. I remem-

11, See "Abolition of Family Debated by Authors," *New York Times*, November 2, 1931, p. 21; and "Shall the Home Be Abolished?" *Literary Digest*, CXI (November 28, 1931), 25–26. Anderson's speech is excerpted in the *New York Times*, November 8, 1931, IX, p. 2.

bered the old saying "Oh that my enemy would write a book," and Russell had written many books. As I was to have the floor during the last ten minutes I planned to take the time reading sentences of his that would refute all he could say on the other side of the question.

Russell was entirely fair and of course I was not. As we stood together in the wings, before going on the stage, he warned me.

"You won't mind if I am a bit rough with you?"

I said I wouldn't mind.

"I am going to be a bit rough myself. I'm going to do you dirt."

My wife, who was present, was bitterly disappointed by my appearance, so disappointed that I am sure she did not hear the debate. I had put on evening clothes but had forgotten to change my socks. I had on red socks. I am very fond of red socks and red neckties. I forgot.

Later I was unable to convince my wife that I had been very brilliant, had annihilated poor Russell.

"I didn't hear you," she said. "I was so ashamed. You looked so grotesque."

Tommy Smith, who was at the time Horace Liveright's editorial chief, wanted to give a party for Russell. It may be that Russell had expressed a desire to see the life of Harlem.

At any rate we went there, had dinner there and Tommy to make the dinner quite complete had invited two very charming negro women to dine with us.

There must have been two or three other men and I remember that the poet Genevieve Taggard,[12] dined with us and was very beautiful and the life of the party.

And there were the two negro women who were no doubt from the very upper crust of Harlem's social and intellectual set. They were very quiet but took part in the dinner conversation and it was evident that they were what is called "well read." No doubt they were the daughters of wealthy negro men. They had been students in one of the more fashionable northern women's colleges, Bryn Mawr or Smith or Wells.

They were also very beautiful, with the strangely soft brown eyes of their race, both slender and tall, both with rich high-brown skins and both beautifully clad.

So we dined and went to a cabaret where there was dancing.

It was a brown and white place. It was the thing you find in Harlem.

12. Genevieve Taggard (1894–1948), American poet interested in political and metaphysial verse.

The men of our party danced but they did not dance with the two negro women and so I did.

We had dined with them. They were our guests. Tommy Smith had arranged it so and it seemed to me rather shabby that, under the circumstances, the two young negro women should be left sitting at the table while man after man of the party danced with Genevieve.

Besides they were wonderful dancers.

And so all evening I danced with them and what amazed me was that Russell was shocked.

He came and spoke to me about it.

"It isn't done, old chap."

He shook his head over my extraordinary behavior.

"But they are our guests. Tommy has invited them. They have dined with us. They are, as you can see, very beautiful. They dance wonderfully."

However he kept insisting that what I was doing was in some way wrong, not the proper thing to do. He was being very English upper class that evening. In spite of all of his radicalism I could feel old Lord John Russell very much taking command of Bertrand for at least that evening.

The American Spectator

Dreiser told me that the scheme was hatched aboard ship, George Jean Nathan, Ernest Boyd and others having thought it up. There was to be this new monthly, having no advertising, to be printed on ordinary news sheets, to sell for five cents. There were these great names of the literary and theatrical world, George Jean Nathan, Eugene O'Neill, Ernest Boyd, Dreiser and Cabell.[13] Nathan later told me that it was, apparently, an immediate success. I was not at that time asked into it. That came later.

13. *The American Spectator* was founded to "replace" *The American Mercury* and ran from 1932 to 1937, but in 1935 the founders sold it to another group. Ernest Boyd (1887–1946), drama and literary critic. In *The American Spectator,* Anderson published: "To Remember," I (May, 1933), 1; "Sherwood Anderson to Theodore Dreiser," I (June, 1933), 1; "Communications," I (September, 1933), 2; "The Nationalist," II (December, 1933), 1; "Winter Day's Walk in New York," II (January, 1934), 3; "Cityscapes," II (February, 1934), 1; "American Spectator," II (February, 1934), 1; "Gertrude Stein," II (April, 1934), 3; "The Line-Up," II (June, 1934), 1; "Samovar," II (July, 1934), 3; and "Motor Trip," II (August, 1934), 9.

It was to be a paper devoted to criticism, with an occasional article and high class short stories, and I dare say the project failed because there were too many editors.

There was an almost immediate misunderstanding between Dreiser and the team of Nathan and Boyd. At that time Nathan and Boyd were inseparable. They were at "21" or some other fashionable restaurant at the cocktail hour every afternoon. They were together at the theatre. Among all the editors they were the men about town, with the Broadway touch.

It irritated Dreiser. In reality Nathan and Boyd were running the paper.

"It is becoming their organ. We are merely giving them the use of our names to back up their Broadway slant on life," Dreiser declared.

Dreiser came to see me.

"Well, what will Cabell do, what will O'Neill do?" The two men were rarely in town, did not come to editorial meetings. He urged me to come in, be one of the editors.

"Sure. Sure O'Neill occasionally writes a short piece or Cabell does the same."

They did nothing to influence the general tone of the paper.

"It is all Broadway, too much Broadway. They are a couple of Broadway boys."

As he does, when he is excited, Dreiser shouted. In a group of people, when there is an argument going on, he can shout down a room full of men.

On the one hand Dreiser can be the most gentle of men. He is, of all American writers I have known, the most essentially tender toward others. If you are hurt Dreiser is hurt with you.

On the other hand Dreiser can become suddenly violent. There are all sorts of stories, going about in the literary world, regarding the man. He was at a dinner given by Ray Long, at that time running the *Cosmopolitan*. I was not invited. Long had no use for my work. Once in an interview he spoke of me as a literary barn yard rooster.

So Lewis, no doubt in his cups, accused Dreiser of plagiarism. It concerned Dreiser's book on Russia. Lewis' wife, Dorothy Thompson, had also written on Russia. Just at that time everyone was doing it.

So there were these accusations and Dreiser immediately slapped Lewis' face.[14] The man can be heavy handed, physically and in his work.

14. On March 19, 1931, Dreiser slapped Sinclair Lewis at a banquet because Lewis charged Dreiser with copying Dorothy Thompson Lewis' book on Russia. See W. A. Swanberg, *Dreiser* (New York: Bantam Books, 1967), pp. 448–50.

And there was that time, when, growing suddenly angry with his publisher, Horace Liveright, he threw a cup of coffee into his face.

An impulsive, generous, tender man. I have always loved him.

So he writes awkwardly, etc.? Well what of it? He can build up an effect, carry you away into other lives. He is a true novelist. I have always thought that he, and not Lewis, among our American writers, should have been given the first Nobel Prize given to an American writer. I have thought that it was given to Lewis because Europe wanted to see Americans as a race of Babbitts.

But to return to *The American Spectator*. I did, persuaded by Dreiser, for a time become one of its editors. I attended one editorial meeting. I wrote for it one of my own better short stories, a story called "The Nationalist" that was later published in the book *Puzzled America.*[15]

I was at the editorial meeting and it was held in Dreiser's rooms at the Hotel Ansonia where he at that time lived. Someone had got a brilliant idea.

There was to be a discussion in which we were all to take part. As Hitler had already become a dominant figure in Germany we were to discuss dictatorship.

"Was it ever advisable to hand government over to a dictator?" Something of that sort was to be discussed. There was to be a stenographer present to take down our words of wisdom. Dreiser brought his secretary.

So we had drinks. The stenographer was brought in and we launched forth. The discussion was, on the whole, pretty stupid. We were all, I dare say, pretty self-conscious. I know I was. I kept trying to think up things to say that would look good in print. The others may have been doing the same thing.

Anyway it was all taken down. It was typed out, a copy provided for each of us, and then the trouble began. It was Nathan's contention that Dreiser, having furnished the stenographer, had seen to it that any good thing said was attributed to Dreiser and I remember sitting with the others on a later occasion, each of us with a copy of the script in our hands.

"But look here. I said this. Dreiser didn't say it."

"The hell I didn't."

A war or an outburst of claims and counter claims. It was all very laughable. Fortunately the script never got into print.[16]

15. *Puzzled America* (New York: Scribner's, 1935), pp. 169–79.
16. A typescript of this conference, owned by The Newberry Library, confirms Anderson's charges. See also *Letters,* ed. Jones and Rideout, Item 360.

As for *The American Spectator* it soon faded. It disappeared. As to whether or not my own joining the editorial staff had anything to do with the fading I can't say.

There were simply too many editors, all of them having too many other interests. It was however an amusing experience. I do not think that it ever added anything to the clearing up of the confusion of the American world.

A Mexican Village at Night

I could not sleep. We had got into the town, some four of us, traveling in two cars, making our way toward Mexico City, on the evening before, a troop of determined soft eyed boys clinging to our running boards.[17] They were like flies clinging. It was when the new paved road, running from Laredo to Mexico City, had just been opened and when the flow of American tourists, south over the great new highway, had just got started and no doubt the boys had been told of the vast wealth of all Americans.

They were determined about pennies or the Mexican five cent pieces and when we had got to a small hotel and as we began to unload our bags each was fought over. There were these boys, with the soft eyes, with such gentle smiles, fighting over each piece while others swarmed over the car itself. They had rags and were wiping off the dust from the car's hood. They wiped the glass, little dirty hands were thrust out.

We fought our way through and into the hotel. We were in our rooms and, at last, after a struggle, our cars were locked and stored for the night.

There was a little gallery onto which you could step and I went out there. I walked up and down. Night had come. I could hear the shuffling sound of soldiers, marching in a street, and there were laborers, returning I dare say from the field, each mounted upon his tiny burro, the legs hanging down, arms swinging and, hanging at the side of each, the long knife, the machete, they use in their work.

There was a party gathered and talking in a neighboring room and they were rich Americans. I stood leaning against a wall, near a window to a room they occupied, and listening. I gathered they were alarmed. There was a woman talking excitedly.

She said that they had come into a wild, a barbarous country.

17. Anderson visited Mexico early in 1938. See his "An Impression of Mexico—Its People," *Southern Literary Messenger,* I (April, 1939), 241–42.

"We will be robbed. Who knows, perhaps we will be murdered," she said. Listening to the voices in the room I gathered that there were two men with the woman and they had been driven to that particular village by a chauffeur. The chauffeur was not in the room. There was, in the particular hotel, a little hotel, a little court into which we had driven our car and I had seen in the court a big car with a New York license tag in which sat a negro.

It was a hot night and I had got a headache. The party with which I was traveling presently went off to find food but I did not go with them. "I will go instead for a walk," I said and went off to walk in the streets of the village and, now that I was alone, having no baggage, getting out of no car before a hotel, the swarms of boys did not bother.

They however kept speaking to me. There were two or three words of English they had learned. "Hello," they cried, when I met a group of them, on some little dark street. "Hello. Good-bye," they said and laughed. There were some of them had got hold of a third word. "Hello, o.k.," they said.

I returned, after my walk, to the little hotel and those of my own party, having managed to dine and being tired from the journey, had retired for the night but, as my head was aching, I could not sleep so I took a chair out to the little balcony and sat smoking. I had come in through the little inner court where cars were stored and had seen the negro chauffeur asleep on the back seat of the big car. He had his legs drawn up and his mouth open. He snored and there was a small man, a native Mexican, quite old, with a blanket about his shoulders and wearing an old straw hat, who walked up and down. I gathered that he was a kind of guard, a night watchman, employed by the hotel to watch the cars. *"Buenos noches,"* he said in his soft voice as I went through the court and up a flight of stairs to my room.

It had grown quite late and I had walked for a long time. I sat on the balcony in silence and, as before, I was near the window of the room where, earlier, I had heard the alarmed voice of the woman but now, for a time, there was silence.

It did not last.

"Did you see him? There has a second one come." It was the woman's voice and, at first, I did not realize that it was my coming, my going to sit on the balcony, that had again alarmed her. She spoke in a loud whisper.

"John," she said, evidently addressing her husband.

"Are you awake?" she asked.

"How in hell can I sleep, in such a place? We may be murdered here.

"There may be a plot to kidnap one of us or even all of us," he added.

"There is that man, sitting out there." It was the woman's voice speaking. "There is that one and another, down in the court." I began to get it. "She is referring to me and to the old man who guards the court," I thought. I became malicious. There was a cock began to crow, somewhere in the village, and he was answered by others. I went softly along the balcony and through a window into my room and presently, as the crowing of the cocks was kept up, I also crowed.

It had begun and it kept up and what a night they had. Occasionally, during the night and as my headache continued and I could not sleep, I went, in my stockinged feet, out upon the balcony to listen and as, from time to time, the cocks again took up their crowing, I joined them.

It was taken, I gathered from words and sentences picked up (A third man having dressed and come into the room with the man and wife. He was quite an old man, with a small grey beard. "Perhaps he is at the head of some big holding company, a kind of Samuel Insull,[18] a multimillionaire, who had been persuaded to come off on this trip," I told myself. I decided he must be the brother of the woman in the room. She called him Joe.), I got it that the figure of the little cloaked man, marching occasionally up and down in the court below, the crowing of the cocks in the village and my answering crows had convinced them that they were surrounded by enemies and that they had gathered in the room, huddled together in there, and were awaiting their fate. There was some talk of the police but, as the man called Joe said, quite sensibly I thought, what was the use?

"We can't talk to them, can't explain if they do come," he said and went on to explain that he had heard that the police, in Mexico, and, for that matter, even the soldiers, were not to be trusted.

"If we had come by train now or if we were in Mexico City," he said. He said that he supposed that, in Mexico City, there was an American consul and began to quarrel with the others for bringing him off, to such a place, in a car.

It went on with them thus, during the night, and once, after a particularly prolonged outbreak of the cock crowing, in which I joined with a kind of savage delight, there was a sudden outbreak of shouts, from several voices, from somewhere over in the Mexican village. It was one of

18. Samuel Insull (1859–1938), utilities executive.

the unaccountable outbreaks of sound that are always occurring, so unexplainedly, at night when you do not sleep, the sudden outbreak of cries, from several voices, then silence and then single voices crying out. It may be there had been a drinking party somewhere in the town and that there were arrests being made. There was the outbreak of sounds, it carried on thus for a time, and then silence and from the neighboring room the wailing voice of the woman.

"Oh, oh," she cried, over and over.

"It is going to happen. They are coming. They are coming," she wailed.

As to what happened later I do not know. There was one of the men who, screwing up courage, went later to arouse the hotel proprietor but, as Joe had suggested, when they got him they could not make him understand their trouble. I slept and at daylight awakened and looking out through the door of my room saw them already in their car. They had got their negro chauffeur awake (no doubt he had been compelled to sleep in the car, to guard their possessions) and he was at the wheel.

They had decided to give up the trip into Mexico I gathered. I saw them, the two old men and the rather fat and fussily dressed woman, get into the car and, going out again to the balcony, saw them drive off into the dawn.

They were however not headed for Mexico City. They were hitting for the border and later when I went down into the court and was passing through it, hoping to find in the village someone awake who would serve me my morning coffee, there was the old man, the guard over the court.

It was evident that he had got the picture of what had gone on, in the breasts of my fellow countrymen, during the night. It may be that he had even heard my attempts to crow like a cock and had sensed my own participation. At any rate he looked at me and laughed. *"Vamos. Vamos,"* he said and threw up his hands so suddenly that the blanket he wore wrapped over his shoulders fell to the ground.

Work Fast, Man

It is an old saying that no man knows himself but surely there is much concerning the self that only the self can know.[19]

19. Anderson's title of this section is "The Purpose." The essay is placed here as a statement of his rededication to finishing the memoirs.

What of this secret life we all lead, the secret thoughts we have, secret acts we do?

There is this man, of whom I have proposed to write. I have been with him since he came from the womb, have walked with him, slept with him, worn his clothes, thought his thoughts. Never has he been able to escape from me or I from him.

Will I dare tell all I know of him?

No. I am quite sure I cannot do that, would not dare do that.

He has too often done things, mean ugly things, he did not quite know he was doing. At such times, often, I have whispered to him, "Do not do it," but he went ahead, driven by some dark impulse.

Then he began justifying his acts, defending himself. An ugly enough act became something almost noble. It would all be quite laughable if it were not so sad.

And why tell all of this, or any part of it, why bother?

But are we not now suddenly passing into a new phase of general life? Individuality is to pass away now. Not the individual but the state is to become all important. Presently we will all be soldiers. We are to become like a swarm of bees in a bee hive or like ants in an ant hill. Every act, every impulse of our lives will be directed.

So, you see, such books as the one I have proposed to write will become historical documents. I am writing of a man, now rapidly becoming an old man. When he was a boy there were no automobiles, no airplanes, no radio. He spent his boyhood in a middle western town where there was but one telephone. There were no chain stores. The great trusts that were to exert such a powerful influence on American life were just forming.

Men were free.

It is true that they were free to lie, to cheat, to gouge one another as well as to live. I shall not try, in preparing this historical document, to set the old life against the new. I shall try instead to be a true historian.

There is something deep down within me that laughs when I say that.

But never mind. I shall try. Courage man! Soon there will be no such thing as individuality left. Hear the soft purr of the new thousands of airplanes far up in the sky. The bees are swarming. New hives are being formed. Work fast, man.

It was several years ago and I was in the city of San Francisco. This was when my friend Lincoln Steffens [20] was still alive and he asked me to go see Mr. Fremont Older. As everyone of the coast knows, Older had made a long fight for the release of Tom Mooncy.[21] Older had been, for many years, the best known and, I'm sure, the best loved newspaper man on the coast.

He was very insistent that I go out to San Quentin to see Tom Mooney. But why?

What could I do for him?

However I went and Ted Lilienthal went with me. He drove me out. Ted, with Leon Gelber, runs a delightful book store in San Francisco and they are also interested in young painters, showing their works in the store.[22] Ted belongs to a family that has been very powerful, I'm told, in banking and financial circles on the coast but is himself not interested in finance.

He is interested in people, in books, in painting, in fine printing. He has his own print shop in a small building behind his house.

So we drove out to San Quentin. It is on a bay. There are great stone prison buildings and on the lawns flowers growing. We went to the office of the warden.

I told him who I was, that I had been sent to him by Older, that I had come to see Tom Mooney.

The warden was a large heavy looking man. He was like the sheriff in a western movie. When I had told him my mission, he sat for a long time looking at me. Then he made a little motion with his hand.

"Another one to see Tom Mooney, eh?" he said.

He leaned forward, pointed a finger at me. Ted, a shy man, had gone into a corner. What the warden said made me feel a little foolish.

"This Tom Mooney," he said, "I know nothing about it. I don't know whether he is guilty or not. I didn't try him. I'm the warden of this prison. People keep coming and coming to see Tom Mooney.

"Hell, man," he said, "I got a lot of other boys in here.

20. Steffens and Anderson were never really close friends. See *Letters,* ed. Jones and Rideout, Item 210. Anderson refers to April, 1932.

21. Thomas J. Zechariah (1882–1942), known as "Tom Mooney," was convicted of murder in 1917 and pardoned in 1939.

22. Gelber and Lilienthal published Anderson's *The Modern Writer* (San Francisco: Lantern Press, 1925).

"Some of them would like to have people coming, now and then, to see them."

It was something to think about. It was no doubt true. What could I do for Tom Mooney?

Then I thought of something. At the time, during the same labor war on the coast, when they had convicted Tom, there had been two others also convicted.

There was the man called "Smitty" and there was one of the McNamara brothers. They were in the prison for life. Not much chance of their getting out.

They had blown up a newspaper office down in Los Angeles.

"Sure we did it."

There had been people killed.

It hadn't been planned that way. There was this bitter labor struggle. They had planned to blow up the building when it was unoccupied but things had gone wrong.

"Sure we're guilty. We did it."

When I mentioned the names of the two men, the warden's face lighted up.

"Sure you can see them. They're a couple of swell eggs.

"About the best two boys we got around here," he added.

He explained about the two men. They were both fine mechanics. He had one of them in charge of the engine room in the prison. The other was in charge of the fire department.

They were brought in, two healthy looking, quiet men, and we began to talk, pulling shy Ted into the conversation, the warden leaning forward to listen.

There was no mention of themselves, of their own fate. There they were, in prison for life, little or no chance of ever leaving the prison.

They were both curiously alive, intellectually alive. They had done something, terrible enough, earlier in their lives, and were paying for it.

As they were in prison for keeps, they had begun reading books. They knew my books, the books of other men of my time. They discussed them with me, asked questions, were filled with intellectual curiosity.

They mentioned some of our outstanding writers. What sort of guys were they? What about Hemingway, Faulkner, Dos Passos,[23] Dreiser? How did these fellows live? What did they look like? Did I know them?

23. John Dos Passos (1896–   ) and Anderson were never close friends. See *Letters,* ed. Jones and Rideout, Item 332.

They spoke of men in political life, of some of the outstanding scientists, gave the curious impression of aliveness, of eager curiosity concerning American life, outside the walls of the prison.

Ted and I both were taken into what seemed to me a kind of warm friendliness, the warden leaning forward to listen, apparently warming himself in it.

They were there and then were gone.

"Well, so long, men."

A kind of warm-heartedness. The warden weakened.

"Oh, I guess I'll have them bring in Tom. Why not?"

He seemed to give the order for Tom's coming a little wearily, like a bar tender humoring a drunken man.

And then Tom came. He was dressed in white, with a black flowing tie.

He marched in. I cannot help what I felt. To me he was a bit the bad actor, let's say, playing the part of Napoleon.

So I was Sherwood Anderson, eh? He strode across the room to me, a finger pointed at my face.

"So you are Sherwood Anderson?" he said again. His finger seemed about to run into my eye and I drew away, but he followed.

"You quit what you are doing," he said.

"You be the American Zola.

"I'm the American Dreyfus." [24]

That was about all. We didn't stay long. I tried to introduce him to Ted Lilienthal but he dismissed poor Ted with a disdainful flourish of his hand.

"A Lilienthal?

"One of my enemies," he said.

As I have suggested, that is about all. There was more, something in the same tone, but I have forgotten.

He had come into the room and he went out, striding out as he had strode in. He left us curiously flat.

It wasn't that we doubted his innocence. Why should we? There was apparently plenty of evidence that he was innocent.

But had his innocence, his martyrdom, done that to him? We had no way of knowing. Ted and I talked about it all the way back to the city.

There were the other two who were guilty. They had said nothing of

24. Anderson was familiar with the case of Albert Dreyfus (1859–1935), Jewish officer in the French army, wrongly convicted of treason in 1894.

their fate, hadn't asked us to sign any petitions, write letters to any governors. They had spoken only of life outside the prison, had wanted us to speak of that.

"Tell us. Tell us. We want to know."

Guilty men, paying for it.

"A couple of swell eggs, Smitty and Mac," the warden had said again as we left his office.

Two guilty men who knew they were stuck.

So warm and friendly.

And then Tom, the innocent one.

"I'm the American Dreyfus.

"You be the American Zola."

Well you, who read this, figure it out, if you can.

Letters, Autographs, and First Editions

I presume that every author of any standing must get a good many letters. They are understanding, silly, pathetic and often helpful. A woman writes to me saying that I am the only writer she has ever read who feels life as she does. I understand the human soul. She would like to be near me. She is very humble. "I could type your manuscripts. I have a little money and can support myself. If you do your own typing and do not want to bother let me come and scrub the floor of the room where you work."

What an opportunity. My floor needs scrubbing all right. However I have grown wise. I do not answer the letter.

There is another who is the daughter of an old friend who was once a benefactor to me. She is married now and lives in a western city. She has no children. She wants to write and, from time to time, sends me manuscripts of stories she has written. My correspondence with her has gone on now for several years. The stories she sends me are almost. They seem to remain almost.

She is, as we all are, absorbed in herself.

"I want to talk about myself," she says and does so often for several pages. She has married a poor man and her husband has a hard time making a living. I think I do understand her a little. She is restless and lonely. She does not have to see me. I am an older man, once her father's friend. Writing to me is a great satisfaction to her. In her letters she pours herself out and, although I cannot do as she does, write long pages, I do always answer her letters.

It does no good. There is no way in which I can help her solve her own particular problem but, as I see it, there is an implied insult in not trying to answer such letters.

There are those who send me manuscripts without asking my permission. Sometimes such manuscripts are sent without return postage. I put such manuscripts aside, I do not look at them. I am upset. I write a postcard.

"What do you mean by sending your manuscript to me? I am not an editor. If you want it back send postage."

Such a manuscript gets lost and I am bothered with letters and even threats. I am even accused of wanting to steal the manuscript.

There is this idea abroad, among many young writers, that certain men have in their pocket a golden key that will unlock all doors.

"Why don't you give me the key? I want into heaven. I will return the key to you."

There is something of that sort in many minds but where is the heaven they seek? I have not found it. You write ten, twenty, fifty books, novels, books of short stories, books of verses, of essays, and still there is the problem of the new books. The struggle is never ending. There is no peace. Always you are dissatisfied, seeking and seeking.

However you know that no one can give you the key. Your life will be spent in searching for it.

Fame, if you attain any fame, is a deceitful bitch. It gets between you and people. I have known fellow writers who having attained some fame were ruined by it. They began to take themselves seriously, became artificial. They lost all touch with the human beings about them.

People do many nice things to you in letters. Someone has read a book of yours. It gave him pleasure and he sat down and wrote to you, expressing thanks for the pleasure given. Often such a one sends no return address. I had, in the book *A Story Teller's Story,*[25] spoken of a certain vice of mine. I had told of an inclination I had to steal pencils, fountain pens and paper. Often when I stopped at a hotel I walked off with all the hotel

25. See *A Story Teller's Story: A Critical Text,* edited by Ray Lewis White (Cleveland: Press of Case Western Reserve University, 1968), pp. 209–10, 212–14.

stationery in sight. Someone came to me and asked me to autograph one of my books.

"But I have no pen."

I was handed a pen and, having autographed the book, pretended absent-mindedness. I put the pen in my pocket. If the person protested I returned the pen. Otherwise I walked off with it.

I was entirely conscious of my vice. I was somewhat ashamed of it but it persisted. I am quite sure that it was all due to a fear that someday, when I most wanted to work, I would find myself without pen, pencil or paper.

Or there might be a forest fire, destroying all the forests from which paper is made. Sometimes I find myself with six or eight bottles of ink hidden away.

I had spoken somewhat of this vice of mine in the book and some very kindly man sent me, by express, a box containing twenty gross of pencils.

I thought it a beautiful gesture. The man also did not send an address. He did not ask for thanks. Perhaps he only wanted to cure me of the one vice in my otherwise spotless life.

There was a woman came to the town where I was living. She hung about. This was when I was running a newspaper in a small Virginia town. I had an apartment over my print shop and was living there with my son.

The woman was very beautiful.

"She is in love with me," I thought. I was a little worried. She went up into my apartment and sat at a window facing the street.

"The town will think that she is my kept woman," I thought.

The editor of a small town weekly is more or less a public figure. He is a sort of preacher, cannot step too obviously aside from the straight and narrow.

Not that I was not willing, had the lady been somewhat more subtle, to step aside but I'll not go into that. She was very beautiful.

I went to an older woman friend in the town, explained the situation to her.

"But it is all right," she said. "She only has a manuscript concealed somewhere about her person. It will come out."

I could not believe it. I was even angry with my woman friend.

"She thinks that I, as a male, and aside from the fact that I am an author, am not attractive enough to fascinate such a woman.

"No. She has no manuscript. Such beautiful women do not write manuscripts. They do not need to."

I really did not want to break the woman's heart. At the moment my own affections were, as we writers say, engaged.

And then, after all, my woman friend was right. She did, after some days, pull out a manuscript on me and I was so upset that I was speechless. I took a train and left town. I called my son my address. "You wire me when she has left town," I said.

There are always books being sent to authors to be autographed and sometimes a good deal of trouble results. There is the question of getting paper and string. You are in the country and the post office is miles away. When the first edition of a book has any value at all its value is raised by the author's signature.

I presume that I am like all authors. Sometimes I am in a friendly mood and often I am not. Such books lie about. They get lost. However I have always felt that if any man or woman puts out money for one of my books and wants my name in it I should be willing to put it in.

However I have always refused to autograph books in order to help sell them. There was a woman book seller in a certain city who asked me to sign a book for her. The book was to sell, let us say, for three dollars.

"I want it for my private library," she said and so I signed the book.

And then, on the same afternoon, I happened to be walking in that street and there was my book in the book store window.

There was a sign put up. The book had been autographed by the author. The price asked for it was ten dollars.

And so I went into the store and there the woman was. I put a ten dollar bill on the counter.

"I'll take that book there in the window," I said. I was very cruel. Although she cried I insisted and I walked out with the book under my arm. I had got an idea. There was a young painter I wanted to help. I wrote a form letter.

"The autographing of books increases their value," I pointed out. I said something about my friend the young painter. I thought him a man of talent. He was broke, had three small children, and his wife was ill.

"If you want me to autograph one of my books send me a dollar and I'll pass it on to him," I said in my letter. I made a mistake. One of the richest men in America sent me seventeen of my books to be signed. They had all been expensively bound in leather. When I opened the package I was sick.

Why hadn't I charged him ten dollars each? The bindings on the books must have cost that much. What a boost for my painter the hundred and seventy dollars would have been.

The letters keep coming. Men write and women write. I go to my desk in the morning and begin answering the letters. Many of the letters are very revealing. Often I say to younger writers who consult me, "Write letters, write many letters to many people." The writing of letters is for me a tuning up for the day's work. Often people are making little pictures out of their lives for me. What is an hour, or two hours, spent thus? The writing of letters is too much with us a lost art. It can also be a way of making friendships, extending thus a little your knowledge of life.

Woman at Night

The night can never be quite gorgeous, to its full possibilities, without the woman and I cannot understand those men who do not want marriage or the men and women who, being married, do not sleep together.

There are the nights that come when you are excessively alive. Now, for this one night, you do not want or need the ultimate intimacy. There is the woman beside you asleep. How quietly and softly she breathes. How excessively alive you are. Now the mind and the fancy both race. You seem to feel and hear, with her breathing, the breathing of the earth under your house, breathing of trees. There is a river just down a short hill from the house. It also breathes softly.

Now the moon is breathing, the stars breathing.

Woman, woman.

How nice to run the hand softly down over your hips, along your legs. You get out of bed and light a candle. An electric light or a lamp would make too much light. You do not want to awaken her.

What you want now is a new way of entering in. You are the male. Now she has become for you all life outside self, become quiet and very beautiful.

I remember once climbing a little hill, above a dark and dense pine forest. It was evening and the light was soft. I threw myself down on the grass. There was a soft grey sky and a new life, a new world was born. The pine forests seemed to hang suspended, downward. Airplane drivers who do stunts, loop the loop, etc., must see the world so.

The hair of the woman in bed is like the tops of dark pine trees in a soft evening light. She has got her head into an uncomfortable position and you go and change it.

Very gently now.

Very very gently.

You do not want to disturb her dreams. You want to enter in a new way, thrust your dreams into her dreams.

Dreams thrust into skies, rivers, mountains, into Mother Earth.

"Woman, you are earth beautiful.

"Now I am a farmer thrusting down seed. Source of life is in you woman."

The dream passes. The night stays. Sometimes terror comes. You have blown out the candle and crept back into bed. In her sleep she draws close to you. There is now a small woman's hand on your hips. How softly touching, softly drawing dreams into self, taking night terrors away.

What fools are men who do not search and search until they find a woman with whom they may lie thus.

Perhaps Women

I wrote a little book called *Perhaps Women* [26] and it had no success. It was so unnoticed that even the critics who have thought least of my work did not bother to speak of it. It was really the work of a metaphysician. The difficulty may have been that I did not write in the dry dusty prose of the metaphysician. I tried merely to show how, as the world becomes more and more highly mechanized, something goes out of men.

It is because man finds his life down through his hands. He finds his life in what he does to the physical world through tools and materials. The male is a doer, whereas that whole natural impulse of the female is to be. It is true that the line between what is male and what is female, in the individual, is never sharply drawn. There are enough half males going about in skirts and half females in trousers.

The female world is the world of fact. All business is female, posses-

26. New York: Horace Liveright, Inc., 1931.

sions are female, all of the material world female. When you get a civilization, such as the one in which I lived my life, devoted to material ends, you have a world in which the female is most at home. The female will always dominate in such a world and that is why America, in my time, was so distinctly a matriarchy.

It is all connected with this mechanization in life. Men lose all touch with the sources of masculine life. There are less good workmen and less real males. I think that one of the best evidences of this is, for example, the worship of obvious power. It is the reason why a fine prose man, like Ernest Hemingway, is so obsessed with killing, with bull fights, etc. This masculinity that must be constantly asserted in this way is always a fake masculinity. All real masculinity and all of the real power that can come out of a true masculinity should be expressed in gentleness. You do not constantly assert what you are sure you have.

Desire for Fame

The woman Tennessee Mitchell, with whom I once lived (I was married to her but it was a marriage that didn't take), told me of Edgar Lee Masters, whose sweetheart she had been.[27] I could never believe all she told me. How can you believe any woman about a man with whom she has been intimate, after the intimacy has come to an end?

However I did believe what she said about his early consuming ambition to become a great literary figure, to get his name up in the world.

In this matter Masters had an odd experience. When he was still a practising lawyer he published several little books of verses, all under pen names, but they got no attention. He wrote his *Spoon River* and it was a great success. His name was up but not as he had wanted it to be. He himself didn't believe in his *Spoon River*.

But to return to this matter of fame. I am convinced that the desire for it keeps many men at work. I remember a conversation on this matter had with Scott Fitzgerald. He said, "I go into the lobby of some big hotel. I walk through. There are crowds of people about. I have a hunger to feel that they all know who I am. If I could be sure that, when I pass through

27. Masters describes his affair with Tennessee Mitchell in *Across Spoon River* (New York: Farrar and Rinehart, 1936), pp. 295–315.

such a public place, people were nudging each other and saying, 'Look. There is Scott Fitzgerald,' I would be happy."

To be sure it is possible that Fitzgerald was pulling my leg but I do not think so. He asked me whether or not I felt the same way and I said I did not. He didn't believe me but what I said was nevertheless true. This desire to be known, to be pointed out, lionized, is quite absent from my nature but, God knows, that is not due to modesty. It may be due rather to a kind of arrogance in me. Except in my time, I have, in my attitude toward my craft, in a certain faith I have kept and in the best of my work, I have been tops.

The Dance Is On

It's a crazy dance of death now. It's in your mind, in your imagination, on the sea, on land, on the air.

We don't come close any more, even to kill another man, or a thousand men, women and children, or to destroy a town or a city. We are far up in the air when we do it or we are at the breach of a huge gun forty or fifty miles away.

Houses, towns and cities are built slowly. What plans men make, how men and women labor, plan, save, dream, to build a house, plant a garden, to a little beautify a street, all of this to pull us all a little more up out of savagery, something achieved beyond bare want, ugliness, brutality.

And then, with a crash, a great column of black smoke, filling the spring air, flying bits of wood, brick, stone, human bodies, it is all gone.

Who has done this thing? Whose bodies are these so mangled, so blown to bits?

There was a young man, there at the breach of a gun. Or he was far up in the sky, in a plane, when he dropped the bomb.

Do you think he is some casual brute, caring nothing? He is the young man with whom you dined one evening last summer. He is that other young man you see there thoughtfully helping an old woman across the street in city traffic. He is the victim of some blind force loose in the world.

Can the dance of death be stopped? It seems a long slow road, back to sanity.

There is something loose in the world, a monster. It is in every factory. Go into a cotton mill, into a silk mill, go look at the presses that print this.

The thing is not a monster here. It is beautiful. Here is a gay dance, a purposeful dance. See the many colored cloth rolling out of the flying machines in the cloth mill. Here is beautiful cloth to clothe all the world. See the newspapers dropping as thick as snow flakes in a new storm, see the graceful streamlined cars coming off the belt in the huge automobile plant.

It is something to make the heart sing, man's amazing skill in destroying distance, making all the world a next door neighbor, man to live richly, proudly, in a proud rich new world man's brains and hands have made.

And now turn the pages, to this other, this horror. Can it be stopped? Can the dance be made, not a dance of death, but of joy and new life?

Can men come out of their selves to others?

What a long road to be traveled.

Years ago I wrote some stories of life in an American middle western town. They were, as best I could make them, studies of little lives, everyday small people in a small town, their lives, their reactions to one another, and for years afterward I got letters, from England, Germany, Turkey, Japan, from South American republics, from France, from many other countries, all saying the same thing.

The stories, they all said, might have been written about people in their own South American, European, Asiatic towns.

So there is this common thing we have, our lives, so essentially alike, deep down, the same dreams, aspirations, hungers.

And then the power hunger, hunger to command other men's lives, that has now changed, perverted this thing we have made. The machine. The machine that can be so beautiful, that can do such wonders for us.

Must the power hunger, also in man, defeat us all, pervert, make horrible all our lives?

It is a dance.

Man never intended it to be the dance of death.

He dreamed of making it a great new dance of life.

Life to be longer, richer, sweeter.

The test of man and the thing he calls "civilization" is on. There is this inanimate monster loose in the world. It can make life infinitely richer. It can destroy all we have built up. It is up to man who made it to control it. Is it all to end in a dance of death or in a dance of new rich life?

The dance is on.[28]

28. Published (revised) in *Rotarian,* LVIII (June, 1941), 7.

Life, not death, is the adventure.

The time will come when men will look back upon my time, speaking of it as another dark age. Any civilization absorbed in economics, the economic interpretation of history, etc., etc. is but a savage and brutal civilization.

There will be a renaissance and then my own work and my own life will be appreciated. For in a muddled time I have lived fully and very richly.

What man of my own time has approached me in this? Who has written so beautifully? In all my experience of men I have never met another who has smelled, tasted, felt, seen as I have. I have been all my life a wanderer but my wandering has been to some purpose. America is a vast country. I have wanted to feel all of it in its thousand phases, see it, walk upon it, its plains, mountains, towns, cities, rivers, lakes, forests and plowed lands. I have been a true son of God in my eager love and appreciation of nature. It is only through nature and art men really live. Man is not woman.

I am very male and do not believe in women artists and these men feminists, how they bore me, how they make my bones ache with boredom.

It is because I am so very male that I can be a real lover of women. To me they have been, when not trying also to be male, the good earth, the sky. In my mind they relate always to the world of nature, the male to the spirit. Although I am essentially male I am not particularly lustful. There has been too much of the male energy in me gone into the effort to produce a beautiful art. I have succeeded sometimes, failed often. To me women are as a flowing stream in which I bathe and clothe myself. They are rich wine drunk, fruit eaten. They have washed me as summer rains wash me.

I speak of women at length because Americans have no understanding of women and because of lack of understanding America has become a matriarchy. In reality women have no desire to DO. Doing is for them a substitute. Their desire is to BE. There was never a real woman lived who did not hunger to be beautiful. The male desires not to be beautiful but to create beauty. No woman can be beautiful without the help of the male. We create their beauty, fertilize it, feed it. If we were a strong race our women would be more beautiful, our land and our cities more beautiful.

All evil, all ugliness, is sign of weakness. Nothing in the end lives on but art. The men in America who build ugly cities, ugly factory towns, who make fields and forests ugly, who make man cry out constantly the word "progress, progress," to cover the fact of their ugly work, these are all weak men. Strong men are always gentle. To them a field is as a woman loved.

In this light what are we to say of the men of our "old south," who cotton cropped all of the fertility out of the most beautiful section of our land? We speak of an old southern aristocracy. We should think only of their ugliness, their terrible weakness. Our Stark Youngs and Allen Tates [29] are our ultimate vulgarisms.

There are many, many vulgarisms. The final proof of it is that we have become a matriarchy.

Oh women, women, how we have defeated you.

But I have lived here. I have been all my life poet here. The matriarchy in which I have lived, the vulgarity of men seeking their so-called "success," the difficulty, the difficulty of going on, living as poet in the midst of this, has only drawn me to shrewdness. It is that has made me a prose man. I write prose only to conceal song, the music of living.

Listen

I remember an old mountain woman, seen over in Grayson County one day. She was the wife of a small farmer over there and had lived with him for forty years. He had died. When I saw that old woman she was coming along a mountain road afoot from the funeral.

There were several people in the road. I happened to be standing in a stream. I was trout fishing. The people came silently along the road. I had stepped behind an over hanging bush. I could see along the road. There was the old mountain woman, two grown daughters and a troup of grandchildren. They were all dressed in the cheap Sunday clothes poor people wear on such occasions. The old wife walked alone behind them all. She had got her a cheap black dress for the occasion.

29. Stark Young attended the University of Mississippi and taught there and at the University of Texas before he moved north. Allen Tate (1899–   ), from Tennessee, was one of the Fugitives and an "agrarian" critic.

The sun was shining. It was late afternoon. The old mountain woman was small and slender. Why had all of her own people left her to walk alone like that?

The reason was pretty obvious. She wanted to be alone. There are times when every human being who has experienced life at all keenly must be alone.

Someone very near to you has died.

Or, if you get life that way, it may be someone not near you, someone you may never have seen. For example, I myself remember what happened to me when I was told one day the writer D. H. Lawrence had died.[30] I had never met Lawrence, the writer, had never seen him, did not know he was ill.

"He's dead," someone said.

"What?"

"Yes. D. H. Lawrence. He died. Hadn't you heard? He died. He's dead."

So, a sudden blackening of the skies. A queer feeling of emptiness, all life empty like that. Why should I try to describe the feeling? Innumerable people have felt it. Have you ever gone into a house or a room in a house where someone you once loved formerly lived? It may have been a man or a woman. It doesn't matter. The thing I am trying to talk about, in this rather disconcerting rambling way, is to say beauty can live in a man as well as in a woman.

There is a man you have known and loved has worked in a certain room for years. You have gone there to sit with him and talk with him. He has left his marks everywhere about the room. Let's say the man was a cigarette smoker. Most modern men are. There is a mark there on his desk, at the edge of his desk. There is in fact a little row of black marks.

He has put his cigarette down there. He was talking, he was absorbed.

Or he was thinking, perhaps, of his work. It doesn't make much difference what the work was. I think that most men, I have thought, as I looked at them, were beautiful men, beautiful because of work, absorption in some kind of work. They were doing something they cared about doing. Let's say they cared rather tremendously.

So there is your friend, standing in a certain room. He has put his

30. D. H. Lawrence died March 2, 1930. Anderson wrote of Lawrence in "A Living Force in Literature," *Brentano's Book Chat,* June, 1921, pp. 17–18; "A Man's Mind," *New Republic,* LXIII (May 21, 1930), 22–23; and "A Man's Song of Life," *Virginia Quarterly Review,* IX (January, 1933), 108–14. See John Peale Bishop, "This Distrust of Ideas (D. H. Lawrence and Sherwood Anderson)," *Vanity Fair,* XXII (December, 1921), 10–12, 118; and James G. Hepburn, "Disarming and Uncanny Visions . . . ," *Literature and Psychology,* IX, No. 1 (Winter, 1959), 9–12.

burning cigarette down on the edge of his desk. He is trying to tell you something. He stands there struggling, let's say for words. Now the cigarette has begun to burn the wood. The desk is varnished and the hot end of the cigarette melts the varnish a little. There is a faint stench in the room. You do not mind.

Afterward, let's say, that friend dies. Such things happen. People you love are always dying or some quality in them that appealed to you, that fed you, that made you love your friend, that quality dies in him. There are little deaths like that as well as the final thing we habitually think of as death.

Friends you have, people you love die and are born again. You know what I mean. It is always happening to everyone you love. When for example you go to a friend's house you take something with you. You take health, the gift of beauty in yourself, give that to your friend, or you take ill health, you take poison. I dare say this sounds like preaching. I don't care. There is something I am trying to say. I am like that man I have tried to describe to you, who stood at his desk lost in thought, trying to find words to say some subtle and difficult thing, his cigarette burning his desk. I am trying to say that all of us go about all the time doing something to others and to things too.

I will speak again of an old wife, an old mountain woman, a poor thin little old working woman I once saw walking in a road.

I speak of her only to show how beauty can exist in the aged, in the tired, in the defeated.

I knew the old woman's story, knew it vaguely. It was simple enough. As a young girl, the daughter of a poor mountain family, she had married a poor and perhaps, as we in the modern world think of education, an uneducated mountain man. He couldn't read or write. He had a little poor mountain land.

They lived there, they raised their children there. In some way they managed.

Their children grew up and married. They lived in other little farms scattered about over the Virginia mountain. For years the little old woman and the old man had lived alone together. Every year they raised and fattened a pig, kept a cow, they worked a few poor fields, on Sunday afternoons sometimes their children and their grandchildren came to see them. Now he was dead. On the day I saw her walking in the road she and the others had just come from the burial.

The old woman was alone, walking behind the others in the mountain road that day. She wanted to be alone. The others of her people were respecting her desire to be alone. They walked ahead of her in silence in the road. Even the children were silent. There was one of the daughters had a tiny babe in her arms. As she walked she suckled it.

The point was the beauty of the old woman. As she walked she braced her shoulders and threw her head back. Her watery little old eyes were fixed and staring.

There is, as everyone knows, a beauty of grief as well as of laughter. It was in her. It came out of her. It seemed to me that day, standing in the water of that creek, near a bridge, near a turn of a mountain road, it seemed to me suddenly that something, a very definite thing (I can't describe it), it seemed to me that it came out of her and ran through trees. It was in the cold waters of the mountain stream that washed my legs. It was in my legs. It sang in distant hills. It was in every tiny particle of dust in all the fields on the sides of the hills.

Dinner in Thessaly

"Not life but the good life."

Didn't Socrates say something like that? It seems to me moral nonsense to go on, in old age, in pain, in uselessness to others, to say nothing of self.

I have always wondered about this whole notion. "Why, if you take your own life you won't go to heaven."

But it's this heaven that I must wonder about. What monstrous egotism that, I, who have lived as I have, so often cruel and brutal to others, selfish, self-centered, only occasionally losing self, becoming impersonal, only at rare rare moments doing any work that means anything to others.

The thought that this life of mine should be perpetuated, go on forever. . . .

By what terrible mischance does it deserve that?

There is this woman, whose death by her own hands, I take it, inspired this discussion.[31] It was, to my seeming, so nice, so clear, what she did and

31. Published (revised) as "The Right to Die: Dinner in Thessaly," *Forum*, XCV (January, 1936), 40–41, as part of a discussion in the euthanasia case of Charlotte Perkins Gilman. See also Zona Gale, "The Right to Die," *Forum*, XCV (February, 1936), 110–12.

her reasons given so sensible. It happens I once met her, sat dining near her, heard her talk. She was one of the living people I have met, full of intense life, energy, of works.

I have, you see, to make this personal, thinking of my own life, grown old, perhaps terribly diseased, myself become a burden on others.

Do you remember Socrates, condemned by the state to die? I remember that his friends came to him. A way of escape could be found. He could flee to Thessaly. There would be friends and admirers in that distant place.

But Socrates had lived in Athens in the day of the glory of Athens. At least it must have seemed so to him. What? To flee all that, friends, comrades, the good talk, the wine of that life for a few more years in the distant place, surrounded perhaps by a few disciples? There were probably ladies' literary clubs out there.

What for a dinner in Thessaly? Bring on the hemlock.

What for an assurance of this heaven no man has ever been able to describe satisfactorily, even to imagine satisfactorily?

I have nothing but respect for the woman Charlotte Gilman. My hat off to her. I wish I also could be assured of the same sort of clean departure, of the courage and sanity of it.

For me it all seems quite clear that all of this clinging to life, giving it so often this vast over estimate, granting always disease, perhaps some quite incurable and loathsome disease. . . . Let the gods explain the existence of such evil in the world. I'll not attempt it. The gods' business for the gods. My business under such circumstances for myself.

Friends who perhaps have loved me, to have this load put on them, coming into my sick room, myself lying there, old and helpless, the stink of that place, the low misery, the mind losing its clean clearness.

"Oh my friends, dear ones, with whom I have walked, talked, made love, seen days and nights. . . .

"To do this to you. . . ."

I think, I must think, that it is past all words, moral nonsense, to say that I must go on, under such circumstances, bringing that much more evil into other lives.

For to me disease is evil, old age, decrepitude, with incurable disease, the final evil.

Springs coming, walks in the forest, love, comradeship—all these gone. "Who took these from me?"

Thanks be to those, scientists or others, who have invented or discovered these poisons.

Perhaps for an almost quiet exit, the door somewhat softly opened.

An end to my being a nuisance to others. Do I want them all to rejoice when I at last die, that sort of rejoicing? [32]

For the End

For years I have been jotting down these impressions, memories, things seen and felt during what has seemed to me a very good life. On all sides now I hear complaints of the quality of life in our times. It may be that I was born one of the lucky ones.

To be sure I have days and, sometimes, even weeks and months of gloom.

What man, at all sensitive to life, doesn't?

I have been a writer now for twenty-five years and on too many days I write badly. I have been panned and praised by critics, have been called a "genius," a "pioneer," a "hazy thinker," a "profound thinker," "clear headed," "muddle headed," a "groper." That last has stuck more persistently than any of the others. If it is meant, by groping, that I do not know the answers, O.K.

During most of my life, to date, I have been healthy and strong. I am no prize fighter, no athlete, but I enjoy thoroughly my friends, women, food, drink, sleep.

There is a kind of persistent youth in some men and I am one of that sort. I rebound quickly from disaster, laugh a good deal, make rather quick and easy connections with others.

When I die I would like this inscription put on my grave:

LIFE NOT DEATH IS THE GREAT ADVENTURE

32. Sherwood Anderson died on a good-will trip to South America, sponsored by the State Department. He became ill on the *Santa Lucia* and died from peritonitis at Colón, Panama Canal Zone, March 8, 1941. On his death, see Freda Kirchwey, "Sherwood Anderson," *Nation,* CLII (March 22, 1941), 313–14. Anderson was buried at Marion, Virginia, March 26. On the burial, see Manuel Komroff, "Procession in the Rain," *Story,* XIX (September–October, 1941), 94–95.

A Selected Bibliography

A SELECTED BIBLIOGRAPHY

I. Books By Sherwood Anderson

Windy McPherson's Son. New York: John Lane Company, 1916; New York: B. W. Huebsch, 1922 (revised); Chicago: University of Chicago Press, 1965, Introduction by Wright Morris.

Marching Men. New York: John Lane Company, 1917; New York: B. W. Huebsch, [1921].

Mid-American Chants. New York: John Lane Company, 1918; New York: B. W. Huebsch, [1921].

Winesburg, Ohio. New York: B. W. Huebsch, 1919; New York: Viking Press, 1960, Introduction by Malcolm Cowley [with critical essays, edited by John Ferres, 1966].

Poor White. New York: B. W. Huebsch, 1920; New York: Viking Press, [1966], Introduction by Walter B. Rideout.

The Triumph of the Egg. New York: B. W. Huebsch, 1921.

Horses and Men. New York: B. W. Huebsch, 1923; New York: Peter Smith, [1933].

Many Marriages. New York: B. W. Huebsch, 1923; New York: Grosset and Dunlap, [1929].

A Story Teller's Story. New York: B. W. Huebsch, 1924; New York: Grove Press, [1958].

Dark Laughter. New York: Boni and Liveright, 1925; New York: Liveright Publishing Corporation, [1960], Introduction by Howard Mumford Jones.

The Modern Writer. San Francisco: Lantern Press, 1925.

Sherwood Anderson's Notebook. New York: Boni and Liveright, 1926.

Tar: A Midwest Childhood. New York: Boni and Liveright, 1926, [1931].

A New Testament. New York: Boni and Liveright, 1927.

Alice and the Lost Novel. London: Elkin Mathews and Marrot, 1929.

Hello Towns! New York: Horace Liveright, 1929.

Nearer the Grass Roots. San Francisco: Westgate Press, 1929.

The American County Fair. New York: Random House, 1930.

Perhaps Women. New York: Horace Liveright, 1931.

Beyond Desire. New York: Liveright, Inc., 1932; New York: Liveright Publishing Corporation, [1961], Introduction by Walter B. Rideout.

Death in the Woods. New York: Liveright, Inc., 1933.

No Swank. Philadelphia: Centaur Press, 1934.

Puzzled America. New York: Charles Scribner's Sons, 1935.

Kit Brandon. New York: Charles Scribner's Sons, 1936.

Plays, Winesburg and Others. New York: Charles Scribner's Sons, 1937.

Five Poems. San Mateo, California: Quercus Press, 1939.

A Writer's Conception of Realism. Olivet, Michigan: Olivet College, 1939.

Home Town. New York: Alliance Book Corporation, 1940.

Sherwood Anderson's Memoirs. New York: Harcourt, Brace and Company, 1942.

The Sherwood Anderson Reader, edited by Paul Rosenfeld. Boston: Houghton Mifflin Company, 1947.

The Portable Sherwood Anderson, edited by Horace Gregory. New York: Viking Press, 1949.

Letters of Sherwood Anderson, edited by Howard Mumford Jones and Walter B. Rideout. Boston: Little, Brown and Company, 1953.

Sherwood Anderson: Short Stories, edited by Maxwell Geismar. New York: Hill and Wang, 1962.

Mid-American Chants, 6 Mid-American Chants by Sherwood Anderson / 11 Midwest Photographs by Art Sinsabaugh. Highlands, N.C.: Nantahala Foundation, 1964, Introduction by Edward Dahlberg.

Return to Winesburg: Selections from Four Years of Writing for a Country Newspaper, edited by Ray Lewis White. Chapel Hill: The University of North Carolina Press, 1967.

A Story Teller's Story: A Critical Text, edited by Ray Lewis White. Cleveland: Press of Case Western Reserve University, 1968.

Tar: A Midwest Childhood, A Critical Text, edited by Ray Lewis White. Cleveland: Press of Case Western Reserve University, 1969.

II. Books About Sherwood Anderson

Anderson, David D. *Sherwood Anderson.* New York: Holt, Rinehart and Winston, 1967.

Burbank, Rex. *Sherwood Anderson.* New York: Twayne Publishers, 1964.

Chase, Cleveland B. *Sherwood Anderson.* New York: R. M. McBride, 1927.

Fagin, Nathan Bryllion. *The Phenomenon of Sherwood Anderson: A Study in American Life and Letters.* Baltimore: Rossi-Bryn, 1927.

Howe, Irving. *Sherwood Anderson.* New York: William Sloane, 1951; Stanford: Stanford University Press, [1966].

The Newberry Library Bulletin, 2d Ser., No. 2 (December, 1948). The Sherwood Anderson Memorial Number.

La Revue des Lettres Modernes, Nos. 78–80 (1963). *Configuration Critique de Sherwood Anderson,* edited by Roger Asselineau.

Schevill, James. *Sherwood Anderson: His Life and Work.* Denver: University of Denver Press, 1951.

Sheehy, Eugene P. and Kenneth A. Lohf. *Sherwood Anderson: A Bibliography.* Los Gatos, California: Talisman Press, 1960; New York: Kraus Reprint Corporation, [1967].

Shenandoah, XIII (Spring, 1962). The Sherwood Anderson Number.

Story, XIX (September–October, 1941). The Sherwood Anderson Memorial Number.

Sutton, William A. *Exit to Elsinore.* Muncie, Indiana: Ball State University, 1967.

Weber, Brom. *Sherwood Anderson.* Minneapolis: University of Minnesota Press, 1964.

White, Ray Lewis, editor. *The Achievement of Sherwood Anderson: Essays in Criticism.* Chapel Hill: The University of North Carolina Press, 1966.

III. Major Area Studies

Aaron, Daniel. *Writers on the Left: Episodes in American Literary Communism.* New York: Harcourt, Brace and World, 1961.

Åhnebrink, Lars. *The Beginnings of Naturalism in American Fiction.* . . . Upsala, Sweden: American Institute in the University of Upsala, 1950.

Berthoff, Warner. *The Ferment of Realism: American Literature, 1884–1919.* New York: Free Press, 1965.

Bridgman, Richard. *The Colloquial Style in America.* New York: Oxford University Press, 1966.

Brooks, Van Wyck. *America's Coming of Age.* New York: B. W. Huebsch, 1915.

————. *The Confident Years: 1885–1915.* New York: Dutton, 1952.

Cargill, Oscar. *Intellectual America: Ideas on the March.* New York: Macmillan Company, 1941.

Curti, Merle. *The Growth of American Thought,* revised edition. New York: Harper's, 1951.

Duffey, Bernard. *The Chicago Renaissance in American Letters: A Critical History.* Lansing: Michigan State University Press, 1954.

Geismar, Maxwell. *The Last of the Provincials: The American Novel, 1915–1925.* Boston: Houghton Mifflin Company, 1947.

————. *Rebels and Ancestors: The American Novel, 1890–1915.* Boston: Houghton Mifflin Company, 1953.

————. *Writers in Crisis: The American Novel between Two Wars.* Boston: Houghton Mifflin Company, 1942.

Herron, Ima Honaker. *The Small Town in American Literature.* Durham: Duke University Press, 1939.

Hoffman, Frederick J. *Freudianism and the Literary Mind,* revised edition. Baton Rouge: Louisiana State University Press, 1957.

————. *The Twenties: American Writing in the Post-War Decade,* revised edition. New York: Free Press, 1962.

————, Charles Allen, and Carolyn Farquhar Ulrich. *The Little Magazine: A History and a Bibliography.* Princeton: Princeton University Press, 1947.

Hofstadter, Richard. *Social Darwinism in American Thought, 1860–1915.* Philadelphia: University of Pennsylvania Press, 1944.

Jones, Howard Mumford. *The Bright Medusa.* Urbana: University of Illinois Press, 1952.

Kazin, Alfred. *On Native Grounds: An Interpretation of Modern American Prose Literature.* New York: Reynal and Hitchcock, 1942.

Kramer, Dale. *Chicago Renaissance: The Literary Life in the Midwest.* New York: Appleton-Century, 1966.

Lillard, Richard Gordon. *American Life in Autobiography: A Descriptive Guide*. Stanford: Stanford University Press, 1956.

Martin, Jay. *Harvests of Change: American Literature, 1865–1914*. Englewood Cliffs, New Jersey: Prentice-Hall, 1967.

Marx, Leo. *The Machine in the Garden: Technology and the Pastoral Ideal in America*. New York: Oxford University Press, 1964.

May, Henry F. *The End of American Innocence: A Study of the First Years of Our Own Time, 1912–1917*. New York: Knopf, 1959.

Rideout, Walter B. *The Radical Novel in the United States, 1900–1954: Some Interrelations of Literature and Society*. Cambridge: Harvard University Press, 1956.

Walcutt, Charles Child. *American Literary Naturalism: A Divided Stream*. Minneapolis: University of Minnesota Press, 1956.

Wector, Dixon. *The Age of the Great Depression, 1929–1941*. New York: Macmillan Company, 1948.

West, Ray B. *The Short Story in America*. Chicago: Regnery, 1956.

West, Thomas Reed. *Flesh of Steel: Literature and the Machine in American Culture*. Nashville: Vanderbilt University Press, 1967.

Index

INDEX